HOME OF HARD-TO-FIND BOOKS

The History of Modern Europe: With an Account
of the Decline and Fall of the Roman Empire
by William Russell

Address:
HardPress
8345 NW 66TH ST #2561
MIAMI FL 33166-2626
USA
Email: info@hardpress.net

CC.3.

940

THE
PACIFIC-UNION
CLUB

SHELF NO. 225

SAN FRANCISCO

EX LIBRIS

405

THE

HISTORY

OF

MODERN EUROPE:

WITH AN

ACCOUNT OF THE DECLINE AND FALL

OF THE

ROMAN EMPIRE;

AND A

VIEW OF THE PROGRESS OF SOCIETY,

FROM THE

RISE OF THE MODERN KINGDOMS TO THE PEACE

OF PARIS, IN 1763;

IN A

SERIES OF LETTERS FROM A NOBLEMAN TO HIS SON.

NEW EDITION,

CONTINUED TO THE DEATH OF WILLIAM IV. OF ENGLAND.

IN FOUR VOLUMES.

VOL. I.

LONDON:

LONGMAN, REES, & CO.; T. CADELL; J. RICHARDSON; J. M. RICHARDSON; BALDWIN & CRADOCK; J. G. & F. RIVINGTON; HATCHARD & SON; HAMILTON & CO.; HARDING & CO.; J. DUNCAN; WHITTAKER & CO.; ALLEN & CO.; SIMPKIN, MARSHALL, & CO.; J. BOHN; COWIE & CO.; J. DOWDING; J. BIGG; J. BAIN; T. & W. BOONE; M. DOYLE; E. HODGSON; GOSLING & EGLEY; SMITH, ELDER, & CO.; T. BUMPUS; R. MACKIE; J. TEMPLEMAN; J. & J. MAYNARD; B. FELLOWES; AND BOOKER & DOLMAN; J. PARKER, OXFORD; J. & J. J. DEIGHTON, CAMBRIDGE; G. & J. ROBINSON, LIVERPOOL; AND A. & C. BLACK, EDINBURGH.

1837.

1 1 2 4 .

LONDON :
GILBERT & RIVINGTON, PRINTERS,
ST. JOHN'S SQUARE

ADVERTISEMENT.

A PERSUASION of the utility of a concise History of Modern Europe induced the author to undertake this work ; and he has had the satisfaction to find his opinion justified by that of the public. The epistolary form was chosen as best calculated, in tracing the concatenation of events, for uniting the accuracy of the chronologer with the entertainment of the memorialist : and the character of a nobleman and a father was assumed, in order to give greater weight to the moral and political maxims, and to entitle the writer to offer, without seeming to dictate to the world, such Reflections on Life and Manners, as are supposed more immediately to belong to the higher orders of society.

To each volume of this Edition is prefixed a chronological table of contents ; and to facilitate reference, an index is subjoined to the work.

ADVERTISEMENT

TO THE

NEW EDITION.

In this edition of Dr. Russell's very popular and interesting work, some important errors have been corrected; but the editor has been scrupulously cautious in making no unnecessary alterations in a work of such established character as the History of Modern Europe. The work has been continued to the commencement of the present year; and the author of the continuation has laboured to be as impartial as is possible for the writer of contemporary history. It is probable that the consequences of the French Revolution and the English Reform are not yet so fully developed as to enable us to judge accurately of their tendency; the writer has therefore passed no judgment on the moral effects of those great events. The characters of the agents are, however, fair subjects of discussion, and he has therefore not scrupled to examine how far the conduct of public men has resulted from purity of motive and rectitude of principle. As he lays no claim to infallibility, he may in some instances be mistaken, and, doubtlessly, some of his readers will dissent from the view he has taken of modern politics. He trusts, however, that, even those who differ from him will give him credit for a sincere desire to discover the truth, and for a sincere expression of his deliberate opinions.

CHRONOLOGICAL TABLE OF CONTENTS

TO

VOLUME I.

PART I.

FROM THE RISE OF THE MODERN KINGDOMS TO THE PEACE OF WESTPHALIA, IN 1648.

LETTER I.

Of the Decline and Fall of the Roman Empire, and the Settlement of the Barbarians.

LETTER II.

Of the System of Policy and Legislation established by the Barbarians in the Provinces of the Roman Empire.

CONTENTS.

LETTER III.

Of the Rise of the French Monarchy, and its Progress under the Kings of the First Race.

LETTER IV.

Of the Affairs of Spain under the Dominion of the Visigoths, and under the Moors, till the Reign of Abdarrahman.

LETTER V.

Of the Dominion of the Ostrogoths in Italy, and the Affairs of the Lombards, till the Reign of Luitprand.

LETTER VI.

Of the Pope's Temporal Power, and the Affairs of Italy in general, the Empire of Constantinople, and the Kingdom of France, from the Time of Charles Martel to that of Charlemagne.

LETTER VII.

Of Britain, from the Time when it was relinquished by the Romans, to the End of the Saxon Heptarchy.

LETTER VIII.

Of the Government and Laws of the Anglo-Saxons.

LETTER IX.

Of the Reign of Charlemagne or Charles the Great, King of France and Emperor of the West.

LETTER X.

Of the Empire of Charlemagne and the Church, from the Accession of Louis the Debonnaire to the Death of Charles the Bald.

CONTENTS.

LETTER XI.

Of the Normans or Danes, before their Settlement in France and England.

LETTER XII.

*Of the Affairs of England, from the End of the Saxon Heptarchy to the
Death of Alfred the Great.*

LETTER XIII.

Of the Empire of Charlemagne and the Church, from the Death of Charles the Bald to that of Louis IV., when the imperial dignity was transferred from the French to the Germans.

LETTER XIV.

Of the German Empire, from the Election of Conrad I. to the Death of Henry the Fowler.

LETTER XV.

Of the Affairs of France, from the Settlement of the Normans to the Extinction of the Carlovingian Race.

LETTER XVI.

Of the German Empire and its Italian Dependencies, under Otho the Great, and his Successors of the House of Saxony.

LETTER XVII.

Sketch of the History of Poland and Russia, and also of the Scandinavian States, to the Death of Magnus the Good, King of Denmark and Norway.

POLAND.

RUSSIA.

THE SCANDINAVIAN REALMS.

LETTER XVIII.

Of the chief Occurrences and Transactions in England, from the Death of Alfred to the Reign of Canute the Great.

LETTER XIX.

Of the Reigns of the French Kings, from the Accession of Hugh Capet to the Invasion of England by William, Duke of Normandy.

LETTER XX.

Of the Government of the Kings of England, from the Danish to the Norman Conquest.

LETTER XXI.

Of the Affairs of Spain, the Saracen Empire, and that of Constantinople, during the Ninth, Tenth, and part of the Eleventh Century.

SPAIN.

LETTER XXII.

Of the Progress of Society in Europe, from the Settlement of the Modern Nations to the Middle of the Eleventh Century.

LETTER XXIII.

Of the German Empire and its Dependencies, under Conrad II. and his Descendants of the House of Franconia.

LETTER XXIV.

Of the Reigns of the first three Norman Kings of England.

CONTENTS.

LETTER XXV.

Sketch of the French History under Philip I. and Louis VI. with some Account of the first Crusade.

CONTENTS.

LETTER XXVI.

Of the German Empire and its Dependencies, from the Death of Henry V. to the Election of Frederic I. surnamed Barbarossa.

LETTER XXVII.

History of France under Louis VII. till the Divorce of Queen Eleanor, with some Account of the second Crusade.

LETTER XXVIII.

Of the Affairs of England during the Reign of Stephen.

LETTER XXIX.

History of England during the Reign of Henry II. with an Account of the Affairs of France.

LETTER XXX.

Of the German Empire and its Dependencies under Frederic I. with some Account of the third Crusade.

LETTER XXXI.

LETTER XXXII.

LETTER XXXIII.

*History of England, from the Grant of the Great Charter to the Reign of
Edward I.*

LETTER XXXIV.

*Sketch of the Affairs of France, from the Death of Philip Augustus, to the
End of the Reign of Louis IX., with some Account of the last Crusade.*

CONTENTS.

LETTER XXXV.

A Survey of the Transactions in Spain, from the Middle of the Eleventh to the End of the Thirteenth Century.

LETTER XXXVI.

Of the Progress of Society in Europe during the Twelfth and Thirteenth Centuries.

LETTER XXXVII.

History of England during the Reign of Edward I., with an Introduction to that of Scotland, and some Account of the Conquest of that Country by the English, as well as of the final Reduction of Wales.

LETTER XXXVIII.

A View of the Reign of Edward II., with an Account of the Affairs of Scotland.

CONTENTS.

LETTER XXXIX.

*Of the German Empire, and its Dependencies, from the Election of Rodolph
of Hapsburgh to the Death of Henry VII.*

LETTER XL.

*History of France, from the Death of Louis IX. till the Accession of the
House of Valois.*

LETTER XLI.

Of the Affairs of England, Scotland, France, and Spain, during the Reign of Edward III.

LETTER XLII.

Of the German Empire and its Dependencies, from the Election of Louis of Bavaria, to the Death of Charles IV.

LETTER XLIII.

History of England from the Death of Edward III. to the Accession of Henry V., with some Account of the Affairs of Scotland.

LETTER XLIV.

Of the German Empire and its dependencies, from the Accession of Wenceslaus to the Death of Sigismund.

LETTER XLV.

Of the Affairs of Poland, Russia, and the Scandinavian States, to the Commencement of the Reign of Margaret over the three northern Kingdoms.

POLAND.

RUSSIA.

SWEDEN, DENMARK, AND NORWAY.

LETTER XLVI.

History of France, from the Death of Charles the Wise, to the Invasion of that Kingdom by Henry V. of England.

LETTER XLVII.

Of the Affairs of England and France, from the Invasion of the latter Kingdom by Henry V., to the Death of Charles VI.

LETTER XLVIII.

Continuation of the History of France and England, from the Accession of Charles VII. to the Expulsion of the English from their Continental Territories, in 1453.

LETTER XLIX.

*Of the German Empire and its Dependencies, from the Election of Albert II.
to that of Maximilian.*

LETTER L.

*Of the Contest in England between the Houses of York and Lancaster, to its
final Extinction in the Accession of the House of Tudor.*

LETTER LI.

Of the Affairs of France, from the Expulsion of the English by Charles VII. to the Invasion of Italy by Charles VIII., in 1494.

LETTER LII.

Of the Progress of the Turks, and the Fall of the Greek Empire.

LETTER LIII.

History of Spain from the Death of Peter the Cruel, in 1369, to the Conquest of Granada, by Ferdinand and Isabella, in 1492.

LETTER LIV.

View of the Reign of Henry VII.

LETTER LV.

A general View of the Continent of Europe, from the Invasion of Italy by Charles VIII. to the League of Cambray, in 1508.

LETTER LVI.

A View of Europe, from the League of Cambray to the Death of Louis XII.

LETTER LVII.

The general View of Europe continued, from the Accession of Francis I. to the Death of the Emperor Maximilian ; including the Rise of the Reformation in Germany.

LETTER LVIII.

Of the Progress of Society in Europe, from the beginning of the Fourteenth to the Middle of the Sixteenth Century, with a retrospective View of the Revival of Letters.

LETTER LIX.

Of the Progress of Navigation, particularly among the Portuguese ; the Discoveries and Settlements of that Nation on the Coast of Africa, and in the East Indies, by the Cape of Good Hope ; the Discovery of America by the Spaniards, the Settlement of the West Indies, and the Conquest of Mexico and Peru ; with some Reflections on the moral and political Consequences of those great Events.

LETTER LX.

A general View of the Affairs of Europe, from the Election of Charles V. in 1519, to the Peace of Cambray, in 1529, including the Progress of the Reformation.

LETTER LXI.

A general View of the Affairs of Europe, and of the Progress of the Reformation on the Continent, from the Peace of Cambray to that of Crespi, in 1544.

LETTER LXII.

*The Domestic History of England during the Reign of Henry VIII., with
some Account of the Affairs of Scotland, and of the Rise of the Reformation in both Kingdoms.*

LETTER LXIII.

*A general View of the Continent of Europe, including the Progress of the
  Reformation in Germany, from the first Meeting of the Council of Trent,
  in 1546, to the Peace of Religion, concluded at Passau, in 1552.*

CONTENTS.

LETTER LXIV.

History of England, from the Death of Henry VIII. until the Accession of Elizabeth, in 1558; with an Account of the Affairs of Scotland, and of the Progress of the Reformation in both the British Kingdoms.

LETTER LXV.

*View of the Continent of Europe, from the Treaty of Passau, in 1552, to the
Peace of Château-Cambresis, in 1559.*

HISTORY

OF

MODERN EUROPE.

PART I.

FROM THE RISE OF THE MODERN KINGDOMS TO THE PEACE OF WESTPHALIA, IN 1648.

LETTER I.

Of the Decline and Fall of the Roman Empire, and the Settlement of the Barbarians.

You have already, my dear Philip, finished your course of Ancient History under your preceptor: in the elements of Modern History I myself will undertake to instruct you. The establishment of the present European nations; the origin of our laws, manners, and customs; the progress of society, of arts, and of letters; demand your particular attention, and were ill committed to the disquisitions of a mere scholar.

Europe is the theatre on which the human character has appeared to the greatest advantage, and where society has attained its most perfect form, both in ancient and modern times. Its history will therefore furnish us with every thing worthy of observation in the study of men and of kingdoms. I shall, however, direct your eye occasionally to the other parts of the globe, that you may have a general idea of the state of the universe. But before I proceed to the history of Modern Europe, it will be proper to say a few words concerning its ancient inhabitants, and its situation at the settlement of the present nations.

The inhabitants of ancient Europe may be divided into three classes, Greeks, Romans, and Barbarians; under which last term we usually comprehend all those nations to whom the two former were pleased to apply it, because they had made less progress in the arts of civilization.   With the Greek and Roman story you are well acquainted.   I shall, therefore, only remind you, that the Greeks, the most polished people of antiquity, inhabited the maritime parts of the country now known by the name of European Turkey; that, when corrupted, they were subdued by the Romans: and that the conquerors then turned their arms against the Gauls, Germans, and other barbarians, whom they in a great measure reduced to subjection, by their superiority in the art of war, but not with the same facility with which they had overcome the voluptuous nations of Asia.   A single battle did not decide the fate of a kingdom.   Those brave and independent people, though often defeated, resumed their arms with fresh valour, and defended with obstinate courage their possessions and their liberties.   But, after a variety of struggles, in which many of them perished in the field, and many were carried into slavery, a miserable remnant submitted to the Romans; while others fled to their mountains for freedom, or took refuge in the inaccessible corners of the North.   There, defended by lakes and rivers, the indignant Barbarians lived, until time had ripened among their enemies the seeds of destruction.   Then, rushing forth, like an impetuous flood, and sweeping every thing before them, they took vengeance on the murderers of mankind; overturned the vast A. D. fabric of the Roman empire, the work and the wonder of 476. ages; established on its ruins new governments and new manners; and accomplished the most signal revolution in the history of nations[1].

Here we must pause, that we may consider the moral and political causes of this great event, and its influence on the state of society.

As soon as the Romans had subdued a particular territory, they prepared to civilize it.   They transferred into each of the conquered countries their laws, manners, arts, sciences, and literature.   And some have thought these a sufficient compensation

---

[1] It was long fashionable with modern writers, especially those of a classical turn, to rail against their rude ancestors, and lament the fall of the Roman empire as a great misfortune to the human race.   This mistake seems to have arisen from an admiration of ancient literature, and an imperfect knowledge of history; from not sufficiently distinguishing between the extinction of Roman liberty and the destruction of Roman despotism.

for the loss of liberty and independence. But you, my dear Philip, will judge very differently, I hope, whatever veneration you may have for the Roman name.

Good laws are essential to good government, arts and sciences to the prosperity of a nation, and learning and politeness to the perfection of the human character. But these, in order to exalt a people, must be the result of the natural progress of civilization, not of any adventitious ferment or external violence. The fruits of summer are ripened in winter by art : but the course of the seasons is necessary to give them their proper flavour, their regular size, and their natural taste. The spontaneous produce of the forest, though somewhat harsh, is preferable to what is raised by such forced culture : and the native dignity, the unsophisticated manners, and rude virtues of the Barbarian, are superior to all that can be taught to the slave. When mankind are obliged to look up to a master for honour and consequence, to flatter his foibles, and to fear his frown, cunning takes place of wisdom, and treachery of fortitude ; the mind loses its vigour, the heart its generosity ; and man, in being polished, is only debased.

This truth was never, perhaps, more strikingly exemplified than in the history of the Roman empire. The degrading influence of its dominion, more than any other circumstance, hastened its dissolution; for, although the conquered nations were by such means more easily kept in subjection, they became unable to resist a foreign enemy, and might be considered as decayed members of the body politic, which increased its size without increasing its strength. An appearance of prosperity, indeed, succeeded to the havoc of war ; the ruined cities were rebuilt, and new ones founded ; population flourished ; civilization advanced ; the arts were cultivated ; but the martial and independent spirit of the people of the northern provinces was so totally extinct in a few centuries, that, instead of preferring death to slavery, like so many of their illustrious ancestors, they patiently submitted to any contribution which a rapacious governor was pleased to levy ; and the descendants of those gallant warriors who had disputed the field with the Roman legions under Cæsar and Germanicus, were unable to oppose the desultory inroads of a troop of undisciplined Barbarians. They were almost incapable either of thinking or acting for themselves. Hence all the countries, which had been subjected to the Roman yoke, fell a prey to the first invader, after the retreat of the imperial forces.

Many other causes contributed to the dissolution of the Roman empire, beside the debility occasioned by its unwieldy corpulence.

Rome owed her dominion as much to the manners as to the arms of her citizens[1]. Their dignity of sentiment, their love of liberty and of their country, their passion for glory, their perseverance in toils, their contempt of danger and of death, their obedience to the laws, and, above all, their civil constitution and military discipline, had extended and cemented the conquests of the Romans. The very usurpations of that sovereign people (for I speak of the times of the republic) were covered with a certain majesty, which rendered even tyranny respectable. But their government carried in its bosom the seeds of destruction. The continual jealousy between the patricians and plebeians, the senate and the people, without any balancing power, made the ruin of the republic inevitable, as soon as the manners were relaxed: and a relaxation of manners was necessarily produced by the pillage of Greece and the conquest of Asia[2], by the contagious refinements of the one, and the influx of wealth from the other.

The fall of Carthage, and the expulsion of the Gauls from central Italy, though seemingly the two most fortunate events in the Roman history, contributed also to a change of manners, and to the extinction of Roman liberty. While Carthage subsisted, the attention of all parties was carried toward that rival state: to defend themselves, or annoy their enemies, was the only care of the Romans: and as long as the Gauls had possessions in the neighbourhood of Rome, her citizens were united by the sense of common danger: but no sooner were their fears from abroad removed, than the people began to be altogether ungovernable. Ambitious men took advantage of their licentiousness; party clashed with party. A master became necessary, in order to terminate the horrors of civil war, as well as to give union and vigour to the state. Interest and vanity made courtiers; force or fear, slaves. The people were disarmed by the jealousy of despotism, and corrupted by the example of an abandoned court. Effeminacy,

---

[1] "Think not," said the younger Cato to the Roman senate, "it was merely by force of arms that our forefathers raised this republic from a low condition to its present greatness:—no! but by things of a very different nature—industry and discipline at home, moderation and justice abroad, a disinterested spirit in council, unblinded by passion, and unbiassed by pleasure." Sallust. *Bell. Catilin.*

[2] It was in the delicious climate and pleasurable groves of Asia (says Sallust) that the Roman soldiers first learned to abandon themselves to wine and women—to admire pictures, statues, and vases of curious workmanship—and to spare nothing civil or sacred in the prosecution of their rapacious aims. *Bell. Catilin.*

debauchery, profligacy, and every atrocious vice, were common upon the throne.

A new source of ruin disclosed itself. Some disputed successions having convinced the troops that the sovereignty was in their hands, they henceforth sold it to the highest bidder. Sporting with the lives of their princes, as formerly with the laws of the republic, they created emperors only to extort money from them, and afterwards massacred them, in order to extort like sums from their successors. Emperors were opposed to emperors, and armies disputed the pretensions of armies. With obedience discipline was lost. Wise princes endeavoured, but in vain, to restore it : their zeal to maintain the ancient military regulations only exposed them to the fury of the soldiery ; the very name of discipline was a signal for revolt. The armies of Rome did not now consist of freemen who had voluntarily chosen a military life, or who, in obedience to the laws, served for a term of years ; but of mercenaries collected from the provinces, or Barbarians bribed into the service, as more able to undergo the fatigues of war. Her soldiers were no longer citizens armed in defence of their country ; they were its oppressors ; they were licensed robbers, insatiably eager for pillage.

To prevent the continual treasons of the soldiery, particularly of the prætorian bands, the emperors associated with themselves, in the supreme power, their sons, their brothers, or such persons as they could trust ; and every emperor after Dioclesian, elected a Cæsar, or successor, whose co-operation was required by the magnitude of the empire. They likewise subdivided, and consequently diminished the power of the prætorian præfects, who were the grand-viziers of their time, appointing four instead of two. By these means the imperial seat was rendered more secure ; the emperors were permitted to die in their beds ; manners were softened, and less blood was shed by ferocity ; but the state was wasted by an enormous expense, and a new species of oppression took place, no less disgraceful to humanity than the former massacres. The tyranny was transferred from the soldiery to the prince ; the cause and the mode were changed, but the effect was the same. Shut up within the walls of a palace, surrounded by flatterers and women, and sunk in the softness of eastern luxury, those masters of empire governed in secret by the dark and subtle artifices of despotism. Iniquitous judgments, under the form of justice, seemed only to set death at a distance, in order to make life more miserable, and existence more precarious. Nothing was said, all was insinuated ; every man of high reputation was accused; and the warrior and the politician daily saw themselves at the mercy of sycophants, who had neither ability to serve the state themselves, nor generosity to suffer others to serve it with honour[1].

The removal of the imperial court to Constantinople, to say nothing of the subsequent division of the empire into Eastern and Western, was a new blow to the grandeur of Rome, and likewise to its security: for the veteran legions, that guarded the banks of the Danube and the Rhine, were also removed to the East, in order to guard another frontier; and Italy, robbed of its wealth and inhabitants, sunk into a state of the most annihilating languor. Changed into a garden by an Asiatic pomp, and crowded with villas, now deserted by their voluptuous owners, this once fertile country was unable to maintain itself: and, when the crops of Sicily and Africa failed, the people breathed nothing but sedition.

The discontents occasioned by the removal of the imperial court were heightened by those of religion. Christianity had long been making progress in the empire; it now ascended the throne of the Cæsars. As the Christians had formerly been persecuted, they, in their turn, became persecutors. The gods of Rome were publicly insulted, their statues were broken, their votaries were harassed. Penal statutes were enacted against the ancient worship: the punishment of death was denounced against the sacrifices formerly ordained by law: the altar of Victory was overturned, the cross was exalted in its stead, and displayed in place of that triumphant eagle under which the world had been conquered[2]. The most dreadful hates and animosities arose. The Pagans accused the Christians of all their misfortunes; they rejoiced in the midst of the greatest calamities, as if the gods had come in person to take vengeance on the destroyers of their altars; while the Christians affirmed, that the remains of Paganism alone had drawn down the wrath of Omnipotence. Both parties were more occupied about their religious disputes than

---

[1] See Montesquieu's *Considérations sur les Causes de la Grandeur des Romains, et de leur Décadence*, chap. xv. xvi. xvii. and the authors there cited, especially Tacitus, Ammianus Marcellinus, and Zosimus.

[2] Four respectable deputations were successively voted to the imperial court, representing the grievances of the priesthood and the senate, and soliciting the restoration of the altar of Victory. The conduct of this important business was intrusted to Symmachus, a noble and eloquent orator, who thus makes Rome herself plead before the imperial tribunal in favour of the ancient worship: "These rites have repelled Hannibal from the city, and the Gauls from the Capitol. Were my grey hairs reserved for such intolerable disgrace? I am ignorant of the new system that I am required to adopt; but I am well assured, that the correction of old age is always an ungrateful and invidious office." Symmach. lib. x. epist. 54.

the common safety ; and, to complete the miseries of the unhappy people, the Christians became divided among themselves.   New sects sprang up ; new disputes took place ; new jealousies and antipathies raged ; and the same punishments were denounced against Heretics and Pagans.   An universal bigotry debased the minds of men.   In a grand assembly of the provinces, it was proposed, that, as there were three persons in the Trinity, there should be three emperors.   Sieges were raised, and cities lost, for the sake of a piece of rotten wood, or withered bone, supposed to have belonged to some saint or martyr.   The effeminacy of the age mingled itself with this infatuation ; and generals, more weak than humane, sat down to mourn the calamities of war, when they should intrepidly have led on their troops to battle[1].

The character of the people with whom the Romans had to contend, was the reverse of their own.   Those barbarians, as they were called, breathed nothing but war.   Their martial spirit was yet in its vigour.   They sought a milder climate, and lands more fertile than their forests and mountains : the sword was their right, and they exercised it without remorse, as the right of nature.   Barbarous they surely were, but they were superior to the people whom they attacked, in virtue as well as in valour.   Simple and severe in their manners, they were unacquainted with the name of luxury ; any thing was sufficient for their extreme frugality.   Hardened by exercise and toil, their bodies seemed inaccessible to disease or pain : they sported with danger, and met death with expressions of joy.   They were, at the same time, remarkable for their regard to the sanctity of the marriage bed, their generous hospitality, their detestation of treachery and falsehood.   They possessed many maxims of civil wisdom, and wanted only the culture of reason to conduct them to the true principles of social life[2].

What could the divided, effeminate, and now dastardly Romans, oppose to such a people ?   Nothing but fear and folly ; or, what was still more ignominious, treachery.   Soon convinced that the combat was unequal, they attempted to appease the invaders by money ; but that peace could not be of long continuance which put those who sold it in a better condition to sell another.   Force is seldom just.   These voluntary contributions

---

[1] Montesq. *Considérat.* &c. chap. xviii.—xxii.   See also Gibbon's *Hist. of the Decline and Fall of the Roman Empire*, vol. iii.—vi. and the authors there quoted.

[2] Tacit. *de Moribus Germ.*—Jornand. *de Reb. Get.*—" As in polished societies," says Ammianus Marcellinus, speaking of the Huns, " ease and tranquillity are courted, they delight in war and dangers.   He who falls in battle is reckoned happy ; while they who die of old age or disease are deemed infamous."   *Hist.* lib. xxxi.

were changed into a tribute, which was demanded as a right ; and war was denounced when it was refused, or fell short of the customary sum. Tributes were multiplied upon tributes, till the empire was drained of its treasure. Another expedient was then adopted : large bodies of the Barbarians were taken into pay, and opposed to other Barbarians. This mode of defence, so contrary to the practice of the first Romans, answered for the moment, but terminated in ruin : those auxiliaries proved the most dangerous enemies to the empire. Already acquainted with the luxuries, the wealth, and the weakness of the Romans, they turned their arms against their masters, inviting their countrymen to come and share with them in the spoils of a people unworthy of so many accommodations. They had likewise become acquainted with what little military skill yet remained among the Romans ; and that, superadded to their natural intrepidity, rendered them irresistible. A third expedient, yet more unworthy of the Roman name, was practised :—assassination was employed by the emperors against those princes or leaders whose arms they feared ; it was even concealed beneath the mask of friendship, and perpetrated under the roof of hospitality—in the convivial hour, and at the festive board[1] !

This diabolical practice, the want of faith, and other unmanly vices of the Romans, not only account for the subversion of their empire, but also for many of the cruelties of the conquerors. Inflamed with the passion of revenge, no less than with the thirst of conquest and the lust of plunder, the inflexible and high spirited, though naturally generous Barbarians, were equally deaf to the offers of treaty and the voice of supplication. Wherever they marched, their route was marked with blood. The most fertile and populous provinces were converted into deserts. Italy was often pillaged, and the metropolis itself did not escape the licentiousness of outrage. New invaders, from regions more remote and barbarous, drove out or exterminated the former colonists : and Europe was successively ravaged, till the countries which had poured forth their myriads were drained of people, and the sword of slaughter was tired of destroying.

The overwhelming progress of the Barbarians soon diffused its powerful effects over Europe. In the course of the fifth century, the Visigoths took possession of Spain ; the Franks, of Gaul ; the Saxons, of the Roman provinces in South Britain ; the Huns, of Pannonia ; the Ostrogoths, of Italy and the adjacent

---

[1] Montesquieu and Gibbon, ubi supra.

provinces. New governments, laws, languages; new manners, customs, dresses; new names of men and of countries prevailed; and an almost total change took place in the state of Europe[1].

How far this change ought to be lamented is not now a point of great dispute. The human species was reduced to such a degree of debasement by the pressure of Roman despotism, that we cannot be displeased at any means, however violent, which removed or lightened the load. But we cannot help lamenting, at the same time, that this revolution was the work of nations so little enlightened by science or polished by civilization; for the Roman laws, though corrupted, were in general the best that human wisdom had framed: and the Roman arts and literature, though they had greatly declined, were still superior to any thing found among rude nations, or which those who spurned them produced for many ages.

The contempt of the Barbarians for the Roman improvements must not, however, be ascribed wholly to their ignorance, nor the suddenness of the revolution to their desolating fury; the manners of the conquered must come in for a share. Had the Romans not been in the lowest state of national degeneracy, they might surely have civilized their conquerors; had they retained any of the virtues of men among them, they might have continued under the government of their own laws. Many of the Gothic leaders were endowed with great abilities, and some were acquainted both with the. policy and literature of the Romans; but they were justly afraid of the contagious influence of Roman example, and therefore avoided every thing allied to that name, whether hurtful or beneficial[2]. They erected a cottage in the neighbourhood of a palace, breaking down the stately building, and burying in its ruins the finest works of human ingenuity; they ate out of vessels of wood, and made the vanquished be served in vessels of silver; they hunted the bear on the voluptuous parterre, the trim garden, and expensive pleasure-ground, where effeminacy was wont to saunter, or indolence to loll; and they pastured their herds where they might have

---

[1] A similar change was soon to occur in the state of Asia, a considerable part of which was still subject to the emperors of Constantinople. These princes, though gradually robbed of their Asiatic provinces by the followers of Mohammed, continued to preserve in the East (as we shall have occasion to see) an image of Roman greatness, long after Rome had been sacked by the Barbarians, and the Roman dominion finally extinguished in the West. The Roman provinces in Africa were already overrun by the Vandals, who had spread desolation with fire and sword.

[2] " When we would brand an enemy," says an enlightened Barbarian, " with disgraceful and contumelious appellations, we call him a *Roman*; a name which comprehends whatever is base, cowardly, avaricious, luxurious,—in a word, falsehood, and all other vices."—Luitprand. *Legat*. ap. Murat. vol. ii.

raised a luxuriant harvest. They prohibited their children from acquiring a knowledge of literature, and of the elegant arts, because they concluded, from the dastardly behaviour of the Romans, that learning tends to enervate the mind, and that he who has trembled under the rod of a pedagogue will never dare to meet a sword with an undaunted eye[1]. Upon the same principles they rejected the Roman jurisprudence. It reserved nothing to the vengeance of man: they, therefore, not unphilosophically, thought that it would rob him of his active powers. Nor could they conceive how the person injured could rest satisfied, but by pouring out his fury upon the author of the injustice. Hence arose all those judicial combats, and private wars, which for many ages desolated Europe.

In what manner light sprang from this darkness, order from this confusion, and taste from this barbarism, we shall have occasion to observe in the course of the history. We shall find that genius and magnificence displayed themselves in a new mode, which prevailed for a time, and was exploded: that the sons, at length, idolized that literature which their fathers had proscribed, and wept over the ruins of those sculptures, paintings, buildings, which they could not restore; digging from dunghills, and the dust of ages, the models of their future imitation, and enervating themselves with the same arts which had enervated the Romans.

In the mean time, we must take a view of the system of policy and legislation established by the Barbarians.

LETTER II.

Of the System of Policy and Legislation established by the Barbarians in the Provinces of the Roman Empire.

THE ancient Germans, Scandinavians, and other nations of Europe, had a certain degree of conformity in their government, manners, and opinions. The same leading character was also observable among the Goths and Vandals who dismembered the Roman empire. Alike distinguished by a love of war and of liberty, by a persuasion that force only constitutes right, and that victory is an infallible proof of justice, they were equally bold in attacking their enemies, and in resisting the absolute domination of any one man. They were free, even in a state of

[1] Procop. *Bell. Goth.* lib. i.

submission.   Their primitive government was a kind of military democracy, under a general or chieftain, who had commonly the title of king.   Matters of little consequence were determined by the principal men ; but the whole community assembled to deliberate on national objects.   The authority of their kings or generals, who owed their eminence entirely to their military talents, and held it by no other claim, was extremely limited ; it consisted rather in the privilege of advising, than in the power of commanding.   Every individual was at liberty to choose whether he would engage in any warlike enterprise.   They therefore followed the chieftain who led them forth in quest of new settlements, from inclination, not control[1], as volunteers who offered to accompany him, not as soldiers whom he could order to march ; and they considered their conquests as common property, in which all had a right to share, as all had contributed to procure them ; nor was any obligation whatever entailed on the possessors of land thus acquired.   Every one was the lord of his own little territory.

Some new arrangements, however, became expedient, when these conquerors had settled in the Roman provinces, where their acquisitions were to be maintained, not only against the ancient inhabitants, but also against the inroads of new invaders. They then saw the necessity of forming a closer union, and of relinquishing some of their private rights for public safety. They continued, therefore, to acknowledge the general who had led them to victory ; he was considered as the head of the colony ; he had the largest portion of the conquered lands ; while every warrior, on receiving a share according to his military rank, tacitly bound himself to appear against the enemies of the community[2].

This new division of property, and the obligations consequent upon it, gave rise to a species of government distinguished by the name of the FEUDAL SYSTEM. The idea of a feudal kingdom was borrowed from that of a military establishment. The victorious army, cantoned in the country which it had seized, continued arranged under its proper officers, who were ordered to hold themselves in readiness to assemble whenever occasion should require their united operations or counsels.

But this system of policy, apparently so well calculated for national defence or conquest, did not sufficiently provide for the

---

[1] Tacit. *de Moribus German.* cap. xi.—xlvi.—Amm. Marcel. lib. xxxi.—Pris. *Rhet.* ap. Byz. Script. vol. i.
[2] Du Cange, *Gloss.* voc. *Miles et Alodis.*

interior order and tranquillity of the state. The bond of political union was feeble; the sources of dissension were many, and corruption was interwoven with the very frame of the constitution. The new partition of the conquered lands, which were chiefly swallowed up by the great officers, gave the few a dangerous ascendency over the many. The king or general, by his superior allotment, had it amply in his power to reward past services, or attach new followers for the purpose of future wars. With this view, he parcelled out his lands, binding those on whom he bestowed them to attend him in all his military enterprises, under the penalty of forfeiture. The nobles, or great officers, followed his example, annexing the same conditions to their benefices or grants of land, and appearing at the head of their numerous vassals, like so many independent princes, whenever their pride was wounded or their property injured. They disputed the claims of the sovereign; they withdrew their attendance, or turned their arms against him[1]. A strong barrier was thus formed against a general despotism in the state; but the nobles themselves, by means of their warlike retainers, were the tyrants of every inferior district, holding the people in servitude, and preventing any regular administration of justice, every one claiming that prerogative within his own domain. Nor was this the only privilege usurped by those haughty chieftains; they also extorted from the crown the right of coining money in their own names, and of carrying on war against their private enemies[2].

In consequence of these encroachments on the royal prerogative, the powerful vassals of the crown obtained grants during life, and afterwards others including their heirs, of such lands as they had originally enjoyed only during pleasure; and they appropriated to themselves titles of honour, as well as offices of power and of trust, which became hereditary in many families. The ties which connected the principal members of the constitution with its head were dissolved; almost all ideas of political subjection were lost, and little appearance of feudal subordination remained. The nobility openly aspired at independence; they scorned to consider themselves as subjects; and a kingdom, considerable in name and extent, was often a mere shadow of monarchy, and really consisted of as many separate principalities as it contained baronies. A variety of feuds and jealousies subsisted among the barons, and gave rise to very frequent wars.

---

[1] Montesquieu, *L'Esprit des Loix*, lib. xxx. xxxi.
[2] Montesquieu, ubi supra.—Robertson's Introd. *Hist. Charles V.*—Hume's *Hist. Eng.* Append. ii.

Hence every country in Europe, wasted or kept in continual alarm by these internal hostilities, was filled with castles and places of strength, in order to protect the inhabitants from the fury of their fellow-subjects.

Kingdoms so divided, and torn by domestic broils, were little capable of any foreign effort. The wars of Europe, therefore, during several centuries, as we shall have occasion to see, resembled more the wild and desultory incursions of pirates, or banditti, than the regular and concerted operations of national force. Happily, however, for posterity, the state of every kingdom was nearly the same; otherwise all must have fallen a prey to one. The independent spirit of the North might have been extinguished for ever, and the present harmonious system of European policy, which so gloriously struggled from the chaos of anarchy, would have sunk in eternal night.

The particular manner in which the Barbarians conducted their judicial proceedings, when they first settled in the provinces of the Roman empire, cannot now be ascertained; but their form of government, their manners, and a variety of other circumstances, lead us to believe that it was nearly the same with that which prevailed in their original countries, where the authority of the magistrate was so limited, and the independence of individuals so great, that they seldom admitted any umpire but the sword[1].

Our most ancient historical records justify this opinion: they represent the exercise of justice in all the kingdoms of Europe, and the ideas of men with respect to equity, as little different from those which prevailed in a state of nature, and deform the first stages of society in every country. Resentment was almost the sole motive for prosecuting crimes, and the gratification of that passion, more than any view to the prosperity and good order of society, was the end, and also the rule, in punishing them. He that suffered the wrong was the only person who had a right to pursue the aggressor—to demand, or remit the punishment; and he might accept a compensation for any offence, how heinous soever. The prosecution of criminals in the name and by the authority of the community, in order to deter others from violating the laws, now justly deemed the great object of legislation, was a maxim of jurisprudence then little understood in theory, and still less regarded in practice. The civil and criminal judges could, in most cases, do no more than appoint the

---

[1] Ferguson's *Essay on Civil Society*, part. ii.

lists, and leave the parties to decide their cause by the sword. Fierce and haughty nobles, unfriendly to the restraints of law, considered it as infamous to give up to another the right of determining what reparation they should accept, or with what vengeance they should rest satisfied; they scorned to appeal to any tribunal but their own right arm. And if men of inferior condition sometimes submitted to award or arbitration, it was only to that of the leader whose courage they respected, and whom in the field they had been accustomed to obey[1]. Hence every chieftain became the judge of his tribe in peace, as well as its general in war. Of the pernicious effects of this power upon government and manners, and the absurd modes of trial established before its abolition, we shall have frequent occasion to take notice in the history of the modern kingdoms.

The feudal system, however, with all its imperfections, and the disorders to which it gave birth, was by no means so debasing to humanity as the uniform pressure of Roman despotism. Very different from that dead calm which accompanies peaceful slavery, and in which every faculty of the soul sinks into a kind of somnolency, it kept the minds of men in continual ferment, and their hearts in agitation. If animosities were keen, friendships also were warm. The commonalty were unfortunately degraded to the condition of slaves, but the nobility were exalted to the rank of princes. The gentry were their associates, and the king, without the form of compact, was in reality but chief magistrate, or head of the community, and could literally do no WRONG; or none, at least, with impunity.

LETTER III.

Of the Rise of the French Monarchy, and its Progress under the Kings of the First Race.

IN history, as in all other sciences, it is necessary to affix certain limits to our inquiries, if we would proceed with certainty; and, where utility more than curiosity is our object, we must even

---

[1] This subject has been finely illustrated by Dr. Robertson (Introd. *Hist. Charles V.*), and by the president Montesquieu (*L'Esprit des Loix*, lib. xviii.—xxxi), who has written a philosophical commentary on the *Laws of the Barbarians*. It has also been treated, with much learning and ingenuity, by Dr. Stuart in his *View of Society*, and by Mr. Gibbon in his *History of the Decline and Fall of the Roman Empire*, chap. xxxviii.

contract these boundaries.   We must not only confine ourselves to those periods where truth can be ascertained, but to those events chiefly which were followed by some civil or political consequence, which produced some alteration in the government or the manners of the people ; and, even of such events, we should be more particularly attentive to those which continue to operate upon our present civil or political system.

In these few words, my dear son, to avoid egotism, I have indirectly given you an account of the manner in which I mean to conduct that *History of Modern Europe* which is intended for your instruction.   The first epochs of modern, as well as ancient history, are involved in fable ; and the transactions of the immediately succeeding periods are handed down to us in barren chronicles, which convey no idea of the characters of the agents, and consequently are destitute alike of instruction and amusement ; while the events of later ages are related with a copiousness so profuse and undistinguishing, that a selection becomes absolutely necessary for such as are unwilling to employ a long course of years in acquiring a knowledge of past transactions.   And, as I would rather have you acquainted with one living than with ten dead statesmen or heroes, I shall be as concise in my narration as is consistent with perspicuity, and as select in my matter as information will allow ; yet always taking care to omit no anecdote which can throw light on the history of the human heart, nor any circumstance that marks the progress of civil society.

Modern History is of little importance before the time of Charle-magne ; and a late celebrated writer has fixed upon the coronation of that prince at Rome, in the year 800, as the proper æra of its commencement.   But for the sake of order, as well as to gratify the natural desire of becoming acquainted with the origin of nations, I shall give you a short sketch of the state of Modern Europe previous to that æra.

The French monarchy first claims our notice : not only on account of its antiquity, but because of its early and continued importance. The Roman power in Gaul had long been declining, when the Franks, a confederation of Germanic tribes, crossed the Rhine, with views of conquest and settlement.   They are said to have founded a kingdom on the Gallic frontiers, under Pharamond ; but of the acts of this prince we have no certain knowledge, and even his existence has been doubted.   With regard to the reign of Clodion there is less doubt ; and he appears to have extended his dominion to the banks of the Somme.

2

Dying in the year 448, he was succeeded by Merovée, who had a share in the great victory obtained over Attila the Hun, on the plains of Châlons. Childeric, though a debauched prince, acquired new territories; and his son Clovis established that kingdom to which he gave the name of *France*, or *the Land of Free Men*. How ill applied in later times!

Clovis, in early life, displayed both valour and prudence. His age did not exceed nineteen years when he crushed the efforts of Syagrius, his Roman competitor: and various circumstances conspired to his farther aggrandizement. The Gauls hated the dominion of the Romans, and were strongly attached to Christianity; Clovis gained on their piety, by favouring their bishops: and his marriage with Clotilda, a Christian princess, induced them to hope that he would speedily embrace their religion. The attachment of his countrymen to their ancient worship was the sole objection: the pious exhortations of the queen had some effect; and the king, having vanquished the Allemanni at Tolbiac, near Cologne, after an obstinate engagement, politically ascribed that victory to the God of Clotilda, whom he said he had invoked at the time of the battle, under a promise of becoming a Christian, if his exertions should be crowned with success. He was A. D. 496. accordingly baptized by St. Remigius, bishop of Rheims; and almost the whole of his subjects followed his example[1].

This was a grand circumstance in favour of Clovis; and he did not fail to take advantage of it. The Gauls were zealous Catholics: but the Arian creed was followed by the Visigoths, who occupied the country between the Loire and the Pyrenées, and also by the Burgundians, who had seized some of the eastern and southern provinces of the Gallic continent. Clotilda herself was a Catholic, though, being a Burgundian, she had been nursed in the bosom of Arianism: and Clovis overflowed with zeal for her faith, when he found that it would second his ambitious views. Under colour of religion, he made war upon Alaric, king of the A. D. 507. Visigoths: the Gallic clergy favoured his pretensions: and the battle of Vouillé, in which that prince was vanquished

[1] *Gest. Franc.* cap. xv.—Greg. Turon. lib. ii. cap. 31.—Of the miracles said to have been wrought on the conversion of Clovis, the author of this work says nothing, as he would not wish to foster pious credulity; but the lovers of the marvellous will find sufficient food for their passion in Hincmar (*Vit. St. Remig.*): It may not, however, be improper to observe, that Clovis, when warmed with the eloquence of the bishop of Rheims, in describing the passion and death of Christ, started up, and, seizing his spear, violently exclaimed, " Had I been there with my valiant Franks, I would have redressed his wrongs!" Fredegarii *Epitom.* cap. xxi.

and slain, added to the kingdom of France a considerable territory to the southward of the Loire [1].

But Clovis, instead of enjoying his good fortune with dignity, disgraced the latter part of his reign by perfidies and cruelties towards the princes of his house, whom he extirpated.   He died at the age of forty-five years, after endeavouring to atone for his crimes by building and endowing churches and monasteries, and assembling a council at Orleans for the regulation of church discipline [2].

The death of Clovis was a severe blow to the grandeur of the French monarchy.   He left four sons, who divided his Nov. extensive dominions among them.   Thierry, the eldest, 511. had the largest share : he was king of Austrasia, which not only comprehended the north-eastern part of France, but included the German conquests of Clovis : Metz was his capital.   Clodomir was king of Orléans, Childebert of Paris, and Clotaire of Soissons. This division of the empire of the Franks, into four independent kingdoms, not only weakened its force, but gave rise to endless broils.   The brothers became enemies whenever their interests jarred : and the most dreadful barbarities were the consequence of their dissensions.

The experience of these evils, however, did not prevent a similar division from taking place after the death of Clotaire, the sole successor of his brothers and nephews.   His four sons divided the four kingdoms by lot [3]. That of Paris fell to Caribert : Soissons A. D. to Chilperic ; Austrasia to Sigebert ; and Orléans to 561. Gontran, in whose lot was also included the Burgundian realm, which had been conquered by the united forces of Childebert and Clotaire.   This new division was followed by consequences still more fatal than the former.   Two queens, who might rather be called furies than women, sacrificed every thing to their bloody ambition—Brunechilda, or Brunehault, princess of Spain, wife to Sigebert, and Fredegonda, first concubine, and afterwards wife to Chilperic.   Their mutual hatred, conjoined with their influence over their husbands, produced a series of crimes, equally ruinous to the royal family and the people.

After the murder of a multitude of princes, and many years of civil war, carried on with the most vindictive spirit, and accompanied with every form of treachery and cruelty, Clotaire II.,

[1] Greg. Tur. lib. ii. cap. 37.
[2] Id. Auct. lib. ii. cap. 40—43.
[3] Id. lib. iv. cap. 22.—Gest. Franc. cap. xxix.

A. D. son of Chilperic and Fredegonda, was left sole king
613. of France[1]. He re-established tranquillity, and gained
the hearts of his people by his justice and generosity; and he
attached the nobles to him by augmenting their consequence.
He committed the government of the provinces of Austrasia
and Burgundy to the Mayors of the Palace, as they were called;
a kind of viceroys, who, daily acquiring power, at last made their
way to the throne.

The vices of Dagobert, the son of Clotaire; the taxes with
which he loaded the people, to furnish his debauches, or to atone
for them, according to the custom of those times, by pious pro-
fusions, weakened the royal authority, at the same time that they
debased it. His two sons, Sigebert II. and Clovis II., were only
the founders of monasteries. They were ciphers in their kingdoms; the mayors were the actual sovereigns.

On the death of Sigebert, Grimoald, mayor of Austrasia,
A. D. placed his own son upon the throne of that kingdom.
654. The usurper was deposed; but the seducing example
remained as a lure to future ambition. The succeeding princes
were as weak as their predecessors; and Pepin d'Heristal, duke
of Austrasia, governed France for twenty-eight years, under the
title of mayor, with great prudence and fortitude. The kings
were no more than decorated pageants, occasionally shown to the
people. The appellation of *fainéans*, which was given to them,
aptly expresses their stupid inactivity.

After the death of Pepin, who, by restoring national assemblies
A. D. (which the despotism of former mayors had abolished), by
714. turning the restless impetuosity of the French against
foreign enemies, and other wise measures, had quietly enjoyed
the supreme power—his authority passed into the hands of his
widow Plectrude, whose grandson, yet an infant, was created
mayor. So high was the veneration of the French for the memory of that great man!—But the government of a woman was
ill suited to those turbulent times, though the insignificant kings
were content to live under the guardianship of a child. Charles
Martel, natural son of Pepin, was suspected of ambitious views
by Plectrude, and imprisoned. He found means, however, to
make his escape, and was received by the Austrasians as their
deliverer. His superior talents soon exalted him to the same
degree of power which his father had enjoyed, and he was no less
worthy of it. By a signal victory, obtained near Tours in 733,

---

[1] Fredeg. cap. xliii.

he saved France from the sword of the Saracens, who had already subjected Spain: and he kept all the neighbouring nations in awe by his wise and vigorous administration; yet he would not assume any higher appellation than that of Duke of France, conscious that the title of King could add nothing to his power. But his son Pepin, less modest, or more vain, assumed the sovereignty in name as well as reality, excluding for ever the A. D. descendants of Clovis, or the Merovingian race, from the 752. throne of France [1].

The circumstances of that revolution I shall soon have occasion to relate.   At present we must take a view of the other states of Europe.

LETTER IV.

Of the Affairs of Spain under the Dominion of the Visigoths, and under the Moors, till the Reign of Abdarrahman.

SPAIN, my dear Philip, next merits your attention, as the second great kingdom on this side of the Alps.   Soon after the Visigoths had founded their monarchy in that Roman province, already over-run by the Vandals and the Suevi, the clergy A. D. became possessed of more power than the prince.   So 467. early was the tyranny of the church in Spain! Almost all causes, both civil and ecclesiastical, were referred to the bishops; they even decided in their councils the most weighty affairs of the nation.   With the nobles, among whom they held the first rank, they often disposed of the crown, which was more elective than hereditary [2].   The kingdom was one theatre of revolutions and crimes.   The number of kings assassinated fills the soul with horror.   The Barbarians, after their establishment, contracted new vices: their ferocity became bloody.   What crimes did not bigotry alone produce!

In order to make you fully sensible of this, as well as inform you of all that is necessary to be known in the history of the Visigoths in Spain, I need only mention the principal reigns.

Leovigild, who died in 586, and who is so much celebrated for his victories over the Suevi, whom he entirely subdued, put to death his son Hermenegild, because he had embraced the Catholic

---

[1] Adon. *Chron.*—*Annal. Metens.*
[2] Geddes's *Tracts*, vol. ii.   See also Saavedra, *Corona Gothica.*

faith, he himself being an Arian. Recared, however, his other son, and successor, abjured Arianism. The Arians were persecuted in their turn. The spirit of persecution daily increased. Sisebut, a prince in other respects wise, and whose valour dispossessed the Greek emperors of what territory they had con-A. D. tinued to hold on the Spanish coasts, obliged the Jews, on 612. pain of death, to receive baptism. In the reign of this monarch, the Visigothic empire was at its height, comprehending not only Spain, but also some neighbouring provinces of Gaul, and part of Mauritania. Chintila, a subsequent king, banished all the Jews; and in an assembly of divines, convoked during his reign, it was declared that no prince should ascend the Spanish throne without swearing to enforce all the laws enacted against that unfortunate people. Under the reign of Recesuint, the election of a king was reserved by a council to the bishops, and to the palatines, or principal officers of the crown. Thus the Spanish nobility lost one of their most essential rights.

Wamba, who defeated the Saracens in an attempt upon Spain, A. D. was deprived of the crown, because he had been clothed 680. in the habit of a *penitent*, while labouring under the influence of poison, administered by the ambitious Erviga! This stroke of priestcraft, the first of the kind that we observe in history, shows at a distance what might be expected from clerical finesse. A council adjudged the throne to Erviga; and another council, holden during his reign, prohibited the kings, under penalty of damnation, from marrying a king's widow. This canon is a sufficient proof of the spirit of legislation which at that time prevailed in Spain. The debauchery, cruelty, and impiety of Witiza, whose wickedness knew no bounds, occasioned a civil war in 710. Roderic, or Roderigo, dethroned this prince, and was himself dethroned by a people whom nothing could withstand [1].

The Mohammedan religion was already established in many countries. Mohammed, who erected at Mecca a spiritual and temporal monarchy, had died in 632; and his countrymen, the Arabs or Saracens, soon after overran great part of Asia, and all that part of Africa which was under the Roman dominion. Animated by the most violent spirit of fanaticism, their valour was altogether irresistible. The Koran promised heaven and eternal sensuality to such as fell in battle, and the conquerors always tendered

---

[1] Ferreras, *Hist. Hisp.* vol. ii.—Mariana *de Rebus Hispaniæ*, lib. vi.—Greg. Turon. lib. vi.

liberty and protection to those who embraced their superstition. They threatened the whole world with subjection. Count Julian, whose daughter king Roderic had dishonoured, invited them, it is said, to land in Spain. Nor can this circumstance be deemed improbable, if we consider the character of the times, revolutions being then more frequently occasioned by the private vices of princes than by any other cause.

The Saracens, already masters of Mauritania, now Barbary (a name derived from the *Berbers*, the original inhabitants), made a descent upon Spain; and by the decisive battle of Xeres, Nov. put an end to the empire of the Visigoths[1]. Mousa, 714. viceroy of Africa, under the khalif Walid, came over to finish the conquest. According to the prudent policy of the Mohammedans (the only enthusiasts who ever united the spirit of toleration with a zeal for making proselytes), he offered the inhabitants their religion and laws, on condition that they should pay to him the same subsidy which they had paid to their former sovereigns; and such as embraced the religion of the conquerors were entitled to all their privileges. Most cities submitted without resistance to the bold invader: others he reduced by force, burning and pillaging them. Oppas, archbishop of Seville, and uncle to the children of Witiza, traitorously joined the Saracens, and sacrificed his country and his religion to his hatred against Roderic. But Pelagius, a prince of the royal blood, remained firm in his faith and duty; and, when he could no longer keep the field against the Infidels, he retired to the mountains of Asturias, followed by a number of faithful adherents. A.D. There he founded a Christian kingdom, which he defended 717. by his valour, and transmitted to his posterity[2].

Unwilling to confine their ambition within the limits of the Pyrenées, the conquerors of Spain invaded France. Though baffled, they renewed their irruptions; and their leader Abdarrahman penetrated to the banks of the Loire. Charles Martel, as you have already seen, put a stop to their career by a memorable battle; and, if we believe the historians of those times, they lost in this action above three hundred thousand men. But such exaggerations are fit only for romance.

Spain was at first very miserable under the dominion of the Moors. The governors, being dependent on the viceroy of

[1] Rod. Tolet. *Hist. Arab. Hist. de l'Afrique et de l'Espagne, sous la Domination des Arabes, par* Cardonne, tome i.
[2] Mariana, lib. vi. et vii.—Ferreras, vol. ii.

Africa, who allowed them to continue but a short time in their government, were more busy in fleecing the Spanish nation than in the administration of justice or the preservation of good order. Civil wars arose among the Moslems themselves; and the khalifs or successors of the pseudo prophet, who had made Damascus the seat of their court, were unable to quell those disorders. The competitions for the khalifate, as might be expected, even favoured the views of the rebels. At length that august dignity, which included both the highest regal and sacer-

A.D. 750.
dotal eminence, passed from the family of the Ommiades to that of the Abassides. This revolution, which was bloody, gave birth to another, truly advantageous to Spain, but injurious to the Christian faith.

A.D. 757.
Abdarrahman, called also Al-Mansour, a prince of the blood royal, who escaped in the massacre of the Ommiades, founded in Spain an independent kingdom, consisting of all those provinces which had been subject to the khalifs[1]. He fixed his residence at Cordova, which became the seat of the arts, of magnificence, luxury, and pleasure. Without persecuting the Christians, he was able, by his artful policy, almost to extinguish Christianity in his dominions, by depriving the bishops of their dioceses, by reserving all honours and offices for the followers of his prophet, and by promoting intermarriages between the Christians and the Moslems. No prince in Europe, of that age, was equal to Abdarrahman in wisdom; nor did any people surpass the Arabs in whatever tends to the aggrandisement of the human soul. Lately enemies to the sciences, they now cultivated them with success, and enjoyed a considerable share both of learning and politeness, while the rest of mankind were sunk in ignorance and barbarism.

I shall afterward have occasion to be more particular on this subject. In the mean time, we must take a survey of Italy, the Grecian empire, and France, from the time of Charles Martel to that of Charle-magne.

---

[1] Abulfeda's *Moslemic Annals.*

LETTER V.

Of the Dominion of the Ostrogoths in Italy and the Affairs of the Lombards till the Reign of Luitprand.

ITALY experienced a variety of fortunes after it lost its ancient masters, before it fell into the hands of Charle-magne. It was first conquered by the Heruli, a people from the extremity A.D. of the Euxine or Black Sea, who held it only a short 476. time, being expelled by the Ostrogoths under Theodoric. Several of the Ostrogothic kings of Italy were princes of great A.D. prudence and humanity. They allowed the Italians (or 493. Romans, as they still affected to be called) to retain their possessions, their laws, their religion, their own government, and their own magistrates, reserving only to the Goths the principal military employments. They acknowledged the emperors of Constantinople as their superiors in rank, but not in jurisdiction. Ravenna was the seat of their court, and in real magnificence vied with ancient Rome, as their equitable administration did with the reigns of Trajan and Antoninus[1]. They were at last subdued by Belisarius and Narses, the generals of Justinian, who having recovered Africa from the Vandals, had the A.D. pleasure of uniting Italy once more to the Eastern or 553. Greek empire.

Soon after the extinction of the Ostrogothic realm, a great part of Italy was seized by Alboin, king of the Lombards, A.D. or Longobards, a Gothic nation. He and his successors 568. made Pavia the place of their residence. The government of Italy was now considerably changed. Alboin established the feudal policy in those countries which he had conquered, settling the principal officers of the army, with the ducal title, in the chief cities of every province. A similar kind of government prevailed in that part of Italy which remained subject to the emperors of Constantinople: the exarch, or supreme governor,

---

[1] Procop. *Bell. Goth.*—Cassiodor. lib. viii.—The lenity of the Ostrogoths, on their settling in Italy, may be attributed to two causes—partly that polish which their manners may be supposed to have received during their intercourse with the Romans, whom they had long served as auxiliaries against the Huns and other barbarous nations; partly to the character of Theodoric the Gothic conqueror, who, having been educated at Constantinople, and initiated in all the learning of the times, retained ever after a just admiration of the Roman laws and arts.

[It is very remarkable that the Goths, even before their intercourse with the Romans, far exceeded the Germanic tribes in knowledge and civilization.—*See Jornandes " De Rebus Geticis."*]

who resided at Ravenna, appointing the dukes or chief magistrates of the other cities, and removing them at pleasure. Even Rome itself was governed by a duke, the very name of the senate and consuls being abolished.

Alboin was one of the greatest princes of his time, and no less A.D. skilled in the science of reigning than in the art of war: 572. but he was slain by the treachery of his wife Rosamond, before he had leisure to perfect the government of his kingdom. Clephis, his successor, was an able, but a barbarous prince. His cruelties gave the Lombards such a disgust to regal power, that they resolved, after his death, to change their form of government; and for the space of twelve years they chose no other king, but lived subject to their dukes. These dukes had hitherto acknowledged the royal authority; but when the kingly power was abolished, each duke became sovereign of his own city and the neighbouring district[1].

The Lombards, during that interregnum, extended their conquests in Italy. But, when they were threatened by foreign enemies, they were sensible of the expediency of restoring their ancient form of government, and committing the management of the war to a single person. For this purpose the heads of the A.D. nation assembled, and with one voice called Autharis, 586. the son of Clephis, to the throne. This prince perfected that form of government which had been introduced by Alboin. Perceiving that the dukes, who had ruled their several districts like independent princes for so many years, were unwilling to part with their authority, he allowed them to continue in their governments, but reserved to himself the supreme jurisdiction. He obliged them to contribute a part of their revenues towards the support of his royal dignity, and take an oath that they would assist him to the utmost of their power in time of war[2]. After settling the government of his kingdom, he enacted several salutary laws for the preservation of tranquillity and good order. He was the first of the Lombard kings who embraced Christianity, and many of his subjects followed his example; but, as he leaned to the Arian system, like most of the Barbarian conquerors, whose simple minds could not comprehend the mysteries of the Trinity and Incarnation, many disputes arose between the Arian and Catholic bishops; for the Romans, or native Italians, were then as zealous Catholics as they are at this day.

Liberty of conscience, however, was allowed under all the

---

[1] Paul Diac. *de Gestis Longob*. lib. ii.   [2] Paul. Diac. lib. iii.

Lombard kings; and Rotharis, who surpassed all his predecessors in wisdom and valour, was so moderate in his principles,
and so indulgent to his people, that during his reign most cities
of Italy had two bishops, one Catholic, and the other Arian.
He was the first prince who gave written laws to the Lombards.
He summoned at Pavia a general diet of the nobles; and A.D.
such regulations as they approved he ordered to be 643.
digested into a code, and observed over all his dominions. His
military talents were not inferior to his civil merits. He greatly
extended the limits of his kingdom, and was so successful over
the imperial forces, that no future hostilities passed between
the exarchs and the kings of the Lombards, till the reign of
Luitprand.

But the eastern emperor Constans, before that time, landed
in Italy with a considerable army, in the hope of expel- A.D.
ling the Lombards and re-uniting their kingdom to his 663.
dominions. He at first gained some inconsiderable advantages;
but his army was afterward totally routed by Romuald, duke of
Benevento, whose father Grimoald had been elected king of the
Lombards.

Grimoald was a prudent prince, and in all respects worthy of
the dignity to which he had been raised. As soon as he A.D.
was free from the alarms of war, he applied himself wholly 668.
to the arts of peace. He reformed the laws of Rotharis, to
which the Italians as well as the Lombards now appealed from
choice. Influenced by the arguments of John, bishop of Bergamo, he renounced the tenets of Arius. His successors following his example, Arianism was at length relinquished by the
whole nation of the Lombards [1].

Luitprand gave strong proofs of his wisdom and valour from
the moment he ascended the throne: but his courage A.D.
sometimes bordered on rashness. Being informed that 712.
two of his attendants had conspired against his life, and only
waited an opportunity of executing their intent, he, in a private
conference, upbraided them with their guilt. Moved by such
heroic firmness, they threw themselves at his feet, as wretches
unworthy of mercy. The king, however, thought otherwise:
he not only pardoned them, but received them into favour and
confidence. Having thus won his domestic enemies by kindness,
and strengthened his interests abroad by marrying the daughter
of the duke of the Boiarii, Luitprand applied himself, in imita-

[1] Paul. Diac. lib. v.

tion of his two illustrious predecessors, Rotharis and Grimoald, to the formation of new laws. In one of these, his sagacity appears highly conspicuous. He blames " the ridiculous custom of trials by duel, in which we would force God to manifest his justice according to the caprice of men:" adding, that " he has only tolerated the abuse, because the Lombards are so much attached to it[1]."

But Luitprand's great qualities were in some measure shaded by his boundless ambition. Not satisfied with the extensive dominions left him by his predecessors, he formed the intention of making himself sole master of Italy; and an opportunity soon offered for attempting the execution of that enterprise.

Leo the Isaurian, then emperor of Constantinople, where theological disputes had long mingled with affairs of state, and where casuists were more common upon the throne than politicians, piously prohibited the worship of images; order-ing all the statues to be broken in pieces, and the paintings in the churches to be pulled down and burned. The populace, whose devotion did not extend beyond such objects— and the monks and secular priests, interested in supporting the mummery—were so highly provoked at this innovation, that they publicly revolted in many places. The emperor, however, took care to have his edict put in force in the East; and he commanded the exarch of Ravenna, and his other officers in the West, to see it as punctually obeyed in their governments. In obedience to that injunction, the exarch began to pull down the images in the churches and public places at Ravenna; a conduct which incensed the superstitious multitude to such a degree, that they openly declared they would rather renounce their allegiance to the emperor than the worship of images. They considered him as an abominable heretic, whom it was lawful to resist by force, and took arms for that purpose[2].

Luitprand, judging this the proper season to put his ambitious project in execution, quickly assembled his forces, and unexpectedly appeared before Ravenna; not doubting that the reduction of that important place would be speedily followed by the conquest of all the imperial dominions in Italy. The exarch, though not fully prepared for such an assault, defended the city with great courage; but finding that he could not long withstand so great a force, and despairing of relief, he privately retired. Luitprand, informed of this, made a vigorous attack,

A.D. 726.

---

[1] *Leges Longob. in Codice Lindenbrog.*   [2] Maimb. *Hist. Iconoclast.*

took the city by storm, and gave it up to be plundered by his soldiers, who found in it an immense booty, as it had been successively the seat of the western emperors, of the Gothic kings, and of the exarchs. Alarmed at the fate of Ravenna, most of the other cities in the exarchate surrendered without resistance [1]. Luitprand seemed, therefore, in a fair way to become master of all Italy. But that conquest neither he nor any of his successors could ever complete: and the attempt proved fatal to the kingdom of the Lombards.

A.D.
728.

LETTER VI.

Of the Pope's temporal Power, and the Affairs of Italy in general, the Empire of Constantinople, and the Kingdom of France, from the time of Charles Martel to that of Charle-magne.

THOUGH Rome was now governed by a duke, who depended on the exarch of Ravenna, the pope, or bishop, had the chief authority in that city. He was yet less conspicuous by his power than the respect which religion inspired for his see, and the confidence which was reposed in his character. St. Gregory, who died in 604, had negociated with princes upon matters of state, and his successors divided their attention between clerical and political pursuits. To free themselves from the dominion of the Greek emperors, without falling a prey to the kings of Italy, was the great object of these ambitious prelates. In order to accomplish this important purpose, they employed with success both religion and intrigue; and at last established a spiritual and temporal monarchy, which of all human institutions, perhaps, most merits the attention of man, whether we consider its nature, its progress, or its prodigious consequences.

Gregory II. had offended the emperor Leo, by opposing his edict against the worship of images: but he was more afraid of the growing power of the Lombards than of the emperor's threats; he therefore resolved to check the career of Luitprand. The only prince in Italy to whom he could have recourse, was Ursus, duke of Venice, the Venetians making already no contemptible figure. Not less alarmed than Gregory at the progress of so powerful a neighbour, Ursus and the Venetians pro-

[1] Paul. Diac. lib. vi.

mised to assist the exarch (who had fled to them for protection) with the whole strength of the republic. They accordingly fitted out a considerable fleet, while the exarch conducted an army by land, and retook Ravenna before Luitprand could march to its relief.

As Ravenna had been chiefly recovered by the interposition of Gregory, he hoped to be able to prevail on the emperor to revoke his edict against the worship of images in the West. Leo, however, sensible that the pope had been influenced on that occasion merely by his own interest, was only more provoked at his obstinacy, and resolved that the edict should be obeyed even in Rome itself. He even ordered the exarch Paul to procure the assassination of the pope, or send him in chains to Constantinople. But Gregory, far from being intimidated by the emperor's threats, solemnly excommunicated the exarch for attempting to put the imperial edict in execution, exhorting all the Italian cities to continue stedfast in the catholic faith. Luitprand, though highly incensed against Gregory, assisted him in his distress; and the populace, rising at Ravenna, murdered the exarch, and made great slaughter of the Iconoclasts, or image-breakers. The duke of Naples shared the same fate with Paul; and, as Leo still required that his favourite edict A.D. should be enforced at Rome, the people of that city, at 730. the instigation of Gregory, withdrew their allegiance from the Greek emperor[1]. Such was the rise of the pope's temporal power.

Informed of this revolt, and not doubting who was the author of it, the emperor levied a powerful army, to chastise the rebels, and take vengeance on the pope. Gregory, alarmed at these warlike preparations, looked round for some power on which he might depend for protection. The Lombards were possessed of sufficient force; but they were too near neighbours to be trusted: the Venetians, though zealous catholics, could not resist with effect the strength of the empire; and the Spanish peninsula was under the yoke of the Saracens. The French seemed the only people to whom it was advisable to apply for aid, as they were at once able to oppose the emperor, and enemies to his edict. France was then governed by Charles Martel, the greatest commander of his age, to whom Gregory sent a solemn embassy, entreating him to defend the Romans and the church against the attempts of Leo. The ambassadors were re-

---

[1] Anastas. *Vit. Greg. II.*—Maimb. *Hist. Iconoclast.*

ceived with extraordinary marks of honour : a treaty was A. D.
concluded[1]: and the French, glad to get any concern in 731.
the affairs of Italy, became the protectors of the church.

In the mean time considerable alterations were made by death.
Gregory II. did not live to see his negociation with France
finished. He was succeeded by Gregory III.; and, ten years
after, Leo was followed on the imperial throne by his son Constantine Copronymus, who not only renewed his father's edict
against the worship of images, but prohibited the invocation of
saints. This new edict confirmed the Romans in the resolution
they had taken of separating themselves entirely from the empire; more especially as, being now under the protection of
France, they had nothing to fear from Constantinople. They
accordingly drove out of their city such of the imperial officers
as had hitherto been suffered to continue in it, and thus abolished the very shadow of subjection to the emperor. A. D.
Soon after Leo, died Charles Martel, and also Gregory 741.
III. The next pope was Zachary, an active and enterprising
prelate, who, immediately after his election, visited Luitprand,
and obtained the restitution of the towns which had been
yielded to that prince as a ransom for Rome, when it was in
danger of falling into his hands[2].

Luitprand henceforth relinquished all ambitious A.D.
thoughts, dying in peace with the church and with men. 748.
Rachis, his successor, confirmed the treaty with the pope; but,
being afterwards inflamed with a thirst of conquest, he invaded
the Roman dukedom, and laid siege to Perugia. Trust- A. D.
ing to the influence of persuasion, Zachary repaired to 750.
the camp of Rachis, and so forcibly represented to him the punishment reserved for those who unjustly invade the property of
others, that the king not only raised the siege, but, being completely subdued by the eloquence of the pontiff, resigned his
crown, and retired to the monastery of Monte Cassino, pros-
trating himself first at Zachary's feet, and taking the habit of
St. Benedict[3].

While affairs were in this situation in Italy, Pepin, son of
Charles Martel, governed France in the character of mayor,
under Childeric III.; and being probably acquainted with the
sentiments of his holiness, proposed to Zachary a case of conscience. which had not hitherto been submitted to the bishop of
Rome. He desired to know, whether a prince incapable of

---

[1] Sigon. *Reg. Ital.*   [2] Paul. Diac. lib. vi.   [3] Paul. Diac. lib. vi.

governing, or a minister who ably supported the weight of royal
authority, ought to have the title of king.   Zachary decided in
favour of the minister; and the French clergy encouraged the
pretensions of Pepin, because he had restored the lands of which
Charles Martel had robbed them.   The nobles respected him,
because he was powerful and brave; and the people despised
the sluggard kings, whom they scarcely knew by name.   The
judgment of the pope, therefore, silenced every scruple.   Chil-
A. D. deric was deposed; or, more properly, degraded, for he
752.   could never be said to reign.   He was shut up in a monastery.   Pepin was raised to the throne; and Boniface, archbishop of Mentz, the famous apostle of the Germans, anointed
him solemnly at Soissons[1].

This ceremony of anointing, borrowed from the Jews, and
hitherto unknown to the French nation, or only used at the
baptism of Clovis, seemed to bestow on the king a kind of divine
character; and so far it was useful, by inspiring respect.   But,
as ignorance abases all things, the bishops soon imagined that
they could confer royalty by anointing princes—an opinion
which was followed by many pernicious consequences.   The
Eastern emperors had long been crowned by the patriarchs of
Constantinople; the popes, in like manner, crowned the emperors of the West.   Crowning and anointing were deemed
necessary to sovereignty.   A pious ceremony, it was imagined
or pretended, gave the church a power of disposing of kingdoms.

These observations, my dear Philip, you will find frequent
occasion to apply.   I offer them here, in order to awaken your
attention.   We must see things in their causes, to reason distinctly on their effects.

Success soon attended the crafty policy of the popes: the new
king of France repaid their favour with interest.   Astulphus,
king of the Lombards, less piously inclined than his brother
Rachis, thought only of conquest.   In imitation of Luitprand,
he resolved to make himself master of all Italy; and while the
emperor was engaged in a war with the Saracens and Bulgarians,
and in a still more hot and dangerous war against images, the
A. D. Lombards invaded the exarchate, took Ravenna, and
753.   subdued the whole province.

Ambition is only increased by accession of dominion.   Astulphus no sooner saw himself master of Ravenna and its ter-

---

[1] Sigon. *Reg. Ital.*

ritory, than he began to lay claim to the Roman dukedom, and to Rome itself. He urged the right of conquest. This, he alleged, entitled him to the same power over the city and its dukedom which the emperors, and also the exarchs, their viceroys, had formerly enjoyed, as he was now in possession of the whole exarchate. To enforce his demand, he led an army towards Rome, reducing many cities in its neighbourhood, and threatening to put the inhabitants to the sword, if they should refuse to acknowledge him as their sovereign. Stephen III., then pope, no less alarmed at the approach of so powerful a prince than at the severity of his message, endeavoured to appease him by a solemn embassy. But presents, prayers, and entreaties, were employed in vain; Astulphus wished to govern Rome.

Stephen now resolved to solicit the aid of France. Pepin, mindful of his obligations to Zachary, and now firmly seated on the throne of Clovis, readily promised his assistance, and sent two ambassadors to conduct the pope to Paris. Astulphus permitted him to pass; and a treaty favourable to the see of Rome was concluded. Pepin and his two sons, on this occasion, received from Stephen the honours of holy unction, and a grant of the title of Patrician[1]. Pepin endeavoured, before he commenced his expedition, to persuade Astulphus to restore what he had conquered, and thus prevent the effusion of Christian blood. But finding the king of the Lombards deaf to his entreaties, he crossed the Alps, and advanced to Pavia. Astulphus now, convinced of his danger, sued for peace, and obtained it on condition that he should deliver up to the pope, not to the emperor, all the places which he had taken. He consented: but instead of fulfilling his engagements, no sooner did he hear of the departure of Pepin, than he again rushed into the Roman territory, took several cities, and laid siege to the capital.

In this extremity, Stephen had recourse to his protector the king of France, writing to him those remarkable letters which are still extant, and in which he artfully introduces St. Peter, to whom a donation of the exarchate had been made in the late treaty, conjuring Pepin, his two sons, and the states of France, to come to his relief; promising them all good things, both in this world and the next, in case of compliance, and denouncing damnation as the consequence of a refusal[2]. Pepin, much affected by this eloquence, wild as it may seem, crossed

---

[1] Leonis Ostiensis, *Hist.* lib. i.   [2] Anastas. *Vit. Steph. III.*

the Alps a second time; and Astulphus again took refuge in Pavia.

The emperor, informed of the treaty, remonstrated by his ambassadors against it, and offered to pay the expenses of the war. But Pepin replied, that the exarchate lately belonged to the Lombards, who had acquired it by right of arms, as the Romans had originally done: and that the right of the Lombards was now in him, so that he could dispose of that territory as he thought proper. He had bestowed it, he said, on St. Peter, that the catholic faith might be preserved in its purity, free from the damnable heresies of the Greeks; and all the money in the world, he added, should never make him revoke that gift, which he was determined to maintain to the church with the last drop of his blood. In consequence of this resolution, the ambassadors were dismissed, without being suffered to reply. Pepin pressed the siege of Pavia; and Astulphus, finding himself unable to hold out, promised to fulfil the former agreement, giving hostages as a pledge of his fidelity, and putting the pope immediately in possession of Comachio, a place of great importance at that time.

Before Pepin returned to France, he renewed his donation to A.D. St. Peter, yielding to Stephen and his successors the 756. exarchate; Æmilia, now Romagna, and Pentapolis, now Marca d'Ancona, to be possessed by them for ever: the kings of France, as patricians or protectors of the Roman people, retaining only an ideal superiority, which was soon forgotten[1]. Thus was the sceptre added to the keys, the sovereignty to the priesthood; and thus were the popes enriched with the spoils of the Lombard kings and the Roman emperors.

Astulphus, soon after he had ratified his treaty with France, was killed by accident, when he was preparing to recover his conquests. Pepin continued to extend his sway and his renown; and, after having imposed tribute on the Saxons and driven the Saracens from Septimania, having exacted an oath of fidelity from the duke of Bavaria, and annexed Aquitaine to his crown, A.D. he died in the fifty-fourth year of his age, equally re-768. spected at home and abroad. He never affected absolute power, but referred all matters of importance to the national assemblies, of which he was the oracle. By the consent of the

---

[1] The nature of Pepin's donation has been disputed, and some writers have even denied that such a grant ever occurred: but, on comparing authorities, and observing the scope of history, the matter seems to have been nearly as represented in the text. The impertinences of Voltaire on this subject, under the form of reasoning, are too contemptible to deserve notice.

nobles, he divided his kingdom between his sons Charles and Carloman.

The reign of Charles, known by the name of Charle-magne or Charles the Great, introduces a new æra, and will furnish the subject of a future Letter. In the mean time, we must trace the settlement of other Barbarians, and the rise of another great kingdom.

LETTER VII.

Of Britain, from the time when it was relinquished by the Romans, to the End of the Saxon Heptarchy.

THE affairs of our own island, my dear son, now claim your attention. It was ultimately evacuated by the Romans about the year 420, after they had been masters of the southern and most fertile part of it above three centuries.

Never, perhaps, was the debasing influence of despotism so fully displayed as in its effect on our ancient countrymen. No people were ever more brave, none more jealous of liberty, than the Britons. With ordinary weapons, and little knowledge of military discipline, they struggled long with the Roman power, and were only subdued at last in consequence of their want of union. But, after a long course of tranquil submission, when the exigencies of the empire obliged the Romans to recall their legions from this island, and resign to the inhabitants their native rights, the degenerate South-Britons were incapable of prizing the gift. Conscious of their inability to protect themselves against their northern neighbours, and wanting resolution to attempt it, they would gladly have lived in security and slavery[1]. They, therefore, repeatedly had recourse to their conquerors: and the Romans, besides occasionally sending over a legion to the aid of the Britons, assisted them in repairing the rampart of Antoninus, which extended between the friths of Forth and

---

[1] Gild. *Hist.*—Bedæ *Hist. Eccles. Gentis Anglorum*, lib. i. Mr. Gibbon, whose historical scepticism is as well known as his theological incredulity, has attempted to controvert the degeneracy of the Britons under the Roman government. But facts will speak for themselves: these he has not been able to destroy. The Britons, who fled before their naked and barbarous neighbours, were surely inferior to those who had intrepidly contended with the Roman legions, under Julius Cæsar, and other great commanders.

Clyde. This wall was deemed by the Romans a necessary barrier against the Scots and Picts.

Much time has been spent in investigating the origin of the Scots and Picts, and warm disputes have arisen on the subject; the detail of which would serve no useful purpose.

The Picts no sooner heard of the final departure of the Romans, than they considered the whole British island as their own. One party crossed the frith of Forth, in boats made of A.D. leather, while another attacked with fury the Roman 421. wall, which the Britons soon abandoned, fleeing like timorous deer, and leaving their country a prey to the enemy. The Picts made dreadful havoc of the fugitives; and, meeting with no opposition, they ravaged the southern parts of the island with fire and sword. Famine followed with all its horrid train; and the mischiefs of pestilence were added.

When the South-Britons had long been harassed with these irruptions, they once more had recourse to Rome. They wrote A.D. to Ætius, then consul for the third time, that memorable 428. letter (entitled *the Groans of the Britons*) which paints their unhappy condition as strongly as it is possible for words: "We know not," said they, "even which way to flee. Chased by the Barbarians to the sea, and forced back by the sea upon the Barbarians, we have only the choice of two deaths: for we must either perish by the sword, or be swallowed up by the waves[1]." What answer they received is uncertain; but it is well known that they obtained no assistance, the empire being threatened by Attila, the most terrible enemy by whom it was ever invaded.

The Britons, however, amidst all their calamities, had one consolation; they had embraced Christianity: a religion which, above all others, teaches the endurance of misfortunes—which encourages its votaries to triumph in adversity, and inspires the soul with joy in the hour of affliction. Many of them fled over to Gaul, and settled in the province of Armorica, to which they gave the name of Britanny, or Bretagne. Some of them submitted to the Picts: while others, collecting courage from despair, sallied from their woods and caves upon the secure and roving invaders, cut many of them to pieces, and obliged the rest to retire into their own country. But the enemy threatening to return with superior forces, the distressed Britons, by the advice of Vortigern (who then possessed the principal authority

[1] Gild. *Hist.*—Bedæ *Hist.*

among them), called the Saxons to their assistance, by a solemn deputation[1].

The Saxons, like all the ancient German tribes, were a free, brave, independent people. They had arrived at that degree of civilization in which the mind has acquired sufficient force for enterprise, and seems to derive energy from the unimpaired vigour of the body. A nation, taken collectively, is never perhaps capable of such great achievements as in this state of half-civilization. The Saxons had spread themselves over an extensive tract of country; and, when the Britons implored their aid, they were masters not only of Holstein, Westphalia, Saxony, East and West Friseland, but also of Holland, and Zealand. They readily complied with the request of Vortigern; and, having fitted out three large transports, about fifteen hundred of them put to sea under the command of the enterprising brothers, Hengist and Horsa. These chieftains landed in the isle A. D. of Thanet, which was assigned to them as a possession; 449. and a league was formed between them and the British prince[2]. Soon after their arrival, they marched against the northern ravagers, who had made a new irruption, and advanced as far as Stamford. Unable to withstand the steady valour of the Saxons, the Picts were routed with great slaughter; and the Britons, felicitating themselves on an expedient by which they had freed their country from so cruel an enemy, hoped thenceforth to enjoy security under the protection of their warlike auxiliaries.

But mankind, in the possession of present good, are apt to overlook the prospect of future evil. The Britons did not foresee that their deliverers were to be their conquerors; though it must have been evident to any disinterested observer, that the day of subjection was nigh. The reflections of Hengist and Horsa, after their late victory, were very different from those of the Britons. They considered with what ease they might subdue an indolent and degenerate people, and sent to their countrymen intelligence of the fertility and opulence of South-Britain, inviting them to come and share in the spoils of the country[3].

The invitation was readily accepted. Seventeen vessels soon arrived with five thousand men, who, joined to those already in

[1] Bed. lib. i.—Gul. Malmesburiens. des Gestis Regum Anglorum, lib. i.
[2] See Gildas and Bede; also the Saxon Chronicle, p. 13.—Mr. Gibbon, on the authority of Nennius, gives a different account of this affair. He represents Hengist and Horsa as two fugitive adventurers, who, in a piratical cruise, were taken into the pay of the British prince.
[3] Ann. Beverl. p. 49.

the island, formed a considerable army [1]. Though now justly alarmed at the number of their allies, the Britons sought security and relief only in passive submission; and even that unmanly expedient soon failed them. The Saxons pulled off the mask: they complained that the promised subsidies were ill paid, and demanded larger supplies of corn and other provisions. These being refused, as exorbitant, they formed an alliance with the Picts, and proceeded to open hostilities against the people whom they had come over to protect.

The Britons were at last under the necessity of taking arms; and having deposed Vortigern, who had rendered himself odious by his vices, and the unfortunate issue of his rash counsels, they put themselves under the command of his son Vortimer. Many battles were fought between the Saxons and Britons with various success, but chiefly to the advantage of the former; and, in one of these conflicts, Horsa was slain. The sole command now devolved upon Hengist; who, reinforced with fresh adventurers from Germany, furiously ravaged the territories of the Britons. Anxious to spread the terror of his arms, he massacred multitudes of all ranks, of both sexes, and all ages [2]. The description is too horrible to read; and for the honour of humanity, I am willing to suppose it to be partly untrue.

Of the unhappy Britons who escaped the general slaughter, some took refuge among rocks and mountains: many perished by hunger: and many, forsaking their asylum, preserved their lives at the expense of their liberty. Others crossing the sea, sought shelter among their countrymen in Armorica. Those who remained at home suffered every species of misery: they were not only robbed of all temporal, but spiritual benefits [3]. In this extremity, a British and a Christain hero appeared. Arthur, prince of the Silures (supposed by some to have been the same with Ambrosius), revived the expiring valour of his countrymen. He defeated the Saxons in several engagements, particularly in

A.D. 520. the famous battle of Badon-hill, which procured the Britons many years of tranquillity. But, the success of Hengist and his followers having excited the ambition of other

A.D. 585. German tribes, successive swarms poured upon the Britons, who ultimately found themselves unequal to the contest,

---

[1] Had Hengist and Horsa been mere exiles, they would not soon have found so many followers.
[2] Bed. lib. i.—Gild. sec. xxiv.—Usserii *Antiq.* p. 226.
[3] Bede, Gildas, Usher, ubi sup.

and therefore retired into Cornwall, Wales, and Cumberland, where they formed independent principalities [1].

The Saxons and Angles, or Anglo-Saxons [2], (for they are mentioned under both these denominations) were now absolute masters of the greater part of South-Britain, which had changed not only its inhabitants, but its language, customs, and political institutions. History affords examples of few conquests more bloody, and few revolutions so violent, as that which was effected by the Saxons. In the course of their long war with the Britons, they established seven kingdoms, namely, those of Kent, Sussex, Essex, Wessex, Mercia, East-Anglia, and Northumberland, which was formed from the union of two minor kingdoms. These realms formed what is commonly called the Saxon Heptarchy [3].

While the Saxons were contending with the Britons for dominion, their several princes, leagued against the common enemy, preserved an union of councils and interests. But, after the wretched natives were shut up in their barren mountains, and the conquerors had nothing to fear from them, the bond of alliance was in a great measure dissolved among the princes of the heptarchy; and although one prince seems still to have assumed, or to have been allowed, some ascendency over the rest, his authority was so limited, that each state acted as if entirely independent. Jealousies and dissensions arose among the Saxon chiefs, and these were followed by perpetual wars; which in Milton's opinion, are no more worthy of a particular narration, than the combats of kites and crows. And, independently of so great an authority, which however it would be presumption to slight, it may be safely affirmed, that the barren records transmitted to us, and the continued barbarities of the times, render it impossible for the most eloquent and discerning writer to make this portion of our history either instructive or entertaining. It will therefore be sufficient for me to observe, that after a variety of inferior revolutions, the seven kingdoms were united by the valour and policy of Egbert, king of Wessex [4]. His dominions were nearly of the same extent with

A.D. 827.

[1] Gul. Malmesb. lib. i.—H. Huntingd. lib. ii. *Chron. Sax.* p. 20.
[2] The Saxons and Angles were originally distinct tribes; but, at the time of their landing in Britain, they were so much incorporated, as to pass sometimes under the one name, sometimes under the other. Hence arose the compound name of Anglo-Saxons. The Jutes had also a considerable share in the conquest of South-Britain.
[3] The extent of each kingdom is of too little importance now to deserve a particular description.
[4] Wessex, or the kingdom of the West Saxons, extended over the counties of Hants, Dorset, Devon, Somerset, Wilts, and Berks.

the territory now called ENGLAND; a name which was given to the empire of the Saxons in Britain at the union of the heptarchy, or, as some suppose, soon after the erection of the seventh kingdom.

The Anglo-Saxons, long before the time of Egbert, had been gradually converted to Christianity by the preaching of Augustine, a Roman monk, and the zeal of Bertha, daughter of Caribert king of Paris, and wife to Ethelbert king of Kent; but, as they received that doctrine through the polluted channels of the church of Rome, though it opened an intercourse with the more polished states of Europe, it had not hitherto been very effectual either in purifying their minds, or in softening their manners. The grossest ignorance and superstition prevailed among them. Reverences to saints and reliques seemed to supplant the worship of the Supreme Being: donations to the church were supposed to atone for every violation of the laws of society; and monastic observances were more esteemed than moral virtues. Even the military virtues so habitual to the Saxons fell into neglect. The nobles themselves began to prefer the indolence and security of the cloister to the toils and tumults of war; and the crown, impoverished by continual benefactions to the church, had no rewards for the encouragement of valour.

This corrupt species of Christianity was attended with another train of inconveniences, proceeding from a superstitious attachment to the see of Rome. The Britons had conducted all ecclesiastical affairs by their own synods and councils, acknowledging no subordination to the Roman pontiff: but the Saxons, having received their religion through the medium of Italian monks, were taught to consider Rome as the capital of their faith. Pilgrimages to that city were accordingly represented as the most meritorious acts of devotion; and not only noblemen and ladies of rank undertook this tedious journey, but kings themselves, resigning their crowns, implored a safe passport to heaven at the foot of St. Peter's chair, and exchanged the purple for the sackcloth [1].

But England, even in those times of British darkness, gave birth to some men equal at least to any of the age in which they lived. Offa, king of Mercia, was thought worthy of the friendship of Charle-magne, the greatest prince that Europe had produced for many centuries; and Alcuin, an English clergyman, had the honour of instructing that illustrious monarch in the

---

[1] Bed. lib. i. ii.—Spelm. Conc.

sciences, at a time when he was surrounded by all the literati of Christendom.

Having mentioned Charle-magne, I think it necessary to observe, that I shall finish the history of that great conqueror and legislator before I treat of the reign of Egbert, the first English monarch—a prince who was educated in the court and in the armies of the new emperor of the West.—Meanwhile, my dear Philip, I must say a few words of the government, laws, and manners, which prevailed among the Saxons after their settlement in Britain.

LETTER VIII.

Of the Government and Laws of the Anglo-Saxons.

If the Saxons, on their settlement in this island, had established the same form of government with the other Gothic nations that seized the provinces of the Roman empire, this letter would have been in a great measure unnecessary; but as they rather exterminated than subdued the natives, and were under few apprehensions from foreign enemies, they had no occasion to subject themselves to feudal services. They therefore retained entire their civil and military institutions : they transplanted into this island those principles of liberty and independence which they had so highly cherished at home, which had been transmitted to them from their ancestors, and which still continue to flourish among their descendants. Their original constitution was a kind of military democracy, in which the protection of the state was the voluntary care of its members, as every free man had a share in the government; and conquest was the interest of all, as all partook of the acquisitions. Their king, or chief, was only the first citizen of the community : his authority depended, as did his station, principally on his personal qualities.—The succession was neither elective nor hereditary. A son who inherited his father's virtues and talents, was sure to succeed to his sway : but, if he happened to be weak or profligate, or was a minor, the next in blood, or the person of the greatest eminence in the state, generally procured an elevation to the throne.

We owe to the masterly pen of Tacitus this account of the primitive government of the Germanic tribes. Unfortunately the Saxon Annals are too imperfect to enable us to delineate exactly the prerogatives of the kings, and the privileges of the

2

people, after the settlement which was effected in Britain. The government might be somewhat different in the different kingdoms of the heptarchy, and might also undergo several changes before the Norman conquest; but of those changes we are in a great measure ignorant. We only know, that at all times, and in all the kingdoms, there was a national council, a Wittena-Gemot, or Assembly of the Wise Men, whose consent was necessary to the enactment of laws, and to give sanction to the measures of public administration. But who the constituent members of that assembly were, has not hitherto been determined with certainty. The most probable conjecture seems to be, that it consisted of the nobility, the dignified clergy, and all possessors of a certain portion of land [1].

The Saxons were divided into three orders of men; the noble, the free, and the servile. The nobles were called *thanes*, and were of two kinds, the principal and the inferior thanes. The latter seem to have had some dependence on the former, as the former had on the king; but of what nature is uncertain. The lower freemen among the Saxons were denominated *ceorles*, and were chiefly employed in husbandry; whence a husbandman and ceorle became synonymous terms. They farmed the lands of the nobility or higher orders, and appear to have been removable at pleasure. But the slaves or villains were by much the most numerous class in the community; and being the property of their masters, were incapable of holding any property themselves. They were of two kinds: household slaves, after the manner of the ancients; and rustic slaves, who were sold or transferred, like cattle, with the soil. The long wars between the Saxons and Britons, and afterwards between the different princes of the heptarchy, seem to have been the cause of the disproportionate number of these unhappy men; for prisoners taken in battle were reduced to slavery by the laws of war, and were entirely at the disposal of their masters [2].

The higher nobility and dignified clergy among the Anglo-Saxons possessed a criminal jurisdiction within their own territories, and could punish without appeal such as they judged worthy of death. This was a dangerous privilege, and liable to the greatest abuse. But although the Anglo-Saxon government seems at last to have become in some measure aristocratical, there were still considerable remains of the ancient

---

[1] At first, five hides were deemed a sufficient qualification: but the required amount gradually rose to forty.
[2] L. Edg. sec. xiv. apud Spelm. *Conc.* vol. i.—*Preface to Brady's Hist.*

democracy. All the freeholders assembled twice a year in the county-court, or *shire-gemot*, to receive appeals from the inferior courts—a practice well calculated for the preservation of general liberty, and for restraining the exorbitant power of the nobles. In these courts were decided all causes, ecclesiastical as well as civil, the bishop and the ealdorman (alderman, or earl) presiding over them. The case was determined by a majority of voices, without much pleading, formality, or delay; the bishop and earl having no farther authority than to keep order among the freeholders, and offer advice [1]. Though it should be granted, therefore, that the wittena-gemot was composed entirely of the greater thanes and dignified clergy, yet in a government where few taxes were imposed by the legislature, and few statutes enacted—where the nation was less governed by laws than by customs, which allowed much latitude of interpretation—the county-courts, where all the freeholders were admitted, and which regulated the daily occurrences of life, formed a wide basis for freedom.

The criminal laws of the Anglo-Saxons, as of most barbarous nations, were far from being severe; a compensation in money being deemed sufficient for murder of any species, and for the lives of persons of any rank, including the king, and the primate, whose head, by the laws of Kent, was estimated at a higher rate than that of the king. The prices of all kinds of wounds were also settled: and he who was detected in adultery with his neighbour's wife, was ordered by the laws of Ethelbert, to pay him a fine, and buy him another wife. The punishments for robbery were various, but none of them capital. If any person could trace his stolen cattle into another's ground, the owner of the ground was obliged to show their tracks out of it, or pay the value of the cattle [2].

But if the punishments for crimes among the Anglo-Saxons were remarkable, their pretended proofs were no less so. When any controversy about a fact was too intricate for the ignorant judges to unravel, they had recourse to what they called the judgment of God, or, in other words, to chance. Their modes of consulting that blind divinity were various; but the most common was the ordeal. This method of trial was practised either by boiling water, or red-hot iron. The water, or iron, was consecrated by prayers, masses, fastings, and exorcisms; after which the person accused either took up with his bare hand a stone sunk in the

---

[1] Hickes' *Dissert.* Epist. ii.—viii.
[2] *Anglo-Saxon Laws*, published by Wilkins.

water to a certain depth, or carried the iron to a particular distance. The hand was immediately wrapped up, and the covering sealed for three days; and if, on examining it, there appeared no marks of burning or scalding, the person accused was pronounced innocent; if otherwise, he was declared guilty [1]. The same kind of proof, or others equally extravagant, prevailed among all the nations of the continent; and money, in like manner, was in every country the atonement for guilt, both in a civil and ecclesiastical sense.

LETTER IX.

Of the Reign of Charle-magne, or Charles the Great, King of France and Emperor of the West.

CHARLES and Carloman, the successors of Pepin in the French monarchy, were men of very different dispositions. Charles was open and generous, Carloman dark and suspicious: it was therefore happy for mankind that Carloman died soon after his father, as intestine wars might have continually resulted from A. D. the opposite tempers and interfering interests of the 770. brothers. Now alone at the head of a powerful kingdom, the great and ambitious genius of Charles soon gave birth to projects which will render his name immortal. A prosperous reign of forty-five years, abounding with military enterprises, political institutions, and literary foundations, offers to our view, in the midst of barbarism, a spectacle worthy of more polished ages.

But before I proceed to the history of this illustrious reign, I must say a few words of the state of Germany at that time.

Germany was formerly possessed by a number of free and independent nations, who bravely defended their liberties against the Romans, and were never totally subjected by them. On the decline of the Roman empire, many of those nations left their country, and founded empires or principalities in other parts; so that the north-western part of Germany at the accession of Charle-magne to the crown of France, was principally occupied by the Saxons. Of their government I have already spoken. They were still Pagans. What was then considered

---

[1] Spelman. in Verb. *Ordeal.*

as their territory, comprehended a vast tract of country extending from Bohemia to the Baltic and the German Ocean. This spacious empire was governed by many independent princes, and inhabited by various tribes, who had become tributary to the French crown. But, whenever the throne of France was vacated by death, or when the kings were engaged either in foreign or domestic wars, the Saxon princes threw off their allegiance and entered the French territories [1]. Charles had occasion to quell one of these revolts immediately after the death of his brother; and the work was imperfectly executed, when his arms were wanted in another quarter.

The two brothers are said to have married two daughters of Didier or Desiderius, king of the Lombards; but this point is doubtful with regard to Carloman. Charles had divorced his consort, under pretence that she was incapable of bearing children, and married Hildegarda, a Suabian princess. Bertha, the widow of Carloman, not thinking herself and her children safe in France after the death of her husband, retired into Italy, and implored the protection of Desiderius, who received her with joy.—Highly incensed against Charles for divorcing his daughter, he hoped by means of these refugees to raise such disturbances in France as might both gratify his revenge, and prevent the French monarch from intermeddling in the affairs of Italy. In this hope he was encouraged by his intimacy with pope A. D. Adrian I., to whom he proposed the crowning and anointing 772. of Carloman's two sons. But Adrian, though disposed to oblige him, refused to comply with the request, as he apprehended that by such conduct he might incur the displeasure of Charles, the natural ally of the church, and the only prince capable of protecting him against his ambitious enemies. Enraged at the refusal, Desiderius ravaged the papal territories, or, as they were called, the *Patrimony of St. Peter*, and threatened to besiege Rome itself. To avert the pressing danger, Adrian privately sent ambassadors to Charle-magne, not only entreating his aid, but inviting him to the conquest of Italy, his friendship for Desiderius being now converted into the most rancorous hatred. The French monarch, who only waited an opportunity to revenge himself on that prince for keeping his nephews, and still more for wishing to crown them, received the pope's invitation with great satisfaction. He immediately left Germany, after a hasty ac-

[1] Eginhardi *Vit. Car. Mag.*

commodation with the Saxons, and collected such an army as evidently showed that his object was nothing less than the extinction of the kingdom of the Lombards [1].

Desiderius now put himself at the head of a great army, and sent troops to guard the passes of the Alps. But Charle-magne, apprised of this precaution, sent a detachment under experienced guides to cross the mountains by a different route. The French completed their march; and, falling unexpectedly upon the A. D. Lombards who guarded the passes, struck them with such 773. terror, that they fled in the utmost confusion. Charles now entered Italy unmolested, and marched in quest of Desiderius. Unable to keep the field, the king of the Lombards retired to his capital, sending his son Adalgisus, as well as Bertha and her two sons, to Verona.

As soon as Charle-magne understood that Desiderius had taken shelter in Pavia, he assembled his whole army, and laid siege to that city, resolving not to withdraw his forces till it should have submitted; but, as the Lombards made a gallant defence, he changed the siege into a blockade, and marched with part of his troops to invest Verona. Adalgisus defended the place, for a time, with great bravery; but, when he was reduced to extremities, he secretly withdrew and fled to Constantinople, where he was cordially received by the emperor. Verona now surrendered to Charles, who, having seized Bertha and her sons, sent them under a strong guard into France.——What afterwards became of them, history has not informed us. It is much to be feared, however, that their fate was little to the honour of the conqueror. Humanity was not the characteristic of those times.

The siege of Pavia was renewed, and pushed with fresh vigour; but before the reduction of the town, Charles repaired to Rome. A. D. The pope received his deliverer in the most pompous 774. manner, the magistrates and judges walking before him with their banners, and the clergy repeating, " Blessed is he that cometh in the name of the Lord!" After Charles had satisfied his curiosity, and confirmed the donation which his father had made to St. Peter, he returned to the camp before Pavia. The Lombards continued to defend that city with obstinate valour: but a plague breaking out among the besieged, the unfortunate Desiderius was obliged at last to surrender his capital, and deliver up himself, his wife, and his children, to

---

[1] Sigon. *Reg. Ital.*—Anast. *Vit. Hadriani.*

Charles, who sent them all into France, where they either died a violent death, or languished out their days in obscurity[1].

Thus ended the kingdom of the Lombards in Italy, after it had subsisted two hundred and six years. They are represented by the monkish historians as a cruel and barbarous people, because they opposed the ambitious views of the popes : but the salutary laws which they left behind them, and which devouring time has still spared, are convincing proofs of their justice, humanity, and wisdom.

Of the state of Italy, at that time, it is proper that I should give you a sketch. It was then shared by the Venetians, the Lombards, the pope, and the Emperor of the East. The Venetians had become very considerable by their trade to the Levant, and bore no small sway in the affairs of Italy, though they had a very small portion of territory on the continent. The pope was master of the exarchate and Pentapolis; the dukedom of Naples, and some cities in the two Calabrian provinces, were ruled by the Emperor of the East. The other parts of Italy belonged to the Lombards ; namely, the dukedoms of Friuli, Spoleto, and Benevento, together with the provinces of Liguria, Venetia, Tuscany, and the Alpes Cottiæ, which were properly called the kingdom of the Lombards. These Charles claimed by right of conquest, and caused himself, in imitation of their princes, to be crowned king of Italy, with an iron crown, which is still preserved in the little town of Monza.

The conqueror thought it necessary to settle the government of his new kingdom before he left Italy ; and, after consulting with the pope, he agreed that the people should be permitted to live under their former laws, and that all things should remain as established by his predecessors. Accordingly he allowed to the dukes of Friuli, Spoleto, and Benevento, the same authority which they had enjoyed under the Lombard kings. He also permitted the other dukes to hold their dukedoms, contenting himself with an oath of allegiance, which he obliged them, as well as the three great dukes, to take annually. It was conceived in these words : " I promise, without fraud or deceit, to be faithful to my sovereign Charles, and his sons, as long as I live : and I swear by these holy Gospels, that I will be faithful to him, as a vassal to his lord and sovereign ; neither will I divulge any thing which, in virtue of my allegiance, he shall commit to me." He never transferred a dukedom from one

[1] Leonis Ostiens. *Hist.*

family to another, unless when the duke broke his oath, or died without male issue. This translation from one to another was called *investiture*; and hence it came, that fiefs were not granted but by investiture[1].

Charles committed the boundaries of his new kingdom, and the territory of cities, to the care of counts, who were invested with great authority. These boundaries were called *Marches*, and those who had the care of them were styled counts of the Marches, or Marquises; whence the title of Marquis had its rise. He also occasionally sent commissaries, who were entrusted with higher powers, and examined the conduct of the counts, whose province it was to administer justice over all his dominions.

That Italy might retain at least some shadow of liberty, he convoked, as often as he returned to that country, a general assembly of the bishops, abbots, and barons, in order to settle affairs of national importance. The Lombards had but one order in their councils, that of the barons; but, as the French had two (the clergy and nobility), he added, in Italy, the order of ecclesiastics to that of the nobles[2].

The affairs of Italy being thus settled, Charles returned to A.D. France, and marched immediately against the Saxons, 776. who had again revolted during his absence. But a detail of his wars with that barbarous though brave people, which continued during the greater part of his reign, can afford little pleasure to a humanized mind. I shall therefore only observe, that, after a number of battles, gallantly fought, and many cruelties, committed on both sides, the Saxons were totally subjected, and Germany became part of the empire of Charle-magne. A desire of converting the Saxons to Christianity seems to have been one of the principal motives for prosecuting this conquest; and, as they were no less tenacious of their religion than of their liberty, persecution marched in the train of war, and stained with blood the fetters of slavery.

Witikind, so deservedly celebrated by his nation, was the most eminent Saxon general during these hostilities. He frequently roused the drooping valour of his countrymen, and revived in their hearts the love of liberty and independence. They requited his gallant exertions with zeal and attachment, for which, however, they severely suffered. After an unsuccessful revolt, when they went to make submission to Charle-magne, he ordered four thousand five hundred of their principal men to be massacred,

---

[1] Sigon. *Reg. Ital.*   [2] Sigon.

because they refused to deliver up their general[1]. An equal instance of severity is scarcely to be found in the history of mankind; especially if we consider that the Saxons were not the natural subjects of Charles, but an independent people struggling for freedom. Witikind at last submitted, and embraced Christianity, continuing ever after faithful to his engagements. But he could never inspire his associates with the same docile sentiments: they were continually revolting; and submitting, that they might have it in their power to revolt again. On the final reduction of their country, the more resolute spirits retired into the north of Europe, carrying with them their vindictive hatred to the dominion and the religion of France[1].

On the subject of religion it may here be observed, that Charle-magne justly considered the mild doctrines of Christianity as the best means of taming a savage people: but he erred in supposing that force would ever make Christians. His Capitulars or ordinances for the Saxons were almost as barbarous as their manners. He obliged them, under pain of death, to receive baptism; he condemned to the severest punishment the breakers of Lent; in a word, he generally substituted force for persuasion. Instead therefore of blaming the obstinacy of these Barbarians, we ought to be filled with horror at the cruel bigotry of the conqueror.

Almost every year of the reign of Charles was signalized by some military expedition, though very different from those of our times. War was then carried on without any settled plan of operations. The troops were neither regularly disciplined nor paid. Every nobleman led forth his vassals, who were only obliged to serve for a certain time; so that there was a kind of necessity for concluding the war with the campaign. The army was dissolved on the approach of winter, and assembled in the next season if necessary. Hence we are enabled to account for some circumstances, which would otherwise appear inexplicable, in the reign of this great prince.

Besides the Lombards and Saxons, whom he conquered, Charles vanquished in several engagements the Avares, or Huns, plundered their capital, and penetrated as far as Raab, on the Danube. He likewise made an expedition into Spain, and carried his arms to the banks of the Ebro[1].

Abdarrahman, the Moorish king, whom I have already mentioned, still reigned with lustre at Cordova. A superb mosque,

---

[1] Eginhardi *Annal.*

now the cathedral of that city, six hundred feet in length, and two hundred and fifty in breadth, supported by three hundred and sixty-five columns of alabaster, jasper, and black marble, continues to manifest the grandeur of this monarch. No other people but the Arabs could then either have conceived or executed such a work. The little Christian king of the Asturias had prudently sued for peace from Abdarrahman; but some of the Moorish governors, having revolted from that prince, offered to acknowledge Charle-magne as their sovereign. Willing to extend his empire on that side, Charles crossed the Pyrenees with all expedition, took Pampeluna and Saragossa, and re-established the Moorish governors under his protection. In repassing the mountains, his rear-guard was defeated by the duke of Gascony, at Roncevaux[1]. Here fell the famous Roland, so much celebrated in romance, and represented as nephew to Charle-magne; though history only tells us that he commanded on the frontiers of Bretagne.

A.D. 778.

Charles, though engaged in so many wars, was far from neglecting the arts of peace, the happiness of his subjects, or the cultivation of his own mind. Government, manners, religion, and letters were his constant pursuits. He frequently convened the national assemblies, for regulating the affairs both of church and state. In these assemblies he proposed such laws as he considered to be of public benefit, and allowed the same liberty to others; but of this liberty, indeed, it would have been difficult to deprive the French nobles, who had been accustomed, from the foundation of the monarchy, to share the legislation with their sovereign. His attention extended even to the most distant corner of his empire, and to all ranks of men. Sensible how much mankind in general reverence old customs, and those constitutions under which they have lived from their youth, he permitted the inhabitants of all the countries that he conquered to retain their own laws, making only such alterations as he judged absolutely necessary for the good of the community. He manifested a particular regard for the common people, and studied their ease and advantage. This benevolence of mind, which can never be sufficiently admired, was both more necessary and more meritorious in those times, as the commonalty were then in a state of almost universal oppression, and were scarcely thought to be entitled to the sympathies of humanity. The same love of mankind led him to repair and form public roads; to build

---

[1] Eginhardi *Annal.*

bridges, where necessary; to make rivers navigable, for the purpose of commerce; and to project that grand canal which would have opened a communication between the German Ocean and the Black Sea, by uniting the Danube and the Rhine[1]. This illustrious project failed in the execution, for want of those machines which art has since constructed. But the greatness of the conception, and the honour of having attempted it, were beyond the power of contingencies; and posterity has done justice to the memory of Charles, by considering him, on account of that and his other public-spirited plans, as one of those few conquerors who did not merely desolate the earth; as a hero truly worthy of the name, who sought to unite his own glory with the welfare of his species.

This great prince was no less amiable in private life than illustrious in his public character. He was an affectionate father, a fond husband, and a generous friend. His house was a model of economy, and his person of simplicity and true grandeur. " For shame!" said he to some of his nobles, who were more finely dressed than the occasion required; " learn to dress like men, and let the world judge of your rank by your merit, not your habit. Leave silks and finery to women, or reserve them for those days of pomp and ceremony when robes are worn for show, not use." On some occasions he himself appeared in imperial magnificence, and freely indulged in every luxury: but in general his dress was plain, and his table was frugal. He had his set hours for study, which he seldom omitted, either in the camp or the court; and, notwithstanding his continual wars, and unremitted attention to the affairs of a great empire, he found leisure to collect the old Frankish poems and historical ballads, with a view to illustrate the history of the monarchy. The loss of this collection is much to be lamented, and could never have happened if every one had been as well acquainted with its importance as Charles. But he was the phœnix of the age; and, though not altogether free from its prejudices, his liberal and comprehensive mind, which examined every thing, and yet found time for all things, would have done honour to the most enlightened period. He was fond of the company of learned men, and assembled them from all parts of Europe, forming in his palace a kind of academy, of which he condescended to become a member. He also established schools, in the cathedrals and principal abbeys, for teaching writing, arithmetic, grammar, and church music[2]; certainly

---

[1] Egin. *Vit. Car. Mag.*   [2] Egin. *Vit. Car. Mag.*

no very elevated sciences, yet considerable at a time when many dignified ecclesiastics could not subscribe the canons of those councils in which they sat as members, and when it was deemed a sufficient qualification for a priest to be able to read the Gospels and understand the Lord's Prayer [1].

Alcuin, our learned countryman, was the companion and particular favourite of Charle-magne, and was at the head of his Royal Academy. A circumstance so much to the honour of this island should not be omitted by a British historian. Three rich abbeys were the reward of the learning and talents of Alcuin. This benevolence has been thought to border on profusion; but in that age of darkness, when even an enthusiastic zeal for learning was a virtue, no encouragement could be too great for the illuminators of the human mind.

Had the religious enthusiasm of this monarch been attended with no worse consequences than his literary ardour, his piety would have been as deservedly admired as his taste. But a blind zeal for the propagation of Christianity, which extinguished his natural feelings, made him guilty of severities that shock humanity; and a superstitious attachment to the see of Rome, which mingled itself with his policy, led him to engage in theological disputes and quibbles unworthy of his character. Only the honours which his father and himself owed to the popes, can render him in any degree excusable. But although the theological part of Charles's character is by no means the brightest, it merits your attention, as it serves to show the prejudices of the age, the littleness of a great man, and the great effects that frequently proceed from little causes.

As Charle-magne was equally a friend to religion and letters, and as any learning which yet remained among mankind, in our quarter of the globe, was monopolised by the clergy, it is not surprising that they obtained strong marks of his favour. Even the payment of tithes, then considered as a grievous oppression, but which he ordered as a compensation for the lands withholden from the church; and the consequence which he gave to churchmen, by admitting them into the national assemblies, and associating them with the counts in the administration of justice; appear less extravagant than his sitting in councils merely ecclesiastical, assembled about the most frivolous points of a vain theology. But, like some princes of later times, Charles seems to have been strongly desirous of being considered not only as

[1] Seg. Brumiens. apud Bruck, *Hist. Philos.*

the protector, but as the head of the church; and from the imposing effect of his power and munificence, this usurpation was overlooked, notwithstanding the height which the papal dignity had then attained.   We accordingly find him seated on A.D. a throne in the council of Frankfort, with one of the 794. pope's legates on each hand, and three hundred bishops waiting his nod.

The purpose of that council was to examine the doctrine of two Spanish bishops, who, in order to refute the accusation of polytheism, brought against the Christians by the Jews and Mohammedans, maintained that Jesus Christ was the son of God only by adoption.   The king opened the assembly himself, and proposed the condemnation of this heresy.   The council decided conformably to his will: and in a letter to the churches of Spain, in consequence of that decision, Charles expressed himself in these remarkable words: " You entreat me to judge of myself: I have done so : I have assisted as an auditor, and an arbiter in an assembly of bishops : we have examined, and, by the grace of God, we have settled, what must be believed !" Neither Constantine nor any other of the Greek emperors, so jealous of their theological prerogative, ever used more positive language.

Charle-magne went still farther in the question of images. Leo IV., the son of Constantine Copronymus, as zealous an image-breaker as his father, had banished his wife Irenè, because she hid images beneath her pillow.   This devout and ambitious princess coming afterwards to the government, during the minority of her son Constantine Porphyrogenitus, with whom she was associated in the empire, re-established that worship which she loved, from policy no less than piety.   The second council of Nice accordingly decreed, that we ought to render to images an *honorary* worship, but not a real *adoration*, which is due to God alone.   Unfortunately, however, the translation of the acts of this council, which pope Adrian sent into France, was so incorrect, that the sense of the article, relating to images, was entirely perverted, running thus: " I receive and honour images according to that adoration which I pay to the Trinity." Charles was so much incensed at this impiety, that he composed, with the aid of the clergy, what are called the *Caroline Books*, in which the council of Nice is treated with the utmost contempt and abuse.   He sent those books to Adrian, desiring him to excommunicate the empress and her son.   The pope prudently excused himself on the score of images, making Charles sensible of the mistake upon which he had proceeded ; but he insinuated at the same time, that he would declare Irenè and Constantine heretics, unless they should restore certain lands which had belonged to the church; artfully hinting at certain projects which he had formed for the *exaltation* of the Romish church and the French monarchy [1]. The exaltation of the monarchy was approaching, though Adrian did not live to be the instrument of it.

Leo III., who succeeded Adrian in the papacy, sent to Charlemagne the standard of Rome, requesting him to send some person to receive the oath of fidelity from the Romans [2]; a most flattering instance of submission, as well as a proof that the sovereignty of Rome, at that time, belonged to the kings of France. Three years after, Pascal and Campule, two relatives of the late pope, not only offered themselves as accusers of Leo, but attacked him in the public streets, and severely wounded him. He made his escape by the assistance of some friends; and the duke of Spoleto, general to the French forces, sent him under an escort to Charle-magne. The king received him with great respect, sent him back with a numerous retinue, and went soon after to Italy to do him justice.

A.D. 796.

At Rome, Charles passed six days in private conferences with the pope; after which he convoked the bishops and nobles to examine the accusation brought against the pontiff. " The apostolic see," exclaimed the bishops, " cannot be judged by man!" Leo, however, spoke to the accusation: he said that the king came *to know the cause;* and no proof appearing against him, he purged himself by oath [3].

A.D. 800.

The trial of a pope was doubtless an uncommon scene; but one soon followed yet more extraordinary. On Christmas-day, as the king assisted at mass in St. Peter's church, in the midst of the ecclesiastical ceremonies, and while he was on his knees before the altar, the supreme pontiff advanced, and put an imperial crown upon his head. As soon as the people perceived it, they cried, " Long life and victory to Charles Augustus, crowned by the hand of God!—Long live the great and pious emperor of the Romans!" The pope then conducted him to a magnificent throne, which had been prepared for the occasion; and as soon as he was seated, paid him those honours which his predecessors had been accustomed to pay to the Roman emperors, declaring, that instead of bearing the title of Patrician,

[1] *Elémens d'Hist. Gén.* par M. l'Abbé Millot, par. II.
[2] Egin. *Vit. Car. Mag.*   [3] Anast. *Vit. Leon.*

he should henceforth be styled Emperor and Augustus. Leo now presented him with the imperial mantle; with which being invested, Charles returned amidst the acclamations of the multitude to his palace [1].

The pope had surely no right to proclaim an emperor: but Charles was worthy of the imperial ensigns; and although he cannot be properly ranked among the successors of Augustus, he is justly considered as the founder of the New Empire of the West.

Charle-magne was no sooner proclaimed emperor than his title was generally acknowledged; and he received several embassies, which must have given him high satisfaction, as they did equal honour to the prince and the man. Irenè, the most artful and ambitious woman of her time, who had deposed her son that she might reign alone, heard with favour the offer of marriage made to her by the new emperor, at the suggestion of pope Leo. This proposal was made with a view of securing her Italian dominions, which she was informed Charles intended to seize; and the matrimonal treaty was actually concluded, when Nicephorus, the patrician, conspired against her, banished her to the isle of Lesbos, and ascended the imperial throne. By a treaty between Charles and this prince, the limits of the A.D. 802. two empires were settled; and Calabria, Sicily, the coast of Naples, Dalmatia, and Venice, were to continue under the Dominion of the Greek emperor [2]. This treaty proves that the Venetians were not yet altogether independent; but they aspired at independence, and soon deservedly attained it.

The renown of Charles extended even into Asia. He kept a correspondence with the famous Haroun Al-Rashid, one of those khalifs who contributed most to enlighten and polish the Arabs. This prince valued the friendship of Charle-magne above that of all other potentates; as a proof of which, he complimented him with an embassy soon after he was proclaimed emperor, and the keys of the holy sepulchre; thus ceding to him—if not the lordship of Jerusalem, as some authors affirm—at least the holy places in that city, whither devotion already led a great number of Christians. Among the presents which the ambassadors of Al-Rashid brought into France were a tame elephant and a striking-clock, the first ever seen in that kingdom; for, notwithstanding the efforts of Charle-magne to enlighten his nation,

---

[1] Anast.— Ægin. Ann.
[2] Egin. Vit. Car. Mag.—Theoph. Chronographia.

his subjects were not equal to those of Haroun in knowledge, or in the arts, either liberal or mechanical. The Arabs might then have been preceptors to all Europe.

I must here say a few words of this surprising pheno-menon.

The Abassides, having ascended the throne of Mohammed, transferred the seat of empire from Damascus to Cufa, and afterwards to Bagdad. Thither the khalif Al-Mansour attracted the arts and sciences. The Greeks had furnished ideas and communicated taste to their barbarous conquerors—a species of triumph reserved for civilized nations, even in a state of servi-tude. Al-Mohdi, successor of Al-Mansour, cultivated these precious seeds : and Al-Rashid, who was the son of Al-Mohdi, augmented their fecundity by his knowledge and attention, being equally liberal and enlightened. Under Al-Mamoun, Al-Motasem, Al-Wathek, and their immediate successors, the sci-ences flourished still more ; but, at length, dissensions and civil wars robbed the Arabs, in their turn, of the fruits of genius and the lights of learning, which are almost inseparable from public tranquillity.

In all nations the same revolutions are produced nearly by the same causes. Nothing merits your attention more in the study of history.

One of the principal causes of the fall of empires has ever been, but more especially in modern times, the error of dividing the same monarchy among different princes. The custom pre-A.D. vailed before the time of Charle-magne : he followed it 806. by a testamentary division of his dominions among his three sons, Charles, Pepin, and Louis. The particulars of this division are of little consequence, as only Louis survived his father. It is necessary, however, to observe, that the Italian provinces had been assigned to Pepin ; a donation which was confirmed to his son Bernard, with the title of King of Italy, and proved the ruin of that prince, as well as the cause of much dis-turbance to the empire.

In the mean time, the emperor was threatened by a new enemy, the most formidable he had ever encountered. The Nor-mans, as the French call them, or the inhabitants of the great northern peninsula of Europe (of whom I shall afterwards more particularly treat), had long harassed the coasts of his extensive dominions with their robberies and piracies ; and, notwithstand-ing the wise measures of Charles, who created a powerful marine, and took every other precaution against their ravages, they not only continued their depredations, but made a formal descent in Friesland, under Godfrey the Dane. Charles assembled A.D. all his forces in the neighbourhood of the Rhine, and was 810. preparing for a decisive battle, which might perhaps have seriously diminished the empire of the Franks, as Godfrey was not inferior to the emperor either in valour or military skill, and had a numerous body of fearless adventurers under his command. But the issue of this battle was prevented by the death of that prince, who was assassinated by one of his followers. His forces were immediately re-embarked ; and a peace was afterwards concluded with his nephew.

The satisfaction which Charles must have received from this deliverance, and the general tranquillity which he now enjoyed, were more than balanced by his domestic misfortunes. He lost his favourite daughter Rotrude, and two of his sons. Soon after the death of his son Charles, he associated Louis with A.D. him in the empire. The ceremony was very solemn. 813. As if this great man had foreseen the usurpations of the church, he placed the imperial crown upon the altar, and ordered the prince to put it on his own head [1] ; intimating thereby, that he held it only of God.

The emperor died at Aix-la-Chapelle, his usual residence, in the seventy-second year of his age, and the forty-sixth of Jan. his reign. The glory of the French empire seemed to 814. expire with him. He possessed all France, the greater part of Germany, a part of Spain, the Low-Countries, and the continent of Italy as far as Benevento. But, to govern such an extent of territory, a monarch must be endowed with the genius of a Charle-magne.

LETTER X.

Of the Empire of Charle-magne and the Church, from the Accession of Louis the Debonnaire to the death of Charles the Bald.

THE history of Europe, for several ages after the death of Charle-magne, is little more than a catalogue of crimes, and a register of the debasing effects of ignorance and superstition.

---

[1] Theogani *Vit. Ludovici Pii.*

His empire soon experienced the same fate with that of Alexander. It had quickly attained its height; and yet, while animated by the superior Genius of Charles, it possessed a surprising degree of strength and harmony. But these not being natural to the feudal system, the discordant elements began to separate under his son Louis the Debonnaire (so called on account of the gentleness of his manners); and that vast body, no longer informed by the same spirit, was in a short time entirely dismembered.

Louis, though a prince of some abilities, was unable to support so great a weight of empire: and his piety and parental fondness, however amiable in themselves, enfeebled a character already took weak, and an authority never respected. He rendered himself odious to the clergy, by attempting to reform certain abuses, without foreseeing that this powerful body would not pay the same submission which had been given to the superior capacity of his father. More religious than politic, he spent less time in settling the affairs of his empire than those of his soul, not considering that true religion consists in fulfilling the duties of our station, and that the practices of the cloister are improperly associated with the functions of the throne. But his greatest error was occasioned by his paternal affection, and a blind imitation of his father's example, in dividing his dominions among his children. Three years after his accession to A.D. 817. the throne, he admitted his eldest son, Lothaire, to a participation of the French and German territories, declared Pepin king of Aquitaine, and created Louis king of Bavaria [1].

Bernard, king of Italy, was offended at this division. He thought his right to the empire superior to the claim of Lothaire, as his father Pepin was elder brother to Louis. The primate of Milan and the bishop of Cremona encouraging his pretensions, he revolted, and levied war against his uncle, in contempt of the imperial authority, to which his crown was subject. Louis acted on this occasion with greater vigour than either his friends or his enemies expected: he immediately raised a powerful army, and was preparing to cross the Alps, when Bernard was abandoned by his troops. That unfortunate prince was made prisoner, and condemned to lose his head; but his uncle, A.D. 818. by a singular kind of lenity, mitigated the sentence to the loss of his eyes. He died three days after the pu-

---

[1] Nithard. *de Dissensionibus Filiorum Ludovici Pii.*

nishment was inflicted; and Louis, to prevent future troubles, ordered three natural sons of Charle-magne to be shut up in a convent [1].

In consequence of these rigours, the emperor was seized with keen remorse; accusing himself of the murder of his nephew, and of tyrannic cruelty to his brothers, inhumanly secluded from the world. He was encouraged by the monks in this melancholy humour; which at last grew to such a height, that he impeached himself in an assembly of the states, and begged the bishops to enjoin him public penance [2]. The clergy, now sensible of his weakness, set no bounds to their usurpations. The popes thought they might do any thing under so pious a prince: they did not wait for the emperor's confirmation of their election, but immediately assumed the tiara, and were guilty of other irregularities. The bishops exalted themselves above the throne, and the whole fraternity of the church claimed an exemption from all civil jurisdiction. Even the monks, while they pretended to renounce the world, seemed to aspire to the government of it.

Louis, by the advice of his ministers, who were desirous of diverting him from his monastic habits, had married a second wife, who was distinguished both by her mental and personal qualities. This princess brought him a son, afterwards known by the name of Charles the Bald, whose birth was the occasion of much joy, but proved the cause of many sorrows. She pressed her husband to put Charles on a footing with his other children, by a new division of his dominions. Lothaire, sensible of the wishes of his indulgent father, and prevailed on by the entreaties of this fond mother, consented to resign a part of his territories to Charles: but he soon repented of his too easy concession; and the three brothers, by a remarkable association, joined in a rebellion against their father [3].

A. D. 824.

A. D. 829.

These disorders were fostered by Walla, abbot of Corbie, a monk of high birth, who had formerly been in the confidence of Louis, but was now in disgrace. He declaimed against the court, and against the empress in particular, accusing her of an adulterous commerce with Count Bernard, the prime minister. His schemes succeeded. The emperor was abandoned by his army, and made prisoner with his wife Judith, and her son Charles. The empress was shut up in a cloister,

A. D. 830.

---

[1] *Vit. Lud. Pii.*   [2] *Vit. Lud. Pii.*
[3] Nithard. *de Dissens. Fil. Lud. Pii.*

and Louis himself would have been obliged to take the monastic habit, had it not been supposed that he would make a voluntary resignation of his crown. He had the courage, however, to insist on the rectitude of his intentions, while he acknowledged his errors, and promised to act with greater circumspection in future. The nobility pitied their humbled sovereign ; and by the intrigues of the monk Gondebaud, who sowed dissensions among the brothers, Louis was restored to his dignity, and seemingly reconciled with his family [1].

The first use that the emperor made of his liberty was to re-call his consort to court, though not without the permission of the pope, as she had formally taken the veil. Bernard was also recalled, and Walla banished: yet Louis did not long enjoy either peace or tranquillity. The monk Gondebaud thought he had a right to be prime minister, as the reward of his services ; and, as women generally repay flattery with favour, they as generally reserve vengeance for insult; the empress brought her animosities to court with her. Walla's friends were per-secuted, and Lothaire was deprived of the title of empe-ror, that the succession might be reserved for young Charles. The three brothers now formed a new league against their father [2]. Count Bernard, dissatisfied with his master's conduct, joined the rebels ; and Gregory IV., then pope, went to France in the army of Lothaire, under pretence of accommodating mat-ters, but really with an intention of employing against the em-peror that power which he derived from him, being pleased with the opportunity of asserting the supremacy and independence of the holy see.

A. D. 832.

The presence of the pope, in those days of superstition, was of itself sufficient to determine the fate of Louis. After a de-ceitful negociation, and an interview with Gregory on the part of Lothaire, the unfortunate emperor found himself at the mercy of his rebellious sons. He was deposed in a tumultuous assem-bly, and Lothaire was proclaimed in his stead [3]. After that infamous transaction, the pope returned to Rome.

A. D. 833.

In order to give permanency to this revolution, as well as to apologize for their own conduct, the bishops of Lothaire's faction had recourse to an artifice like that which had been used for the degradation of king Wamba in Spain. " A penitent," said they, " is incapable of all civil offices; a royal penitent must therefore

[1] *Vit. Lud. Pii.*   [2] Nithard. *de Dissens. Fil. Lud. Pii.*
                              [3] *Vit. Lud. Pii.*

be incapable of reigning: let us subject Louis to a perpetual penance, and he can never re-ascend the throne." He was accordingly arraigned in the assembly of the states, by Ebbo, archbishop of Rheims (who had been raised by his bounty from the condition of a slave) and condemned to do penance for life [1].

Louis was then a prisoner in a monastery at Soissons ; and, being much intimidated, he patiently submitted to a ceremony no less solemn than debasing. He prostrated himself on a haircloth, which was spread before the altar, and owned himself guilty of the charges brought against him, in the presence of many bishops, canons, and monks ; Lothaire being also present, in order to enjoy the sight of his father's humiliation. But this acknowledgment was not deemed sufficient: he was obliged to read aloud a written confession, in which he was made to accuse himself of sacrilege and murder, and to number among his crimes the marching of troops in Lent, calling an assembly on Holy-Thursday, and taking arms to defend himself against his rebellious children !—for superstition can transform into crimes the most innocent, and even the most necessary actions. After having finished his confession, this unhappy prince, by order of the ungrateful archbishop, laid aside his sword and belt, divested himself of the royal robes, put on the penitential sackcloth, and had a cell assigned to him.

But the feelings of nature, and the voice of humanity, prevailed over the prejudices of the age, and the policy of the clergy. Lothaire became an object of general abhorrence, and his father of compassion : his two brothers united against him, in behalf of that father whom they had contributed to humble. The nobility returned to their obedience : they paid homage to Louis, as their lawful sovereign ; and the ambitious Lothaire was obliged to crave mercy, in the sight of the whole army, at the feet of a parent and an emperor, whom he had lately insulted in the habit of a penitent [2]. He received it, and was permitted to retain the kingdom of Italy, which he had enjoyed from the time of Bernard's death.

A. D. 834.

Louis immediately demanded absolution (such was his weakness!) and in a general assembly at Thionville, he was formally restored to his dignity. He might now have ended his days in peace, but for the intrigues of Judith, who, still ambitious of the aggrandisement of her son, again entered into a negociation with

---

[1] *Vit. Lud. Pii.*   [2] Nithard. *de Dissens. Fil. Lud. Pii.*

A. D. Lothaire, in consequence of the death of his brother
839. Pepin. An assembly was convoked at Worms, to which
he was invited. His father received him kindly; the empress
loaded him with caresses. The kingdom of Neustria[1] had lately
been added to the dominions of her son: and her present object
was, to engage Lothaire in a scheme by which Charles should
also become possessed of Aquitaine, at the expense of Pepin's
children. Lothaire assented to what he was not in a condition to
dispute. But Louis, king of Bavaria, though not injured by this
new division of the empire, was so much incensed at its supposed
injustice, that he assembled the whole force of his dominions.
His father marched against him, but became suddenly indisposed; and, an eclipse of the sun happening at the same time,
the superstitious old man had the vanity to think that Heaven
had taken the trouble to foretell to mankind the death of a prince,
whose very virtues seemed almost to dishonour the throne, and
who ought never to have stirred beyond the walls of a cloister.
He therefore repeatedly received the communion, and scarcely
took any other nourishment, till his piety fulfilled the prediction
which his folly had suggested[2].

June, Louis died near Mentz, in the sixty-fourth year of his
840. age and the twenty-seventh of his reign. He left a crown,
a sword, and a very rich sceptre to Lothaire, by which it was
supposed he also left him the empire, on condition that he should
fulfil his engagements to Judith and Charles. The bishop of
Mentz, observing that he had left nothing to his son Louis, then
in arms against him, reminded him that forgiveness at least was
his duty. " Yes, I forgive him!" cried the dying prince, with
great emotion; " but tell him from me, that he ought to seek
forgiveness of God, for bringing my grey hairs in sorrow to the
grave."

A bad son, my dear Philip, cannot be expected to make a
good brother; for the natural feelings in the second relation are
necessarily weaker than in the first; you will not, therefore, be
surprised to find the sons of Louis the Debonnaire armed against
each other. No sooner was Lothaire informed of his father's
death, than he considered himself as emperor in the most extensive sense of the word, and resolved to make himself master of
the whole imperial dominions, regardless of his engagements in
favour of Charles the Bald, or the right of his brother Louis to

---

[1] The north-western part of France, including Paris, was so called.
[2] *Vit. Lud. Pii.*

the kingdom of Bavaria. And he seemed likely to attain the object of his ambition. He was a prince of great subtlety and address, could wear the complexion of the times, and was possessed of an extensive territory, beside the title of emperor, which was still much respected; he therefore assured himself of success against his brothers: Charles being only a youth of seventeen, under the tuition of his mother, and Louis a prince of no high reputation. He was deceived, however, in his conjectures. These two princes, united by a sense of common interest, gave him battle at Fontenai, in Burgundy, where fraternal hatred appeared in all its horrors. Few engagements have been so bloody, if (as it is said) 100,000 men fell on the spot: but this is a manifest exaggeration, for a cotemporary writer calculates the number of the slain at 40,000, and there is reason to believe that even his estimate is overcharged. Lothaire and his nephew Pepin (who had joined him to assert his right to the crown of Aquitaine) were totally defeated[1]. Pepin fled to Aquitaine, and his uncle towards Italy, abandoning France to the victorious army.

June 25, 841.

Nothing now remained for Louis and Charles but to secure their conquests. For this purpose they applied to the clergy; and with hopes the more flattering, as Lothaire, in order to raise troops with greater expedition, had promised the Saxons the liberty of renouncing Christianity, or, in other words, liberty of conscience, the very idea of which was abhorred by the church of Rome. Several bishops assembled at Aix-la-Chapelle; and, after examining the misconduct of the emperor, asked the two princes, whether they chose to follow his example, or govern according to the laws of God. Their answer may easily be imagined. " Receive then the kingdom by the divine authority," added the prelates: " we exhort you, we command you to receive it[2]."

This command would have taken effect in its most comprehensive meaning, if Lothaire had respected it as much as his brothers. But that artful prince, by means of his indulgence to the Saxons, and other politic expedients, was enabled to procure a new army. He again became formidable. The two victorious princes, therefore, thought it advisable to negociate with him. By a new treaty of division, he was left in possession of the kingdom of Italy, with the imperial dignity, and the countries situated between the Rhône and the Alps, the Meuse and the Rhine. Charles retained Neustria and Aquitaine; and

---

[1] Nithard. *de Dissens. Fil. Lud. Pii.*   [2] Nithard.—*Annal. Metens.*

Louis, afterwards styled the German, had all the provinces on the other side of the Rhine, and some cities on this side of it [1].

The extinction of the civil war made but one evil less in the empire of Charle-magne, ravaged in different parts by the Normans, and by the Saracens, who pillaged Italy. The turbulent independence of the nobles, accustomed during the last reign to despise the prince and the laws—the discontents of the clergy—and the ambitious projects of both—were the sources of new troubles. Every thing threatened the most fatal revolutions; every thing tended to anarchy.

To lessen these evils, the three brothers entered into an association, the effect of weakness more than affection, by which the enemies of one were to be considered as the enemies of all; (so low was the empire of the great Charles!) and, in an assembly A.D. at Mersen, on the Meuse, they settled certain constitu-851. tions relative to the succession, and other public matters. By these it was established, that the children of the reigning prince, whether of age or under age, should succeed to his dominions, and owe nothing to the other princes of the monarchy but the respect due to the ties of blood [2]—a regulation well calculated to prevent civil wars, though it proved ineffectual in those disorderly times. But other constitutions of the same assembly tended to enfeeble the royal authority, which had already too much need of support. They imported, that the crown vassals should no longer be obliged to follow the king, unless in general wars, occasioned by foreign invasions; and that every free man should be at liberty to choose whether he would be the vassal of the king or of a subject. The first of these regulations increased the independence of the crown vassals, and the second their power, by augmenting the number of their retainers; for many persons chose rather to depend upon some neighbouring nobleman, whose immediate protection they might claim (at a time when protection was necessary, independent of the laws), than on the sovereign, whose attention they had less reason to expect, and whose aid was more distant or doubtful.

Lothaire, some years after, took the habit of a monk, that, according to the language of those times, he might atone for his crimes, and, though he had lived a tyrant, die a saint. In this pious disguise he expired, before he had worn it for a week. He Sept. had divided his dominions among his three sons; and, by 855. virtue of the treaty of Mersen, they quietly succeeded to

---

[1] Nithard. [2] *Annal. Bertinian.*

their allotments. Louis had Italy, with the title of emperor: Lothaire ruled over that country which from him received the appellation of the kingdom of Lotharingia, a more extensive territory than the subsequent Lorrain: Charles became king of Provence, and also governed the district since called Dauphiné, as well as a part of Burgundy. As if these kings were not sufficient, Charles the Bald declared his infant son Charles king of Aquitaine[1].

Thus was the empire of Charle-magne weakened by subdivisions, till it became, to use the language of Shakspeare, only " a stage to feed contention on." Foreign invasions conspired with civil dissensions to spread terror and disorder in every quarter, but more especially through the dominions of Charles the Bald— a prince as weak as his father, and restless as his mother. The Normans carried fire and sword into the heart of his kingdom, to Rouen, and even to the gates of Paris. Young Pepin, son of the last king of Aquitaine, joined the invaders, and ravaged that country over which he had been born to reign. Nomenoge, duke of Bretagne, usurped the title of king, which Charles was obliged to confirm to his son Herispée, by whom he had been totally defeated. The spirit of revolt became every day more general. Some factious nobles invited Louis the German to usurp his brother's kingdom. He came at the head of a powerful army, and received the homage of the principal nobility. A.D. Venilon, archbishop of Sens, and other prelates of the 858. party of Louis, at the same time declared that Charles had forfeited his dignity by mal-administration, and crowned his brother[2].

Charles, however, recovered his kingdom as quickly as he had lost it. The prelates who were his friends, excommunicated those who had dethroned him ; which brought the rebels into contempt and even abhorrence. Louis sent back his army into Germany, that he might not give umbrage to the French, and he was afterwards obliged to take the same route himself. Charles no sooner appeared than he was universally acknowledged : his restoration did not cost a single blow. The most terrible anathemas were now denounced against Louis by the French clergy, unless he should submit to the rigours of the church ; and he was weak enough to reply, that he must first consult the bishops of his own kingdom[3].

The weakness of Charles the Bald was still more extraor-

---

[1] *Annal. Fuldens.*   [2] *Annal. Bertinian.—Concil. Gal.* vol. ii.
[3] *Annal. Bertin.*

dinary. Having assembled a council to judge the traitor Venilon, he presented a memorial against him, in which is the following singular passage : " I ought not to have been *deposed*, or at least not before I had been *judged* by the *bishops*, who *gave* me the *royal authority!* I have always *submitted* to their *correction*, and am ready now to *submit* to it!" Venilon escaped punishment by making his peace with the prince : and the bishops of the council bound themselves by a canon to remain united, " for the *correction* of *kings*, the *nobility*, and the *people*[1]!"

Various circumstances show, that the clergy now aspired to the right of disposing of crowns, which they founded on the custom of anointing kings. They employed fictions and sophisms to render themselves independent : they refused the oath of fealty, " because sacred hands could not, without abomination, submit to hands impure[2]!" One usurpation led to another ; abuse constituted right—a quibble appeared a divine law. Ignorance sanctified every thing ; and we may safely conclude, from the abject language of Charles, in publicly acknowledging the right of the bishops to depose him, and other examples of a similar nature, that the usurpations of the clergy were in a great measure occasioned by the slavish superstition of the laity, equally blind, wicked, and devout.

The zeal of the bishops to establish their independence was favourable to the projects of the court of Rome. Sergius II. had taken possession of the apostolic see, in 844, without the approbation of Lothaire, then emperor ; who, incensed at such an insult, sent his son Louis to Rome with troops and prelates. The pope having conducted the prince to St. Peter's gate, said to him, " I permit you to enter if your intentions are good ; if not, I will not suffer you to enter!" and the French soldiers being guilty of some irregularities, he actually ordered the gates to be shut. Lothaire complained! Sergius was cited to appear before a council ; he appeared, and justified himself in the eye of the priesthood[3]." Leo IV., celebrated for the courage with which he defended Rome against the Saracens, and Benedict III., elected in spite of the emperor, lived in peace with royalty ; but Nicholas I., more bold than any of his predecessors, made himself the judge of kings and of bishops, and realized the chimera of lying decretals.

---

[1] *Concil. Gal.* vol. ii.—*Hist. Eccles. par* Fleury.
[2] *Hist. de l'Eglise Gallic.*
[3] *Concil. Gal.* vol. ii.—Fleury, *Hist. Eccles.*

[Before I adduce any instances of the spirit of pope Nicholas, I will take cursory notice of the story of a female, vulgarly called Pope Joan, who is said to have filled the papal chair between the pontificates of Leo and Benedict. It has been affirmed, that a woman of English extraction, but of German birth, studied at Rome for some years in the disguise of a man; and, having acquired the reputation of an able theologian, was unanimously elected pontiff, in the year 855; that she governed the church above a twelvemonth; but, having been criminally connected with one of her domestics, felt the pains of childbirth in a public procession, and died soon after she had been delivered. This story does not appear to have been mentioned before the lapse of four centuries from the period to which it is assigned. It was obviously fabricated with a view of exposing the Romanists to ridicule and odium: and it is disbelieved by every man of candour and judgment.]

A grand occasion offered in France for Nicholas to exercise that authority which he attributed to himself. Lothaire, A. D. king of Lorrain, divorced his wife Theutberge on a charge 860. of incest with her own brother. She was cleared by the trial of boiling water, but afterwards convicted by her own voluntary confession. A council at Aix-la-Chapelle authorized Lothaire to espouse Valdrade, a young lady to whom he had been ar- A. D. dently attached from his early years. The guilty individuals 862. were equally desirous of this marriage; but the pope, affecting to be shocked at the criminal amour, endeavoured to force the king to take back his first wife. For this purpose he A. D. ordered the bishops to hold a council at Metz with his 863. legates, and to cite and judge Lothaire. They confirmed the divorce, contrary to the expectations of the pontiff—a decree which so much enraged him, that he deposed the bishops of Treves and Cologne, relations of Valdrade, who had been appointed to present to him the acts of the council. These prelates complained to the emperor Louis II. He went immediately to Rome, displayed his authority, and seemed determined to repress the papal power. But he was seized with an indisposition, and also with superstitious fears; and he retired, after having approved the conduct of Nicholas, who became still more imperious. Lothaire offered to justify himself in person before the pope; but his holiness insisted that Valdrade should first be dismissed; and a legate threatened the king with immediate excommunication, if he continued in disobedience. The intimidated prince now submitted; he recalled Theutberge, and even consented that the legate should lead Valdrade in triumph to Rome. She set out on that mortifying journey, but fearing the violence of the pope, refused to proceed; and, in a short time, resumed her place both as mistress and queen. The unfortunate Theutberge, sinking beneath the weight of persecution and neglect, at last desired to be separated from Lothaire, protesting that her marriage was void, and that Valdrade's was legitimate. But nothing could move the inflexible Nicholas: he continued obstinate [1].

We may consider this pope as the forerunner of Gregory VII.; and, in the same circumstances, he would probably have carried his ambition to the same height. The bishops of Treves and Cologne accused him, in an invective, of making himself *emperor* of the whole world; and that expression, though somewhat strained, was not altogether without foundation. He asserted his dominion over the French clergy, by re-establishing Rothade of Soissons, who had been deposed by a provincial council; and he received appeals from all ecclesiastics dissatisfied with their bishops. By these means he accustomed the people to acknowledge a supreme tribunal at a distance from their own country, and consequently a foreign sway. He gave orders for the succession to the kingdom of Provence, which Charles the Bald disputed with the emperor Louis, brother to the deceased king. " Let no one prevent the emperor," said he, in a letter on that subject, " from governing the kingdoms which he holds in virtue of a succession confirmed by the holy see, and by the crown which the sovereign pontiff has set upon his head."

Nicholas died in 867; but his principles had taken such deep root, that Adrian II., his successor, though more moderate, and desirous of peace, thought his condescension great in permitting the king of Lorrain to come to Rome, in order to justify himself, A. D. or do penance. Charles the Bald and Louis the German 868. waited with impatience for the excommunication of their nephew, being persuaded that they should then have a right to seize his dominions. Thus the blind ambition of princes favoured the exercise of a power, which they ought to have foreseen might be turned against themselves; which afterwards became the scourge of royalty, and made every crowned head tremble.

Lothaire, while at Rome, employed all possible means to soften the pope; he received the communion from his hand, after

---

[1] Hincmar de *Divort. Lothar. et Theutberg.*

having sworn that he would in future avoid all criminal commerce with Valdrade, according to the prohibition of Nicholas. He soon after died at Placentia. His death was considered as a just vengeance, as a mark of the Divine displeasure against perjury; and it rendered the proof by the eucharist still more important.

The emperor Louis II. ought legally to have succeeded to the dominions of the deceased king; but he being at that time employed in expelling the Saracens, who had invaded Italy, and consequently not in a condition to assert his right by arms, Charles the Bald seized the succession, and retained it notwithstanding the remonstrances of the pope. " The *arms* which God has put into our hand," said Adrian, " are prepared for his defence [1]!" Charles was more afraid of the arms of his brother the German, with whom he found it necessary to share the kingdom, though the nobility and clergy of Lorrain had voluntarily submitted to him.

The pope still continued his remonstrances in favour of the emperor, hoping at least to obtain something for him; but they were disregarded by the French king, who had now thrown off much of his piety, and answered in a spirited maner by the famous Hincmar, archbishop of Rheims. This bold and independent prelate desired the pope to call to mind that respect and submission which the ancient pontiffs had always paid to princes, and to reflect that his dignity gave him no right over the government of kingdoms; that he could not be at the same time pope and king; that the choice of a sovereign belongs to the people; that anathemas ill applied have no effect upon the soul; and that *free* men are not to be enslaved by a bishop of Rome [2].

Adrian affected to despise these arguments, and continued for some time his menaces, both against Hincmar and the king; but finding them ineffectual, he changed his tone, and wrote several flattering letters to Charles, promising him the empire on the death of his nephew, then in a languishing condition. This project in favour of the French king was executed under John VIII., Adrian's successor. The emperor dying without A. D. male heirs, Louis the German claimed the succession 875. and the imperial dignity, as elder brother to Charles; but the pope preferred the claim of the latter for political reasons, which, with the court of Rome, never failed to take place of equity.

---

[1] *Epist. Adriani.*   [2] Fleury, *Hist. Eccles.*

Louis seemed approaching to his end, and had three sons, among whom his dominions would be divided.   Charles was a younger man, and had only one son; he therefore appeared the most proper person to choose as a protector.   He crossed the Alps at the head of his army, and accordingly received the imperial crown as a *present* from the pope; but nearly in the same manner that many presents of the like kind are obtained in our A. D. days, by paying a considerable sum for it.   In an assem-876. bly at Pavia, the bishops, abbots, and Italian nobles, re-cognised him in the following words; " Since the Divine favour, through the merits of the holy apostles, and of their vicar pope John, has raised you to the empire, according to the judgment of the Holy Ghost, we elect you unanimously for our protector and lord [1]."

On the death of Louis the German, a prince of some merit both as a warrior and politician, Charles the Bald, always am-bitious and imprudent, attempted to seize that part of Lorrain which he had granted to his brother, and was deservedly de-feated [2].   His three nephews, Carloman, Louis, and Charles, preserved their possessions by maintaining a strict union among themselves.   The first had Bavaria, the second Saxony, and the third Suabia.

The Saracens renewing their ravages in Italy, the pope had recourse to the new emperor; and desired him " to remember the hand that had given him the empire, lest," added he, " if driven to despair, we should change our opinion!"   This me-nace, sufficiently intelligible, had its effect.   Though France was then overrun by the Normans, whom Charles was unable to resist, he undertook to expel the Saracens; and he had scarcely arrived in Italy, when he received intelligence of a new enemy. Carloman had advanced against him, with an intention of seizing the imperial crown and the kingdom of Italy, in virtue of his father's will and the right of primogeniture.   Charles, be-Oct. trayed by his nobles, retired with precipitation, and died 877. in a miserable cottage, on Mont Cenis, in the fifty-fifth year of his age [3].

An ordinance in the last year of his reign permitted the nobility to transmit their employments to their sons, or other male heirs.   This privilege, extorted from the crown, as I have already observed, was one of the principal sources of disorder

[1] Fleury. *Hist. Eccles.*   [2] *Annal. Fuldens.*
[3] Sigon. *Reg. Ital.*—*Annal. Berlin.*

in the feudal government; and tended, as we shall have occasion to see, to the abolition of all political subjection.　In the mean time I must speak of a people who deserve your attention, no less on account of their manners than their warlike achievements.

LETTER XI.

Of the Normans or Danes, before their Settlement in France and England.

THE bravest and most liberal-minded of the Saxons, my dear Philip, on the final reduction of their country by Charle-magne, having fled from the dominion and persecutions of the conqueror into the ancient Scandinavia, or that part of Europe which comprehends the present kingdoms of Sweden, Denmark, and Norway, carried with them their vengeance and violent aversion against Christianity.　There, meeting with men of dispositions similar to their own, and of the same religion with themselves, they were cordially received, and soon stimulated the natives to deeds of arms; to enterprises which at once promised revenge to the fugitives, and subsistence to the inhabitants of countries then overstocked with people.

In their various incursions on the continent, these ferocious adventurers were known by the general name of Normans, from their northern situation; and, in their attacks upon Britain, by the common appellation of Danes, to whatever country they might belong.　They became the terror of all the maritime parts of Europe.　But, before I speak of their depredations, I must say a few words of their religion and manners.

The manners of a people, and the popular superstition, depend on each other.　Religion takes its complexion originally from the manners; men form a deity according to their own ideas, their prejudices, their passions: and the manners are, in a great measure, continued or altered by the established religion of any country, especially when it is calculated to affect the imagination. The religion of the ancient Scandinavians was highly so, and was preserved entire among the Normans, who also retained their unadulterated manners.　They were worthy of each other: equally bloody and barbarous, but formed to inspire the most enthusiastic courage, and the most unremitted perseverance in toil. Odin, whom the Saxons called Woden, was their supreme divinity. They painted him as the god of *terror*—the author of *devastation*—the father of *carnage!*—and they worshipped him accordingly. They sacrificed to him, when they were successful, some of the captives taken in war; and they believed that those heroes would stand highest in his favour who had killed most enemies in the field; that, after death, the brave would be admitted into his palace, and there have the happiness of drinking ale (the favourite liquor of the northern nations) out of the skulls of their slaughtered foes [1].

In consequence of this belief, fatigues, wounds, combats, and perils, were the exercises of infancy and the sports of youth. They were forbidden to pronounce the word fear, even on the most trying occasions. Education, prejudice, manners, example, habit—all contributed to subdue in them the sensation of timidity: to make them covet danger, and seem greedy of death. Military discipline was only requsite to enable them to enslave the whole Christian world, then sinking under the weight of a debasing superstition, and cringing beneath the rod of priestly tyranny.

Though Charle-magne took many wise precautions against the Normans, he was not able wholly to prevent their irruptions, and was only freed by the death of their leader from a dangerous competition. Under Louis the Débonnaire, they threw all France into alarm; and, under Charles the Bald, they committed horrible devastions. Their fleets, which were composed of light barks, braved the storms of the ocean, and penetrated every creek and river; so that they landed sometimes on the coasts and sometimes in the interior parts of the kingdom. As the government took no effectual measures for repelling them, the unprotected people knew nothing but fear. Fire and sword, on all hands, marked the route of the ravagers. With their booty they carried off women, to whom they were much addicted, and boys to recruit their predatory bands. Their irruptions were renewed with alarming frequency. They repeatedly pillaged Rouen; they surprised and burnt Paris; they laid waste Aquitaine and other provinces, and reduced the French king to the greatest distress.

---

[1] See the *Edda*; or System of Runic Mythology. In that state of festivity the departed warriors were supposed to be served at table by beautiful virgins called Valker, who ministered to other pleasures besides those of the feast. (*Edda Mythol.* xxxi.) And war and arms, the delight of the Scandinavians in this life, were believed to be their amusements in another world. *Edda*, xxxv.

Shut up at St. Denis, while his capital was in flames, Charles the Bald was less anxious about saving his people than the reliques. Instead of encountering the enemy, he bought a peace ; or, in other words, he furnished the Normans with the means, while he inspired them with the motive, of a new war. They returned accordingly ; and Charles, to complete his disgrace, published, when going to assist the pope, in the last year of his reign, a capitular to regulate the contributions to be paid to the Normans [1].

England had also experienced a variety of calamities from the incursions of these plunderers, when it found a protector in the great Alfred. But before I exhibit the exploits, or consider the institutions of that illustrious prince, we must take a view of the reigns of his predecessors from the end of the Saxon Heptarchy.

LETTER XII.

Of the Affairs of England, from the End of the Saxon Heptarchy to the Death of Alfred the Great.

EGBERT, the founder of the English monarchy, was a prince of eminent abilities and great experience. He had enjoyed a considerable command in the armies of Charle-magne, by whom he was much respected, and had acted with success against the Normans and other enemies of the empire. After his return to Britain, he was engaged in a variety of contests with some of the contemporary princes before he obtained the supreme dominion : but, having surmounted those difficulties, he found himself without a rival. As he was the only remaining decendant of Cerdic, one of the first Saxon leaders who landed in this island, and who were all supposed to have sprung from Woden, the hero or the god, the people readily transferred their allegiance to a prince who appeared to merit it equally by his birth and talents. A union of government seemed to promise internal tranquillity ; and the Saxons, from their insular situation and their power, had little reason to be afraid of foreign enemies. Egbert, therefore, flattered himself with the hopes of peace and security. But human foresight is very limited; a

A.D. 827.

---

[1] *Capit. Carol. Calvi.*

fleet of those northern adventurers, whom we have already seen
ravaging France under the name of Normans, soon gave the
English monarch reason to alter his opinion. Though they had
previously made some minor incursions, historians usually date
their ravages from their appearance in the Isle of Sheppey, which
they pillaged, and carried off their booty with impunity. They
A.D. soon returned in thirty-five ships. The king gave them
833. battle at Charmouth in Dorsetshire, where they were
worsted, after an obstinate dispute, but made good their retreat
to their ships. Now sensible what an enemy they had to deal
with, they entered into an alliance with the Britons of Cornwall;
A.D. and, landing in that country, they and their confederates
835. rushed forward, till they were met by Egbert, at Hen-
gesdown, and totally defeated[1]. But while England was threatened by new alarms from the same quarter, this warlike monarch,
A.D. who alone was able to oppose the invaders, unfortunately
838. died, and left the kingdom to his son Ethelwolf, a prince
better fitted to wear the cowl than the crown.

Ethelwolf began his reign with dividing his dominions, according to the absurd custom of those times; delivering over to his
eldest son Athelstan, the counties of Essex, Kent, and Sussex.
But no inconveniences seem to have arisen from this partition,
the terror of the Danish invaders preventing all domestic dissensions. Time proved that this terror was but too just. The Danes
returned with redoubled fury; and though often repulsed, and
sometimes defeated, they always obtained their end, by committing plunder, and carrying off their booty. They avoided coming
to a general engagement, which was not suited to their plan of
operations. Their vessels, being small, ran easily up the creeks
and rivers; they drew them ashore, and formed an entrenchment
around them, leaving them under a guard. They scattered themselves over the face of the country in small parties, making spoil
of every thing that came in their way—goods, cattle, and women.
If opposed by a superior force, they retired to their vessels, set
sail, and invaded some distant quarter not prepared for their
reception. All England was kept in continual alarm; and the
inhabitants of one part would not venture to assist another, lest
their own families and possessions should be exposed to the fury
of the ravagers. Every season of the year was alike: no man
could be certain of a day's safety.

Encouraged by their past successes, the Danes at length

---

[1] *Chron. Sax.*

landed in so large a body as seemed to threaten the whole A.D.
island with subjection. But the Anglo-Saxons, though 851.
labouring under the weight of superstition, were still a gallant
people : they roused themselves with a vigour proportioned to
the necessity, and defeated their invaders in several engagements[1]. A body of Danes, however, now ventured, for the first
time, to take up their winter-quarters in England ; and other
parties renewed their inhuman ravages.

The harassed state of his kingdom did not hinder Ethelwolf
from making a pilgrimage to Rome, with his favourite A.D.
son Alfred. In his return, after a twelvemonth spent in 854.
devotions and benefactions to the see of Rome, he married Judith,
daughter of Charles the Bald ; and soon after his arrival in
England, he conferred a perpetual and very important donation
on the church, by granting to the clergy a tenth out of A.D.
all the produce of land. This enormous tax upon in- 855.
dustry had been long claimed by the servants of the altar, as a
perpetual property belonging to the priesthood—a jargon founded
on the practice of the Jews. Charle-magne had ordered the tithe
to be paid in consideration of the church-lands seized by the
laity ; but, in England, no such invasion had been made. The
church enjoyed many lands, and was enriched by the continual
oblations of the people : the English clergy, therefore, had not
hitherto been able to obtain their demand. But an opportunity
now offered itself, and religion furnished the motive ; a weak
and superstitious prince, and an ignorant people, dejected by
their losses, and in terror of future invasions, eagerly adopted any
means, however costly, of bribing the protection of heaven[2].

After the death of Athelstan, Ethelbald, the king's second
son, had formed the project of excluding his father from the
throne. This unnatural attempt gave the pious monarch little
concern. He complied with most of his son's demands, and the
kingdom was divided between them. He lived only two A.D.
years after his return to England, which he left by his 857.
will to be shared between Ethelbald and Ethelbert.

Ethelbald was said to be a profligate prince ; but, if so, his
reign was happily short ; and his brother Ethelbert suc- A.D.
ceeding to the government of the whole kingdom, con- 860.
ducted himself in a manner more suitable to his rank. England was still infested by the depredations of the Danes, who,
in his reign, sacked Winchester, but were there defeated.

[1] *Chron. Sax.* [2] Selden's *History of Tithes*, chap. viii.

Ethelbert was succeeded by his brother Ethelred, whose
A.D. whole reign was one continued struggle with the Danes.
866. He defended his kingdom with much bravery, and was
gallantly seconded in all his efforts by his younger brother
Alfred, who, though excluded from a large inheritance left to
him by his father, generously sacrificed his resentment to the
A.D. public good. Ethelred died in the midst of these troubles,
871. and left his disordered kingdom to Alfred.

The new monarch was now twenty-two years of age, and a
prince of very promising talents. He had no sooner buried his
brother than he was obliged to take the field against the Danes.
They had seized Wilton, and were ravaging the neighbouring
country. He gave them battle, and at first gained some advantage over them; but, pursuing his victory too far, he was
worsted by means of the enemy's numbers. The loss of the
Danes, however, was so considerable, that, fearing Alfred might
suddenly receive reinforcements from his subjects, they stipulated
for a safe retreat under a promise of quitting Wessex. But
they were no sooner freed from danger than they renewed their
A.D. ravages. A new swarm of Danes landed, and Alfred,
875. after various conflicts, again condescended to treat with
them, and was again deceived. While he was expecting the
execution of the agreement, another swarm from the northern
hive landed on this island, and reduced the Saxons to despair.
They believed themselves abandoned by Heaven, and devoted to
destruction; since, after all their vigorous efforts, fresh invaders
still poured in upon them, as greedy of spoil and slaughter as
the former. Some left their country; others submitted to the
conquerors; but none would listen to the exhortations of
Alfred, who, still undismayed, begged them to make another
effort in defence of their possessions, their liberties, and their
prince[1].

A.D. Thus abandoned by his subjects, this illustrious mo-
878. narch relinquished, for a time, the ensigns of his dignity,
and assumed the habit of a peasant. In that mean disguise he
eluded the pursuit and the fury of his enemies; and, in order
to save his country, he even condescended to live for some time
as servant to a grazier. But the human mind is as little suited
to employments beneath as above its capacity: the great Alfred
made a bad swine-herd. His guardian genius was occupied with
higher cares; and, as soon as he found that his enemies were

_____

[1] *Chron. Sax.* — Alur. Beverl. *Annal.*

more remiss in their search, he collected some of his adherents, and retired to a morass, formed by the stagnating waters of the Thone and Parret; where finding some firm ground, he erected a small fortress. This place was called *Æthlinga-ige*, or the Isle of Nobles; and it now bears the name of Athelney. Here, for some months, Alfred lay concealed, but not inactive; he made occasional sallies upon the Danes, who often felt the vigour of his arm, but knew not whence the blow came, or by whom it was directed. At length a prosperous event emboldened the royal fugitive to leave his retreat, and enter on a scene of action more worthy of himself.

Oddune, governor of Devonshire, being besieged in his castle by Hubba, a celebrated Danish general, made an unexpected sally upon his adversaries, routed them, and pursued them with great slaughter; killed Hubba himself, and gained possession of the famous *Reafen*, or Raven, an enchanted standard, in which the Danes put great confidence[1]. Alfred hearing of this victory, was happy to find the seeds of valour beginning to revive among his subjects; but before he would assemble them in arms, he resolved to inspect the situation of the enemy, and judge of the probability of success, as an unfortunate attempt in the present state of national despondency might be ruinous and fatal. In consequence of this resolution, he entered the Danish camp under the disguise of a harper, and passed unsuspected through every quarter. He observed the supine security of the ravagers, their contempt of the English, and their neglect of all military regulations. Encouraged by these propitious appearances, he sent secret intelligence to his most powerful subjects, and summoned them to attend with their vassals on the borders of Selwood forest. The English, who, instead of ending their calamities by submission, as they fondly hoped, had found the insolence and rapine of the conquerors more intolerable than the dangers and fatigues of war, joyfully resorted to the place of rendezvous. They saluted their beloved monarch with bursts of applause: they could not satiate their eyes with the sight of a prince whom they had believed dead, and who now appeared as their deliverer; they urged him to lead them to liberty and vengeance. Alfred did not suffer their ardour to cool: he conducted them instantly to Edington, where the Danes lay encamped; and, taking advantage of his previous knowledge of the enemy's situation, he directed his attack against the most un-

[1] *Chron. Sax.*—Abb. Rieval.

2

guarded quarter. Surprised to see an army of Englishmen, whom they considered as totally subdued, and still more to find Alfred at their head, the Danes still maintained their military fame, and made a desperate resistance. After an obstinate battle they were at length broken, and routed with great slaughter[1].

Alfred, no less generous than brave, and who knew as well how to govern as to conquer, took the surviving Danes, and their prince Guthrun or Gothrum, under his protection. He granted them their lives on submission, and liberty to settle in East-Anglia, on condition that they should embrace Christianity. Many consented, and were baptized: others passed over to the continent[2].

After this success, Alfred employed himself in establishing civil and military institutions; in composing the minds of men to industry and justice, and in providing against the return of like calamities. He rebuilt the towns which had been ruined by the Danes, and formed a regular militia for the defence of the kingdom. He took care that all his subjects should be armed and registered, and assigned to them a regular round of duty; he distributed one part into the castles and fortresses, which he erected in proper places; he appointed another to take the field on any alarm, and assemble at stated places of rendez-vous; and he left a sufficient number at home, who were employed in the cultivation of the lands, and afterwards took their turn in military service. The whole kingdom was like one great garrison: the Danes, who occasionally re-appeared on the coasts, could no sooner land in any quarter than a sufficient force was ready to oppose them, without leaving the other parts naked or defenceless[3].

But Alfred did not trust solely to his land forces: he may be deemed the creator of the English navy, as well as the establisher of the monarchy. Sensible that ships form the most natural bulwark of an island, a circumstance hitherto overlooked by the English (as the Saxons were now generally called), he provided himself with a naval force, and met the Danes on their own element. A hundred and twenty armed vessels were stationed upon the coasts, and being provided with warlike engines and expert seamen, both Frisians and English, maintained a supe-

---

[1] *Chron. Sax.*—Sim. Dunelm.—Alur. Beverl.
[2] Asserii *Annal.*—Hen. Huntingd.
[3] Spelman's *Life of Alfred.*

riority over the enemy, and gave birth to that claim which England still supports—to the sovereignty of the ocean.

Thus did Alfred provide for the security of his kingdom ; and the excellent posture of defence every where established, together with the wisdom and valour of the prince, at length restored peace and tranquillity to England, and communicated to it a consequence hitherto unknown in the monarchy.   But I should convey to you, my dear son, a very imperfect idea of Alfred's merit, by confining myself to his military and political talents.   His judicial institutions, and his zeal for the encouragement of arts and sciences, demand your particular attention. We must now, therefore, consider him in a character altogether civil—as the father of English law and English literature.

Though Alfred in the early part of his reign had subdued, settled, or expelled the Danes as a body, straggling bands of that people afterwards continued to infest the kingdom with their robberies; and even the native English, reduced to extreme indigence by these and former depredations, abandoned themselves to a like disorderly life.   They joined the robbers in pillaging the more wealthy part of their fellow-citizens. Those evils required redress, and Alfred took means effectually to remove them.   In order to render the execution of justice more strict and regular, he divided all England into counties ; these counties he subdivided into hundreds, and the hundreds into tithings.   Every householder was answerable for the behaviour of his family, of his slaves, and even of his guests, if they resided above three days in his house.   Ten neighbouring householders, answerable for each other's conduct, were formed into one corporation under the name of a tithing, decennary, or friburgh, over which a person called a tithing-man, head-borough, or bors-holder, presided.   Every man who did not register himself in some tithing was punished as an outlaw ; and no man could change his habitation without a certificate from the head of the tithing to which he previously belonged [1].

These regulations may seem rigorous, and are not perhaps necessary in times when men are habituated to obedience and justice.   But they were well calculated to reduce a fierce and licentious people under the salutary restraints of law and government: and Alfred took care to temper their severity by other institutions favourable to the freedom and security of the subject.   Nothing can be more liberal than his plan for the admi-

---

[1]   *Fœdas Alfredi et Gothurn.* cap. iii. cap. Wilkins.

nistration of justice. The bors-holder summoned his whole decennary to assist him in the decision of smaller differences among the members of the corporation : in controversies of greater moment, the dispute was brought before the hundred, which consisted of ten decennaries or a hundred families of freemen, and regularly assembled once in four weeks, for the trying of causes [1]. Their mode of decision claims your attention : twelve freeholders were chosen, who, having sworn with the chief magistrate of the hundred to administer impartial justice, proceeded to the examination of the cause that was submitted to them. In this simple form of trial you will perceive the origin of Juries, or judgment by equals, an institution almost peculiar to the English nation, admirable in itself, and the best calculated for the preservation of man's natural rights, and the administration of justice, that human wisdom ever devised [2].

Besides these monthly meetings of the hundred, there was an annual meeting appointed for the more general inspection of the police of the district, for inquiring into crimes, correcting the misconduct of magistrates, and obliging every person to show the decennary in which he was registered. In imitation of their ancestors, the ancient Germans, the people on those occasions assembled in arms : whence a hundred was sometimes called a wapentake, and its court served for the support of military discipline, as well as the administration of justice.

The next superior court to that of the hundred was the county-court, which met twice a-year, and consisted of all the freeholders of the county, who had an equal vote in the decision of causes ; but of this court I have already spoken in treating of the laws and government of the Saxons. I shall therefore only add here, that to the alderman and bishop, Alfred added a third judge in each county, under the name of sheriff, who enjoyed equal authority with the two former [3]. His office also empowered him to guard the rights of the crown in the county, and levy the fines imposed : which, in an age when money atoned for almost every violation of the laws of society, formed no inconsiderable branch of the public revenue.

In default of justice from all these courts, an appeal lay to the

---

[1] *Foedas Alfredi et Gothurn.* cap. iii. cap. Wilkins.
[2] Trial by jury was known to the Saxons, at least in criminal cases, before their settlement in Britain. But among the nations of the continent, it was not necessary that the members of a jury should be unanimous in their decision ; a majority was sufficient to acquit or condemn the person accused. Stiernhook *de Jure Sueon. et Gothor. Vetust.* lib. i.
[3] Ingulph. Hist.

king himself in council : and, as the wisdom and justice of Alfred were universally revered, he was soon overwhelmed with appeals from all parts of his dominions.   In order to remedy this inconvenience he chose the earl and sheriffs from among the men most celebrated for probity and knowledge in the kingdom ; he punished severely all malversation in office ; he removed all whom he found unequal to the trust[1]; and the better to guide magistrates of all kinds in the administration of justice, he A. D. framed a code of law, which, though now lost, served long 890. as the basis of English jurisprudence, and is generally esteemed the origin of our COMMON LAW.

Alfred appointed regular meetings of the states of England twice a-year in the city of London, which he had repaired and beautified, and which thenceforth became the capital of the kingdom.   Every thing soon wore a new aspect under his wise and equitable government.   Such success attended his legislation, and so exact was the general police, that he is said to have hung up, by way of trial, golden bracelets near the high roads, and no man dared to touch them[2]. But this great prince, though rigorous in the administration of justice, which he wisely considered as the best means of repressing crimes, preserved the most sacred regard to the liberty of his people.   His concern on this subject extended even to future times, and ought to endear his memory to every Englishman.   " It is just," says he in his will, " that the English should for ever remain FREE AS THEIR OWN THOUGHTS[3]."

After providing for the security of his kingdom, and taming his subjects to the restraints of law, Alfred extended his care to those things which aggrandize a nation, and make a people happy. Sensible that good morals and knowledge are almost inseparable in every age, though not in every individual, he gave great encouragement to the pursuit of learning.   He invited the most celebrated scholars from all parts of Europe: he established schools for the instruction of the ignorant: he founded, or at least repaired, the university of Oxford, and endowed it with many privileges and revenues ; he enjoined by law all freeholders, possessed of two hides of land[4], to send their children to school : and he gave preferment, either in church or state, to such only as had made some proficiency in knowledge.   But the most effectual

[1] *Le Miroir de Justice*, chap. ii.
[2] Gul. Malmesb. lib. ii.
[3] Asser. p. 2.
[4] A hide contained land sufficient to employ one plough.   Gervase of Tilbury says, it commonly consisted of a hundred acres.

expedient employed by Alfred for the encouragement of learning
was his own example.   Notwithstanding the multiplicity of civil
objects which engaged his attention, and although he is said to
have fought in person fifty-six battles by sea and land, this illustrious hero and legislator was able to acquire by his unremitted
industry, during a life of no extraordinary length, a greater portion of knowledge, and even to produce more books, than most
speculative men, in more fortunate ages, who have devoted their
whole time to study.   He composed a variety of poems, fables,
and apt stories, to lead the untutored mind to the love of letters,
and bend the heart to the practice of virtue.   He also gave
Saxon translations of the histories of Orosius and Bede, and of
the Consolation of Philosophy, by Boëtius.

Alfred was no less attentive to the propagation of those mechanical arts, which have a more sensible though not a more
intimate connexion with the welfare of a state.   He introduced
and encouraged manufactures of all kinds, and suffered no in-
ventor or improver of any useful or ingenious art to go unre-
warded.   He prompted men of activity and industry to apply
themselves to navigation, and to push commerce into the most
distant countries; and he set apart a seventh portion of his own
revenue for maintaining a number of workmen, whom he employed in rebuilding or repairing towns and castles.   The ele-
gancies of life are said to have been brought to him even from
the Mediterranean and the Indies [1]; and his subjects, seeing
these desirable productions and the means of acquiring riches by
trade, were taught to respect those peaceful virtues by which
alone such blessings can be earned or ensured.

This extraordinary man, who is justly considered, both by
natives and foreigners, as the greatest prince after Charle-magne
that Europe saw for several ages, and as one of the wisest and
Oct.   best that ever adorned the annals of any nation, died in
900.   the vigour of his age and the full strength of his faculties,
after a life of fifty-one years, and a glorious reign of twenty-nine
years and a half.   His merit both in public and private life, may
be set in opposition to that of any sovereign or citizen in ancient
or modern times.   He seems indeed, as is observed by an elegant
and profound historian [2], to be the complete model of that perfect character, which under the denomination of a sage, or truly
wise man, philosophers have been so fond of delineating without
the hope of ever seeing it realized.

---

[1] Gul. Malmesb. lib. ii.   [2] Hume, vol. i.

LETTER XIII.

Of the Empire of Charle-magne, and the Church, from the Death of Charles the Bald to that of Louis IV., when the Imperial Dignity was transferred from the French to the Germans.

THE continent of Europe, my dear Philip, toward the close of the ninth century, offers nothing to our view but calamities, disorders, revolutions, and anarchy. Louis the Stammerer, son of Charles the Bald, may be said to have purchased the crown of France at the price, and on the conditions, which the A.D. bishops and nobles were pleased to impose on him. He 887. was not acknowledged before he had heaped lands, honours, and offices, on the nobility, and had promised that the clergy should enjoy the same emoluments and privileges which they had possessed under Louis the Débonnaire [1].

Pope John VIII. eagerly wished that Louis should be elected emperor in the room of his father, by the Italian states; but not being able to carry his point, he retired into France, and held a council at Troyes, where he excommunicated the duke of Spoleto, and the duke of Tuscany, for opposing his measures, and attacking the ecclesiastical state. One of the canons of this council is very remarkable: it expressly asserts, that " the *powers of the world* shall not dare to seat themselves in the presence of bishops unless desired [2]."

Louis the Stammerer died after a reign of eighteen months, and left his queen Adelaide pregnant. He was succeeded A.D. by Louis III. and Carloman II., two sons by a wife whom 879. he had divorced. Duke Boson, father-in-law to Carloman, promoted the accession of those princes, that he might afterwards share the monarchy. By his intrigues with the pope and the clergy, he procured from a council a declaration of the necessity of erecting a new kingdom; and the members bestowed, by the Divine inspiration (to use their own language), the kingdom of Arles, or Provence, upon this ambitious duke. Italy was in possession of Carloman, king of Bavaria, who had also seized part of Lorrain; and the French nobility already enjoyed most of the lands; so that a king of France retained little more than the mere shadow of royalty.

[1] Aimon. de Rebus Gestis Francorum, lib. v.　　　[2] Concil. Gal. vol. iii.

On the death of the joint kings of France, who lived in harmony notwithstanding their confined situation, their brother Charles, born after his father's death, and known by the name of the Simple, ought to have succeeded to the monarchy, by the right
A.D. 884. of birth; but as he was very young, the nobles elected Charles the Fat (son of Louis the German), already emperor, successor to his two brothers [1]. He re-united in his person all the French empire, except the kingdom of the usurper Boson; and proved what those who elected him had not sufficiently attended to, that a prince may conduct his affairs with judgment, while confined within a moderate compass, and yet be very unfit for the government of a great empire.

The incapacity, and even the cowardice of Charles, soon became too obvious to be denied. Though he had governed his paternal dominions without any visible defect of judgment, and raised himself to the empire by his reputation and address, his mind, instead of expanding itself to its new object, even shrank from it, and contracted itself, till every mark of ability disappeared. After disgracing himself by ceding Friesland to the Normans, and promising them a tribute for forbearance, he roused them by his perfidy, while he encouraged them by his weakness. Enraged at the death of their king, who had been invited to a conference and murdered, they entered France, burned Pontoise, and besieged Paris [2].

This siege is much celebrated by the French historians: prodigies are related of both parties. Eudes, count of Paris, whom we shall soon see on the throne of France; his brother Robert; bishop Gosselin; and his nephew, abbot Eble; were particularly distinguished by their valour and patriotism. The besieged defended themselves for a whole year against an army of thirty thousand men, and the combined efforts of courage and stratagem, before the emperor came to their relief. At length Charles ap-
A.D. 887. peared with all the military force of his realm, fully persuaded that the Normans would retire at the sight of his standards [3]. But he soon found his mistake; for they did not show the smallest alarm. Preferring a shameful negociation to a doubtful victory, he engaged to pay them a large ransom for his capital and the safety of his kingdom; and (what was still more disgraceful) not being able to raise the money till the spring, he permitted the Normans to winter in Burgundy, which had not yet acknowledged his authority; or, in other

[1] Aimon. lib. v.　　　　　　[2] Chron. Gest. Norm.
[3] Paul. Æmil. de Gest. Franc.

words, to continue their ravages, which they did with the most insatiable fury [1].

This ignominious treaty, and its consequences, entirely ruined the emperor's reputation, which was already low. He had no minister in whom he could confide ; for he was neither loved nor feared. The Germans first revolted. Charles had incurred the hatred of the nobility by attempting to limit the hereditary fiefs ; and he made the clergy his enemies, while he exposed himself to universal contempt, by prosecuting Ludard, bishop of Verceil, his prime minister, and the only person of authority in his service, on a suspicion of a criminal correspondence with the empress Richilde, whom he imprisoned, and who completed his disgrace. She affirmed, that she was innocent of the crime laid to her charge ; and, in support of this asseveration, she offered to undergo any trial that should be assigned to her, according to the superstitious custom of those times, when an appeal to Heaven was preferred to a judicial process. Ludard fostered the general discontent; and Charles was deposed in a diet of the empire, and neglected to such a degree as to be obliged to subsist by the liberality of the archbishop of Mentz [2].

A.D. 888.

Arnolf, the bastard son of Carloman the Bavarian king, and grandson to Louis the German, was now raised to the imperial dignity. Italy submitted alternately to Berengarius, duke of Friuli, and Guido, duke of Spoleto, both of the family of Charlemagne by the mother's side. Their competitions were long and bloody. Count Eudes, whose valour had saved Paris, and whose father Robert the Strong, had been no less brave and illustrious, was chosen king of Neustria or Roman France ; a dignity which he agreed to hold in trust for Charles the Simple, yet a minor [3].

Notwithstanding the courage and talents of Eudes, France was still a scene of contention and disorder. A faction pretended to assert the right of the lawful heir, who was not really injured : and Eudes ceded to him as an appanage, a considerable portion of the kingdom. Count Rodolph established the kingdom of Transjurane Burgundy (so called from its situation beyond mount Jura), which comprehended nearly the present Switzerland and part of Savoy. A council confirmed to Louis, the son of Boson, the kingdom of Arles, as a council had given it to his father [4]. History would be a mere chaos, were it to comprehend all the acts of violence, treachery, and outrage, that dis-

[1] *Gest. Norm.*   [2] *Annal. Fuldens.*
[3] *Annal. Metens.*   [4] Regin. *Chron.*

graced this period. I shall therefore only notice the leading circumstances, which alone deserve your attention.

Eudes died before he was able to remedy the disorders of the A.D. state; and Charles the Simple (too justly so named), now 898. acknowledged king of France in his own right, increased by his weakness the prevailing evils. The nobles openly aspired to independence. They usurped the governments with which they had been entrusted, and extorted confirmations of them from Charles for themselves and their heirs, on the easy condition of an empty homage [1]. A large and once well-regulated kingdom was divided into a multitude of separate principalities, altogether independent of the crown, or dependent only in name, whose possessors waged continual wars with each other, and exercised an insupportable tyranny over their vassals. By these means the people were either reduced to a state of absolute servitude, or to a condition so precarious and wretched, that they were often happy to exchange it for protection and slavery [2].

The Normans took advantage of this state of weakness and anarchy to establish themselves in France. Rollo, one of their most illustrious leaders, and truly a great captain, after having spread terror over all the maritime provinces of Europe, sailed A.D. up the Seine, took Rouen, fortified it, and made it his 905. head-quarters. Now sure of a safe retreat, he set no bounds to his depredations; and soon became so formidable, that Charles offered him his daughter in marriage, with a part of the Neustrian realm as her dowry. Francon, Archbishop of Rouen, was charged with the negociation. He only demanded that Rollo should acknowledge Charles as his superior, and become a good Christian; and in order to induce the Norman to embrace the faith, the prelate preached of a future state, of hell, and of heaven. Interest, not superstition, determined Rollo. After consulting the soldiers, who like most gentlemen of the sword, were very easy on the article of religion, he agreed to the treaty; on condition that the province of Bretagne should also be ceded A.D. to him, till Neustria, then entirely laid waste by the 912. ravages of his countrymen, could be cultivated. His request was granted, he was baptized, and did homage for his crown, less as a vassal than a conqueror [3].

---

[1] *Orig. des Dignitez et des Magist. de France*, par Fauchet.
[2] Montesquieu, *L'Esprit des Loix*, liv. xxx.
[3] When he came to the last part of the ceremony, which was that of kneeling and kissing the king's toe, he positively refused compliance; and it was with much difficulty that he could be persuaded to make that compliment, even by one of his officers. At length, however, he agreed to the alternative. But all the Normans,

Rollo was worthy of his good fortune: he sunk the soldier in the sovereign, and proved himself no less skilled in the arts of peace than in those of war.   The country ceded to him (which thenceforth took the name of Normandy, in honour of its new inhabitants), soon became happy and flourishing under his laws. Sensible that the power of a prince is always proportioned to the number of his subjects, he invited a great number of Scandinavians to colonise his dominions.   He encouraged agriculture and industry; was particularly severe in punishing theft, robbery, and every species of violence; and rigidly exact in the administration of justice, which he saw was the great basis of policy, and without which his people would naturally return to their former irregularities [1].   A taste for the sweets of society increased with the conveniences of life, and the love of justice with the benefits derived from it; and in a short time not only was the new duchy populous and well-cultivated, but the Normans were regular in their manners, and obedient to the laws.   A band of pirates became good citizens, and their leader the ablest prince and the wisest legislator of the age in which he lived!

While these things passed in France, great alterations took place in the neighbouring states, and among the princes of the blood of Charle-magne: but only the most remarkable claim our attention.   The emperor Arnolf was succeeded by his son Louis IV., only seven years of age.   Rodolf II., king of Arles, crossed the Alps, and obtained the crown of Lombardy: but he was driven out of Italy in his turn, by Hugh count of Provence, who afterwards ceded to him that country, and thus the provinces of the kingdom of Arles, were again united under one head [2]. On the decease of the son of Arnolf, the empire departed A.D. from the French to the Germans; from the family of 912. Charle-magne to those Saxons whom he had subdued and persecuted, who became in their turn the protectors of that religion for which they had suffered, and the persecutors of other pagans. But this revolution deserves a particular letter.

it seems, were bad courtiers; for the officer commissioned to represent Rollo, despising so unwarlike a prince as Charles, caught his majesty by the foot, and, pretending to carry it to his mouth that he might kiss it, overturned both him and his chair before all his nobility.   This insult was passed over as an accident, because the French nation was in no condition to revenge it.   Gol. Gemet. *Chron. Norm.*

[1] Gol. Gemet.—Dudon *de Morib. et Act. Duc. Norm.*
[2] *Annal. Metens.*

LETTER XIV.

*Of the German Empire, from the Election of Conrad I. to the
Death of Henry the Fowler.*

SOME historians are of opinion, that the German empire does
not properly commence till the reign of Otho the Great, when
Italy was re-united to the imperial dominions; but the extinc-
A.D. tion of the race of Charle-magne in Germany, when the
912. empire was wholly detached from France, and the imperial dignity became elective, seems to me the most natural period to fix its origin, though the first two emperors never received the papal sanction.   I shall therefore begin with Conrad,
the first German who ruled the empire after it ceased to be
considered as an appendage of France.

Though the successors of Charle-magne possessed that empire
which he had formed by virtue of hereditary descent, they had
usually procured the consent of the nobles to their testamentary
deeds, that no dispute might arise with regard to the succession.
This precaution was highly necessary in those turbulent times,
especially as the imperial dominions were generally divided
among the children of the reigning family, who were thus put
in a better condition to contest a doubtful title.   What was at
first no more than a politic condescension of the emperors, the
public gradually interpreted into a privilege of the nobility; and
hence originated the right of those electors, by whom the emperor is still invested with the imperial power and dignity.
They had already deposed Charles the Fat, and raised Arnolf
to the empire.

Thus authorized by custom, the German nobles assembled at
Worms, on the death of Louis IV., and, not judging Charles
the Simple worthy to govern them, they offered the imperial
crown to Otho, duke of Saxony.   But he declined it, on account of his age; and, with a generosity peculiar to himself,
recommended to the electors Conrad, duke of Franconia, though
his enemy: Conrad was accordingly chosen by the diet.   The
empire then comprehended not only the present German circles,
but also Holland, Flanders, and Switzerland.

The reign of Conrad I. was one continued scene of troubles,
though he took every necessary measure to support his authority, and preserve the tranquillity of the empire.   He was no

sooner elected than he had occasion to march into Lorrain, where the nobility, being attached to the family of Charlemagne, acknowledged Charles the Simple as their sovereign, and offered to put him in possession of that country.   Before Conrad could settle the affairs of Lorrain, he was recalled by the revolt of several powerful dukes, who envied his promotion.   One rebellion succeeded another; and, to complete his misfortunes, the Hungarians invaded the empire.   They had for some time been accustomed to pass the entrenchments formed by Charlemagne along the Raab in order to restrain their incursions; and, no less fierce than the ancient Huns, they had widely diffused their devastations.   They had several times pillaged Italy; and now in their way from that country, where they had humbled Berengarius (taking advantage of the troubles of the em-   A.D. pire), they made irruptions into Saxony, Thuringia,   917. Franconia, Lorrain, and Alsace, which they desolated with fire and sword, and obliged Conrad to purchase a peace on dishonourable terms [1].   This prince died without male heirs, after recommending to the Germanic body, as his successor, Henry, duke of Saxony, son of that Otho to whom he owed his crown.

Henry I., surnamed the Fowler, because he delighted in the pursuit of birds, was elected with universal approbation   A.D. by the assembled states, composed of the dignified clergy,   919. the principal nobility, and the heads of the army.

This right of choosing an emperor, originally common to all the members of the Germanic body, was afterwards confined, as we shall have occasion to see, to seven of the chief members of that body, considered as representatives of the whole, and of all its different orders; namely, the archbishops of Mentz, Cologne, and Treves, chancellors of the three great districts into which the German empire was anciently divided, the king of Bohemia, the duke of Saxony, the marquis of Brandenburg, and the count palatine of the Rhine [2].

It was still undecided whether Lorrain should belong to France or Germany.   Henry, as soon as the situation   A.D. of his affairs would permit, entered it with a powerful   925. army, and subdued the whole country.   His next objects were the internal peace and prosperity of the empire.   He published a general amnesty in favour of all thieves and banditti, provided

[1] *Annal. German.* ap Struv. *Corp. Hist.* vol. i.
[2] Goldast. *Politic. Imperial.* init.

they would enlist in his armies, and actually formed them into a troop. He created marquises, in imitation of Charle-magne, to guard the frontiers of the empire against the Barbarians, and obliged all vassals and sub-vassals to furnish soldiers, and corn for their subsistence '. He likewise ordered the principal towns to be surrounded with walls, bastions, and ditches; and that the nobility might be habituated to the use of arms, even in time of peace, he instituted certain military games, or tournaments, in which they vied with each other in displaying their valour and address.

After taking these wise measures for the welfare of the state, Henry began to prepare for war against the Hungarians, whom he had exasperated by refusing to gratify them with an annual tribute (a disgrace to which Louis IV. had submitted), and by A.D. other marks of disdain and defiance. Enraged at his 932. firmness, they entered Germany with a very numerous army, breathing vengeance. But Henry, being supported by the whole force of his dominions, defeated them with great slaughter at Mersburg, and rescued the empire from a barbarous enemy, and an ignominious tribute '.

Having thus subdued his enemies, and secured the tranquillity of his subjects, both at home and abroad, the emperor began to taste the fruits of his wisdom and valour, when the pope and the citizens of Rome invited him to the conquest of Italy, still A.D. distracted by civil wars; offering him the holy unction, 936. and the title of Augustus. Henry, who wished to be master of Italy, and was also desirous of the papal sanction to the imperial crown, set out immediately for that country, at the head of his troops; but, being seized with an apoplexy on his march, he was obliged to return, and died at Mansleben in Thuringia. Before his death, he convoked the princes of the empire, who settled the succession on his son Otho.

Henry was universally allowed to be the ablest statesman and the greatest prince of Europe in his time: but his successor Otho, afterwards styled the Great, surpassed him both in power and renown, though not perhaps in valour or abilities. For, as Voltaire well observes, the acknowledged heir of an able prince, who has been the founder or restorer of a state, is always more powerful than his father, if not greatly inferior in courage and talents:—and the reason is obvious: he enters on a career already opened to him, and begins where his predecessor ended.

---

[1] *Ann. Sax.*   [2] Engelhus. p. 174.

Hence Alexander went farther than Philip, Charle-magne than Pepin, and Otho the Great than Henry the Fowler. But, before I proceed to the reign of Otho, we must take a view of the troubles of France under Charles the Simple, and his unhappy successors of the Carlovingian race.

LETTER XV.

Of the Affairs of France, from the Settlement of the Normans to the Extinction of the Carlovingian Race.

You have already, my dear Philip, seen the usurpations of the nobles, and the settlement of the Normans in France, under Charles the Simple. He gave continual proofs of his weakness, and became equally contemptible to the French and Normans. A violent attempt was made to dethrone him by Robert, duke of France, brother to Eudes, the late king. This rebellion was defeated, in the first instance, by the unexpected answer of Rollo, duke of Normandy, who generously declared, when solicited to join in it, that he was equally incapable of abetting or suffering injustice[1].—Yet Rollo, as we have seen, was once a robber by profession. But then, as we ought to observe in his vindication, he was under engagements to no prince, and claimed the protection of no laws : he was then on a footing with the Cæsars and the Alexanders, and now only inferior in power to the Alfreds and Charle-magnes.

After the death of Rollo, duke Robert renewed his intrigues. He obliged the king to dismiss Haganon, his favourite counsellor ; and then seized that minister's treasures, with which he gratified his adherents. They declared Charles incapa- A.D. ble of reigning, and proclaimed Robert king of France. 922. He was soon after killed in battle ; yet his party triumphed ; and his son Hugh the Great, (or the Abbot, as he is styled by some writers, on account of the number of rich abbeys which he held,) had the crown in his power. But he chose to place A.D. it on the head of Rodolph, duke of Burgundy, who as- 923. sumed the title of king, and was almost universally acknowledged.

Charles was soon after decoyed into a fortress by the trea-

---

[1] Flodoardi *Chron.*

cherous friendship of the powerful count of Vermandois, and detained prisoner. He now became the sport of the ambition of his own rebellious subjects. The count released him, and paid homage to him as his sovereign, when he wished to obtain a grant from Rodolph, and shut him up when he had succeeded in his object. The unfortunate prince died in confinement[1].

A.D. 929. After the death of Charles the Simple, Rodolph acted with great spirit and resolution. He repelled the incursions of some new tribes of Normans, restrained the licentiousness of the nobles, and restored both tranquillity and vigour to the kingdom. But, as this prince died without issue, France was again involved in troubles, and a kind of interregnum ensued. At length Hugh the Great, still disdaining the title of king, or afraid to usurp it, recalled Charles's son, Louis (surnamed the Stranger), from England, whither he had been carried by his mother Edgiva, grand-daughter of the great Alfred[2].

A.D. 936.

The prince who was thus recalled, was in a great measure unacquainted with the affairs of France; yet he conducted himself with a spirit becoming his rank, though not without some degree of that imprudence which was natural to his age. He attempted to rescue himself from the tyranny of duke Hugh, who allowed him little more than the name of king. But, after a variety of struggles, he was obliged to make peace with his vassal, and cede to him the county of Laon.

Louis the Stranger died at the age of thirty-eight years, and left a shadow of royalty to his son Lothaire; or rather Hugh the Great was pleased to grant him the title of king, that he himself might enjoy the power. This ambitious nobleman, no less formidable than the ancient mayors, died in 956, and was succeeded in consequence and abilities by his son Hugh Capet.

A.D. 954.

Lothaire wanted neither courage nor ambition. He attempted to recover Lorrain, which had been for some time in the possession of the emperors of Germany. But Otho II., by an artful stroke of policy, disconcerted his measures, and ruined his reputation. He ceded the disputed territory to the king's brother Charles, on condition that he should hold it as a fief of the empire. Lothaire, incensed at this donation, by which his brother was benefited at the expense of his character, his interest, and the honour of his crown, assembled a powerful army,

---

[1] Glab. *Hist. sui Temp.*   [2] Flodoardi *Chron.*

and marched suddenly to Aix-la-Chapelle, where he surprised the emperor, and put him to flight. He himself was vanquished, in his turn, and was again victorious. But, at the end A.D. of the contest, he was obliged to resign Lorrain, which 980. was divided between Charles and Otho[1].

He died in 986, and was quietly succeeded by his son Louis V., who governed under the direction of Hugh Capet, during a short and turbulent reign. With him ended the sway A.D. of the Carlovingians, or descendants of Charle-magne, 987. the second race of French kings. The affairs of the empire now claim your attention.

LETTER XVI.

Of the German Empire and its Italian Dependencies under Otho the Great, and his Successors of the House of Saxony.

OTHO I., the most powerful emperor since Charle-magne, and who had the honour of re-uniting Italy to the imperial dominions, was elected at Aix-la-Chapelle by the unanimous consent of the diet, according to the promise made to his father, A.D. Henry the Fowler[2]. He began his reign with the most 936. upright administration, and seemed desirous of living in peace and tranquillity. But his quiet was soon interrupted by wars both foreign and domestic, which he had sufficient abilities to manage, and which terminated in his aggrandisement.

The Hungarians, according to custom, invaded the empire, committing every species of barbarity. Otho, however, soon

[1] Aimon. lib. v.
[2] The diets of the German empire were originally the same with the national assemblies convoked by the kings of France. They met at least once a year, and every freeman had a right to be present. They were great councils, in which the sovereign deliberated with his subjects concerning their common interests. But when the nobles and dignified clergy acquired, with the rank of princes, territorial and independent jurisdiction, the diet became an assembly of the separate states that formed the confederacy, of which the emperor was the head ; and, if any member possessed more than one of those states, he was allowed to have a proportional number of suffrages. On the same principle the imperial cities, as soon as they became free, and acquired supreme and independent jurisdiction within their own territories, were received as members of the diet. (Alrum. *de Comitiis Rom. German. Imperii.*) The powers of the diet extend to every thing relative to the common interests of the Germanic body, as a confederacy, but not to the interior government of the different states, unless when domestic disorders disturb or threaten the peace of the empire.

put a stop to their ravages. He came up with them on the plain of Dortmund, in Westphalia, and defeated them with great slaughter. But the Hungarians were not the only enemies whom Otho had to encounter. Immediately after his return from this victory, he was informed that the Bohemians had re-

A.D. volted. Bohemia was then entirely barbarous, and
937. mostly pagan. Otho, after a variety of struggles, rendered it tributary to Germany, and also obliged the inhabitants to embrace Christianity[1].

In the mean time the emperor was engaged in many disputes with his own rebellious subjects. On the death of Arnold, duke of Bavaria, his son Everard refused to do homage to Otho, on pretence that he was not his vassal, but his ally. This struggle between the crown and the great fiefs—between the power which always seeks increase, and liberty which aims at independence—for a long time agitated Europe. It subsisted in Spain, while the Christians had to contend with the votaries of Mohammed; but after the expulsion of the Moors, the sovereign authority gained the ascendant. It was this competition that involved France in troubles till the reign of Louis XI., when the feudal lordships were gradually circumscribed and weakened, and the nobles reduced to a dependence on the prince; that established in England the mixed government, to which we owe our present greatness, and cemented in Poland the liberty of the nobles with the slavery of the people. The same spirit hath, at different times, troubled Sweden and Denmark, and founded the republics of Holland and Switzerland: the same cause hath almost every where produced different effects! The prerogatives of the prince have, in some instances, as in that of the German empire, been reduced to a mere title, and the national union itself preserved only in the observance of a few insignificant formalities. The duke of Bavaria was not willing to observe even these formalities: Otho therefore entered that country with an army, expelled Everard, and bestowed the duchy upon his uncle Bertolf, who willingly did homage for such a present[2]. The emperor at the same time created one of Everard's brothers count Palatine of Bavaria, and the other count Palatine of the Rhine.

This dignity of count palatine was revived from the counts of the palace of the Roman and French emperors. These palatines were at first supreme judges, and gave judgment in the

---

[1] Dubra. *Hist. Bohem.*   [2] Barre, *Hist. d'Allemagne*, tome iii.

last appeal, in the name of the emperor. They were also en-trusted with the government of the imperial domains.

Otho, having thus settled the internal tranquillity of the em-pire (which, however, was soon disturbed by the rebel- A. D. lion of his brother), assembled a diet at Arensberg, 940. where among other things, it was debated, whether inheritance should descend in a direct line ; whether, for example, a grand-son, heir to an eldest son, should succeed, on the death of his grand-father, in preference to his uncles. The diet not being able to come to any determination on this point, though so clear according to our present ideas of inheritance, it was agreed that the cause which had suggested the doubt should be decided by duel. An equal number of combatants were accordingly chosen on both sides ; aud the suit was determined in favour of the grandson, his champions being victorious [1]. The decision by arms was, for once, consistent with equity ; the law is now uni-versal. This mode of trial soon became general over Europe ; and under the following reign a diet ordained that doubtful cases should no longer be decided upon oath, but by the sword [2]. The base were thus deprived of the advantages which they might have reaped from perjury, whatever inconveniences might attend the ordinance [3]. And the regulation itself proves the baseness as well as the ignorance of the age.

In order to counterbalance the power of the nobility, Otho augmented the privileges of the German clergy. He A. D. conferred on them duchies and counties, with all the 943. rights of other princes and nobles ; and, like Charle-magne, the founder of the empire, whose lustre he restored, he propa- A. D. gated Christianity by force of arms. He obliged the 948. Danes to pay him tribute, and receive baptism, as an earnest of their good behaviour [4].

Pleased with his success in the north, Otho directed his at-tention to the south ; and an opportunity of gratifying his ambition without injury to his humane feelings, now presented itself to his view. Italy was torn by factions, and ruled by tyrants. Rodolph II., king of the two Burgundies, had de-throned Berengarius, and was himself dethroned by Hugh, mar-quis of Provence, whose son Lothaire was also dethroned by Be-rengarius II. This Berengarius kept Adelaide, the widow of

[1] Barre, *Hist. d'Allemagne*, tome iii.
[2] *Leg. Longob.* lib. ii.
[3] This reason is actually assigned, in a Barbarian code, in favour of the judicial combat, in cases where an oath might settle the dispute. *Leg. Burgund,* tit. xlv.
[4] *Ann. Sax.*

A. D. Lothaire, in confinement. She invited Otho to her relief.
952. He entered Italy, at the head of a powerful army, rescued Adelaide, married her, and obliged Berengarius to take an oath of fealty, generously leaving him in possession of his kingdom [1].

The pleasure which Otho must have received from the conquest of Italy was allayed by the revolt of his son Ludolph, who, though already declared successor to the empire, was so much chagrined at his father's second marriage, that he engaged in a rebellion against him with the duke of Franconia, and other German noblemen. Pursued by the vigilance of the emperor, Ludolph took refuge in Ratisbon, where he was soon reduced to extremity. At the intercession of his friends, however, he was permitted to
A. D. retire with his followers. He again rebelled; but re-
955. turning soon after to a sense of his duty, he took an opportunity, when Otho was hunting to throw himself at his feet, and implored forgiveness in the most humiliating language. " Have pity," said he (after a pathetic pause) " on your child, who returns, like the prodigal son, to his father. If you permit him to live, who has so often deserved to die, he will be faithful and obedient for the future, and have time to repent of his folly and ingratitude." The emperor, equally surprised and affected at this moving spectacle, raised his son from the ground, while the tears flowed from his eyes, received him into favour, and forgave all his followers [2].

The young prince afterwards died in Italy, whither he had been sent by his father, to humble the ungrateful Berengarius, who had broken his faith with the emperor, and tyrannized
A.D. over his countrymen. The untimely death of Ludolph,
959. which greatly affected Otho, gave Berengarius time to breathe. He was soon absolute master of the ancient kingdom of Lombardy, but not of Rome, which was then governed by Octavian, grandson of the celebrated Marozia, concubine of Sergius III. By the great interest of his family, he had been elected pope at the age of eighteen, when he was not even in orders. He took the name of John XII. out of respect to the memory of his uncle, John XI., and was the first pope who changed his name on his accession to the pontificate [3].

This John XII. was a patrician, or nobleman of Rome, and consequently united in the papal chair the privileges of temporal

---

[1] Flodoard. lib. iv.   [2] *Annal. Germ.*
[3] Sigon. *Reg. Ital.* lib. vi.

and spiritual authority, by a right whose legality could not be disputed.	But he was young, sunk in debauchery, and unable to oppose the tyranny of Berengarius and his son Adelbert; he therefore conjured Otho, " by the love of God and A. D. of the holy apostles, to come and deliver the Roman 960. church from the fangs of two monsters." This flattering invitation was accompanied with an offer of the papal sanction to the imperial crown, and of the kingdom of Lombardy, from the Italian states.

In compliance with the request of the pope, or rather with the occasion which it afforded of gratifying his own ambition, the emperor assembled a powerful army, and marched into Italy, after having convoked a diet at Worms, where Otho, his son by Adelaide, was elected his successor—a necessary precaution in those troublesome times for securing the crown in a family. Berengarius fled before him: he entered Pavia without opposition, and was crowned king of Lombardy at Milan, by A. D. the archbishop of that city, in presence of the nobility and 962. clergy, who had formally deposed Berengarius.	Rome also opened its gates to Otho: and the pope crowned him emperor of the Romans, dignified him with the title of Augustus, and swore allegiance to him on the tomb where the body of St. Peter is said to be deposited[1].	The emperor at the same time confirmed to the apostolic see the donations made by Pepin and Charle-magne, " saving in all things," says he, " our authority, and that of our son and descendants[2];" expressions by which it appears that, in this grant, Otho reserved to the empire the supreme jurisdiction over the papal territories.

Otho now marched in pursuit of Berengarius, whom he seized, and condemned to perpetual imprisonment.	Meanwhile the pope, finding that he had given himself a master in a protector, repented of his conduct, violated his oath to the emperor, and entered into a league with Adelbert, the son of Berengarius. Otho suddenly returned to Rome; Adelbert fled; and a council deposed John XII. for his debaucheries, as was pretended, but in reality for revolting from the emperor, though his licentiousness was sufficiently enormous to render him unworthy of any civil or ecclesiastical dignity.	Leo VIII., a layman, but a man of virtue, was elected his successor; and the clergy and A. D. citizens of Rome took anew the oath of allegiance to 963.

---

[1] *Scriptor. Rerum Germanicarum, edit.* Meibom.
[2] *Exemplar. Diplom. Othon.* ap. Baron.

Otho, and bound themselves neither to elect nor consecrate a pope without the consent of the emperor [1].

But Otho having occasion to quell some disturbances in Spoleto, a faction reinstated John XII., a new council deposed A. D. Leo; and a canon was enacted, declaring " that no in-
964. ferior can degrade a superior [2];" the framers of which not only meant to intimate, that the bishops and cardinals had no power to depose a pope, but that the emperor, as a layman, owed to the church that very allegiance which he exacted from her.

Soon after this revolution, pope John was assassinated in the arms of one of his mistresses. His party, however, still refused to acknowledge Leo, and proceeded to the election of Benedict V., who was accordingly promoted to the chair of St. Peter. Informed of these audacious and faithless proceedings, Otho marched back to Rome, which he reduced, and restored Leo VIII. to his dignity. Benedict appeared before a council: owned himself guilty of usurpation; stripped himself of the pontifical robes; implored compassion, and was banished to Hamburg. Leo. VIII., with all the clergy and Roman people, enacted at the same time a celebrated decree, which was long considered as a fundamental law of the empire; " That Otho, and his suc-cessors in the kingdom of Italy, should always have the power of choosing a successor, of naming the pope, and of giving investi-ture to bishops [3]."

The affairs of Italy being thus settled, Otho returned to Ger-
A. D. many; where he had scarcely arrived, when the Italians
965. again revolted, and expelled John XIII., who had been elected in the presence of the imperial commissioners, after the death of Leo VIII. Enraged at so many instances of perfidy, Otho once more entered Italy, and marched to Rome, which he treated with a severity somewhat bordering on revenge, but justly merited. He banished the consuls, hanged the tribunes, and caused the prefect of Rome, who aimed at the character of a second Brutus, to be whipped naked through the streets on an
A. D. ass [4]. These ancient dignities subsisted only in name,
966. and the people were destitute of every virtue. They had repeatedly broken their faith to the prince, whose protection they had craved, and to whom they had sworn allegiance: an attempt therefore to restore the republic, which had at one time been considered as the height of patriotism, was now deservedly

---

[1] Sigon. lib. vii.　　　　[2] Luitprand. lib. vi.
[3] *Extract.* in Grat.　　　[4] Sigon. lib. vii.

punished as a seditious revolt—though a person of no less eminence than Voltaire seems to consider both in the same light.

After re-establishing the pope, and regulating the police of
Rome, Otho retired to Capua, where he received ambassadors
from Nicephorus the Greek emperor, who wished to A.D.
renew the old alliance between the eastern and western 967.
empires, and also proposed a marriage between the princess
Theophania and Otho's son, lately associated with his father in
the supreme power. In the course of this negociation, however,
the Greek grew jealous of the German, and ordered the nobles
to be assassinated who came to receive the princess. Incensed
at so enormous a perfidy, Otho directed his Generals to enter
Calabria, where they defeated the Greek army, cut off A.D.
the noses of their prisoners, and sent them in that condi- 968.
tion to Constantinople [1].

But peace was soon afterwards established between the empires.
Nicephorus being put to death by his subjects, John Tzimisces,
his successor, sent Theophania into Italy, where her marriage with
young Otho was consummated, and all differences were A.D.
accommodated [2]. The emperor returned to Germany, 970.
covered with glory and success, and lived to enjoy the fruits of
his victories two years in his native Saxony. He died May,
after a reign of thirty-six years; during which he had 973.
justly acquired the appellation of the GREAT, the Conqueror of
Italy, and the restorer of the Empire of Charle-magne.

Otho II., surnamed the Sanguinary, on account of the blood
spilled under his reign, succeeded his father at the age of eighteen.
His youth occasioned troubles, which his valour enabled him to
dissipate. Henry, duke of Bavaria, and several other noblemen,
rebelled, but were all reduced in a short time. Denmark and
Bohemia felt his power, and Rome, by new crimes, offered a
theatre for his justice. The consul Crescentius, son of the abandoned Theodora, who had been concubine to pope John X.,
revived the project of restoring the republic, and caused Benedict VI., who adhered to the emperor, to be murdered in prison.
His faction elected Boniface VII., another faction elected Benedict VII., and a third chose John XIV., who was put to death
by Boniface [3].

These horrors succeeded one another so rapidly that chronolo-
gists have not been able to ascertain the date, nor historians
accurately to settle the names of the pontiffs. The pope of one

---

[1] Sigon. lib. vii.   [2] *Annal. de l'Emp.* vol. i.
                [3] Sigon. lib. vii.

party was the anti-pope of another. But Benedict VII., and the imperial party prevailing, Boniface went to Constantinople, and implored the Greek emperors, Basil and Constantine, to come and restore the throne of the Cæsars in Italy, and deliver the Romans from the German yoke.

This circumstance, my dear Philip, merits your attention. The popes, in order to increase their power, had formerly renounced their allegiance to the Greeks, and called in the Franks. They afterwards had recourse to the Germans, who confirmed the privileges granted to them by the French; and now they seemed ready to receive their ancient masters, or rather to acknowledge no master at all: and hence they have been accused of boundless ambition. But in these proceedings I can see no foundation for such a charge. It is natural for man to desire sway; and, when obtained, to seek to increase it. When the popes had become temporal princes, they would consequently seek to secure and extend their dominion. If they had acted otherwise, they would not have been men. I am much more offended at that dominion of blind belief, which they endeavour to extend over the human mind. The one was a generous, the other an ignoble ambition; the first made only a few men change their sovereign, the latter subjected millions to a debasing superstition, and was necessarily accompanied with hypocrisy and fraud.

I have already mentioned, in the history of France, the dispute about Lorrain, which Otho II. politically shared with Lothaire's brother Charles, on condition that the French prince should do homage for it after the custom of those times, with bended knee, A.D. 981. and closed hands. That war being finished, and the affairs of Germany settled, Otho marched into Italy, entered Rome without opposition, and severely chastised the rebels; but, in attempting to wrest Calabria from the Greeks his troops were routed by the Saracens, whom the Greeks had called to their assistance [1]. He died at Rome, while he was preparing to take revenge on the enemy.

A.D. 983. Otho III. succeeded his father at twelve years of age; and his uncle and his mother disputing the administration, Germany was disquieted by a turbulent regency, while Rome became a prey to new factions, and the scene of new crimes. Crescentius blew again the trumpet of liberty, and persuaded the Romans they were still free, that he might have it in his power to enslave them.

---

[1] Leonis Catiensis *Hist.* lib. ii.

When the emperor began to act for himself he displayed considerable abilities both in war and peace. He defeated the Danes, who had invaded the empire, and entered into A.D. a friendly alliance with Eric, king of Sweden, on con- 989. dition that German missionaries should be allowed to preach the Gospel in his dominions [1]; a great concession in those times, and highly mortifying to the zealots of the religion of Odin.

He afterwards marched into Italy at the intercession of John XV., who was persecuted by Crescentius. Alarmed at the name of Otho, which had so often proved fatal to their A.D. confederates, the rebels returned to their duty, and Cres- 996. centius was pardoned. But as soon as the emperor had left Rome, that licentious spirit again revolted ; expelled Gregory V., the successor of John XV., and elevated to the papal chair a creature of his own, under the name of John XVI. Enraged at this fresh insult, Otho returned with a powerful army to A.D. Rome, which he took by assault; ordered Crescentius to 998. be beheaded, and the anti-pope to be thrown from the top of the castle of St. Angelo, after his eyes had been put out, and his nose cut off [2]. Having restored Gregory, and again received the allegiance of the citizens of Rome, Otho returned to Germany.

The Saracens afterwards making an irruption into the Campania of Rome, the emperor was again obliged to march A.D. into Italy. He expelled the ravagers, and repaired with 1001. a small body of troops to Rome, where his life was endangered by a conspiracy; and while he was assembling forces to punish the rebels, he is said to have been poisoned by a pair of gloves sent to him by the widow of Crescentius, whom he had subjected to the most infamous treatment [3].

The empire sustained a great loss in the death of this prince, who was equally brave, resolute, and just, and, by a glo- Jan. rious reign of eighteen years, changed the surname of In- 1002. fant, which had been given him at his accession, into that of the Wonder of the World.

As Otho died without children, many candidates for the imperial dignity arose. The prince who obtained it was Henry duke of Bavaria, who, after he had passed some years in adjusting the disordered affairs of Germany, found it necessary to march into Italy,

---

[1] *Annal. de l'Emp.* tome i.   [2] Ibid.—Heiss' *Hist. de l'Emp.* tome i.
[3] Auct. supra citat.

A.D. where Ardouin, marquis of Ivrea, had assumed the sove-
1005. reignty.   The usurper retired at the approach of Henry,
who was crowned king of Lombardy, at Pavia, by the archbishop
of Milan ; but the marquis having some partisans in that city,
they inflamed the populace to such a degree, that the emperor
was in danger of being sacrificed to their fury.   The tumult was
at last quelled by the imperial troops.   Those within the city
defended the palace, while detachments from the camps caled
the walls, and committed terrible slaughter in the streets, till
Henry ordered them to desist, and retired to the fortress of
St. Peter.   Thither the principal citizens repaired in a body ;
implored the emperor's clemency ; protested their loyalty, and
laid the blame of the sedition on the partisans of Ardouin, who
had practised on the ignorance of the vulgar.   Henry generously
admitted their apology : "Mercy," said he, " is my favourite
virtue ; and I would much rather find your obedience the result
of affection than the consequence of fear [1]."

The troubles of Germany obliged the emperor to leave Italy
without visiting Rome.   But, when he had quelled those disturbances, he returned to Italy with his wife Cunegunda, and
A.D. was crowned by Benedict VIII.   He at the same time
1014. again defeated Ardouin, and quieted the disorders of
Lombardy.

Weary of human greatness or of the toils of empire, and
charmed with the tranquillity of a monastic life, Henry had
for some time expressed a desire of retiring from the world, and
now actually assumed the religious habit.   But the abbot of
St. Val, when he received the emperor as a brother, wisely imposed the following command on him : " Monks owe obedience
to their superior," said he : " I order you to continue at the
helm of government [2]."

In consequence of this injunction, Henry consented to wear
A.D. the crown, and increased in prosperity to the hour of his
1024. death.   Yet he seems to have been a prince of a weak
mind ; for besides his monastic whim, it appears that he had
made a vow of chastity.   And, when he felt his end approaching,
he sent for the parents of his wife Cunegunda, and said, " You
gave her to me a virgin, and I restore her a virgin !"—Can a
restraint on the natural inclinations be a virtue, where their
indulgence does not interfere with the welfare of society?   Do

---

[1] Heiss, lib. ii.—Barre, tome iii.   [2] *Annal. de l'Emp.* tome i.

not think so. Such a declaration from a husband is almost
sufficient to make us credit the charge of adultery adduced
against Cunegunda, though she is said to have proved her innocence by handling red-hot iron.

LETTER XVII.

*Sketch of the History of Poland and Russia, and also of the
Scandinavian States, to the Death of Magnus the Good, King
of Denmark and Norway.*

IN a survey of European occurrences and transactions, my
dear son, the northern states are far from being unworthy of
notice, though their history may be thought less interesting than
that of the southern realms and nations.

Before I treat of Russia and the Scandinavian states, I will
give you a short view of the history of Poland, which, though not
strictly in the north of Europe, was formerly so connected or
involved with Russia in politics and war, besides the community
of origin, that I may without impropriety, on this occasion,
offer some remarks respecting its early state.

The people were of Sarmatian, that is, Sclavonian origin; and
the first rulers of the country, after the formation of several
petty states into one, bore the title of duke. Lech was long
considered by historians as the founder of the state: but we
have so little authority for the accounts given of this prince and
some of his reputed successors, that, in pretending to inform you
of the acts of their government, I should rather seem to bewilder
you in the darkness of fable and of error, than open to your view
the light of genuine history.

Several centuries after the time assigned for the death of Lech,
Piast, said to have been a wheelwright, was elevated to the dignity of duke of Poland, on the extinction of the former A.D.
line of princes. He governed with mildness, yet not with- 830.
out spirit, and left his dominions in peace to his son, by whose
active valour they were considerably extended. The two succeeding dukes were not destitute of political ability; but
Mieczslaus, the first Christian sovereign of Poland, was more fit
to slumber in a monastery than to govern a state, though he
deserves our praise for his zeal in promoting the conversion of
his subjects. His son Boleslaus possessed greater ability, but
was inclined to deviate into an opposite extreme, being too

A.D. fond of war and bloodshed.   Soon after his accession, he
999. was honoured by the emperor Otho III. with the title
of king [1].

Boleslaus diffused the terror of his arms through Russia,
Bohemia, Moravia, Saxony, and Prussia, and obtained the
epithet of Great by his talents, his exploits, and his power.   He
A.D. was succeeded by his son Mieczslaus II., who was imme-
1025. diately engaged in a war with the Russians, which he
closed with honour; but he was less successful against the Bohemians and other nations who attempted to shake off the tributary
yoke imposed by his warlike predecessor.

The tyranny and rapacity of Rixa, who acted as regent for
Casimir, filled the country with confusion; and the fierce hostilities of the Bohemians and the Russians completed the misery
of the nation.   Casimir, who had been driven out of the realm
A.D. during these commotions, was at length recalled.   He
1040. conciliated the Russians by marrying a princess of their
nation : and, by his indefatigable exertions, he restored peace
and order to the state.

Boleslaus II. was a brave but cruel and profligate prince.
While he was carrying on a war against the Russians, a rebellion arose in his kingdom.   He quelled it by the vigour of his
arms, and punished it with inordinate severity.   Having embroiled himself with the clergy by the murder of the bishop of
Cracow, he was excommunicated by Pope Gregory VII., and
forced by the public hatred to quit his throne and country.
Ladislaus, brother of the exiled prince, was for some time excluded from all power by the incensed pontiff: but his patient
submission ultimately procured his elevation to the sovereignty,
though he was not suffered to enjoy the royal title [2].

Proceeding to a review of the Russian history, I find myself
authorized to inform you, that about the year 862, Ruric, the
enterprising leader of a body of Scandinavians, who were more
fierce and warlike than the Sarmatians, changed into a principality the republican government which the latter had long
maintained in the territory of Novogorod [3].   He preserved till
his death the power which he thus acquired; and Oleg, one of
his relatives, added the town and district of Kiow to the Russian
possessions.   Encouraged by this success, he invaded the dominions of the Greek emperor, Leo the Philosopher, whom he

[1] Matth. Michov. *Chron.* lib. ii.—Mart. Cromeri. *Hist.*
[2] Michov. *Chron.* Guagnin.—*Sarmat. Europ. Descript.*
[3] Muller, *Sammlung, Russischer, Geschichte,* vol. i.

compelled to submit to dishonourable terms of peace; for philosophers in general, my dear Philip, are unable to withstand the energy of barbarian warriors.

Igor, the son of Ruric, ravaged in the year 941 some of the Asiatic provinces of the Greeks; but the invaders were so severely chastised by the troops of Constantine Porphyrogenitus, that scarcely a third part of their number returned to Russia. After Igor had fallen a victim to the resentment of the Drevlians, whom he had treated with insult and outrage, his widow Olga, who acted as regent for his son, subdued and cruelly punished the offending tribe. She more honourably distinguished herself in the sequel, by building towns and promoting commerce, as well as by introducing the Christian faith among the Russians, though they did not generally embrace it in her time. Svetoslaus, or Sviatoslaf, signalized his courage against the Bulgarians, but was unfortunate in a war with the Greeks, and was killed in 973 by the Petchenegans, whom he had endeavoured to bring under his yoke. He was so imprudent as to divide his territories among his three sons; but, after bloody dissensions, they were reunited by Wolodimir or Vladimir, who became a great and successful prince, recovering the obedience of revolted tribes, and extending his frontiers at the expense of his neighbours. He endeavoured to civilize and polish his subjects; but their minds were not then ripe for general improvement, though they consented to become Christians in imitation of his example. His latter days were embittered by the contumacy of his son Jaroslaus or Yaroslaf; and he is said to have died of grief in 1015, while he was marching against the rebellious prince. Sviatopolk now endeavoured to deprive his brother Jaroslaus of his share of the succession : but he was baffled in his schemes, and obliged to quit the country. He was reinstated by Boleslaus I., king of Poland, whose daughter he had espoused; but, being defeated by his brother, he died in his retreat from the field of battle [1].

The reign of Jaroslaus was honourable to himself, and beneficial to his subjects. He framed a code of laws, encouraged arts and manufactures, and provided for the diffusion of religious and moral principles. He died at the age of seventy-six years, distributing his dominions among four of his sons, whom he had by a Swedish princess. A.D. 1054.

Sweden now claims some degree of attention; but it is not

---

[1] Nest. *Chron.* Muller, *Sammlung Russ. Gesch.* vol. i.

necessary that I should dwell long upon the subject.   The early history of that kingdom is doubtful and obscure.   After a series of Gothic rulers of the state, we hear of its being subdued, about the year 760, by Ivar, king of Denmark[1].   Another cloud hangs over the realm till the appearance of Biorn, who seems to have reigned before the middle of the ninth century.   Under his government, the Swedes were enlightened with Christian knowledge.   Near the close of that century, their king Olaus or Olaf II. conquered Denmark: but how long he or his posterity retained it, we cannot clearly discover.   From that time to the reign of Ingo the Pious we meet with no certain accounts or memorable incidents.   This prince was murdered by some pagan malcontents for his Christian zeal; but his brother Alstan, being more popular, died in peace[2].

With regard to Denmark, we hear of the reign of Skiold in that country about the beginning of the sixth century; but we cannot depend on the information.   After a long list of supposed princes, we observe the name of Godfrey, who is styled king of Denmark by the historian of Charle-magne.   Heming succeeded him in 810; and on the death of this prince, a bloody conflict ensued, by which Harold and Regenfroy obtained possession of the throne.   These associated kings invaded Norway with success in 813, but were soon after deprived even of their former kingdom by the sons of Godfrey[3].   Harold, however, recovered a part of his realm, and enjoyed the favour and friendship of Louis the Débonnaire, at whose court he was baptized in the Christian faith.   Other princes followed, whose subjects, like the Swedes and Norwegians, were more addicted to piracy than attached to the peaceful arts of civilized society.

Early in the tenth century, another prince of the name of Harold, one of the descendants of a Gothic chieftain who had emigrated from Sweden when it was over-run by the victorious Ivar, reduced some principalities, and became king of all Norway.   On the death of his grandson in 977, the kingdom was degraded into an earldom under the Danish sovereign; but its dignity was soon restored, and the people were converted from the absurdities of paganism[4].

Sweyn, king of Denmark, of whose success in England you will soon be informed, appears to have exercised some authority

[1] Snorronis Sturlonidis *Hist. Regum Septentrion.*
[2] Adami Bremensis *Hist.*—Puffendorf.
[3] Eginhardi *Annal.*
[4] Snorronis *Hist. Regum Septent.*

in Norway; and his successor, Canute the Great, obtained possession of that kingdom. Olaus, in attempting to recover the crown, lost his life in 1030. Canute's son, Sweyn, governed for some years the Norwegian territories; but on his father's death, he was removed from his high station by the efforts of the people, who placed on their throne Magnus, the son of Olaus. The new king concluded an agreement with Hardi-canute, the Danish monarch, importing that the survivor should be sovereign of both realms. The death of the Dane, in 1042, gratified the Norwegian prince with that honour and benefit; and he reigned with reputation till the year 1047, when the kingdoms were again divided.

From this necessary survey of the Sarmatian and Gothic states, I now lead you to a renewed consideration of the affairs of your own country.

LETTER XVIII.

Of the chief Occurrences and Transactions in England, from the Death of Alfred to the Reign of Canute the Great.

ENGLAND, my dear Philip, from the reign of Alfred to the Danish conquest, affords few objects to arrest the attention of the scholar, the gentleman, or the politician. Little attention was paid to arts or letters; which, with manners, suffered a decline. The constitution remained nearly the same. A concise account of the principal reigns will therefore be sufficient for your purpose; more especially as England, during this period, had no connexion with the affairs of the continent.

Alfred was succeeded by his son Edward the Elder, being the first of that name who sat on the English throne. Though inferior to his father in genius and erudition, he equalled him in military talents: and he had occasion for them. Ethelwald, his cousin, disputed the crown, and called in the Danes to support his claim. The death of this claimant, who fell in A.D. a battle with the Kentish men[1], decided the quarrel; 905. but Edward's wars with the Danes continued during the greater part of his reign, though he was successful in almost every engagement.

Athelstan, Edward's natural son, obtained the kingdom, in

[1] *Chron. Sax.*

A. D. preference to his legitimate children. As he had arrived
925. at an age more suited to the cares of government, and as
the nation, exposed to foreign and domestic wars, required a
prince of vigour and abilities, the stain in his birth was overlooked.

No sooner was he securely seated on the throne, than he endeavoured to give it stability by providing against the insurrections of the domestic Danes. With this view he marched into
Northumberland, their most considerable settlement; and finding that they bore with impatience the English yoke, he judged
it prudent to confer on Sithric, a Danish nobleman, the title of
king, and to give him his sister Editha in marriage, as a farther
motive of attachment. But this policy, though apparently wise,
proved the source of many troubles.

Sithric died within a twelvemonth after his elevation; and his
two sons by a former marriage, Anlaf and Guthfred, founding
pretensions on their father's rank, assumed the sovereignty,
without waiting for the approbation of Athelstan. But they
were soon expelled by that powerful monarch, who was no less
brave than politic. The former took shelter in Ireland, the
latter in Scotland; where he was protected for some time by
the clemency of Constantine, who then swayed the Scottish
sceptre. Continually solicited, however, and even menaced by
the English monarch, Constantine at last promised to deliver up
his guest; but, secretly detesting such treachery, he gave him a
hint to make his escape. Incensed at Constantine's behaviour,
though the death of the fugitive had freed him from all appre-
A.D. hensions, Athelstan entered Scotland with a numerous
934. army, and reduced the Scots to such distress, that their
king was happy to preserve his crown by the most humble submission[1].

Athelstan afterwards defeated the Scots, Welsh, and Danes,
A.D. in a general engagement at Brunsbury, in Northumber-
938. land. In consequence of this victory he enjoyed tranquillity during the rest of his reign. He appears to have been
one of the most able and active of our ancient princes; and his
memorable law for the encouragement of commerce, discovers a
liberality of mind worthy of the most enlightened ages: That a
merchant, who had made two voyages on his own account to
distant lands, should be admitted to the rank of a gentleman[2].

Athelstan was succeeded by his brother Edmund; who, on

---

[1] Hoved. *Annal.* Gul. Malmesb.   [2] Brompt. *Chron.*

his accession, met with some disturbance from the Nor- A.D.
thumbrian Danes, whom he reduced to obedience. He 941.
also conquered Cumberland from the Britons, and conferred
that principality on Malcolm, king of Scotland, on condi- A.D.
tion that he should do homage to England for it, and 945.
protect the northern counties from all future incursions of the
Danes[1].

Edmund's reign was short, and his death violent. As he
was solemnizing a feast in Gloucestershire, a notorious A.D.
robber, named Leolf, whom he had sentenced to banish- 947.
ment, audaciously entered the hall where his sovereign dined,
and seated himself at one of the tables. Enraged at such insolence, Edmund ordered him to be seized ; but, observing that
the ruffian was preparing to resist, the indignant monarch
sprang up, and catching him by the hair, dragged him out of
the hall. Meanwhile Leolf, having drawn his dagger, lifted his
arm with a furious blow, and stabbed the king, who immediately
expired on the bosom of his murderer[2].

Edmund left male issue ; but, as his eldest son was too young
to govern the kingdom, his brother Edred was raised to the
throne. The beginning of Edred's reign was disturbed by a
revolt of the Northumbrian Danes. Though frequently humbled, they were never entirely subdued, nor had they ever paid
a sincere allegiance to the English crown : their obedience lasted
no longer than the present terror. Edred, instructed by experience, took every precaution to prevent their future insurrections. He settled English garrisons in their most considerable
towns, and placed over them an English governor, to A.D.
watch their motions, and check the first appearance of 952.
revolt.

Edred, though a brave and active prince, lay under the influence of the lowest superstition, and had blindly delivered over
his conscience to the guidance of St. Dunstan, abbot of Glastonbury, whom he advanced to the highest offices of state, and who
concealed beneath an appearance of sanctity the most insatiable
and insolent ambition. In order to impose on the credulity of
mankind, this designing monk had long secluded himself from
the world in a miserable cell, where he is said to have had frequent conflicts with the devil ; but at length, when the infernal
spirit attempted to seduce him in the shape of a woman, Dunstan seized him by the nose with a pair of red-hot pincers, and

[1] Gul. Malmesb. lib. ii.   [2] Gul. Malmesb. lib. ii.—H. Huntingd. lib. v.

held him till the whole neighbourhood resounded with his bel-
lowings[1].   Satan, thus vanquished, never more dared to show
his face.   This story, and others of the like nature, then seriously
believed, procured the abbot a reputation, both with prince and
people, which no real piety or virtue could have obtained for
him.   Soon after his return from solitude, he was placed by
Edred at the head of the treasury; and, sensible that he owed
his advancement solely to the opinion of his austerity, he professed himself a friend to the rigid monastic rules, which about
this time began to prevail, and by which monks were excluded
from all commerce with the world and with women.   He introduced them into the convents of Glastonbury and Abingdon,
and endeavoured to render them universal in the kingdom[2].

There had been monasteries in England from the first introduction of Christianity among the Saxons, and those establishments had been greatly multiplied by the mistaken piety of the
English princes and nobles, who sought to bribe Heaven by
donations to the church.   But the monks had hitherto been a
species of secular priests, who were at liberty either to marry or
continue single, and who lived after the manner of our present
canons or prebendaries.   They both intermingled with the
world, in some degree, and endeavoured to render themselves
useful to it.   A superstitious devotion, however, had produced
in Italy a new species of monks, who secluded themselves entirely from the world, renounced all claim to liberty, and made
a merit of the most inviolable chastity.   The popes had favoured
the doctrine from motives of general policy, as detaching the
ecclesiastical from the civil power : Dunstan, equally artful,
embraced it for his own aggrandizement.   Celibacy was therefore extolled as the universal duty of priests ; and, in England,
the minds of men were already prepared for such an innovation,
though it militates against the strongest propensities in human
nature.

The first preachers of Christianity among the Saxons had carried to the most extravagant height the praises of inviolable
chastity ; the pleasures of love had been represented as incom-
patible with Christian perfection ; and an abstinence from all
commerce with the softer sex was deemed a sufficient atonement for the greatest enormities.   It was a natural consequence
of this doctrine, that those who officiated at the altar should at
least be free from such pollution.   And Dunstan and his re-

---

[1] Osberne, in *Anglia Sacra*, vol. ii.   [2] Ibid.

formed monks knew well how to avail themselves of these popular topics, and set off their own character to the best advantage. On the other hand, their rivals the secular clergy, who were numerous and rich, and had possession of the ecclesiastical dignities, defended themselves with vigour, and boldly maintained the sanctity of the institution of marriage [1]. The whole nation was thrown into a ferment.

In the mean time the power of the monks received a check by the death of Edred, the dupe of their ambition. He left children, but in an infant state : the crown was therefore conferred on Edwy, one of the sons of Edmund. A. D. 955.

This prince, who was only seventeen years of age at his accession, possessed an elegant person, and the most amiable and promising virtues. But neither the graces of his figure nor the accomplishments of his mind could screen him from the fury of the monks, whom he unhappily offended in the beginning of his reign. The beautiful Elgiva, his second or third cousin, had made an impression on his susceptible heart ; and, as he was at an age when the tender passions are most keenly felt, he ventured to marry her, though within the degrees of consanguinity prohibited by the church. The austerity of the monks made them particularly violent on this occasion : the king therefore entertained a strong aversion against them, and resolved to oppose their project of expelling the seculars from the convents. But he soon had reason to repent his rashness in provoking such dangerous enemies. On the day of his coronation, while the nobility, assembled in the great hall, were indulging themselves in riot and disorder, after the example of their German ancestors, Edwy, attracted by the gentler pleasures of love, retired to the queen's apartment, and gave a loose to his fondness, which was feebly checked by the presence of her mother. Dunstan conjectured the reason of the king's absence ; and accompanied by Odo, archbishop of Canterbury, over whom he had gained an absolute ascendant, he burst into the royal privacy, drew Edwy from the arms of his consort, and pushed him back ignominiously into the company of the nobles, abusing the queen with the most opprobrious epithets [2].

Though Edwy was young, and had the prejudices of the age to encounter, he found means to revenge this public insult. He accused Dunstan of malversation in office while at the head of the treasury ; and as that minister did not clear himself of the

---

[1] Spelm. *Concil.* vol. i.　　　　　[2] Gul. Malmesb. lib. ii.

charge, the king banished him. But Dunstan's partisans were not idle during his absence. They poisoned the minds of the people to such a degree by declamations against the king, and panegyrics on the abbot's sanctity, that the royal authority was despised, and even outrageously insulted. Archbishop Odo ordered the queen to be seized; and after her face had been seared with a red-hot iron, in order to destroy that fatal beauty which had ensnared the king, she was carried into Ireland, there to remain in perpetual exile[1].

Edwy finding resistance ineffectual, was obliged to consent to a divorce, which was pronounced by the imperious Odo. But these were not the only evils which attended this unfortunate prince and his consort. The amiable Elgiva was made prisoner by her persecutors, and cruelly murdered in returning to the embraces of the king, whom she still considered as her husband. Nothing less than her death could satisfy the archbishop and the monks. Edwy, by the same influence, was deposed from the sovereignty of all England to the northward of the Thames, in order to make room for his brother Edgar, a boy of thirteen years of age. Dunstan returned to England; took upon him the government of the young king and his party; was soon installed in the see of Worcester, and afterwards in that of Canterbury. In the mean time the unhappy Edwy was excommunicated, and pursued by his enemies with unrelenting ven-

A. D. geance[2]. But his early death freed them from all in-
959. quietude, and left Edgar in peaceable possession of the monarchy.

The reign of Edgar is one of the most fortunate in the English annals. Though he was very young when he ascended the throne, he soon discovered an excellent capacity for government. He manifested no dread of war; he took the wisest precautions for public safety; and, by his vigilance and foresight, he was enabled to indulge his natural inclination for peace. He maintained a body of soldiers in the north, to keep the mutinous Northumbrians in awe, and to repel the inroads of the Scots. He also built and supported a powerful navy; and, in order to habituate the seamen to the practice of their profession, as well as to intimidate his enemies, he stationed three squadrons off the coast of his kingdom, and commanded them to make by turns the circuit of his dominions. The foreign Danes durst not approach a country which was so strongly defended: the do-

---

[1] Osberne, ubi sup.   [2] Brompt. *Chron.*

mestic Danes foresaw that destruction would be the inevitable consequence of insurrection ; and the princes of Wales, of Scotland, and even of Ireland, were happy to appease so potent a monarch by submission[1].

But the politic Edgar more especially maintained his authority at home, and preserved public tranquillity, by paying court to Dunstan and the monks, who had violently placed him on the throne, and whose claim to superior sanctity gave them an ascendant over the people. He favoured their scheme of pretended reformation ; he consulted them in the administration of all ecclesiastical and even of many civil affairs ; and although the vigour of his genius prevented him from being entirely guided by them, he took care never to disoblige them. Hence he is represented by the monkish writers not only as an able politician, a character which he seems to have merited, but also as a saint and a man of virtue, though he was licentious in the highest degree, and violated every law human and divine. His very amours are a compound of barbarity and brutality. He broke into a convent, carried off a nun, and even committed violence on her person. Struck also with the charms of a nobleman's daughter, in whose house he was entertained, he demanded that she should pass that very night with him, without once consulting the young lady's inclinations[2]. But his most remarkable amour was with the beautiful Elfrida, and as it is connected with the history of the following reign, I shall relate it circumstantially. It will give you at once an idea of the manners of the age and of the character of Edgar.

Elfrida, the only daughter and sole heiress of Ordgar earl of Devon, though educated in the country, and a stranger at court, had filled all England with the fame of her beauty. The amorous king sent Athelwold, his favourite, to ascertain, by a personal view, the truth or the falsehood of the rumour. The courtier no sooner saw Elfrida than he was inflamed with love, and determined to sacrifice to it his fidelity to his master: he therefore told Edgar, on his return, that the fortune and quality of Elfrida had alone been the cause of the adulation paid to her ; and that her charms, far from being extraordinary, would have

---

[1] Spelm. *Conc.* vol. i.
[2] This demand was made to the mother, who, being a woman of virtue, sent secretly to the king's bed, instead of her daughter, her maid Elfleda. Edgar, not displeased, forgave the old lady for her pious deceit, and transferred his love to Elfleda, who became his favourite mistress. *Gul. Malmes.* lib. ii.

been entirely overlooked in a woman of inferior condition. " But," added he, when he found that he had blunted the keen edge of the king's curiosity, " though she has nothing to claim the attention of a sovereign, her immense wealth would, to a subject, be a sufficient compensation for the homeliness of her person ; and although it could never produce on me the illusion of beauty, it might make her a convenient wife !" Edgar, willing to establish his favourite's fortune, not only gave his approbation to the projected match, but forwarded its success, by recommending him so strongly to the Earl of Devon, that he was soon made happy in the possession of his beloved Elfrida. Dreading, however, the eyes of the king, he still found some pretence for detaining his wife in the country. But all his cautions were insufficient to conceal his treachery. Royal favourites are never without enemies ; Edgar was soon informed of the truth ; but, before he would punish Athelwold, he resolved to satisfy himself fully in regard to Elfrida's beauty. He therefore told his deceiver that he intended to pay him a visit at his castle, and be introduced to his wife. Athelwold was thunderstruck at the proposal ; but, as he could not refuse such an honour, he only begged leave to go a few hours before his royal guest, that he might make due preparations for his reception. On his arrival, he fell at his wife's feet, discovered the whole secret, and conjured her, if she valued either her own honour or his life, to disguise as much as possible that fatal beauty which had tempted him to deceive his prince and friend. Elfrida promised compliance, though nothing appears to have been farther from her thoughts. She adorned her person with the most exquisite art, and called forth all her charms ; not despairing, it should seem, yet to reach that exalted station of which Athelwold's fondness had deprived her. The event was answerable to her wishes : she excited at once in Edgar's bosom the warmest love, and the keenest desire of revenge. The king, however, who could dissemble those passions, as well as feel them, beheld her with seeming indifference ; and having seduced Athelwold into a wood, under pretence of hunting, he stabbed him with his own hand, took Elfrida to court, and soon after publicly married her[1].

This reign is remarkable for the extirpation of wolves from England. Edgar took great pleasure in pursuing those ravenous animals ; and when he found that they had all taken

---

[1] Gul. Malmesb.—Brompt.

shelter in the mountains and forests of Wales, he changed the tribute of money imposed on the Welsh princes by Athelstan into an annual tribute of three hundred wolves' heads—a policy which occasioned so much diligence in hunting them, that the breed soon became extinct in the island.

Edgar was followed on the throne by his son Edward, commonly called the Martyr, whose succession, however, did A. D. not take place without much opposition. Elfrida, his 975. step-mother, had a son named Ethelred, only eight years old, for whom she endeavoured to procure the crown. But the principal nobility, dreading her imperious temper, opposed a measure which must increase her authority, if not put her in possession of the regency; and Dunstan, to whom it was of great importance to have a king favourable to his cause, resolutely crowned and anointed Edward, over whom he had already gained an absolute ascendant. His short reign was remarkable for nothing but a continual struggle between the monks and the A.D. secular clergy. He was treacherously murdered at the 979. instigation of Elfrida, whose son was then placed on the throne.

Soon after the accession of Ethelred, a prince without courage or capacity, England was again visited by the Danes. The wise regulations of Alfred, and the valour of his immediate successors, had long deterred those ravagers from approaching the British shores; and their settlement in France had required, for a time, most of their superfluous hands. But a new race of men having now sprung up in the northern regions, who could no longer disburthen themselves on Normandy, and England not being at this time governed by an Alfred or an Edgar, they ventured to renew their depredations. Ethelred, instead of rousing A.D. his people to defend with courage their prince and their 991. property, meanly compounded with the enemy for his safety, by bribing them to retire from the kingdom [1].

This shameful expedient, which invited assailants instead of repelling them, was attended with the success that might have been expected: the Danes returned and were again bribed to depart. In the mean time, Ethelred, from a policy incident to weak princes, embraced the cruel resolution of massacring all the Danes who had settled in his dominions. Secret orders were given for this inhuman purpose, and the obnoxious A.D. colonists were destroyed without mercy. Even Gunilda, 1002.

[1] Gul. Malmesb. lib. ii.

sister to Sweyn king of Denmark, who had married earl Palling, and embraced Christianity, was seized and put to death, after having seen her husband and son brutally murdered [1].

This unhappy princess foretold, in the agonies of despair, that her murder would soon be revenged by the ruin of the English nation. Never was prophecy better fulfilled, nor ever did barbarous policy prove more fatal to its projectors! The king of A.D. Denmark, breathing vengeance for the slaughter of his 1003. countrymen, landed in the west of England, and soon reduced the greater part of the realm. The English, sensible of what they had to expect from a barbarous and enraged enemy, attempted several times to make a stand; but they were successively betrayed by the Mercian earls Alfric and Edric. The base and imprudent expedient of money was again tried, till the nation was entirely drained of its treasure, but without effect. The Danes continued their ravages; and Ethelred, equally afraid A.D. of the violence of the enemy, and the treachery of his own 1013. subjects, fled over to his brother-in-law, Richard duke of Normandy, who received him with a generosity that does honour to his memory [2].

Sweyn died soon after Ethelred left England, and before he A.D. had time to establish himself in his newly-acquired do-1014. minions. Ethelred was recalled: but his misconduct was incurable. On resuming the government, he discovered the same incapacity, indolence, cowardice, and credulity, which had so often exposed him to the insults of his enemies: and the English found in Canute, the son of Sweyn, an enemy no less formidable than his father. An army was assembled against him under the command of Edric and prince Edmund. Edric, whom the infatuated king still trusted, continued his perfidious A.D. machinations. After endeavouring in vain to get the 1015. prince into his power, he found means to disperse the army, and then openly revolted to Canute with forty vessels [3].

Notwithstanding this misfortune, Edmund, whose intrepidity never failed him, collected the remaining force of the kingdom,

[1] Gul. Malmesb. lib. ii.—Hen. Hunting. lib. vi. Contrary to the testimony of most of our old historians, who represent the massacre of the Danes as universal, Wallingford says that it affected only a military body in the pay of the king. After so great a lapse of time, it is impossible to decide upon the matter with certainty; but as the kingdoms of Northumberland and East-Anglia were chiefly peopled with Danes, Wallingford's account may possibly be true.

[2] Hen. Hunting. lib. vi.

[3] Gul. Malmesb. lib. ii.

and was soon in a condition to give the enemy battle.   But the king had so often experienced the perfidy of his subjects, that he had lost all confidence in them : he therefore refused to take the field : so that the prince's vigorous measures were rendered altogether ineffectual, the army being discouraged by the timidity of the sovereign.   As the north had already submitted to Canute's power, Edmund retired to London, determined to A.D. maintain the small remains of English liberty.   In the 1016. mean time his father died, after an inglorious reign of thirty-seven years.

Edmund, who received the name of Ironside from his hardy valour, possessed courage and abilities sufficient to have saved his country, if many of the nobles had not been infected with treachery and disloyalty.   But this disaffection rendered his best concerted schemes abortive, and his noblest efforts fruitless.   The traitor Edric pretended to return to his duty ; and Edmund was induced to give him a considerable command in the army.   A battle was soon after fought at Assington, in Essex.   Edric deserted to the enemy in the beginning of the day, and occasioned the total defeat of the English army, with a great slaughter of the nobility.

The indefatigable king, however, still had resources.   He assembled a new army at Gloucester, and was again in a condition to dispute the field ; when the Danish and English nobility, equally tired of the struggle, obliged their two leaders to come to terms.   The kingdom was divided between them by treaty.   Canute reserved to himself the provinces of Mercia, East-Anglia, and Northumberland ; the southern parts A.D. were assigned to Edmund, who did not long survive the 1016. agreement.   He is said to have been murdered at Oxford by two of his chamberlains, accomplices of Edric, whose treachery made way for the accession of the Danish prince to the throne of England [1].

[1] Gul. Malmesb.—Hen. Huntingd.

LETTER XIX.

Of the Reigns of the French Kings, from the accession of Hugh Capet, to the invasion of England, by William Duke of Normandy.

WHILE England changed its line of sovereigns, and Germany its form of government, France also had changed its reigning family, and had become, like Germany, a government entirely feudal. Each province had its hereditary counts or dukes. He who could only seize two or three small villages, paid homage to the usurper of a province ; and he who had only a castle held it of the possessor of a town. The kingdom was a monstrous assemblage of members, without any compact body.

A.D. 987.

Of the princes, or nobles, who held their lands immediately of the crown, Hugh Capet was not the least powerful. He possessed the dukedom of France, which extended as far as Touraine: he was also count of Paris; and the vast domains which he held in Picardy and Champagne gave him great authority in those provinces. He therefore seized the crown on the death of Louis V. [1], and brought more strength to it than he derived from it; for the royal domain was now reduced to the cities of Laon and Soissons, with a few other disputed territories.

The right of succession belonged to Charles duke of Lorrain, uncle to Louis V.; but the condition of vassal of the empire appeared to the French nobility a sufficient reason for excluding him; and Hugh secured the favour of the clergy by resigning to them the abbeys which had been hereditary in his family. An extreme devotion, real or assumed, recommended him to the people ; force and address seconded his ambition ; and the national aversion against his rival completed its success. He was acknowledged in an assembly of the nobles ; he was anointed at Rheims ; and he farther established his throne, by associating his son Robert in the government of the kingdom, and investing him with those ensigns of royalty which he prudently denied to himself, as what might give umbrage to men who were lately his equals [2].

A.D. 988.

Disgusted at this usurpation, the duke of Lorrain entered

---

[1] Glab. *Hist. sui Temp.* lib. ii.   [2] Glab. *Hist. sui Temp.*

France, made himself master of Laon by assault, and of A. D.
Rheims by the treachery of archbishop Arnolf, his relative. 989.
But this unhappy prince was afterwards himself betrayed by the
bishop of Laon, and made prisoner for life[1].

A council was assembled for the trial of Arnolf. He was
degraded ; and Gerbert, a man of learning and genius, who had
been tutor to the emperor Otho III. and to the king's son
Robert, was elected archbishop of Rheims. But the court of
Rome not being consulted in this transaction, the election was
declared void, Arnolf was re-established, and Gerbert deposed.
The former, however, remained in prison till the death of Hugh,
who was more afraid of Arnolf's intrigues than of the thunder
of the Vatican ; while the other, having found an asylum in
the court of his pupil Otho, became archbishop of Ravenna, and
afterwards pope, under the name of Silvester II.

No other memorable incidents distinguished the reign of
Hugh, who conducted all his affairs with great prudence and
moderation ; and had the extraordinary honour of establishing
a new family, and in some measure a new form of government,
with few circumstances of violence, and without the effusion of
blood. He died in the fifty-seventh year of his age, and A. D.
the tenth of his reign, and was quietly succeeded by his 996.
son Robert, a prince of a less vigorous genius, though not of a
less amiable disposition.

The most remarkable circumstance in the reign of Robert,
and the most worthy of our attention, is his excommunication
by the pope. This prince had espoused Bertha, his cousin in
the fourth degree—a marriage not only lawful according to our
present ideas, and justified by the practice of all nations, ancient and modern, but expedient for the welfare of the state,
she being the sister of Rodolph king of Burgundy. But the
clergy, among their other usurpations, had about this time made
a sacrament of marriage, and laid the most essential of civil engagements under spiritual prohibitions, which extended even to
the seventh degree of consanguinity. The popes politically
arrogated to themselves a special jurisdiction over this first object
of society, and that on which all the rest hang. Gregory V.
therefore undertook to dissolve the marriage between Robert
and Bertha, though it had been authorized by several bishops ;
and, without examining the cause or hearing the parties, he
published an arbitrary decree, which strictly enjoined the sepa-

[1] Sigeberti *Chron.*

ration of the king and queen. As Robert persisted in keeping his wife, he incurred the sentence of excommunication; which, according to cardinal Peter Damien, an historian of those times, had such an effect on the minds of men, that the king was abandoned by all his courtiers, and even by his own domestics, two servants excepted; and these threw to the dogs all the victuals which their master left at meals, and purified, by fire, the vessels in which he had been served: so fearful were they of what had been touched by an excommunicated person[1]! The same credulous author adds, that the queen was delivered of a monster, which had a neck and head like those of a goose—a certain proof and punishment of incest!—But, as Voltaire justly observes, there was nothing monstrous in all this affair, but the insolence of the pope, and the weakness of the king; who, giving way to superstitious terrors, or afraid of civil commotions, at last repudiated his wife Bertha, and married Constance, daughter to the count of Arles, in whom he found an imperious termagant, instead of an amiable consort. Gregory also obliged him to restore the traitor Arnolf to the see of Rheims[2].

In the mean time Robert had it in his power to have been master of the popes, if he had possessed the ambition and the vigour necessary for such an enterprise. After the death of A.D. Henry II., the last emperor of the house of Saxony, the 1024. Italians offered their crown and the imperial dignity to the king of France. Robert, however, had the resolution to refuse it; and not only his own subjects, but Europe in general, were soon convinced that he had acted wisely; for those who made the proposal deserted the person who accepted it[3].

The latter years of Robert's reign were rendered very unhappy by the disorders of his family. He was unfortunate in losing his eldest son Hugh, whom he had associated in the sovereignty; and he was harassed by the attempts of his queen Constance to regulate the succession. Having an aversion against her son Henry, she wished to place her younger son Robert on the throne. But the king, by the advice of a national

---

[1] Let us not, however, with certain sarcastical historians, represent this mode of inspiring religious terrors as an invention of the Christian priesthood. For Cæsar tells us that, among the ancient Gauls, if any one, whether magistrate or private person, refused to submit to the sentence of the Druids, he was excluded from the sacrifices; and that, while under such prohibition, all men shunned him, lest they should suffer by the contagion of his impiety. (Cæs. *Bell. Gall.* lib. vi.) The power of EXCOMMUNICATION, or the authority of debarring the vicious and refractory from religious privileges, is necessary indeed to every body of priests. But it ought to extend no farther, to affect no legal right or civil privilege.
[2] Aimon. *Hist.* lib. v.   [3] Id. ibid.

council, confirmed the succession to Henry, his eldest surviving son.   Provoked at this measure, the queen endeavoured to embroil the brothers; but they, being united by a sincere friendship, withstood all her irritations.   At length, becoming equally the object of her hatred, they retired from court, and took arms in order to obtain a separate establishment[1].   In the July 20, mean time the king died, and was succeeded by Henry.   1031.

There is not any monarch in the French history more generally or more highly commended than Robert (notwithstanding his weakness of temper), or on whose death the lamentations of all ranks of people were louder or more sincere.   The monks spoke the sense of the whole nation, when they deplored his death in these words; "We have lost a father who governed us in peace.   We lived under him in security: for he did not oppress, or suffer others to be guilty of oppression: we loved him, and there was nobody whom we feared."

Henry I. was twenty-five years of age at his accession to the throne, and, with all the spirit of a young man, he had the sagacity and prudence of one more advanced in years; without which the crown would have been shaken from his head almost as soon as it was placed upon it.   Constance, who hated him, as has been observed, and who was ambitious still to govern, had drawn over to her party a number of lords and bishops, under pretence of supporting the cause of young Robert.   Henry, therefore, after some ineffectual struggles, was obliged to take refuge in Normandy, where he was received with all possible respect by Duke Robert, who assured him that the treasures and forces of the duchy were at his disposal.   Nor were these mere expressions of civility; an army of Normans entered France on one side, while the king and the royal party invaded it on the other. The queen-dowager and her faction were humbled, and Henry recovered all that he had lost.   But although this contest ended gloriously for the king, it proved prejudicial to the monarchy; for as the success of the war was chiefly the consequence of the exertions of the Normans, Henry added to the duchy Gisors, Chaumont, Pontoise, and that part of the Vexin which yet remained to the crown[2].

The next affair of importance that occupied the king's attention, was the succession to the duchy of Normandy.   Duke Robert had thought fit, in compliance with the fashionable devotion of those times, to make a pilgrimage to Jerusalem.   But

---

[1] Glab. *Hist. sui Temp.* lib. iii.   [2] Gul. Gemet. lib. vi.

before his departure, as he was a prudent prince, though now old and superstitious, he assembled his nobles : and informing them of his pious purpose, the length of the journey, and the dangers to which he must be exposed, he engaged them to swear allegiance to his natural son William, whom he tenderly loved, and intended for his successor, as he had no legitimate issue. He also recommended the guardianship of this son to two persons in whom he placed the greatest confidence—the king of France, and Alain duke of Bretagne[1]. But these precautions did not prevent many disorders, which a mind not hoodwinked by superstition must have foreseen ; arising from the habitual turbulence of the great, the illegitimacy of William, and the pretensions of other branches of the ducal family.

Robert died, as he had apprehended, in his pilgrimage ; and A. D. 1035. left his son rather the heir of his wishes than of his dominions. The licentious nobles, freed from the awe of sovereign authority, broke out into personal quarrels, and made the whole duchy a scene of war and devastation. The duke of Bretagne came to appease their animosities ; but, being very roughly treated, he returned home, and was soon after carried off by slow poison, supposed to have been given him in Normandy. Various pretenders to the succession arose ; and the king of France, forgetting what he owed to Robert, seemed willing to deprive his infant son of his inheritance, by taking advantage of these troubles. He accordingly invaded the Norman frontier, and reduced several places ; but not finding the conquest so easy as A. D. 1046. he expected, or influenced by the returning sentiments of friendship and generosity, he united his forces with those of the young duke, and the malcontents were totally routed in the battle of Val de Dunes, which gave William quiet possession of his dominions[2].

Aug. 4, 1060. Henry was succeeded by his son Philip, whom he had by his second wife, the daughter of Jaroslaus or Yaroslaf, grand duke of Russia—a circumstance truly remarkable in an age when no very familiar intercourse prevailed between distant nations. But the prohibitions of marriage were so multiplied, and the example of his father so alarming, that Henry is supposed to have sought a wife in a remote country, in order to avoid the crime of incest, and the danger of excommunication. What must the disorders of society have been, when even a king did not know whom he might lawfully marry !

[1] Gul. Gemet. lib. vi.   [2] Id. Ibid.

Philip I. was only eight years of age at the time of his accession; and, instead of being put under the guardianship of his mother or his uncle, one of whom, it might naturally be supposed, would have been called to the regency, he was committed by his father to the care of Baldwin the Pious, earl of Flanders—a man of strict honour, and brother-in-law to Henry. Baldwin gave his pupil an education suitable to his rank: he kept the nobles in awe, without giving them just cause of offence; and he maintained peace, by being always prepared for war. History, in a word, scarcely furnishes us with an instance of a minority more quiet or more happy—an example the more remarkable, from the delicacy of the times and circumstances.

The only colour that Baldwin gave for censure, was in his conduct towards William duke of Normandy, who was preparing to invade England, and whom he permitted to raise forces in France and Flanders—a liberty which, from the event, was judged impolitic. But the duke being his son-in-law, he could not refuse him with a good grace; and there was yet a farther motive for compliance. The fortunate and enterprising William might have entered France with that army which he had assembled against England, where he succeeded more speedily and with greater ease than could have been expected. But the particulars of that invasion, and its consequences, belong to the history of our own country. I shall therefore only here observe, that, to balance in some measure the increase of William's power, a close alliance was concluded between the crowns of France and Scotland. Soon after that negociation A.D. Baldwin died, and left his pupil Philip in peaceable pos- 1067. session of his kingdom, when he had completed his fifteenth year.

LETTER XX.

Of the Government of the Kings of England, from the Danish to the Norman Conquest.

You have already, my dear Philip, seen Edmund Ironside inhumanly murdered, and England exposed to the ambition of Canute the Dane, a prince both active and brave, and at the head of a numerous army, ready to take advantage of the A.D. minority of Edward and Edmund, the sons of the late 1017.

king. The English could therefore expect nothing but total subjection from Canute. But the Danish monarch, commonly so little scrupulous, showed, on this occasion, an anxiety to conceal his injustice under plausible pretence. Before he seized the inheritance of the two young princes, he summoned a general assembly of the states of England, in order to fix the succession; and, when he had suborned some noblemen to depose that, in the treaty of Gloucester, it was agreed, "That Canute, in case of Edmund's decease, should succeed to the whole kingdom," the states, convinced by this evidence, or overawed by his victorious arms, put the Dane in full posssession of the government [1].

But although Canute had now attained the great object of his ambition in the undivided sovereignty of England, he was at first obliged to make many sacrifices to it, and to gratify the chief nobility, by bestowing on them extensive governments and jurisdictions. He also thought himself obliged, from political motives, to exercise some severities. In order to reward his Danish followers, he loaded the people with oppressive taxes; and jealous of the two young princes, but sensible that he should render himself detested if he ordered them to be murdered in England, he sent them to his ally the king of Sweden, whom he desired to put them to death. But the Swedish monarch was too generous to comply with such a barbarous request. Afraid, however, to draw on himself the displeasure of Canute, by protecting the English princes, he sent them to be educated in the Hungarian court—a strange place surely to seek for a preceptor. But the defenceless seek only a protector; and the sons of Edmund found one in the king of Hungary [2].

The removal of Edmund's children into a distant country was regarded by Canute, next to their death, as the greatest security of his government. But he was still under alarm on account of Alfred and Edward, the sons of Ethelred, who were protected and supported by their uncle, Richard duke of Normandy. Richard had even fitted out a fleet with a view of procuring the English crown for one of these princes. To avert the storm, and secure himself on that side, Canute paid his addresses to Emma, the duke's sister, and the mother of those princes who disputed his sway. He was listened to: Richard sent over Emma to England, where she was soon after married to Canute, the enemy of her former husband's family, and the conqueror of

---

[1] Hoved. *Annal.*   [2] Hoved. *ad annum* 1017.

that country which her children had a right to rule. But Canute promised that her children should still rule it, though not the children of Ethelred; and, although the English disapproved the match, they were pleased to find at court a princess to whom they were accustomed; so that the conqueror, by this marriage, not only secured the alliance of the Normans, but acquired the confidence of his new subjects. Having thus freed himself from the danger of a revolution, Canute determined, like a truly wise prince, to reconcile the English to the Danish yoke by the equity of his administration. He sent back to their own country as many of his followers as could safely be spared; he restored the Saxon customs; he made no distinction between the Danes and the English in the distribution of justice; and he took care, by a strict execution of law, to protect the lives and properties of all his subjects[1]. The Danes were gradually incorporated with the native English; and both were glad to breathe a little from those multiplied calamities which the conquerors, no less than the conquered, had experienced in their struggle for dominion.

The first use that Canute made of this tranquillity was to visit Denmark, where he obtained a victory over the Swedes, chiefly by the valour of the English under the command of earl A.D. Godwin. In another voyage to Denmark, he made him- 1019. self master of Norway, by expelling Olaus the Saint from his kingdom. Canute seems thus to have attained the A.D. height of his ambition: for from this period, he appears 1028. not only to have relinquished all thoughts of future conquest, but to have despised all the glories and pleasures of the world—a necessary consequence, my dear Philip, of assigning to human enjoyments a satisfaction which they cannot yield, and more especially of pursuing them (another effect of the same cause) at the expense of justice and humanity.

During this change of mind it must have been that Canute, the most powerful prince of his time, being sovereign of Denmark, Norway, and England, put to the blush his flattering courtiers, who exclaimed, in admiration of his grandeur, that every thing was *possible* for him. He ordered a chair to be brought, and seated himself on the sea-shore, while the tide was rising; and as the waves approached, he said, in an imperious tone, " Thou, sea, art under my dominion, and the land upon which I sit is mine: I charge thee, approach no farther! nor

---

[1] Gul. Malmesh. lib. ii.

dare to wet the feet of thy sovereign." He even sat some time in seeming expectation of submission; but as the sea still advanced towards him, and at last began to wash him with its billows, he turned to his courtiers, and observed, that every creature in the universe is feeble and impotent; and that power resides only with ONE Being, in whose hands are the elements of nature, and who can say to the ocean, " Thus far shalt thou go, and no farther [1]!"

But although Canute, weary of worldly greatness, began to turn his eyes towards a future state of existence, the spirit which prevailed in that age unfortunately gave a false direction to his piety. Instead of making reparation to the persons whom he had injured by former acts of violence, he built churches, endowed monasteries, and appointed prayers to be said for the souls of those who had fallen in battle against him; and (what was thought by many to be still more meritorious) he undertook a pilgrimage to Rome.

After his return from the continent, he performed nothing memorable, except an expedition against Malcolm, king of A.D. Scotland, whom he humbled. He left the crown of 1035. England to Harold Harefoot, his son by his first wife Elgiva, daughter to the earl of Hants, in prejudice of Hardicanute, his son by queen Emma, to whom he had promised the succession [2].

Harold, after a short reign, was succeeded by his brother, A.D. Hardi-canute, whose reign was yet shorter. Neither of 1040. these princes had any striking qualities; nor did any thing worthy of your notice happen during their reigns. It will therefore A.D. be sufficient to observe, that on the death of Hardi-1042. canute, who fell a sacrifice to his brutal intemperance, the English shook off the Danish yoke, and placed Edward, son of Ethelred and Emma, on the throne of his ancestors.

This revolution was effected with great facility; and the mild and equitable government of Edward soon reconciled the Danes, no less than the English, to his sway. The distinction between the two nations vanished. But the English in vain flattered themselves that they were for ever delivered from foreign masters. A little time convinced them that the evil was rather suspended than removed.

Edward had been educated in Normandy; and, as he had contracted a friendship with many of the natives of that country,

---

[1] *Anglia Sacra,* vol. i.   [2] *Chron. Sax.*—Hoved.

and a predilection for their manners, the court of England was soon filled with Normans, who were distinguished by the royal favour, and had great influence in the national councils. He had also, it appears, though married to a beautiful woman, made an indiscreet vow of virginity, which rendered his bed sterile, but procured to him from the monks the title of Saint and Confessor : and he is said to have given his kinsman, William duke of Normandy, hopes of succeeding to the English crown. What use that enterprising prince made of this promise, real or pretended, we shall afterward have occasion to see.

In the mean time the English, and particularly the opulent and powerful earl Godwin, became jealous of the preference shown to foreigners, and openly revolted. The rebels were humbled: the estates of Godwin and his sons were confiscated ; and they were obliged to quit the realm. But they soon A.D. after returned, and reduced the king to conditions; of 1051. which the most important was, that all foreigners should be banished[1].

Godwin's death, which happened about two years after this treaty, prevented him from establishing that authority which he had acquired at the expense of the crown. But his son Harold, who succeeded him in his estates and offices, and who, with an ambition equal to that of his father, was superior to him in address and insinuation, proved no less dangerous to the unsuspecting and unwarlike Edward, whose confidence he had obtained. And the death of Siward, earl of Northumberland, while A.D. it enfeebled the royal authority, gave still more conse- 1055. quence to the ambitious Harold. Siward, beside his loyalty and exploits in behalf of the crown, had acquired honour to England by his successful conduct in the only foreign enterprise undertaken during this reign : and as it is connected with a memorable circumstance in the history of a neighbouring kingdom, as well as with the intrigues of Harold, it doubly deserves our attention.

Duncan, king of Scotland, a prince of a gentle disposition, and some talents, but not possessed of sufficient vigour to govern a turbulent nation distracted by the animosities of the great, had laid himself open to the designs of Macbeth, a potent nobleman, nearly allied to the crown ; who, not contented with opposing the king's authority, carried yet farther his traitorous ambition. He murdered his sovereign, usurped the crown, and chased Malcolm, the prince and heir, into England. Siward, whose daughter

---

[1] Sim. Dunelm.—Hoved.

was married to Duncan, undertook, by Edward's orders, the protection of this unhappy family. He marched with an army into Scotland, defeated and killed the bold usurper, and restored Malcolm to the throne of his ancestors. This service, added to his former connexions with the royal family of Scotland, brought great accession to the authority of Siward in the north, and enabled him to be highly useful to Edward, in restraining the ambition of Godwin and his powerful family ; but as he had lost his eldest son Osbern in the action with Macbeth, it proved eventually fatal to his house, and hurtful to the crown. His second son, Waltheof, appeared too young, on his father's death, to be intrusted with the government of Northumberland; and Harold's influence obtained that dukedom for Tosti, his own brother[1].

There are two anecdotes related of Siward, which strongly mark his character, and are eminently expressive of that enthusiasm of valour, long so predominant in the house of Northumberland. When informed of his son Osbern's death, he was at first inconsolable. But when, having inquired how he fell, he found that the youth had behaved with great gallantry, and that his wound was in the *breast,* the feelings of the father seemed lost in those of the soldier ; his grief was transformed into joy : " Would to God," exclaimed he, " that I had as many sons as I have hairs, that I might lose them thus!" And when his own death approached, he ordered himself to be clothed in a suit of complete armour ; and, sitting erect on a couch, with a spear in his hand, " In this posture," said he, " the only one worthy of a warrior, I will meet the tyrant : if I cannot conquer, I shall at least *face* my enemy[2]."

Tosti behaved so tyrannically in his government of Northumberland, that the people rose against him, and expelled him by force of arms—a circumstance which contributed much to his brother's aggrandisement. Harold was appointed by the king to punish the Northumbrians, and advanced with an army for that purpose; but being met by a deputation from Morcar, whom the provincials wished to have for their governor, and finding that Tosti had acted in a manner unworthy of his station, he returned to the king, and generously persuaded him not only to pardon the rebels, but to confer the earldom on Morcar. He afterward married the sister of that nobleman, for whose brother Edwin he procured the earldom of Mercia. He also undertook an expedi-

---

[1] Gul. Malmesb. lib. ii.—Hoved.   [2] H. Huntingd. lib. vi.

tion against the Welsh, over whom he placed such princes as he approved.

By these politic and fortunate steps, Harold soon found himself in a condition openly to aspire to the royal succession. He had gained the affections of his countrymen by his lenity to the Northumbrians; he had raised their admiration of his valour by his success in Wales; and so great was his influence, that almost all England was under the command of himself or his friends. His competitors for the succession were Edgar Atheling, the off-spring of king Edmund's son Edward, the lawful heir to the crown, and William duke of Normandy, the king's cousin. But the first was a youth, whose imbecility was thought sufficient to set aside his claim, and the second a foreigner. Edward's pre-possessions rendered him unwilling to support the pretensions of Harold : and his irresolution prevented him from securing the crown to the duke of Normandy, whom he secretly favoured. He therefore died without appointing a successor, being worn A.D. out with age and infirmities, and more anxious about ob- 1066. taining a heavenly than settling his earthly inheritance.

Edward the Confessor was the first who *touched* for the scrofula, hence denominated the King's Evil. The opinion of his sanctity procured belief, among the superstitious vulgar, to this mode of cure; and his successors regarded it as a part of their royalty to support the same idea. The practice was first dropped by the princes of the house of Brunswick, who wisely considered, that such a pretension must be attended with ridicule in the eyes of all men of cultivated minds, and even become the scorn of an en-lightened populace. Posterity are more indebted to Edward for the body of laws which he compiled, and which, on account of their mildness, were long dear to our ancestors.

Though this prince left the succession undecided, it did not long continue so. Harold immediately stepped into the vacant throne; and so well had he taken his measures, that his succes-sion was attended with as little opposition or disturbance as if he had succeeded by the most indisputable hereditary title. The right of Edgar Atheling was scarcely ever mentioned, and still less the claim of the duke of Normandy; the whole nation seemed joyfully to swear allegiance to the new king [1].

The first danger that Harold experienced was from abroad, and from his own brother. Tosti, when expelled from the government of Northumberland, had submitted to a voluntary

[1] Gul. Pictav.—Order. Vital.

banishment in Flanders; but no sooner did he hear of the accession of Harold, to whose fortunate ambition he considered himself as having fallen a sacrifice, than he entered into a league with Hardrada king of Norway, who invaded England with a fleet of three hundred sail. Tosti himself had collected about sixty vessels in the ports of Flanders, with which he put to sea; and, after committing some depredations on the southern and eastern coasts of England, he sailed to Northumberland, where he was joined by the Norwegian armament. The invaders disembarked at the mouth of the Humber, and defeated the earls of Northumberland and Mercia[1].

Harold was no sooner informed of this disaster than he hastened to the northward, anxious for the safety of his people, and eager to show himself worthy of that crown which had been conferred upon him by his countrymen. The English flocked from all quarters to his standard; so that he found himself in a condition to give battle to his foes, as soon as he reached them.

The two armies engaged at Stanford-bridge, near York. The action, which was long and bloody, terminated in the total rout of the enemy, and in the death of Tosti and Hardrada[2]. Harold, however, had scarcely time to rejoice on account of this victory, before he received intelligence that the duke of Normandy had landed with a formidable force in the south of England.

The Norman prince founded his claim to the English crown on a pretended will of Edward the Confessor in his favour. This claim he fortified with an oath extorted from Harold when shipwrecked on the coast of France, importing that he would never aspire to the succession, and that he would even support the pretensions of William. The will Harold knew to be void of foundation, and the oath he entirely disregarded, as it had been drawn from him by the fear of violence. He therefore replied to the Norman ambassadors, who summoned him to resign the kingdom, that he was determined strenuously to maintain those national liberties with which he had been intrusted, and that the same moment should put a period to his life and his sway[3].

This was such an answer as William expected. He knew the valour of Harold, and the power of the English nation; but he consulted only his ambition, and his courage. The boldness of the enterprise, he thought, would astonish his adversaries, and

[1] H. Huntingd. lib. vii.   [2] Gul. Malmesb. lib. ii.
[3] R. Higdeni *Poly-Chronicon.*—Matth. Westm.

inspire his soldiers with resolution from despair, as well as from a desire of supporting the military reputation of their countrymen.

A martial spirit had at this time diffused itself over Europe; and the feudal nobles, whose minds were elated by their princely situation, eagerly embraced the most hazardous enterprises, how little soever they might be interested in the failure or success. Hence arose their passion for chivalry, and their ambition to outshine each other in exertions of strength and prowess. William had long been distinguished among those haughty chieftains by his power, his courage, and his address in all military exercises; and all who were ambitious of acquiring renown in arms repaired to the court of Normandy, where they were entertained with that hospitality and courtesy which dignified the age. The fame of the intended invasion of England had been widely propagated; and the more perilous the attempt appeared the more it suited the genius of the times. Multitudes of adventurers, therefore, crowded to tender their service to William, who selected from the whole number as many as, when added to the Norman troops, swelled his army to the amount of 60,000 men.

The continental monarchs could surely have obstructed those supplies. But Philip of France (whose interest was most likely to be affected by the scheme) being a minor, Baldwin, earl of Flanders, William's father-in-law, who then held the reigns of government, favoured the duke's levies, as I have had occasion to observe, both in France and Flanders; and the emperor Henry IV., besides giving all his vassals leave to embark in this expedition, promised to defend Normandy during the absence of the duke, and thereby enabled him to draw his whole strength to the attack of England.

But William's most important ally was pope Alexander II., who had an extraordinary influence over the warriors of that age; and who, besides being flattered by an appeal which William had made to the court of Rome on the subject of his undertaking, at a time when this pontiff wished to be the arbiter of princes, foresaw that if the French and Norman barons should be successful in their enterprise, they would import into England, which still maintained some degree of independence in ecclesiastical matters, a more devoted reverence to the holy see. He therefore declared immediately in favour of William's claim; pronounced Harold a perjured usurper; denounced excommunication against him and his adherents; and in order more particularly to encourage the duke, he sent him a consecrated banner, and a ring with one of St. Peter's hairs in it. Thus, as the sagacious Hume remarks, all the ambition and violence of this invasion were covered safely over with the broad mantle of religion.

The Norman fleet, which consisted of three thousand vessels, had been assembled early in the summer, and put to sea soon after; but being long detained by contrary winds, the troops began to imagine that Heaven had declared against them, and that, notwithstanding the pope's benediction, they were destined to destruction. The wind, however, fortunately changed on the eve of the feast of St. Michael, the tutelary saint of Normandy; and the soldiers and their bold leaders, who had an equal contempt of real and dread of imaginary dangers, fancying they saw the hand of Providence in the cause of their former terrors, set out with the greatest alacrity; and safely arrived at Pevensey in Sussex, where the troops quietly disembarked. The duke himself had the misfortune to fall, as he leaped on shore—a circumstance which, by his superstitious followers, might have been construed to his disadvantage, but which he had the presence of mind to turn in his favour, By calling aloud, " I have taken possession of England[1]!"

Harold's late victory proved his ruin. Many of his bravest officers and veteran soldiers fell in the action ; many retired from fatigue, and a great number withdrew from discontent, because he had refused to distribute the spoils of the field among them— a conduct little suited to his usual generosity, and which can only be ascribed to a desire of relieving his people in the war that hung over them from Normandy, and which he foresaw must be attended with great expense.

From the smallness of the king's force, and other circumstances, his brother Gurth, a man of bravery and conduct, began to entertain apprehensions of the event, and represented to him that it would be more prudent to prolong the war than to risk a general action, as the winter was approaching, when the enemy would suffer many hardships, while the English, better sheltered, and becoming every day more incensed against their invaders, would hasten from all parts to his assistance, and render his army invincible: or, if he thought it necessary to hazard a battle, he ought at least not to expose his person, that some resource might still be left for the liberty and independence

---

[1] Wace, *Histoire des Ducs de Normandie*.

of the kingdom. Harold, however, rejected this advice with disdain, and advanced without delay against the Normans, who had removed their camp to Hastings. He affected to be so confident of success, that he sent a message to the duke of Normandy, offering him a sum of money if he would retire from the kingdom without effusion of blood; and William, equally elate, commanded him to resign the crown of England, to submit their cause to the arbitration of the pope, or to fight him in single combat. Harold replied, that the God of Battles would soon be the arbiter of all their differences [1].

Both armies now impatiently expected the awful decision. In the night which preceded the battle, the scene was very different in the two camps. The English passed the time in rioting and feasting; the Normans in prayer and preparation for the conflict. As soon as the day began to appear, the duke harangued his principal officers in terms suitable to the occasion, and divided his army into three lines. The first consisted of archers and light-armed infantry; the second was composed of his bravest battalions, heavy-armed, and ranged in close order. The cavalry, at the head of which William placed himself, formed the third line, and were so disposed, that they stretched beyond the infantry, and flanked each wing of the army. He commanded the signal to be given: and the whole army moving at once, and singing the celebrated song of Roland, the supposed nephew and renowned captain of Charle-magne, advanced in order of battle [2]. Oct. 14.

In the arrangement of the English army, Harold seized the advantage of a rising ground, and drew some trenches to secure his flanks. The Kentish men were placed in the front, a post which they had always claimed as their due; the Londoners guarded the standard: and the king, dismounting, placed himself in the centre, at the head of his infantry, expressing his resolution to conquer or die. The first attack of the Norman infantry was terrible; the archers severely galled their adversaries; and, as the English ranks were close, the arrows did great execution. But Harold's army received the shock undismayed; and after a furious struggle, which long remained undecided, the Nomans began to give ground. Confusion was spreading from rank to rank; when William, who found himself on the brink of ruin, hastened with a select band to the relief of his broken forces. His presence restored the battle; and

[1] Gul. Pictav.—Wace.
[2] Gul. Malmesb. lib. iii.—Du Cange in *Gloss*. Verb. *Cant. Roland*.

the English were obliged to retire in their turn. Finding that they still made a vigorous resistance, the duke ordered his troops to make a hasty retreat, and allure their antagonists from their station by the appearance of flight. The artifice succeeded. Impelled by the enthusiasm of valour and the heat of action, the troops of Harold precipitately followed the Normans into the plain; while William directed his infantry to face about on their pursuers, and the cavalry to make an assault upon their wings. The English were thrown into disorder, and driven back with loss to the hill; where being rallied by the address of Harold, they were again able to maintain the combat. William tried the same stratagem a second time, and with equal success. Yet he still found a large body of English forces that remained firm around their prince, and seemed determined to dispute the field to the last man; when fortune decided a victory which valour had left doubtful. The king was pierced in the brain with an arrow, while bravely defending the royal standard at the head of his guards; and his two gallant brothers, Gurth and Leofwin, were also slain. Dispirited by the loss of their leaders, the English now gave way on all sides, and were pursued with great slaughter by the victorious Normans[1].

Such were the chief features of the battle of Hastings, which terminated the Anglo-Saxon monarchy, and which, by the heroic valour displayed on both sides, seemed worthy to decide the fate of a mighty kingdom. Fifteen thousand of the Normans fell, and a much greater number of the English forces[2].——But we must take a view of the other nations of Europe, and also throw a glance on those of Asia and Africa, before we consider the consequences of this victory, and the influence of the revolution by which it was followed, upon the laws, government, and manners of England. In the mean time, however, it will not be improper to take a slight survey of the state of England at the Norman conquest.

POSTSCRIPT.

No territory of so small an extent has ever so much engaged the attention of mankind, for so long a series of ages, as the island of Britain. From the most remote antiquity it was visited by the Phœnicians and Carthaginians, on account of its

[1] Gul. Malmesb. ubi sup.—Gul. Pict.—Hoved.—Order. Vital.
[2] Gul. Gemet. lib. vii.

tin and other valuable productions. The Romans, in the height of their power, made themselves masters of the southern part of it, at a great expense of blood and treasure ; and they thought the acquisition of sufficient importance to induce them to preserve their footing in this distant and transmarine province for three hundred years, by maintaining in it a considerable naval and military force. The ancient Britons lost their courage and their independent spirit under the Roman dominion, but received from their enlightened governors some knowledge of art and letters [1]. The Saxons, in achieving their sanguinary conquests, destroyed every trace of ingenuity which the Romans had introduced into the island, without bringing one peaceful art, with which the Britons were not better acquainted: and the wars between the princes of the Heptarchy afterward obstructed among their people the usual progress of civilization. But no sooner was England united into one kingdom, under Egbert, than commerce and manufactures began to be cultivated in a country so highly favoured by Nature; abounding in the materials of industry, and favoured on three sides by the proximity of the sea, which forms on its coasts many commodious bays and safe harbours [2].

The Anglo-Saxon commerce, however, was cruelly injured by the piratical cruises and predatory invasions of the Danes; yet did England then contain many large trading towns, and a greater number of inhabitants both in the towns and in the country, than could have been expected in such a turbulent and hostile period. London, York, Bristol [3], Exeter, and Norwich, were great and populous cities ; and as the labours of husbandry were chiefly performed by slaves or villains, who were excluded from military service, the number of freemen in England, *habituated*

---

[1] If the Britons had any knowledge of letters before the arrival of the Romans, that knowledge was confined chiefly, if not solely, to their priests, the mysterious Druids.

[2] The principal English exports, during the Anglo-Saxon times, were tin, lead, wool, hides, horses, and *slaves!* These slaves consisted not solely of such unhappy persons as the laws of war or other causes had reduced to the condition of perpetual servitude. The Anglo-Saxons are accused by some contemporary writers, of making merchandise even of their nearest relatives—" a custom," adds a respectable historian who lived in the reign of the first Henry, " which prevails in Northumberland even in our own days." Gul. Malmesb. lib. i.

[3] The Bristol traders were distinguished, even in those early ages, by their mercantile sagacity. " The people of this town," says an author of undoubted veracity, " were cured of a most odious and inveterate custom by Wulfstan (bishop of Worcester at the Norman conquest), *of buying men and women in all parts of England, and exporting them for the sake of gain. The young women they commonly got with child, and carried them to market in their pregnancy, that they might bring a better price!*" *Anglia Sacra*, vol. ii.

to the *use* of *arms*, if not greater, must have been as great at the Norman invasion as in any former or subsequent period[1]. But let us not hence conclude, that sixty thousand men, under an experienced leader, have at all times been sufficient to overturn the constitution of this vigorous kingdom. William was ultimately indebted for his good fortune, less to the rashness of the English monarch, his own conduct, or the valour of his troops, than to the unsettled state of the succession to the crown. Harold had owed his exaltation to the throne as much to fear as affection ; and, on his death, the English nobility, who had borne with impatience the sway of an equal, naturally looked up to his conqueror and competitor, the kinsman of the last prince, as their sovereign, their head, and centre of union. The duke of Normandy, at Hastings, had triumphed over their elected king, but not over their liberties. These, when a spirited resistance was yet in their power, they imprudently put into his hands (as we shall afterwards have occasion to see), in the hope that he would not abuse their generosity.

LETTER XXI.

Of the Affairs of Spain, the Saracen Empire, and that of Con-stantinople, during the ninth, tenth, and part of the eleventh Century.

THE death of Abdarrahman, the Moorish king, whom we have seen reign with so much lustre at Cordova, was followed by dissensions among his children, which procured some relief to the

---

[1] To that exemption from rustic labour, which was friendly to the use of arms, may also perhaps be ascribed the dissolute manners of the Anglo-Saxons. Unless when employed in war or in hunting, their whole time was spent in drinking and feasting. This licentious life seems to have much impaired the native courage of the English nation, before the Danish conquest. The wars which introduced and accompanied that conquest revived their martial spirit : and under the Danish princes, the Anglo-Saxons appear to have emulated their conquerors in all acts of prowess and valour. But both were alike given to long and excessive drinking, in large societies or clubs : and the Danes added to this convivial intemperance an inordinate passion for women ; in which they seem to have gloried, and which they often gratified in a manner shocking to humanity. Violence in love was with them as common as in war. Yet they sometimes made use of other means to accomplish their purpose—they affected gallantry ; and by their attention to dress and cleanliness, are said to have seduced many English wives. That cleanliness, however, by which they were distinguished, consisted only in combing their hair once a day, and washing themselves once a week. Wallingford, ap. Gale, vol. i.—*Anglia Sacra*, vol. ii.

Spanish Christians. The little kingdom of the Asturias (or of Leon, as it was afterwards called), founded by Pelagius, increased under Alphonso III., surnamed the Great, who began to reign in the year 862. About thirty-four years prior to that date, Eneco count of Bigorre had founded the kingdom of A.D. Navarre, which became one of the most considerable 828. Christian principalities in Spain.

The Moors, however, still possessed more than three-fourths of Spain, and the most fertile provinces. Among them, as among the Christian nations, a crowd of too powerful nobles affected independence, and the sovereign was obliged to contend with his subjects for dominion. This was the time to have crushed the Mohammedan power : but the Spanish Christians were not more united than their enemies. Though continually at war with the Moors, they were always destroying each other. The reign of Alphonso the Great abounded with conspiracies and revolts : his wife and his two sons were among the number of the rebels. He resigned his crown to Garcias, the elder of those princes ; A.D. he even generously fought under his command ; and died 910. in 911, with the glory of a hero, and the piety of a saint [1].

Ramiro II., king of Leon, another Spanish hero, gained the celebrated victory of Simancas, where the Moors, under Aug. Abdarrahman III., lost thirty-thousand men [2]. He had 938. promised to St. James, in a pilgrimage to Compostella, that if he should be victorious, all his subjects should offer annually a certain measure of wheat to the church of that saint. The church was enriched, and the name of St. James became the alarm to battle among the Spaniards.

Men are chiefly indebted for all their heroic achievements to their passions ; hence nothing is so irresistible as the valour inspired by enthusiasm, while it continues. The name of St. James was long terrible to the Moors, and long the companion to victory. Mohammed Al-Mansour, however, the celebrated general and prime-minister of Hashem II., king of Cordova, found means, by another artifice, to turn the tide of success. Seeing his troops begin to fly, in a battle fought on the A.D. banks of the river Ezla, he dismounted from his horse, sat 995. down in the field, threw his turban on the ground, and laying his arms across his breast, declared that he would in that posture meet his fate, since he was abandoned by his army. This stratagem had the desired effect : his troops returned to the charge,

[1] Ferreras.—Mariana.   [2] Mariana, lib. viii.

and obtained a complete victory.   The Moors became sensible
that they could conquer in spite of St. James ; and the Christians
in their turn trembled at the name Al-Mansour.

That great man, who was no less a politician than a warrior,
is said to have vanquished the Christian princes in fifty engagements.   He took the city of Leon by assault ; sacked Compostella ; pillaged the church of St. James, and carried the gates in
triumph, on the shoulders of his army, to Cordova. This triumph
proved his ruin.   A flux breaking out among his troops, the
A.D.   Christians considered that distemper as a punishment
998.   inflicted by St. James : the flame of enthusiasm was rekindled, and Al-Mansour was defeated.   But what was infinitely
more advantageous to the Christians, as well as more fatal to
himself, he was so much ashamed of his misfortune, that he would
neither eat nor drink, and obstinately perished of hunger [1].

Before the middle of the eleventh century, the race of Abdarrahman being extinct, the kingdom of Cordova was dismembered
by the ambition of a number of noblemen who usurped the regal
title.   Toledo, Valencia, Seville, Saragossa, and almost all the
great cities, had their independent sovereigns.   The provinces
were changed into kingdoms, which multiplied in the same manner among the Christians, who had a king of Leon, of Navarre,
of Castile, of Arragon : and Sancho, surnamed the Great, king
A.D.   of Navarre, was so imprudent as to subdivide his domi-
1035.   nions among his four sons.   Perpetual jealousies, with all
the crimes that accompany them, were the consequence of these
divisions of territory—treachery, poisonings, assassinations ! the
common weapons of petty neighbouring and rival princes, who
have much ambition and small means of gratifying it.   Hence the
history of Spain becomes less important, in proportion to the
increase of the number of kingdoms.   One circumstance, however, merits our attention, both on account of its nature and its
singularity.

In this dark and oppressive period, when the commonalty of
Europe in general were in a degraded and wretched state, the
people of Arragon shared the government with their sovereign.
The representatives of cities and towns had a place in their *cortès,*
or national assembly.   But the Arragonians, not satisfied with
this check on the royal prerogative, nor willing to trust the preservation of their liberties solely to their representatives, elected
a *justiza,* or grand judge, who was the supreme interpreter of the

---

[1] Rod. Tolet. de *Reb. Hisp.*—*Annal. Compostel.*

laws, and whose particular business it was to restrain the encroachments of the crown, and protect the rights of the subject. He was chosen from among the *cavalleros*, or second order in the state, answering to our gentry, that he might be equally interested in curbing the oppressive spirit of the nobles, and setting bounds to the ambition of the prince. His person was sacred, and his jurisdiction almost unbounded : his power was exerted in superintending the political administration, no less than in regulating the course of justice. He had a right to review all the royal proclamations and patents, and to declare whether they were agreeable to law, and ought to be carried into execution : and he could, by his sole authority, exclude any of the king's ministers from the management of affairs ; and call them to answer for their conduct in office, while he himself was answerable to the *cortès* alone. He had also the singular privilege of administering the coronation oath, in the name of the people; when, holding a naked sword opposite to the king's heart, he repeated these remarkable words : " We, who are your equals, make you our sovereign, and promise obedience to your government, on condition that you maintain our rights and liberties ; if not—not !" And it was accordingly an established maxim in the constitution of Arragon, that, if the king should violate his engagements, it was lawful for the people to depose him, and to elect another in his stead[1].

From the Arabs in Spain we pass naturally to those of Asia, and the neighbouring continent of Africa. The great empire of the Arabs, as well as its branches, had experienced those revolutions which war and discord usually produce, and which sooner or later overturn the best founded governments. The glory of the khalifate was obscured about the beginning of the tenth century. Under weak or wicked princes, the African governors shook off their allegiance. Religious quarrels augmented those of ambition. The Ismëlians or Fatimites, a Mohammedan sect, were inflamed with all the fury of fanaticism. They over- A. D. threw the Aglabite dynasty, which governed Tunis and 909. Tripoli ; and, after an interval of sixty years, they founded a principality in Egypt. Cairo, the capital, then became the A. D. seat of a new khalif, and a flourishing city of commerce. 969.

Another sect of fanatics, persuaded that the abuses introduced into the religion of Mohammed required reformation, delivered

---

[1] Zurit. *Annal. de Arrag.* Hier. Blanca, *Comment. de Rebus Arrag.*

themselves up to the transports of enthusiasm, and acquired strength by being persecuted. They revolted, obtained several victories, and seized the provinces on the north-western coast of Africa, which form the present kingdom of Morocco ; where their chief, like the other khalifs, uniting the royalty with the priest-hood, governed his new empire under the appellation of Emir-al-Moumenin, or Commander of the Faithful, a title implying his claim to the khalifate.

Other circumstances conspired to dismember the empire of the Arabs. The khalifs of Bagdad had received into their armies a body of Turks, or Turcomans, a Tartar tribe. These auxiliaries, on account of their valour, were soon employed as the royal guard, and subjected those whom they were hired to protect. They took advantage of the civil wars raised against the khalifate to make themselves lords of the Asiatic states : they gradually deprived the khalifs of the sovereignty, but permitted them to retain the pontificate, which they affected to revere ; prudently submitting to the religion of the country, and kneeling to the priest while they despoiled the king[1].

A variety of sovereigns sprang up under the name of sultans, who were invested with their dominions by the khalifs, but took care to leave them very little authority ; so that the successors of Mohammed found themselves, towards the middle of the eleventh century, in much the same situation with those of St. Peter under the first German emperors, or with the kings of Europe about the same time, whose power declined in propor-tion to the increase of their vassals.

While the Saracen empire was thus nearly overturned, and that of Charle-magne falling to pieces, the empire of Constanti-nople, to borrow a simile from Voltaire, still stood like a large tree, vigorous though old, stripped of its branches, and even of some of its roots, and buffeted on every side by storms and tempests. Though considerably diminished on the eastern fron-tier, it yet extended over all Greece, Macedonia, Epirus, Thes-saly, Thrace, Illyricum : it was contracted indeed, but not dis-membered ; often changing its emperors, but always united under the person who swayed the sceptre. How unworthy were these princes, in general, of the imperial dignity ! and what a people had they to govern !

Nicephorus, whom we have seen dethrone Irene, was an exe-

[1] Leunclav. *Annal. Turcic.* Elmacin. *Histor. Saracen.*

crable tyrant.   The Saracens robbed him of the isle of Cyprus;
and the Bulgarians, the scourge of Thrace, after having A. D.
cut off his arm, beheaded him, and threw his body to 811.
the beasts of the field, while they made a drinking cup of his
skull[1].

Stauratius, the son of Nicephorus, rendered himself so odious
in the beginning of his reign, that he was abandoned by his
people, and obliged to become a monk.

Michael, who succeeded, refused to make peace with the
Bulgarians, because a monk declared that he could not in conscience deliver up the deserters.   In consequence of this refusal,
the Greeks were defeated by the Bulgarians; the emperor betook himself to flight, and the officers, incensed at his behaviour,
proclaimed Leo the Armenian.

Leo attempted to assassinate the king of the Bulgarians, who,
in revenge, pillaged the suburbs of Constantinople.   The emperor could conceive nothing more effectual to save the state
than the extirpation of idolatry; that is to say, the suppression
of images.   He accordingly commanded a new persecution; and
eight hundred and twenty persons were massacred in one
church.

Michael II., called the Stammerer, at first tolerated the worship of images: but he afterwards changed his system, persecuted those whom he had formerly protected, and would even
have had the sabbath observed, and the passover celebrated in
the manner of the Jews.   The Saracens took advantage of his
weakness to make themselves masters of the isle of Crete, A. D.
now Candia; they also conquered almost all Sicily, and 823.
ravaged Apulia and Calabria[2].

During the reign of Theophilus, though more worthy of the
imperial throne, the persecution was redoubled, and the Saracens
extended their conquests.   But after his death, the em- A. D.
press Theodora, governing during the minority of Michael 842.
III., re-established the worship of images, as Irene had formerly
done.   Afterward, desirous of converting the Manicheans by
terror, she caused them to be destroyed in thousands.   Those
who escaped went over to the Bulgarians; and the empire was
obliged to contend with its own subjects.   Michael confined
Theodora in a convent; and, delivering himself up to vice and
criminality, carried his impiety so far, as to sport with the eccle-

---

[1] Theophan. *Chronograph.*   [2] Cedreni *Compend.*

A. D. siastical ceremonies.   He was assassinated by Basil, whom
867. he had associated in the empire, and imprudently would
have deposed.

Basil, originally a beggar, now found himself emperor.   He is
celebrated for his justice and humanity ; but he was a dupe to
the patriarch Photius, whom he favoured with his confidence,
even after he had exiled him.   His reign is the æra of the grand
schism which for ever divided the Greek and Latin churches.

This schism, which took its rise from a jealousy between the
primates of the East and West, was brought to a crisis by the
conversion of the Bulgarians.   As Bulgaria had formerly belonged to the eastern empire, it was disputed, whether the new
Christians ought to be subject to the pope, or to the patriarch of
Constantinople.   Other reasons were assigned for the rupture
that followed ; but this is the true one, and the only one which
A. D. it is necessary for you to know.   The council of Con-
879. stantinople gave judgment in favour of the patriarch ;
but the pope's legates protested against the decision.   New
circumstances widened the breach.   The two primates excommunicated each other ; and although the quarrel was sometimes
moderated by the interposition of the emperors, the schism continued.

The Saracens took Syracuse, while Basil was employed in
founding a church ; and his son Leo composed sermons, while
the empire was attacked on all sides.   Leo, however, was styled
the Philosopher, because he loved learning, and favoured learned
men, not from being an Alfred or a Marcus Aurelius.

Constantine Porphyrogenitus, the son and successor of Leo,
merits the eulogies bestowed on him, as a protector of the sciences,
which he himself cultivated with success.   Men of the first rank
taught philosophy, geometry, and rhetoric, at Constantinople,
during his reign, which commenced in 912, and ended in 959.
But the affairs of the empire were not, in general conducted
better than they had formerly been.   They were still worse conducted under Romanus, the son of Constantine, who poisoned
his father, and was the tyrant of his people.

Nicephorus Phocas had the honour of vanquishing the Saracens, and of recovering from them Crete, Antioch, and other
places.   His avarice and tyranny, however, rendered him odious :
A. D. his wife joined in a conspiracy against him ; and he was
969. murdered in bed.

John Zimisces, one of the assassins, seized the empire, and

defended it against the Russians and Saracens, whom he defeated in several engagements. This brave prince was A.D. poisoned by his chamberlain, after a short reign. 975.

Basil II. was a warrior, but a barbarous one. Having vanquished the Bulgarians, he caused the eyes of five thousand prisoners to be put out. His subjects, loaded with taxes, could not enjoy his triumphs. He fought for himself, not for A.D. them. His death was followed by a train of the blackest 1025. crimes of which we have any example in history[1].

The princess Zoë, daughter of Constantine, the brother and colleague of Basil, had espoused Romanus Argyropulus, who was proclaimed emperor. Zoë afterwards became en- A.D. amoured of Michael the Paphlagonian, a man of low 1028. birth. She poisoned her husband, in order to give the throne to her lover ; and the poison not operating so quickly as she wished, she caused him to be drowned in a bath. The A.D. patriarch of Constantinople at first scrupled to marry the 1034. empress to Michael : but a sum of money quieted his conscience, and the grant of the crown followed the sanction of the church.

The emperor Michael, a prey to diseases and remorse, died in the habit of a monk ; and Zoë procured the imperial A.D. crown for Michael Calaphates, the son of a ship-caulker, 1041. by a sister of the other Michael, hoping that he would be the slave of her will. But, on the contrary, the new emperor soon put her in confinement. The people revolted : they released Zoë and her sister Theodora, and put out the eyes of Calaphates[2].

The two sisters reigned together about three months, and employed themselves only upon trifles. The people would have a prince ; and Zoë then married Constantine Monomachus, one of her ancient lovers, who was placed on the throne. The upstart emperor neglected his wife for a young mistress. The Greeks, incensed at his conduct, seized him in a procession, and declared that they would only obey the two empresses. He would have been cut in pieces, if the princesses had not interposed.

Monomachus augmented the miseries of the empire by his rapacity. The inhabitants of the frontier provinces had been exempted from taxes, on condition that they should defend themselves against the barbarians. The emperor pretended that he would protect them, and compelled them to pay like the rest

---

[1] Zonaræ *Annal.*—Cedreni *Compend.*   [2] Zonar.—Cedren.

of his subjects; but they were poorly defended, notwithstanding the taxes.

These particulars will be sufficient to enable you to judge of the state of Constantinople. If at any time we find an able and warlike prince upon the throne, we always find the same reigning spirit of superstition and rebellion. Isaac Comnenus, one of the best Greek emperors, was hated by the monks, because he applied to the public exigences the excess of their wealth. Lamed A.D. 1059. by a fall from his horse, he gave himself up to devotion, resigned his crown in favour of Constantine Ducas, and took the habit of a monk.

Ducas, too much a friend to peace, abandoned the provinces to the ravages of the Turks. He made his three sons emperors, and left the regency to their mother Eudoxia, exacting from her a promise that she would never marry; and this promise he obliged her to confirm in writing. Eudoxia, however, soon resolved to marry Romanus Diogenes, whom she had condemned to death, but whose fine person subdued her heart. Her promise, deposited in the hands of the patriarch, now gave her great uneasiness. In order to recover it, she artfully pretended to have fixed her choice on the patriarch's kinsman. This amorous deceit had the desired effect. The writing was restored; and A.D. 1069. the empress, absolved from her promise of widowhood, did not fail to take advantage of her release. She immediately married Romanus, and procured him the empire[1].

Could ignorant savages have acted more absurdly? or ruffians obnoxious to public justice more atrociously?—Yet the Greeks were still the most learned and polished people in Europe; and Constantinople, notwithstanding all its misfortunes, its revolutions, and crimes, having never felt the destructive rage of the barbarians, continued to be the largest and most beautiful European city, after the fall of Rome, and the only one where any image of ancient manners or ingenuity remained.

Thus, my dear Philip, we rapidly traverse the wilds of history, where the objects are often confused, rude, and uninteresting. But it is necessary to travel these first stages, in order to arrive at more cultivated fields. We shall soon meet with a new set of objects highly interesting and important; and then a more deliberate survey will be required. In the mean time we must take a review of past ages.

---

[1] Annæ Comnenæ *Alex.*—Nicet. *Hist.*

LETTER XXII.

*Of the Progress of Society in Europe, from the Settlement of the
Modern Nations to the Middle of the Eleventh Century.*

I HAVE already given you, in a particular letter, a sketch of the
system of policy and legislation established by the barbarians on
their settlement in the provinces of the Roman empire[1]: and I
have endeavoured, in the course of my general narration, to mark
the progress of society, as it regards religion, laws, government,
manners, and literature.   But as the history of the human mind
is infinitely more important than the detail of events, this letter,
my dear Philip, shall be entirely devoted to such circumstances
as tend more particularly to throw light upon that subject.   I
shall also pursue the same method, at different intervals, during
the subsequent part of your historical studies.

Though the invaders wanted taste to value the Roman arts,
laws, or literature, they generally embraced the religion of the
conquered people.   And the mild and benevolent spirit of
Christianity would doubtless have softened their savage manners,
had not their minds been already infected by a barbarous superstition.   Their former religion, mingling itself with the Christian
principles and ceremonies, produced that absurd mixture of
violence, devotion, and folly, which so long disgraced the Romish
church, and which formed the character of the middle ages.
The clergy were gainers, but Christianity was a loser, by the
conversion of the barbarians.   They rather changed the object
than the spirit of their religion.

The druids among the Gauls and Britons, the priests among
the ancient Germans, and among all the nations of Scandinavia,
possessed an absolute dominion over the minds of men.   These
people, after embracing Christianity, preserved their veneration
for the priesthood.   And unhappily the clergy of those times
had neither virtue enough to prevent them from abusing, nor
knowledge sufficient to enable them to make a proper use of
their power.   They blindly favoured the superstitious homage:
and such of the barbarians as entered into holy orders retained
their ignorance and their original prejudices.

The Christian emperors of Rome and Constantinople had

[1] See Letter I.

enriched the church : they had lavished on it privileges and immunities; and these seducing advantages had contributed to a relaxation of discipline, and the introduction of disorders, more or less hurtful, which had altered the spirit of the Gospel. Under the dominion of the barbarians the degeneracy increased, till the pure principles of Christianity were lost in a gross superstition, which, instead of aspiring to virtuous sanctity, the only sacrifice that can render a rational being acceptable to the great Author of order and excellence, endeavoured to conciliate the favour of God by the same means that satisfied the justice of men, or by those which were employed to appease their fabulous deities[1].

As the punishments due for civil crimes, among the barbarian conquerors, might be bought off by money, they attempted in like manner to bribe Heaven, by benefactions to the church, in order to supersede all future inquest. And the more they gave themselves up to their brutal passions, to rapine, and to violence, the more profuse they were in this species of good works. They seem to have believed, says the abbé de Mably, that avarice was the first attribute of the Divinity, and that the saints made a traffic of their influence and protection. Hence the *bon mot* of Clovis : " St. Martin serves his friends very well ; but he also makes them pay well for his trouble !"

" Our treasury is poor," said Chilperic, the grandson of Clovis: " our riches are gone to the church: the bishops are the kings !" And indeed the superior clergy, who, by the acquisition of lands, added the power of fortune to the influence of religion, were often the arbiters of kingdoms, and disposed of the crown while they regulated the affairs of the state. There was a necessity of consulting them, because they possessed all the knowledge that then remained in Europe. The acts of their councils were considered as infallible decrees, and they spoke usually in the name of God ; but, alas ! they were only men.

As the interest of the clergy clashed with that of the laity, opposition and jealousy produced new disorders. The priests made use of artifice against their powerful adversaries : they invented fables to awe them into submission : they employed the spiritual arms in defence of their temporal goods, and changed the mild language of charity into terrific anathemas. To the thunder of the church, the instrument of so many wars and revolutions, they joined the assistance of the sword. Warlike

[1] Mosheim, *Hist. Eccles.* vol. i. ii.

prelates, clad in armour, combated for their possessions, or to usurp those of others; and, like the heathen priests, whose pernicious influence was founded on the ignorance of the people, the Christian clergy sought to extend their authority by confining all knowledge to their own order. They made a mystery of the most necessary sciences; truth was not permitted to see the light, and reason was fettered in the cell of superstition. Many of the ecclesiastics themselves could scarcely read, and writing was chiefly confined to the cloisters[1], where a blind and interested devotion, equally willing to deceive and to believe, held the quill, and where false chronicles and fabulous legends were composed, which contaminated history, religion, and the principles and the laws of society.

Without arts, sciences, commerce, policy, principles, the European nations were all in a barbarous and wretched state. Charle-magne indeed in France, and Alfred the Great in England, endeavoured to dispel this darkness, and tame their subjects to the restraints of law: and they were so fortunate as to succeed. Light and order distinguished their reigns. But the ignorance and barbarism of the age were too powerful for their liberal institutions: the darkness returned, after their time, more thick and heavy than formerly, and settled over Europe; and society again fell into chaos.

The ignorance of the West was so profound, during the ninth and tenth centuries, that the clergy, who alone possessed the important secrets of reading and writing, became necessarily the arbiters and judges of almost all secular affairs. They comprehended within their jurisdiction, marriages, contracts, wills, which they took care to involve in mystery, and by which they opened to themselves new sources of wealth and power[2]. Every thing wore the colour of religion; temporal and spiritual concerns were confounded; and from this unnatural mixture sprang numerous abuses. The history of that period forms a satire on the human soul; and also on religion, if we should impute to it the faults of its ministers.

"Redeem your souls from destruction," says St. Egidius, bishop of Noyon, "while you have the means in your power: offer presents and tithes to churchmen; come more frequently to church; humbly implore the patronage of the saints; for, if

---

[1] Persons who could not write made the sign of the cross in lieu of their names, in confirmation of any legal deed. (Du Cange, Gloss. ad vocem *Crux*.) Hence the phrase *signing* instead of *subscribing* a paper.

[2] Fleury, *Hist. Eccles.* tome xix. *Disc. Prelim.*

you observe these things, you may come with security in the day of the tribunal of the Eternal Judge, and say, Give unto us, O Lord, for we have given unto thee [1] ?"

In several churches of France a festival was celebrated in commemoration of the Virgin Mary's flight into Egypt. It was called the Feast of the Ass. A young girl richly dressed, with a child in her arms, was placed upon an ass superbly caparisoned. The ass was led to the altar in solemn procession. High mass was said with great pomp. The ass was taught to kneel at proper places; a hymn, no less childish than impious, was sung in his praise: and when the ceremony was ended, the priest, instead of the usual words with which he dismissed the people, brayed three times like an ass: and the people, instead of the usual response, brayed three times in return [2].

Letters began to revive in the eleventh century, but made small progress till near its close. A scientific jargon, a false logic, employed about words, without conveying any idea of things, composed the learning of those times. It confounded all things, in endeavouring to analyse every thing. As the new scholars were chiefly clergymen, theological matters engaged the greatest share of their attention; and as they neither knew history, philosophy, nor criticism, their labours were as futile as their inquiries, which were equally disgraceful to reason and religion. The conception of the blessed Virgin, and the digestion of the eucharist, were two of the principal objects of their speculation: and out of the last a third arose, which was, to know whether it was voided again [3].

The disorders of government and manners kept pace, as they always will, with those of religion and learning. These disorders seem to have attained their utmost height about the middle of the tenth century. Then the feudal policy, the defects of which I have pointed out [4], was almost universal. The dukes or governors of provinces, the marquises employed to guard the marches or borders, and even the counts entrusted with the administration of justice, all originally officers of the crown, had made themselves masters of their duchies, marquisates, and counties. The king, indeed, as superior lord, still received homage from them for those lands which they held of the crown, and which, in default of heirs, returned to the royal domain. He had the right of calling them out to war, of judging them in his court by their assembled peers, and of confiscating their

[1] *Spicileg. Vet. Script.* vol. ii.   [2] Du Cange, ad voc. *Festum.*
[3] *Hist. Littéraire de France.*   [4] Letter II.

estates in case of rebellion ; but, in all other respects, they themselves enjoyed their rights of royalty.   They had their sub-
vassals, or subjects : they made laws, held courts, coined money
in their own names, and levied war against their private enemies [1].

The most dreadful disorders arose from this state of feudal
anarchy. Force decided disputes of every kind. Europe seemed
to be one great field of battle, where the weak struggled for
freedom, and the strong for dominion. The king was without
power, and the nobles without principle : they were tyrants at
home and robbers abroad. Nothing remained to be a check
upon ferocity and violence. The Tartars in their deserts could
not be less indebted to the laws of society than the Europeans
during the period under review. The people, the most numerous
as well as the most useful class in the community, were either
actual slaves, or exposed to so many miseries, arising from pillage
and oppression, that many of them made a voluntary surrender
of their liberty for bread and protection [2]. What must have
been the state of that government where slavery was an eligible
condition !

But, conformably to the observation of the philosophic Hume,
there is a point of depression as well as of exaltation, beyond
which human affairs seldom pass, and from which they naturally
return in a contrary progress. This utmost point of decline
society seems to have attained in Europe, as I have already said,
about the middle of the tenth century ; when the disorders of
the feudal government, together with the corruption of taste and
manners consequent upon these, had arrived at their greatest
excess. Accordingly from that æra we can trace a succession
of causes and events, which, with different degrees of influence,
contributed to abolish anarchy and barbarism, and introduce
order and politeness.

Among the first of these causes we must rank chivalry, which,
as the elegant and inquisitive Dr. Robertson remarks, though
commonly considered as a wild institution, the result of caprice
and the source of extravagance, arose naturally from the state of
society in those times, and had a very serious effect in refining
the manners of the European nations.

The feudal state, as has been observed, was a state of perpetual war, rapine, and anarchy. The weak and unarmed were
constantly exposed to insults or injuries. The power of the

---

[1] Du Cange, ad voc. *Feudum*.   [2] Marculf. lib. ii. cap. 8.

sovereign was too limited to prevent these wrongs, and the legislative authority too feeble to redress them.　There was scarcely any shelter from violence and oppression, except what the valour and generosity of private persons afforded: and the arm of the brave was the only tribunal to which the helpless could appeal for justice.　Traders could no longer travel in safety, or bring unmolested their commodities to market.　Every possessor of a castle laid them under contribution; and many not only plundered the merchants, but carried off all the women that fell in their way.　Slight inconveniences may be overlooked or endured: but when abuses grow to a certain height, the society must be reformed or go to ruin.　It becomes the business of all to discover and to apply such remedies as will most effectually remove the prevailing disorders.　Humanity sprang from the bosom of violence, and relief from the hand of rapacity.　Those licentious and tyrannic nobles, who had been guilty of every species of outrage and every mode of oppression; who equally unjust, unfeeling, and superstitious, had made pilgrimages, and had been guilty of pillage! who had massacred, and had done penance! touched at last with a sense of natural equity, and swayed by the conviction of a common interest, formed associations for the redress of private wrongs, and the preservation of public safety[1].　So honourable was the origin of an institution generally represented as whimsical.

Among the ancient Germans, as well as among the modern knights, the young warrior was armed, for the first time, with certain ceremonies proper to inspire martial ardour; but chivalry, considered as a civil and military institution, is as late as the eleventh century.　The previous discipline and solemnities of initiation were remarkable.　The novice in chivalry was educated in the house of some knight, commonly a person of high rank, whom he served first in the character of a page, and afterwards of esquire: nor was he admitted to the supreme honour of knighthood, until he had given many striking proofs of his valour and address.　The ceremony of initiation was very solemn.　Severe fastings, and nights spent in a church or chapel in prayer; confession of sins, and the receiving of the sacraments with devotion; bathing, and putting on white robes, as emblems of the purity of manners required by the laws of chivalry, were necessary preparations for this ceremony.

When the candidate for knighthood had gone through these

---

[1] *Mém. sur l'Ancienne Chevalerie*, par M. de la Curne de St. Palaye.

and other formalities, he fell at the feet of the person from whom he expected that honour, and on his knees delivered to him his sword.   When he had answered suitable questions, the usual oath was administered to him ; namely, to serve his prince, defend the faith, protect the persons and reputations of virtuous ladies, and to rescue, at the hazard of his life, widows, orphans, and all unhappy persons groaning under injustice or oppression. Then the knights and ladies, who assisted at the ceremony, adorned the candidate with the armour and ensigns of chivalry ; first putting on the spurs, and, after intermediate investments and decorations, girding him with the sword.   Seeing him thus accoutred, the king, or some nobleman who was to confer the honour of knighthood, gave him the *accolade,* or dubbing, by three gentle strokes with the flat part of the sword on the shoulder, or with the palm of the hand on the neck, saying, " In the name of God, St. Michael, and St. George, I make thee a knight ! be thou loyal, brave, and hardy [1]."

Valour, humanity, courtesy, justice, honour, were the characteristics of chivalry ; and to these we may add religion, which by infusing a large portion of enthusiastic zeal, carried them all to a romantic excess, wonderfully suited to the genius of the age, and productive of the greatest and most permanent effects both upon policy and manners.   War was carried on with less ferocity, when humanity, no less than courage, began to be deemed the ornament of knighthood, and knighthood a distinction superior to royalty, and an honour which princes were proud to receive from the hands of private gentlemen ; more gentle and polished manners were introduced, when courtesy was recommended as the most amiable of knightly virtues, and every knight devoted himself to the service of some lady ; and violence and oppression decreased, when it was accounted meritorious to check and to punish them.   A scrupulous adherence to truth, with the most religious attention to the performance of all engagements, particularly those between the sexes, as more easily violated, became the distinguishing character of a gentleman ; because chivalry was regarded as the school of honour, and inculcated the most delicate sensibility with respect to that point [2].   And

[1] *Mém. sur l'Ancienne Chevalerie,* par M. de la Curne de St. Palaye.
[2] This sentiment became reciprocal.   Even a princess, says Tirant le Blanc, declares, that she submits to lose all right to the benefits of chivalry, and consents that never any knight shall take arms in her defence, if she keeps not the promise of marriage, which she has given to the knight who adored her.   And a young gentlewoman, whose defence was undertaken by Gerard de Nevers, beholding the ardour with which he engaged in it, took off her glove, we are told, and delivered it to him, saying, " Sir, my person, my life, my lands, and my honour, I deposit in

valour, seconded by so many motives of love, religion, and virtue, became altogether irresistible.

That the spirit of chivalry often rose to an extravagant height, and had sometimes a pernicious tendency, must however be allowed. In Spain, under the influence of a romantic gallantry, it gave birth to a series of wild adventures, which have been deservedly ridiculed; in the train of Norman ambition, it extinguished the liberties of England, and deluged Italy in blood; and we shall soon see it, at the call of superstition, and as the engine of papal power, desolate Asia under the banner of the cross. But these violences, resulting from accidental circumstances, ought not to be considered as arguments against an institution laudable in itself, and necessary at the time of its establishment. And they who pretend to despise it, the advocates of ancient barbarism and ancient rusticity, ought to remember, that chivalry not only first taught mankind to carry the civilities of peace into the operations of war, and to mingle politeness with the use of the sword, but roused the human soul from its lethargy; invigorating the human character, even while it softened it; and produced exploits which antiquity cannot parallel. Nor ought they to forget, that it gave variety and elegance, and communicated an increase of pleasure, to the intercourse of life, by making woman a more essential part of society; and is therefore entitled to our gratitude, though the point of honour, and the refinements in gallantry, its more doubtful effects, should be excluded from the improvements in modern manners.

But the beneficial effects of chivalry were strongly counteracted by other institutions of a less social kind. Some persons of both sexes, of most religions and most countries, have in all ages secluded themselves from the world, in order to acquire a reputation for superior sanctity, or to indulge a melancholy turn of mind, affecting to hold converse only with the Divinity. These solitary devotees, however, in ancient times, were few; and the spirit of religious seclusion, among the Heathens, was confined chiefly to high southern latitudes, where the heat of the climate favours the indolence of the cloister. But the case has been very different in more modern ages: for although the monastic life had its origin among the Christians in Egypt, Syria, and Pales-

---

the care of God and you; praying for such assistance and grace, that I may be delivered out of this peril." (M. de la Curne de St. Palaye, ubi sup.) Many similar examples might be produced of this mutual confidence, the basis of that elegant intercourse between the sexes, which so remarkably distinguishes modern from ancient manners.

tine, it rapidly spread not only over all Asia and Africa, but also over Europe, and penetrated to the most remote corners of the North and West, almost at the same time that it reached the extremities of the East and South; to the great injury of population and industry, and the obstruction of the natural progress of society [1].

Nor were these the only consequences of the passion for pious solitude. As all who put on the religious habit, after the monastic system was completely formed, took a vow of perpetual chastity, the commerce of the sexes was represented by those holy visionaries as inconsistent with Christian purity; and the whole body of the clergy, in order to preserve their influence with the people, found themselves under the necessity of professing a life of celibacy. This condescension, which was justly considered as a triumph by the monks, increased their importance, and augmented the number of their fraternities. Nothing was esteemed so meritorious, at this period, as the building and endowing of monasteries. And multitudes of men and women of all conditions, but especially of the higher ranks, considering the pleasures of society as seducers to the pit of destruction, retired to mountains and deserts, or crowded into cloisters, where, under the notion of mortifying the body, and shutting all the avenues of the soul against the allurements of external objects, they affected an austerity that gained them universal veneration, and threw a cloud over the manners of the Christian world.

The extravagance to which both sexes are said to have carried that austerity, during the first fervours of monastic zeal, seems altogether incredible to cool reason, unenlightened by philosophy. In attempting to strip human nature of every amiable and ornamental quality, in order to humble pride, and repress the approaches of loose desire, or, in their own phrase, " to deliver the *celestial spirit* from the *bondage* of *flesh* and *blood*," they in a manner divested themselves of the human character. They not only lived among wild beasts, but, after the manner of those savage animals, ran naked through the lonely deserts with a furious aspect, and lodged in gloomy caverns; or grazed in the fields like the common herd, and like cattle took their abode in the open air [2]. It is even said, that some monks and holy virgins, by the habit of going naked, became so completely covered with hair, as to require no other veil to modesty. Many chose their rugged

---

[1] Mosheim, *Hist. Eccles.* vol. i. ii.
[2] Mosheim. vol. ii.—Tillemont, *Mém. Eccles.* tome viii.

dwelling in the hollow side or narrow cleft of some rock, which obliged them to sit or stand in the most painful and emaciating posture, during the remainder of their wretched lives; while others, with no small exultation, usurped the den of some ferocious brother-brute, whom they affected to resemble; and not a few under the name of Stylites, or Pillar-saints, ascended the top of some lofty column, where they remained for years, night and day, without any shelter from heat or cold[1].

Even after religious houses had been provided for the devout solitaries of both sexes, and endowed with ample revenues by the profuse superstition of the newly converted barbarians, they attempted in their several cells to extinguish every spark of sensuality, by meagre fastings, bloody flagellations, and other cruel austerities of discipline. But no sooner did the monastic fury subside, than nature began to assert her empire in the hearts of the deluded fanatics, and to tell them that, in abandoning society, they had relinquished the most essential requisites of human happiness. The discovery of this important truth did not tend to promote that purity of conduct, or that strictness of self-denial, which their engagements required; and libertinism and profligacy gradually crept into those foundations from which every kind of corruption ought to have been systematically excluded.

The ignorance of the times, however, favoured by certain circumstances, continued the veneration for religious solitude, notwithstanding the licentiousness which prevailed among the pretended devotees. Many new monastic orders were instituted in the eleventh century, under various rules of discipline; but all with a view to greater regularity of manners. And monks were called from the lonely cell to the most arduous and exalted stations; to fill the papal chair, and support the triple crown; or to discharge the office of prime-minister in some mighty kingdom, and regulate the interests of nations. Though utterly ignorant of public transactions, their reputation for superior sanctity, which was easily acquired, by real or affected austerity, in ages of rapine and superstition, made them be thought fit to direct all things. This spiritual reputation even enabled them to trample upon the authority, and insult the persons, of the princes whose government they administered; especially if the lives of such princes, as was very commonly the case, happened to be stained with any atrocious acts of lust, violence, or oppression.

---

[1] Tillemont, *Mém. Eccles.* tome viii.

In order to stay the uplifted arm of Divine justice, and render the Governor of the World propitious, the king knelt at the feet of the monk and the minister—happy to commit to the favourite of Heaven the sole guidance of his spiritual and temporal concerns[1].   And if chivalry, by awakening a spirit of enterprise, had not roused the human powers to deeds of valour, and revived the passion for the softer sex, by connecting it with arms, and separating it from gross desire, Europe might have sunk under the tyranny of a set of men, who pretended to renounce the world and its affairs, and Christendom have become but one great cloister.

LETTER XXIII.

*Of the German Empire and its Dependencies, under Conrad II.
and his Descendants of the House of Franconia.*

WE now, my dear Philip, return to the great line of history, which I shall endeavour to trace with accuracy, that you may be able to keep in view the train of events, without which you will neither be able to reason distinctly on them yourself, nor to understand clearly the reasonings of others.   I shall therefore bring down the history of the German empire to the death of Henry V., when the quarrel between the popes and the emperors came to a stand, before I speak of the affairs of France and England, which, from the Norman conquest, became inseparably interwoven, but had little influence for some centuries on the rest of Europe.

Great disputes ensued on the death of Henry II., about the nomination of a successor to the empire, as that prince died without issue.   The princes and states assembled in the open fields,

---

[1] Beside the wealth and influence acquired by the monks in consequence of the superstitious ignorance of the great, who often shared not only their power, but the fruits of their rapine, with their pious directors, a popular opinion which prevailed towards the close of the tenth century contributed greatly to augment their opulence. The thousand years, from the birth or death of Christ, mentioned by St. John in the book of Revelation, were supposed to be nearly accomplished, and the day of judgment at hand.   Multitudes of Christians therefore, anxious only for their eternal salvation, delivered over to the monastic orders all their lands, treasures, and other valuable effects, and repaired with precipitation to Palestine, where they expected the appearance of Christ on Mount Sion.   Mosheim, vol. ii.

A.D. between Mentz and Worms, no hall being sufficient to
1024. hold them; and after six weeks' encampment and deliberation, they elected Conrad, duke of Franconia, surnamed the
Salic, because he was born on the banks of the river Sala[1].

Being informed of a revolt of the Lombards, the new emperor
marched into Italy: and having reduced the rebels by force of
A.D. arms, he went to Rome, where he was consecrated and
1027. crowned by pope John XX. He was soon obliged to
return to Germany, as an insurrection had broken out in his
absence. Before he attempted to humble the insurgents, he
procured the sanction of the diet to the succession of his son
Henry, who was solemnly crowned at Aix-la-Chapelle. The
rebellion was quickly suppressed by the valour of Conrad, who
defeated the authors of it in several engagements; in one of
which, Ernest, duke of Suabia, who had been put to the ban of
the empire, was slain[2].

The word *ban* originally signified banner, afterwards edict, and
lastly, a declaration of outlawry, which was intimated thus:
" We declare thy wife a widow, thy children orphans, and send
thee, in the name of the devil, to the four corners of the earth."
This is one of the first examples of that proscription.

The emperor next turned his arms against the Poles, and afterwards against the Hungarians, and obliged both to subscribe to
his own conditions. In the mean time, Rodolph III., the last
king of Transjurane Burgundy, and Provence, dying without
issue, left his dominions to Conrad. While he was employed in
taking possession of his new territories, the Poles again took up
arms. When he had met with success against them, he was
called into Italy to suppress a revolt, excited by Hubert, bishop
of Milan, whom he had loaded with favours. He was so quick
A. D. in his motions, that he took Milan by surprise. The
1039. bishop was condemned to perpetual banishment; and the
emperor died soon after his return to Germany, with the character
of a just, generous, and magnanimous prince[3].

Henry III., surnamed the Black, now became emperor. In
the earlier part of his reign, he was engaged in wars with
Bohemia, Poland, and Hungary; which, however, produced no
very remarkable incidents. Rome and Italy, as usual, were
involved in confusion, and distracted by factions, particularly
those of the Pandolphi and the Ptolemei. The Pandolphi had
thrust Benedict IX., a boy of twelve years of age, into the

---

[1] *Annal. de l'Emp.* tome i.　　　[2] Heiss. lib. ii.　　　[3] Id. ibid.

papacy.   He was deposed by the Ptolemei and the people, who substituted in his place Sylvester III.   This pontiff was deposed, in his turn, by the Pandolphi, and his rival re-established. A. D. Benedict, however, finding himself universally despised, 1044. sold his right to John, arch-priest of the Roman church ; but afterwards repenting of his bargain, he aimed at the resumption of his dignity.

These three popes, supported by their several partisans, and living peaceably with each other, maintained themselves each upon a different branch of the revenues of the holy see.   One resided at St. Peter's, another at Santa Maria Major, and the third in the palace of the Lateran, all leading the most profligate and scandalous lives.   A priest, called Gratian, at last put an end to this extraordinary triumvirate.   Partly by artifice, partly by presents, he prevailed upon all three to renounce their pretensions to the papacy ; and the people of Rome, out of gratitude for so signal a service to the church, elected him as an assistant to John, who had taken the name of Gregory VI.

Henry III. took umbrage at this election, in which he had not been consulted, and marched with an army into Italy.   No emperor ever exercised more absolute authority in that country. He deposed Gregory, as having been guilty of simony, and filled the papal chair with his own chancellor, Suideger, bishop A.D. of Bamberg, who assumed the name of Clement II., and 1046. afterward consecrated at Rome, Henry and the empress Agnes[1]. After this ceremony, the Romans having sworn never to elect a pope without the approbation of the reigning emperor, Henry proceeded to Capua, where he was visited by Drogo or A.D. Draco, Rainulphus, and other adventurers, who, having 1047. left Normandy at different times, had made themselves masters of a great part of Apulia and Calabria, at the expense of the Greeks and Saracens.   Henry entered into a treaty with them ; and not only solemnly invested them with those territories which they had acquired by conquest, but prevailed on the pope to excommunicate the Beneventines, who had refused to open their gates to him, and bestowed that city and its dependencies, as fiefs of the empire, upon the Norman princes, provided they took possession by force of arms[2].   What use they made of the imperial favour we shall afterwards have occasion to see.   At present the papacy claims our whole attention.

---

[1] Muratori, *Annal. d'Ital.*—Mosheim, *Hist. Eccles.* vol. ii.
[2] *Hist. Conq. Norm.*

Clement II. was succeeded in the apostolic see by Da-
A.D. masus II.; on whose death Henry nominated Bruno,
1048. bishop of Toul, to the vacant chair.　Bruno immediately
assumed the pontificals; but being a modest and pious prelate,
he threw them off, by the persuasion of Hildebrand, an aspiring
monk, and went to Rome as a private man.　" The emperor
alone," said Hildebrand, " has no right to create a pope."　He
accompanied Bruno to Rome, and secretly retarded his election,
that he might arrogate to himself the merit of obtaining it[1].　The
scheme succeeded to his wish.　Bruno, who took the name of
Leo IX., believing himself indebted to Hildebrand for the pontificate, favoured him with his particular friendship and confidence; and hence originated the power of this enterprising monk,
of obscure birth, but boundless ambition, who so long governed
Rome, and whose zeal for the exaltation of the church occasioned
so many troubles to Europe.

Leo, soon after his elevation, waited on the emperor at Worms,
to crave assistance against the Norman princes, who were become
the terror of Italy, and treated their subjects with great severity.
Henry furnished the pope with an army; at the head of which
his holiness marched against the Normans, after having excom-
A.D. municated them, accompanied by a great number of
1053. bishops and other ecclesiastics, who were all either killed
or made prisoners, the Germans and Italians being totally routed.
Leo himself was led captive to Benevento, of which the Normans
were now masters, and which Henry had granted to the pope in
exchange for the fief of Bamberg in Germany.　The Norman
chiefs, however, who had a right to that city by a prior grant,
restored it, in the mean time, to the princes of Lombardy; and
the holy father was treated with so much respect by the conquerors, that he revoked the sentence of excommunication, and
joined his sanction to the imperial investiture for the lands which
they held in Apulia and Calabria[2].

Leo died soon after his release; and the emperor, about the
A.D. same time, caused his infant son, afterwards the famous
1054. Henry IV., to be declared king of the Romans, a
title in use for the acknowledged heir of the empire, until the
subversion of the ancient Germanic constitution by Napoleon.
Gebhard, a German bishop, was elected pope under the name of
Victor II., and confirmed by the address of Hildebrand, who

---

[1] Leonis Ostiens. *Hist.* lib. ii.—Dithmar. *Vit. Greg. VII.*
[2] Giannone, *Hist. di Napol.*

visited the emperor for that purpose, though he disdained to consult him previously on the subject. Perhaps Hidebrand would not have found this task so easy, had not Henry been involved in a war with the Hungarians, who severely harassed him, but whom he obliged at last to pay a considerable tribute, and furnish him annually with a certain number of fighting men.

As soon as the emperor had finished this war, and others to which it gave rise, he marched into Italy to inspect the conduct of his sister Beatrice, widow of Bonifice marquis of Mantua, and made her prisoner. She had married Gozelo, duke of Lorrain, without the emperor's consent; and contracted Matilda, her daughter by the marquis of Mantua, to Godfrey duke of Spoleto and Tuscany, Gozelo's son by a former marriage. This formidable alliance justly alarmed Henry; he therefore attempted A. D. to dissolve it by carrying his sister into Germany, where 1056. he died soon after his return.

This emperor, in his last journey to Italy, concluded an alliance with Contarini, doge of Venice. That republic was already rich and powerful, though it had only been enfranchised in the year 998 from the tribute of a mantle of cloth of gold, which it formerly paid as a mark of subjection, to the emperors of Constantinople. The Genoese were the rivals of the Venetians, in power and in commerce, and were already in possession of the island of Corsica, which they had taken from the Saracens [1].

Henry IV., surnamed the Great, was only five years old at his father's death. He was immediately acknowledged emperor in a diet of the princes convoked at Cologne, and the care of his education was committed to his mother Agnes, who also governed the empire. She was a woman of spirit and address, and discharged both her public and private trust with diligence and ability.

Germany, during the first years of this reign, was harassed with civil wars; so that the empress Agnes, notwithstanding her strong talents, found it difficult to maintain her authority. And at length the dukes of Saxony and Bavaria, uncles of the A.D. young emperor, took him from her by stratagem, accusing 1062. her of having sacrificed the public welfare to the will of the bishop of Augsburg, her minister and supposed gallant. Thus divested of the regency, she fled to Rome, and there took the veil [2].

Henry was now put under the tuition of the archbishops of

[1] Muratori, *Annal. d'Ital.* vol. vi.   [2] *Annal. de l'Emp.*

Cologne and Bremen, who discharged their trust in a very oppo-site manner. The first endeavoured to inspire him with a love of learning and virtue, while the second sought only to acquire an ascendancy over his passions, by indulging him in all the pleasures of youth. This indulgence produced a habit of licentiousness which he could never afterwards restrain.

Italy was a prey, as usual, to intestine disorders. After a variety of troubles, excited on account of the pontificate, Nicholas II., the creature of Hildebrand, passed a famous decree, by which it was ordained, in a council of a hundred and thirteen bishops, that for the future the cardinals only should elect the pope, and that the election should be confirmed by the rest of the Roman clergy and the people: " saving the honour," he added, " due to our dear son Henry, now king ; and who, if it please God, shall one day be emperor, according to the privilege which we have already conferred upon him ; and saving the honour of his successors on whom the apostolic see shall confer the same high privilege [1].

The same pope, after having in vain excommunicated the Norman princes, made protectors and vassals of them ; and they, who were feudatories of the empire, less afraid of the popes than the emperors, readily did homage for their lands to Nicholas, in 1059, and agreed to hold them of the church [2].

This mode of tenure was very common in those days of rapacity, both for princes and private persons, the only authority then respected being that of the church : and the Normans wisely made use of it as a safeguard against the emperors. They gave their lands to the church under the name of an oblation or offer-ing, and continued to possess them on paying a slight acknow-ledgment. Hence arose the pope's claim of superiority over the kingdoms of Naples and Sicily.

Robert Guiscard, the Norman warrior, one of the gallant sons of Tancred of Hauteville, received from the pope the ducal crown of Apulia and Calabria ; and Richard, count of Aversa, was con-firmed prince of Capua, a title which he had already assumed. The pope also gave the Normans a right to hold Sicily in the same manner with their other possessions, provided they could

---

[1] *Chronicon Farsense* in Murat. *Script. Rer. Ital.* vol. ii.—To this edict the cardi-nals owe the extensive authority and important privileges which they still enjoy. Under the name of *Cardinals* the pope comprehended the seven Roman bishops, who were considered as his suffragans, and also the twenty-eight presbyters, or parish priests, who officiated in the principal churches. Mosheim, *Hist. Eccles.* vol. ii.

[2] Giannone, *Hist. di Napol.*

expel the Saracens from it[1] : and Robert and his brother Roger made themselves masters of that island about the year 1070.

When Henry IV. had assumed the reins of government, he resolved to repress the robberies and extortions, which A.D. the subjects of the duke of Saxony exercised upon 1072. strangers, as well as upon each other. But the princes and nobles, who were gainers by these abuses, particularly by the infamous practice of imprisoning travellers, and making them pay for their ransom, opposed the intended reformation, and entered into an association against the emperor, under pretence that their liberties were in danger. In this rebellious disposition they were encouraged by the arrogance of pope Alexander II., who, at the instigation of Hildebrand, summoned Henry to appear before the tribunal of the holy see, on account of his loose life, and to answer to the charge of having exposed the investiture of bishops to sale[2].

Henry treated the pope's mandate with contempt, and carried on the war with vigour against the Saxons, whom he totally routed in a bloody engagement, which was followed by the A.D. conquest of Saxony. The leaders of the rebellion asked 1074. pardon of the emperor in public, and begged to be restored to his favour : he generously accepted their submission, and peace was restored to Germany.

But Henry was not suffered long to enjoy the fruits of his valour. A new storm threatened him from Italy, which afterwards fell with violence on his head, and shook all the thrones in Christendom. On the death of Alexander II., in 1073, Hildebrand had been elected pope, under the name of Gregory VII. ; and, although he had not asked the emperor's voice, he prudently waited for his confirmation before he assumed the tiara. He obtained it by this mark of submission : Henry confirmed his election ; and Gregory then pulled off the mask. He began his pontificate with excommunicating every ecclesiastic who should receive a benefice from a layman, and every layman by whom such benefice should be conferred. This was engaging the church in an open war with the sovereigns of all the Christian nations. But the thunder of the holy see was more particularly directed against the emperor ; and Henry, sensible of his danger, and willing to avert it, wrote a submissive letter to Gregory, who pretended to take him into favour, after having severely

---

[1] Giannone, *Hist. di Napol.*
[2] Leonis Ostiens. *Hist.* lib. iii.—Dithmar. *Vit. Greg. VII.*

reprimanded him for the crimes of simony and debauchery, of which he now confessed himself guilty [1].

Gregory, at the same time, proposed a crusade, in order to deliver the holy sepulchre from the hands of the infidels : offering to head the Christians in person, and desiring Henry to serve as a volunteer under his command [2] !—a project so wild and extravagant, that nothing but the prevailing spirit of the times, the double enthusiasm of religion and valour, can save the memory of its author from the imputation of insanity.

Gregory's project of making himself lord of Christendom, by not only dissolving the jurisdiction which kings and emperors had hitherto exercised over the various orders of the clergy, but also by subjecting to the papal authority all temporal princes, and rendering their dominions tributary to the see of Rome, seems no less romantic ; yet this he undertook, and not altogether without success.   Solomon, king of Hungary, dethroned by his cousin Geysa, had fled to Henry for protection, and renewed the homage of Hungary to the empire.   Gregory, who favoured Geysa, exclaimed against this act of submission ; and said, in a letter to Solomon, " You ought to know, that the kingdom of Hungary belongs to the Roman Church ; and learn, that you will incur the indignation of the holy see, if you do not acknowledge that you hold your dominions of the pope, and not of the emperor [3]."

This presumptuous declaration, and the neglect with which it was treated, brought the quarrel between the empire and the church to a crisis.   It was directed to Solomon, but intended for Henry.   And if Gregory could not succeed in one way, he was resolved that he should in another ; he therefore resumed the claims of investitures, for which he had a more plausible pretence ; and as that dispute and its consequences merit particular attention, I shall be more circumstantial than usual.

The predecessors of Henry IV. as well as other princes of Christendom, had enjoyed the right of nominating bishops and abbots, and of giving them investiture by the ring and crosier. The popes had been accustomed, on their part, to send legates to the emperors, to entreat their assistance, to obtain their confirmation, or desire them to come and receive the papal sanction, but for no other purpose.   Gregory, however, sent two legates to summon Henry to appear before him as a delinquent, because

[1] *Annal. de l'Emp.* tome i.—Dithmar. *Vit. Greg. VII.*
[2] Dithmar. *Vit. Greg. VII.*
[3] Goldast, *Apologia pro Hen. IV.*—Thomas. *Content. inter Imp. et Sacerdot.*

he still continued to bestow investitures, notwithstanding the apostolic decree to the contrary; adding, that if he should fail to yield obedience to the church, he must expect to be excommunicated and dethroned.

Incensed at this arrogant message from one whom he considered as his vassal, Henry abruptly dismissed the legates, and convoked an assembly of princes and dignified ecclesiastics at   A.D. Worms; where, after mature deliberation, they concluded,   1076. that Gregory, having usurped the chair of St. Peter by indirect means, infected the church of God with many novelties and abuses, and deviated from his duty to his sovereign in several scandalous attempts, the emperor, by the supreme authority derived from his predecessors, ought to divest him of his dignity, and appoint another in his place [1].

In consequence of this determination, Henry sent an ambassador to Rome, with a formal deprivation of Gregory; who, in his turn, convoked a council, at which were present a hundred and ten bishops, who unanimously agreed that the pope had just cause to depose Henry, to dissolve the oath of allegiance which the princes and states had taken in his favour, and to prohibit them from holding any correspondence with him on pain of excommunication; and that sentence was immediately fulminated against the emperor and his adherents. " In the name of Almighty God, and by your authority," said Gregory, addressing the members of the council, " I prohibit Henry, the son of our emperor Henry, from governing the Teutonic kingdom, and Italy; I release all Christians from their oath of allegiance to him: and I strictly forbid all persons to serve or attend him as king [2]."

This is the first instance of a pope's pretending to deprive a sovereign of his crown; but it was too flattering to ecclesiastical pride to be the last. No prelate from the foundation of the church, had ever presumed to use so imperious a language as Gregory; for, although Louis the Debonnaire had been deposed by his bishops, there was at least some colour for that step. They condemned Louis, in appearance, only to do public penance.

The circular letters written by this pontiff breathe the same spirit with his sentence of deposition. In these he repeatedly asserts, that " bishops are superior to kings, and made to judge them!"—expressions alike artful and presumptuous, and calcu-

[1] Schilter *de Libertat. Eccles. German.* lib. iv.
[2] Dithmar. *Hist. Bell. inter Imp. et Sacerdot.*

lated for bringing in all the churchmen of the world to his standard. Gregory's purpose is said to have been, to engage in the bonds of fidelity and allegiance to the Vicar of Christ, as King of kings and Lord of lords, all the potentates of the earth, and to establish at Rome an annual assembly of bishops, by whom the contests that might arise between kingdoms and sovereign states were to be decided, the rights and pretensions of princes to be examined, and the fate of nations and empires to be determined [1].

The haughty pontiff knew well what consequences would follow the thunder of the church. The German bishops came immediately over to his party, and drew with them many of the nobles; the brand of civil war still lay smouldering, and a bull properly directed was sufficient to set it in a blaze. The Saxons, Henry's old enemies, made use of the papal displeasure as a pretence for rebelling against him. Even his favourite Guelf, a nobleman to whom he had given the duchy of Bavaria, supported the malcontents with that power which he owed to his sovereign's bounty; and the very princes and prelates who had assisted in deposing Gregory, gave up their monarch to be tried by the pope, who was requested to come to Augsburg for that purpose [2].

Willing to prevent this odious trial at Augsburg, Henry took the unaccountable resolution of suddenly passing the Tyrolese Alps, accompanied only by a few domestics, in order to ask absolution of Gregory, his tyrannical oppressor, who was then in Canosa, on the Apennines; a fortress belonging to the countess or duchess Matilda, whom I have already had occasion to mention. At the gates of this place the emperor presented himself as a humble penitent. He alone was admitted within the outer court, where, being stripped of his robes, and wrapped in sack-cloth, he was obliged to remain three days, in the month of January, barefooted and fasting, before he was permitted to kiss the feet of his holiness, who was then shut up with the devout Matilda, whose spiritual director he had long been. So strong was the attachment of this lady to Gregory, or her hatred against the Germans, that she assigned all her territories to the apostolic see; and this donation is perhaps the true cause of almost all the wars which subsequently raged between the emperors and the popes. She possessed in her own right, great

A.D. 1077.

---

[1] Mosheim, *Hist. Eccles.* vol. ii. et par. ii. cent. xi. Auct. cit. in loc.
[2] Dithmar. ubi sup.—*Annal.*—*German.* ap. Struv.

part of Tuscany; Mantua, Parma, Reggio, Placentia, Ferrara, Modena, Verona, and almost the whole of what is now called the patrimony of St. Peter, from Viterbo to Orvieto; with part of Umbria, Spoleto, and the Marche of Ancona [1].

The emperor was at length permitted to throw himself at the feet of the haughty pontiff, who condescended to grant him absolution, after he had sworn obedience to his holiness in all things, and promised to submit to his solemn decision at Augsburg—so that Henry reaped no other fruit than disgrace by his journey, while Gregory, elate with his triumph, and now considering himself as the lord and master of all the crowned heads in Christendom, said in several of his letters, that it was his duty, " to pull down the pride of kings."

This extraordinary accommodation disgusted the princes of Italy. They never could forgive the insolence of the pope or the abject humility of the emperor. Happily, however, for Henry, their indignation at Gregory's arrogance overbalanced their detestation of *his* meanness. He took advantage of this temper : and by a change of fortune hitherto unknown to the German emperors, he found a strong party in Italy, when abandoned in Germany. All Lombardy took up arms against the pope, while he was raising all Germany against the emperor.

Gregory, on the one hand, made use of every art to procure the election of another emperor in Germany ; and Henry, on his part, left nothing undone to persuade the Italians to make choice of another pope. The Germans chose Rodolph A. D. duke of Suabia, who was solemnly crowned at Mentz; 1078. and Gregory, hesitating on this occasion, behaved truly like the supreme judge of kings. He had deposed Henry ; but it was still in his power to pardon that prince : he therefore affected to be displeased that Rodolph was consecrated without his order ; and declared, that he would acknowledge as emperor and king of Germany that claimant who should be most submissive to the holy see [2].

Henry, however, trusting more to the valour of his troops than to the generosity of the pope, set out immediately for Germany, where he defeated his enemies, in several engagements; A.D. and Gregory, seeing no hopes of submission, thundered 1080. out a second sentence of excommunication against him, confirming at the same time the election of Rodolph, to whom he sent a

---

[1] Franc. Mar. Florent. *Mem. della Contessa Matilde.*
[2] Dithmar. *Hist. Bell. intrr Imp. et Sacerdot.*—Muratori, *Annal. d'Ital.*

golden crown, on which the following well-known verse, equally haughty and puerile was engraven :

Petra dedit Petro, Petrus diadema Rodolpho.

This donation was accompanied with a prophetic anathema against Henry, so wild and extravagant as to make one doubt whether it was dictated by enthusiasm or priestcraft.   After depriving him of *strength in combat*, and condemning him *never to be victorious*, it concludes with the following remarkable apostrophe to St. Peter and St. Paul : " Make all men sensible, that, as you can bind and loose every thing in heaven, you can also upon earth take from, or give to, every one according to his deserts, empires, kingdoms, principalities : let the kings and princes of the age instantly feel your power, that they may not dare to despise the orders of your church ; and let your justice be so speedily executed upon Henry, that nobody may doubt of his falling by your means, and not by chance [1]."

To avoid the effects of the second excommunication, Henry took a step worthy of himself.   He assembled at Brixen about twenty German bishops, who, acting also for the bishops of Lombardy, unanimously resolved, that the pope, instead of having power over the emperor, owed him obedience and allegiance; and that, having rendered himself unworthy of the papal chair by his misconduct and rebellion, he ought to be deposed.   They accordingly degraded Hildebrand, and elected in his room Guibert, archbishop of Ravenna, a person of undoubted merit, who took the name of Clement III.

Henry promised to put the new pope in possession of Rome. But he was obliged, in the mean time, to shift the scene of action, and to employ all his forces against his rival Rodolph, who had re-assembled a large body of troops in Saxony.   The two armies met near Mersburg, and both fought with great fury.   Victory remained long doubtful : but the fortune of the day seemed inclined to Rodolph, when his hand was cut off by the famous Godfrey of Bouillon, then in the service of Henry, and afterwards renowned by the conquest of Jerusalem.   Discouraged by the misfortune of their chief, the rebels immediately gave way ; and Rodolph, perceiving his end approaching, ordered the hand that was cut off to be brought to him, and made a speech to his officers on the occasion, which could not fail to have a favourable influence on the emperor's affairs.   " Behold," said he, " the hand

[1] Hardouin, *Concil.*—Fleury, *Hist. Eccles.*

with which I took the oath of allegiance to Henry—an oath which, at the instigation of Rome, I have violated, in perfidiously aspiring to an honour that was not my due[1]."

The emperor, thus delivered from his formidable antagonist, soon dispersed the rest of his enemies in Germany, and set out for Italy, in order to settle Clement III. in the papal chair. But the gates of Rome being shut against him, he was obliged to attack the city in form. After a siege of two years, it was taken by assault, and with difficulty saved from being pillaged: but Gregory retired into the castle of St. Angelo, and thence defied and excommunicated the conqueror. A.D. 1081.

The new pope being consecrated with the usual ceremonies, expressed his gratitude by crowning Henry, with the concurrence of the Roman senate and people. The siege of St. Angelo was in the mean time prosecuted: but the emperor being called into Lombardy, Robert Guiscard took advantage of his absence to release Gregory, who died soon after at Salerno. His last words, borrowed from the Scripture, were worthy of the greatest saint: " I have loved justice, and hated iniquity; therefore I die in exile[2]." A.D. 1084.
A.D. 1085.

Henry did not long enjoy the success of his Italian expedition, or that tranquillity which might have been expected from the death of Gregory. Germany was involved in new troubles: thither he rapidly marched. The Saxons had elected a king of the Romans, whom he defeated in several conflicts, and whose blood atoned for his presumption. Another pretender shared the same fate. Every thing yielded to the emperor's valour.

But while Henry was thus victorious in Germany, his enemies were busy in embroiling his affairs in Italy. Not satisfied with the emperor's pope, they had elected the abbot of Monte Casino, under the name of Victor III., and, he dying in a short time, they chose in his room Urban II., who, in conjunction with the countess Matilda, seduced the emperor's son, Conrad, into a rebellion against his father.

Conrad, assuming the title of king of Italy, was crowned by Anselmo, archbishop of Milan; and soon after this ceremony, he married the daughter of Roger, count of Sicily. He succeeded so well in his usurpation, that the greater part of the Italian cities and nobles acknowledged him as their sovereign. Despairing of being able to reduce him to obedience by arms, A.D. 1090.

[1] *Chron. Magdeb.*
[2] Dithmar. *Vit. Greg. VII.*—Murat ubi sup.

A.D. Henry at length assembled the German princes, who put
1099. the delinquent to the ban of the empire, and declared his
brother Henry king of the Romans [1]. An accommodation was
now made with the Saxons and other adversaries of the emperor;
and he hoped to spend the latter part of his life in peace.

Pascal II., another Hildebrand, succeeded Urban in the see
of Rome. This pontiff no sooner found himself safely seated in
the papal chair, than he called a council, to which he summoned
A.D. the emperor; and, as Henry did not obey the citation, he
1101. excommunicated him anew for the schisms which he had
introduced into the church. But that vengeance, though sufficiently severe, was gentle in comparison of what Pascal meditated and accomplished. After the death of Conrad, he excited
young Henry to rebel against his father, under pretence of defending the cause of orthodoxy; alleging that he was bound to
take upon himself the reins of government, as he could not
acknowledge an excommunicated king or father [2].

In vain did the emperor use every paternal remonstrance to
dissuade his son from proceeding to extremities: the breach
became wider; and both prepared for the decision of the sword.
But the son, dreading his father's military superiority, and con-
fiding in his tenderness, made use of a stratagem as base as it
was effectual. He threw himself unexpectedly at the emperor's
feet, and implored pardon for his undutiful behaviour, which he
imputed to the advice of evil counsellors. In consequence of
this submission, he was taken into favour by his deceived parent,
who immediately dismissed his army. The ungrateful youth
now bared his perfidious heart: he ordered his father to be confined; and assembled a diet of his own confederates, at which
the pope's legate presided, and repeated the sentence of excom-
A.D. munication against the obnoxious emperor, whose dignity
1105. was instantly transferred to his rebellious son [3].

The archbishops of Mentz and Cologne were sent as deputies
to the old emperor, to intimate his deposition, and demand the
regalia. Henry received this deputation with equal surprise and
concern; and finding that the chief accusation against him was
" the scandalous manner in which he had set bishoprics to sale,"
he thus addressed the audacious ecclesiastics: " If I have pros-
tituted the benefices of the church for hire, you yourselves are
the most proper persons to convict me of that simony. Say,

[1] Chron Magdeb.   [2] Dithmar. *Hist. Bel. inter Imp. et Sacerdot.*
                                  [3] Id. Ibid.

then, I conjure you, in the name of the eternal God! what have
I exacted, or what have I received, for having promoted you to
the dignities which you now enjoy?"   They acknowledged that
he was innocent as far as regarded their preferment:—" and
yet," continued he, " the archbishoprics of Mentz and Cologne
being two of the best in my gift, I might have filled my coffers
by exposing them to sale.   I bestowed them, however, on you,
out of free grace and favour ; and a worthy return you make to
my benevolence!—Do not, I beseech you, become abettors of
those who have lifted up their hands against their lord and
master, in defiance of faith, gratitude, and allegiance."

As the two archbishops, unmoved by that pathetic address,
insisted on his compliance with the purport of their errand, he
retired, and put on his royal ornaments; then returning to the
apartment he had left, and seating himself on a chair of state, he
renewed his remonstrance in these words ; " Here are the marks
of that royalty with which I was invested by God and the
princes of the empire : if you disregard the wrath of Heaven,
and the eternal reproach of mankind, so much as to lay violent
hands on your sovereign, you may strip me of them.   I am not
in a condition to defend myself."

Regardless of these expostulations, the unfeeling prelates
snatched the crown from his head, and, dragging him from his
chair, pulled off his robes by force.   While they were thus employed, Henry exclaimed, " Great God!"—the tears flowed
down his venerable cheeks—" thou art the God of vengeance,
and wilt repay this outrage.   I have sinned, I own, and merited
such shame by the follies of my youth ; but thou wilt not fail
to punish those traitors, for their insolence, ingratitude, and
perjury [1]."

To such a degree of wretchedness was this prince reduced by
the barbarity of his son, that, destitute of the common necessaries of life, he entreated the bishop of Spire, whom he had
promoted to that see, to grant him a canonry for his subsistence ;
representing that he was capable of performing the office of
" chanter or reader !"   Disappointed in that humble request, he
shed a flood of tears, and turning to those who were present,
said, with a deep sigh, " My dear friends, at least have pity on
my condition, for I am touched by the hand of the Lord !"
The hand of man, at least, was heavy upon him ; for he was not
only in want but under confinement.

---

[1] Dithmar. ubi sup.—Heiss. lib. ii. cap. ix.

In the midst of these distresses, when every one thought his courage was utterly extinguished, and his soul overwhelmed by despondence, Henry found means to escape from custody, and reach Cologne, where he was recognised as lawful emperor. He then repaired to the Low Countries, where he found friends, who raised a considerable body of men to facilitate his restoration; and he sent circular letters to the princes of Christendom, in order to interest them in his cause. He even wrote to the pope, giving him to understand, that he was inclined to an accommodation, provided it could be settled without prejudice to his crown. But before any thing material could be executed Aug. 7, in his favour, he died at Liege, in the fifty-sixth year of 1106. his age, and the forty-ninth of his reign. He was a prince of great courage, and excellent endowments both of body and mind. There was an air of dignity in his appearance that spoke the greatness of his soul. He possessed a natural fund of eloquence and vivacity; was of a mild and merciful temper; extremely charitable; and an admirable pattern of fortitude and resignation [1].

Henry V. put the finishing stroke to his barbarous, unnatural, and hypocritical conduct, by causing his father's body, as the carcass of an excommunicated wretch, to be dug out of the grave where it was buried, in the cathedral of Liege, and be carried to a cave at Spire [2]. But, notwithstanding his obligations and seeming attachment to the church, this parricidal zealot no sooner found himself established upon the imperial throne, than he maintained that right of investiture in opposition to which he had taken arms against his father, and the exercise of which was thought to merit anathemas so frightful as to disturb the sacred mansions of the dead.

In order to terminate that old dispute, Henry invited the pope into Germany. But Pascal, who was well acquainted with the new emperor's haughty and implacable disposition, thought proper to take a different route, and put himself under the protection of Philip I. king of France, who undertook to mediate an accommodation between the empire and the holy see. A conference accordingly took place at Chalons, but without effect.

After this unsuccessful meeting, the pope held a council at A.D. Troyes, and Henry convoked a diet at Mentz: the former 1107. supported Pascal's pretensions, and the latter declared for the emperor's right of investiture. But more weighty affairs

---

[1] Leonis Ostiens. *Hist.—Chron. Magdeb.*   [2] *Annal. de l'Emp.* tome i.

demanding Henry's attention, the dispute subsided for a time. He was engaged for several years in wars with Hungary and Poland, which ended without any very remarkable incidents, and left things nearly as at the beginning.

When he was weary of fighting, Henry thought of disputing : he was desirous of settling his contest with the pope ; and therefore entered Italy with such an army as he thought would A. D. intimidate the pontiff. Pascal received him with an ap- 1111. pearance of cordiality, but would not renounce the claim of investiture ; and Henry, finding himself deceived in his expectations, ordered the pope to be seized. The citizens now took up arms, and a battle was fought within the walls of Rome. The Romans were defeated ; and the carnage was so great, that the waters of the Tiber were stained with blood. Pascal was taken prisoner, and became less inflexible. He crowned Henry, and confirmed him in the right of investiture ; dividing the host with him, at the same time, in token of perfect reconciliation, and pronouncing the following anathema : " As this part of the vivifying body is separated from the other, let the violator of this treaty be separated from the kingdom of Christ[1]."

But Henry had no sooner left Italy than it appeared that the court of Rome was by no means sincere in the concessions it had made ; for, although Pascal himself still preserved the exteriors of friendship and good faith, a council of the Lateran, A.D. called by him, annulled the bull for the royal investiture 1112. of benefices, and ordered the emperor to be excommunicated.

A rebellion broke out in Saxony, which Henry was enabled to quell by the valour of his nephew, Frederic duke of A. D. Suabia and Alsace, whom he had promoted to the su- 1114. preme command of his army. On the death of the countess Matilda, the emperor, as her nearest relative, claimed the A.D. succession, notwithstanding the steps she had taken in 1115. favour of the holy see, alleging that it was not in her power to alienate her estates, which depended immediately upon the empire. He therefore set out for Lombardy, and sent ambassadors to Rome, beseeching the pope to revoke that sentence of excommunication which, in defiance of their last agreement, had been fulminated against him.

Pascal would not even favour the ambassadors with an audience, but convoked a council, in which his treaty with the

[1] *Chron. Abb. Petriburgens.*—Padre Paolo, *Benef. Eccles.*

A.D. emperor was a second time condemned. Incensed at
1116. such arrogance, Henry advanced towards Rome, determined to make his authority respected ; and the pope, alarmed at his approach, took shelter among the Norman princes in Apulia, the new vassals and protectors of the church.

The emperor entered Rome in triumph, and was crowned by
A. D. Burden, bishop of Braga, who attended him in this ex-
1117. pedition. But Henry's presence being necessary in Tuscany, Pascal privately returned to Rome, where he died
A. D. after a pontificate unusually long. Cardinal Cajetan was
1118. elected his successor, without the assent of the emperor, under the name of Gelasius II.

Enraged at this presumption, Henry declared the election void, and ordered the substitution of Burden, who, assuming the name of Gregory VIII., revoked the sentence of excommunication against his patron, and confirmed his right of investiture. Gelasius, though supported by the Norman princes, was
A. D. obliged to take refuge in France, where he died; and
1119. the archbishop of Vienne was elected in his room, by the cardinals then present, under the name of Calixtus II.

Calixtus attempted an accommodation with Henry, which not succeeding, he called a council, and excommunicated both the
A. D. emperor and the antipope. He then set out for Rome,
1120. where he was honourably received, and Gregory VIII. retired to Sutri, a strong town garrisoned by the emperor's troops. They were not, however, able to protect him from the fury of his rival. Calixtus, assisted by the Norman princes, besieged Sutri ; and the inhabitants, dreading the consequences, delivered up Gregory, who was placed by his competitor upon a camel, with his face towards the tail, and conducted through the streets of Rome, amid the scoffs and insults of the populace, as a prelude to his confinement for life[1].

The states of the empire, wishing for a termination of this long contest between the popes and the emperors, unanimously supplicated Henry for peace. He referred himself entirely to their decision ; and, a diet being assembled at Worms, it was decreed that an embassy should immediately be sent to the pope, desiring that he would convoke a general council at Rome,
A. D. by which all disputes might be determined. Calixtus
1123. accordingly called the famous council, which was opened

---

[1] Dithmar. *Hist. Bell. inter Imp. et Sacerdot.*

during Lent, and at which were present three hundred bishops and about seven hundred abbots.

The imperial ambassadors being heard before this grand assembly, the affair of investiture was at length settled, with their consent, on the following conditions :—" That, for the future, the bishops and abbots should be chosen by the monks and canons ; but that this election should be made in presence of the emperor, or of an ambassador appointed by him for that purpose : that, in case of a dispute among the electors, the decision of it should be left to the emperor, who was to consult with the bishops on that subject ; that the bishop or abbot elect should take an oath of allegiance to the emperor, receive from his hand the *regalia*, and do homage for them ; that the emperor should no longer confer the *regalia* by the ceremony of the ring and crosier, which were the ensigns of a spiritual dignity, but by that of the sceptre, as more proper to invest the person elected in the possession of rights and privileges merely temporal[1]."

Thus, in substituting the *sceptre* for the *ring* and *crosier*, ended one of the most bloody quarrels that ever desolated Christendom. But as no mention had been made, in this accommodation, of the emperor's right to create popes, or to intermeddle in their election, Calixtus was no sooner dead, than the cardinals, clergy, and people of Rome, without the A. D. participation of Henry, proceeded to a new election, 1124. which was carried on with so much disorder, that two persons were chosen at the same time ; Theobald, called Celestine, and Lambert, bishop of Ostia, who assumed the name of Honorius II. The latter was confirmed in the papacy on the voluntary resignation of his competitor.

Henry died at Utrecht, at the age of forty-four years. He was a wise, politic, and resolute prince ; and, exclusive May, of his unnatural behaviour to his father, was worthy of 1125. the imperial throne. As he had no children by his wife Matilda, who was the daughter of Henry I. of England, a contest arose for the succession. But a variety of objects demand your attention, before I proceed with the history of Germany.

---

[1] Padre Paolo, ubi sup.—Schilt. *de Libertat. German.* lib. iv.

LETTER XXIV.

Of the Reigns of the first three Norman Kings of England.

You have already, my dear Philip, seen the Norman duke victorious at Hastings. Nothing could exceed the astonish-
A. D. ment of the English nation at the issue of that unfortu-
1066. nate battle—the death of their king, and the slaughter of their principal nobility. And William, in order to terminate an enterprise which required celerity and vigour to render it completely successful, instantly put his army in motion, and advanced by forced marches to London. His approach increased the general alarm, and the divisions already prevalent in the English councils. The superior clergy, many of whom even then were French or Normans, began to declare in his favour; and the pope's bull, by which his undertaking was avowed and consecrated, was now offered as a reason for general submission.

Other causes rendered it difficult for the English, destitute as they were of a leader, to defend their liberties in this critical emergency. The body of the people had, in a great measure, lost their ancient pride and independent spirit, during their subjection to the Danes; and as Canute had, in the course of his administration, much abated the rigours of conquest, and governed them equitably by their own laws, they regarded with less terror a foreign sovereign; and deemed the inconveniences of admitting the pretensions of William less dreadful than those of bloodshed, war, and resistance. A repulse, which a party of Londoners received from five hundred Norman horse, renewed the terror of the great defeat at Hastings: the easy submission of all the inhabitants of Kent was an additional discouragement; and the burning of Southwark made the citizens of London dread a like fate for their capital. Few men longer entertained any thoughts but of immediate safety and self-preservation.

Stigand, archbishop of Canterbury, met the conqueror at Berkhamsted, and made submissions to him: and before he reached London, all the chief nobility, with the weak Edgar Atheling, their lawful but deservedly neglected prince, came into William's camp, and declared their intention of yielding to his authority. They requested him to accept the crown which they now considered as vacant; and orders were immediately issued to prepare every thing for the ceremony of his coronation. It was accordingly performed in Westminster-abbey, in presence of the most considerable nobility and gentry, both English and Norman, with seeming satisfaction[1]. This appearance of satisfaction on the part of the former, if it contained any sincerity, must have been the effect of the conciliating manner in which the ceremony was conducted. The duke took the usual oath administered to the Anglo-Saxon kings at their inauguration ; namely, " to preserve inviolate the constitution, and govern according to the laws," before the crown was placed upon his head, and after the consent of all present had been asked and obtained[2].

William thus possessed of the throne by a pretended will of king Edward, and an irregular election of the people, A.D. abetted by force of arms, retired to Barking, in Essex, 1067. where he received the submissions of all the nobles who had not attended his coronation, and whom he generally confirmed in the possession of their lands and dignities, confiscating only the estates of Harold and those of his most active partisans. Every thing wore the appearance of peace and tranquillity. The new sovereign seemed solicitous to unite the English and Normans by intermarriages and alliances ; and all his subjects who approached his person were received with affability and respect. He confirmed the liberties and immunities of London, and all the other cities of England ; and seemed desirous of resting every thing on ancient foundations. In his whole administration he bore the semblance of the lawful prince, not of the conqueror: so that the English began to flatter themselves they had only changed the succession of their sovereigns—a point which gave them little concern—without injury to the form of their government.

But, notwithstanding this seeming confidence and friendship, which he expressed for his English subjects, he took care to place all real power in the hands of the Normans, and still to keep possession of that sword to which he was chiefly indebted for

---

[1] Gul. Pictav.—Orderic. Vital.

[2] Aware that such an oath would be demanded, and conscious that he must either violate it or relinquish the rights of conquest, William is said to have hesitated, whether he should accept the offer of the English crown from the nobility and clergy, or owe it solely to the sword. But his most experienced officers advised him to moderate his ambition ; sensible that the people of England, when they saw they had to contend for their free constitution, and not merely for the person who should administer their government, would fight with double fury, when they found that their dearest interests, their liberty and property, were at stake.—*Gul. Pictav.*

his crown.   He every where disarmed the inhabitants; he built fortresses in the principal towns, where he quartered Norman soldiers; he bestowed the forfeited estates on the most powerful of his captains, and established funds for the payment of his troops.   While his civil administration seemed to be that of the legal magistrate, his military institutions were those of a master and a tyrant.   By this mixture of rigour and lenity he so subdued and composed the minds of the people of England, that he ventured to visit his native country within six months after he had left it.

Various reasons have been assigned by historians for this extraordinary journey; for extraordinary it certainly was in William, as Normandy remained in tranquillity, to absent himself so soon after the exterior submission of a great nation.   Some have ascribed it to an ostentatious desire of displaying his pomp and magnificence among his ancient courtiers; while others, supposing him incapable of such weakness, affirm that in this step, apparently so extravagant, he was guided by a concealed policy: that finding he could neither satisfy his rapacious officers, nor secure his unstable government without seizing the possessions of the English nobility and gentry, he left them to the mercy of an insolent and licentious army, in order to try their spirit, to provoke them to rebellion, and to give a colour to his intended usurpations.   William, perhaps, was influenced by both these motives in undertaking his journey to Normandy.   But, whatever was the cause, the effect is certain: many of the English gentry revolted in consequence of the king's absence; and he thenceforth either embraced, or was more fully confirmed in, the resolution of reducing them to the most abject condition.

But although the natural violence and austerity of William's temper prevented him from feeling any scruples in the execution of his tyrannical purpose, he had art enough to conceal his intention, and still to preserve some appearance of justice in his oppressions.   He was prevailed on to pardon the rebels who submitted to his mercy; and he ordered that all his English subjects, who had been arbitrarily expelled from their possessions by the Normans during his absence, should be reinstated.   The public discontents, however, daily increased; and the injuries committed and suffered on both sides, highly embittered the quarrel between the victors and vanquished.   The insolence of imperious masters, dispersed through the kingdom, seemed intolerable to the natives, who took every opportunity of gratifying their vengeance by the private slaughter of their enemies. Meanwhile an insurrection in the northern counties drew general attention, and seemed pregnant with the most important events.

Edwin and Morcar, the potent earls of Mercia and A.D. Northumberland, were the conductors of this attempt to 1068. shake off the Norman yoke. Before they took arms, they had stipulated for aid from Blethin, prince of North Wales, Malcolm, king of Scotland, and Sweyn, king of Denmark. Aware of the importance of celerity in crushing a rebellion supported by such powerful leaders, and in a cause so agreeable to the wishes of the body of the people, William, who had always his troops in readiness, marched northward with speed; and reached York before the hostile chieftains were prepared for action, or had received any succours, except a small reinforcement from Wales. Edwin and Morcar, therefore, found it necessary to have recourse to the clemency of the king : and their adherents, thus deserted, were unable to make any resistance. But the treatment of the chieftains and their followers, after submission, was very different. William observed religiously the terms granted to the former, and allowed them for the present to keep possession of their estates ; but he punished the latter with the rigours of confiscation [1].

The English were now convinced that their final subjection was intended. The early confiscation of the estates of Harold's followers seemed iniquitous, as the proprietors had never sworn fealty to the duke of Normandy, and fought only in defence of that government which they themselves had established. Yet that rigour, however repugnant to the spirit of the Anglo-Saxon laws, was excused on account of the urgent necessities of the victor; and such as were not involved in those forfeitures hoped to enjoy unmolested their possessions and their dignities. But the subsequent confiscation of so many estates in favour of the Normans, convinced the people that William intended to rely solely, for the maintenance of his authority, on the support and affection of foreigners. And they foresaw that new forfeitures and attainders would necessarily ensue from this destructive plan of policy.

Impressed with a sense of their melancholy situation, many of the English fled into foreign countries, with an intention of passing their lives abroad free from oppression, or of returning at an early opportunity to assist their friends in recovering their

---

[1] Orderic Vital.—Sim. Dunelm.

native liberties. Edgar Atheling himself, though caressed by William, retired into Scotland with his sisters Margaret and Christina. They were well received by Malcolm III., who soon after espoused Margaret; and partly with a view of strengthening his kingdom by the accession of so many strangers, partly in the hope of employing them against the growing power of William, he gave great countenance to all the English exiles[1]. Many of them settled in Scotland, and there laid the foundations of families which afterward made a figure in that kingdom.

While the people of England laboured under these oppressions, new attempts were made for the recovery of their liberties. Godwin, Edmund, and Magnus, sons of Harold, had sought a retreat in Ireland, after the defeat at Hastings; and, having met with a kind reception from the princes of that island, they projected an invasion of England, and hoped that all the exiles from Denmark, Scotland, and Wales, assisted by forces from these several countries, would at once commence hostilities, and rouse the resentment of the English nation against their haughty A.D. conquerors. They landed in Devonshire, but found a 1069. body of Normans ready to oppose them; and, being defeated in several encounters, they were obliged to seek shelter in their ships.

The struggle, however, was not yet over; all the north of England was soon in arms. The Northumbrians, impatient of servitude, had attacked Robert de Comyn, governor of Durham, and put him and seven hundred of his followers to death. This example animated the inhabitants of York, who slew Robert Fitz-Richard their governor, and besieged in the castle William Malet, on whom the chief command had devolved. About the same time a Danish army landed, under the command of Osberne, brother to king Sweyn; and Edgar Atheling also reappeared with some English noblemen who had shared his exile, and who easily excited the warlike and discontented Northumbrians to a general insurrection.

To provide more effectually for the defence of the citadel of York, Malet set fire to some neighbouring houses. The flames quickly spreading, reduced the greater part of the city to ashes; and the enraged inhabitants, aided by the Danes, took advantage of the confusion to attack the fortress, which they carried by assault, and put the garrison, amounting to three thousand men, to the sword. This success served as a signal of revolt to many

---

[1] Matth. Par. *Hist. Maj.*—Hoved. *Annal.*

other parts of the kingdom. The English, repenting of their former too easy submission, seemed determined to make one great effort for the recovery of their liberty and the expulsion of their oppressors [1].

Undismayed amidst these alarms, William marched against the insurgents in the north, whom he considered as most formidable. Not choosing, however, to trust entirely to force, he endeavoured to weaken the rebels by detaching the Danes from them. He prevailed upon Osberne, by large presents, and the liberty of plundering the coast, to desert his engagements. Many English noblemen, in despair, followed the unworthy example, and made submissions to the Conqueror. Malcolm, coming too late to support his confederates, was obliged to retire; and the Normans again triumphed. Prince Edgar escaped A. D. to the court of that monarch; but he afterwards submitted 1070. to his enemy, and was permitted to live unmolested in England [2].

William's seeming clemency proceeded only from political considerations, or from his esteem of individuals : his heart was hardened against all compassion toward the English as a people ; and he scrupled at no measure, however violent, which seemed requisite to support his plan of tyrannical administration. To punish the Northumbrians, and incapacitate them evermore from molesting him, he issued orders for laying waste the whole country between the Humber and the Tyne [3]. The houses were reduced to ashes by the unfeeling Normans ; the cattle were seized and driven away ; the instruments of husbandry were destroyed ; and the inhabitants were compelled either to seek a subsistence in the southern parts of Scotland, or to perish miserably in the woods from cold and hunger. The lives of a hundred thousand persons are computed to have been sacrificed to this stroke of barbarous policy [4]; which by seeking a remedy for a temporary evil, inflicted a lasting wound on the power and population of the country.

The insurrections and conspiracies, in different parts of the kingdom, had involved the bulk of the landholders in the guilt of treason ; and the king rigorously executed against them the laws of forfeiture and attainder. Their lives were commonly spared ; but their estates were either annexed to the royal domain, or conferred with the most profuse bounty on the Normans and other foreigners. Against a people thus devoted to destruction,

---

[1] Ord. Vital.—Gul. Gemet.—Sim. Dunelm. [2] Gul. Gemet.—Hoved.
[3] *Chron. Sax.*—Sim. Dunelm. Flor. Vigorn. [4] Order. Vital.

any suspicion served as the most undoubted proof of guilt. It was a sufficient crime in an Englishman to be opulent, noble, or powerful : and the policy of the king concurring with the rapacity of needy adventurers, produced an almost total revolution in the landed property of the kingdom. Ancient and honourable families were reduced to beggary. The nobles were treated with ignominy and contempt; they had the mortification to see their castles and manors possessed by Normans of the meanest condition, and to find themselves excluded from every road that led either to riches or preferment [1].

Power naturally follows property. This change of landholders alone, therefore, gave great security to the Norman government. But William also took care, by the new institutions that he established, to retain for ever the military authority in those hands which had enabled him to acquire the kingdom. He introduced into England the feudal polity, which he found established in France and Normandy; and which, during that age, was the foundation both of the stablity and of the disorders in most of the monarchical governments of Europe. He divided all the lands of England, with few exceptions, into baronies; and he conferred these, with the reservation of stated services and payments, on the most considerable of his followers. The barons, who held immediately of the crown, assigned parts of their lands to other foreigners, who were denominated knights or vassals, and who paid their lord the same duty and submission in peace and war, which he owed to his sovereign. As scarcely any of the native English were admitted into the first rank, the few who retained any landed property were glad to be received into the second, and, under the protection of some powerful Norman, to load themselves and their posterity with a grievous servitude for estates which had been transmitted free to them from their ancestors [2].

William's next regulations regarded the church. He deposed Stigand, the primate, and several other English bishops, by the assistance of Ermenfroy, the pope's legate; and as it was a fixed maxim in his reign, as well as in some of the subsequent, that no native of the island should be advanced to any dignity, eccle-

---

[1] M. Westm.—Order. Vital.
[2] M. Westm.—M. Par.—Bracton, lib. i. cap. 11.—Fleta, lib. i. cap. 8. The proprietors of land, under the Anglo-Saxon princes, were only subjected to three obligations ; namely to attend the king with their followers in military expeditions, to assist in building or defending the royal castles, and to keep the highways and bridges in a proper state of repair. These were emphatically called the *three necessities*, as they certainly were, in a government without regular troops, and almost without revenue. Spelm. Reliq.—Hickessii *Dissert.*

siastical, civil, or military, he promoted Lanfranc, a Milanese monk, to the see of Canterbury. That prelate professed the most devoted attachment to Rome, whose power thenceforth daily increased in England, and became very dangerous to some of William's successors; but the arbitrary power of the Conqueror over the English, and his extensive authority over the Normans, prevented him from feeling its inconvenience. He retained the clergy in great subjection, as well as his lay subjects, and would allow no person of any condition or character to dispute his absolute will and pleasure. None of his ministers or barons, whatever might be their offences, could be subjected to spiritual censures, until his consent was obtained. He prohibited his people from acknowledging any one as pope, whom he himself had not recognised; and he ordered that all ecclesiastical canons, voted in any synod, should be submitted to him, and ratified by his authority, before they could be valid. The same sanction was required for bulls or letters from Rome, before they were produced. And when the imperious Gregory VII., whom we have seen tyrannizing over kings and emperors, wrote to this monarch, requiring him to fulfil his promise of doing homage for the kingdom of England to the see of Rome, and to send him that tribute which his predecessors had been accustomed to pay to the vicar of Christ (meaning *St. Peter's Pence*, a charitable donation of the Saxon princes, which the court of Rome, as usual, was inclined to construe into a badge of subjection acknowledged by the kingdom), William coolly replied, that the money should be remitted as formerly, but that he neither promised to do homage to Rome, nor entertained any thoughts of imposing that servitude on his kingdom [1].

The following anecdote shows, in a still stronger light, the contempt of this prince for ecclesiastical dominion. Odo, bishop of Bayeux, the king's maternal brother, whom he had created earl of Kent, and entrusted with a great share of power, had amassed immense riches; and agreeably to the usual progress of human wishes, he began to regard his present eminence as only a step to future grandeur. He even aspired to the papacy, and had resolved to transmit all his wealth to Italy, and go thither with several noblemen, whom he had persuaded to follow his example, in hopes of establishments under the future pope. William was no sooner informed of this scheme, than he accused Odo of treason, and ordered him to be arrested; but nobody

[1] *Ang. Sacra.*—Ingulph. Order. Vital.

N 2

would lay hands on the bishop. The king was therefore obliged to seize him ; and when Odo insisted that, as a prelate, he was exempt from all temporal jurisdiction, William boldly replied, " I arrest not the bishop, but the earl !" and accordingly sent him prisoner into Normandy, where he was long detained in custody, notwithstanding the remonstrances and menaces of the pope [1].

The English had the cruel mortification to find, that their king's authority, however worthy of a sovereign in some instances, generally tended to their oppression, or to perpetuate their subjection. He had even entertained the difficult project of totally abolishing their language. He ordered the English youth to be instructed in the French tongue, in all the schools throughout the kingdom. The pleadings in the supreme courts of judicature were in French : the deeds were often drawn in the same language : the laws were composed in that idiom. No other tongue was used at court : it became the language of all fashionable societies : and many of the natives themselves affected to excel in it [2]. To this attempt of the Conqueror, and to the foreign dominions so long annexed to the crown of England, we owe the great mixture of French at present to be found in our language.

While William was thus wantonly exercising his tyranny over England, his foreign affairs fell into disorder ; and the oppressed English assisted him in their retrieval. Fulk, count of Anjou, had seized the province of Maine, which had fallen under the A.D. dominion of the duke of Normandy, by the will of Her-1073. bert, the last count. But William, by the assistance of his new subjects, soon obliged the inhabitants, who had revolted, to return to their duty, and the count of Anjou to renounce his pretensions [3].

The king now passed some time in Normandy, where his presence was become necessary on account of the turbulent disposition of his eldest son Robert, who openly aspired to inde-A.D. pendence, and demanded immediate possession of Nor-1076. mandy and Maine. William gave him a positive refusal, repeating that homely saying, that he never intended to throw off his clothes till he went to bed. He accordingly called over an army of Englishmen, under his ancient captains, who bravely expelled Robert and his adherents. The prince took shelter in the castle of Gerberoy, in the Beauvoisis, which the king of

[1] *Ang. Sacra.* Order. Vital.
[2] *Chron. Rothom.*—Ingulph. *Hist.*—Warton's *Hist. of Eng. Poetry.*
[3] *Chron. Sax.*—Order. Vital.

France, who secretly favoured his pretensions, had provided for him. In this fortress he was closely besieged by his father, against whom he made a gallant defence; and many rencounters passed, which resembled more the single combats of chivalry than the military operations of armies. One was too remarkable, by its circumstances and its event, to be omitted. Robert, encountering the king, who was concealed by his helmet, A.D. wounded and dismounted him, when, calling for assist- 1079. ance, his voice discovered him to his son, who, struck with a sense of remorse, duty, and the dread of greater guilt, instantly threw himself at William's feet, craved pardon for his offences, and offered to purchase forgiveness by any atonement. A return of kindness, however, did not immediately ensue. William's military pride was wounded, and his resentment was too obstinate at once to yield; but a reconciliation was affected by the interposition of the queen and the nobles [1].

The peaceable state of William's affairs now gave him leisure to finish an undertaking, which proves his great and extensive genius, and does honour to his memory. It was a general survey of all the lands of England; their extent in each district, their proprietors, tenures, value; the quantity of mea- A.D. dow, pasture, wood, and arable land, which they con- 1081. tained; and in some counties, the number of tenants, cottagers, and slaves of all denominations, who lived upon them. This valuable piece of antiquity, called the Doomesday book, is still preserved in the Exchequer, and contributes to the illustration of the ancient state of England.

William, like all the Normans, was much attached to the manly amusement of hunting: and his passion for this sport he cruelly indulged at the expense of his unhappy subjects. Not content with those large forests which the Saxon kings possessed in all parts of England, he resolved to make a new forest near Winchester, the usual place of his residence. For that purpose he laid waste the country for an extent of thirty miles in Hampshire, expelling the inhabitants from their houses, seizing their property, and demolishing churches and convents, without making the sufferers any compensation for the injury [2].

The death of this prince was occasioned by a quarrel not altogether worthy of his life. A witticism gave rise to war. William, who was become corpulent, had been detained in bed

---

[1] Hoved. *Annal.*   Order. Vital.
[2] H. Huntingd. lib. vi.—Gul. Malmesb. lib. iii.

by sickness, while in Normandy—a circumstance which gave the French king occasion to say, with the vivacity natural to his country, that he was surprised his brother of England should be so long in being delivered of his big belly. William, enraged at this levity, swore, " by the brightness and resurrection of God?" his usual oath, that, at his rising, he would present so many *lights* at the church of Notre Dame, as would give little pleasure to the king of France;—alluding to the usual practice, at that time, of carrying a torch to church after child-birth. On his recovery, he led an army into the Isle of France, and laid every thing waste with fire and sword. But the progress of this hostility was stopped by an accident which put an end to the English monarch's life. His horse suddenly starting aside, he bruised his belly on the pommel of the saddle; and this bruise, joined to his former bad habit of body, brought on a mortification, of which he died, at the age of sixty-one, or (as some say) sixty-four years [1]. He left Normandy and Maine to Robert: he wrote to Lanfranc, desiring him to crown his second son William king of England; and he bequeathed to Henry the possessions of his mother Matilda.

Sept. 9, 1087.

The characters of princes are best seen in their actions: I shall, however, give you a concise character of the Conqueror; for such he ultimately proved, though little more than a conditional sovereign when he first received the submissions of the English nation [2]. The spirit of William I., says a philosophic historian, was bold and enterprising, yet guided by prudence; and his exorbitant ambition, which lay little under the restraints of justice, and still less under those of humanity, ever submitted to the dictates of reason, and sound policy. Though not insensible to generosity, he was hardened against compassion; and he seemed equally ostentatious and ambitious of *éclat*, in his clemency and in his vengeance.

William II. (surnamed *Rufus*, or the Red, from the colour of his hair) was quickly crowned king of England, in consequence of his father's recommendatory letters to the primate; and Robert, at the same time, took peaceable possession of Nor-

---

[1] Wace.—Order. Vital.

[2] William acted so uniformly like a conqueror, that before the end of his reign, there was scarcely one Englishman, who was either earl, baron, bishop, or abbot, (Gul. Malmesb. lib. iii.—Ingulph.) Perhaps no revolution was ever attended with so complete and sudden a change of power and property, as that which was effected by the duke of Normandy. Nor was the administration of any prince ever more absolute than that of William I., though the government which he established was not exteriorly a despotism, but a feudal monarchy.

mandy. But this partition of the Conqueror's dominions, though apparently made without any violence or opposition, occasioned in England many discontents, which seemed to promise a sudden revolution. The Norman barons, who possessed large estates both in England and their own country, were uneasy at the separation of those territories, and foresaw that, as it would be impossible for them to preserve long their allegiance to two masters, they must necessarily resign either their ancient property or their new acquisitions. Robert's title to Normandy they esteemed incontestible; his claim to England they thought plausible; they therefore wished that this prince, who alone had any pretensions to unite the duchy and kingdom, might be put in possession of both [1].

A comparison between the personal qualities of the two princes, also led the mal-contents to prefer the elder. Robert was brave, open, sincere, generous; whereas William, though not less brave than his brother, was violent, haughty, tyrannical, and seemed disposed to govern more by fear than the love of his people. The bishop of Bayeux, who had been released from prison on the death of the Conqueror, en- A.D. forced all these motives with the dissatisfied barons, and 1088. engaged many of them in a formal conspiracy to dethrone the king.

Expecting immediate support from Normandy, the conspirators hastened to put themselves in a military posture: and William, sensible of his perilous situation, endeavoured to provide against the threatened danger by gaining the affections of the English, who zealously embraced his cause, upon receiving some general promises of good treatment, and permission to hunt in the royal forests, having now lost all hopes of recovering their ancient liberties. By their asssistance the king was enabled to subdue the rebels: but those Norman barons, who had remained faithful to him, were the only gainers. He paid little regard to the promises made to his English subjects, who still found themselves exposed to the same oppressions which they had experienced during the reign of the Conqueror, and which were augmented by the tyrannical temper of the present monarch [2]. Even the privileges of the church formed but a feeble rampart against the usurpations of William; yet the

[1] Order. Vital.
[2] *Chron. Sax.*—Gul. Malmesb. lib. iv. The application of William, however, and the service they had rendered him, made the natives sensible of their import-

terror of his authority, confirmed by the suppression of the late insurrections, kept every one in subjection, notwithstanding the murmurs of the clergy, and preserved general tranquillity in England.

William even thought himself sufficiently powerful to disturb his brother in the possession of Normandy, and bribed several Norman barons to favour his unjust claim. The duke had also reason to apprehend danger from the intrigues of his brother Henry, who inherited more of his father's money than his other possessions, and had furnished Robert, during his preparations against England, with the sum of three thousand marks; in return for which slender supply, he had been put in possession of the Cotentin, almost one-third of the duke's dominions. But these two brothers, notwithstanding their mutual jealousies,

A.D. 1090. now united, in order to defend their territories against the ambition of the king of England, who appeared in Normandy at the head of a numerous army; and affairs seemed to be hastening to extremity, when an accommodation was brought about by the interposition of the nobility.

Prince Henry, however, disgusted at the terms of that agreement, in which he thought himself treated with neglect, retired to St. Michael's Mount, a strong fortress on the coast of Normandy, and infested the neighbouring country with his incursions. Robert and William, his two brothers, besieged him in this place, and had nearly obliged him to surrender by reason of the scarcity of water; when the elder, hearing of his brother's distress, granted him permission to obtain a supply, and also sent him some pipes of wine for his own table—a conduct which could only have been dictated by the generous but romantic spirit of chivalry that prevailed in those times, and with which the duke was strongly infected. Being reproved by William for this imprudent generosity, Robert replied, " What! shall I suffer my brother to die of thirst?—Where shall we find another brother when he is gone?"

Willam, during this siege, also performed an act of generosity less suited to his character. Riding out alone to survey the fortress, he was attacked by two soldiers and dismounted. One of the assailants drew his sword, in order to despatch the king. " Hold, knave!" cried William, " I am the king of England."

ance by reason of their numbers; and they gradually recovered their consequence in the course of the struggles between the king and the nobles.

The soldier suspended his blow, and raised the king from the ground; who, charmed with the fellow's behaviour, rewarded him handsomely, and took him into his service [1].

Prince Henry was at last obliged to capitulate : and being despoiled of all his dominions, wandered about for some time with very few attendants, and often in great poverty.   A.D. 1091.

William was afterwards engaged in humbling the Scots and Welsh, who had infested England with their incursions. He had also occasion to quell a conspiracy of his own barons, who were desirous of exalting to the throne Stephen, count of Aumale, nephew of the Conqueror.   A.D. 1095. But the noise of these petty wars and commotions was quite sunk in the tumult of the Crusades, which then engaged the attention of all Europe, and have since attracted the curiosity of mankind, as the most extraordinary examples of human folly that were ever exhibited on the face of the globe. The cause and consequences of these pious enterprises I shall afterwards have occasion to consider; at present I shall only speak of them as they affect the history of England.

The duke of Normandy, impelled by the bravery and mistaken generosity of his spirit, early enlisted himself in the first crusade; but being always unprovided with money, he found that it would be impossible for him, without some supply, to appear in a manner suitable to his rank at the head of his numerous vassals, who, transported with the general fury, were desirous of following him into Asia. He therefore resolved to mortgage his dominions, which he had not prudence to govern; and he offered them to his brother William, who kept aloof from all those fanatical and romantic warriors, for so small a sum as ten thousand marks [2]. The bargain was concluded, and William took possession of Normandy and Maine;   A.D. 1096. while Robert set out for the Holy Land in pursuit of glory, and in full hopes of securing his eternal salvation.

In the mean time, William, who regarded only the things of this world, was engaged in a quarrel with Anselm, archbishop of Canterbury, a Piedmontese monk, whom he wished to deprive of his see for refractory behaviour. Anselm appealed to Rome against the king's injustice : and affairs came to such extremities, that the primate, finding it dangerous to remain in the kingdom, desired permission to retire beyond sea. It was

---

[1] Gul. Malmesb. lib. iv.—M. Paris.   [2] Hoved. *Annal.*

A.D. granted to him; but all his temporalities were confiscated,
1097. He was received with great respect by Urban II., who considered him as a martyr in the cause of religion, and even threatened the king with the sentence of excommunication for his proceedings against the primate [1].

Anselm afterwards distinguished himself in the council of Bari, where the famous dispute between the Greek and Latin churches, relative to the *procession* of the third person of the Trinity, was agitated; namely, whether the Holy Ghost proceeded from the Father and the Son, or from the Father only.

A.D. He also assisted in a council at Rome, where spiritual
1099. censures were denounced against all ecclesiastics who did homage to laymen for their benefices, and all laymen who exacted such homage. The arguments used on that occasion, in favour of the clergy, are worthy of the ignorance of the age, and strongly mark the gross superstition into which the human mind was sunk.

The ceremony of feudal homage I have already mentioned. The Romish council now declared, that such submission was inconsistent with the dignity of the sacerdotal character, as well as with the independence of the church; " For," said Urban, " it is a most execrable thing, that holy hands, appointed to perform what was never granted to any angel, to create God the Creator, and offer him to God his Father, for the salvation of mankind, should be reduced to the humiliating baseness of slavishly mingling with profane hands, which are soiled with impurity, rapine, and bloodshed [2]."

The fanaticism of the times afforded the king of England a second opportunity of increasing his dominions. Poictou and Guienne were offered to be mortgaged to him, for the same pious purpose that had induced his brother Robert to put him in possession of Normandy and Maine. The terms were adjusted; but, before they were fulfilled, an accident put an end
Aug. 2, to William's life, and all his ambitious projects. Walter
1100. Tyrrel, a French knight, remarkable for his address in archery, attended him in the New Forest, for the purpose of hunting : and, as the king had dismounted after the chase, his companion, eager to show his dexterity, discharged an arrow at a stag which suddenly started before him. The arrow, glancing against a tree, struck William to the heart, and instantly killed

---

[1] Eadm. *Hist. Novorum.* lib. ii.—Order. Vital.
[2] Fleury, *Hist. Eccles.*—*Anglia Sacra*, vol. i.—Sim. Dunelm.

him : while Tyrrel, without informing any one of the accident, put spurs to his horse, hastened to the sea-shore, embarked for France, and joined in the crusade—a penance which he imposed on himself for this involuntary crime, and which was deemed sufficient to expiate crimes of the blackest dye [1].

William II., though a man of sound understanding, appears to have been a violent and tyrannical prince, a perfidious, encroaching, and dangerous neighbour, and an unkind and ungenerous relative. His vices, however, have probably been exaggerated by the monkish writers, the only historians of those times, as he was utterly void of superstition, and had not even a decent respect for religion. Of this many examples might be adduced; but one will be sufficient. When the body of the clergy presented a petition, that he would give them leave to send a form of prayer to be used in all the churches of England, " That God would move the heart of the king to appoint an archbishop !" (for he had kept the revenues or temporalities of the see of Canterbury in his own hands for the space of four years) he carelessly replied, " You may pray as you please, and I will act as I please [2]." Had he lived a few years longer, he might greatly have enlarged his dominions; and, as he was the most powerful and politic prince in Europe, he might perhaps have become its arbiter. He built the Tower, Westminster-hall, and London-bridge, monuments of his greatness which still remain. His most liberal measure was the sending of an army into Scotland, in order to restore Edgar, the true heir of that crown, the son of Malcolm Canmore by Margaret, sister of Edgar Atheling. The enterprise was successful.

As William Rufus was never married, and consequently could leave no lawful issue, the crown of England now belonged to his brother Robert, both by the right of birth and of solemn compact, ratified by the nobility. But as prince Henry was hunting in the New Forest when Rufus fell, he immediately galloped to Winchester, secured the royal treasure, was saluted king, and proceeded to the exercise of the sovereign authority. Sensible, however, that a crown usurped against all the rules of justice would sit very unsteady on his head, he resolved, by fair professions at least, to gain the affections of his subjects. Besides taking the usual coronation oath, to maintain the constitution, and to execute justice, he granted a charter, which was calculated to remedy many of the grievous oppressions complained of during

---

[1] *Chron. Sax.*—Sim. Dunelm.   [2] Gul. Malmesb. lib. iv.

the reign of his father and his brother; and he promised a general confirmation and observance of the laws of Edward the Confessor[1].

To fix himself more firmly on the throne, the king recalled archbishop Anselm, and reinstated him in the see of Canterbury. He also married Matilda, daughter of Malcolm, and niece to Edgar Atheling. And this marriage, more than any other measure of his reign, tended to endear Henry to his English subjects, who had felt so severely the tyranny of the Normans, that they reflected with infinite regret on their former liberty, and hoped for a more equal and mild administration, when the blood of their native princes should be united with that of their new sovereigns. But the policy and prudence of Henry were in danger of being frustrated by the sudden appearance of Robert, who returned from the Holy Land about a month after the death of William II., took possession of Normandy without resistance, and made preparations for asserting his claim to the English throne.

The great reputation which Robert had acquired in the East favoured his pretensions; and the Norman barons, still impressed with apprehensions of the consequences of the separation of the duchy and kingdom, manifested the same discontent which had appeared on the accession of Rufus. Henry was therefore in danger of being dethroned: and it was only through the exhortations of archbishop Anselm that a considerable number of his subjects were engaged to oppose Robert, who had landed at Portsmouth. The two armies continued some days in sight of each other without coming to action; and, by the persuasion of the same prelate, a treaty was concluded between the brothers.

A.D. 1101.

It was agreed, that Robert should resign his pretensions to the crown of England, for an annual pension of three thousand marks; that, if either of the princes should die without issue, the other should succeed to his dominions; that the adherents of each should be reinstated in their honours and possessions; and that neither the king nor the duke should thenceforth countenance the enemies of each other[2]. But these conditions, though so favourable to Henry, were soon violated by his rapacity and ambition. He indeed restored the estates of Robert's adherents, but took care that they should not remain long in undisturbed possession; and various pretences were formed for

[1] M. Paris.—Hoved.   [2] Chron. Sax.—Order. Vital.

despoiling and humbling all who, in his opinion, had either inclination or abilities to disturb his government.

Enraged at the fate of his friends, Robert imprudently ventured into England, but met with such an unfavourable reception, that he was alarmed for his own safety, and glad to purchase his escape with the loss of his pension.　One indiscretion followed another.　The affairs of Normandy fell into confusion ; Henry went over by invitation, to regulate them ; but instead of supporting his brother's authority, he increased the discontent by every art of bribery, intrigue, and insinuation, and at length made himself master of the duchy.　The unfortunate Robert, who seemed born only to be the sport of fortune, was defeated at Tenerchebrai, and carried prisoner into England.　He A.D. remained in custody above twenty-seven years, and died 1106. a captive in the castle of Cardiff, in Glamorganshire [1].

The acquisition of Normandy was a great point of Henry's ambition, not only as it was the ancient inheritance of his family, but as it gave him considerable weight on the continent.　The injustice of the usurpation, however, was a source of inquietude ; and the jealousy of the French monarch gave rise to those wars which were to prove so injurious to posterity.　Louis VI., in concert with the counts of Anjou and Flanders, supported the claim of William, son of Robert, to the duchy of Normandy : he even craved the assistance of the church for the true heir, and reprobated the enormity of detaining in prison so brave a prince as Robert, one of the most eminent champions of the cross.　But Henry knew how to defend the rights of his crown with vigour, and yet with dexterity.　He detached the count of Anjou from the alliance, by contracting his son William to that prince's daughter, while he gained the pope and his favourites by liberal presents and promises.　Calixtus II., who was A.D. then in France, declared, after a conference with Henry, 1119. that of all men whom he had ever seen, the king of England was beyond comparison, the most *eloquent* and *persuasive* [2]. The complaints of the Norman prince were thenceforth disregarded.

The military operations of Louis proved as unsuccessful as his intrigues.　The French and English armies engaged near Andeli, in Normandy, where William, the son of Robert, behaved with great bravery.　Henry himself was in imminent danger.　He

---

[1] Gul. Malmesb. lib. v.　The story of his being deprived of his sight appears to be ill-founded.
[2] Gul. Malmesb.

was wounded in the head by a gallant Norman, named Crispin, who had followed the fortunes of William; but rather roused than intimidated by the blow, the king collected all his might, and beat his antagonist to the ground. The English, animated by the example of their sovereign, put the French to a total rout: and an accommodation soon after took place between the two monarchs, in which the interests of young William were entirely neglected [1].

Henry's public prosperity was overbalanced by a domestic A.D. misfortune. His son William had accompanied him 1120. into Normandy, but perished in his return. He was anxious to get first to land; and the captain of his vessel being intoxicated with liquor, heedlessly ran her on a rock, where she was dashed to pieces. Beside the prince, above one hundred and forty young noblemen or knights were lost on this occasion [2]. The king was so much affected at the intelligence, that he is said never to have smiled more.

Henry had now no legitimate issue, except Matilda, the A.D. widow of the emperor Henry V., whose hand he afterwards 1127. bestowed on Geoffrey Plantagenet, son of the count of Anjou. He endeavoured to secure her succession to all his domi- A.D. nions, and obliged the barons of Normandy and England 1133. to swear fealty to her. After six years she was delivered of a son, who received the name of Henry; and the king, farther to ensure the succession, ordered all the nobles to renew the oath which they had taken, and also to swear fealty to her infant son [3].

The joy of this event, and the pleasure of his daughter's com- Dec. 1, pany, induced Henry to remain in Normandy, where he 1135. died, in the sixty-eighth year of his age, and the thirty-sixth of his reign. He was one of the most able and accomplished princes that ever filled the English throne, possessing all the qualities, both mental and personal, that could adorn his high station, or fit him for the government of an extensive territory. His learning, which procured him the name of *Beauclerc*, or the *fine scholar*, would have distinguished him in private life, and his talents would have given him an ascendant in any condition.

The affairs of France, my dear Philip, and the crusades, which took their rise in that kingdom, claim your attention before I

[1] H. Huntingd. lib. vii.—Dicet. *Hist*.   [2] Hoved. *Annal*.
[3] Walsingh. *Hypodigma Neustriæ*.—M. Paris.

speak of the disputed succession of Matilda, and of her son Henry Plantagenet, whose reign affords some of the most interesting spectacles in the history of England. In the mean time it will be proper to take a slight review of the change produced in our ancient constitution, and in the condition of our Saxon ancestors, by the Norman conquest or revolution.

POSTSCRIPT.

Having informed you, in my eighth letter, of the chief points of the Anglo-Saxon government, and recounted in the twelfth the improvements introduced by the great Alfred, I proceed to observe that this happy constitution was almost entirely subverted by the tyranny of the first William. The government which he substituted was a rigid feudal monarchy, or military aristocracy, in which a regular chain of subordination and of service was established, from the sovereign or commander-in-chief, to the serf or villain: and which, like all feudal governments, was attended with a grievous depression of the body of the people, who were daily exposed to the insults, violences, and exactions of the nobles, whose vassals they all were, and from whose oppressive jurisdiction it was difficult and dangerous for them to appeal.

This depression, as might be expected, was more complete and humiliating in England, under the first Anglo-Norman princes, than in any other feudal government. The Conqueror, by his artful and tyrannical policy, by attainders and confiscations, had become, in the course of his reign, proprietor of almost all the lands in the kingdom. These lands, however, he could not retain, had he been even willing, in his own hands: he was under the necessity of bestowing the greater part of them on his Norman captains, or nobles, the companions of his conquest, and the instruments of his tyranny, who had led their own vassals to battle[1]. But those grants he clogged with heavy feudal services, and prestations or payments, which no one dared to refuse. He was the general of a victorious army, which was still obliged to continue in a military posture, in order to secure the possessions it had seized. And the Anglo-Norman barons,

---

[1] Nothing can more strongly indicate that necessity than the following anecdote. Earl Warrenne, when questioned, in a subsequent reign, concerning his right to the land he possessed, boldly drew his sword, "This," said he, " is my title!—William the Bastard did not conquer England himself: the Norman barons, and my ancestors among the rest, were joint adventurers in the enterprise."—Dugdale's *Baronage*, vol. i.

and tenants *in capite*, by knight-service, who with the dignified clergy, formed the *national assembly*, imposed obligations yet more severe on their vassals, the inferior landholders (consisting chiefly of English gentlemen) as well as on the body of the people, for whom they seemed to have no compassion [1].

But the rigour of the Anglo-Norman Government, and the tyrannical and licentious spirit of the nobles, proved ultimately favourable to general liberty. The oppresed people looked up to the king for protection; and circumstances enabled them to obtain it. The defect in the title of William II. and of Henry I. induced them to listen to the complaints of their English subjects, and to redress some of their grievances. The people, pleased even with the partial relief afforded to them, became sensible of their consequence, and of their obligations to the crown; while the barons, finding themselves in quiet possession of their English estates, and apprehending no future disturbance from the natives, bore with impatience the burthens imposed upon them by William I., and to which they had readily sub-

---

[1] The state of England, at the death of William the Conqueror, is thus described by one of our ancient historians, who was almost contemporary with that prince. " The Normans," says he, " had now fully executed the wrath of Heaven upon the English. There was hardly any one of that nation who possessed any power; they were all involved in servitude and sorrow; insomuch that to be called an Englishman was considered as a reproach. In those miserable times many oppressive taxes and tyrannical customs were introduced. The king himself, when he had let his lands at their full value, if another tenant came and offered more, and a third offered still more, violated his former engagements, and gave them to him who offered most; and the great men were inflamed with such a rage for money, that they cared not by what means it was acquired. The more they talked of justice, the more injuriously they acted. Those who were called justiciaries were the fountains of all iniquity. Sheriffs and magistrates, whose peculiar duty it was to pronounce righteous judgments, were the most cruel of all tyrants, and greater plunderers than common thieves and robbers." (Hen. Huntingd. lib. vii.) And the author of the Saxon Chronicle, in speaking of the miseries of a subsequent reign, says, that the great barons " grievously oppressed the poor people with building castles; and, when they were built, they filled them with wicked men, or rather devils, who seized both men and women supposed to be possessed of any money, threw them into prison, and put them to more cruel tortures than the martyrs ever endured." (*Chron. Sax.* p. 238.) The truth of this melancholy description is corroborated by the testimony of William of Malmesbury.

The great power and success of the Normans rendered them licentious as well as tyrannical. This licentiousness was so great, that the princess Matilda, daughter of Malcolm Canmore, who had received her education in England, and was afterwards married to Henry I., thought it necessary to wear the religious habit, in order to preserve her person from violation. Before a great council of the Anglo-Norman clergy, she herself declared that she had been induced by no other motive to put on the veil. And the council admitted her plea, in the following memorable words:—" When the great king William conquered this land, many of his followers, elate with their extraordinary success, and thinking that all things ought to be subservient to their will and pleasure, not only seized the possessions of the vanquished, but invaded the honour of their matrons and virgins. Hence many young ladies, who dreaded such violences, were induced to seek shelter in convents, and even to take the veil as a farther security to their virtue."—Eadm. *Hist.* lib. iii.

mitted in the hour of conquest and of danger. They saw the necessity of being more indulgent to their vassals, in order to obtain sufficient force to enable them to retrench the prerogatives of the sovereign, and to connect their cause with that of the people. And the people, always formidable by their numbers, courted by both parties, and sometimes siding with one, sometimes with the other, in the bloody contests between the crown and the barons, recovered by various progressive steps, which I shall have occasion to trace in the course of my narration, their ancient and natural right to a place in the parliament or national assembly.

Thus restored to a share in the legislature, the English commonalty felt more fully their own importance ; and, by a long and vigorous struggle, maintained with unexampled perseverance, they wrested from both the king and the nobles all the other rights of a free people, of which their Anglo-Saxon ancestors had been robbed by the violent invasion and cruel ·policy of William the Norman. To those rights they were entitled as men, by the great law of nature and reason, which declares the *welfare* of the *whole* community to be the end of all civil government ; and, as Englishmen, by inheritance. In whatever light, therefore, we view the privileges of the commons, they are RESUMPTIONS, not USURPATIONS.

In order to establish this important political truth, some of our popular writers have endeavoured to prove, that the people of England were by no means robbed of their liberty or property by William I., and that the *commons* had a *share* in the *legislature* under *all* the Anglo-Norman princes. But as this position cannot be maintained without violating historical testimony, the advocates for prerogative have had greatly the advantage in that dispute[1]. I have therefore made the usurpations of William, in violation of his coronation oath, the basis of my argument. Usurpation can create no right, nor the exercise of illegal authority any prerogative.

---

[1] Mr. Hume, in particular, has triumphed over every adversary. His collected arguments, supported by facts, to prove " that the commons originally formed no part of the Anglo-Norman parliament," are strong and satisfactory. But the following clause in the Great Charter is of itself sufficient to determine the dispute. " We will cause to be summoned," says the king, " as a COMMON COUNCIL of the KINGDOM, the *archbishops*, *bishops*, *earls*, and *great barons*, personally, by our letters ; and besides, we will cause to be summoned, in general, by our sheriffs and bailiffs, all *others*, who HOLD OF US IN CHIEF." (*Mag. Chart.* Sec. xiv.) This testimony, so full and conclusive, when duly weighed, must preclude all future controversy on the subject.

LETTER XXV.

Sketch of the French History, under Philip I. and Louis VI.,
with some Account of the first Crusade.

PHILIP I., as I have already observed, had been well educated,
and was not deficient in capacity ; but his mind had acquired a
wrong bias, which prompted him too frequently to prefer his
interest, or his inclinations, to his honour. His reign is not so
remarkable for any thing as his marrying Bertrade de Montfort,
duchess of Anjou, while her husband and his queen were both
alive. For this irregularity he was excommunicated by Urban
II. in the famous council of Clermont, where the first Crusade
was preached for the recovery of the Holy Land[1],—a circumstance
which naturally leads me to speak of that extravagant expedition, its causes, and consequences.

Gregory VII. among his other vast ideas, had formed, as we
have seen, the project of uniting the western Christians against
the Mohammedans, and of recovering Palestine from the hands
of those infidels[2] ; and nothing but his quarrel with the emperor
Henry IV., by which he declared himself an enemy to the civil
power of princes, could have obstructed the progress of this undertaking, conducted by so able a politician, at a time when the
minds of men were fully prepared for such an enterprise. The
work, however, was reserved for a meaner instrument ; for a man
whose condition could excite no jealousy, and whose head was
as weak as his imagination was warm. But before I mention
this man, I must say a few words of the state of the East at that
time, and of the passion for pilgrimages which then prevailed in
Europe.

We naturally view with veneration and delight those places
which have been the residence of any illustrious personage, or
the scene of any great transaction. Hence arises the enthusiasm with which the literati still visit the ruins of Athens and
Rome ; and hence flowed the superstitious devotion with which
Christians, from the earliest ages of the church, were accustomed
to visit that country where their religion had commenced, and
that city in which the Messiah had died for the redemption of
those who believe in his name. Pilgrimages to the shrines of

---

[1] Harduin. *Concil.* vol. xi.   [2] See Letter XXIII.

saints and martyrs were also common; but as this distant pere-grination could not be performed without considerable expense, fatigue, and danger, it appeared more meritorious than all others, and was soon considered as an expiation for almost every crime.   And a prevailing opinion, which I before stated[1], re-specting the Millennium, increased the number and the ardour of the credulous devotees that undertook this tedious journey.   A general consternation seized the minds of Christians.   Many relinquished their possessions, abandoned their friends and fami-lies, and hurried with precipitation to the Holy Land, where they imagined Christ would suddenly appear to judge the quick and the dead[2].

But the Christians, though ultimately undeceived in regard to the day of judgment, had the mortification, in these pious journeys, to see the holy sepulchre, and the other places sanctified by the presence of the Saviour, in the hands of infidels.   The followers and the countrymen of Mohammed had early made themselves masters of Palestine, which the Greek empire, far in its decline, was unable to protect against so warlike an enemy.   They gave little disturbance, however, to those zealous pilgrims who daily flocked to Jerusalem : they even allowed all strangers, after paying a moderate tribute, to visit the sepulchre, perform religious duties, and return in peace.   But when the Turks, a Tartar tribe who had embraced the Moslem creed, had wrested Syria from the Saracens, and taken Jerusalem, pilgrims were exposed to outrages of every kind from these fierce barbarians.   And this change coinciding with the panic of the consummation of all things, and the supposed appearance of Christ on Mount Sion, filled Europe with alarm and indignation.   Every pilgrim who returned from Palestine related the dangers he had encountered in visiting the holy city, and described, with exaggeration, the cruelty and vexations of the Turks, who, to use the language of those zealots, not only profaned the sepulchre of the Lord by their presence, but derided the sacred mysteries in the very place of their completion[3].

While the minds of men were thus roused, a fanatical monk, commonly known by the name of Peter the Hermit, a native of Amiens in Picardy, revived the project of Gregory VII. of leading all the forces of Christendom against the infidels, and of

---

[1] See the last note to Letter XXII.
[2] *Chron.* Will. Godelil. ap. Bonquet, *Recueil des Hist. de France*, tome x. Eccard. *Corp. Script. Medii Ævi*, vol. i.

driving them out of the Holy Land.   He had made the pilgrimage to Jerusalem, and was so deeply affected with the danger to which that act of piety now exposed Christians, that he ran from province to province on his return, with a crucifix in his hand, exciting princes and people to this holy war ; and wherever he came he kindled the same enthusiastic ardour with which he himself was animated.

Urban II., who had at first been doubtful of the success of such a project, at length entered into Peter's views, and summoned at Placentia a council, which was holden in the open fields, as no hall was sufficient to contain the multitude : it consisted of four thousand ecclesiastics, and thirty thousand laymen, who all declared for the war against the infidels ; but none of them heartily engaged in the enterprise. Urban therefore found it necessary to call another council in the same year at Clermont, in Auvergne, where the greatest prelates, nobles, and princes attended ; and when the pope and the hermit had concluded their pathetic exhortations, the whole assembly, as if impelled by an immediate inspiration, exclaimed with one voice : " It is the will of God !—It is the will of God !"— words which were deemed so memorable, and believed to be so much the result of a divine influence, that they were employed as the motto on the sacred standard, and as the signal of rendezvous and battle in all the future exploits of the champions of the *Cross*, the symbol chosen by the devout combatants, in allusion to the death of Christ, as the badge of union, and affixed to their right shoulder, whence their expedition derived the name of a Crusade.[1]

A.D. 1095.

Persons of all ranks flew to arms with the utmost ardour. Not only the gallant nobles of that age, with their martial followers, whom the boldness of a romantic enterprise might have been apt to allure, but men in the more humble and pacific stations of life, ecclesiastics of every order, and even women, concealing their sex beneath the disguise of armour, engaged with emulation in an undertaking which was deemed so sacred and meritorious.   The greatest criminals were forward in a service, which they regarded as a propitiation for all their crimes. If they succeeded, they hoped to make their fortune in this world ; and if they died, they fondly expected a crown of glory in the world to come.   Devotion, passion, prejudice, and habit, all contributed to the same end ; and the combination of so

---

[1] Theod. Ruinart. in *Vit. Urbani II.*—Baron. *Annal. Eccles.* vol. xi.

many causes produced that wonderful emigration by which Europe, loosened from its foundations, and impelled by its moving principle, seemed in one united body to precipitate itself upon Asia [1].

The adventurers soon became so numerous, that their more experienced leaders, the counts of Vermandois, Toulouse, and Blois, the duke of Normandy, and Godfrey of Bouillon, prince of Brabant, apprehended, from the unwieldy magnitude of the force, a defeat of the grand object of the expedition. They therefore permitted a vast and undisciplined multitude A.D. to go before them, under the command of Peter the 1096. Hermit, Walter the Moneyless, and other wild fanatics.

Peter and his army, before which he walked with sandals on his feet, a rope about his waist, and every other mark of monkish austerity, took the road to Constantinople, through Hungary and Bulgaria. Godescald, a German priest, and his banditti, took the same route ; and trusting that Heaven, by supernatural means, would supply all their necessities, they made no provision for subsistence on their march. But they soon found it expedient to obtain by plunder what they had vainly expected from miracles. Want is ingenious in suggesting pretences for its supply. Their fury first discharged itself upon the Jews. As the soldiers of Jesus Christ, they thought themselves authorised to take revenge upon his murderers : they accordingly fell upon those unhappy people, and put to the sword without mercy such as would not submit to baptism, seizing their effects as lawful prize. In Bavaria alone twelve thousand Jews were massacred, and many thousands in the other provinces of Germany. But Jews not being every where found, these pious robbers, who had tasted the sweets of plunder, and were under no military regulations, pillaged without distinction, until the inhabitants of the countries through which they passed rose and cut off many thousands of their number. The Hermit, however, and the remnant of his army, at length reached Constantinople, where he received a fresh supply of German and Italian vagabonds, who were guilty of the greatest disorders, pillaging even the very churches [2].

Alexis Comnenus, the Greek emperor, who had applied to the princes of the Latin church for succour against the Turks, entertained a hope of obtaining such aid as might enable him

---

[1] These are the expressions of the Greek princess and historian, Anna Comnena.
[2] Maimbourg, *Hist. des Croisades*, tome i.

to repulse the enemy.   He was, therefore, astonished to see his dominions overwhelmed by an inundation of licentious barbarians, strangers alike to order and discipline, and to hear of the multitudes that were following, under different leaders.   He contented himself, however, with freeing himself, as soon as possible, from such troublesome guests, by furnishing them with vessels to transport themselves to the other side of the Bosphorus; and Peter soon saw himself in the plains of Asia, at the head of a Christian army, ready to give battle to the infidels. Soliman, soltan of Nice, fell upon the disorderly crowd, and slaughtered a great number almost without resistance.   Walter the Moneyless, and many other leaders, of equal distinction, were slain; but Peter the Hermit found his way back to Constantinople, where he was considered as a maniac, who had enlisted a multitude of madmen to follow him [1].

In the mean time the more disciplined armies arrived at the A.D. imperial city, and were there joined by Boëmond, son 1097. of Robert Guiscard, from motives of policy rather than piety.   Having no other inheritance than the small principality of Tarentum, and his own valour, he took advantage of the epidemic enthusiasm of the times to assemble under his banner ten thousand horsemen, well armed, and some infantry, with which he hoped to conquer a few provinces either from the Christians or Moslems.   His presence alarmed the emperor Alexis, with whom he had been formerly at war.   But the refined policy of that prince, who harassed those rapacious allies whom he wished to ruin, diverted all his apprehensions of injury from Boëmond, or the other leaders of the crusade.   He furnished them with provisions, and transported them safely into Asia; after having conciliated their affections by presents and promises, and engaged them to do him homage for the lands they should conquer from the Turks [2].   Asia, like Europe, was then divided into a number of little states, comprehended under the great ones.   The Turkish princes paid an empty homage to the khalif of Bagdad, but were in reality his masters; and the sultans, who were very numerous, weakened still farther the empire of Mohammed by continual wars with each other, the necessary consequence of divided sway.   The soldiers of the cross, therefore, who, when mustered on the banks of the Bosphorus, are said to have amounted to one hundred thousand horsemen, and six hundred thousand foot, were sufficient (even if

---

[1] Annæ Comnenæ *Alex.*   [2] Maimbourg, ubi sup.

we subtract a very large number from this exaggerated account)
to have conquered all Asia, had they been united under one
head, or commanded by leaders that observed any concert in
their operations.   But they were unhappily conducted by men
of the most independent, intractable spirit, unacquainted with
discipline, and enemies to civil or military subordination.   Their
zeal, however, their bravery, and their irresistible force, still
carried them forward, and advanced them to the great end of
their enterprise, in spite of the scarcity of provisions, the excesses of fatigue, and the influence of unknown climes.   After
an obstinate siege, they took Nice, the seat of old Soliman,   A.D.
whose army they had twice defeated : they made them-   1098.
selves masters of Antioch, the seat of another sultan, and greatly
impaired the strength of the Turks, who had so long tyrannized
over the Arabs [1].

The khalif of Egypt, whose alliance the Christians had
hitherto courted, now recovered his authority in Jerusalem, and
sent ambassadors to the leaders of the crusade, informing them,
that they might perform their religious vows, if they would
come disarmed to that city.   His overtures, however, were
rejected.   He was required to yield up the city to the Christians ;
and on his refusal, the champions of the cross advanced to the
siege of Jerusalem, the acquisition of which they considered as
the consummation of their labours.

The principal force of these pious adventurers being greatly
diminished by detachments which had been sent off, and by a
variety of disasters, did not (it is said) exceed twenty thousand
foot, and fifteen hundred horse, while the garrison of Jerusalem
consisted of forty thousand men.   But after a siege of   A.D.
five weeks, they took the city by assault, and put the gar-   1099.
rison and inhabitants to the sword without distinction.   Arms
protected not the brave, nor submission the timid : no age or sex
received mercy ; infants perished by the same sword that pierced
their mothers.   The streets of Jerusalem were covered with heaps
of slain ; and the shrieks of agony or despair still resounded from
every house; when these triumphant warriors, glutted with
slaughter, threw aside their arms, yet streaming with blood, and
advanced with naked feet and bended knees to the sepulchre of
the Prince of Peace, sang anthems to that Redeemer, who had
purchased their salvation by his death ; and while dead to the
calamities of their fellow-creatures, dissolved in tears for the suf-

---

[1] Gul. Malmesb. lib. iv.—H. Huntingd. lib. vii.—Maimbourg, tome i.

ferings of the Messiah [1].   So inconsistent is human nature with itself; and so easily, as the philosophic Hume remarks, does the most effeminate superstition associate both with the most heroic courage and with the fiercest barbarity.

About the same time that this great event happened in Asia, where Godfrey of Bouillon was chosen king of Jerusalem, and some other Christian leaders settled in their new conquests, Urban II. the author of the crusade, and the queen of France, died in Europe.   In consequence of these deaths, Philip I., who still continued to live with the countess of Anjou, was absolved by the new pope from the sentence of excommunication denounced in the council of Clermont.   But although this absolution quieted in some measure his domestic troubles, his authority, which the thunder of the church, together with his indolent and licentious course of life, had ruined, was far from being restored.   The nobles more and more affected independence : they insulted him every hour; plundered his subjects; and entirely cut off the communication between Paris and Orleans [2].

In order to remedy these evils, Philip associated his son Louis A.D. in the government, or at least declared him, with the 1100. consent of the nobility, his successor.   This young prince was, in all respects, the reverse of his father : active, vigorous, affable, generous, and free from the vices incident to youth.   He saw that in a state so corrupted nothing could be done but by force ; he therefore remained almost continually in the field, with a small body of troops about him, and these he employed against all the nobles who would not listen to the dictates of justice and equity, but treated the laws of their country with A.D. derision. He demolished their castles : he compelled them 1102. to make restitution to such as they had pillaged, and forced them to abandon the lands they had usurped from the clergy ; yet all these rigours he executed in a manner so disinterested, and with so indisputable a zeal for the public welfare, that he gained the affections of the virtuous part of the nobility, and the reverence of the people, while he restored order to the state, and preserved the monarchy from subversion [3].

This prince, who is commonly called by the old historians Louis the Gross, from his great size in the latter part of his life, July 29, succeeded his father when he was about thirty years of 1108. age.   He engaged in a long and desultory war against

---

[1] M. Paris.—Order. Vital.—Vertot, *Hist. des Chev. de Malt.* tom. i.
[2] Order. Vital.
[3] Order. Vital.—Sug. *Vit. Lud. Grossi.*

Henry I. of England, a powerful vassal, whom it was his interest to humble. The war was carried on with a variety of fortunes, but without producing any remarkable event (except what I have related in the history of England), or any alteration in the state of either kingdom [1].

A peace was at length concluded between the rival princes; after which Louis VI. devoted himself to the regulation of A.D. the interior polity of his kingdom, and humbled or over- 1128. awed the great vassals of the crown, so as to procure universal tranquillity. This he accomplished, by establishing the commons or third estate, by enfranchising the bondmen, and by diminishing the exorbitant authority of the seignorial jurisdictions; sending commissaries into the provinces to receive the complaints and redress the wrongs of such as had been oppressed by the dukes and counts, and everywhere encouraging appeals to the royal judges. But, in the midst of his prosperity, he fell into a languishing disorder occasioned by his excessive corpulence; and when his death seemed to approach, he ordered his son to be called to him, and gave him the following excellent advice: " By this sign," said he (drawing the signet from his finger, and putting it on that of the prince,) " I invest you with sovereign authority; but remember, that it is nothing but a public employment to which you are called by Heaven, and for the exercise of which you must render an account in the world to come [2]."

The king unexpectedly recovered: but he would never afterwards use any of the ensigns of royalty. He afterwards procured a considerable accession of territory to the French crown. William duke of Guienne, and earl of Poictou, desirous of making a pilgrimage to the shrine of St. James of Compostella, bequeathed his extensive territories to his daughter Eleanor, on condition of her marrying young Louis, already crowned king of France: and the duke dying in that pilgrimage, the marriage was celebrated with great pomp at Bourdeaux, where Louis VII. was solemnly inaugurated as lord of Guienne and Poictou [3].

After a reign of twenty-nine years, Louis VI. died at Aug. 4, Paris, in the sixtieth year of his age. A better man, his- 1137. torians agree, never graced the throne of France: but with the addition of certain qualities, his countrymen say, he might have made a better king. Posterity, however, may not perhaps be inclined to think worse of his character, when they are told that

---

[1] See Letter XXIV.
[2] Sug. *Vit. Lud. Grossi.* — Henault, *Hist. Chronologique,* tome i.
[3] Id. Ib.

the qualities he wanted were hypocrisy and dissimulation, and that his vices were honesty and sincerity, which led him to despise flattery, and indulge himself in a manly freedom of speech.

We should now, my dear Philip, return to the history of England; but the second crusade, which was conducted by the sovereigns of France and Germany, makes it necessary to carry farther the affairs of the continent.

LETTER XXVI.

Of the German Empire and its Dependencies, from the Death of Henry V. to the Election of Frederic I. surnamed Barbarossa.

AT the death of Henry V. it was generally supposed that the states would confer the empire on one of his nephews, Conrad, duke of Franconia, or Frederic, duke of Suabia, who were princes of great merit; but Albert, archbishop of Mentz, found means to influence the German chiefs to give their suffrages in favour of
A. D. Lothaire, duke of Saxe-Supplembourgh, who had sup-
1125. ported him in all his contests with the late emperor. This prince was accordingly crowned at Aix-la-Chapelle, in presence of the pope's nuncio. His two competitors neglected nothing in their power to obtain the throne. But after a spirited opposition, they dropped their pretensions, and were reconciled to Lothaire, who honoured them with his regard and friendship[1].

The first expedition of the new emperor was against the Bohemians, whom he obliged to sue for peace, and do homage to the empire. He next marched into Italy, where the affairs of the
A.D. church were in disorder. Innocent II. had succeeded
1130. Honorius II. by virtue of a canonical election; notwithstanding which Peter Leo, the grandson of a wealthy Jew, was also proclaimed pope by the name of Anacletus, and kept possession of Rome by means of his money, whilst his rival was obliged to retire into France, the common asylum of distressed
A.D. popes. Lothaire espoused the cause of Innocent, with
1132. whom he had an interview at Liege; accompanied him to

---

[1] *Annal. de l'Emp* tome i.—Heiss, lib. ii. cap. xi.

Rome, at the head of an army, and re-established him in the papal chair, in spite of all the efforts of Anacletus [1].

After being solemnly crowned at Rome, the emperor returned to Germany ; where, by the advice of Ernerius, a learned professor of the Roman law, he ordered that justice should be administered in the empire according to the Digest of Justinian, a copy of which was, about this time, found in Italy [2].   In the mean time Roger, duke of Apulia, who had become king of Sicily, raised an army in favour of Anacletus, and made himself master of almost all the places belonging to the holy see. Innocent retired to Pisa, which was then one of the most considerable trading cities in Europe, and again implored the assistance of Lothaire.   The emperor did not desert him in his adversity ; he put himself at the head of a powerful army, and, by the help of the Pisans, soon recovered all the patrimony of St. Peter.   The pope was re-conducted in triumph to Rome ; a circumstance which so much affected Anacletus, that he fell a martyr to the success of his competitor, literally dying of grief.

The emperor afterwards attacked the king of Sicily with success, and deprived him of Apulia and Calabria, which he transferred to Renaud, one of his own relatives [3].   On his return to Germany, he was seized with a dangerous distemper, Dec. which carried him off, near Trent.   He was distinguished 1137. by a passionate love of peace, and an exact attention to the administration of public justice.

Conrad, duke of Franconia, was now elected emperor ; but the throne was disputed by Henry the Haughty, duke of Bavaria, the name of whose family was Welf or Guelph : hence those who espoused his party were called Guelphs.   Henry died during this contest, after being divested of his dominions by the A.D. princes of the empire ; but the war was still carried on 1140. against the emperor by Guelph, the duke's brother, and Roger king of Sicily.   The imperial army was commanded by Frederic, duke of Suabia, who, being born at the castle of Weiblingen, gave to his soldiers the name of Ghibelins ; an epithet by which the imperial party was distinguished in Italy, while the pope's adherents became famous under that of Guelphs [4].

Duke Guelph and his principal followers were besieged in the castle of Weinsberg, and having sustained great loss in a sally,

[1] Jean de Launes, *Hist. du Pontificat du Pape Innocent II.*
[2] On this subject, which is involved in controversy, see Hen. Brenchmann. *Hist. Pandect.*, and Murat. *Antiq. Ital.* vol. ii.
[3] *Annal. de l'Emp.* tome i.
[4] Murat. *Dissertat. de Guelph. et Guibel.*—Sigon. lib. xi.— Krant. *Sax.* lib. viii.

were obliged to surrender at discretion. The emperor, however, instead of using his good fortune with rigour, granted the duke and his chief officers permission to retire unmolested. But the duchess, suspecting the generosity of Conrad, with whose enmity against her husband she was well acquainted, begged that she, and the other women in the castle, might be allowed to come out with as much as each of them could carry, and be conducted to a place of safety. Her request was granted, and the evacuation was immediately performed; when the emperor and his army, who expected to see every lady loaded with jewels, gold, and silver, beheld, to their astonishment, the duchess and her fair companions staggering beneath the weight of their husbands. A.D. The tears ran down Conrad's cheeks; he applauded their 1141. conjugal tenderness, and an accommodation with Guelph and his adherents was the consequence of this act of female heroism [1].

While these incidents occurred in Germany, new disorders broke out in Italy. The people of Rome formed a design of re-establishing the commonwealth, retrieving the sovereignty of their city, and abolishing the temporal dominion of the popes. Lucius A.D. II. marched against the rebels, and was killed at the foot 1145. of the Capitol; but Eugenius III., his successor, found means to reduce them to obedience, and preserve the authority of the apostolic see [2].

This pontiff afterwards countenanced the second crusade against the Saracens, preached by St. Bernard, in which the emperor and the king of France engaged, as you will soon A.D. more particularly learn. Another crusade was preached 1147. against the Moors of Spain, in which a great number of Germans, from the neighbourhood of the Rhine and Weser, engaged; and the Saxons, about the same time, undertook a crusade against the pagans of the North, whom they cut off in thousands, without making one convert [3].

Nothing remarkable happened in the empire, after the return of Conrad III. from the East, except the death of prince Henry, his eldest son, who had been elected king of the Romans. This Feb. 15, event greatly affected the emperor, who died soon after; 1152. and his nephew Frederic, duke of Suabia, surnamed Barbarossa, was raised to the imperial throne by the unanimous voice of the princes and nobles both of Italy and Germany.

---

[1] Heiss, lib. ii. cap. xii.
[2] Fleury, Hist. Eccles. vol. xiv.—Mosheim, Hist. Eccles. vol. iii.
[3] Id. ibid.

LETTER XXVII.

*History of France under Louis VII. till the Divorce of Queen
Eleanor, with some account of the second Crusade.*

Louis VII. (frequently called the Young), after he had enjoyed some years of peace, found himself engaged in one of those
civil wars which the feudal government rendered unavoid-   A.D.
able ; and having, in an expedition into Champagne, made   1143.
himself master of the town of Vitri, he ordered it to be set on
fire.   In consequence of this inhuman order, thirteen hundred
persons, who had taken refuge in the church, perished in the
flames[1].   This unjustifiable act made a deep impression upon
the king's mind, and prepared the way for a second crusade,
which now demands our attention.

The power of the Christians of the East gradually declined
in those countries which they had conquered.   The little kingdom of Edessa had already been taken by the Turks, and Jerusalem itself was threatened.   Europe was solicited for a new
armament : and as the French had begun the first inundation,
they were again applied to, in hopes of a second.

Pope Eugenius III., to whom the deputies from the East had
been sent, wisely fixed upon Bernard, abbot of Clairvaux,   A.D.
as the instrument of this pious warfare.   Bernard was   1145.
learned for those times, naturally eloquent, austere in his life,
irreproachable in his morals, enthusiastically zealous, and inflexible in his purpose.   He had long enjoyed the reputation of
a saint, was heard as an oracle, and revered as a prophet.   It is
not very surprising, therefore, that he found means to persuade
the king of France, that there was no other method of expiating
his guilt but by an expedition to the Holy Land.

At Vezelai, in Burgundy, a scaffold was erected in the market-
place, on which St. Bernard appeared by the side of   A.D.
Louis VII.   The saint spoke first; the king seconded   1146.
him, after taking the cross ; and the holy example was followed
by all present, among whom were many of the chief nobility[2].

Suger, abbot of St. Denis, then prime minister, a man very
different from Bernard, endeavoured in vain to dissuade the king

---

[1] Gul. Tyr. *Gest. Ludovic. VII.*   [2] *Epist. Ludovic. ad Suger.*

from abandoning his dominions, by telling him that he might make a much more suitable atonement for his guilt by remaining at home, and governing his kingdom in a wise and prudent manner. The eloquence of St. Bernard, and the madness of the times, prevailed over reason and sound policy. Suger, however, retained his opinion, and made no scruple of foretelling the inconveniences that would attend an expedition into Palestine ; whilst Bernard made himself answerable for its success, and extolled it with an enthusiasm that passed for inspiration.

From France this fanatical orator went to preach the crusade in Germany ; where, by the force of his irresistible eloquence, he prevailed on the emperor Conrad III., his nephew Frederic, and an infinite number of persons of all ranks, to take the cross, promising them, in the name of God, victory over the infidels. He ran from city to city, every where communicating his enthusiasm, and, if we believe the historians of those times, working miracles. It is not indeed pretended that he restored the dead to life ; but the blind received sight, the lame walked, the sick were healed. And to these bold assertions we may add the extraordinary circumstance, that while St. Bernard's eloquence operated so powerfully on the minds of the Germans, he always preached to them in French, a language which they did not understand ! or in Latin, equally unintelligible to the body of the people [1].

The hope of certain victory drew after the emperor and the king of France the greater part of the knights of their dominions ; and it is said that in each army there were reckoned seventy thousand men in complete armour, with a prodigious number of light horse, besides infantry, so that we cannot well reduce this second emigration to less than three hundred thousand persons.

The Germans took the field first, the French followed ; and A. D. 1147. the same excesses that had been committed by the warriors of the first crusade were renewed by those of the second. Hence Manuel Comnenus, who now filled the throne of Constantinople, was disquieted with the same apprehensions which the former enterprise had raised in the mind of his grandfather Alexis. If the Greek emperor behaved ungenerously to them it must therefore be ascribed to the irregularity of their own conduct, which made craft necessary where force was unequal, especially as Manuel is represented, on all other occasions, as a prince of great generosity and magnanimity. But the mortality

[1] Henault, *Hist. Chronol.* tome i.—*Annal. de l'Emp.* tome i.

which prevailed in the German army, near the plains of Constantinople, may be fully accounted for from intemperance and the change of climate, without supposing that the wells were poisoned, or that lime was mingled with the flour.

After Conrad had passed the Bosphorus, he acted with that imprudence which seems inseparable from such romantic expeditions. As the principality of Antioch was yet in being, he might have joined those Christians who remained in Syria, and there have waited for the king of France. Their numbers united would have ensured them success. But, instead of such a rational measure, the emperor, jealous both of the prince of Antioch, and the king of France, marched immediately into the middle of Asia Minor, where the soltan of Iconium, a more experienced general, drew his heavy German cavalry among the rocks, and cut A.D. his army in pieces. Conrad fled to Antioch; went to 1148. Jerusalem as a pilgrim, instead of appearing there as the leader of an army; and returned to Europe with a very small force[1].

The king of France was not more successful in his enterprise. He fell into the same snare that had deceived the emperor; and, being surprised among the rocks near Laodicea, was worsted, as Conrad had been. But Louis met with a domestic misfortune that gave him more uneasiness than the loss of his army. Queen Eleanor was suspected of an amour at the court of her uncle, the prince of Antioch, where her husband had taken refuge. She is even said to have forgotten her fatigues in the arms of a young Turk: and the conclusion of the expedition was, that Louis, like Conrad, returned to Europe with the wreck of a great army, after visiting the holy sepulchre, and being dishonoured by his pious consort. Thousands of ruined A.D. families in vain exclaimed against St. Bernard for his de- 1149. luding prophecies: he excused himself by the example of Moses; who, like him, he said, had promised to conduct the Israelites into a happy country, and yet saw the first generation perish in the desert[2].

Louis, more delicate than politic, annulled (soon after his return) his marriage with Eleanor, who immediately espoused Henry Plantagenet, presumptive heir to the crown of England; an inheritance which the accession of power arising from this alliance enabled him to obtain, while France lost the fine pro-

---

[1] Otho de Frising.—Gul. Tyr.
[2] Gul. Tyr. *Gest. Ludovic. VII.*—Henault, *Hist. Chronol.* tome i.

vinces of Guienne and Poictou, the hereditary possessions of the queen. But, before I treat of that subject, we must take a view of England during the introductory reign.

LETTER XXVIII.

Of the Affairs of England during the Reign of Stephen.

HENRY I., my dear Philip (as you have had occasion to see), left his dominions to his daughter Matilda; and as the nobility, both of England and Normandy, had sworn fealty to her, she had reason to expect the inheritance of both states. But the repugnance of the feudal barons to female succession prevailed over their good faith, and paved the way for the usurpation of Stephen, count of Boulogne, son of the count of Blois, and grandson of the Conqueror by his daughter Adela.

A.D. 1135.

Stephen was a prince of vigour and ability; but the manner in which he obtained the crown of England obliged him to grant exorbitant privileges to the nobility and clergy, who might be said to command the kingdom. The barons erected numerous castles; garrisoned them with their own troops; and, when offended, bade defiance to their sovereign, while wars among themselves were carried on with the utmost fury in every quarter. They even assumed the right of coining money, and of exercising, without appeal, every act of jurisdiction; and the inferior gentry and the people, finding no guardianship from the laws during this total dissolution of sovereign authority, were obliged to pay court to some neighbouring chieftain, and to purchase his protection, not only by yielding to his exactions, but by assisting him in his rapine upon others[1].

A.D. 1136.

While affairs continued in this distracted situation, David king of Scotland appeared at the head of a considerable army, in defence of his niece Matilda's title; and, penetrating into Yorkshire, ravaged the whole country. These barbarous outrages incensed the northern nobility, who might otherwise have been inclined to join him, and proved the ruin of Matilda's cause. The earl of Albemarle, and other powerful nobles, assembled an

---

[1] Gul. Malmesb. *Hist. Novel.* lib. i.

army at Northallerton, where a great battle was fought, Aug. 22, called the *Battle of the Standard*, from a high crucifix 1138. erected by the English on a waggon, and carried along with the army as a military ensign.   The Scots were routed with great slaughter, and the king narrowly escaped falling into the hands of the English army[1].

This success overawed the malcontents in England, and might have given stability to Stephen's throne, had he not been so elated by prosperity as to engage in a contest with the clergy, who were at that time an over-match for any monarch.   They acted entirely as barons : built castles, employed military power against their sovereign or their neighbours, and thereby increased those disorders which it was their duty to prevent, while they claimed an exemption from all civil jurisdiction, and attracted popularity by the sacredness of their character.   The bishop of Salisbury, whose castle had been seized by order of the A.D. king, appealed to the pope ; and, if Stephen and his par- 1139. tisans had not employed menaces, and even shown a disposition to execute vengeance by the hands of the soldiery, affairs would soon have come to extremity between the crown and the mitre.

Matilda, encouraged by these discontents, and invited by the rebellious clergy, landed in England, accompanied by Sept. Robert earl of Gloucester, natural son of the late king, and 30. a retinue of a hundred and forty knights.   She fixed her residence at Arundel castle, whose gates were opened to her by Adelaide of Louvain, the relict of king Henry.   Her party daily increased ; she was soon joined by several barons : war raged in all parts of the kingdom ; and it was carried on with so A.D. much fury, that the land was left uncultivated, and the 1140. instruments of husbandry were destroyed or abandoned.   A grievous famine, the natural consequence of such disorders, equally affected both parties, and reduced the spoilers, as well as the defenceless people, to extreme want[2].

Such was the wretched state of the nation, when an unexpected event seemed to promise some mitigation of the public calamities.   The royal army was defeated near the castle Feb. 2, of Lincoln ; and Stephen himself, surrounded by the 1141. enemy, and borne down by numbers, was made prisoner, after displaying extraordinary valour.   He was conducted to Gloucester, thrown into prison, and ignominiously fettered.   But he

---

[1] R. Hagulst.—Ailred. de *Bell. Standardi.*
[2] *Chron. Sax.*—*Gest. Reg. Stephani.*

was soon released in exchange for earl Robert, Matilda's brother, who was no less the soul of one party than Stephen was of the other; and the civil war was prosecuted with greater fury than ever[1].

The weakness of both parties, however, at last produced a tacit cessation of arms: and the empress Matilda retired into A.D. Normandy. But an event soon after happened, which 1148. threatened a revival of hostilities in England. Prince Henry, the son of Matilda and Geoffrey Plantagenet, had en-A.D. tered his seventeenth year, and was desirous of receiving 1149. the honour of knighthood from his grand-uncle, the king of Scotland. For this purpose he passed through England with a great retinue, and was visited by the most considerable of his partisans, whose hopes he roused by his dexterity and vigour in all manly exercises, and his prudence in every occurrence. He remained some time in Scotland, where he increased in reputation; and on his return to Normandy, he was invested in that duchy, with the consent of his mother. On his father's death, A.D. he took possession of Anjou, Touraine, and Maine, and, 1151. soon after, espoused the heiress of Guienne and Poictou, whom Louis VII. had divorced, as I have already observed, on account of her gallantries. This marriage rendered the young duke a formidable rival both to Louis and Stephen, and the prospect of his rising fortune had such an effect in England, that the archbishop of Canterbury refused to anoint Eustace, Stephen's son, as his successor, and retired beyond sea, to avoid the fury of the enraged monarch[2].

As soon as Henry was informed of these dispositions in the A.D. people, he invaded England. Stephen advanced with a 1153. superior force to meet him; and a decisive action was daily expected, when the nobles of both parties, terrified with the prospect of farther bloodshed and confusion, interposed with their good offices, and set on foot a negociation between the contending princes. The death of Eustace, which happened during the course of the treaty, facilitated its conclusion; and a convention was at length adjusted, by which it was agreed, that Stephen should possess the crown during his life; that justice should be administered in his name, even in the provinces which had submitted to his rival; and that Henry, on Stephen's death, should succeed to the kingdom of England, and William, Stephen's son, to Boulogne and his patrimonial estate[3].

[1] Gul. Malmesb. *Hist. Nov.* lib. ii.—H. Huntingd. lib. viii.   [2] Id. Ibid.
[3] *Annal. Waverl.*—Brompton.

All the barons swore to the observance of this treaty, and did homage to Henry as heir of the crown. He soon after retired from the kingdom ; and Stephen's death, which quickly followed, prevented those jealousies and feuds which were likely to Oct. 25, have ensued in so delicate a situation. The character of 1154. Stephen is differently represented by historians ; but all allow that he possessed industry, activity, and courage to a great degree ; and, if he had succeeded by a just title, he seems to have been well qualified to promote the happiness and prosperity of his subjects, notwithstanding the miseries that England suffered in his reign[1].

LETTER XXIX.

History of England, during the reign of Henry II.; with an Account of the Affairs of France.

I HAVE already observed, my dear son, that before the conquest of England by the duke of Normandy, this island was as distinct from the rest of the world in politics as in situation. The English had then neither enemies nor allies on the continent. But the foreign dominions of William and his successors connected them with the kings and great vassals of France ; and while the opposite pretensions of the popes and the emperors in Italy produced a continual intercourse between Germany and that country, the two great monarchs of France and England formed, in another part of Europe, a separate system, and carried on their wars and negociations, without meeting either with opposition or support from their neighbours ; the extensive confederacies by which the European potentates were afterwards united, and made the guardians of each other, being then totally unknown. We may therefore suppose that Louis VII. observed with terror the rising greatness of the house of Anjou or Plantagenet, whose continental dominions nearly added one-third of the whole French monarchy to the possessions of the new

---

[1] These miseries are thus described by a contemporary historian : " All England wore a face of desolation and wretchedness. Multitudes abandoned their beloved country, and went into voluntary exile : others, forsaking their own houses, built wretched huts in the church-yards, hoping for protection from the sacredness of the place. Whole families, after sustaining life as long as they could, by eating herbs, roots, and the flesh of dogs and horses, at last died of hunger ;—and you might see many pleasant villages without a single inhabitant of either sex."—*Gest. Reg. Steph.*

king of England. The jealousy occasioned by this alarming circumstance, however, as we shall have occasion to see, not only
saved France from falling a prey to England, but exalted that
kingdom to the height of grandeur which it long enjoyed. The
king of England soon became a kind of foreigner in his continental dominions ; and the other powerful vassals of the French
crown were less offended at the oppression of a co-vassal, than
pleased at the expulsion of the Anglo-Normans.

But as these important consequences could not be foreseen by
human wisdom, the king of France had maintained a strict union
with Stephen, in order to prevent the succession of Henry. The
sudden death of the usurper, however, disappointed the hopes of
Louis. Henry was received in England with the acclamations of
all classes of people ; and he began his reign with re-establishing
justice and good order, to which the kingdom had been long a
stranger. He dismissed the foreign mercenaries retained by
Stephen ; and, that he might restore authority to the laws, he
caused the new castles, which had proved so many sanctuaries to
rebels and freebooters, to be demolished[1]. To conciliate still
farther the affections of his subjects, he voluntarily confirmed
that charter of liberties which had been granted by his grandfather Henry I.[2]

Tranquillity was no sooner restored to England, than Henry
had occasion to visit his foreign dominions. Having settled the
affairs of those provinces, he returned to repress the incursions of the Welsh, who gave him much trouble, but at
length submitted. A quarrel afterwards broke out between Louis
and Henry, relative to the county of Toulouse ; and a
war commenced between the two monarchs. But these
hostilities produced no memorable event, were stopped by a cessation of arms, and soon terminated in a peace, through the
mediation of the pope.

A. D. 1157.

A. D. 1159.

This war, so insignificant in itself, is remarkable for the manner in which it was conducted. An army formed of feudal vassals, as I have had occasion to observe, commonly proved very
intractable and undisciplined, both on account of the independent spirit of the men who composed it, and because the commissions were not bestowed by the choice of the sovereign, in
reward of the military talents and services of the officers. Each
baron conducted his own vassals, and his rank in the army was

[1] Gervas. *Chron.*—Gul. Neubrig. lib. ii.
[2] See Blackstone's *Law Tracts*, vol. ii.

greater or less, in proportion to the value of his property. Even the chief command, under that of the prince, was often attached to birth; and as the military vassals were obliged to serve only forty days at their own charge, the state reaped very little benefit from their attendance. Henry, sensible of these inconveniences, levied upon his vassals in Normandy, and other provinces remote from the seat of war, a sum of money in lieu of their service; and this commutation, by reason of the greater distance, was still more advantageous to his English vassals. He therefore imposed a *scutage* of three pounds upon each knight's fee; a condition to which, though it was unusual, the military tenants readily submitted. With this money he levied an army which was more at his disposal, and whose service was more durable and constant: and in order to facilitate those levies, he enlarged the privileges of the people, and rendered them less dependent on the barons.

Having thus regulated his civil and military affairs, and accommodated his differences with Louis, Henry began to cast his eye upon the church, where abuses of every kind A.D 1162. prevailed. The clergy, among their other inventions to obtain money, had inculcated the necessity of penance as an atonement for sin. They had also introduced the practice of paying large sums of money as a composition for such penances. Thus the sins of the people became sources of revenue to the priests; and the king computed, that by this invention alone, they levied more money from his subjects than flowed into the royal treasury by all the methods of public supply [1]. Feeling for his oppressed people, he required that a layman, nominated by him, should for the future be present in all ecclesiastical courts, and that the consent of this officer should be necessary to every composition made by sinners for their spiritual offences.

But the grand difficulty was, how to carry this order into execution, as the ecclesiastics in that age had renounced all immediate subordination to the civil power. They openly claimed exemption, in cases of criminal accusation, from a trial before courts of justice. Spiritual penalties alone could be inflicted on their offences; and, as the clerical habit was thus become a protection for all enormities, they could not fail to increase. Accordingly crimes of the deepest dye were frequently committed with impunity by ecclesiastics; and it was found upon inquiry that no less than a hundred murders had been perpetrated since

---

[1] Fitz-Stephen. *Vit. Sancti Thomæ.*

the king's accession, by men in holy orders, who had never been called to account for these offences against the laws of nature and society [1].

In order to bring such criminals to justice, as the first step towards his projected reformation of the church, and in the hope of restoring union between the civil and ecclesiastical powers, so necessary in every government for the maintenance of peace and harmony, Henry exalted Thomas Becket, his chancellor, and the first man of English descent who had occupied an eminent station since the Norman conquest, to the see of Canterbury, on the death of archbishop Theobald ; rightly judging, that if the present opportunity should be neglected, and the usurpations of the clergy allowed to proceed, the crown would be in danger, from the predominating superstition of the people, of falling under subjection to the mitre.

Becket, while chancellor, was pompous in his retinue, sumptuous in his furniture, and luxurious in his table, beyond what England had seen in a subject. His house was a place of education for the sons of the chief nobility; and the king himself frequently condescended to partake of his chancellor's entertainments. His amusements were as gay as his manner of life was splendid and elegant. He employed himself at leisure hours in hunting, hawking, gaming, and horsemanship. His complaisance and good-humour had rendered him agreeable, and his industry and abilities useful to his master. He was well acquainted with the king's intention of retrenching, or rather confining within ancient bounds, all ecclesiastical privileges ; and, as he had hitherto seemed disposed to comply with every advance to that purpose, Henry considered him as the most proper person whom he could place at the head of the English church. But no prince of so much penetration ever so little understood the character of his minister.

Becket was no sooner installed in the see of Canterbury, which rendered him the second person in the kingdom, than he secretly aspired at being the first in real power, and totally altered his manner of life. He affected the greatest austerity, and the most rigid mortification : he wore sackcloth next his skin, which he changed so seldom that it was filled with dirt and vermin. His usual diet was bread, his drink water : he tore his back with the frequent discipline which he inflicted upon it ; and he daily washed on his knees, in imitation of Jesus

[1] Gul. Neubr. lib. ii.

Christ, the feet of thirteen beggars, whom he afterwards dismissed with presents [1].   Every one who made profession of sanctity was admitted to his conversation, and returned full of panegyrics on the humility as well as piety and mortification of the primate, whose aspect now wore the appearance of intense thought and profound devotion.   And all men of penetration saw that he was meditating some great design, and that the ambition and ostentation of his character had taken a new and more dangerous direction.

This champion of the church (for such he now declared himself) did not even wait till the king had matured his projects for the diminution of ecclesiastical power : he himself began hostilities, and endeavoured to overawe his sovereign by the intrepidity and boldness of his measures.   But although Henry found that he had mistaken the character of the person whom he had promoted to the primacy, he determined not to desist from his former intention of retrenching clerical usurpations : and an event soon occured which gave him a plausible pretence for putting his design in execution, and brought matters to a crisis with the archbishop.

A clergyman in Worcestershire having debauched a gentleman's daughter, had proceeded to murder the father.   The A.D. general indignation against so enormous a crime, made 1163. the king insist that the ecclesiastical assassin should be delivered up to the civil magistrate, and receive condign punishment : but Becket maintained that no greater punishment ought to be inflicted upon him than degradation.   Henry took advantage of the incident to attack all the usurpations of the clergy, and to determine at once those controversies, which daily multiplied between the civil and ecclesiastical jurisdictions.   He summoned an assembly of all the prelates of England, and put to them this concise question : " Are you, or are you not, willing to submit to the ancient laws and customs of the kingdom ?" As the bishops answered in equivocal and unsatisfactory terms, he convoked at Cla- A.D rendon a general council, for the decision of that important 1164. question.   The barons were gained to the king's party, either by the reasons he urged or by his superior authority, while the bishops were overawed by the general combination against them.   And the following laws, among others, commonly called the constitutions of Clarendon, were voted without opposition : " That no chief tenant of the crown should be excommunicated

---

[1] Fitz-Steph. *Vit. S. Thom.*

or have his lands put under an interdict, without the king's consent; that no appeals in spiritual causes should be carried before the holy see, nor any clergyman be suffered to leave the kingdom, unless with the king's permission; that laymen should not be accused in spiritual courts, except by legal and reputable promoters and witnesses; and lastly," which was the great object aimed at, " that churchmen, accused of any crime, should be tried in the civil courts [1]."

These articles were well calculated to prevent the principal abuses in ecclesiastical affairs, and to put a final stop to the usurpations of the church; and, having been passed in a national and civil assembly, they fully established the superiority of the legislature over all papal decrees and spiritual canons. But as Henry knew that the bishops would take the first opportunity to deny the authority which had enacted these constitutions, he resolved that they should affix their seals to them, and give a promise to observe them. With this view they were reduced to writing; and none of the prelates dared to oppose the king's will except Becket, who peremptorily refused to set his seal to the constitutions, though he promised *legally*, with *good faith*, and without *fraud* or *reserve*, to regard them, and even took an oath to that purpose [2].

Henry thinking he had now finally prevailed in this great contest, sent the constitutions of Clarendon to Alexander III. to be ratified. But the pope, unfriendly to the king's wishes, annulled those anti-clerical ordinances. When the archbishop found that he might depend on the papal support in an oppotion to regal authority, he expressed the deepest sorrow for his concessions. He redoubled his austerities as a punishment for his criminal compliance; and he refused to exercise any part of his ecclesiastical function, until he should receive absolution from the pope; a favour which was readily granted to him.

Incensed at the behaviour of Becket, the king summoned him to give an account of his administration of the office of chancellor, and to pay the balance due from the revenues of all the prelacies, abbeys, and baronies, which had been subject to his management during that time. This prosecution, which seems to have been more dictated by passion than by justice, or even by sound policy, threw Becket and all the clergy of England into the utmost confusion. Some bishops advised him to resign his see on receiving an acquittal; others were of opinion that he ought

[1] Gervas. *Chron.*—Matth. Par.   [2] Hoved. *Annal.*—Gervas. *Chron.*

to submit himself entirely to the king's mercy; for they were fully sensible that accounts of so much intricacy could not be readily produced, so as to satisfy a tribunal resolved to ruin and oppress him.   But the primate had too much courage to yield: he determined to brave all his enemies, to trust to the sacredness of his character for protection, and to defy the utmost efforts of royal indignation, by involving his cause with that of God and the church.   He therefore strictly prohibited his suffragans from assisting at any such trial, or giving their sanction to any sentence against him : he put himself and his see under the immediate protection of the vicegerent of Christ, and appealed to his holiness against any penalty which his iniquitous judges might think proper to inflict upon him.   " The indignation of a great monarch," added he, " with his sword, can only kill the body ; while that of the church, intrusted to the primate, can kill the soul, and throw the disobedient into infinite and eternal perdition [1]."

Appeals to Rome, even in spiritual causes, had been prohibited by the constitutions of Clarendon, and consequently were become criminal by law ; but an appeal in a civil cause, such as the king's demand upon Becket, was altogether new and unprecedented, and tended to the subversion of the English government.   Henry, therefore, being now furnished with a better pretence for his violence, would probably have pushed this affair to the utmost against the primate, had he not retired beyond sea, and found patrons and protectors in the pope and the king of France.

The violent prosecution carried on against Becket at home, had a natural tendency to turn the public favour on his side, and to make men forget his former ingratitude towards the king, and his departure from all oaths and engagements, as well as the enormity of those ecclesiastical privileges of which he affected to be the champion: and political considerations conspired with sympathy to procure him countenance and support abroad.   The king of France and the earl of Flanders, jealous of the rising greatness of Henry, were glad of an opportunity of embroiling his government.   They pretended to pity extremely the condition of the persecuted archbishop; and the pope, whose interests were more immediately concerned in abetting his cause, honoured Becket with the highest marks of distinction.   A residence was assigned to him in the abbey of Pontigny, where he

---

[1] M. Paris.   Hoved.—*Epist. S. Thom.*

lived for some years in great magnificence, partly by a pension out of the revenues of the abbey, and partly by the generosity of the French monarch [1].

The exiled primate filled Europe with exclamations against the violence he had suffered. He compared himself to Christ, who had been condemned by a lay tribunal, and who was crucified anew in the present oppressions under which his church laboured. But mere complaint did not sufficiently accord with the vehemence of Becket's temper. Having resigned his see into the hands of the pope, as a mark of submission, and received it again from the head of the church, with high encomiums on his piety and fortitude, he fulminated a sentence of excommunication against the king's chief ministers by name, as well as against every one who had favoured or obeyed the constitutions of Clarendon: he abrogated those profane laws, absolving all persons from the oaths which they had taken to observe them; and he suspended the spiritual thunder over Henry, only that he might avoid the blow by a timely repentance [2].

Henry, on the other hand, employed the temporal weapons A.D. still in his power. He suspended the payment of St. 1165. Peter's Pence, and made some advances towards an alliance with the emperor. But he at length became weary of contention, and earnestly wished for an accommodation, which, however, continued to be obstructed by mutual jealousy. When A.D. all differences seemed to be adjusted the king offered to 1168. sign the treaty, with a salvo to his *royal dignity*—a reservation which so disgusted the primate, that the negociation became fruitless. On another occasion, Becket, imitating Henry's example, offered to make his submissions with a salvo of the *honour of God* and the *liberties of the Church*—a proposal which, for a like reason, was offensive to the king, and rendered the treaty abortive. A third conference was broken off in the same manner. And even in a fourth, when all things were settled, A.D. and the primate expected to be introduced to the king, 1169. Henry refused to grant him the kiss of peace, under pretence that he had made a vow to the contrary. The want of this formality, insignificant as it may seem, prevented the conclusion of the treaty, it being regarded in those times as the only sure mark of forgiveness.

In one of these conferences, at which the French king was present, Henry said to that monarch, " There have been many

---

[1] *Epist. S. Thom.*   [2] M. Paris.—Hoved.—Fitz-Steph.

kings of England, some of greater, some of less authority than myself: there have also been many archbishops of Canterbury, holy and good men, and entitled to every kind of respect:—let Becket only act towards me with the same submission which the greatest of his predecessors paid to the least of mine, and there shall be no controversy between us [1]."

Louis was so much struck with this state of the case, and with an offer which Henry made to submit his cause to the French clergy, that he could not forbear condemning Becket and withdrawing his friendship for a time. But their common animosity against Henry soon produced a revival of their former intimacy; and the primate renewed his threats and excommunications. All difficulties between the parties, however, were at last surmounted, and Becket was permitted to return on condi- A.D. tions both honourable and advantageous—a certain proof, 1170. not only that Henry was alarmed at the interdict to which his dominions would have been subjected, if he had continued in disobedience to the church, but also that the thunder of the church must then have been truly formidable, since it could humble a prince of so haughty a spirit.

This accommodation with Becket, however, did not procure Henry even that temporary tranquillity which he had hoped to reap from it. Instead of learning moderation in the school of adversity, the primate was only animated with a spirit of revenge. Elated by the victory which he had obtained over his sovereign, he set no bounds to his arrogance. On his arrival in England, where he went from town to town in a sort of triumphal cavalcade, he notified to the archbishop of York the sentence of suspension, and to the bishops of London and Salisbury that of excommunication, which, at his solicitations, the pope had pronounced against them, because they had assisted at the coronation of prince Henry, whom the king had associated in the royalty, during the absence of the primate, and when an interdict was ready to be laid upon his dominions—a precaution thought necessary to ensure the succession of that prince. By this violent measure, Becket in effect declared war against the king himself; yet, in so doing, he appears to have been guided by policy as well as passion. Apprehensive that a prince of such profound sagacity might in the end prevail, he resolved to take all the advantage which his present victory gave him, and to disconcert the cautious measures of the king by the vehemence

[1] *Vit. S. Thom.* lib. ii.

and vigour of his own conduct. Assured of support from Rome, he had little fear of dangers which his courage taught him to despise, and which, though followed by the most fatal consequences, would still gratify his thirst of glory, and reward his ambition with the crown of martyrdom.

The suspended and excommunicated prelates visited the king at Bayeux in Normandy, and complained to him of the violent proceedings of Becket; and Henry apprehending that his whole plan of operations would be overturned, and the contest revived, which he had endeavoured by so many negociations to appease, was thrown into the most violent agitation. " Will my servants," exclaimed he, " still leave me exposed to the insolence of this imperious and ungrateful priest?"—These words seemed to call for vengeance; and four gentlemen of the king's household, Reginald Fitz-Urse, William de Tracy, Hugh de Morville, and Richard Brito, communicating their thoughts to each other, and swearing to revenge their sovereign's quarrel, secretly withdrew from court, and hastened to England. Henry informed of some menacing expressions which they had thrown out, dispatched a messenger after them, charging them to attempt nothing against the person of the primate. But these orders came too late to prevent their fatal purpose. Though they took different routes to avoid suspicion, they arrived nearly about the same time at Canterbury, where they found the primate in perfect security; and on his refusing, with his usual insolence and ob-
Dec. stinacy, to take off the excommunication and suspension
29. of the bishops, they murdered him in the cathedral, during the evening service [1].

Such was the tragical death of Thomas Becket—a prelate of the most lofty, intrepid, and inflexible spirit, who was able to cover from the world, and probably from himself, the efforts of pride and ambition, under the disguise of sanctity, and of zeal for the interests of Christ and his church. His death confirmed to the clergy those privileges which his opposition could not obtain. Though Henry had proposed to have him arrested, when informed of his renewed insolence, he no sooner heard of the murder, than he was filled with the utmost consternation. Interdicts and excommunications, weapons in themselves so terrible, would now, he foresaw, be armed with double force; in vain would he plead his innocence, and even his total ignorance of the fact; he was sufficiently guilty, if the church thought him

---

[1] *Vit. S. Thom.* lib. iii.—M. Paris.— Gervas. *Chron.*

so. These considerations gave him the deepest and most un-affected concern. He shut himself up from the light of the sun for three days, denying himself all manner of sustenance; and as soon as he recovered, in any degree, his tone of mind, A. D. he sent a solemn embassy to Rome, maintaining his inno- 1171. cence, and offering to submit the whole affair to the decision of the holy see [1].

The pope, flattered by this unexpected condescension, forbore to proceed to extremities against Henry, particularly as he was sensible that he could reap greater advantages from moderation than from violence. The clergy, in the mean time, were not idle in magnifying the sanctity of the murdered primate. Other saints had borne testimony, by their sufferings, to the general doctrine of Christianity; but Becket had sacrificed his life for the power and privileges of the church. This peculiar merit challenged (not without a ready concurrence) a tribute of grati-tude to his memory from the whole clerical body. Endless were the panegyrics on his virtues; and the miracles pretended to be wrought by his reliques were more numerous, more absurd, and more impudently attested, than those which ever filled the legend of any saint or martyr. His shrine not only restored dead men to life! it also restored cows, dogs, and horses. Presents were sent, and pilgrimages performed, from all parts of Christ-endom, in order to obtain his intercession with Heaven: and it was computed that, in one year, above a hundred thousand pil-grims arrived at Canterbury, and paid their devotions at his tomb [2].

As Henry found, however, that he was in no immediate danger from the thunder of the Vatican, he undertook the conquest of Ireland—an enterprise which he had long meditated, and for which he had obtained a bull from pope Adrian IV., but which had been deferred on account of his quarrels with the primate. Of that island something must here be said.

Ireland was probably first peopled from Britain, as Britain was from Gaul; and its first inhabitants were of Celtic origin. After the introduction of Christianity, the Irish made rapid progress in the arts of civilized life, and their ecclesiastical schools were celebrated throughout Europe. But the invasions of the Danes proved fatal to the prosperity of the unfortunate island; their best and bravest fell in the numerous battles that were fought, and at length the death of Brian Bom in the arms of victory left the country without a head; none of his successors could com-

---

[1] M. Paris.—Hoved. [2] Gul. Neubrig.—Brompt.—Hoved.

mand the obedience of all the septs, there was no longer a central government, " every man did that which seemed right in his own eyes." The chieftains of the small principalities, into which the island was divided, exercised perpetual hostilities against each other ; and the uncertain succession of the Irish princes was a continual source of domestic convulsion, the usual title of each petty sovereign to his principality being the murder of his predecessor. Courage and force, though exercised in the commission of injustice, were more honoured than pacific virtues ; and the most simple arts of life were scarcely known to the rude natives of the island.

From this short account of the state of the country, you will not be surprised, my dear Philip, when I inform you, that earl Strongbow and other enterprising knights had great success with a very inconsiderable force, and that Henry, in a progress which he made through the island, had little other occupation than to receive the homage of his new subjects. He left most of the Irish chieftains or princes in possession of their ancient terri-
A. D. tories : he bestowed lands on some of his English ad-
1172. venturers ; and after a stay of a few months, returned to Britain [1].

The pope's two legates, Albert and Theodine, to whom was committed the trial of Henry's conduct in regard to the death of Becket, had arrived in Normandy before his return, and had sent frequent letters to England, full of menacing expressions. The king hastened over to meet them; and was so fortunate as to conclude an accommodation with them on terms more easy than could have been expected. He cleared himself by oath of all concern in the murder of Becket. But as the passion which he had expressed on account of that prelate's conduct had probably been the cause of his violent death, he promised to serve three years against the infidels, either in Spain or Palestine, if the pope should require him ; and he agreed to permit appeals to the holy see, in ecclesiastical causes, surety being given that nothing should be attempted against the rights of his crown [2].

Henry seemed now to have reached the pinnacle of human grandeur and felicity. His dangerous controversy with the church was at an end, and he appeared to be equally happy in his domestic situation and his political government. But this
A. D. tranquillity was of short duration. Prince Henry, at the
1173. instigation of Louis VII., his father-in-law, insisted that

[1] M. Paris.—Giraldi Cambrensis *Hibernia Expugnat.* lib. i.
[2] M. Paris.—Hoved.

his father should resign to him either the kingdom of England on the duchy of Normandy : and the king's sons, Geoffrey and Richard, also leagued with the court of France, by the persuasions of their mother, queen Eleanor, whose jealousy, when in years, was as violent as her amorous passions in youth.

Thus Europe saw, with astonishment, the best and most indulgent of parents obliged to maintain war against his wife and his sons ; and what was still more extraordinary, several princes not ashamed to support this unnatural rebellion !—Not only the French monarch, but William king of Scotland, the earl of Flanders, and some other princes, besides many barons, both English and Norman, espoused the quarrel of young Henry and his brothers.

In order to break this alarming confederacy, the king of England humbled himself so far as to supplicate the court of Rome. Though aware of the danger of the interference of ecclesiastical authority in temporal disputes, he applied to the pope to excommunicate his enemies, and thus reduce to obedience his undutiful children, whom he was unwilling to punish by the sword. The bulls required were issued by the pontiff; but as they had not the desired effect, Henry was obliged to have recourse to arms; and he carried on war with success against the French, the Scots, and his rebellious barons in England and Normandy.

Meanwhile, sensible of his danger, and of the effects of superstition on the minds of the people, he went barefooted to Becket's tomb; prostrated himself before the shrine of the saint; remained in fasting and prayer during a whole day; watched all night the holy reliques; and, assembling a chapter of the monks, put scourges into their hands, and presented his bare shoulders to the lashes which these incensed ecclesiastics not sparingly inflicted upon him!—The next morning he received absolution; and his generals obtained, on the same day, a great victory over the Scots, which was regarded as a proof of his final reconciliation with the sainted primate and with Heaven [2].

A.D. 1174.

July 13.

The victory over the Scots was gained near Alnwick, where their king was made prisoner; and, the spirit of the English rebels being broken by this blow, the whole kingdom was restored to tranquillity. It was deemed impious longer to resist a prince who seemed to be under the immediate protection of

[1] Gul. Neubrig.—Hoved.
[2] Benedict. Abb. de Rebus Gestis Hen. II.—Hoved.

Heaven. The clergy exalted anew the merits and the powerful intercession of Becket; and Henry, instead of opposing their superstition, politically propagated an opinion so favourable to his

A.D. interests. Victorious in all quarters, crowned with glory, 1175. and absolute master of his English dominions, he hastened to Normandy, where a peace was concluded with Louis, and an accommodation adjusted with his sons.

Having thus, contrary to all expectation, extricated himself from a situation in which his throne was exposed to the utmost danger, Henry occupied himself for several years in administering justice, enacting laws, and guarding against those inconveniences which either the past convulsions of the state, or the political institutions of that age, rendered unavoidable. The success which had attended him in his wars discouraged his neighbours from making any attempts against him, so that he was enabled to complete his internal regulations without disturbance from any quarter. Some of these regulations deserve particular notice.

As the clergy, by the constitutions of Clarendon, which Henry endeavoured still to maintain, were subjected to a trial by the civil magistrate, it seemed but just to afford them the protection of that power to which they owed obedience : he therefore enacted a law, that the murderers of a clergyman should be tried before the justiciary, in the presence of the bishop, or his official ; and besides the usual punishment for murder, should be subjected to a forfeiture of their estates, and a confiscation of their goods and chattels[1]. He also passed an equitable law, that the goods of a vassal should not be seized for the debt of his lord, unless the vassal was surety for the debt ; and that in cases of insolvency, the rents of vassals should be paid to the creditors of the lord, not to the lord himself[2].

The division of England into six circuits, and the appointment of itinerant judges to each, after the example of the commissaries of Louis VI. and the *missi* of Charle-magne, formed another important ordinance of the English monarch—a measure which had a direct tendency to curb the oppressions of the barons, and to protect the inferior gentry or small landholders, and the common people in their property[3].

Not neglecting the defence of the realm, Henry published a

A.D. famous decree, called an *Assize of Arms*. He required 1181. that every person possessed of a single knight's fee should

---

[1] Gervas. *Chron.*—R. Dicet. [2] Benedict. Abb. [3] Hoved. *Annal.*

have a coat of mail, a helmet, a shield, and a lance: and that the same accoutrements should be provided by every one, for whatever number of knights' fees he might hold.   Every free layman, who had rents or goods to the value of sixteen marks, was to be armed in like manner : every one, who had ten marks, was obliged to have an iron gorget, a cap of iron, and a lance ; and all burgesses were to have a cap of iron, a lance, and a coat thickly quilted with wool, tow, or cotton, called a *Wambais* [1].

While Henry was thus employed in providing for the happiness and security of his subjects, the king of France had fallen into a most abject superstition; and was induced, by a devotion more sincere than that of his powerful rival, to make a pilgrimage in 1179 to the tomb of Becket, in order to obtain his intercession for the recovery of Philip, his son and heir.   Louis (as the sagacious Hume remarks, with no less ingenuity than pleasantry) probably thought himself entitled to the favour of that saint, on account of their ancient intimacy ; and hoped that Becket, whom he had protected while on earth, would not, now that he was so highly advanced in heaven, forget his old friend and benefactor.   The young prince was restored to health ; and, as was supposed, through the intercession of Becket.   But the king himself, soon after his return, was struck with an apoplexy, which deprived him of his judgment; and Philip II., afterwards surnamed Augustus, took upon him the administration, though he was only in his fifteenth year.   His father's death, which happened in the following year, opened his way to the throne; Sept. 18, and he proved the ablest and greatest monarch that had 1180. governed France since the reign of Charlemagne.   The superior age and experience of Henry, however, while they moderated his ambition, gave him such an ascendant over this prince, that no dangerous rivalry, for some time, arose between them.   The English monarch, instead of taking advantage of Philip's youth, employed his good offices in composing the quarrels which arose in the royal family of France : and he was successful in mediating an accommodation between the king, his mother, and uncles.   But these services were ill-requited by Philip, who when he came to man's estate, encouraged Henry's sons in their ungrateful and undutiful behaviour towards their father.

The quarrels between the king of England and his family, however, were in some measure quieted by the death of his two sons, young Henry and his brother Geoffrey; and the rivalry

---

[1] *Annal. Waverl.*—Bened. Abb.

between the elder Henry and Philip seemed, for a time, to give place to the general passion for the relief of the Holy Land.
A.D. Both assumed the cross, and imposed a tax, amounting 1188. to the tenth of all moveables, on such of their subjects as remained at home [1].

Before this great enterprise, however, could be carried into execution, some obstacles were to be surmounted. Philip, still jealous of Henry's greatness, entered into a private confederacy with prince Richard, now heir apparent to the English crown; and, by working on his ambitious and impatient temper, persuaded him to seek present power and independence at the expense of filial duty, and of the grandeur of that monarchy which he was one day to inherit. The king of England was therefore obliged, at an advanced age, to defend his dominions by arms,
A. D. and to enter on a war with France, and with his eldest 1189. surviving son—a prince of great valour and popularity, who had seduced the chief barons of Poictou, Guienne, Anjou, and Normandy. Henry, as might be expected, was unsuccessful, a misfortune which so much subdued his spirit, that he concluded a treaty on very disadvantageous terms. He agreed that Richard should receive the homage and fealty of all his subjects, and that all his associates should be pardoned; and he engaged to pay the king of France a compensation for the charges of the war [2].

But the mortification which Henry, who had been accustomed to give law to his enemies, received from these humiliating conditions, was light in comparison of what he experienced from another cause. When he demanded a list of the persons to whom he was to grant an indemnity for confederating with Richard, he was astonished to find at the head of them the name of his son John, who had always shared his confidence, and whose influence over the king had often excited the jealousy of Richard. Overloaded with cares and sorrows, and robbed of his last domestic comforts, this unhappy father broke out into expressions of the utmost despair: he cursed the day of his birth; and bestowed on his undutiful and ungrateful children a malediction which he could never be brought to retract [3]. The more his heart was disposed to friendship and affection, the more he resented the barbarous return which his four sons had successively made to his parental care; and this fatal discovery, by depriving

[1] Benedict. Abb.—Hoved.   [2] M. Paris.—Bened. Abb.
[3] Hoved.—*Annal.*

him of all that made life desirable, quite broke his spirit, and threw him in a fever, of which he soon after expired, in the fifty-seventh year of his age, at the castle of Chinon, in Anjou.

The character of Henry, both in public and private life, was almost without a blemish; and his natural endowments were equal to his moral qualities. He seems to have possessed every mental and personal accomplishment that could render him either estimable or amiable. He was of a middle stature, strong, and well proportioned; his countenance was lively and engaging; his conversation affable and entertaining; his elocution easy, persuasive, and ever at command. He loved peace, but was courageous and skilful in war; was provident without excessive caution, severe in the execution of justice without inhumanity, and temperate without austerity. He is said to have been of a very amorous complexion, and historians mention two of his natural sons by Rosamond, the fair daughter of Lord Clifford—namely, William Long-sword, and Geoffrey, archbishop of York. The other circumstances of the story commonly told of that lady seem to be fabulous, though adopted by many historical writers.

Like most of his predecessors of the Norman line, Henry spent more of his time on the continent than in England. He was surrounded by the English nobility and gentry when abroad; and the French nobles and gentry attended him when he returned to this island. All foreign improvements, therefore, in literature and politeness, in laws and arts, seem to have been then transplanted into England: and the spirit of liberty, which continued to animate the breasts of the native English, communicated itself to the Anglo-Norman barons, and rendered them not only more desirous of independence for themselves, but also more willing to concede it to the people, whom they had at first affected to despise.

The effects of this secret revolution in the sentiments of men we shall afterwards have occasion to trace. At present I must return to the affairs of Germany; remarking by the way, that Henry II. left only two legitimate sons, Richard who succeeded him, and John, who was denominated Lack-land, because he inherited no territory, though his father, at one time, had intended to leave him a large share of his extensive dominions.

LETTER XXX.

*Of the German Empire and its dependencies under Frederic I.,
with some account of the third Crusade.*

I HAVE already stated, my dear Philip, that Frederic Barbarossa, a brave and able prince, was unanimously chosen em-
A.D. peror on the death of Conrad III. His elevation seemed
1152. to give general satisfaction to Europe; but he was soon
involved in troubles, which required all his courage and capacity
to surmount, and which it would be tedious circumstantially to
relate. I shall therefore only observe, that, after having settled
the affairs of Germany, by restoring Bavaria to Henry the Lion,
A.D. duke of Saxony, he marched into Italy, in order to com-
1155. pose the disturbances of that country, and to be crowned
by the pope, in imitation of his predecessors.

Adrian IV., who then filled St. Peter's chair, was an Englishman, and a great example of what may be done by personal
merit and good fortune. The son of a mendicant, and long a
mendicant himself, strolling from country to country, he was
received as a servant to the canons of St. Rufus in Provence.
He was afterwards admitted a monk, was raised to the rank of
abbot and general of the order, and at length to the pontificate.
He was inclined to crown a vassal, but afraid of giving himself a
master: he therefore insisted upon the Roman ceremonial, which
required, that the emperor should prostrate himself before the
pope, kiss his feet, hold his stirrup, and lead the holy father's
white palfrey by the bridle the distance of nine Roman paces.

Frederic looked upon the whole ceremony as an insult, and
refused to submit to it; but the officers of the Roman chancery,
who kept a register of every thing of this kind, assured him that
his predecessors had always complied with these forms. The
ceremony of kissing the pope's feet, which he knew to be the
established custom, did not so keenly wound the emperor's pride
as that of holding the bridle and the stirrup, which he considered as
an innovation: and indeed it does not appear that any emperor,
except Lothaire II., had complied with this part of the formality.
Frederic, however, at length submitted to these affronts, as
empty marks of Christian humility, though the court of Rome
viewed them as proofs of real subjection [1].

---

[1] Bunau, *Hist. Fred. I.*—Murat. *Antiq. Ital.*

But the emperor's difficulties were not yet over. The citizens of Rome sent him a deputation, demanding the restoration of their ancient form of government, and offering to stipulate with him for the imperial dignity. " Charlemagne and Otho conquered you by their valour," replied Frederic, " and I am your master by right of succession : it is my business to prescribe laws, and yours to receive them." With these words he dismissed the deputies, and was inaugurated without the walls of the city by the pope, who put the sceptre into his hand, and the crown upon his head.

The nature of the imperial dignity was then so little understood, and the pretensions were so contradictory, that, A.D. on the one hand the Roman citizens mutinied, and a **1156.** great deal of blood was shed, because the pope had crowned the emperor without the consent of the senate and the people ; and, on the other hand, Adrian repeatedly declared, that he had conferred the *benefice* of the Roman empire on Frederic I., " *beneficium imperii Romani*" (the word *beneficium* literally signifying a fief, though his holiness explained it otherwise). Adrian also exhibited publicly in Rome a picture of the emperor Lothaire on his knees before pope Innocent II., holding both his hands joined between those of the pontiff, which was the distinguishing mark of vassalage ; and on the picture was this inscription :

Rex venit ante fores, jurans prius urbis honores ;
Post homo fit papæ, sumit quo dante coronam[1].

" Before the gates the king appears ;
  Rome's honours to maintain he swears ;
  Then to the pope sinks lowly down,
  Who grants him the imperial crown."

Frederic was at Besançon, when he received information of Adrian's insolence ; and when he expressed his displeasure at it, a cardinal then present said, " If he does not hold the empire of the pope, of whom does he hold it ?" Enraged at this impertinent speech, Otho, count Palatine, would have pierced the author of it with the sword which he wore as marshal of the empire, had not Frederic prevented him. The cardinal immediately fled, and the pope entered into a treaty. The Germans then made use of no argument but force, and the court of Rome sheltered itself under the ambiguity of its expressions. Adrian declared that *benefice*, according to his idea, signified a *favour*, not a *fief;* and he promised to put out of the way the painting of the consecration of Lothaire.

A few observations will not here be improper. Adrian IV., besieged by William, king of Sicily, in Benevento, gave up to him several ecclesiastical pretensions. He consented that Sicily should never have any legate, nor be subjected to any appeal to the see of Rome, except with the king's permission. Since that time, the kings of Sicily, though the only princes who are vassals of the pope, are in a manner popes in their own island. The Roman pontiffs, thus at once adored and abused, somewhat resembled, to borrow a remark from Voltaire, the idols which the Indians scourge to obtain favours from them.

Adrian, however, fully revenged himself upon other princes who required his occasional aid. He wrote in the following manner to Henry II. of England. "There is no doubt, and you acknowledge it, that Ireland, and all the islands which have received the faith, appertain to the Roman Church; but, if you wish to take possession of that island, in order to banish vice from it, to enforce the observance of the Christian doctrines, and with an intent of paying the yearly tribute of St. Peter's penny for every house, we with pleasure grant you our permission to conquer it[1]." Thus an English beggar, who had become bishop of Rome, bestowed Ireland, by his sole authority, upon an English king, who was desirous of gaining possession of that country, and who had power to accomplish the ambitious scheme.

The intrepid activity of Frederic Barbarossa had not only to subdue the pope, who disputed the empire; Rome, which refused to acknowledge a master; and many other cities of Italy, that asserted their independence : he had, at the same time, the Bohemians, who had mutinied against him, to humble[2] : and also the Poles, with whom he was at war. Yet all this he A.D. effected. He was successful in Poland : he quelled the 1158. tumults in Bohemia : he secured the fidelity of the German princes, by rendering himself formidable to foreign nations; and then hastened to Italy, where hopes of independence had

---

[1] M. Paris.—Girald. Cambr.

[2] [It is not improper, in this place, to state briefly the origin and progress of the kingdom erected in Bohemia by the Sarmatians or Sclavonians. For many centuries the country was governed by dukes, whom Charlemagne rendered tributary to the empire. At length, in 1086, duke Ladislaus was permitted, by the imperial diet, to assume the regal title. The country was long harassed by intestine divisions, of which the emperors took advantage for the establishment of their feudal superiority over the kings. Of nine princes who governed from the year above-mentioned to the time of Frederic Barbarossa, two died by the hand of violence, and two were deposed.]—COOTE.

arisen, in consequence of his troubles and perplexities.   In that country he found great confusion, arising not so much from the efforts of several cities to recover their freedom, as from that party rage which constantly prevailed at the election of a pope.

On the death of Adrian, two opposite factions tumultuously elected two persons, known by the names of Victor IV. and Alexander III.   The emperor's allies necessarily acknowledged the pope chosen by him ; and those princes who were A.D. jealous of the emperor acknowledged the other.   What 1159. was the shame and scandal of Rome, therefore, became the signal of division over all Europe.   Victor, Frederick's pope, had Germany, Bohemia, and one half of Italy on his side.   The other kingdoms and states submitted to Alexander III., in honour of whom the Milanese, who were avowed enemies to the emperor, built the city of Alexandria.   In vain did Frederic's party endeavour to have it called Cæsaria; the pope's name prevailed : and it was afterwards called, out of derision, *Alexandria della Paglia*, or *Alexandria built of straw*, on account of the meanness of its buildings [1].

Happy had it been for Europe if that age had produced no disputes attended with more fatal consequences ; but unfortunately this was not the case.   Milan, for maintaining its independence, was, by the emperor's orders, razed to the A.D. foundations, and salt was strewed upon its ruins ; Brescia 1162. and Placentia were dismantled by the conqueror ; and the other cities which had aimed at independence were deprived of their privileges.

Pope Alexander, who had excited these revolts, and had been obliged to take refuge in France, returned to Rome after the death of his rival ; and the civil war was renewed.   The emperor caused another pope to be elected, under the appellation A.D. of Pascal III. ; on whose decease a new pontiff was 1164. nominated by Frederic, under the title of Calixtus III.   Meanwhile Alexander was not intimidated.   He solemnly A.D. excommunicated the emperor ; and the flames of civil 1168. discord continued to spread.   The chief cities of Italy, supported by the Greek emperor and the king of Sicily, entered into an association for the defence of their liberties ; and the pope, at length, proved stronger by negociating than the emperor by fighting.   The imperialists, worn out by fatigue and disease, were routed by the confederates at the celebrated A.D. battle of Legnano ; and Frederic himself narrowly escaped 1176.

[1] Murat. *Antiq. Ital.*

being made prisoner. About the same time his eldest son was defeated at sea by the Venetians, and fell into the hands of the enemy. Alexander, in honour of this victory, sailed into the Adriatic Sea, or Gulf of Venice, accompanied by the whole senate, and after having pronounced many benedictions on that element, threw into it a ring as a mark of his gratitude and affection. Hence originated that ceremony which is annually performed by the Venetians, under the notion of espousing the Adriatic.

These misfortunes disposed the emperor to an accommodation with the pope; but his pride would not permit him to make any humiliating advances. He therefore exerted himself with so much vigour in repairing his losses, that he was soon enabled to risk another battle, in which his enemies were worsted; and being no less a politician than a general, he seized this fortunate moment to signify his desire of peace to Alexander, who received the proposal with great joy. Venice had the honour of being the place of reconciliation. The emperor, the pope, and a number of princes and cardinals repaired to that city, then A. D. mistress of the sea, and one of the wonders of the world. 1177. There Frederic put an end to his bloody dispute with the see of Rome, by acknowledging the pope, kissing his feet, and holding his stirrup while he mounted his mule [1].

This reconciliation was attended by the submission of all the towns in Italy, which had entered into an association for their mutual defence. They obtained a general pardon, and were left at liberty to use their own laws and forms of government, but were obliged to take the oath of allegiance to the emperor, as their superior lord.

Calixtus, the anti-pope, finding himself abandoned by the emperor, in consequence of that treaty, made his submissions to A.D. Alexander, who, to prevent future schisms, called a 1179. general council, in which it was decreed, that no pope should be deemed duly elected without having the votes of two-thirds of the college of cardinals in his favour [2].

The affairs of Italy being thus settled, the emperor returned to Germany, where Henry the Lion, duke of Saxony, had raised fresh troubles. He was a proud, haughty, and turbulent prince, like most of his predecessors, and not only oppressed his own subjects, but committed violences against all his neighbours. His natural pride was not diminished by his alliance with the

---

[1] Bunau, *Hist. Fred.*   [2] Mosheim, *Hist. Eccles* vol. iii.

king of England, whose daughter he had married.　Glad of an opportunity of being revenged upon Henry, who had abandoned him in his Italian expedition, Frederic convoked a diet at　A.D. Goslar, where the duke was put to the ban of the empire;　1180. and, after a variety of struggles, the sentence was put in execution.　He was divested of all his dominions, which were bestowed upon different vassals of the empire.

Sensible of his folly when too late, the degraded duke threw himself at the emperor's feet, and begged with great humility, that some of his territories might be restored.　Frederic,　A.D. touched with his unfortunate condition, referred him to　1181. a diet of the empire at Erfort.　There Henry endeavoured to acquit himself of the crimes laid to his charge.　But as it was impracticable immediately to withdraw his fiefs from the present possessors, the emperor advised him to reside in England, until the princes who had shared his dominions could be persuaded to relinquish them; and he promised that, in the mean time, no attempt should be made upon the territories of Brunswick or Lunenburg, which he would protect in behalf of Henry's children.　In compliance with this advice, the duke retired to England, where he was hospitably entertained by his father-in-law, Henry II.; and there his wife bore him a fourth son, the ancestor of the present house of Brunswick, and consequently of the family now reigning in Great Britain [1].

While tranquillity was, in this manner, happily restored to Italy and Germany, the Oriental Christians were in the utmost distress.　The celebrated Saladin, or Salaheddin, born in the small country of the Curds, (a nation always warlike, and always free,) having fixed himself by his bravery and conduct on the throne of Egypt, began to extend his conquests over the East: and finding the settlements of the Christians in Palestine a great obstacle to the progress of his arms, he bent the whole force of his policy and valour to subdue that small and barren, but important territory.　Taking advantage of the dissensions which prevailed among the champions of the Cross, and having secretly, it is said, gained the count of Tripoli, who commanded their armies, he invaded Palestine with a mighty force; and, aided by the treachery of that count, gained at Tiberias a complete victory over them, which utterly broke the power of the already languishing kingdom of Jerusalem.　The holy city itself　A.D. fell into his hands, after a feeble resistance; the kingdom　1187.

---

[1] *Annal. de l'Emp.* tome i.

of Antioch also was almost entirely subdued by his arms; and, except some maritime towns, nothing of importance remained of those boasted conquests, which, near a century before, had cost the efforts of all Europe to acquire [1].

Alarmed at this intelligence, pope Clement III. ordered a crusade to be preached through all the countries in Christendom. Europe was filled with grief and astonishment at the progress of the infidels in Asia. To give a check to it seemed the common cause of Christians. Frederic Barbarossa, who was at that time employed in making regulations for the preservation A.D. of the peace and good order of Germany, assembled a 1188. diet at Mentz, in order to deliberate with the states of the empire on this subject. He took the cross; and his example was followed by his son Frederic, and the most distinguished of the German nobles, ecclesiastics as well as laymen. The rendezvous was appointed at Ratisbon; and, to prevent the inconvenience of too great a multitude, the emperor decreed, that no person should take the cross who could not afford to expend three marks of silver. But notwithstanding this regulation, wisely calculated to prevent those necessities which had ruined the former armies, so great was the zeal of the Germans, that adventurers assembled to the number of one hundred and fifty thousand fighting men, well armed, and provided with necessaries for the expedition [2].

Before his departure, Frederic made a progress through the principal cities of Germany, accompanied by his son Henry, to whom he intended to commit the government of the empire; and that he might omit nothing necessary to the preservation of peace and harmony during his absence, he endeavoured so to regulate the succession to his dominions that none of his children should have cause to complain, or any pretext to disturb A.D. the public tranquillity. He then marched at the head of 1189. thirty thousand men, by the way of Vienna, to Presburg, where he was joined by the rest of his army. He thence proceeded through Hungary, into the territories of the Greek emperor, Isaac Angelus, who, notwithstanding his professions of friendship, had been detached from the interest of Frederic by Saladin's promises and insinuations, and took all opportunities of harassing the Germans in their march. Incensed at this perfidy, Frederic laid the country under contribution; defeated a body of Greeks that attacked him by surprise; and compelled

---

[1] Maimbourg, *Hist. des Croisades.*   [2] Id. Ibid.—Bunau.

Isaac to sue for peace. He wintered at Adrianople : crossed the Hellespont in the spring; defeated the infidels in A. D. several battles; pillaged the city of Iconium, and crossed 1190. Mount Taurus. All Asia was filled with the terror of his arms. He seemed to be among the soldiers of the cross what Saladin was among the Turks—an able politician, and a good general, tried by fortune. The Oriental Christians therefore flattered themselves with certain relief from his assistance. But their hopes were suddenly blasted. This great prince, while leading his army over a narrow bridge that crossed the Selef or Calocadnus, unfortunately fell into the river, and being hurried away by its rapid stream, was drowned. The bold enterprise he had undertaken was consequently frustrated.

Thus perished Frederic I., in the sixty-ninth year of his age, and the thirty-ninth of his reign—a prince of a firm spirit and strong talents, who had the good of his country always at heart, and who supported the dignity of the empire with great courage and reputation. He was succeeded on the imperial throne by his son Henry VI. surnamed the Severe. But before entering on the reign of this prince, I must carry forward the history of the third crusade, continued by the kings of France and England.

LETTER XXXI.

Of the affairs of France and England, from the death of Henry II. to the grant of the Great Charter by King John, with a farther account of the third Crusade.

THE death of Henry II. was an event esteemed equally fortunate by his son Richard, and by Philip Augustus, king of France. Philip had lost a dangerous and implacable enemy, and Richard acquired that crown which he had long wished to A.D. possess. Both seemed to consider the recovery of the 1189. Holy Land as the sole purpose of their government; yet neither was so much impelled to that pious undertaking by superstition, as by the love of military glory. The king of England, in particular, carried so little appearance of sanctity in his conduct, that, when advised by a zealous preacher of the crusade (who from that merit had acquired the privilege of speaking the boldest

2

truths) to disengage himself from his pride, avarice, and volup-
tuousness, which the priest affectedly called the king's favourite
daughters, Richard promptly replied, "You counsel well! and
I hereby dispose of the first to the Templars, of the second to
the Benedictines, and the third to my bishops[1]."

The reiterated calamities attending the former crusades taught
the kings of France and England the necessity of trying another
route to the Holy Land. They determined to conduct their
armies thither by sea; to carry provisions with them; and, by
means of their naval power, to maintain an open communication
with their own states, and with all the western parts of
Europe. The first place of rendezvous was the plain of
Vezelay, where Philip and Richard found their armies amount to
one hundred thousand men. They renewed their promises of
mutual friendship; pledged their faith not to invade each other's
dominions during the crusade, and exchanging the oaths of all
their barons and prelates to the same effect, then separated. Philip
took the road to Genoa; Richard directed his course to Marseilles; both with a view of meeting their fleets, whichwer e
severally appointed to assemble in those harbours[2]. They put
to sea together; and both, nearly about the same time, were
obliged by stress of weather to take shelter in Messina, where
they were detained during the whole winter. This event laid
the foundation of animosities between them, which were never
afterwards entirely removed, and proved ultimately fatal to their
enterprise.

A.D.
1190.

But before I proceed to that subject, a few words relative to
the characters and circumstances of the two princes will be necessary. Philip and Richard, though professed friends, were, by
the situation and extent of their dominions, rivals in power; by
their age and inclinations, competitors for glory; and these causes
of emulation, which might have stimulated them to martial
efforts, had they been acting in the field against the common
enemy, soon excited quarrels, during their present leisure, between monarchs of such fiery tempers. Equally haughty, ambitious, intrepid, and inflexible, they were irritated at the least
appearance of injury, and did not endeavour, by mutual condescension, to efface those occasions of complaint which arose between them. Other sources of discord were added to the natural
rivalry of their characters.

William II., king of Naples and Sicily, had married Joan,

---

[1] M. Westminst.   [2] G. Vinis. *Iter. Hierosol.* lib. ii.

sister to Richard; and that prince, dying without issue, had bequeathed his dominions to his paternal sister Constantia, the
only legitimate surviving offspring of Roger the First, king of
Sicily of the race of Guiscard, the Norman hero.   The emperor
Henry VI. had married this princess, in expectation of that rich
inheritance; but Tancred, her natural brother, by his interest
among the Sicilian nobles, had gained possession of the throne.
The approach of the crusaders gave him apprehensions for his
unstable government: and he was uncertain whether he had
most reason to dread the presence of the French or English
monarch.   Philip was engaged in strict alliance with the emperor, Tancred's competitor; Richard was disgusted at his rigour
towards the queen-dowager, whom he confined in Palermo, because she had opposed his succession to the crown.   Sensible,
therefore, of the delicacy of his situation, Tancred resolved to
pay his court to both these princes; and he was not unsuccessful
in his endeavours.   He persuaded Philip, that it would be highly
improper to interrupt theexpedition against the infidels by any
attack upon a Christian prince: he restored queen Joan to her
liberty, and even found means to form an alliance with her
brother.   But before this friendship was cemented, Richard,
jealous both of Tancred and the inhabitants of Messina, had
taken up his quarters in the suburbs, and possessed himself of a
small fort which commanded the harbour.   The citizens took
umbrage.   Mutual insults and injuries passed between them and
the English soldiers.   Philip, who had quartered his troops in
the town, endeavoured to accommodate the quarrel, and held a
conference with Richard for that purpose.

While the two kings, who met in the open fields, were engaged
in discourse on this subject, a body of the Sicilians seemed to be
drawing towards them.   Richard, always ardent and impatient,
pushed forward, in order to learn the cause of that extraordinary
movement: and the English adventurers, insolent from their
power, and inflamed by former animosities, wanting only a pretence to attack the Messinese, chased them from the field, and
drove them into the town, and entered with them at the gates.

The king employed his authority to restrain them from pillaging or massacring the defenceless inhabitants; but he gave
orders that the standard of England, in token of his victory
should be erected on the walls.   Philip, who considered the city
of Messina as his quarters, exclaimed against the arrogance of
the English monarch, and ordered some of his men to pull down

the standard. But Richard informed him by a mesenger, that although he would willingly himself remove that ground of offence, he would not permit it to be done by others; and if the French king attempted such an insult on his dignity, he should not succeed but by the utmost effusion of blood. Philip, satisfied with this species of haughty condescension, recalled his orders, and the difference was seemingly accommodated; but the seeds of rancour and jealousy still remained in the breasts of the two monarchs[1].

After leaving Sicily, the English fleet was assailed by a furious tempest. It was driven on the coast of Cyprus, and some of the vessels were wrecked. Isaac Comnenus, despot of Cyprus, who had assumed the magnificent title of emperor, pillaged the ships that were stranded, and threw the seamen and passengers into prison. But Richard, who arrived soon after, took ample vengeance on him for the injury. He disembarked his troops; defeated the tyrant, who opposed his landing; entered Limisso by storm; obtained a second victory; obliged Isaac to surrender at discretion; established governors over the island; and afterwards conferred it as a sovereignty upon Guy de Lusignan, the expelled king of Jerusalem. Thrown into prison, and loaded with irons, the Greek prince complained of the little respect with which he was treated. Richard ordered silver fetters to be made for him; and this phantom of an emperor, pleased with the distinction, expressed a sense of the generosity of his conqueror[2].

A.D. 1191.

Before the two kings arrived in Asia, Ptolemais, or Acre, had long been besieged by a numerous Christian army, and defended by the utmost efforts of Saladin. Of the German crusaders, so many had retired from the imperial ensigns, and such a number had fallen by pestilence and famine, that only a very small force had joined the besiegers of Acre, whose zeal began sensibly to decline. But the appearance of Philip and Richard inspired them with new life; and emulation between the rival kings and rival nations produced extraordinary acts of valour. Richard especially, animated by a courage more precipitate than that of Philip, and more agreeable to the romantic spirit of the age, drew the attention of all the religious and military world, and acquired a great and splendid reputation. Ptolemais was taken. The garrison, reduced to extremity, surrendered the place; and the governor engaged that Saladin, besides paying a large sum as

---

[1] Bened. Abb.—M. Paris.—G. Vinis.　　　[2] Bened Abb.—M. Paris.

a ransom, should release two thousand five hundred Christian prisoners, and restore the wood of the true cross [1].

Thus was this famous siege, which had so long engaged the attention of all Europe and Asia, brought to the desired close, after the loss of three hundred thousand men, exclusive of persons of superior rank; six archbishops, twelve bishops, forty earls, and five hundred barons. But the French monarch instead of pursuing the hopes of farther conquest, and redeeming the holy city from slavery, being disgusted with the ascendant assumed and acquired by the king of England, and having views of many advantages which he might reap by his presence in Europe, declared his resolution of returning to France; and he pleaded his ill state of health as an excuse for his desertion of the common cause. He left however to Richard ten thousand of his men, under the command of the duke of Burgundy, and he renewed his oath not to commit hostilities against that prince's territories during his absence. But no sooner did he reach Italy than he applied to pope Celestine III. for a dispensation from his vow; and though that request was not granted, he still proceeded, but after a more concealed manner, in his unjust projects. He seduced prince John, king Richard's brother, from his allegiance, and did every thing possible to blacken the character of that monarch himself, representing him as privy to the murder of the marquis de Montferrat, who had been taken off by an Asiatic chief, called *The old Man of the Mountain*, the prince of the *Assassins*—a word which has found its way into most European languages, from the practice of these bold and determined ruffians, against whom no precaution was sufficient to guard any man, however powerful [2].

But Richard's heroic actions in Palestine formed the best apology for his conduct. The Christian adventurers, under his command, resolved to attempt the siege of Ascalon, in order to prepare the way for that of Jerusalem; and they marched along the sea-coast with that intention. Saladin took measures to obstruct their passage; and on this occasion was fought one of the greatest battles of that age, and the most celebrated for the military genius of the commanders, for the number and valour of the troops, and for the variety of events which attended it. The right and left wings of the Christian army were broken in the beginning of the day, and in danger of being totally

A.D. 1192.

---

[1] Benedict. Abb.—Saladin delayed to ratify the treaty; and the Saracen prisoners, to the number of 2700, were inhumanly butchered.—*Vinisauf*, lib iv.
[2] Walt. Hemingf.—Brompt.—Vinis.

defeated, when Richard, who commanded the centre, and led on the main body, restored the battle. He attacked the enemy with admirable intrepidity and presence of mind; performed the part of a consummate general and gallant soldier; and not only gave the two wings leisure to recover from their confusion, but obtained a complete victory over the Saracens, eight thousand of whom are said to have been slain in the field [1]. Ascalon soon after fell into the hands of the Christians; other sieges were carried on with success; and Richard was even able to advance within sight of Jerusalem, the great object of his hopes and fears, when he had the mortification to find, that he must abandon all thoughts of immediate success, and put a stop to the career of victory.

Animated with an enthusiastic ardour for these holy wars, the champions of the cross, at first, laid aside all regard to safety or interest in the prosecution of their pious purpose; and, trusting to the immediate assistance of heaven, set nothing before their eyes but fame and victory in this world, and a crown of glory in the next. But long absence from home, fatigue, disease, famine, and the varieties of fortune which naturally attend war, had gradually abated that fury which nothing was able instantly to allay or withstand. Every leader, except the king of England, expressed a desire of speedily returning to Europe; so that there appeared an absolute necessity of abandoning, for the present, all hopes of farther conquest, and of securing the acquisitions of the adventurers by an accommodation with Saladin. Richard therefore concluded a truce with that monarch; stipulating that Ptolemais, Joppa, and other sea-port towns of Palestine, should remain in the hands of the Christians, and that every one of that religion should have liberty to perform his pilgrimage to Jerusalem unmolested [2]. This truce was concluded for three years, three months, three weeks, three days, and three hours, a magical number, suggested by a superstition well suited to the object of the war.

A. D. 1193. Saladin died at Damascus, soon after he had concluded the truce with the crusaders. He was a prince of great generosity and valour; and it is truly memorable, that, during his fatal illness, he ordered his winding-sheet to be carried as a standard through every street of the city, while a crier went before the person who bore that ensign of mortality, and proclaimed with a loud voice, "This is all that remains to the

---

[1] G. Vinis. lib. iv.   [2] W. Hemingf. lib. ii.—G. Vinis. lib. vi.

mighty Saladin, the conqueror of the East!" His last will is also remarkable. He ordered alms to be distributed among the poor, without distinction of Jew, Christian, or Mohammedan, intending by this bequest to intimate, that all men are brethren, and that when we would assist them, we ought not to inquire what they believe, but what they feel—an admirable lesson to Christians, though from an infidel. But the advantage of science, of moderation, and humanity, seemed at that time to be on the side of the Saracens.

After the truce Richard had no farther business in Palestine; and the intelligence which he received of the intrigues of his brother John and the king of France made him sensible that his presence was necessary in Europe. Not thinking it safe to pass through Philip's dominions, he sailed to the Adriatic; and being shipwrecked near Aquileia, he assumed the habit of a pilgrim, with an intention of taking his journey secretly through Germany. But his liberality and expenses betrayed him. He was arrested and thrown into prison by Leopold, duke of Austria, whom he had offended at the siege of Ptolemais, and who sold him to the emperor Henry VI., who had taken offence at Richard's alliance with Tancred, king of Sicily, and was glad to have him in his power[1]. Thus the gallant king of England, who had filled the world with his renown, found himself, during the most critical state of his affairs, confined to a dungeon, in the heart of Germany, loaded with irons, and entirely at the mercy of his enemy, the basest and most sordid of mankind[2].

While the high spirit of Richard suffered every insult and indignity in Germany, the king of France employed force, intrigue, and negociation, against the dominions and the person

---

[1] Gul. Neubr.—M. Paris.
[2] *Chron.* T. Wykes.—The vindictive enemies of Richard, if we believe the literary history of the times, carefully concealed not only the place of his confinement, but even the circumstance of his captivity; and both might have remained unknown but for the grateful attachment of a Provençal bard, or minstrel, named Blondel, who had shared that prince's friendship, and experienced his bounty. Having travelled over the European continent to learn the history of his beloved patron, who was a poet as well as a hero, Blondel accidentally gained intelligence of a certain castle in Germany, where a prisoner of distinction was confined, and guarded with great vigilance. Persuaded, by a secret impulse, that this prisoner was the king of England, the minstrel repaired to the place. But the gates of the castle were shut against him, and he could obtain no information relative to the name or quality of the unhappy person whom it secured. In this extremity, he thought of an expedient for making the desired discovery. He chanted, with a loud voice, some verses of a song which had been composed partly by himself, partly by Richard; and to his unspeakable joy, on making a pause, he heard it re-echoed and continued by the royal captive. To this discovery the English monarch is said to have eventually owed his release.—*Histoire des Troubadours.* But historians now regard this account as fabulous.

of his unfortunate rival.   He made large offers to the emperor, if he would deliver into his hands the royal prisoner: he formed an alliance by marriage with Denmark, desiring that the ancient Danish claim to the crown of England might be transferred to him; he concluded a treaty with prince John, who is said to have done homage to him for the English crown; and he invaded Normandy, while the traitor John attempted to make himself master of England [1].

Richard, being produced before a diet of the empire, made such an impression on the German princes by his spirit and eloquence, that they exclaimed loudly against the conduct of the emperor.   The pope also threatened him with excommunication; and, although Henry had listened to the proposals of the king of France and prince John, he found that it would be impracticable for him to execute his and their base purposes, or to detain the king of England longer in captivity.   He therefore concluded a treaty with Richard for his ransom, and agreed to restore him to his freedom for one hundred and fifty thousand marks of silver [2], about three hundred thousand pounds of our present money; an enormous sum in those days.

As soon as Philip heard of Richard's release, he wrote to his confederate John in these emphatical words; " Take care of yourself! the devil is let loose."   How different on this occasion were the sentiments of the English!—Their joy was extreme on the appearance of their king, who had acquired so much glory, and spread the reputation of their name to the farthest East.   After renewing the ceremony of his coronation, amid the acclamations of all ranks of people, and reducing the fortresses which still remained in the hands of his brother's adherents, Richard passed over with an army into Normandy, eager to make war upon Philip, and to revenge himself for the injuries he had sustained from that monarch [3].

A. D. 1194.

When we consider two such powerful and warlike monarchs, inflamed with personal animosity, enraged by mutual injuries, excited by rivalry, impelled by opposite interests, and instigated by the pride and violence of their own tempers, our curiosity is naturally raised, and we expect an obstinate and furious war, distinguished by the greatest events, and concluded by some remarkable catastrophe.   We find ourselves, however, entirely disappointed; the reduction of a castle, the surprisal of a straggling party, a rencounter of horse, resembling more a rout than a battle,

---

[1] M. Paris.—W. Hemingf.—Hoved.
[2] Rym. Fœdera, vol. i.   [3] Hoved. *Annal.*

comprehend the whole of the exploits on both sides! a certain proof, as a great historian observes, of the weakness of princes in that age, and of the little authority which they possessed over their refractory vassals [1].

During this war, which continued, with short intervals, till Richard's death, prince John deserted Philip, threw himself at his brother's feet, craved pardon for his offences, and was received into favour, at the intercession of his mother. " I forgive him with all my heart," said the king; " and hope I shall as easily forget his offences as he will my pardon [2]."

Peace was ready to be concluded between England and France, when Richard was unfortunately slain before an inconsiderable castle which he had invested. The story is thus related:

Vidomar, viscount of Limoges, had found a treasure, of which he sent part to the king, as a present. But Richard claimed the whole: and, at the head of some Brabançons, besieged the castle of Chalus, to enforce the viscount's compliance with his demand. The garrison offered to surrender; but the king replied, that since he had taken the trouble of besieging the place in person, he would take it by force, and hang every one of them. While he was surveying the castle, one Bertrand de Gourdon, an archer, took aim at him, and pierced his shoulder with an arrow. The king, however, gave orders for an assault; took the place, and ordered all the garrison to be hanged, except Gourdon, whom he reserved for a more cruel execution [3].

Richard's wound was not in itself dangerous, but the unskilfulnes of the surgeon rendered it mortal. When April 6, he found his end approaching, he sent for Gourdon, and de- 1199. manded the reason why he sought his life. " My father and my two brothers," replied the undaunted soldier, " fell by your sword, and you intended to have put me to death. I am now in your power, and you may do your worst; but I shall endure the most severe torments with pleasure, provided I can think that Heaven has afforded me such great revenge, as, with my own hand, to be the cause of your death." Struck with the boldness of this reply, and humbled by his approaching dissolution, Richard ordered the prisoner to be set at liberty, and a sum of money to be given to him. But the Brabançon leader Marcadée, a stranger to such generosity, seized the unhappy man, flayed him alive, and then hanged him [4].

[1] Hume's *Hist. of Eng.* vol. ii. [2] M. Paris.
[3] Hoved.—Brompton.
[4] Hoved.—The Brabançons were ruffian mercenaries, formed out of the numerous

The military talents of Richard formed the most shining part of his character. No man, even in that romantic age, carried personal courage or intrepidity to a greater height; and this quality obtained him the appellation of *Cœur de Lion*, or the *Lion-hearted hero*. As he left no issue, he was succeeded by his brother John.

The succession was disputed by Arthur, duke of Bretagne, son of John's elder brother Geoffrey; and the barons of Anjou, Maine, and Touraine, declared in favour of this young prince's title. The king of France also assisted him; and every thing A.D. promised success, when Arthur was unfortunately taken 1203. prisoner by his uncle John, and inhumanly murdered.

The fate of this unhappy prince is differently related; but the following account seems the most probable. After having employed unsuccessfully different assassins, John went in a boat by night to the castle of Rouen, where Arthur was confined, and ordered him to be brought forth. Aware of his danger, and subdued by the continuance of his misfortunes, and by the approach of death, the brave youth, who had before gallantly maintained the justice of his cause, threw himself on his knees before his uncle, and begged for mercy. But the barbarous tyrant, making no reply, stabbed his nephew to the heart, and, fastening a stone to the dead body, threw it into the Seine[1].

John's misfortunes commenced with his crime. He was from that moment detested by his subjects, both in England and on the continent. The Bretons, disappointed in their fondest hopes, waged implacable war against him, in order to revenge the murder of their duke: and they carried their complaints before the French monarch, as superior lord, demanding justice for the inhuman violence of John. Philip received their application with pleasure: he summoned John to be tried before him and his peers; and on his non-appearance, he was declared guilty of felony and parricide, and all his foreign dominions were declared to be forfeited to the crown of France[2].

Nothing now remained but the execution of this sentence to complete the glory of Philip, whose active and ambitious spirit had long with impatience borne the neighbourhood of so power-

bands of robbers, who, during the middle ages, infested every country of Europe, and set the civil magistrate at defiance. Excluded from the protection of general society, these banditti formed a kind of government among themselves. Troops of them were sometimes admitted into the service of princes or barons, and they often acted in an independent manner, under leaders of their own. *Gul. Neubrig.*

[1] T. Wykes.—W. Hemingf.—M. Paris.—H. Knighton.
[2] *Annal. Margan.*—M. Westm.

ful a vassal as the king of England. He therefore embraced with eagerness and joy the present opportunity of annexing to the French crown the English dominions on the continent; a project which the sound policy of Henry II. and the military genius of Richard I. had rendered impracticable to the most vigorous efforts, and most dangerous intrigues, of this able A.D. and artful prince. But the general defection of John's 1204. vassals rendered every enterprise easy against him; and Philip not only re-united Normandy to the crown of France, but successively reduced Anjou, Maine, Touraine, and part of Poictou, under his dominion [1]. Thus, by the baseness of one prince, and the intrepidity of another, the French monarchy received, in a few years, such an accession of power and grandeur as, in the ordinary course of affairs, it might have required several ages to attain.

John's arrival in England completed his disgrace. He saw himself despised by the barons, on account of his pusillanimity and baseness: and a quarrel with the clergy drew upon him the contempt of that order, and the indignation of Rome. The papal chair was then filled by Innocent III., who, having been exalted to it at a more early period of life than usual, and being endowed with a lofty and enterprising genius, gave full scope to his ambition; and attempted, perhaps more openly than any of his predecessors, to convert that spiritual superiority which was allowed to him by the European princes, into a real dominion over them; strongly inculcating that extravagant maxim, " that no princes or bishops, civil governors, or ecclesiastical rulers, have any lawful power in church or state, but what they derive from the pope." To this pontiff an ap- A.D. peal was made relative to the election of an archbishop of 1206. Canterbury. Two primates had been elected; one by the monks or canons of Christ-Church, Canterbury, and one by the suffragan bishops, who had the king's approbation. The pope declared both elections void; and commanded the monks to choose cardinal Langton, an Englishman by birth, but educated in France, and connected by his interests and attachments with the see of Rome. The monks complied; and John, in- A. D. flamed with rage at such an usurpation of his prerogative, 1207. expelled them from the convent; swearing by God's teeth, his usual oath, that if the pope should give him any further disturbance, he would banish all the bishops and clergy of England [2].

---

[1] Nic. Triverti *Annal.* [2] M. Paris.

Innocent, however, knew his weakness, and laid the kingdom under an interdict, the grand instrument of vengeance and policy employed against sovereigns by the court of Rome.

The execution of this sentence was artfully calculated to strike the senses in the highest degree, and to operate with irresistible force on the superstitious minds of the people. The nation was suddenly deprived of all exterior exercise of its religion: the altars were despoiled of their ornaments; the crosses, the reliques, the images, the statues of the saints, were laid on the ground; and, as if the air itself had been profaned, and might pollute them by its contact, the priests carefully covered them up, even from their own approach and veneration. The use of bells entirely ceased in the churches: bells themselves were removed from the steeples, and laid on the ground with the other sacred utensils. Mass was celebrated with shut doors, and none but the priests were admitted to that holy institution. The laity partook of no religious rite, except baptism of new born infants, and the communion to the dying. The dead were not interred in consecrated ground; they were thrown into ditches, or buried in the common fields; and their obsequies were not attended with prayers, or any hallowed ceremony. The people were prohibited the use of meat, as in Lent, and debarred from all pleasures and amusements. Every thing wore the appearance of the deepest distress and of the most immediate apprehensions of Divine vengeance and indignation [1].

While England groaned under this dreadful sentence, a very extraordinary scene disclosed itself on the continent. The pope published a crusade against the Albigenses, a species of sectaries in the south of France, whom he denominated heretics, because they neglected the established ceremonies of the church, and A.D. opposed the power and influence of the clergy. Moved 1209. by that mad superstition, which had hurried such armies into Asia, and by the reigning passion for wars and adventures, people flocked from all parts of Europe to the standard of Simon de Montfort, the general of this crusade. The count of Toulouse, who protected the Albigenses, was stripped of his dominions; and these unhappy people, though

[1] John, besides banishing the bishops, and confiscating the estates of all the ecclesiastics who obeyed the interdict, took a very singular and severe revenge upon the clergy. In order to distress them in the tenderest point, and at the same time expose them to reproach and ridicule, he threw into prison all their concubines. (M. Paris—*Ann. Waverl.*) These concubines were a sort of inferior wives, politically indulged to the clergy by the civil magistrate, after the canons of the church had enjoined celibacy to the members of that sacred body. Padre Paolo, *Hist. Conc. Trid.* lib. i.

the most inoffensive of mankind, were exterminated with all the circumstances of the most unfeeling barbarity [1].

Innocent, having thus made trial of his power, prosecuted his ecclesiastical vengeance against the king of England, by giving authority to the bishops of London, Ely, and Worcester, to denounce against him the sentence of excommunication. His subjects were absolved from their oath of allegiance, and a A.D. sentence of deposition soon followed. As the last sentence 1212. required an armed force to execute it, the pontiff fixed on the French king as the person into whose hands he could most properly intrust so terrible a weapon : and he offered to that monarch, besides the remission of all his sins, and endless spiritual benefits, the kingdom of England as the reward of his labour [2].

Seduced by the prospect of present interest, Philip accepted the pope's liberal offer, although he thereby ratified an authority which might one day hurl him from his throne, and which it was the common concern of all princes to oppose. Partly by the zeal of the age, partly by the personal regard universally paid to him, he prepared a force which seemed equal to the greatness of his enterprise. John, on the other hand, issued out writs, requiring the immediate attendance of his military vassals at Dover, and even the service of all able-bodied men, to defend the kingdom in this dangerous extremity. An infinite number appeared, out of which he selected an army of sixty thousand men. He had also a formidable fleet at Portsmouth, and he might have relied on the fidelity of both ; not indeed from their attachment to him, but from that spirit of emulation which has so long subsisted between the natives of England and France.

A decisive action was expected between the two kings, when the pope artfully tricked them both, and took to himself A.D. that tempting prize which he had pretended to hold out 1213. to Philip. This extraordinary transaction was negociated by Pandolfo, the pope's legate. In his way through France, he observed Philip's great preparations, and highly commended his zeal and diligence. He thence passed to Dover, under pretence of treating with the barons in favour of the French king, and had a conference with John on his arrival. He magnified to that prince the number of the enemy, and the disaffection of his own subjects ; intimating, that there was yet one way, and but one, to secure himself from the impending danger ; namely, to put himself under the protection of the pope, who, like a kind

---

[1] *Hist. Albig.*   [2] M. Paris.—M. Westminst.

and merciful father, was still willing to receive him into his bosom.

John, labouring under the apprehensions of present terror, listened to the insidious proposal, and abjectly agreed to hold his dominions as a feudatory of the church of Rome. In consequence of this agreement, he did homage to the pope in the person of his legate Pandolfo, with all the humiliating rites which the feudal law required of vassals. He came disarmed into the presence of the legate, who was seated on a throne : he threw himself on his knees before it : he lifted up his joined hands, and put them between those of Pandolfo, and swore fealty to the pope in the following words : " I John, by the grace of God, king of England and lord of Ireland, for the expiation of my sins, and out of my own free will, with the advice and consent of my barons, give to the church of Rome, and to pope Innocent III. and his successors, the kingdoms of England and Ireland, with all the rights belonging to them ; and I will hold them of the pope, as his vassal. I will be faithful to God, to the church of Rome, to the pope my lord, and to his successors lawfully elected : and I bind myself to pay him a tribute of one thousand marks of silver yearly ; namely, seven hundred for the kingdom of England, and three hundred for Ireland[1]."

Part of the money was immediately paid to the legate, as an earnest of the subjection of the kingdom ; after which the crown and sceptre were delivered to him. The insolent Italian trampled the money under his feet, to intimate the pope's superiority and the king's dependent state, and kept the *regalia* five days ; then returned them to John, as a favour from the pope.

During this disgraceful negociation, Philip waited impatiently at Boulogne for the legate's return, in order to put to sea. The legate at length returned ; and the monarch, to his great astonishment, was desired to relinquish all thoughts of attacking England, as it was then a fief of the church of Rome, and its king a vassal of the holy see. Philip was enraged at this intelligence : he swore that he would not be a dupe to such hypocritical pretences ; nor would he have desisted from his enterprise but for more weighty reasons. His fleet was nearly destroyed by the navy of England ; and Otho IV., who at once disputed the empire with Frederic II., and Italy with the pope, had entered into alliance with his uncle, the king of England, in order to oppose the designs of France, now become formidable

---

[1] Rym. Fœdera, vol. i.—M. Paris.

to the rest of Europe. With this view he put himself at the head of a numerous host; and the French monarch seemed in danger of being crushed for having grasped at a present proffered to him by the pope.

Philip, however, advanced undismayed to meet his enemies, with an army of forty thousand men, commanded by the chief nobility of France. Otho was attended by Longsword the gallant earl of Salisbury, the count of Flanders, the duke of Brabant, and some German princes; and his force doubled that of Philip. The two armies met near the village of Bou- July 27, vines, between Lisle and Tournay, where the allies were 1214. totally routed, and thirty thousand Germans are said to have been slain [1].

This victory established the glory of Philip, and gave full security to all his dominions. John could therefore hope for nothing farther than henceforth to rule his own kingdom in peace; and his close alliance with the pope, which he was determined at any price to maintain, ensured him, as he imagined, the attainment of that felicity. How much was he deceived! A truce was indeed concluded with France, but the most grievous scene of this prince's misfortunes still awaited him. He was doomed to humble himself before his own subjects, that the rights of Englishmen might be restored, and the privileges of humanity secured and ascertained.

After the invasion of England by William the Norman, the necessity of devolving great power into the hands of a prince, who was to maintain a military dominion over a vanquished nation, had induced the barons to subject themselves to a more absolute authority than men of their rank commonly submitted to in other feudal governments; so that England, from the time of the Conquest, had groaned under a tyranny unknown to all the kingdoms founded by the Gothic conquerors. Prerogatives once exalted are not easily reduced. Different concessions had been made by the succeeding princes, in order to serve their temporary purposes. These, however, were soon disregarded, and the same authority continued to be exercised. But the feeble reign of John, who had rendered himself odious and contemptible to the whole nation, seemed to afford, to all ranks of men, a happy opportunity of recovering their natural and constitutional rights;—and it was not neglected.

The barons entered into a confederacy, and formally demanded

1 Rigord. *de Gestis Phil. August.*—P. Æmil.

A. D. a restoration of their privileges; and, that their cause
1215. might wear the greater appearance of justice, they also
included those of the clergy and the people. They took arms
to enforce their request: they ravaged the royal domains: and
John, after employing a variety of expedients in order to divert
the blow aimed at the prerogatives of the crown, was obliged to
treat with his subjects.

A conference took place between the king and the barons at
Runnemede, between Windsor and Staines; a spot ever since
deservedly celebrated, and even hallowed by every zealous lover
June of liberty. There John, after a debate of some days,
15. signed and sealed the famous *Magna Charta*, or GREAT
CHARTER; which granted or rather secured very important privileges to every order of men in the kingdom—to the barons,
to the clergy, and to the people.

What these privileges particularly were you will best learn,
my dear Philip, from the charter itself, which deserves your
most early and continued attention, as it involves all the great
outlines of a legal government, and provides for the equal distribution of justice, and free enjoyment of property; the chief
objects for which political society was first founded by men,
which the people have a perpetual and inalienable right to recall,
and which no time, precedent, statute, or positive institution,
ought to deter them from keeping ever uppermost in their
thoughts[1].

The better to secure the execution of this charter, the barons
stipulated with the king for the privilege of choosing twenty-five
members of their own order, as conservators of the public liberties: and no bounds were set to the authority of these noblemen,
either in extent or duration. If complaint should be made of a
violation of the charter, any four of the conservators might admonish the king to redress the grievance; and, on the refusal of
satisfaction, they might assemble the whole number. These
guardians of freedom, in conjunction with the great council of
the nation, were empowered to compel him to observe the charter; and, in case of resistance, might levy war against him.

[1] The most valuable stipulation in this charter, and the grand security of the
lives, liberties, and property of Englishmen, was the following concession: " No
freeman shall be apprehended, imprisoned, disseized, outlawed, banished, or in any
way destroyed; nor will WE *go upon him*, nor will WE *send* upon him, except by the
legal judgment of his peers, or by the law of the land." The stipulation next in importance seems to be this: " To no man will we *sell*, to no man will we *deny*, or
delay, right and *justice*." These concessions show, in a very strong light, the iniquitous practices and violent sway of the Anglo-Norman princes.

All men throughout the kingdom were bound, under penalty of confiscation, to swear obedience to the twenty-five barons ; and the freeholders of every county were to choose twelve knights, who should make report of such evil customs as required redress [1].

In what manner John acted under these regulations, to which he seemed passively to submit, together with their influence on the English constitution, and on the affairs of France, we shall afterwards have occasion to see. At present we must attend to the concerns of the other states of Europe.

LETTER XXXII.

Of the German Empire and its Dependencies, from the Accession of Henry VI. to the Election of Rodolph of Hapsburg, Founder of the house of Austria; with a Continuation of the History of the Crusades.

It is necessary, my dear Philip, that I should here recapitulate a little ; for there is no portion of modern history more perplexed than that under review.

The emperor, Frederic Barbarossa, died, as you have seen, in his expedition to the Holy Land ; and Henry VI. received almost at the same time intelligence of the death of his A.D. father and his brother-in-law, William king of Naples 1190. and Sicily, to whose dominions he was heir in right of his wife. After settling the affairs of Germany, he levied an army, and marched into Italy, in order to be crowned by the pope, and go with the empress Constantia to recover the succession of Sicily, which had been bestowed on her nephew Tancred, by the voluntary vote of the nobility. With this view he endeavoured to conciliate the affections of the Italians, by enlarging the privileges of Genoa, Pisa, and other cities, in his way to Rome. There the ceremony of coronation was performed by Celes- A.D. tine III., and was accompanied with a very remarkable 1191. circumstance. That pope, who was then in his eighty-sixth year, had no sooner placed the crown upon Henry's head, than he kicked it off again, as a testimony of the power residing in the sovereign pontiff, to make and unmake emperors [2].

---

[1] M. Paris.—Rymer, vol. i.   [2] Hoved. *Annal.*—Heiss, lib. ii.

Henry now prepared for the conquest of Naples and Sicily, in which he was opposed by the pope. For, although Celestine considered Tancred as an usurper, and wished to see him deprived of the crown, which he claimed, in imitation of his predecessors, as a fief of the holy see, he was still more unwilling to suffer the emperor to possess that kingdom, because such an accession of territory would render him too powerful in Italy for the interests of the church. He dreaded so formidable a vassal. Henry, however, without paying any regard to the threats and remonstrances of his holiness, took almost all the towns of Campania, Apulia, and Calabria; invested the city of Naples, and sent for the Genoese fleet, which he had engaged to form a blockade by sea. But, before its arrival, he was obliged to raise the siege, in consequence of a dreadful mortality among his troops; and all future attempts upon the kingdom of Naples and Sicily proved ineffectual during the life of Tancred [1].

The emperor, after his return to Germany, incorporated the A.D. 1192 Teutonic knights into a regular order, religious and military, and built a house for them at Coblentz. These Teutonic knights, and also the Knights Templars, and Knights Hospitalers, were originally monks who settled in Jerusalem when it was first taken by the champions of the Cross. They were established into religious fraternities for the relief of distressed pilgrims, and for the care of the sick and wounded, without any hostile purpose. But the holy city being afterwards in danger, they took up arms, and made a vow to combat the infidels, as they had formerly done to combat their own carnal inclinations. The enthusiastic zeal of the times increased their number; they became wealthy and honourable; were patronised by several princes, and formed a militia of conquerors [2]. Their exploits I shall have occasion to relate.

In what manner Richard I., king of England, was arrested on his return from the Holy Land, by Leopold duke of Austria, and detained prisoner by the emperor, we have already seen. As soon as Henry had received the money for that prince's A.D. 1193. ransom, he made new preparations for the conquest of Sicily; and, Tancred dying about the same time, he effected his purpose by the assistance of the Genoese. The queen-dowager surrendered Salerno, and her right to the crown, on condition that her son William should possess the principality of Tarentum. But Henry, joining the most atrocious cruelty

[1] Sigon. *Reg. Ital.* lib. xv.   [2] Helyot, *Hist. des Ordres.*

to the basest perfidy, no sooner found himself master of the place, than he ordered the infant prince to be castrated, deprived of his sight, and confined in a dungeon. The royal treasure was transported to Germany, and the queen and her daughters were shut up in a convent[1].

During these transactions in Sicily, the empress, though near the age of fifty, was delivered of a son named Frederic. And Henry, in the plenitude of his power, assembled soon after a diet of the German princes, to whom he explained his intention of rendering the imperial crown hereditary, in order to prevent those disturbances which attended the election of emperors. A decree was passed for that purpose; and Frederic II., A. D. yet an infant, was declared king of the Romans[2]. 1196.

In the mean time the emperor was solicited by the pope to engage in a new crusade, for the relief of the Christians in the Holy Land. He obeyed, but took care to turn it to his advantage. He convoked a diet at Worms, where he solemnly declared his resolution of employing his whole power, and even of hazarding his life, for the accomplishment of so holy an undertaking: and he expatiated on the subject with such eloquence, that almost the whole assembly took the cross. And such multitudes, from all the provinces of the empire, enlisted themselves, that Henry divided them into three large armies: one of which, under the command of the bishop of Mentz, took the route of Hungary, where it was joined by Margaret, queen of that country, who entered herself in this pious expedition, and ended her days in Palestine. The second army was assembled in Lower Saxony, and embarked in a fleet furnished by the inhabitants of Lubec, Hamburg, Holstein, and Friseland; and the emperor in person conducted the third into Italy, in order to take vengeance upon the Normans of Naples and Sicily, who had risen against his government[3].

The rebels were humbled, and their chiefs condemned to perish by the most excruciating tortures. One Jornandi, of the house of the Norman princes, was tied naked on a chair of red-hot iron, and crowned with a circle of the same burning metal, which was nailed to his head. The empress, shocked at such cruelty, renounced her faith to her husband, and encouraged her countrymen to recover their liberties. Resolution sprang from despair. The inhabitants took arms; the empress headed them; and

---

[1] Sigon. *Reg. Ital.* [2] Lunig. *Arch. Imp.*—Heiss, lib. ii.
[3] Giannone, *Hist. di Napol.*

Henry having dismissed his troops, no longer thought necessary to his bloody purposes, and sent them to pursue their
expedition to the Holy Land, (blessed atonement for his and
their crimes !) was obliged to submit to his wife, and to the conditions which she was pleased to impose on him in favour of the
Sept. 28, Sicilians.   He died at Messina soon after this treaty;
1198.   and, as was supposed, of poison administered by the empress, who saw the ruin of her country hatching in his perfidious
and vindictive heart.

Henry, amidst all his baseness, possessed some great qualities.
He was active, eloquent, brave ; his administration was vigorous,
and his policy deep.   Of all the successors of Charle-magne, no
one was'more feared and obeyed, either at home or abroad.

His son Frederic was now chosen emperor ; but as he was yet
a minor, the government was committed to his uncle, Philip
duke of Suabia, both by the will of Henry and by an assembly
of the German princes.   Other princes, however, incensed to see
an elective empire become hereditary, held a new diet at Cologne, and chose Otho duke of Brunswick, son of Henry the
Lion.   Frederic's title was confirmed in a general assembly at
Arnsburgh ; and his uncle Philip was declared king of the
Romans, to give greater weight to his administration[1].

The two elections divided the empire into two powerful
factions.   Pope Innocent III. threw himself into the scale of
Otho, and excommunicated Philip and his adherents.   This able
and ambitious pontiff was a determined enemy to the house of
Suabia ; not from any personal animosity, but out of a principle
of policy.   That house had long been an object of dread to the
popes, from its continued possession of the imperial crown : and
the accession of the kingdom of Naples and Sicily rendered it
still more formidable.   Innocent, therefore, joyfully embraced
the present opportunity of divesting the house of Suabia of the
empire, by supporting the election of Otho, and sowing divisions
among the Suabian party.   Otho was also patronised by his
uncle, the king of England ; a circumstance which naturally inclined the king of France to the side of his rival.   Faction clashed
with faction ; friendship with interest ; caprice, ambition, or
resentment, gave the sway ; and nothing was beheld on all hands
but the horrors and miseries of civil war[2].

The empress Constantia remained in Sicily, where all was
peace, as a regent and guardian for her infant son Frederic, who

---

[1] Krantz, *Hist. Sax.* lib. viii.—Heiss, libii.   [2] Id. ibid.—*Annal. de l'Emp.* vol. i.

had been crowned king of that island, with the consent of pope
Celestine III. But she also had her troubles. A new investiture from the holy see being necessary on the death of Celestine,
Innocent took advantage of the critical situation of affairs to
aggrandize the papacy at the expense of the kings of Sicily.
They possessed, as we have seen, the privilege of filling up vacant
benefices, and of judging all ecclesiastical causes in the last appeal;
they were really popes in their own island, though vassals of his
holiness. Innocent pretended that these powers had been surreptitiously obtained; and demanded, that Constantia should
renounce them in the name of her son, and do pure and simple
homage for Sicily. But before any thing was settled A.D.
relative to this affair, the empress died, leaving the 1200.
regency of the kingdom to the pope; so that he was enabled
to prescribe what conditions he thought proper to young
Frederic [1].

The troubles of Germany still continued; and the pope redoubled his efforts to detach the princes and prelates from the
cause of Philip, king of the Romans, in defiance of the expostulations of the king of France. To these remonstrances he
proudly replied, "Either Philip must lose the empire, or I the
papacy [2]."

But all these dissensions and troubles in Europe did not prevent the formation of another crusade, or expedition into Asia,
for the recovery of the Holy Land. The adventurers who took
the cross were chiefly French and Germans. Baldwin, count of
Flanders, was their commander; and the Venetians, as greedy of
wealth and power as the ancient Carthaginians, furnished them
with ships, for which they took care to be amply paid both in
money and territory. The Christian city of Zara, in Dalmatia,
had withdrawn itself from the government of the republic: the
army of the cross undertook to reduce it to obedience; A. D.
and it was besieged and taken, notwithstanding the threats 1203.
and excommunications of the pope [3]. Nothing can show in a
stronger light the reigning spirit of those *pious* adventurers.

The storm next broke upon Constantinople. Isaac Angelus
had been dethroned, and deprived of his sight, in 1195, by his
brother Alexis. Isaac's son, named also Alexis, who had made
his escape into Germany, and was then in the army of the
crusade, implored the assistance of its leaders against the usurper:

[1] Murat. *Antiq. Ital.* vol. vi. [2] *Gest. Innocent. III.*
[3] Maimbourg, *Hist. des Croisades.*

engaging, in case of success, to furnish them with provisions, to pay them a large sum of money, and to submit to the jurisdiction of the pope. By their means the lawful prince was restored. He ratified the treaty made by his son, and died; when young Alexis, who was hated by the Greeks for having called in the Latins, became the victim of a new faction. One of his relatives, surnamed Murzufle, strangled him, and usurped the imperial throne [1].

Baldwin and his followers, who sought only an apology for their intended violence, had now a good one; and, under pretence of revenging the death of Alexis, made themselves masters of

A. D. 1204. Constantinople. They met with little resistance; put every one who opposes them to the sword, and indulged in all the excesses of avarice and fury. The booty of the French lords alone was valued at four hundred thousand marks of silver; the very churches were pillaged! And what strongly marks the character of that giddy nation, which has been at all times nearly the same, we are informed by Nicetas, that the French officers danced with the ladies in the sanctuary of the church of St. Sophia, after having robbed the altar, and drenched the city in blood.

Thus was Constantinople, the most flourishing Christian city in the world, plundered by the Christians themselves, who had vowed to fight only against infidels!—Baldwin, the most powerful of these ravagers, procured the dignity of emperor; and this new usurper condemned the other usurper, Murzufle, to be thrown headlong from the top of a lofty column. The Venetians had, for their share of the conquered empire, Peloponnesus, the island of Candia, and several cities on the coast of Phrygia; and the marquis of Montferrat seized Thessaly; so that Baldwin had little left except Thrace and Moesia. The pope gained, for a time, the whole Eastern church: and, in a word, an acquisition was made of much greater consequence than Palestine. Of this, indeed, the conquerors seemed fully convinced; for notwithstanding the vow they had taken, to succour Jerusalem, only a very inconsiderable number of the many knights who had engaged in this pious enterprise went into Syria, and those were such as could obtain no share in the spoils of the Greeks [2].

Innocent III., speaking of this conquest, says, in one of his letters, " God, willing to console his church by the re-union of the schismatics, has made the empire pass from the proud, super-

---

[1] Nicet. *Chron.*   [2] Nicet.—Cantacuzen.

stitious, disobedient Greeks, to the humble, pious catholic, and submissive Latins." So easy it is by words to give to persons and things that complexion which most favours our interests and our prejudices!

I should now, my dear Philip, return to the affairs of Germany; but a few more particulars, consequent on the reduction of Constantinople, require first to be noted, as they cannot afterward be so properly brought under review.

There still remained many princes of the imperial house of Comnenus, who did not lose their courage with the destruction of their empire. One of these, named Alexis, took refuge on the coast of Colchis, and erected a petty state, which he styled the empire of Trebisond ; so much was the word *empire* abused! Theodore Lascaris retook Nice, and settled himself in Bithynia, by opportunely making use of the Arabs against the Turks. He also assumed the title of emperor, and caused a patriarch to be elected of his own communion. Other Greeks entered iuto an alliance with the Turks, and even invited their ancient enemies, the Bulgarians, to assist them against the emperor Bald- A.D. win, who being overcome by those barbarians, near 1206. Adrianople, had his legs and arms cut off, and was left a prey to wild beasts [1]. Henry, his brother and successor, was poisoned in 1216; and, in 1261, the imperial city, which had declined under the Latins, returned to the Greeks.

Diverting our attention from the East, we find Philip and Otho desolating the West. At length Philip prevailed ; and Otho, obliged to abandon Germany, took refuge in England. Philip, who was now crowned emperor, proposed an accommodation with the pope; but before it could be adjusted, he was assassinated by the count Palatine of Bavaria, in consequence of a A.D. private dispute [2].   1208.

Otho returned to Germany on the death of Philip, married that prince's daughter, and was crowned at Rome, after A.D. yielding to the holy see the long-disputed inheritance of 1209. the countess Matilda, and confirming the rights and privileges of the Italian cities.

But these concessions, as far at least as they regarded the pope, were only a sacrifice to present policy. Otho no sooner found himself in a condition to act offensively, than he resumed his grant; and not only recovered the possessions of the empire,

[1] Nicet. Cantacuzen.   [2] Heiss, lib. ii. cap. xv.

A.D. 1210. but made hostile incursions into Apulia, ravaging the dominions of young Frederic, king of Naples and Sicily, who was under the protection of the holy see. Hence we may A.D. 1211. date the ruin of Otho. The pope excommunicated him; and Frederic was re-elected emperor by the German princes [1].

Otho, however, on his return to Germany, finding his party still considerable, and not doubting that he should be able to A.D. 1213. humble his rival by means of his superior force, entered into an alliance with the king of England against the French monarch. The unfortunate battle of Bouvines, where A.D. 1214. the confederates were defeated, as we have seen, completed the ruin of Otho. Abandoned by all the princes of Germany, and altogether without resource, he retired to Brunswick, where he lived above three years as a private man, dedicating his time to the duties of religion. He was not deposed, but forgotten; and if it be true that, in the excess of his humility, he ordered himself to be thrown down, and trodden upon by his kitchen-boys, we may well say with Voltaire, that the kicks of a turn-spit can never expiate the faults of a prince [2].

Frederic II., being now universally acknowledged emperor, A.D. 1215. was crowned at Aix-la-Chapelle with great magnificence; and, in order to preserve the favour of the pope, he added to the other solemnities of his coronation a vow to go in person to the Holy Land [3].

About this time pope Innocent died, and was succeeded by A.D. 1216. Honorius III., who expressed great eagerness in forwarding the crusade, which he ordered to be preached through all the provinces of Germany, Sweden, Denmark, Bohemia, and Hungary; and his endeavours were crowned with success. The emperor indeed excused himself from the performance of his vow, until he should have regulated the affairs of Italy; and other European monarchs were likewise unwilling to embark personally in the expedition. But an infinite number of private noblemen and their vassals took the cross, under the dukes of Austria and Bavaria, the archbishop of Mentz, and the bishops of Munster and Utrecht; and Andrew II., king of Hungary, was declared generalissimo of the crusade [4].

---

[1] Heiss, lib. ii. cap. xvi.
[2] Heiss, lib. ii. cap. xvii.
[3] *Annal. de l'Emp.* vol. ii.
[4] *Annal. Paderborn.*—[It may here be observed, that Hungary (which, though its name refers to the Huns, was chiefly inhabited by the Igours, a colony from Finland,

While the adventurers of Upper Germany marched towards Italy, in order to embark at Venice, Genoa, and Messina, A.D. a fleet was equipped in the ports of Lower Saxony, to 1217. transport the troops of Westphalia, Saxony, and the teritory of Cologne.   These, joining the squadron of the Frieslanders, Flemings, and subjects of Brabandt, commanded by the counts of Holland, Weerden, and Berg, set sail for the strait of Gibraltar, on their voyage to Ptolemais.   But, being driven by a tempest into the road of Lisbon, they were prevailed upon to assist Alphonso II., king of Portugal, against the Moors.   They defeated the infidels, and took from them the city of Alcazar [1].

The king of Hungary and his army, having joined the king of Cyprus, landed at Ptolemais, where he was joyfully received by John de Brienne, titular king of Jerusalem.   After refreshing and reviewing their forces, the two kings marched against the Saracens, with the wood of the true cross carried before them. The troops of Saifeddin, Soltan of Egypt and Syria, being greatly out-numbered by the Christians, retired without giving battle; and the champions of the cross undertook the siege of Thabor, in which they miscarried.   They now separated themselves into four bodies for the conveniency of subsisting.   The king A.D. of Cyprus died; and the Hungarian monarch returned to 1218. his own dominions, in order to quiet some disturbances which had arisen during his absence [2].

The fleet from the coast of Portugal arrived in Palestine soon after the departure of the king of Hungary; and it was resolved in a council of war to besiege Damietta in Egypt, which was accordingly invested by sea and land.   During the siege Saifeddin died; and his son Al-Kamel Nasereddin, who came to the relief of the town, was defeated.   The duke of Austria, with a considerable body of men, returned soon after to Germany; and a reinforcement arrived from the emperor under the con- A.D. duct of Cardinal Albano, legate of the holy see [3].   1219.

This cardinal, who was a Spanish Benedictine, pretended that he, as representative of the pope, the natural head of the crusade, had an incontestable right to be general; and that, as the

the Sclavonians, and the Germans) being a kingdom in the year 1000, under Stephen, the son of duke Geysa, who had embraced the Christian religion.   His brother-in-law Ovo was defeated and slain in 1044, by the emperor Henry III.   Ladislaus I., who distinguished himself by his victories and conquests, died in 1095, and was afterwards canonised.   The crown continued to be enjoyed by the family of Geysa, though the monarch had been declared elective.   The nineteenth king was the above-mentioned leader of the crusaders.]

[1] *Annal. Paderborn.*   [2] Jac. de Vitri.—Maimbourg.
[3] Vertot, *Hist. des Chev. de Malthe,* vol. i.—Maimbourg, vol. ii.

king of Jerusalem held his crown only by virtue of the pope's license, he ought in all things to pay obedience to the legate of his holiness. Much time was spent in that dispute, and in writing to Rome for his advice. At length the pope's answer came, by which he ordered the king of Jerusalem to serve under the Benedictine; and his orders were punctually obeyed. John de Brienne resigned the command; and the monkish general led the army of the cross between two branches of the Nile, just at the time when that river, which fertilizes and defends Egypt, began to overflow its banks. The soltan, informed of the exact state of affairs, flooded the camp of the Christians, by opening the sluices; and while he burned their ships on the one side, the Nile increasing on the other, threatened to swallow up their whole army. The legate now saw himself and his troops in a similar extremity to that in which the Egyptians under Pharaoh are described, when they beheld the sea ready to rush in upon them.

A.D. 1221. In consequence of this pressing danger, Damietta, which had been taken after a long siege, was restored; and the leaders of the crusade were obliged to conclude a dishonourable treaty, by which they bound themselves not to serve against the soltan of Egypt for eight years [1].

The Christians of the East had now no hopes left but in Frederic II., who was about this time crowned at Rome by Honorius, whose friendship he had purchased, by promising to detach Naples and Sicily from the empire, and bestow them on his son Henry, as fiefs of the holy see. He also promised to pass into Asia with an army, at any time the pope should appoint: but this promise he was not inclined to perform. He was indeed more worthily employed in embellishing and aggrandizing Naples; in establishing an university in that city, where the Roman law was taught; and in expelling the vagrant Saracens, who still infested Sicily [2].

In the mean time the unfortunate leaders of the crusade arrived in Europe; and the pope, incensed at the loss of Damietta, wrote a severe letter to the emperor, taxing him with A.D. 1225. having sacrificed the interest of Christianity by the neglect of his vow, and threatening him with immediate excommunication if he did not instantly depart with an army into Asia. Frederic, exasperated at these reproaches, renounced all correspondence with the court of Rome; renewed his ecclesiastical

---

[1] Vertot, *Hist. des Chev. de Malthe*, vol. i.—Maimbourg.
[2] Signon. *Reg. Ital.*—Giannone, *Hist di Napol.*

jurisdiction in Sicily ; filled up vacant sees and benefices ;　A.D.
and expelled some bishops, who were creatures of the 1226.
pope, on pretence of their being concerned in practices against
the state.

Honorius at first attempted to combat rigour with rigour,
menacing the emperor with the thunder of the church, for presuming to lift up his hand against the sanctuary ; but finding that
Frederic was not to be intimidated by such threats, his holiness
became sensible of his own imprudence, in wantonly incurring
the resentment of so powerful a prince, and thought proper to
soothe him by submissive apologies and gentle exhortations.　A
reconciliation soon took place ; and after a conference at Veroli,
the emperor, as a proof of his sincere attachment to the church,
published some very severe edicts against heresy, which seem to
have authorised the tribunal of the inquisition [1].

A solemn assembly was afterwards holden at Ferentino, where
both Frederic and the pope were present, together with John de
Brienne, who had returned to Europe to demand succours
against the soltan of Egypt.　John had an only daughter named
Yolanta, whom he proposed as a wife to the emperor, with the
kingdom of Jerusalem as her dowry, on condition that Frederic
should, within two years, perform the vow he had made to lead
an army into the Holy Land.　Frederic married her on these
terms, because he wished to please the pope ; and since that time
the kings of Sicily have taken the title of king of Jerusalem.
But the emperor was not very eager to attempt the conquest of
his wife's portion, having other business to perform.　The chief
cities of Lombardy had entered into a secret league, with　A. D.
a view to throw off his authority.　He convoked a diet at 1227.
Cremona, where all the German and Italian noblemen were summoned to attend.　A variety of subjects were there discussed ;
but nothing of consequence was settled.　An accommodation,
however, resulted from the mediation of the pope, who, as umpire of the dispute, decreed, that the emperor should lay aside
his resentment against the confederate towns, and that the towns
should furnish and maintain four hundred knights for the relief
of the Holy Land [2].

Peace being thus concluded, Honorius reminded the emperor
of his vow : Frederic promised compliance : but his holiness died
before he could see the execution of a project which he seemed
to have so much at heart.　He was succeeded by Gregory IX.,

[1] Petr. de Vignes, lib. i.　　　　　[2] Richardi *Chron.* ap. Murat.

who, pursuing the same line of policy, urged the departure of Frederic for the Holy Land, and, finding him still backward, declared him incapable of holding the imperial dignity, as having incurred the sentence of excommunication.　Frederic, incensed at such insolence, ravaged the patrimony of St. Peter, and was A.D. actually excommunicated.　The animosity between the 1228. Guelphs and Ghibellines revived; the pope was obliged to quit Rome; and Italy became a scene of war and desolation, or rather of numerous civil wars, which, by inflaming the minds, and exciting the resentment of the Italian princes, unfortunately accustomed them to the horrid practices of poisoning and assassination.

To remove the cause of so many troubles, and gratify the prejudices of a superstitious age, Frederic resolved to perform his vow.　He accordingly embarked for the Holy Land, leaving the affairs of Italy to the management of Rinaldo duke of Spoleto. The pope prohibited his departure, before he was absolved from the censures of the church.　But Frederic went in contempt of the church, and succeeded better than any commander who had gone before him.　He did not indeed desolate Asia, and gratify the barbarous zeal of the times, by shedding the blood of infidels; A.D. but he concluded a treaty with the soltan of Egypt, by 1229. which the end of his expedition seemed fully answered. The soltan ceded to him Jerusalem, and its territory, as far as Joppa; Bethlehem, Nazareth, and all the country between A.D. Jerusalem and Ptolemais; Tyre, Sidon, and the neigh-1230. bouring districts.　In return for these concessions, the emperor granted the Saracens a truce for ten years[1].

His reign, after his return from the East, was one continued quarrel with the popes.　The cities of Lombardy had revolted during his absence, at the instigation of Gregory IX.; and, before they could be reduced, the same pontiff excited the em-A.D. peror's son Henry, who had been elected king of the 1235. Romans, to rebel against his father.　The rebellion was suppressed, the prince was confined, and Frederic obtained a complete victory over the associated towns; but his troubles were A.D. not yet at an end.　The pope again excommunicated him, 1237. and, to sow division between him and the princes of the empire, sent a bull into Germany, in which are the following remarkable words: "A beast of blasphemy, abounding with names, is risen from the sea, with the feet of a bear, the face of a lion, and members of other different animals : which, like the proud, hath opened its mouth in blasphemy against the holy name ; not even fearing to throw the arrows of calumny against the tabernacle of God, and the saints that dwell in heaven. This beast, desirous of breaking every thing in pieces with his iron teeth and nails, and of trampling all things under his feet, hath already prepared private battering-rams against the wall of the catholic faith ; and now raises open machines, in erecting soul-destroying schools of Ishmaelites : rising, according to report, in opposition to Christ the Redeemer of mankind, the table of whose covenant he attempts to abolish with the pen of wicked heresy.   Be not therefore surprised at the malice of this blasphemous beast, if we, who are the servants of the Almighty, should be exposed to the arrows of his destruction.—This king of plagues was even heard to say, that the whole world has been deceived by three impostors ; namely, Moses, Jesus Christ, and Mohammed.   But he makes Jesus Christ far inferior to the other two : ' They,' says he, ' supported their glory to the last, whereas Christ was ignominiously crucified.'   He also maintains," continues Gregory, " that it is folly to believe the ONE only God, Creator of the Universe, could be born of a *woman*, especially of a *virgin*[1]."

Frederic, on the other hand, in his apology to the princes of Germany, calls Gregory the *Great Dragon*, the *Antichrist*, of whom it is written, " and another Red Horse arose from the sea, and he that sat upon him took Peace from the Earth[2]."

The emperor's apology was sustained in Germany ; and finding that he had nothing to fear from this quarter, he resolved to take ample vengeance on the pope and his associates.   With that view he marched to Rome, where he thought his A.D. party was strong enough to procure him admission.   But 1239. this favourite scheme was defeated by the activity of Gregory, who ordered a crusade to be preached against the emperor, as an enemy of the Christian faith ; a step which so incensed Frederic, that he ordered all his prisoners who wore the cross, to be exposed to the most cruel tortures[3].

The two factions of the Guelphs and Ghibellines continued to rage with greater violence than ever ; involving cities, districts, and even private families, in troubles, divisions, and civil butchery, no quarter being given on either side.   Meanwhile

---

[1] Gob. Pers. *Cosmod.* cap. lxiv.   [2] Id. ibid.
[3] Krantz, lib. vii.—Murat. *Annal. Ital.* vol. vii.

A.D. Gregory IX. died, and was succeeded by Celestine IV., 1243. and afterwards by Innocent IV., formerly cardinal Fieschi, who had always expressed the greatest regard for the emperor and his interest. Frederic was accordingly congratulated upon this occasion; but, having a greater degree of penetration than those about him, he replied, " I see little reason to rejoice. The cardinal was my friend; but the pope will be my enemy."

Innocent soon proved the justice of this conjecture. He ambitiously attempted to negociate a peace for Italy. But not being able to obtain from Frederic his exorbitant demands, and apprehensive of danger to his own person, he fled into France, A.D. assembled a general council at Lyons, and deposed the 1245. emperor. " I declare," said he, " Frederic II., attainted and convicted of sacrilege and heresy, excommunicated and dethroned: and I order the electors to choose rather another emperor, reserving to myself the disposal of the kingdom of Sicily [1]."

Frederic was at Turin when he received the news of his deposition, and behaved in a manner that seemed to border upon weakness. He called for the casket in which the imperial ornaments were kept; and opening it, and taking the crown in his hand, " Innocent," he cried, " has not yet deprived me of thee: thou art still mine! and, before I part with thee, much blood shall be spilled [2]."

Conrad, the emperor's second son, had been declared king of the Romans, on the death of his brother Henry, which soon followed his confinement; but the imperial throne being now declared vacant by the pope, the German bishops (for none of A.D. the princes were present,) at the instigation of his holi-1246. ness, proceeded to the election of a new emperor; and they chose Henry, landgrave of Thuringia, who was styled in derision, " The King of Priests."

Innocent now renewed the crusade against Frederic. It was proclaimed by the preaching friars, since called Dominicans, and the minor friars, known by the name of Cordeliers or Franciscans, a new militia of the court of Rome, which, about this time, began to be established in Europe. The pope, however, did not confine himself to these measures, but engaged in conspiracies against the life of an emperor who had dared to resist the decree of a council, and oppose the whole body of monks and zealots.

---

[1] Gob. Pers. ubi sup.   [2] M. Par. *Hist. Maj.*

Frederic's life was several times in danger from these plots, which induced him, it is said, to make choice of Mohammedan guards, who, he was certain, would not be under the influence of the prevailing superstition.

On the decease of the landgrave of Thuringia, the same prelates who had taken the liberty of creating one emperor A.D. chose another : namely, William, count of Holland, a 1248. young nobleman of twenty years of age, who bore the same contemptuous title as his predecessor [1].

Fortune, which had hitherto favoured Frederic, seemed now to desert him. He was defeated before Parma, which he had long besieged ; and to complete his misfortunes, he soon after learned, that his natural son Entius, whom he had made king of Sardinia, was worsted and taken prisoner by the Bolognese. In this extremity, he retired to his kingdom of Naples, A.D. in order to recruit his army : and there died of a fever, in 1250. the fifty-seventh year of his age. He was a prince of great genius, erudition, and fortitude ; and notwithstanding all the turmoils of his reign, he built towns, founded universities, and gave, as it were, a new life to learning in Italy.

After the death of this prince, the affairs of Germany fell into the utmost confusion, and Italy continued long in the same distracted state in which he had left it. The clergy took arms against the laity, the weak were oppressed by the strong, and laws divine and human were disregarded. But a particular history of that unhappy period would fill the mind with disgust and horror : I shall therefore only observe, that after the death of Frederic's son Conrad (who had assumed the imperial A.D. dignity as successor to his father) and of his competitor, 1256. William of Holland, many candidates appeared for the empire, and several were elected by different factions ; among whom was Richard earl of Cornwall, brother to Henry III. king of England. But no emperor was properly acknowledged till the year 1273, when Rodolph, count of Hapsburg, was unanimously raised to the vacant throne.

During the interregnum which preceded the election of Rodolph, the king of Hungary and the count of Holland entirely freed themselves from the homage which they had been accustomed to pay to the empire : and nearly about the same time, several German cities erected a municipal form of government, which still continues. Lubeck, Cologne, Brunswick, and Dantzic,

---

[1] *Annal. Boior.*

united for their mutual defence against the encroachments of the great lords, by a famous association, called the Hanseatic League ; and these towns were afterwards joined by eighty others, belonging to different states, which formed a kind of commercial republic. Italy also, during this period, assumed a new form of government. That freedom for which the cities of Lombardy had so long struggled was confirmed to them for a sum of money ; they were emancipated by the fruits of their industry. Sicily likewise changed its government, and its prince, as will be related in the history of France, which furnished a sovereign to the Sicilians.

I next propose to carry forward the affairs of England, to the reign of Edward I., a period at which the history of our own island becomes peculiarly interesting to every Briton.

LETTER XXXIII.

History of England, from the Grant of the Great Charter, to the Reign of Edward I.

You have already seen, my dear Philip, in what manner king John was forced by his barons to grant the Great Charter of English liberty, and to accede to such regulations as were A.D. 1215. deemed necessary for preserving it. He went still farther ; he dismissed his forces, and promised that his government should be as gentle as his people could wish it. But he only dissembled, in the expectation of an opportunity of revoking all his concessions; and in order to accelerate such an event, he secretly sent emissaries to enlist foreign soldiers, and to invite the rapacious Brabançons into his service, by the prospect of sharing the spoils of England. He also despatched a messenger to Rome, to lay the Great Charter before the pope, who considering himself as superior lord of the kingdom, was incensed at the presumption of the barons, and issued a bull annulling the charter, absolving the king from his oath to observe it, and denouncing excommunication against all who should persevere in maintaining such treasonable pretensions [1].

[1] Rymer, vol. i.—M. Paris.

John now pulled off the mask; he recalled his concessions; and, as his foreign mercenaries arrived with the bull, he expected nothing but universal submission. But our gallant ancestors were not so easily frightened out of their rights. Langton, the primate, though he owed his elevation to an encroachment of the court of Rome, refused to obey the pope in publishing the sentence of excommunication against the barons. Persons of all ranks, among the clergy as well as laity, seemed determined to maintain, at the expense of their lives, the privileges granted in the Great Charter. John had therefore nothing to rely on for the re-establishment of his tyranny, but the sword of his Brabançons: and that unfortunately proved too strong, if not for the liberties of England, at least for its prosperity.

The barons, after obtaining the Great Charter, had sunk into a kind of fatal security. They not only dismissed their vassals, but did not take proper measures for re-assembling them on any emergency; so that the king found himself master of the field, without an adequate force to oppose him. Castles were defended, and skirmishes risked, but no regular opposition was made to the progress of the royal arms; while the ravenous mercenaries, incited by a cruel and incensed prince, were let loose against the houses and estates of the barons, and spread devastation over the whole face of the kingdom. Nothing was to be seen, from Dover to Berwick, but the flames of villages, castles reduced to ashes, and the consternation and misery of the helpless inhabitants [1].

In this desperate extremity, the barons, dreading the total loss of their liberties, their lives, and their possessions, had recourse to a remedy no less desperate. They offered to A.D. acknowledge, as their sovereign, prince Louis, eldest son 1216. of the king of France, provided he would protect them from the fury of their enraged monarch. The temptation was too great to be resisted by a prince of Philip's ambition. He sent over instantly a small army to the relief of the barons, and afterwards a more numerous body of forces, with his son at their head; although the pope's legate threatened him with interdicts and excommunications, if he should presume to invade the dominions of a prince who was under the immediate protection of the holy see. As Philip was assured of the fidelity of his subjects, these menaces did not deter him from his purpose. He took care, however, to preserve appearances in his acts of violence.

[1] M. Paris.— *Chron. Mailros.*

He pretended that his son had accepted the offer from the English barons without his advice, and against his inclinations, and that the armies sent into England were levied in that prince's name. But these artifices were not employed by Philip to deceive. He knew that the pope had too much penetration to be so easily imposed upon, and that they were too gross even to gull the people: but he knew, at the same time, that the manner of conducting any measure is nearly of as much consequence as the measure itself, and that a violation of decency, in the eye of the world, is more criminal than a breach of justice.

Louis no sooner landed in England than John was deserted by his foreign troops, who being principally levied in the French provinces, refused to serve against the heir of their monarchy; so that the barons had the melancholy prospect of succeeding in their purpose, and of escaping the tyranny of their own king, by imposing on themselves and the nation a foreign yoke. But the imprudent partiality of Louis to his countrymen increased that jealousy, which it was so natural for the English to entertain in their present situation, and did great injury to his cause. Many of the dissatisfied barons returned to the king's party; Oct. 19. and John was preparing to make a last effort for his crown, when death put an end to his troubles and his crimes in the fifty-first year of his age, and the eighteenth of his reign. His character was a complication of vices, equally mean and odious; ruinous to himself and destructive to his people. But a sally of wit upon the usual corpulence of the priests, more than all his enormities, made him pass with the clergy of that age for an impious prince. "How plump and well-fed is this animal!" exclaimed he, on having caught a very fat stag;— "and yet I dare swear he never heard mass [1]."

John was succeeded by his son Henry III., who was then only nine years old; and for once a minority proved of singular service to England. The earl of Pembroke, who by his office of marechal was at the head of the military power, and consequently, in perilous times, at the head of the state, determined to support the authority of the infant price. He was chosen protector; and fortunately for the young monarch and for the nation, the regency could not have been committed to more able or more faithful hands. In order to reconcile all classes of men to the government of Henry, he persuaded him to renew and confirm the Great Charter. And he wrote letters in the king's

[1] M. Paris.

name to all the mal-content barons, representing that whatever animosity they might have harboured against John, they ought to retain none against his son, who, though he inherited his throne, had not succeeded either to his resentments or his principles, and was resolved to avoid the paths which had led to such dangerous extremities; exhorting them, at the same time, by a speedy return to their duty to restore the independence of the kingdom, and secure that liberty for which they had so zealously contended [1].

These arguments, enforced by the character of Pembroke, had a great influence on the barons. Most of them secretly negociated with him, and many of them openly returned to their duty. Louis, therefore, who had passed over to France and brought fresh succours from that kingdom, found his party much weakened on his return; and that the death of John, con- A.D. trary to all expectation, had blasted his favourite scheme. 1217. He laid siege, however, to Dover, which was gallantly defended by Hubert de Burgh. In the mean time the French army, commanded by the count de Perche, was totally defeated by the earl of Pembroke, near Lincoln; and four hundred knights, with many persons of superior rank, were made prisoners by the English. Louis, when informed of this disastrous event, retired to London, which was the centre and life of his party. He there received intelligence of a new misfortune, which extinguished all his hopes. A French fleet, having a considerable reinforcement on board, had been repulsed in the channel with great loss [2].

The English barons now hastened from all quarters to make peace with the protector, and prevent, by an early submission, those attainders to which they were exposed on account of their rebellion; while Louis, whose cause was now totally desperate, began to be anxious for the safety of his person, and was glad, on any tolerable conditions, to make his escape from a country in which every thing had become hostile to him. He accordingly concluded a treaty with Pembroke, by which he promised to evacuate the kingdom; only stipulating, in return, an indemnity to his adherents, a restitution of their honours and fortunes, and the free and equal enjoyment of those liberties which had been granted to the rest of the nation [3]. Thus, my dear Philip, was happily terminated a civil war, which seemed to spring from

---

[1] Rymer, vol. i.—Brady, *Append.* No. 143.   [2] M. Paris.
[3] Rymer, vol. i.

the most incurable hatred and jealousy, and had threatened to reduce England to a province of France.

The prudence and equity of the protector, after the expulsion of the French, contributed to cure entirely those wounds which had been made by intestine discord. He received the rebellious barons into favour, strictly observed the terms of peace which he had granted to them; and endeavoured, by an equal behaviour, to bury all past animosities in perpetual oblivion. But, unfortunately for the kingdom, this great and good man did not long survive the pacification; and as Henry, when he reached the age of adolescence, proved a weak and contemptible prince, England was again involved in civil commotions, which it would be idle and impertinent to relate, as they were neither followed, during many years, by an event of importance to society, nor attended with any circumstances which can throw light upon the human character. Their causes and consequences were alike insignificant.

It is necessary, however, to observe, that the king having married Eleanor, daughter of the count of Provence, was surrounded by a multitude of strangers, from that and other countries, whom he caressed with the fondest affection, and enriched by an imprudent generosity. The insolence of these foreigners, it is said, rose to such a height, that when, on account of their outrages or oppressions, an appeal was made to the laws, they scrupled not to say, " What do the laws of England signify to us? We mind them not." This open contempt of the English constitution roused the resentment of the barons, and highly aggravated the general discontent arising from the preference shown to strangers, as it made every act of violence committed by a foreigner appear not only an injury, but an insult. Yet no remonstrance or complaint could prevail on the king to abandon them, or even to moderate his attachment towards them.

Henry's profuse bounty to his foreign relatives, and to their friends and favourites, would have appeared less intolerable to the English, had any thing been done for the benefit of the nation, or had the king's enterprises in foreign countries been attended with any success or glory to himself or the public. Neither of these, however, was the case. As imprudence governed his policy, misfortune marked his measures. He declared war against France, and made an expedition into Guienne, upon the invitation of his father-in-law, who promised to join him with all his forces; but being worsted near

A.D. 1242.

Saintes, he was deserted by his allies, lost what remained to him of Poictou, and was obliged to return with disgrace to England [1].

Want of economy, and an ill-judged liberality, were the great defects in Henry's domestic administration. These kept him always indigent, and obliged him continually to harass his barons for money, under different pretences. Their discontents were thus increased, and he was still a beggar. Even before his foreign expedition, his debts had become so troublesome, that he sold all his plate and jewels in order to discharge them. When this expedient was first proposed to him, he asked where he should find purchasers. " In the city of London," it was replied. " On my word," said he, " if the treasury of Augustus were brought to sale, the citizens are able to be the purchasers. These clowns, who assume to themselves the name of barons, abound in every thing, while I am reduced to extreme necessity [2]." And he was thenceforth observed to be more greedy in his exactions from the citizens.

The grievances, however, of which the English during this reign had reason to complain in their civil government, seem to have been less burthensome than those which proceeded from spiritual usurpations and abuses, and which Henry, who relied on the pope for the support of his tottering authority, never failed to countenance. The chief benefices of the kingdom were conferred on Italians; and non-residence and pluralities were carried to so enormous a height, that Mansel the king's chaplain, is said to have enjoyed, at one time, seven hundred ecclesiastical livings. The pope exacted the revenues of all vacant benefices; the twentieth of all ecclesiastical revenues, without exception; the third of such as exceeded one hundred marks a year; and the half of such as were possessed by non-residents. He also claimed the goods of all intestate clergymen; and pretended a right to inherit all money gained by usury.

But the most oppressive expedient employed by the court of Rome, in order to drain money from England, was that A.D. of embarking Henry on a project for the conquest of 1250. Sicily. On the death of the emperor Frederic II. the succession of that island devolved to his son Conrad, and afterwards to his grandson Conradin, yet an infant; and as Mainfroy, the emperor's natural son, under pretence of governing the kingdom during the minority of the prince, had formed an intention of usurping the sovereignty, Innocent IV. had a good apology for

---

[1] M. Paris.—W. Heming.—*Chron. Dunst.*   [2] M. Paris.

exerting that superiority which the popes claimed over Sicily, and at the same time an opportunity of gratifying his hatred against the house of Suabia. He accordingly attempted to make himself master of the kingdom; but being disappointed in all his enterprises by the activity and artifices of Mainfroy, and finding that his own force was not sufficient for such a conquest, he made a tender of the crown to Henry's brother, Richard earl of Cornwall, one of the richest subjects in Europe. The earl had the prudence to reject the dangerous present, but not the power to prevent the evil. The same offer being afterwards made to the king, in favour of his second son Edmund, that weak monarch was led, by the levity and thoughtlessness of his disposition, to embrace the insidious proposal; and immense sums were drawn from England, under pretence of carrying this project into execution; for the pope took that upon himself. But the money was still found insufficient: the conquest of Sicily was as remote as ever. Henry, therefore, sensible at length of the delusion, was obliged to resign into the pope's hands that crown which he had more than purchased, but which it was never intended either he or his family should inherit [1].

A.D. 1255.

The earl of Cornwall had reason to value himself on his foresight, in refusing the fraudulent bargain with Rome, and in preferring the solid honours of an opulent and powerful prince of the blood in England, to the empty and precarious glory of a foreign dignity; but he had not always firmness sufficient to adhere to this resolution. His immense wealth induced some of the German princes to propose him as a candidate for the empire, after the death of William of Holland; and his vanity and ambition for once prevailed over his prudence and his avarice. Hs went over to Germany, was tempted to expend vast sums on his election, and succeeded so far as to be chosen by a faction, and crowned at Aix-la-Chapelle; but, having no personal or family connexions in that country, he never could attain any solid power. He therefore found it necessary to return to England, after having lavished the frugality of a whole life in the vain pursuit of a splendid title [2].

A. D. 1256.

England, in the mean while, was involved in new troubles. The weakness of Henry's government, and the absence of his brother, gave reins to the factious and turbulent spirit of the barons. They demanded an extension of their privileges; and,

[1] Rymer, vol. i.—M. Paris, *Chron. Dunst.*   [2] M. Paris.

if we may credit the historians of those times, had formed a plan of so many limitations of the royal authority, as would have reduced the king to a mere cipher. Henry would agree to nothing but a renewal of the Great Charter; which, at the desire of the barons, was ratified in the following manner. All the prelates and abbots were assembled: they held burning tapers in their hands; the charter was read before them; they denounced the sentence of excommunication against every one who should violate that fundamental law; they threw their tapers on the ground, and exclaimed, " May the soul of every one, who incurs this sentence, so stink and corrupt in hell!" The king also bore a part in the ceremony, and subjoined, " So help me God! I will keep all these articles inviolate, as I am a man, as I am a Christian, a knight, and a king crowned and anointed [1]."

This tremendous ceremony had no effect on the king, who instantly forgot his engagements; and the barons boldly renewed their pretensions. At the head of the malcontents was Simon de Montfort, earl of Leicester, a man of great talents and boundless ambition, who had married Eleanor, the king's sister, and hoped to wrest the sceptre from the feeble and irresolute hand that held it. He represented to his associates the necessity of reforming the state, and of putting the execution of the laws into other hands than those which had hitherto been found, from repeated experience, unfit for that important charge. After so many submissions and fruitless promises, the king's word, he said, could no longer be relied on; and only his inability to violate national privileges could thenceforth insure their preservation.

These observations, which were founded in truth, and entirely conformable to the sentiments of those to whom they were addressed, had the desired effect. The barons resolved to take the administration into their own hands: and Henry, having A.D. summoned a parliament at Oxford, found himself a pri- 1258. soner in his national council, and was obliged to submit to the terms prescribed to him, called the Provisions of Oxford. According to these regulations, twelve barons were selected from among the king's ministers; twelve more were chosen by the parliament; and to these twenty-four noblemen unlimited authority was granted to reform the state. Leicester was at the head of this legislative body, to which the supreme power was in reality transferred: and their first step seemed well calculated for the

---

[1] W. Heming.—M. Paris.—M. West.

end which they professed to have in view. They ordered that
four knights should be chosen by each county; that they should
make inquiry into the grievances of which their neighbourhood
had reason to complain, and should attend the ensuing parliament, in order to give information of the state of their particular counties [1].

Instead of continuing in the same popular course, the earl and
his associates studiously provided for the extension and prolonga-
tion of their own exorbitant authority, at the expense both of
the king and the people. They enjoyed the supreme power
three years; and had visibly employed it, not for the reformation
of the state, their original pretence for assuming it, but for the
aggrandisement of themselves and their families. The breach
of trust was notorious; all felt it, and murmured against
it; and the pope, in order to gain the favour of the nation,
absolved the king and his subjects from the oath which they had
taken to observe the Provisions of Oxford.

A.D.
1261.

As soon as Henry received the pope's absolution from his oath,
accompanied with threats of excommunication against all his
opponents, he resumed the government; offering, however, to maintain all the regulations made by the reforming barons, except those which entirely annihilated the royal
authority. But these haughty chieftains could not peaceably
resign that uncontrolled power which they had so long
enjoyed. Many of them adopted Leicester's views, which
held in prospect nothing less than the throne itself. The civil war
was renewed in all its horrors: and after several fruitless
negociations, the collected force of the two parties met
near Lewes, in Sussex, where the royal army was totally defeated,
and the king and his brother were made prisoners [2].

A.D.
1262.

A.D.
1263.

May 14,
1264.

No sooner had Leicester obtained this victory, than he acted as
sole master, and even tyrant of the kingdom. He seized the
estates of no less than eighteen barons, as his share of the spoil
gained in the late battle: he engrossed to himself the ransom of
all the prisoners; and told his barons, with wanton insolence,
that it was sufficient for them that he had saved them by that
victory, from the forfeitures and attainders which hung over
them. All the officers of the crown were named by him; the
whole authority, and the arms of the state, were lodged in his
hands [3].

[1] Rymer, vol. i.—*Chron. Dunst.*   [2] W. Hemingf. lib. iii.—*Chron. Wikes.*
[3] Rymer, vol. i.—Hemingf.

But it was impossible that things should remain long in this equivocal situation. It became necessary for Leicester, either to descend to the rank of a subject, or mount up to that of a sovereign; and he could do neither without peril. He summoned a new parliament; which, for his own purposes, he fixed on A.D. a more democratical basis than any called since the Nor- 1265. man conquest, if not from the foundation of the monarchy. He ordered returns to be made not only of two knights from every shire, but also of deputies from the boroughs [1]; and thus introduced into the national council a second order of men, hitherto regarded as too mean to enjoy a place in those august assemblies, or to have any share in the government of the state.

But although we are indebted to Leicester's usurpation for the first rude outline of the House of Commons, his policy only forwarded by some years an institution for which the general state of society had already prepared the nation; and that house, though derived from so invidious an origin, soon proved, when it was summoned by legal princes, one of the most useful members of the constitution, and gradually rescued the kingdom, as we shall have occasion to see, both from aristocratical and regal tyranny. It is but just, however, to observe, that as this necessary and now powerful branch of our constitution owed its rise to usurpation, it is the only one that has latterly given an usurper to the state. The person to whom I allude is Oliver Cromwell; and I may venture to affirm, that, if ever England should be again subjected to the absolute will of any ONE man, unless from abroad, that man must be a member of the House of Commons. The people are alike jealous of the power of the king and of the nobles; but they are themselves greedy of dominion, and can only possess it through their representatives. A popular member of the lower house, therefore, needs only ambition, enterprise, and a favourable conjuncture, to overturn the throne; to strip the nobles of their privileges and dignities; and while he blows the trumpet of liberty, to tell his equals that they are slaves.

Leicester's motive for giving this form to the parliament was a desire of crushing his rivals among the powerful barons: and trusting to the popularity acquired by such a measure, he ordered the earl of Derby to be accused in the king's name, and committed to prison without being brought to a legal trial. Several other barons were threatened with the same fate, and

---

[1] Rymer, vol. i.

therefore deserted the confederacy. The royalists flew to arms; prince Edward made his escape from a confinement into which he had been insidiously drawn; and the joy at this young hero's appearance, together with the oppressions under which the nation laboured soon procured him a force which Leicester was

Aug. 4. unable to resist. A battle was fought near Evesham, where the earl was slain, and his army totally routed. When that nobleman, who possessed great military talents, observed the vast superiority in numbers, and excellent disposition of the royalists, he exclamed, " The Lord have mercy on our souls! for I see our bodies are prince Edward's : he has learned from me the art of war[1]." Another particular deserves to be noticed. The old king, disguised in armour, having been placed by the rebels in the front of the battle, had received a wound, and was on the point of being put to death, when he weakly, but opportunely, cried out " Spare my life; I am Henry of Winchester, your king[2]!" His brave son flew to his rescue, and put him in a place of safety.

The victory of Evesham proved decisive in favour of the royal party; but it was used with moderation. Although the suppression of an extensive rebellion commonly produces a revolution in government, and strengthens as well as enlarges the prerogatives of the crown, no sacrifices of national liberty were exacted upon this occasion. The clemency of this victory is also remarkable : no blood was shed on the scaffold. The mild disposition of the king, and the prudence of the prince, tempered the insolence of power, and gradually restored order to the several members of the state.

The affairs of England being thus settled, prince Edward, seduced by a thirst of glory, undertook an expedition into the

A.D. 1270. Holy Land, where he signalized himself by many acts of valour, and struck such terror into the Saracens, that they employed an assassin to murder him. The ruffian wounded Edward in the arm, but paid for his temerity with his life[3]. Meanwhile the prince's absence from England was productive of many pernicious consequences, which the old king, unequal to the burden of government, was incapable of preventing[4]. He therefore implored his gallant son to return, and assist him in swaying that sceptre which was ready to drop from his feeble

---

[1] Hemingf. lib. lii.   [2] Ibid.   [3] Heming.—Wikes.
[4] The police was so loose during the latter part of Henry's reign, that not only single houses, but whole villages were often pillaged by bands of robbers.—*Chron. Dunst.*

hands.   Edward obeyed : but before his arrival the king ex- pired, in the sixty-sixth year of his age, and the fifty- Nov. 16, seventh of his reign.   1272.

The most obvious feature in the character of Henry III. is his weakness.   From this source, rather than from insincerity or treachery, arose his negligence in observing his promises; and hence, for the sake of present convenience, he was easily induced to sacrifice the lasting advantages arising from the trust and con- fidence of his people.   A better head, with the same dispositions, would have prevented him from falling into so many errors : but (every good has its alloy!) with a worse heart, it would have enabled him to maintain them.

Prince Edward had reached Sicily, in his return from the Holy Land, when he received intelligence of the death of his father, and immediately proceeded homeward.   But a variety of objects, my dear Philip, claim your attention, before I carry farther the transactions of our own island, which now became truly im- portant.   The reign of Edward I. forms a new æra in the history of Britain.

LETTER XXXIV.

Sketch of the Affairs of France, from the Death of Philip Augustus to the End of the Reign of Louis IX., with some Account of the last Crusade.

THE reign of Philip Augustus has already engaged our atten- tion.   We have had occasion to observe the great abilities of that prince, both as a warrior and a politician : we have seen him re-unite some considerable provinces to the kingdom of France at the expense of the English monarchy; we have seen him attempt the conquest of England itself: and we have also seen in what manner prince Louis was obliged to abandon that project, notwithstanding the power and the intrigues of Philip. July 14. Soon after the return of Louis, his father died, and left 1223. the kingdom of France twice as large as he had received it ; so that future acquisitions became easy to his successors.

Louis VIII., however, did not enlarge the monarchy.   His short reign was chiefly spent in a crusade against the Nov. 8. Albigenses, in the prosecution of which he died : he was 1226.

succeeded by his son Louis IX. commonly called St. Louis. During the minority of this prince, various disorders arose in France, occasioned chiefly by the ambition of the powerful vassals of the crown. But all these were happily composed by the prudence and firmness of Blanche of Castile, the regent and queen-mother.

Louis no sooner came of age than he was universally acknow-
A.D. ledged to be the greatest prince in Europe; and his cha-
1235. racter is perhaps the most singular in the annals of history.
To the mean and abject superstition of a monk he not only united all the courage and magnanimity of a hero, but (what may be deemed still more wonderful) the justice and integrity of the sincere patriot, and where religion was not concerned, the mild-ness and humanity of the true philosopher. So far was he from taking advantage of the divisions among the English, during the reign of Henry III., or attempting to expel those dangerous rivals from the provinces which they still possessed in France, that he entertained many scruples in regard to the sentence of attainder pronounced against the king's father; and had not his bishops, it is said, persuaded him that John was justly punished for his barbarity and felony, he would have gladly restored the conquests of Philip Augustus [1].

When Gregory IX., after excommunicating Frederic II.,
A.D. offered the empire to the count of Artois, brother of St.
1240. Louis, this pious prince acted in the same disinterested
manner. He did not indeed refuse that gift as what the pope had no right to bestow; but he, or rather his barons, replied, that Frederic had always appeared to him a good catholic; that ambassadors ought first to be sent to know his sentiments touch-ing his faith; that, if orthodox, there could be no reason for attacking him; but, if heretical, war ought to be carried on against him with violence: and, in such case, even against the pope himself [2].

This was the foible of Louis. Persuaded that heretics, or those who did not hold the established belief, deserved the punishment of death, he favoured the tribunal of the Inquisition;
A.D. and the same turn of thinking led him to ascribe merit to
1244. a war against infidels. His humane heart became a prey
to the barbarous devotion of the times. When a dangerous illness had deprived him of his senses, and almost of his life, his heated imagination took fire, and he thought he heard a voice

---

[1] Nang. *Vit. Ludovici IX.*   [2] Ibid.

commanding him to shed the blood of infidels. He accordingly made a vow, as soon as he recovered, to engage in a new crusade, and immediately took the cross. Nor could any remonstrances engage him to forego his purpose: he considered his vow as a sacred and indissoluble obligation [1].

But Louis, though not to be dissuaded from his Eastern expedition, was in no hurry to depart. He spent four years in making preparations, and in settling the government of his kingdom, which he left to the care of his mother; and, at length, set sail for Cyprus, accompanied by his queen, his three A.D. brothers, and almost all the knights of France. At 1248. Cyprus it was resolved to make a descent upon Egypt, as it was supposed that Jerusalem and the Holy Land could not be preserved while that country remained in the hands of the infidels. But before I speak of the transactions of Egypt, I must say a few words of the state of the East in those times.

Asia, my dear Philip, from the earliest ages, has been the seat of enormous monarchy, and the theatre of the most astonishing revolutions. You have seen with what rapidity it was overrun by the Arabs, and afterwards by the Turks; you have seen those conquering people, for a time, borne down by the champions of the cross, and Saladin himself sink beneath the arms of our illustrious Richard. But neither the zeal of the Christians, nor the enthusiasm of the Mohammedans, seem to have proved so successful as the hardy valour of the Moguls, or Western Tartars, under Genghiz-Khan, who, in a few years, reduced Persia, and pushed his conquests as far as the Euphrates; subdued a part of Hindostan and of China; all Tartary, and the frontier provinces of Russia.

This wonderful man died in 1227, when he was preparing to complete the conquest of China. His empire was divided among his four sons, whose names it is unnecessary here to mention. Houlakou, one of his grandsons, extended his conquests, and put an end to the long declining dominions of the khalifs of Bagdad. Another prince of his family carried terror into Poland and Hungary, and to the very gates of Constantinople [2].

These Western Tartars, accustomed from their birth to brave hunger, fatigue, and death, were irresistible, while they preserved their savage austerity of manners. The offspring of the same deserts which had produced the Huns and the Turks, they were

---

[1] Joinville, *Hist. de St. Louis.*
[2] Vie de Genghiz-Can, par P. de la Croix—*Mod. Univ. Hist.* vol. iii. fol. edit.

more fierce than either; and as the Goths had formerly seized Thrace, when expelled by the Huns from their native habitations, the Kowarasmians, in like manner, flying before the Moguls, overran Syria and Palestine, and made themselves masters of Jerusalem in 1244, putting the inhabitants to the sword. The Christians, however still possessed Tyre, Sidon, Tripoli, and Ptolemais; and, though generally divided among themselves, they united in imploring the assistance of Europe against this danger.

Such was the situation of the East, and of the Oriental Christians, when St. Louis set out for their relief. But instead of sailing immediately for Palestine, he made a descent upon Egypt. As the sovereign of that territory was not now in possession of Jerusalem, this invasion must have proceeded from the king's ignorance of the affairs of the East, or from an ambition of conquering so fine a country, rather than from any hope of advancing the interests of Christianity.

A. D. 1249. Louis and his army landed near the city of Damietta; which, contrary to all expectations, was abandoned to them. He afterwards received fresh succours from France; and found himself in the plains of Egypt at the head of sixty thousand men (the flower of his kingdom), by whom he was both obeyed and loved. What might not have been expected from such a force, under such a general! Not only Egypt, but Syria, should have yielded to their arms. Yet this crusade, like all the rest, terminated in sorrow and disappointment. One half of these fine Dec. 1250. troops fell a prey to sickness and debauchery, the other part was defeated by the soltan, at Massoura: where Louis beheld his brother Robert of Artois killed by his side, and himself taken prisoner with his two other brothers, the counts of Anjou and Poictiers, and all his nobility [1].

The French, however, were still in possession of Damietta. There the queen was lodged: and thinking her safety doubtful, as the place was besieged, she addressed herself to the Sieur Joinville, a venerable knight, and made him promise, on the faith of chivalry, to cut off her head, if ever her virtue should be in danger. "Most readily," answered Joinville, in the true spirit of the times, "will I perform at your request what I thought indeed to do of myself, should misfortune make it necessary." But he had happily no occasion to put his promise into execution. Damietta held out, and a treaty was concluded with the sultan;

[1] Joinville, *Hist. de St. Louis.*

by which that city was restored in consideration of the king's liberty, and a thousand pieces of gold paid for the ransom of the other prisoners [1].

Louis was now solicited to return to Europe with the remnant of his fleet and army; but devotion led him to Palestine, where he continued above three years without effecting any thing of consequence.   In the mean time the affairs of France were in great confusion.   The queen-mother, during the king's captivity, had unadvisedly given permission to a fanatical monk to preach a new crusade for her son's release; and this man, availing himself of the pastoral circumstances in the Nativity, assem- A.D. bled near one hundred thousand people of low condition, 1251. whom he called shepherds.   It soon appeared, however, that they might with more propriety have been styled wolves.   They robbed and pillaged wherever they came; and it was found necessary to disperse them by force of arms.   Nor was that effected without much trouble [2].

The death of the queen-mother determined Louis, at last, to revisit France.   But he only returned in order to prepare A.D. for a new crusade; so strongly had that madness infected 1254. his mind!—Meanwhile his zeal for justice, his care to reform abuses, his wise laws, his virtuous example, soon repaired the evils occasioned by his absence.   He established, on a solid foundation, the right of appeal to the royal judges, one of the best expedients for reducing the exorbitant power of the nobles.   He absolutely prohibited private wars, which the feudal anarchy had tolerated; he substituted juridical proofs, instead of those by duel; and, no less enlightened than pious, he rescued France from the exactions of the court of Rome.

In his transactions with his neighbours, he was alike exemplary.   Equity and disinterestedness formed the basis of his policy.   If he sometimes carried those virtues too far as a prince, they always did him honour as a man: they even procured him respect as a sovereign; and secured to his subjects the greatest blessings that a people can enjoy—peace and prosperity.   He ceded to James I. of Arragon his incontestable right to Roussillon and Catalonia, which had been subject to France from the time of Charlemagne, in exchange for certain claims of that monarch to some fiefs in Provence and Languedoc; and he restored A.D. to the English crown Querci, Perigord, and the Limosin, 1259.

[1] Joinville, *Hist. de St. Louis.*
[2] Fontenay, *Hist. de l' Eglise Gallic.* tome xi.—Boulay, *Hist. Acad. Parisiensis.* vol. iii.

for no higher consideration than that the king of England should renounce all right to Normandy, Maine, and the other forfeited provinces, which were already in the possession of France. But Louis, as has been observed, was doubtful of the right by which he held those provinces. And although an ambitious prince, instead of making this compromise, might have taken advantage of the troubles of England under Henry III., to seize Guienne, and all that remained to that monarchy in France; such a prince might also, by these means, have drawn on himself the jealousy of his neighbours, and in the end have fallen a sacrifice to his rapacity; whereas Louis, by his moderation, acquired the confidence of all Europe, and was chosen arbiter between the king

A.D. 1264.

of England and his barons, at a time when it was his interest to have ruined both; an honour never conferred upon any other rival monarch, and with which, perhaps, no other could ever have been safely trusted. He determined in favour of the king without prejudice to the people; he annulled the Provisions of Oxford, as derogatory to the rights of the crown, but enforced the observance of the Great Charter. And although this sentence was rejected by Leicester and his party, it will remain an eternal monument of the equity of Louis[1].

The most reprehensible circumstance in this great monarch's conduct, and perhaps the only one that deserves to be considered in that light, was his approbation of the treaty between his brother and the pope, relative to Sicily. When that kingdom was offered to the count of Anjou, he accepted it; and Louis

A.D. 1266.

permitted a crusade to be preached in France against Mainfroy, who had now actually usurped the Sicilian throne, in prejudice to his nephew Conradin. The count of Anjou marched into Italy at the head of a numerous army. Mainfroy was defeated and slain in the plains of Benevento, and Conradin appeared in vindication of his native rights. He also

A.D. 1268.

was routed, and taken prisoner, together with his uncle, the duke of Austria; and both were executed at Naples, upon a scaffold, at the request of the pope, and by the sentence of a pretended court of justice[2]; an indignity not hitherto offered to a crowned head.

In consequence of the revolution that followed this barbarity, by which Charles, count of Anjou, established himself on the Sicilian throne, the ancient rights of that island were annihilated,

---

[1] Rymer, vol. i.—*Chron.* Wikes.—*Chron. Dunst.*
[2] Giannone, *Hist. di Nap.*

and it fell entirely under the jurisdiction of the pope. Meanwhile St. Louis, who, either out of respect to his holiness, or complaisance to his brother, thus beheld with indifference the liberties of mankind sacrificed, and the blood of princes unjustly shed, was preparing to lead a new army against the infidels. He hoped to make a convert of the king of Tunis; and, for that purpose, landed on the coast of Africa, sword in hand, at the head of his troops. But the Tunisine prince refused to embrace Christianity: the French troops were seized with an epidemical distemper, of which Louis beheld one of his sons expire, and another at the point of death, when he himself caught the infection, and died in the fifty-sixth year of his age. His son Aug. 25, and successor, Philip, recovered; kept the field against 1270. the Moors; and saved the remains of the French army, which procured him the name of the Hardy[1]. But the reign of this prince must not at present engage our attention; we must return to the affairs of Spain, which had still little connection with the rest of Europe, but was gradually rising into consequence.

LETTER XXXV.

A Survey of the Transactions in Spain, from the Middle of the Eleventh to the End of the Thirteenth Century.

WE left Spain, my dear Philip, towards the middle of the eleventh century, dismembered by the Moors and Christians, and both nations harassed by civil wars. About that time Ferdinand, son of Sancho the Great, king of Navarre and Arragon, united to his dominions Old Castile, together with the kingdom A.D. of Leon, which he took from his brother-in-law, Vere- 1036. mond, whom he slew in battle. Castile then became a kingdom, and Leon one of its provinces[2].

In the reign of the son of this Ferdinand flourished Don Roderigo, surnamed the Cid, who actually married Chimene, whose father he had murdered. They who know nothing of his history, but from the celebrated tragedy written by Corneille, suppose that Ferdinand was in possession of Andalusia. The

---

[1] Joinville, ubi sup.—Mezeray, vol. iii.
[2] Mariana, *de Rebus Hispaniæ*, lib. ix.

Cid began his famous exploits by assisting Sancho, Ferdinand's
A.D. eldest son, to deprive his brothers and sisters of the
1072. inheritance left to them by their father; but the death of
Sancho, in one of these unjust expeditions, secured the observance of Ferdinand's will.

A short digression will be here necessary. Besides the many
kings at this time in Spain, who nearly amounted to the number
of twenty, there were many independent lords, who came on
horseback, completely armed, and followed by several esquires,
to offer their services to the princes and princesses engaged in
war. The princes with whom these lords engaged, girded them
with a belt, and presented them with a sword, with which they
gave them a slight blow on the shoulder; and hence the origin
of knights errant, and of the number of single combats, which so
long desolated Spain.

One of the most celebrated of these combats followed the
murder of that king Sancho, whose death I have just mentioned,
and who was assassinated while he was besieging his sister Urraca
in the city of Zamora. Three knights maintained the honour of
the infanta against Don Diego de Lara, who had accused her.
Don Diego overthrew and killed two of the infanta's knights;
the horse of the third, having the reins of his bridle cut, carried
his master out of the lists; and the combat was declared undecided.

Of all the Spanish knights, the Cid distinguished himself most
eminently against the Moors. Several knights ranged themselves
under his banner; and these, with their esquires and horsemen,
composed an army covered with iron, and mounted on the most
beautiful steeds in the country. With this force he overcame
several Moorish kings; and having fortified the city of Alcassar,
he there erected a petty sovereignty.

But of the various enterprises in which the Cid and his followers
were engaged, the most gallant was the siege of Toledo, which
A.D. his master Alphonso VI., king of Old Castile, undertook
1084. against the Moors. The fame of this siege, and the Cid's
reputation, drew many knights and princes from France and
Italy; particularly Raymond, count of Toulouse, and two princes
of the blood-royal of France, of the branch of Burgundy. The
Moorish king, named Hiaya, was the son of Al-Mamoun, one of
the most generous princes mentioned in history, who had afforded
an asylum, in this very city, to Alphonso, when persecuted by his
brother Sancho. They had lived together for a long time in
strict friendship; and Al-Mamoun was so far from detaining

Alphonso when he became king by the death of Sancho, that he gave him part of his treasures, and they shed tears, it is said, at parting. But the spirit of those times made every thing seem lawful against infidels, and even meritorious. Several Moorish chiefs went out of the city to reproach Alphonso with his ingratitude, and many remarkable combats were fought under the walls.

When the siege had continued a whole year, Toledo capitulated, on condition, that the Moors should enjoy their A.D. religion and laws, and suffer no injury in their persons or 1085. property [1]. All New Castile, in a short time, yielded to the Cid, who took possession of it in the name of Alphonso; and Madrid, a small place, which was one day to become the capital of Spain, fell into the hands of the Christians.

Immediately after the reduction of Toledo, Alphonso called an assembly of bishops, who without the concurrence of the people, formerly thought necessary, promoted a priest named Bernard, to the bishopric of that city; and pope Urban II., at the king's request, made him primate of Spain. The king and the pope were also anxious to establish the Romish liturgy and ritual, in place of the Gothic, or Mosarabic, hitherto in use. The Spaniards contended zealously for the ritual of their ancestors; the pope urged them to receive that to which he had given his infallible sanction: a violent contest arose; and, to the disgrace of human reason, a religious opinion was referred to the decision of the sword. Two knights accordingly entered the lists in complete armour. The Mosarabic champion was victorious; but the king and the archbishop had sufficient influence to procure a new trial, though contrary to all the laws of combat. The next appeal was to God by fire. A fire being prepared for that purpose, a copy of each liturgy was cast into the flames. The fire, we may suppose, respected neither; but authority prevailed. The Romish liturgy was ordered to be received; yet some A.D. churches were permitted to retain the Mosarabic [2]. 1087.

Alphonso, either from policy, or inclination, augmented the dominions which he had acquired through the valour of the Cid, by marrying Zaid, daughter of Ebn-Abad, the Mohammedan king of Seville, with whom he received several towns in dowry: and he is reproached with having, in conjunction with his father-in-law, invited the sovereign of Morocco into Spain. But be that

[1] Rod. Tolet. *de Reb. Hisp.*—Mariana, ubi sup.—Ferreras, *Hist. de Espana.*
[2] Id. ibid.

as it may, the *Emir-al-Moumenin* came; and, instead of assisting the king of Seville in reducing the petty Moorish
princes, he turned his arms against him, took the city of
Seville, and became a dangerous neighbour to Alphonso [1].

In the mean time the Cid, at the head of his army of knights,
subdued the kingdom of Valencia. Few kings in Spain were,
at that time, so powerful as he ; yet he never assumed the regal
title, but continued faithful to his master Alphonso, while he
governed Valencia with the authority of a sovereign. After his
death, which happened in 1096, the kings of Castile and Arragon continued their wars against the infidels; and Spain was
more drenched in blood than ever, and more desolated.

Alphonso, surnamed the Battle-giver, king of Navarre and
Arragon, took Saragossa from the Moors ; and that city,
which afterwards became the capital of the kingdom of
Arragon, was never again subjected to the dominion of the
infidels. He was continually at war either with the Christians
or Mohammedans; and the latter gained a complete victory over
him, which mortified him so much, that he died of chagrin, leaving his kingdom by will to the Knights Templars. This was bequeathing a civil war as his last legacy. The
testament was esteemed valid; but fortunately these knights
were not in a condition to enforce it; and the states of Arragon
chose for their king Ramiro, brother to the deceased prince.
He had led a monastic life for upwards of forty years, and
proved incapable of governing. The people of Navarre therefore chose another king, descended from their ancient monarchs;
and, by this division, both these states became a prey to the
Moors. They were saved by the timely assistance of Alphonso
VIII., king of Castile, who had obtained many victories over
the infidels, and in return for his protection received the city of
Saragossa from the Arragonese, and the homage of the king of
Navarre. This success so much elated Alphonso, that he assumed the title of Emperor of Spain [2].

Alphonso Henriquez, count of Portugal, received about this
time the title of king from his soldiers, after a victory obtained
over the Moors; and he took Lisbon from them by the assistance of an army of crusaders, who had been driven up the Tagus
by tempestuous weather. On this occasion pope Alexander III., steady to the policy of his predecessors, took

A.D. 1097.

A.D. 1118.

A.D. 1134.

A.D. 1147.

---

[1] Rod. Tolet. *de Reb. Hisp.*—Mariana, ubi sup.—Ferreras, *Hist. de España.*
[2] Rod. Tolet. *de Reb. Hisp.*

advantage of the papal maxim, that all countries conquered from the infidels belong to the holy see, to assert his superiority over Portugal; and Alphonso politically allowed him an annual   A.D. tribute of two marks of gold, on receiving a bull from   1179. Rome, confirming his regal dignity and his infallible right to that territory [1].

Very few efforts would now have been sufficient to have driven the Moors entirely out of Spain: but for that purpose it was necessary that the Spanish Christians should be united among themselves, whereas they were engaged in almost perpetual wars one with another. They united, however, at   A.D. length from a sense of common danger, and also implored   1211. the assistance of other Christian princes of Europe.

Mohammed Al-naser, the Emir-al-Moumenin, having crossed the sea with an army of near one hundred thousand men, and being joined by the Moors in Andalusia, assured himself of making an entire conquest of Spain. The rumour of this great armament roused the attention of the whole European continent. Many adventurers came from all quarter. To these the kings of Castile, Arragon, and Navarre united their forces: the   A.D. kingdom of Portugal also furnished a body of troops; and   1212. the Christian and Mohammedan armies met in the defiles of the Sierra Morena, or Black Mountain, on the borders of Andalusia, and in the province of Toledo. Alphonso IX., king of Castile, commanded the centre of the Christian army: the archbishop of Toledo carried the cross before him. The African prince occupied the same place in the Moorish army: he was dressed in a rich robe, with the Koran in one hand, and a sabre in the other. The battle was long and obstinately disputed: but at length the Christians prevailed [2]; and the 16th of July, the day on which the victory was gained, is still celebrated in Toledo.

The consequences of this victory, however, were not so great as might have been expected. The Moors of Andalusia were strengthened by the remains of the African army, while that of the Christians immediately dispersed. Almost all the knights who had been present at the battle returned to their respective homes as soon as it was over. But although the Christians seemed thus to neglect their true interests, by allowing the Mohammedans time to recruit themselves, the Moors employed that time more to their own hurt than the Christians could if

---

[1] Neufville, *Hist. Gén. de Port.*   [2] Rod. Tolet. *de Reb. Hisp.*

united against them.   All the Moorish states, both in Spain
and Africa, were rent in pieces by civil dissensions, and a variety
of new sovereigns sprang up, which entirely broke the power of
the infidels.

The period seemed therefore arrived, to use the language of
that haughty and superstitious nation, marked out by Heaven
for the glory of Spain, and the expulsion of the Moors.   Fer-
A.D. dinand III., styled by his countrymen St. Ferdinand,
1236. took from the infidels the famous city of Cordova, the
residence of the first Moorish kings; and James I. of Arragon
A.D. dispossessed them of the island of Majorca, and drove
1238. them out of the fine kingdom of Valencia.   St. Ferdi-
dand also subdued the province of Murcia, and made himself
A.D. master of Seville, the most opulent city belonging to the
1248. Moors [1].   Death at length put an end to his conquests:
and if divine honours are due to those who have been the de-
A.D. liverers of their country, Spain justly reverences the name
1252. of Ferdinand III.

Alphonso, surnamed the Astronomer, or the Wise, the son
of St. Ferdinand, likewise exalted the glory of Spain; but in a
manner very different from that of his father.   This prince, who
rivalled the Arabians in the sciences, digested the celebrated
Spanish code called *Las Partidas;* and under his inspection those
astronomical tables were drawn up, which still bear his name,
and do honour to his memory.   In his old age he saw his son
Sancho rebel against him, and was reduced to the disagreeable
A.D. necessity of leaguing with the Moors against his own
1283. blood, and his rebellious Christian subjects.   This was
not the first alliance which Christians had formed with infidels
against Christians; but it was certainly the most excusable.

Alphonso invited to his assistance the Emir-al-Moumenin,
who immediately crossed the sea; and the two monarchs met
at Zara, on the confines of Granada.   The behaviour and speech
of the Moorish prince, on this occasion, deserve to be recorded.
He gave the place of honour to Alphonso at meeting: " I treat
you thus," said he, " because you are unfortunate; and enter
into an alliance with you to support the common cause of all
kings and all fathers [2]."

The rebels were vanquished; but the good old king died before
he had time to enjoy the fruits of his victory: and, the Emir-

---

[1] Rod. Tolet. *de Reb. Hisp.*   [2] Ferreras et Mariana, ubi supra.

al-Moumenin being obliged to return to Africa, the unnatural Sancho succeeded to the crown, in prejudice to the off- A.D. spring of a former marriage. He even reigned happily ; and 1284. his son Ferdinand IV. was not unsuccessful against the Moors.

This Ferdinand is called by the Spanish historians, the Summoned ; and the reason assigned for it is somewhat remarkable. When he had ordered two noblemen, in a fit of anger, to be thrown from the top of a rock, they summoned him to appear in the presence of God within a month ; at the end of which he died[1].   It is to be wished, as Voltaire very justly ob- A.D. serves, that this story were true, or at least believed to 1312. be so by all princes who think they have a right to follow their own imperious wills at the expense of the lives of their fellow-creatures.

These are the circumstances most worthy of notice in the history of Spain, during the period here examined.   We must now take a view of the progress of society.

LETTER XXXVI.

Of the Progress of Society in Europe during the Twelfth and Thirteenth Centuries.

You have already, my dear Philip, seen letters begin to revive, and manners to soften, about the middle of the eleventh century.   But the progress of refinement was slow during the two succeeding centuries, and often altogether obstructed by monastic austerities, theological disputes, ecclesiastical broils, and the disorders of feudal anarchy.   Society, however, made many beneficial advances before the close of this period.   These I shall endeavour distinctly to trace.

The influence of the spirit of chivalry on manners, as we have seen, was great and singular : it enlarged the generosities of the human heart, and soothed its ferocity.   But, being unhappily blended with superstition, it became itself the means of violence, armed one half of the species against the other, and precipitated Europe upon Asia.   I allude to the crusades.   Yet these romantic expeditions, though barbarous and destructive in them-

[1] Ferreras, *Hist. Espana.*

selves, were followed by some important consequences, equally
conducive to the welfare of the community and of the individual.
The crusaders being taken under the immediate protection of
the church, and its heaviest anathemas denounced against all
who should molest their persons or their property, private hostilities were for a time suspended or extinguished; the feudal
sovereigns became more powerful, and their vassals less turbulent; a more steady administation of justice was introduced,
and some advances were made towards regular government.

The commercial effects of the crusades were not less considerable than their political influence. Many ships were necessary
to transport the prodigious armies which Europe poured forth,
and also to supply them with provisions. These ships were
principally furnished by the Venetians, the Pisans, and the
Genoese; who accquired, by that service, immense sums of
money, and opened to themselves, at the same time, a new
source of wealth, by importing into Europe the commodities of
Asia. A taste for these commodities became general. The
Italian cities grew rich and powerful, and obtained extensive
privileges. Some of them erected themselves into sovereignties,
others into corporations or independent communities[1]; and the
establishment of those communities may be considered as the
first great step towards civilization in Modern Europe.

This subject requires your particular attention. The feudal
government, as I have had occasion to observe, had degenerated
into a system of oppression. Not only the inhabitants of the
country, but even whole cities and villages, held of some great
lord, on whom they depended for protection; and the citizens
were not less subject to his arbitrary jurisdiction than those who
were employed in cultivating the estates of their masters. Services of various kinds, equally disgraceful and oppressive, were
exacted from them without mercy or moderation: and they
were deprived of the most natural and inalienable rights of
humanity. They could not dispose of their effects by will,
appoint guardians to their children, or even marry, without the
consent of their superior lord[2].

As men in such a condition had few motives to industry, we
find all the cities of Europe, before their enfranchisement,
equally poor and wretched. But no sooner were they formed
into bodies politic, governed by magistrates chosen from among

[1] Murat. *Antiq. Ital.* vol. ii.
[2] *Ordon. des Rois de France,* tome i.—D'Ach. Spicileg. vol. xi.—Murat. *Antiq.*
Ital. vol. iv.

their own members, than the spirit of industry revived, and commerce began to flourish. Population increased with independence; the conveniences of life with the means of procuring them: property gave birth to statutes and regulations; a sense of common danger enforced them: and the more frequent occasions of intercourse among men and kingdoms gradually led to a greater refinement in manners, and tended to wear off those national and local prejudices which created dissension and animosity between the inhabitants of different states and provinces.

The mode in which these immunities were obtained, varied in the different kingdoms of Europe. Some of the Italian cities acquired their freedom by arms, others by money; and in France and Germany many of the great barons were glad to sell charters of liberty to the towns within their jurisdiction, in order to repair the expense incurred by the crusades. The sovereigns also granted, or sold, similar privileges to the towns within the royal domain, with a view of creating some power that might counter-balance their potent vassals, who often gave law to the crown [1]. The practice quickly spread over Europe; and before the end of the thirteenth century its beneficial effects were generally felt.

These effects were no less extensive upon government than upon manners. Self-preservation had obliged every man, during several centuries, to court the patronage of some powerful baron, whose castle was the common asylum in times of danger; but towns surrounded with walls, and filled with citizens trained to arms, bound by interest as well as the most solemn engagements to protect each other, afforded a more commodious and secure retreat. The nobles became of less importance when they ceased to be the sole guardians of the people; and the crown acquired an increase of power and consequence, when it no longer depended entirely upon its great vassals for the supply of its armies. The cities contributed liberally towards the support of the royal authority, as they deemed the sovereigns the authors of their liberty, and their protectors against the domineering spirit of the nobles. Hence flowed another consequence of corporation charters.

The inhabitants of cities having obtained personal freedom, and municipal jurisdiction, soon aspired to civil liberty and political power. And the sovereigns in most kingdoms found it necessary to admit them to a share in the legislature, on account

---

[1] Du Cange, voc. *Communia*.

of their utility in raising the supplies for government; it being
a fundamental principle in the feudal policy, that no free man
could be taxed but with his own consent. The citizens were
now free; but the wealth, power, and consequence, which they
acquired on recovering their liberty, added weight to their claim
to political eminence, and seemed to mark them out as an
essential branch in the constitution. They had it much in their
power to supply the exigencies of the crown, and also to
repress the encroachment of the nobles. In England, Germany,
and even in France, where the voice of liberty is heard no more,
the representatives of communities accordingly obtained, by different means, a place in the national council, as early as the
beginning of the fourteenth century [1].

Thus, my dear Philip, an intermediate power was established
between the king and the nobles, to which each had recourse alternately, and which sometimes opposed the one and sometimes the
other. It tempered the rigour of aristocratical oppression with
a mixture of popular liberty, while it restrained the usurpations
of the crown: it secured to the great body of the people, who
had formerly no representatives, active and powerful guardians
of their rights and liberties; and it entirely changed the spirit
of the laws, by introducing into the statutes and the jurisprudence of the European nations ideas of equality, order, and
public good.

To this new power, the villains or slaves, who resided in the
country and were employed in agriculture, looked up for freedom. They obtained it, though contrary to the spirit of the
feudal polity. The odious names of master and slave were
abolished. The husbandman became farmer of the same fields
which he had been compelled to cultivate for the benefit of
another. He reaped a share of the fruits of his own industry.
New prospects opened, new incitements were offered to ingenuity and enterprise. The activity of genius was awakened;
and a numerous class of men, who formerly had no political existence, were restored to society, and augmented the force and
riches of the state.

The second great advance which society made, during the
period under review, was an approach towards a more regular
administration of justice. The barbarous nations who over-ran

---

[1] M. l'Abbé Mably, *Observat. sur l'Hist. de France*, tome ii.—Henault, tome i.—
Pfeffel *Abregé de l'Hist. du Droit d'Allemagne*. Brady's *Treatise of Boroughs.*—
Madox, *Firma Burgi.*

the Roman empire, and settled in its provinces, rejected the Roman jurisprudence with the same contempt with which they spurned the Roman arts. Both respected objects of which they had no conception, and were adapted to a state of society with which they were then unacquainted. But as civilization advanced, they became sensible of the imperfection of their own institutions, and even of their absurdity. Trials by ordeal and by duel were abolished in most countries before the close of the thirteenth century ; and various attempts were made to restrain the practice of private war, one of the greatest abuses of feudal polity, and which struck at the foundation of all government.

As the authority of the civil magistrate was found ineffectual to remedy this evil, the church interposed ; and various regulations were published, in order to set bounds to private hostilities. But these all proving insufficient, supernatural means were employed : a letter was sent from heaven to a bishop of Aquitaine, commanding men to cease from violence, and be reconciled to each other. This revelation was published during a season of public calamity, when men were willing to perform any thing in order to avert the wrath of an offended God. A general reconciliation took place ; and a resolution was formed, that no man should in future attack or molest his adversaries during the seasons appropriated for the celebration of the great festivals of the church, or from the end of Thursday in each week to the beginning of Monday in the week ensuing : the three intervening days being considered as particularly holy, Christ's passion having happened on one of those days, and his resurrection on another. This cessation from hostility was called " The Truce of God ;" and three complete days, in every week, allowed such a considerable space for the passions of the antagonists to cool, and for the people to enjoy a respite from the calamities of war, as well as to take measures for their own security, that if the Truce of God had been strictly observed, it would have gone far towards putting an end to private wars. That, however, was not the case ; the nobles prosecuted their quarrels as formerly, till near the end of the twelfth century, when a carpenter of Guienne gave out, that Jesus Christ had appeared to him, and having commanded him to exhort mankind to peace, had given him, as a proof of his mission, an image of the Virgin holding her Son in her arms, with this inscription : " Lamb of God, who takest away the sins of the world, give us peace !" This low fanatic was received as an inspired messenger of Heaven. Many prelates and barons assembled at Puy, and took an oath, not only to make peace with all their own enemies, but to attack such as refused to lay down their arms and to be reconciled to their adversaries. They formed an association for that purpose, and assumed the honourable name of " The Brotherhood of God." Associations of the same kind were formed in other countries; and these, together with civil prohibitions enforced by royal power, contributed to remove this pernicious evil [1].

When society was thus emerging from barbarism, and men were become sensible of the necessity of order, a copy of Justinian's Pandects was discovered at Amalphi, in Italy, and although the age had still too little taste to relish the beauty of the Roman classics, it immediately perceived the merit of a system of laws, in which all the points most interesting to mankind were settled with precision, discernment and equity. All men of letters were struck with admiration at the wisdom of the ancients; the code of Justinian was studied with eagerness; and professors of civil law were appointed, who taught this new science in most countries in Europe.

The effects of studying and imitating so perfect a model, were, as might be expected, great. Fixed and general laws were established; the principles and forms by which judges should regulate their decisions were ascertained; the feudal law was reduced into a regular system; the canon law was methodised; the loose uncertain customs of different provinces or kingdoms were collected and arranged with order and accuracy. And these improvements in the system of jurisprudence had an extensive influence on society. They gave rise to a distinction of professions.

Among rude nations no profession is honourable but that of arms; and as the functions of peace are few and simple, war is the only study. Such had been the state of Europe during several centuries. But when law became a science, the knowledge of which required a regular course of studies and long attention to the practice of courts, a new order of men naturally acquired consideration and influence in society. Another profession, beside that of arms, was introduced, and reputed honourable among the laity; the talents requisite for discharging it were cultivated; the arts and virtues of peace were placed in their proper rank; and the people of Europe became accustomed

---

[1] Du Cange, *Gloss.* voc. *Truega.*—Du Mont, *Corps Diplomatique*, tome i.—Robertson's *Introd. Hist. Charles V.* sec. i.—Hume's *Hist. England*, Append. i.

to see men rise to eminence by civil as well as military employment [1].

The study of the Roman law had also a considerable influence upon letters. The knowledge of a variety of sciences became necessary, in order to expound with judgment the civil code; and the same passion which impelled men to prosecute the juridical science with so much ardour, rendered them anxious to excel in every branch of literature. Colleges and universities were founded, a regular course of study was planned, and a regular set of professors established. Privileges of great value were conferred upon masters and scholars; academical titles and honours were invented, as rewards for the different degrees of literary eminence; and an incredible number of students, allured by these advantages, resorted to the new seats of learning.

But a false taste unhappily infected all those seminaries; for which a learned and inquisitive writer thus ingeniously accounts. Most of the persons who attempted to revive literature in the twelfth and thirteenth centuries had received instruction, and derived their principles of science, from the Greeks in the Eastern empire, or the Arabs in Spain and Africa. Both those people, acute and inquisitive to excess, corrupted the sciences which they cultivated. The Greeks rendered theology a system of speculative refinement, or endless controversy; and the Arabs communicated to philosophy a spirit of metaphysical and frivolous subtilty. Misled by these guides, the persons who first applied to science were involved in a maze of intricate inquiries. Instead of allowing their fancy to take its natural range, and produce such works of elegant invention as might have improved the taste and refined the sentiments of the age; instead of cultivating those arts which embellish human life, and render it delightful; they spent the whole force of their genius in speculations as unavailing as they were difficult [2].

But, fruitless and ill-directed as these speculations were, their novelty roused, and their boldness engaged, the human mind; and although science was farther circumscribed in its influence, and prevented during several ages from diffusing itself through society, by being delivered in the Latin tongue, its progress deserves to be mentioned, as one of the great causes which contributed to introduce a change of manners into modern Europe.

[1] Montesquieu, *l'Esprit de Loix*, liv. xxviii. — Hume. — Robertson.
[2] Robertson's *Introduc.* sec. i.

That ardent though mistaken spirit of inquiry which prevailed, gave a *stimulus* to ingenuity and invention : it led men to a new employment of their faculties, which they found to be agreeable as well as interesting ; it accustomed them to exercises and occupations that tended to soften their manners, and to give them some relish for those gentle virtues which are peculiar to nations among whom science has been cultivated with success.

Some ages indeed elapsed before taste, order, and politeness, were restored to society : but anarchy and barbarism gradually disappeared with ignorance ; the evils of life, with its crimes; and public and private happiness began to be better understood ; until Europe (wisely governed) attained the enjoyment of all advantages, pleasures, amusements, and tender sympathies, which are necessary to alleviate the pains inseparable from existence, and soothe the sorrows allied to humanity.

LETTER XXXVII.

History of England during the Reign of Edward I., with an Introduction to that of Scotland, and some Account of the Conquest of that Country by the English, as well as of the final Reduction of Wales.

THE reign of Edward I., my dear Philip, as I have already observed, forms a new æra in the history of Britain. I must now make you sensible what entitles it to that distinction.

As soon as Edward returned to England (where his authority A.D. 1274. was firmly established, by his high character both at home and abroad,) he applied himself assiduously to the correction of those disorders which the civil commotions, and the loose administration of his father, had introduced into every part of government. By an exact distribution of justice, and a rigid execution of the laws, he at once gave protection to the inferior orders of the state, and diminished the arbitrary power of the nobles. He made it a rule in his own conduct to observe, except upon extraordinary occasions, the privileges secured to the barons by the Great Charter; and he insisted on their observance of the same charter towards their vassals. He took measures for attracting reverence to the crown as the grand fountain of justice, and the general asylum against violence and oppression.   By these judicious proceedings, the state of the kingdom was soon wholly changed: order and tranquillity were restored to society, and vigour to government [1].

Now it was that the enterprising spirit of Edward began more remarkably to show itself.   He undertook an expedition A.D. against Llewellyn, prince of Wales, who had formerly 1277. joined the rebellious barons, and whose two brothers, David and Roderic, had fled to Edward for protection, craving his assistance to recover their possessions, and seconding his attempts to en- slave their native country.

The Welsh prince had no resource against the superior force of Edward but the inaccessible situation of his mountains, which had protected his forefathers against all the attempts of the Saxon and Norman conquerors. He accordingly retired with the bravest of his subjects among the hills of Snowdon. But Edward, no less vigorous than cautious, pierced into the heart of the country, and approached the Welsh army in its last retreat.   Having carefully secured every pass behind him, he avoided putting to trial the valour of a nation proud of its ancient independence. He was willing to trust to the more slow but sure effects of famine for success; and Llewellyn was at length obliged to submit, and receive the terms imposed upon him by the English monarch [2].

These terms were ill observed by the victors, who oppressed and insulted the inhabitants of the districts which were yielded to them.   The indignation of the Welsh was roused; they flew to arms; and Edward again entered Wales with an army, not displeased with the occasion of making his conquest final.   This army he committed to the command of Roger Mortimer, while he himself waited the event in the castle of Rhudlan; and Llewellyn, having ventured to leave his mountainous posts, was defeated by Mortimer, and slain, with two thousand of A.D. his followers.   All the Welsh nobility submitted to 1282. Edward, and the laws of England were established in the prin- cipality [3].

In order to preserve his conquests, Edward had recourse to a barbarous policy.   He ordered David, brother to Llewellyn, and his successor in the principality of Wales, to be hanged, A.D. drawn, and quartered, as a traitor, for taking arms in 1283. defence of his native country, which he had once unhappily

----

[1] M. Westm.—T. Walsingh. *Hist. Brev.*   [2] *Chron.* Wikes.
[3] T. Wals.—*Annal. Wave.*—Powel's *Hist. Wales.*

deserted, and for maintaining by force his own hereditary authority. He also ordered all the Welsh bards to be put to death;
from a belief, and no absurd one, that he should more easily
subdue the independent spirit of the people, when their minds
ceased to be roused by the ideas of military valour and ancient
glory, preserved in the traditional poems of those minstrels, and
recited or sung by them on all public occasions and days of
festivity [1].

Edward's conduct in regard to Scotland, at which his ambition now pointed, is little more excusable. But some points
must be premised, my dear Philip, before I proceed to his
transactions with that country.

After the final departure of the Romans from this island, the
Scots, who had colonized some of its northern districts, were
driven to Ireland by the Picts : but about the beginning of the
sixth century, Fergus and Lorn, two enterprising brothers,
emigrated with an army from their Hibernian settlements, and
erected a kingdom in Argyleshire and the neighbouring territories. Wars were occasionally carried on between the successors of Fergus and the Pictish kings, till Kenneth the Scot,
either by inheritance or by conquest, united into one monarchy
the whole country at present known by the name of North
Britain. The Scots thenceforth became more formidable ; and,
having less business on their hands at home, were always ready
to join the English malecontents, and made frequent incursions
into the bordering counties. In one of these inroads, William,
king of Scotland was taken prisoner ; and Henry II., as the
price of his liberty, not only extorted from him an exorbitant
ransom, and a promise to surrender the places of greatest
strength in his dominions, but compelled him to do homage for
his whole kingdom. Richard I., a more generous but less
politic prince than his father, solemnly renounced his claim of
homage, and absolved William from the other severe conditions
which Henry had imposed. The crown of Scotland was therefore again independent ; and the northern potentate only did
homage for the fiefs which he enjoyed in England, (a circumstance which has occasioned various mistakes and much dispute
among historians,) in the same manner as the king of England
himself swore fealty to the French monarch, for the fiefs which
A.D. he inherited in France. But on the death of Alexander
1286. III., above a century after the captivity of William,

---

[1] Sir J. Wynne.

2

Edward I., availing himself of the situation of affairs in Scotland, revived the claim of sovereignty which had been renounced by Richard [1].

This is the real state of the controversy concerning the independence of Scotland, which took its rise about this time, and in the following manner.   As Alexander left no male issue, nor any descendant except Margaret of Norway, his grand-daughter, who did not long survive him, the right of succession belonged to the descendants of David earl of Huntingdon, third son of king David I.   Of that line, two illustrious competitors for the crown appeared : Robert Bruce, son of Isabel, earl David's second daughter; and John Baliol, grandson of Margaret, the eldest daughter.   According to the rules of succession now established, Baliol's right was preferable : he would succeed as the representative of his mother and grandmother, and Bruce's plea of being one degree nearer the common stock would be disregarded.   But in that age the question appeared no less intricate than important : the sentiments of men were divided : each claim was supported by a powerful faction ; and arms alone, it was feared, must terminate a dispute too weighty for the laws to decide.

In this critical situation the parliament of Scotland, in order to avoid the miseries of civil war, embraced the dangerous resolution of appealing to Edward I.   He was accordingly chosen arbitrator; and both parties agreed to acquiesce in his decree. Now it was that this ambitious and enterprising prince, already master of Wales, resolved to make himself lord of the whole island of Britain, by reviving his obscure claim of feudal superiority over Scotland.   Under pretence of examining the question with the utmost solemnity, he summoned all the A.D. Scottish barons to attend him at Norham on the southern 1291. banks of the Tweed ; and having gained some, and intimidated others, he prevailed on all who were present, not excepting Bruce and Baliol, the two competitors for the succession, to acknowledge Scotland a fief of the English crown, and swear fealty to him as their sovereign or liege lord [2].

This step led to another still more important.   As it was in vain to pronounce a sentence which he had not power to execute, Edward demanded possession of the disputed kingdom, that he might be able to deliver it to him whose right should be found

[1] Buchan. *Rerum Scoticarum Hist.* lib. viii. — Robertson's *Hist. of Scotland*, book i.
[2] Rymer, vol. ii. — W. Heming. vol. i.

preferable : and with that exorbitant demand the barons and the
A.D. claimants complied. He soon after gave judgment in
1292. favour of Baliol, as being the least formidable of the competitors, in the opinion of a respectable historian[1]; but, in
justice to Edward, I am bound to say, that his award, which
was no less equitable than solemn, seemed to proceed merely
from the state of the question. He not only referred it to the
consideration of a hundred and forty commissioners, partly
English and partly Scotch, but proposed it to all the celebrated
lawyers in Europe, who returned an uniform answer conformable to the king's decree. Baliol renewed the oath of fealty to
England, and was put in possession of the kingdom[2].

Edward having thus established his unjust claim of feudal
superiority over Scotland, aimed at the absolute sovereignty
and dominion of that kingdom. He attempted to provoke
Baliol by indignities ; to rouse him to rebellion, and to rob him
of his crown, as the punishment of his pretended treason and
A.D. felony. Even the passive spirit of Baliol began to
1295. mutiny ; and he entered into a secret alliance with
France, which was already engaged in a war with England, the
more effectually to maintain his independence.

The expenses attending these multiplied wars of Edward,
and his new preparations for reducing Scotland, obliged him to
have frequent recourse to parliamentary supplies, and introduced
the lower orders of the state into the public councils. This
period, therefore, the twenty-third year of his reign, seems to
be the true æra of the House of Commons : for the former
precedent of representatives from the boroughs, summoned by
the earl of Leicester, was regarded as the irregular act of a
faction, and had been discontinued in all the subsequent parliaments. But when the multiplied necessities of the crown produced a greater demand for money than could be conveniently
answered by the common mode of taxation, Edward became sensible, that the most expeditious way of obtaining supplies would
be, to assemble the deputies of all the boroughs, inform them
explicitly of the exigencies of the state, and desire their consent
to the demands of their sovereign. He therefore issued writs
to the sheriffs, enjoining them to send to parliament, with two
knights of the shire, two deputies from each borough within
their county, provided with sufficient powers from their community, to consent to such imposts as might seem necessary for the

---

[1] Robertson.   [2] Rymer, vol. ii.—W. Heming. vol. i.

support of government—"as it is a most equitable rule," says he, in his preamble to his writ, "that what concerns all should be approved by all, and common dangers be repelled by united efforts[1]." Such a way of thinking implies a generosity of mind much superior to what might be expected from Edward's general conduct.

The different corporations, after the election of these deputies, gave security for their attendance before the king and parliament; and their charges were borne by the borough that sent them[2]; how different in that, as well as in other respects, from our more modern representatives!—instead of checking and controlling the authority of the king, they were naturally induced to adhere to him, as the great fountain of justice, and to support him against the power of the nobles, who at once oppressed them, and disturbed him in the execution of the laws. The king, in his turn, gave countenance to an order of men so useful, and so little dangerous. The peers also were obliged to treat them with some respect, on account of their consequence as a body. By these means the commons, or third estate, long so abject in England, as well as in all other European countries, rose gradually to their present importance; and, in their progress, made arts and commerce, the necessary attendants of liberty and equality, flourish in Britain.

Edward employed the supplies granted by his people in warlike preparations against his northern neighbour. He cited Baliol, as his vassal, to appear in an English parliament at Newcastle. But that prince having now received pope Celestin's dispensation from his oath of fealty, renounced his homage to England, and set Edward at defiance. This bravado was ill supported by the military operations of the Scots. Edward crossed the Tweed without opposition, at the head of thirty thousand foot, and four thousand horse. Berwick was taken by assault; the Scots were totally routed near Dunbar; the whole southern part of the kingdom was subdued; and the timid Baliol, discontented with his own subjects, and over-awed by the English, instead of making use of those resources which were yet left, hastened to make his submissions to the conqueror. He expressed the deepest penitence for his disloyalty to his liege lord; and he made a solemn and irrevocable renunciation of his crown into the hands of Edward[3].

A.D. 1296.

---

[1] Brady's *Treatise of Boroughs*, from the Records.
[2] Id. Ibid.—*Reliquiæ* Spelm.
[3] Rymer, vol. ii.—Heming, vol. i.—Triverti *Annal.*

The English monarch marched as far north as Aberdeen and Elgin without meeting a single enemy. No Scot approached him, but to do homage. Even the turbulent Highlanders, ever refractory to their own princes, and insubmissive to the restraints of law, endeavoured by a timely obedience to prevent the devastation of their country : and Edward, flattering himself that he had now attained the great object of his wishes, in the final reduction of Scotland, left earl Warrenne governor of the kingdom, and returned with his victorious army into England[1].

Here a few particulars are necessary. There was a stone, to which the popular superstition of the Scots paid the highest veneration. All their kings were seated on it when they received inauguration. Ancient tradition assured them, that their nation should always govern where this stone was placed ; and it was carefully preserved at Scone, as the true palladium of their monarchy, and their ultimate resource under all misfortunes. Edward gained possession of it, and carried it with him into England. He also gave orders for the destruction of the records, and of all documents calculated to preserve the memory of the independence of the kingdom of Scotland, and refute the English claims of superiority. The great seal of Baliol was broken, and that prince himself was brought to London, and committed to close custody in the Tower[2]. Two years after, he was restored to liberty, and submitted to a voluntary banishment in France ; where without making any farther attempt for the recovery of his royalty, he died in a private station.

Edward was not so successful in an effort which he made for the recovery of Guienne. Philip the Fair had robbed England of this province, by an artifice similar to that which Edward had practised against the Scots. He had cited the English monarch, as his vassal, to answer in the court of peers to the charge of treason against his sovereign, for having permitted his subjects to seize some Norman vessels, and denied satisfaction : and Edward, refusing to comply, was declared guilty of treason, and the duchy of Guienne confiscated. An English army was sent over to recover it, under the earl of Lancaster, who died in a short time; and the earl of Lincoln, who succeeded him in the command, failed in the attempt. But the active and ambitious spirit of Edward could not rest satisfied so long as the ancient patrimony A.D. of his family remained in the hands of his rival. He there-1297. fore entered into an alliance with the earls of Holland and

---

[1] Heming.—Trivet.   [2] W. Heming.—T. Walsingham.

Flanders[1]; and hoped that, when he should enter the frontiers of France at the head of English, Flemish, and Dutch armies, the French king would purchase peace by the restitution of Guienne.

To set this vast machine in motion, considerable supplies were necessary from parliament; and these Edward readily obtained both from the lords and commons. He was not so fortunate in his impositions on the clergy, whom he always hated, and from whom he demanded a fifth of all their moveables, as a punishment for their adherence to the Montfort faction. They urged the pope's bull in opposition to all such demands; and Edward instead of applying to Boniface VIII., then pontiff, for a relaxation of his mandate, boldly told the ecclesiastics, that since they refused to support the civil government, they were unworthy of receiving any benefit from it, and he would accordingly put them out of the protection of the laws.

This rigorous measure was immediately carried into execution. Orders were issued to the judges to receive no cause brought before them by the clergy; to hear and decide all causes in which they were defendants; to do every one justice against them, but to do them justice against nobody. The ecclesiastics soon found themselves in a very miserable situation. They could not remain always in their own houses or convents for want of subsistence: if they went abroad in quest of necessaries, they were robbed and abused by every ruffian, and no redress could be obtained by them for the most violent injury. The spirit of the clergy was at last broken by this harsh treatment. They all either publicly or privately complied with the king's demands, and received the protection of the laws[2]. Not one ecclesiastic, as the sagacious Hume remarks, seemed willing to suffer, for the sake of religious privileges, this new species of martyrdom, the most tedious and languishing of any; the most mortifying to spiritual pride, and not rewarded by that crown of glory which the church holds up with such ostentation to her faithful sons.

But all these supplies were not sufficient for the king's necessities. He therefore had recourse to arbitrary power, and exacted contributions from every order of men in the kingdom. The people murmured, and the barons mutinied, notwithstanding their great personal regard for Edward. He was obliged to

[1] Rymer, vol. ii.
[2] W. Heming. vol. i.—*Chron. Dunst.* vol. ii.

make concessions; to promise all his subjects a compensation for the losses they had sustained; and to confirm the Great Charter, with an additional clause, in order to secure the nation for ever against all impositions and taxes without consent of parliament[1]. These concessions, my dear Philip, our ancestors had the honour of extorting, by their boldness and perseverance, from the ablest, the most warlike, and the most ambitious monarch that ever sat upon the throne of England. The validity of the Great Charter was never afterwards formally disputed.

These domestic discontents obstructed the king's embarkation for Flanders: so that he lost the proper season for action, and after his arrival made no great progress against the enemy. The French monarch, however, proposed a cessation of arms; and peace was soon after concluded by the mediation of the pope, in consequence of which Guienne was restored to England.

In the mean time the Scots rebelled. Earl Warrenne, having returned to England, on account of his ill state of health, had left the administration entirely in the hands of Ormsby and Cressingham, the officers next in rank, who, instead of acting with the prudence and moderation necessary to reconcile the Scots to a yoke which they bore with such extreme reluctance, exasperated all men of spirit by the rigour of their government. Among these William Wallace, whose heroic exploits are worthy of just panegyric, but to whom the fond admiration of the Scots has ascribed many fabulous acts of prowess, undertook and accomplished the difficult project of delivering his native country from the dominion of foreigners. He had been provoked by the insolence of an English officer to put him to death; and finding himself on that account obnoxious to the conquerors, he fled into the woods, and offered himself as a leader to all whom the oppressions of the English governors had reduced to the like necessity. He was of a gigantic stature, and endowed with wonderful strength of body, invincible fortitude of mind, disinterested magnanimity, incredible patience, and ability to bear hunger, fatigue, and all the severities of the seasons; so that he soon acquired, among his desperate associates, that authority to which his virtues so eminently entitled him. Every day brought accounts of his gallant actions, which were received with no less favour by his countrymen than terror by the enemy. All men who thirsted after military fame were desirous to partake of his

---

[1] T. Walsingham.—W. Hemingford.

renown; his successful valour seemed to vindicate the nation from the ignominy under which it had fallen by its tame submission to the English; and although no nobleman of eminence ventured yet to join the party of Wallace, he had gained a general confidence and attachment which birth and fortune alone are not able to confer.

So many fortunate enterprises brought the valour of the Scottish chieftain's followers to correspond with his own: and he determined to strike a decisive blow against the English government. Ormsby, apprised of this intention, fled hastily into England; and all the other officers of his nation imitated his example. Their terror added courage to the Scots, who took arms in every quarter. Many of the principal barons openly countenanced Wallace's party; and the nation, shaking off its fetters, prepared to defend, by one united effort, that liberty which it had so unexpectedly recovered from the hands of its oppressors.

Warrenne having collected an army of forty thousand men in the north of England, in order to re-establish his authority, suddenly entered Annandale before the Scots had united their forces, or put themselves in a posture of defence; and many of the nobles, alarmed at the danger of their situation, renewed their oaths of fealty, and received a pardon for past offences. But Wallace, still undaunted, continued obstinate in his purpose. As he found himself unable to give battle to the enemy, he marched to the northward, in the hope of prolonging the war, and of turning to his advantage the situation of that mountainous and barren country. Warrenne attacked him in his camp near Stirling, on the banks of the Forth, where the English were totally routed. Cressingham, whose impatience Sept. urged this attack, was slain; and Warrenne was obliged to 11. retire into England, and the principal fortresses in Scotland surrendered to the conquerors [1].

Wallace was now universally revered as the deliverer of his country, and received from his followers the title of Regent or guardian of the kingdom, a dignity which he well deserved. Not satisfied with expelling the enemy, he urged his army to march into England, and revenge all past injuries by retaliating on that hostile nation. The Scots, who deemed every thing possible with such a leader, joyfully attended his call. They

[1] W. Heming.—T. Walsingham.

rushed into the northern counties during the winter, and having extended their ravages on all sides, returned into their own country with ample spoils.

Edward, who was in Flanders when he received intelligence
A.D. of these events, hastened to England, in assured hopes,
1298. not only of wiping off every disgrace, but of recovering the important conquest of Scotland, which he had always considered as the chief glory of his reign. With this view he collected the military force of England, Wales, and Ireland; and with an army of eighty thousand combatants, entered the devoted kingdom. Scotland was at no time able to withstand such a force. At present it was without a head, and was convulsed by intestine jealousies. The elevation of Wallace was the object of envy to the nobility, who repined to see a private man raised above them by his rank, and still more by his reputation. Sensible of these evils, Wallace resigned his authority; and the chief command devolved upon men more eminent by birth, though less distinguished by abilities, but under whom
July the nobles were more willing to serve in defence of their
22. country. They fixed their station at Falkirk, where Edward came up with them, and defeated their army with great slaughter [1].

The subjection of Scotland, however, was not yet accomplished. The English, after reducing all the southern provinces, were
A.D. obliged to retire for want of provisions; and the Scots,
1299. no less enraged at their present defeat than elevated by their past victories, still maintained the contest for liberty. They were again victorious, and again subdued. Wallace alone maintained his independence amidst the general slavery of his countrymen. But he was at length betrayed to the English by his friend Sir John Monteith: and Edward, whose natural bravery and magnanimity should have led him to respect the like qualities in an enemy, ordered this illustrious patriot to be carried in chains to London; to be tried as a rebel and traitor, though he had never made submission or sworn fealty to Eng-
A.D. land, and to be executed on Tower Hill [2]. He did not
1305. think his favourite conquest secure whilst Wallace lived. Policy, therefore, as well as revenge, urged him to sacrifice a hero, who had defended for many years, with signal valour and perseverance, the liberties of his native country.

---

[1] T. Walsingh.—T. Wilkes.—W. Heming.   [2] Triveti. *Annal.*

But the barbarous policy of Edward failed of the purpose to which it was directed. The cruelty and injustice exercised upon Wallace, instead of breaking the spirit, only roused more effectually the resentment of the Scots. All the envy which, during his life, had attended that gallant chieftain, being now buried in his grave, he was universally regarded as the champion of Scotland, and equally lamented by all ranks of men. The people were every where disposed to rise against the English government; and a new and more fortunate leader soon presented himself, who conducted them to liberty, to victory, and to vengeance.

Robert Bruce, grandson of that Robert who had been one of the competitors for the crown of Scotland, had formerly served in the English army; but the example of Wallace excited his emulation, and the wrongs inflicted on his countrymen roused him to revenge. Bruce regretted his engagement with Edward, and secretly determined to take measures for rescuing from slavery his oppressed country. The death of Wallace and Baliol seemed to offer the desired opportunity. He hoped that the Scots, without a leader, and without a king, would unanimously repair to his standard, and seat him on their throne. Inflamed with the ardour of youth, and buoyed up by native courage, his high spirit saw alone the glory of the enterprise, or regarded the difficulties that must attend it as the source only of greater glory: the miseries and oppressions which he had beheld his countrymen suffer in their unequal contests for independence, the repeated defeats and misfortunes which they had undergone in the struggle, proved to him but so many incentives to bring them relief, and to lead them boiling with revenge against the haughty victors.

In consequence of this resolution, Bruce suddenly left the English court, and arrived at Dumfries, where many of the nobles happened to be assembled, and among the rest A.D. John Comyn, to whom he had communicated his designs, and 1305. who had basely revealed them to Edward. The noblemen were astonished at the appearance of Bruce, and yet more when he told them that he was come to live or die with them in defence of the liberties of his country, and that he hoped, with their assistance, to redeem the Scottish name from all the indignities which it had so long suffered from the tyranny of their imperious masters. It would be better, he said, if Heaven should so decree it, to perish at once like brave men, with swords in their hands, than to dread long, and at last undergo, the fate of the unfortunate Wallace [1].

The spirit with which this discourse was delivered, the bold sentiments which it conveyed, the novelty of Bruce's declaration, assisted by the graces of his youth, and manly deportment, made deep impression on the minds of the nobles, and roused all those principles of indignation and revenge with which they had long been secretly actuated. They declared their resolution to use the utmost efforts for delivering their country from bondage, and to second the courage of Bruce, with zeal and alacrity. Comyn alone, who had privately taken his measures with Edward, opposed the general determination, by representing the great power of the English nation; and Bruce, already informed of his treachery, followed him out of the assembly, stabbed him, and left him for dead. Sir Thomas Kirkpatrick, one of Bruce's friends, asked him, on his return, if the traitor was slain. " I believe so," replied Bruce. " And is that a matter," cried Kirkpatrick, " to be left to conjecture? I will secure him." He according drew his dagger, ran to Comyn, and pierced him to the heart [2].

This assassination, which contains circumstances justly condemned by our present manners, was regarded in that age as an effort of manly vigour and just policy. Hence the family of Kirkpatrick took for the crest of their arms a hand with a bloody dagger, and, as a motto, the words employed by their ancestor, when he executed that violent action: " I make sicker," i. e. *surer*.

The murder of Comyn affixed the seal to the conspiracy of the Scottish nobles. They had now no resource left, but to shake off the yoke of England or perish in the attempt. The genius of the nation roused itself from its long dejection. Bruce fiercely attacked the dispersed bodies of the English; gained possession of many castles; and was solemnly crowned at Scone. The English were again driven out of the kingdom, except such as took shelter in the fortresses still in their hands; and Edward found that the Scots, already twice conquered by his valour, were yet unsubdued.

Conscious, however, of his superior power and skill in arms, this great monarch thought of nothing but victory and vengeance.

[1] M. Westm.—Buchanan.
[2] W. Heming.—M. Westm.—T. Walsingham.

He sent a body of troops into Scotland under Aymer de Valence, earl of Pembroke; who, falling unexpectedly upon Bruce, threw his army into disorder, and obliged him to take shelter in the Western Isles. Edward himself was advancing with a mighty force, determined to make the now defenceless Scots the victims of his severity, when he unexpectedly sickened and died July 7, at Carlisle; enjoining with his latest breath his son and 1307. successor to prosecute the war, and not to desist before he had completely subdued the kingdom of Scotland [1].

The character of Edward I., as a warrior and politician, has already been sufficiently delineated. I shall therefore forbear touching again on those particulars, and conclude this letter with his merit as a legislator, which has justly secured to him the honourable appellation of the English Justinian. The numerous statutes passed during his reign settle the chief points of jurisprudence; and, as Sir Edward Coke observes, truly deserve the name of establishments, because they have been more constant and durable than any of the laws subsequently enacted. The regular order maintained in his administration also gave the common law an opportunity to refine itself; brought the judges to a certainty in their determinations, and the lawyers to precision in their pleadings. He regulated the jurisdiction of all courts, established the office of justice of the peace, and completed the division of the court of Exchequer into four distinct courts, each of which managed its separate branch, without dependence upon any one magistrate; and as the lawyers afterwards invented a method of carrying business from one court to another, the several courts became rivals and checks on each other; a circumstance which tended greatly to improve the practice of the law in this country [2]. But although Edward took so much care that his subjects should do justice to each other, we cannot ascribe it to his love of equity; for in all his transactions, either with them or with his neighbours, he always desired to have his own hands free:—and his violences upon both were not few.

---

[1] T. Walsingham.—Trivet.
[2] *Hist. of English Law*, by Sir Matthew Hale.

LETTER XXXVIII.

A View of the Reign of Edward II., with an Account of the Affairs of Scotland.

From the critical situation of affairs between England and Scotland at the death of Edward I., it will be advisable, my dear Philip, to carry farther the history of our own island, before we return to the transactions of the continent.

No prince ever ascended the English throne with more promising advantages than Edward II. He was in the twenty-fourth year of his age, and universally beloved by the people, both on account of the sweetness of his disposition, and as the son and successor of their illustrious monarch. He was at the head of a great army, ready to subject the whole island to his sway; and all men seemed to expect tranquillity and happiness under his government. But the first act of his reign blasted all these hopes, and showed him totally unqualified for his high station. Instead of prosecuting the conquest of Scotland, according to the desire of his father, he returned to England after some feeble efforts, and disbanded his forces; although Robert Bruce had emerged from his retreat, and had become sufficiently formidable to render more vigorous measures necessary.

The next step taken by Edward was no less weak and imprudent. He recalled Piers Gaveston, a youthful favourite, whom the late king had banished on account of his ascendancy over this prince, and whom, on his death-bed, he had made him promise never more to encourage. Gaveston was the son of a Gascon knight of some distinction, and by his shining accomplishments had early insinuated himself into the affections of young Edward, whose heart was easily caught by appearances, and strongly disposed to friendship and confidence. He was endowed with the utmost elegance of shape and person; had a fine mien and easy carriage; had distinguished himself in all warlike and genteel exercises, and was celebrated for those quick sallies of wit in which his countrymen usually excel. We therefore need not be surprised at his being thought necessary to a gay monarch, whose foibles he was able to flatter: but a wise king will have no public favourite, and still less a foreign one. Edward experienced this danger.

Gaveston no sooner arrived at court than he was loaded with benefits, and exalted to the greatest honours. The king bestowed upon him the earldom of Cornwall; gave him his niece Margaret in marriage; and seemed to enjoy no pleasure in his royalty but as it served to add lustre to this object of his fond idolatry. The haughty barons, already dissatisfied with Edward's conduct in regard to Scotland, were enraged at the superiority of a minion whom they despised; nor did they endeavour to conceal their animosity.

The favourite, instead of disarming envy by the moderation and modesty of his behaviour, displayed his power and influence with the utmost ostentation. Every day multiplied his enemies, who only waited for an opportunity of cementing their union, so as to render it fatal both to him and his master. This union being at length effected, by Thomas earl of Lancaster, cousin-german to the king, the confederate nobles bound them- A.D. selves by oath to expel Gaveston; they took arms for 1308. that purpose, and Edward was obliged to banish him. But he was afterwards recalled, reinstated in his former consequence, and became more than ever, by his continued insolence, the object of general detestation among the nobility. The confederacy against him was renewed; he was again banished, and again recalled by the fond, deluded monarch. A universal A.D. revolt took place: Edward and his favourite were hunted 1312. from corner to corner; and Gaveston at last fell by the hands of the public executioner [1].

After this sacrifice, the king's person became less obnoxious to the people. The discontents of all men seemed to be much appeased; the animosities of faction no longer prevailed; and England, it was hoped, would now be able to take vengeance on all her enemies, but especially on the Scots, whose progress was the object of general resentment and indignation.

Soon after Edward's retreat from Scotland, Robert Bruce made himself master of the whole kingdom, except a few fortresses. He daily reconciled the minds of the nobility to his dominion: he enlisted under his standard every bold spirit, and he enriched his followers with the spoils of the enemy. Sir James Douglas, in whom commenced the greatness and renown of that warlike family, seconded Robert in all his enterprises. Edward Bruce, the king's brother, also distinguished himself by his valour: and the dread of the English power being now

---

[1] T. Walsingham.—T. de la More.—W. Hemingf.

abated by the feeble conduct of Edward, even the least sanguine of the Scots began to entertain hopes of recovering their independence. They obtained a truce, which was of short duration, and ill observed on both sides. But, short as it was, it served to consolidate the power of the king, and introduce order into the civil government. War was renewed with greater fury than ever. Not content with defending himself, Robert made successful inroads into England, supported his needy followers by the plunder of the country, and taught them to despise the military genius of a nation which had long been the object of their terror.

Edward, at length aroused from his lethargy, had marched with an army into Scotland; and Robert, determined not to risk too much against a superior force, had retired amidst the mountains. The English monarch advanced beyond Edinburgh; but being destitute of provisions, and ill supported by his nobility, he was obliged to return home, without gaining any advantage over the enemy. The seeming union, however, of all parties in England, after the death of Gaveston, opened again the prospect of reducing Scotland, and promised a happy conclusion to a war in which both the interests and the passions of the nation were so deeply engaged.

Edward assembled forces from all quarters, with a view of finishing at one blow this important enterprise. He summoned the most warlike of his vassals from Gascony: he enlisted troops in Flanders and other foreign countries: he invited over great numbers of the disorderly Irish, as to a certain prey: he joined to them a body of Welsh, who were actuated by like motives: A.D. he collected a considerable force in England, and entered 1314. Scotland at the head of an army of about eighty thousand men. The Scottish host did not exceed thirty thousand combatants; but being composed of men who had distinguished themselves by many acts of valour, who were rendered desperate by their situation, and who were inured to all the varieties of fortune, they might justly, under such a leader as Bruce, be esteemed equal to a far more numerous body. Robert, however, left as little as possible to the superior gallantry of his troops. He posted himself strongly at Bannockburn, near Stirling: he had a rivulet in front, a hill on his right flank, and a morass on his left.

As soon as the English army appeared, a smart conflict arose June between two bodies of cavalry; and Robert, engaging in 14. a single combat with Henry de Bohun, at one stroke cleft the head of his antagonist with a battle-axe, in sight of the two armies.   The English horse fled with precipitation to their main body, and night suspended hostilities.   Encouraged by this favourable event, and glorying in the prowess of their king, the Scots prognosticated a happy issue to the contest of the ensuing day ; and the English, confident in their numbers, and elated by past successes, longed for an opportunity of revenge.   The darkness was borne with impatience : and Edward, as soon as light appeared, drew up his forces and advanced against the Scots. Both armies engaged with great ardour, and the dispute was fierce and bloody.   Sir James Douglas had broken the English cavalry : but their line of infantry was still firm, when a stratagem decided the fortune of the field.   Bruce had collected a number of waggoners and sumpter-boys, and furnished them with standards.   They appeared upon the heights towards the left.   The English mistook them for a fresh army coming to surround them ; a panic seized them ; they threw down their arms and fled.   The Scots pursued with great slaughter, as far as Berwick ; and besides an inestimable booty, took many persons of quality prisoners, with above four hundred gentlemen, whom Robert treated with great humanity, and whose ransom was a new accession of wealth to the victorious army.   Edward himself narrowly escaped by taking shelter in Dunbar, whence he passed by sea to Berwick [1].

Such was the great and decisive battle of Bannockburn, which secured the independence of Scotland, fixed Bruce on the throne of that kingdom, and may be deemed the most signal blow that the English monarchy has received since the Norman invasion. The number of slain is not certainly known ; but it must have been very great : for the impression of this defeat on the minds of the English was so strong, that for some years no superiority of force could encourage them to keep the field against the Scots.

In order to avail himself of his present success, Robert entered England ; ravaged all the northern counties without opposition ; and, elate with his continued prosperity, now entertained hopes of making the most important conquests at the expense of the English.   He sent over his brother Edward with six A. D. thousand men into Ireland ; and he himself soon followed 1315. after with a more numerous body of troops.   But a grievous famine, which harassed both islands, obliged Robert to return to Britain.   His brother, who assumed the title of king of

[1] Mon. Malms.—T. de la More —Walsingh. Ypod. Neust.

A. D. Ireland, was defeated and slain by the English near
1318. Dundalk; and Robert became sensible that he had
attempted projects too extensive for the force of his narrow
kingdom.

Edward, besides the disasters which he suffered from the
invasion of the Scots, and the opposition to his government in
Ireland, was harassed with a rebellion in Wales; and the factions
of his nobility troubled him yet more than all these. They took
advantage of the public calamities to insult his fallen fortunes,
and endeavoured to establish their own independence on the
ruins of the throne. His unhappy situation obliged him to
comply with all their demands. The administration was new-
modelled by the direction of Lancaster, and that prince was placed
at the head of the council. Edward himself was evidently by
nature unfit to hold the reins of government. He was sensible
of his own defects, and sought to be governed; but all the
favourites (for such they were rather than ministers) whom he
successively chose were regarded as fellow-subjects exalted above
their rank and station, and became the objects of envy to the
chief nobility. His principal favourite, after the death of Gaveston, was Hugh le Despenser, or Spenser, who was of a noble
family, and possessed all the exterior accomplishments of person
and address that were fitted to engage the weak mind of Edward,
but was destitute of that moderation and prudence which might
have qualified him to mitigate the envy of the great, and conduct
himself quietly through the perils of the dangerous station to
which he was advanced.

No sooner was Edward's attachment declared for Spenser,
than the turbulent Lancaster and most of the great barons
regarded him as their rival, and formed violent plans for his ruin.
A.D. They withdrew themselves from parliament, took arms,
1321. and demanded the banishment of the favourite and his
father. The father was then abroad, the son at sea; and both
were employed in executing different commissions. The king
replied, that his coronation oath, by which he was bound to
observe the laws, restrained him from giving his assent to so
illegal a demand, or condemning noblemen who were accused of
no crime, nor had any opportunity of giving answer. But equity
and reason proved a feeble barrier against men who had arms in
their hands, and who, being already involved in guilt, saw no
safety but in success and victory. They entered London with
their troops; and adducing before the parliament a charge against
the Spensers (of which they did not attempt to prove one article),

they procured by menaces and violence, a sentence of perpetual exile against those ministers [1].

This act of violence, in which the king was obliged to acquiesce, rendered his person and authority so contemptible, that every one thought himself entitled to treat the royal family with neglect. The queen was publicly insulted; but, as that princess was then popular, Edward was permitted to take vengeance on the offender. Having now some forces on foot, and having concerted measures with his friends throughout England, he ventured to pull off the mask; to attack all his enemies; and to recall the two Spensers, whose sentence he declared illegal, unjust, and contrary to the tenor of the Great Charter [2].

The king had now anticipated the movements of the barons; an advantage which, in those times, was generally decisive. It proved so in the present instance. Lancaster alone made resistance; he was taken at Boroughbridge, condemned by a A.D. court martial, and beheaded at Pontefract. About twenty 1322. of the most notorious offenders were afterwards condemned by legal trial, and executed. Many were thrown into prison; some made their escape beyond sea; and most of the forfeitures were seized by young Spenser, whose rapacity was insatiable. The barons of the king's party were disgusted with this partial division of the spoils; the envy against the favourite rose higher than ever. To the people, who always hated him, he became still more the object of aversion: all the relatives of the attainted barons vowed revenge; and although tranquillity was in appearance restored to the kingdom, the general contempt of the king, and odium of Spenser, engendered future revolutions and convulsions.

In such a situation no success could be expected from foreign wars. Edward, therefore, after making one more fruitless attempt against Scotland, whence he retreated with dishonour, A.D. found it necessary to terminate hostilities with that king- 1323. dom by a truce of thirteen years. This truce was so much the more seasonable for England, as the nation was at that time threatened with hostilities from France. Charles the Fair had some grounds of complaint against the English ministers in Guienne, and seemed desirous of profiting in a territorial view by the indolence and weakness of Edward.

After an embassy by the earl of Kent had been tried in A.D. vain, queen Isabella obtained permission to go over to 1325.

[1] Tyrrel, from the Register of C. C. Canterbury—T. Walsingh.—Rymer, vol. iii.
[2] Rymer, ubi sup.

Paris, and endeavour to adjust the dispute with her brother Charles. She there found a number of English fugitives, the remains of the Lancastrian faction; and their common hatred of young Spenser soon produced a secret friendship and correspondence between them and that princess, who envied the favourite his influence with the king. Among these refugees was Roger Mortimer, a potent baron of the Welsh marches, who had been condemned for high treason, but had made his escape from the Tower. His consequence introduced him to queen Isabella, and the graces of his person and address advanced him quickly in her affections. He became her confident and counsellor in all her measures; and, gaining ground daily upon her heart, he engaged her to sacrifice at last, to her passion, all the sentiments of honour and fidelity to her husband. Hating now the man she had injured, and whom she never loved, she entered ardently into all Mortimer's conspiracies; and having artfully secured the person and acquiescence of the heir of the monarchy, she resolved on the utter ruin of the king, as well as of his favourite. She engaged her brother to take part in the same criminal purpose: her court was daily filled with exiled barons: Mortimer lived in the most declared intimacy with her, and a correspondence was secretly carried on with the malcontent party in England [1].

When Edward was informed of these alarming circumstances, he ordered the queen to return speedily with the prince. But Isabella publicly replied, that she would never set foot in the kingdom, while Hugh Spenser was suffered to influence and advise the king. This declaration increased her popularity in England, and threw a decent veil over her treasonable enterprises. She no sooner arrived in England with her son than the king was entirely deserted. He fled into Wales. The elder Spenser, now earl of Winchester, and governor of the castle of Bristol, was delivered by the garrison into the hands of his enemies; and, A. D. 1326. being instantly condemned, without any trial, witness, or accusation, to suffer death, he was hanged on a gibbet in his armour. His unhappy but more criminal son soon after shared the same fate: and the king, disappointed in his expectation of succours from the Welsh, was seized among their mountains, where he had endeavoured to conceal himself, and confined in Kenilworth castle. Taking advantage of the prevailing delusion, the queen summoned, in Edward's name, a parliament at

---

[1] T. Walsingham.—T. de la More.

Westminster, where the king was accused of incapacity for government, and by the authority of her partisans deposed. A.D. The prince, a youth of fourteen years of age, was placed 1327. on the throne, and the queen was appointed regent during his minority .

The great body of the people are seldom long in the wrong with respect to any political measure. Corrupted as they now were by the licentiousness of the times, and inflamed by faction, they could not in the present instance remain insensible to the voice of nature. A wife had dishonoured her husband, invaded his kingdom with an armed force, and insisted on his dethronement: she had made her infant son an instrument in this unnatural treatment of his father; and had, by false pretences, seduced the nation into rebellion against their sovereign, whose weakness was his only crime. All these circumstances were so odious in themselves, and formed such a complicated scene of guilt, that the least reflection sufficed to open men's eyes, and make them detest so flagrant an infringement of every public and private duty.

The earl of Lancaster (formerly earl of Leicester), to whose custody the deposed prince had been committed, was soon touched with sentiments of compassion and generosity towards his sovereign; and besides using him with gentleness and humanity, he was supposed to have entertained more honourable intentions in his favour. The king was therefore taken out of his hands, and delivered over to lord Berkeley, Maltravers, and Gournay, who were intrusted alternately, each for a month, with the charge of guarding him. While in the custody of Berkeley, Edward was treated with respect; but when the turn of Maltravers and Gournay came, every species of indignity was offered him, as if their intention had been to break entirely the unhappy prince's spirit, and to employ his sorrows and afflictions, instead of more violent and more dangerous means, as the instruments of his murder. That method of destroying him, however, appearing too slow to the impatient Mortimer, he sent orders to the two ruffians to despatch the king secretly. Taking advantage of the indisposition of Berkeley, they seized Edward in that nobleman's castle, threw him on a bed, held him down violently, and thrust into his fundament a horn, through which they burned his bowels with a red-hot iron. Although outward marks of violence were prevented by this expedient, the atro-

---

[1] Ypod. Neust.—T. de la More.—Rymer, vol. iv.

cious deed was discovered to all the guards and attendants by the screams of the agonized king [1].

Thus perished the unfortunate Edward II. It is not easy for imagination to conceive a man more innocent and inoffensive, or a prince less fitted for governing a fierce and turbulent people. The vigour and capacity of the son made ample amends for his father's weakness. But a variety of objects must occupy our attention before we consider the reign of Edward III.

LETTER XXXIX.

Of the German Empire and its Dependencies, from the Election of Rodolph of Hapsburg to the Death of Henry VII.

THE German empire, my dear Philip, as I have already had occasion to observe, could not properly be said to have a head, A.D. 1273 from the death of Frederic II. till the election of Rodolph count of Hapsburg. This great captain, who had for some time exercised the office of grand marshal to Ottocarus king of Bohemia, and was raised to the imperial dignity on account of his military talents, no sooner found himself in possession of the august throne, than he employed his authority in suppressing the disorders which had prevailed during the interregnum; and he succeeded so well in his endeavours, that peace and security were soon generally re-established in Germany. He destroyed in Thuringia sixty castles, which were the retreats of banditti, and ordered ninety-nine highwaymen to be hanged at one time in the city of Erfort [2].

Having thus in some measure settled the interior police of the empire, Rodolph assembled a diet at Mentz, where he A. D. granted new privileges to Goslar and other cities, and 1274 confirmed those which had been granted by his predecessors. Here also the deliberations of the assembly turned upon the conduct of certain princes who had protested against the election of the count of Hapsburg. Of these, one was his former master, the king of Bohemia, against whom the diet had other causes of dissatisfaction. He had seized the duchy of

[1] T. Walsingham.—T. de la More.
[2] *Annal. Boior.*—Heiss. liv. ii. c. 22.

Austria, after the death of Frederic, the last duke; and the states complained of the oppressions which they suffered under this usurper, from whom they begged to be delivered.

A second diet was summoned on this subject at Augsburg; where Ottocarus not appearing, or doing homage by his ambassadors, was declared a rebel to the empire. His possession of Austria, Stiria, Carniola, and Carinthia, was adjudged illegal; and the emperor was desired to divest him of those territories. A.D. 1275.

When this sentence was notified to the king, he boldly exclaimed, "To whom should I do homage?—I owe Rodolph nothing: he was formerly my servant, and I paid him his wages. My possessions I will maintain with the point of my sword[1]."

Having formed this resolution, he associated himself with several other German princes, and among the rest with the duke of Bavaria. But they were all at last obliged to submit; and the proud Ottocarus himself not only relinquished the contested territories, but did homage for Bohemia and Moravia.

This homage was performed in the island of Camberg in the Danube, under a close canopy, in order to save Ottocarus from a public humiliation. He repaired to the place covered with gold and jewels. Rodolph, by a superior pride, received him in the most coarse and simple dress; and in the midst of the ceremony, either by accident or design, the curtains of the canopy fell back, and exposed to the eyes of the people, and the armies that lined the banks of the river, the haughty king on his knees, with his hands joined between those of his conqueror, whom he had so often called his steward, and to whom he now became cup-bearer. A.D. 1276.

The wife of Ottocarus, a Russian princess, and no less haughty than her husband, was so much hurt by this mortifying circumstance, that she persuaded him to renounce the treaty he had concluded with Rodolph, and again have recourse to arms for the recovery of Austria. The emperor immediately marched against him; and a battle ensued, in which Ottocarus was slain. A.D. 1278.

Rodolph now discovered himself to be no less a politician than a warrior. He gave the government of Austria and its appendages to his eldest son, count Albert; whom he afterwards, in a diet at Augsburg, publicly invested with that duchy, which was incorporated with the college of the princes: A.D. 1282.

---

[1] Æn. Sylv. *Hist. Bohem.*

2

hence arose the Austrian power and grandeur. Rodolph, at the same time, invested another son with the county of Suabia, which belonged to him in right of his wife. He also wisely resolved to adhere to the articles of the treaty with Ottocarus; and accordingly put his infant son Wenceslaus under the tutelage of the marquis of Brandenburg[1].

But although Rodolph's authority was now fully established in Germany, he was far from being master in Italy. The imperial crown had indeed been confirmed to him by Gregory X., on his ceding to the holy see lands of the countess Matilda, and all the territories mentioned in the grants made to the church by former emperors. In so doing, Rodolph properly yielded nothing but the right of receiving homage from noblemen, who never submitted to it without reluctance, and cities which it was not in his power to command. Venice, Genoa, and Pisa, had a greater number of ships than the emperor could muster of ensigns: Florence had become considerable, and was already the nurse of the liberal arts.

Rodolph spent the latter part of his reign in establishing the grandeur of his family in Austria. He granted privileges to the clergy; bestowed new dignities upon the noblemen; diminished the taxes; built and repaired public edifices; and behaved with such generosity and moderation, as won the hearts of all men. But, notwithstanding his popularity, he could not procure the election of his son Albert, as king of the Romans; a disappointment Sept. 30, which, together with the death of his son Rodolph, so 1291. much chagrined him, that he died soon after. He was a prince of great valour, sagacity, and probity; and raised the empire, from a state of misery and confusion, to the enjoyment of peace, policy, and opulence[2].

After an interregnum of nine months, which was productive of many disorders, the German princes raised to the imperial A.D. throne Adolphus of Nassau, on the same principle which 1292. had made them choose his predecessor. He seemed capable of maintaining the glory of the empire at the head of its armies, without being able to enslave it.

---

[1] Heiss, ubi sup.—Du Mont. *Corp. Diplom.* tome i.
[2] Heiss, lib. ii. cap. 22.—Barre, tome vi.—*Annal. de l'Emp.* tome ii.—Nothing can show in a stronger light Rodolph's resolution and presence of mind than his behaviour at his coronation. The absence of the imperial sceptre, (supposed *to be* that of Charlemagne,) which had been mislaid, seemed to afford some disaffected noblemen a pretext for refusing the oath of allegiance:—" This is my sceptre," said Rodolph, seizing a crucifix, and all the princes and nobles instantly took the oath, and did him homage as emperor.

The reign of this prince was one continued scene of troubles, and at last terminated in his deposition. He had been hurried by his necessities into the commission of several acts of injustice : which Albert, duke of Austria, dissatisfied at not succeeding to the imperial throne, took care to represent in the worst light. A confederacy was formed against Adolphus; and he A.D. was deposed by the archbishop of Mentz, in the name of 1298. the princes of the empire.

" Six years ago," said the archbishop, "the empire being vacant, we canonically elected Adolphus count of Nassau, king of the Romans, knowing at that time no person more worthy of the dignity. At first, he conducted himself wisely, following the counsels of the most prudent electors, and princes of his court. But he began by degrees to despise their advice, and listen to the counsels of young persons, without either sense or experience; then he found himself destitute of means and friends to assist him sincerely in bearing the burthen of government. The electors perceiving his indigence, and swayed by many other motives, have demanded the pope's consent to depose him, and choose another emperor. We are told that our envoys have obtained the consent of his holiness; though those of Adolphus affirm the contrary : but we, having no regard to any authority except that which is vested in ourselves, and finding Adolphus incapable of governing the empire, do depose him from the imperial dignity, and elect Albert, duke of Austria, king of the Romans [1]."

Adolphus, apprised of this election, raised the siege of Ruffach, in Alsace, and marched towards Spire, where he encamped. He was reinforced by the count Palatine Rodolph, Otho duke of Bavaria, and the cities of Spire and Worms, which had never deserted his cause. Albert advanced towards him, in order to dispute the imperial crown by arms. They engaged between Gelnsheim and the cloister of Rosendal, and the battle was maintained with much obstinacy on both sides. In the heat of action Adolphus, singling out his rival, attacked him hand to hand, haughtily exclaiming, "Here you shall resign to me the empire and your life!"—"Both," replied Albert, "are in the hands of God !" and immediately struck his competitor with such violence in the face, that he fell from his horse, and was instantly slain.

During the reign of Adolphus, and also of Rodolph, the Jews

---

[1] *Chron. Colm.*

were persecuted in the empire with great cruelty, on a supposition that they had slain several Christian children, and committed other crimes, which excited the hatred of the public. They were accused of having stolen a consecrated host : and the credulous and vindictive inhabitants of Nuremberg, Rotenberg, and other towns, seized all the Israelites who fell in their way, committed them to the flames, and drove the rest to such despair, that numbers chose rather to destroy themselves and their families than run the hazard of falling into the hands of the merciless Christians [1].

Though Albert had been elected king of the Romans before his victory over Adolphus, and consequently became emperor on the death of that prince, he chose to have his title confirmed by a new diet at Frankfort; and he was afterwards solemnly crowned at Aix-la-Chapelle. The concourse of people on this occasion was so great, that the duke of Saxony, the emperor's brother, and several other persons, were squeezed to death in the crowd [2].

The first years of Albert's reign were disquieted by a quarrel with the pope and the ecclesiastical electors. Boniface VIII., the last pontiff who pretended to dispose of crowns, and who carried the pretensions of the apostolic see as high as any of his predecessors, took part with the three German archbishops, who had refused to answer the emperor's summons. They were at length, however, obliged to submit ; and Boniface confirmed the election of Albert, when he wished to make him the instrument of his vengeance against Philip the Fair. But the emperor did not obtain this confirmation, it is said, before he had declared, that " the empire was transferred by the holy see from the Greeks to the Germans ; that the sovereign pontiff had granted to certain ecclesiastical and secular princes the right of electing a king of the Romans, destined to the empire; and that emperors and kings derive their regal power from the pope [3]."

A.D. 1303.

The most remarkable event in this reign is the rise of the republic of Switzerland. Fortified by their natural situation, surrounded with mountains, torrents, and woods, the Swiss, having

---

[1] *Annal. Steron.*—Mosheim, *Hist. Eccles.* vol. iii.—Dr. Mosheim leaves it doubtful whether the accusations against the Jews were true or false ; but his learned and judicious translator, in a note, gives reason to believe that they were insidiously forged.

[2] Heiss. liv. ii. cap. xxiv.

[3] *Hist. des Démêléz de Bonif. VIII. avec Philippe le Bel.*—Mosheim, *Hist. Eccles.* vol. iii.

nothing to fear from strangers, had lived happily in a rugged country, suited only to men who were accustomed to a frugal and laborious course of life. Equality of condition was the basis of their government. They had been free from time immemorial ; and when any of their nobility attempted to tyrannize, they were either expelled, or reduced within bounds by the people. But although the Swiss were extremely jealous of their liberty, they had always been submissive to the empire, on which they depended ; and many of their towns were free and imperial.

When Rodolph of Hapsburg was elected emperor, several lords of castles formally accused the cantons of Ury, Schwitz, and Underwald, of having withdrawn themselves from their feudal subjection. But Rodolph, who had formerly fought against these petty tyrants, decided in favour of the citizens ; and thenceforth these three cantons were under the patronage, but not the dominion, of the house of Austria.

Rodolph always treated the Swiss with great indulgence, and generously defended their rights and privileges against the noblemen that attempted to infringe them. Albert's conduct in this respect was just the reverse of his father's : he wanted to govern the Swiss as an absolute sovereign, and had formed a scheme for erecting their country into a principality for one of his sons. In order to accomplish this purpose, he endeavoured to persuade the cantons of Ury, Schwitz, and Underwald, to submit voluntarily to his dominion. In case of compliance, he promised to rule them with great lenity ; but finding them tenacious of their independence, and deaf to all his solicitations, he resolved to tame them by rougher methods , and appointed governors who domineered over them in the most arbitrary manner.

Tradition relates the following romantic anecdote of the cruelty of Geisler, governor of Ury. He ordered his hat to be fixed upon a pole in the market-place of Altdorf, and every passenger was commanded, on pain of death, to pay obeisance to it. But the independent spirit of William Tell, who, among others, had projected the deliverance of his country, disdained to pay that absurd homage. On this the governor ordered him to be hanged ; but remitted the punishment, on condition that he should strike an apple from his son's head with an arrow. Tell, who was an excellent marksman, accepted the alternative, and had the good fortune to strike off the apple, without hurting his son. But Geisler perceiving a second arrow under William's coat, inquired for what purpose that was intended ? " It was designed for thee," replied the indignant Swiss, " if I had killed my son." For that heroic answer he was doomed to perpetual imprisonment; though fortune happily put it out of the governor's power to carry his sentence into execution.

This, and other acts of wanton tyranny, determined Arnauld Melchtat, a native of Underwald; Werner Straffacher, of Schwitz; and Walter Furtz, of Ury, to put in execution those measures which they had concerted for delivering themselves and their country from the Austrian dominion. Naturally bold and enterprising, and united by a long intimacy of friendship, they had frequently met in private to deliberate upon this in-

A. D. teresting subject: each associated three others; and these
1308. twelve men accomplished their important enterprise without the loss of a single life. Having prepared the inhabitants of their several cantons for a revolt, they surprised the Austrian governors; conducted them to the frontiers, obliging them to promise upon oath never more to serve against the Helvetic nation; and then dismissed them; an instance of moderation not perhaps to be equalled in the history of mankind, of a people incensed against their oppressors, and who had them in their power [1].

Thus, my dear Philip, these three cantons procured their freedom; and the other provinces soon engaged in this confederacy, which gave birth to the republic of Switzerland. Never did any people fight with greater spirit for their liberty than the Swiss. They purchased it by above fifty battles against the Austrians; and they well deserved the prize for which they fought; for never were the beneficial effects of liberty more remarkable than in Switzerland.

When Albert was ready to hazard his forces against that courage which is inspired by the enthusiam of new-born freedom, he fell a sacrifice to his rapacity and injustice. His nephew John, who could not obtain from him the enjoyment of his patrimony, was inflamed with a thirst of revenge. This injured

May youth, confederating with three others, stabbed the em-
1. peror in the presence of his court and army, on the banks of the river Rus, in the neighbourhood of Switzerland [2]. No sovereign was ever less regretted. He did not want valour or abilities; but a desire of aggrandizing his family influenced his whole conduct, and made him violate every public and private tie.

---

[1] Stefler. *Annal. Helvetic.*   [2] Rebdorf, ad ann. 1308.

The imperial throne continued vacant for seven months after the assassination of Albert. At length the electors assembled at Frankfort, and chose Henry, count of Luxemburg; A.D. 1309. who was crowned, without opposition, at Aix-la-Chapelle. Soon afterward, in a diet at Spire, sentence of death was pronounced against prince John, for the murder of his uncle, the late emperor; whose sons, at the same time, demanded the investiture of Austria and the other hereditary dominions of their father, which Henry intended to seize. They obtained their demand, on making him sensible that, as the house of Austria had already sent two emperors out of the world, it might yet prove fatal to a third, if he did not desist from his unjust pretensions [1].

At this assembly also appeared Eiizabeth, daughter and heiress of Wenceslaus, king of Bohemia. She had been contracted to John, count of Luxemburg, son of the emperor; but the marriage had been delayed under different pretences. The princess therefore demanded, that the contract might be fulfilled, or cause shown why the nuptials should not be solemnized; and, understanding that a report had been spread to the disadvantage of her chastity, she defied her accusers to the proof. As the charge could not be substantiated, the nuptials were solemnized with great magnificence, in presence of the electors and other princes and noblemen of the diet [2].

The emperors, from the time of Frederic II., seemed to have lost sight of Italy. But Henry VII., as soon as he had settled the affairs of the North, resolved to re-establish the imperial authority in that country. With this view a diet was A.D. 1310. convoked at Frankfort; where proper supplies being granted for the emperor's journey, well known by the name of the Roman Expedition, he set out for Italy, accompanied by the dukes of Austria and Bavaria, the archbishop of Treves, the bishop of Liege, the counts of Savoy and Flanders, with other noblemen, and the militia of all the imperial towns.

Italy was still divided by the factions of the Guelphs and Ghibelines, who butchered one another without humanity or remorse. Bnt their contest was no longer the same : it was not now a struggle between the empire and the priesthood, but between faction and faction, inflamed by mutual jealousies and animosities. Pope Clement V. had been obliged to leave Rome,

---

[1] Heiss. lib. ii. cap. 25.   [2] Id. Ibid.

which was distracted by the anarchy of popular government. The Colonna and Ursini families and the Roman barons divided the city : and this division was the cause of the long abode of the popes in France, as we shall have occasion to see in the history of that kingdom ; so that Rome seemed equally lost to the popes and the emperors. Sicily was in the possession of the house of Arragon, in consequence of the famous massacre, called the Sicilian Vespers, which delivered that island from the tyranny of the French, as will be afterward more fully related. Carobert, king of Hungary, disputed the kingdom of Naples with his uncle Robert, son of Charles II. of the house of Anjou. The house of Esté had established itself at Ferrara ; and the Venetians aimed at the possession of that country. The old league of the Italian cities no longer subsisted. It had been formed with no other view than to oppose the emperors : and since they had neglected Italy, the cities were wholly employed in aggrandizing themselves at the expense of each other. The Florentines and the Genoese made war upon the republic of Pisa. Every city was also divided into factions within itself ; Florence, between the Blacks and the Whites, and Milan, between the Visconti and the Turriani.

In the midst of these troubles, Henry VII. appeared in Italy, A.D. and caused himself to be crowned king of Lombardy, at 1311. Milan. The Guelphs had concealed the old iron crown of the Lombard kings, as if the right of reigning were attached to a particular circlet of metal. But Henry, contemning such a thought, ordered a new crown to be made, with which the ceremony of inauguration was performed [1].

Cremona was the first place that ventured to oppose the emperor. He reduced it by force, and subjected it to heavy contributions. Parma, Vicenza, and Placentia, made peace with him on reasonable conditions. Padua paid a hundred thousand crowns, and received an imperial officer as governor. The Venetians presented Henry with a large sum of money, an imperial crown of gold enriched with diamonds, and a chain of very curious workmanship. Brescia made a desperate resistance, and sustained a very long siege ; in the course of which the emperor's brother was slain, and his army diminished to such a degree, that the inhabitants ventured to march out, under the command of their prefect, Thibault de Drussati, and gave him

---

[1] Struv. period. ix. sect. iv.

battle. But they were repulsed with great loss after an obstinate engagement, and at last obliged to submit. Their city was dismantled.

From Brescia Henry marched to Genoa, where he was received with expressions of joy, and splendidly entertained. A.D. He next proceeded to Rome, where, after much blood- 1312. shed, he received the imperial crown from the hands of the cardinals. Clement V., who had originally invited Henry into Italy, growing jealous of his success, had leagued with Robert, king of Naples, and the Ursini, to oppose his entrance into Rome. He entered it in spite of them, by the assistance of the Colonna party [1].

Now master of that ancient city, Henry appointed a governor of it; and ordered that the cities and states of Italy should pay him an annual tribute. In this order he comprehended the kingdom of Naples, to which he was preparing to en- Aug. 25, force his claim of superiority, when he died at Benevento 1313. of poison (as it is commonly supposed), given him by a Dominican friar in the consecrated wine of the sacrament [2].

During the last years of the reign of Henry VII., who was a valiant and politic prince, the knights of the Teutonic order aggrandized themselves by making war upon the Pagans of the North. They possessed themselves of Samogitia, after butchering all the inhabitants who refused to embrace Christianity; they took Dantzic, and purchased Pomerella of the marquis of Brandenburg. But while the order was making these acquisitions in Europe, it lost all its possessions in Asia [3].

The affairs of France now claim our attention.

LETTER XL.

History of France, from the Death of Louis IX. till the Accession of the House of Valois.

You have already, my dear Philip, seen the pious Louis IX. perish on the coast of Africa, in a second expedition against the

---

[1] Struv. ubi sup.—Cuspin. *Vit. Hen. VII.*   [2] Cuspin. *Vit. Hen. VII.*
[3] Petit de Duisburgh, *Chronic. Prussiæ.*

A.D. 1270. infidels. The most remarkable circumstance in the reign of his son Philip III. surnamed the Hardy, a prince of some merit, but much inferior to his father, is the interest he took in the affairs of his uncle Charles of Anjou, king of Naples and Sicily. This circumstance naturally leads us to an account of the Sicilian Vespers, and of the war between France and Arragon.

Charles, by the severity of his government, had not only rendered himself but his family odious to the Sicilians; and the insolence and debauchery of the French troops had excited an irreconcilable aversion against the whole nation. At the same time, the boundless ambition of this prince, who was actually preparing to attack the Greek emperor, Michael Palæologus, and was suspected of having an eye to the German empire, raised a general jealousy of him among his neighbours. Of that number was Pope Nicholas III., who particularly dreaded Charles's power; and, if he is not slandered by the French historians, contrived the scheme of his humiliation, though it did not take effect till after the death of his holiness. It was conducted by John di Procida, a Sicilian nobleman, who had secretly prepared the minds of his countrymen for a revolt; and an accident gave it birth.

On the evening of Easter-day, as the French and Sicilians A.D. 1282. were going in procession to the church of Montreale, in the neighbourhood of Palermo, a bride happened to pass with her train; when one Droguet, a Frenchman, instantly ran to her, and began to use her in a rude manner, under pretence of searching for concealed arms. A young Sicilian, flaming with resentment, stabbed Droguet to the heart; a tumult ensued, and two hundred Frenchmen were slain on the spot. The enraged populace now ran to the city, crying aloud, "Kill the French!"—and, without distinction of age or sex, murdered every person of that nation found in Palermo. The same fury spread itself through the whole island, and produced a general massacre. The enraged conspirators, brutally cruel, did not even spare their own relatives, but ripped up women who were pregnant by Frenchmen, and dashed the half-formed infants against the walls, while the priests, catching the general frenzy, butchered all the French penitents [1].

Peter king of Arragon, who had married the daughter of Mainfroy, the former usurper of Sicily, supported the Sicilians

[1] Giannone, *Hist. di Napol.*—Giov. Villani—Spondan.

in their rebellion, and openly claimed the kingdom in right of his wife. The Sicilians received him with open arms. He was crowned at Palermo; and Charles of Anjou was obliged to abandon the island, after having besieged Messina for six weeks in vain. He had now no hopes but from France, where the nobility in general were well affected to him, and readily offered to furnish troops for his support. In this disposition they were encouraged by Philip. Pope Martin IV. was also entirely in the interest of Charles; who might probably have recovered Sicily, had he not imprudently agreed to decide the dispute with Peter by single combat.

The king of Arragon, who had the duel very little at heart, was thus enabled to amuse his rival, and fix his own family on the throne of Sicily, which became a separate kingdom from Naples. In the mean time, the pope excommunicated Peter, and gave his dominions to any of the younger sons of France that the king should choose to name. Philip, flattered by A.D. this proposal, declared his son Charles of Valois king of 1283. Arragon and Valencia, and count of Barcelona. He put himself at the head of a numerous army, in order to realise these honours; and he furnished, at the same time, his uncle Charles with a fleet and army for the recovery of Sicily. Splendid projects! which proved the ruin of both.

Charles had left his son of the same name at Naples, with strict orders to incur no risk until his arrival with succours from France. But that young prince, provoked by the Arragonese fleet, sailed out with the force under his command, and A.D. was defeated and taken prisoner before his father's return; 1284. a circumstance which so much affected the king, that he is said to have strangled himself with a halter—a death sufficiently mild for such a tyrant[1].

Meanwhile the French army, under the command of Philip, had penetrated into Catalonia, and laid siege to Girona, which made a gallant defence. The king of Arragon, being in the neighbourhood with a small army, attacked a convoy going to the French camp, and received a mortal wound. Girona surrendered; and Philip having put a good garrison into it, dismissed part of his fleet, which had been principally hired from the Italian states. Roger di Loria, the Arragonese admiral, who durst not attack the French fleet while entire, burned and destroyed it when divided, seizing all the money and provisions

[1] Spondan. Giannone, *Hist. di Napol.*

intended for the support of the army; and these losses sunk so
Oct. 5, deeply into the mind of Philip, that he repassed the Py-
1285. renees, and died a few days after at Perpignan[1].   Philip
III. was the first French monarch who granted letters of
nobility, which he bestowed on Ralph the Goldsmith.   In so
doing, he only restored the ancient constitution of the Franks,
who, being all of one blood, were esteemed equally noble, and
alike capable of the highest offices.   The notion of a particular
and distinct noblesse took its rise towards the close of the second
race, when many of the officers of the crown had usurped, and
converted into hereditary dignities, the offices and jurisdictions
which they received from royal favour[2].

The reign of Philip IV. surnamed the Fair, the son and successor of Philip the Hardy, forms an æra in the history of France,
by the civil and political regulations to which it gave birth; the institution of the supreme tribunals, called Parliaments; and the
formal admission of the commons, or third estate, into the general assemblies of the nation.   How the French commons came
afterwards to be excluded from these assemblies, we shall have
occasion to see in the course of our narration.

The first care of Philip was to compose all differences with his
neighbours, as he found his finances exhausted: and this he was
enabled to effect by the mediation of Edward I. of England,
against whom he afterwards ungenerously commenced hostilities,
while that monarch was engaged in a war with Scotland.   Philip
also attempted, at the expense of much blood and treasure, to
seize Flanders, when the count was an ally of the king of England.   But as these wars were neither distinguished by any remarkable event, nor followed by any consequence that altered
the state of either country, I shall proceed to the transactions
between Philip and the see of Rome, and the extinction of the
order of Knights Templars.

Pope Boniface VIII. had prohibited the clergy in general
from granting any aids or subsidies to princes without his leave.
Philip IV., who was no less haughty than his holiness, and very
needy, thought the clergy, as being the richest order of the
state, ought to contribute to the wants of the crown, when the
situation of affairs made it necessary, and without any application to Rome; he therefore encountered the pope's bull by an edict,
forbidding any of the French clergy to send money abroad without the royal permission.   This was the first cause of the famous

---

[1] Nang. *Chron.*   [2] Henault, tome i.

quarrel between Boniface and Philip; and the insolence of the bishop of Pamiers threw things into a still greater ferment.

This man, named Bernard Saissetti, who had rebelled against the king in his diocese, was appointed by Boniface legate to the French court. An obnoxious subject thus invested with a A. D. dignity, which, according to the see of Rome, made him 1303. equal to the sovereign himself, came to Paris and braved Philip, threatening his kingdom with an interdict. A layman who had behaved in such a manner would have been punished with death; but the person of a churchman was sacred; and Philip was satisfied with delivering this incendiary into the hands of his metropolitan, the archbishop of Narbonne, not daring to treat him as a criminal.

The pope, enraged at the confinement of his legate, issued a bull declaring that the vicar of Christ was invested with full authority over the kings and kingdoms of the earth; and the chief French ecclesiastics received, at the same time, an order from his holiness to repair to Rome. A French archdeacon carried this bull and these orders to the king; commanding him, under pain of excommunication, to acknowledge the pope as his temporal sovereign. This insolence was answered with a moderation little suited to the character of Philip. He contented himself with ordering the pope's bull to be thrown into the fire, and prohibiting the departure of the bishops from the kingdom. Forty of them, however, with many of the heads of religious orders, went to Rome, notwithstanding the king's prohibition. For this trespass he seized all their temporalities.

While Boniface and his council were considering the conduct of Philip, and by means of his confessor brought his most secret thoughts under review, that politic prince assembled the states of his kingdom. They acknowledged his independent right to the sovereignty of France, and disavowed the pope's claim. It was on this occasion that the representatives of cities were first regularly summoned to the national assembly[1].

Philip was now at full liberty to treat the pope as an open enemy. He accordingly leagued with the family of Colonna, and sent William de Nogaret, a celebrated lawyer, into Italy, with a sum of money, in order to raise troops. With a body of desperadoes suddenly and secretly collected, William and Sciarra Colonna surprised Boniface at Anagni, a town in his own territories, and the place of his birth, exclaiming, "Let the pope

[1] Henault, ubi sup.—Du Chesne.—Polyd. Virg.

die! and long live the king of France!"   Boniface, however, did
not lose his courage.   He dressed himself in his cope ; put the
tiara upon his head ; and holding the keys in one hand and the
cross in the other, presented himself with an air of majesty before his conquerors.   On this occasion, it is said, Sciarra had the
brutality to strike him, crying out, " Tyrant! renounce the pontificate, which thou hast dishonoured."—" I am pope," replied
Boniface, with a look of intrepidity, " and will die pope!"   This
gallant behaviour had such an effect on the minds of the inhabitants, that they rose against his enemies, and rescued him from
their hands.   But Boniface was so much affected by the indignities which had been offered him, that he did not long survive[1].

The next pope, Benedict IX., was a mild and good man ; and
being desirous of using his power for the promotion of peace, he
revoked the sentence of excommunication which his predecessor
had fulminated against Philip the Fair.   He also pardoned the
Colonnas, and showed a great disposition to reform that corruption which had spread itself through the dominions of the church.
But these proceedings excited the hatred of his licentious and
vindictive countrymen, who suddenly took him off by poison.

A.D. 1305.   He was succeeded by Clement V., who being a Frenchman, and entirely in the interest of Philip, fixed his residence in France.   By means of this pope the French monarch
united the city of Lyons to his kingdom ; but although this was
considered as a valuable acquisition, he had occasion for the
assistance of Clement in an affair that lay nearer his heart.   I
allude to the suppression of the order of Knights Templars.
That religious and military order, which took its rise, as has
been already observed, during the first fervour of the crusades,
had made rapid advances in credit and authority ; and had acquired, from the piety of the faithful, ample possessions in every
Christian country, but more especially in France.   The great
riches of those knights, and other concurring causes, had however relaxed the severity of their discipline.   Convinced by experience, by fatigues, and by dangers, of the folly of their fruitless expeditions into Asia, they chose rather to enjoy in ease
their opulent fortunes in Europe ; and being all men of respectable families, they scorned the ignoble occupations of a monastic
life, and passed their time wholly in the fashionable amusements
of hunting, gallantry, and the pleasures of the table.   By these
means the Templars had in a great measure lost that popularity

---

[1] A. Baillet, *Hist. des Démélez de Boniface VIII. avec Philippe le Bel.*

which first raised them to honour and distinction. But the immediate cause of their destruction proceeded from the cruel and vindictive spirit of Philip the Fair.

The severity of the taxes, and the mal-administration of Philip and his council in regard to the coin, which they had repeatedly altered in its value, occasioned a sedition in Paris. The Knights Templars were accused of being concerned in the tumult. They were rich, as has been observed; and Philip was no less avaricious than vindictive. He determined to involve the whole order in one undistinguished ruin; and on no better information than that of two knights condemned by their superiors to perpetual imprisonment for their vices, he ordered all the Templars in France to be committed to prison in one day, and imputed to them such enormous and absurd crimes as are sufficient of themselves to destroy all the credit of the accusation. They were charged with robbery, murder, and the most unnatural vices; and it was pretended, that every one whom they received into their order was obliged to renounce his Saviour, to spit upon the cross, and to join to this impiety the superstition of worshipping a gilded head, which was secretly kept at one of their houses at Marseilles. The novice was also said to be initiated by many infamous rites, which could serve no other purpose than to degrade the order in his eyes; and, as Voltaire justly observes, it shows a very imperfect knowledge of mankind, to suppose there can be any societies that support themselves by the badness of their morals, or who make a law to enforce the practice of impudence and obscenity. Every society endeavours to render itself respectable to those who are desirous of becoming members of it.

Absurd, however, as these accusations appear, above one hundred knights were put to the rack, in order to extort from them a confession of their guilt. The more obstinate perished in the hands of their tormentors. Several, in the violence of their agonies, acknowledged whatever was desired of them. Forged confessions were imputed to others; and Philip, as A.D. if their guilt had now been certain, proceeded to a confis- 1311. cation of all their treasures. But no sooner were these unhappy men relieved from their tortures than they disavowed their forced confessions, exclaimed against the forgeries, justified the innocence of their order, and appealed to the many gallant actions performed by them as a full apology for their conduct.

Enraged at this disappointment, and thinking himself bound

in honour to proceed to extremities, Philip ordered fifty-four Templars, whom he branded as relapsed heretics, to perish by the punishment of fire in his capital.   Great numbers expired, after a like manner, in different parts of the kingdom : and when the tyrant found that the perseverance of those unhappy victims, in justifying to the last their innocence, had made deep impression on the minds of the people, he endeavoured to overcome the constancy of the Templars by new inhumanities.   Jacques de Molai, the grand-master of the order, and another great officer, brother

A.D. 1312. to the sovereign of Dauphiné, were conducted to a scaffold, erected before the church of Nôtre-Dame at Paris. A full pardon was offered them on one hand ; a fire, destined for their execution, was shown to them on the other.   But these gallant noblemen persisted in the protestation of their own innocence and that of their order ; and, as the reward of their fortitude, they were instantly hurried into the flames by the public executioner [1].

In all this barbarous injustice Clement V. fully concurred ; and by the plenitude of his apostolic power, in a general council at Vienne, without examining a single witness, or making any inquiry into the truth of facts, he abolished the whole order. The Templars all over Europe were thrown into prison ; their conduct underwent a strict scrutiny, and the power of their enemies still pursued and oppressed them.   But no where, except in France, were the smallest traces of their guilt pretended to be found.   Some countries sent ample testimony of their piety and morals ; but, as the order was now annihilated, their lands in France, Italy, England and Germany, were given to the Knights Hospitalers.   In Spain, they were given to the knights of Calatrava, an order established to combat the Moors [2].

Philip, soon after the suppression of this order, revived his quarrel with the count of Flanders, whose dominions he again unsuccessfully attempted to unite to the crown of France.   The failure of that project, together with some domestic misfortunes,

Nov. 29, 1314. threw him into a languishing consumption, which carried him off in the thirtieth year of his reign, and the forty-seventh of his age.   He was certainly a prince of great talents ; and, notwithstanding his vices, France ought to reverence his memory.   By fixing the parliaments, or supreme courts of judi-

[1] Puteau, *Hist. de la Condamnat. des Templiers.*—Nic. Gartler. *Hist. Templar.*— Steph. Baluz. *Vit. Pontif. Avenion.*
[2] Id. Ibid.—Rymer, vol. iii.—Vertot, *Hist. des Chev. de Malthe,* tome ii.

cature, he secured the ready execution of justice to all his subjects; and though his motive for admitting the third estate into the national council might not be the most generous, he by that measure put it in the power of the French nation to have established a free government.

Louis X., surnamed Hutin or the Wrangler, the son and successor of Philip the Fair, began his reign with an act of injustice. At the instigation of his uncle, the count of Valois, he caused his prime minister Marigni to be executed, on account of A.D. many pretended crimes, and magic among the rest; but 1315. in reality on account of his supposed riches, which were confiscated to the crown.   But the acquisition of the effects of Marigni and his reputed accomplices not being sufficient for the king's wants, he extorted money from the nobility, under various pretences : he levied a tenth upon the clergy : he sold enfranchisements to the slaves employed in cultivating the royal domains; and when they could not purchase their freedom June. 8. he declared them free, and levied the money by force[1]! 1316. He died, like his father, after an unsuccessful attempt upon Flanders.

On the death of Louis X., a violent dispute arose in regard to the succession.   The king had one daughter by his first wife Margaret of Burgundy, and left his queen Clemence of Hungary pregnant.   Clemence was brought to bed of a son, who lived only eight days.   It had long been a prevailing opinion, that the crown of France could never descend to a female ; and as nations, in accounting for principles which they regard as fundamental, and as peculiar to themselves, are fond of grounding them on primary laws rather than on blind custom, it had been usual to derive this maxim (though according to the best antiquaries falsely) from a clause in the Salian code, the body of laws of an ancient tribe among the Franks.   In consequence of this opinion, and precedents founded on it, Philip V., surnamed the Long, brother to Louis X., was proclaimed king; and as the duke of Burgundy made some opposition, and asserted the right of his niece, the states of the kingdom, by a solemn and deliberate decree, excluded her, and declared all females for ever A.D. incapable of succeeding to the crown of France[2].   The 1317. wisdom of this decree is too evident to need being pointed out. It not only prevents those evils which necessarily proceed from

[1] Le Gendre.—Dupleix.   [2] Mezeray.—Du Tillet.—Henault.

female caprices and tender partialities, so apt to make a minister from love and degrade him from whim, but is attended with this peculiar advantage, that a foreigner can never become sovereign of France by marriage; a circumstance always dangerous, and often productive of the most fatal revolutions.

The reigns of Philip the Long and his brother Charles the Fair, were short; nor did any memorable event occur under the sway of either. Charles left only one daughter, and consequently no heir to the crown; but, as his queen was pregnant, A.D. Philip de Valois, the next male heir, was appointed regent, 1328. with a declared right of succession, if the issue should prove female.

The queen of France was delivered of a daughter: the regency ended; and Philip de Valois ascended the throne of France.

This prince was cousin-german to the deceased king, and incontestably the nearest male heir descended from a male; but Edward III., as we shall soon have occasion to see, asserted the superiority of his own claim. In the mean time, I must make you acquainted with the more early part of the reign of that illustrious monarch.

LETTER XLI.

Of the Affairs of England, Scotland, France, and Spain, during the Reign of Edward III.

THE reign of Edward III., my dear Philip, opens a wide field of observation, and involves whatever is great or interesting in A.D. the history of Europe during that period. But before we 1327. enter on the foreign transactions of this prince, I must inform you of the domestic; and, for this purpose, some recapitulation may be necessary.

You have already been informed of the murder of the second Edward, by the inhuman emissaries of Roger Mortimer, the queen's gallant; and you may easily suppose that he and Isabella were then the objects of public odium. Conscious of this, they subjected to their vengeance whomsoever they feared, in order to secure their usurped power. The earl of Kent, the young king's uncle, was iniquitously condemned and executed; the earl of

Lancaster was thrown into prison; and others of the nobility were prosecuted under different pretences [1].

These abuses could not long escape the observation of a prince of so much discernment as young Edward, nor fail to rouse his active spirit against the murderer of his father, and the dishonourer of his mother. But he was besieged in such a manner by the creatures of Mortimer, that it became necessary to conduct the project of bringing that felon to justice with as much secrecy and caution as if he had been forming a conspiracy against his sovereign. He communicated his intentions, however, to A.D. 1330. some of the nobles, who readily entered into his views; and they surprised the usurper in the castle of Nottingham, and dragged him from an apartment adjoining to that of the queen, while she, in the most pathetic manner implored her son to spare the *gentle* Mortimer ! A parliament was immediately summoned for his condemnation ; and he was sentenced to die, from the supposed notoriety of his crimes, without any form of trial. He perished by the hands of the hangman, at the Elmes, near London ; and the queen was confined, during life, to her house at Risings ; where she languished out twenty-five years of sorrow rather than of penitence [2].

Edward having now taken the reins of government into his own hands, applied himself, with industry and judgment, to redress all those grievances which had either proceeded from want of authority in the crown, or the late abuses of it. He issued writs to the judges, enjoining them to ad- A.D. 1331. minister justice, without paying any regard to the arbitrary orders of the great: and as thieves, murderers, and criminals of all descriptions, had multiplied to an enormous degree during the public convulsions, and were openly protected by the powerful barons, who made use of them against their enemies, the king began seriously to remedy the evil, after exacting from the peers a solemn promise in parliament, that they would break off all connexion with such malefactors [3]. The ministers of justice, animated by his example, employed the utmost diligence in discovering, pursuing, and punishing criminals: and the disorder was by degrees corrected.

In proportion as the government acquired authority at home, it became formidable to the neighbouring nations; and the ambitious spirit of Edward sought and soon found an occasion of

---

[1] W. Hemingf.—T. Walsingham.　　　[2] Knighton.—Walsingham.
[3] Cotton's *Abridgment.*

exerting itself. The wise and valiant Robert Bruce, king of Scotland, who had recovered by arms the independence of his country, and fixed it by treaty, was now dead, and had left his son David, a minor, under the guardianship of Randolph earl of Murray, the companion of his victories. About this time, Edward Baliol, son of John, formerly crowned king of Scotland, was discovered in a French prison by lord Beaumont, an English baron, who, in the right of his wife, claimed the earldom of Buchan in Scotland ; and who, deeming Baliol a proper instrument for his purpose, procured him his liberty, and persuaded him to assert his claim to the Scottish crown.

Many other English noblemen, who had obtained estates during the subjection of Scotland, were in the same situation with Beaumont. They also saw the utility of Baliol, and began to think of recovering their possessions by arms : and they applied to Edward for his concurrence and assistance. The king was ashamed to avow their enterprise. He apprehended that violence and injustice would every where be imputed to him, if he should attack with superior force a minor king, and a brother-in-law, whose independent title had been solemnly acknowledged : but he secretly encouraged Baliol in his claim, conniving at his assembling forces in the North, and gave countenance to the nobles who were disposed to join him. Near three thousand men were assembled, with whom Baliol and his adherents landed on the coast of Fife.

A.D. 1332.

Scotland was now in a very different state from that in which it had appeared under the victorious Robert. Besides the loss of that great monarch, whose genius and authority preserved entire the whole political fabric, and maintained union among the unruly barons, lord Douglas, impatient of rest, had gone over to Spain in a crusade against the Moors, and there perished in battle. The earl of Murray, long declining through years and infirmities, had lately died, and was succeeded in the regency by Donald earl of Mar, a man much inferior in talents ; so that the military spirit of the Scots, though still unbroken, was left without an able guide. Baliol had valour and activity, and his followers, being firmly united by the common object, drove back the Scots who opposed his landing. He marched into the heart of the country; and with his small party defeated an army of thirty thousand men, under the earl of Mar, of whom twelve thousand are said to have been slain [1].

---

[1] Hemingf.—Walsingham.

Baliol, soon after this victory, made himself master of Perth, and was crowned at Scone. Scotland was thus easily conquered; but Baliol lost the kingdom by a revolution as sudden as that by which he had acquired it. His imprudence, or his necessities, prompting him to dismiss the majority of his English followers, he was unexpectedly attacked near Annan by Sir Archibald Douglas, and other chieftains of Bruce's party. He was routed: his brother John Baliol was slain; and he himself was chased into England in a miserable condition [1].

In this extremity Baliol again had recourse to the English monarch, without whose assistance he could neither recover nor keep possession of his throne. He offered to acknowledge Edward's superiority; to renew the homage for Scotland; A.D. and to espouse the princess Jane, if the pope's consent 1333. could be obtained for dissolving her marriage with David Bruce, which was not yet consummated. Ambitious of retrieving the important superiority relinquished by Mortimer during his minority, Edward willingly accepted the offer, and put himself at the head of a powerful army, in order to reinstate Baliol in his throne. The Scots met him with an army more numerous, but less united, and worse supplied with arms and provisions. July. A battle was fought at Halidown-hill, near Berwick; 19. where about twenty thousand of the Scots fell, and the chief nobility were either killed or taken prisoners [2].

After this fatal blow, the Scottish nobles had no resource but in submission. Baliol was acknowledged king by a parliament assembled at Edinburgh; the superiority of England was again recognized; many of the Scottish barons swore fealty to Edward; who, leaving a considerable body of troops with Baliol to complete the conquest of the kingdom, returned to England A.D. with the remainder of his army. But the English forces 1334. had no sooner retired than the Scots revolted from Baliol, and returned to their former allegiance under Bruce. Edward was again obliged to assemble an army, and to march into Scotland. The Scots, taught by experience, withdrew to their hills A.D. and fastnesses. He destroyed the houses, and ravaged 1335. the estates, of those whom he called rebels. But this severity only confirmed them in their antipathy to England and to Baliol: and being now rendered desperate, they soon re- A.D. conquered their country from the English. Edward 1336. again made his appearance in Scotland, and with like success.

---

[1] Knight.—Buchanan.   [2] Mon. Malmesb.—Walsingham.

He found every thing hostile in the kingdom, except the spot on which he was encamped ; and although he marched uncontrolled over the low countries, the nation itself seemed farther than ever from being broken or subdued. Besides being supported by their pride or anger, passions difficult to tame, the Scots were encouraged amidst all their calamities by promises of relief from France : and as a war was now likely to break out between that kingdom and England, they had reason to expect a division of the force which had so long harassed and oppressed them [1].

These transactions naturally bring us back to Edward's claim to the crown of France ; on which depended the most memorable events, not only of this long and active reign, but of the whole English and French history, during more than a century. His pretensions were weak and ill-founded. He admitted the general principle, that females could not inherit the crown of France. But, in so doing, he only set aside his mother's right, to establish his own ; for although he acknowledged females incapable of inheriting, he asserted that males descending from females were liable to no such objection, but might claim by right of propinquity. This plea, however, was not only more favourable to Charles king of Navarre, descended from a daughter of Louis X., but contrary to the established rules of succession in every European country. Edward's claim was therefore disregarded, and the title of Philip of Valois was generally acknowledged [2].

But although the youthful and ambitious mind of Edward had rashly entertained this false idea, he would not, in support of his claim, engage in immediate hostilities with so powerful a monarch as Philip VI. On the contrary, he went to Amiens and did homage for Guienne [3]. By that compliance he indirectly acknowledged Philip's title to the crown of France. His own claim indeed was so unreasonable, and so thoroughly disavowed by the French, that to insist on it was no better than to pretend to the violent conquest of the kingdom ; and it probably would not have been farther thought of, had not some incidents afterwards arisen which excited an animosity between the two kings.

Robert of Artois, a prince of great talents and credit, who had married Philip's sister, had fallen into disgrace at the court of France. His brother-in-law not only abandoned him, but persecuted him with violence. He came over to England, and was favourably received by Edward. Now resigning

A.D. 1337.

---

[1] Rymer, vol. iv.—Leland's *Collect.* vol. ii.—Heming.
[2] Froissard, tome i. D'Arb. Spicileg. vol. iii.   [3] Rymer, vol. iv.

himself to all the movements of rage and revenge, he endeavoured to revive in the mind of the English monarch his supposed title to the crown of France; and even flattered, him, that it was not impossible for a prince of his valour and abilities to render this claim effectual. "I made Philip de Valois king of France," added he: "and with your assistance, I will depose him for his ingratitude [1]."

Edward was the more disposed to listen to such suggestions, as he had reason to complain of Philip's conduct with regard to Guienne, and was also displeased at the encouragement given by that prince to the Scots. Resentment gradually filled the breasts of both monarchs, and made them incapable of hearkening to any terms of accommodation. Philip thought himself bound by policy to assist the Scots; and Edward pretended that he must renounce all claim to generosity, if he should withdraw his protection from Robert of Artois. Alliances were formed on both sides, and great preparations were made for war.

On the side of England appeared the count of Hainault (the king's father-in-law), the duke of Brabant, the archbishop of Cologne, the duke of Gueldres, the marquis of Juliers, and the count of Namur. These princes could supply, either from their own states, or from the bordering countries, great numbers of warlike troops; and nothing seemed requisite to make Edward's alliance in that quarter truly formidable but the accession of Flanders, which he obtained by means somewhat extraordinary.

The Flemings, the first people in the north of Europe that successfully cultivated arts and manufactures, began now to emerge from that state of vassalage, or rather slavery, into which the common people had been universally thrown by the abuses of the feudal polity; and the lower class of men among them had risen to a degree of riches unknown elsewhere to those of their station in that comparatively barbarous age. It was impossible for such men not to resent any act of tyranny; and acts of tyranny were likely to be practised by a sovereign and nobility accustomed to domineer. They had risen in tumults; they had insulted the nobles, and driven their earl into France.

In every such revolution there is some leader, to whose guidance the people blindly deliver themselves; and on his character depends the happiness or misery of those who have put

---

[1] Froissard, liv. i.—*Mem. de Robert d'Artois.*

themselves under his care, for every such man has it in his power to be a despot; so narrow are the boundaries between liberty and slavery. The present Flemish demagogue was James van Arteveld a brewer of Ghent, who governed the people with a more absolute sway than had been assumed by any of their lawful sovereigns. He had placed and displaced the magistrates at pleasure. He was constantly attended by a guard, who on the least signal from him, instantly assassinated any man that happened to fall under his displeasure. He had a multitude of spies in all the towns of Flanders; and it was immediate death to give him the smallest umbrage. This was the man to whom Edward addressed himself for bringing over the Flemings to his interest[1].

Proud of advances from so great a prince, and sensible that the Flemings were naturally inclined to maintain connexions with A.D. the English on account of the advantages of trade, their 1338. leader embraced the cause of Edward, and invited him over to the Low-Countries. The king repaired to Flanders, attended by several of his nobility, and a body of English forces; but before the Flemings, who were vassals of France, would take up arms against their liege lord, Edward was obliged to assume the title of king of France, and to challenge their assistance for dethroning Philip de Valois, the usurper of his throne[2]. This step, which was taken by the advice of Arteveld, as he knew it would produce an irreconcilable breach between the two monarchs (an additional motive for joining the cause of Edward), gave rise to that animosity which the English and French nations, but more especially the former, have ever since borne against each other—an animosity which had, for some centuries, so visible an influence on all their transactions, and which still continues to inflame the heart of many an honest Englishman.

Let philosophers blame this prejudice as inconsistent with the liberality of the human mind; let moralists mourn its severity, and weak politicians lament its destructive rage. You, my dear Philip, as a lover of your country, will ever, I hope, revere a passion that has so often given victory to the arms of England, and humbled her haughty rival; which has preserved, and continues to preserve, the independence of Great Britain!

The French monarch made great preparations against the attack from the English; and his foreign alliances were both more

---

[1] Froissard, liv. i.   [2] W. Heming.—Walsingham.—Rymer, vol. v.

natural and powerful than those which were formed by his antagonist.   The king of Navarre, the duke of Bretagne, the count
of Bar, were entirely in the interest of Philip; and on the side
of Germany, he was favoured by the king of Bohemia, the palatine of the Rhine, the dukes of Lorrain and Austria, the bishop
of Liege, the counts of Deuxponts, Vaudemont, and Ge-   A.D.
neva.   A mighty army was brought into the field on   1339.
each side.   Conferences and mutual defiances, however, were
all that the first campaign produced; and Edward, distressed for
want of money, was obliged to disband his army, and return to
England.

But this illustrious prince had too high a spirit to be discouraged by the first difficulties of an undertaking.   He was
anxious to retrieve his honour by more successful and   A.D.
more gallant enterprises; and the next season proved   1340.
somewhat more fortunate.   The English, under the command of
Edward, gained an important advantage over the French   June
by sea.   Two hundred and thirty French ships were taken,   24.
and above twenty thousand Frenchmen were killed, with two of
their admirals.   The lustre of this victory increased the king's
reputation among his allies, who assembled their forces with expedition, and joined the English army; and Edward marched to
the frontiers of France at the head of a hundred thousand men.
The French monarch had collected an army still more numerous;
yet he continued to adhere to the prudent resolution he had
formed of putting nothing to hazard, thus hoping to weary out
the enemy.   This conduct had in some measure the desired
effect.   Edward, fatigued with fruitless sieges, and irritated at
the disagreeable prospect that lay before him, challenged Philip
to decide their claim to the crown of France by single combat,
by an action of one hundred against one hundred, or by a general
engagement.   Philip replied with his usual coolness, that it did
not become a vassal to challenge his liege lord; and Edward
found it necessary to conclude a truce for one year[2].

This truce would in all probability have been converted into
a solid peace, and Edward would have dropped his claim, had
not an unexpected circumstance opened to him more promising
views, and given his enterprising genius full opportunity to display itself.   The count de Montfort, the heir male of Bretagne,

[1] Froissard, ubi sup.—Walsingham.
[2] R. de Avesb.—Ad de Murim.—Froissard.

had seized that duchy in opposition to Charles of Blois, the
A.D. French king's nephew, who had married the daughter of
1341. the late duke. Sensible that he could expect no favour
from Philip, Montfort made a voyage to England, on pretence
of soliciting his claim to the earldom of Richmond, which had
devolved to him by his brother's death; and then offering to do
homage to Edward, as king of France, for the Breton duchy, he
proposed a close alliance.

Little negociation was necessary to conclude a treaty between
two princes connected by their immediate interests. But the
captivity of the count de Montfort, which happened soon after,
seemed to put an end to all the advantages which might naturally
have been expected from such an alliance. The affairs of Bretagne, however, were unexpectedly retrieved by Jane of Flanders, countess of Montfort, the most extraordinary woman of
her time. Roused by the captivity of her husband from those
domestic cares to which she had hitherto confined herself, she
A.D. boldly undertook to support the fallen fortunes of her
1342. family. She went from place to place, encouraging the
garrisons, providing them with every thing necessary for subsistence, and concerting the proper plans of defence; and after
having put the whole province in a good posture, she shut herself up in Hennebonne, where she waited with impatience the
arrival of those succours which Edward had promised her.

Charles of Blois, anxious to make himself master of this important fortress, and still more to get possession of the person of
the countess, sat down before the place with a great army, and
conducted the attack with indefatigable industry. The defence
was no less vigorous. The besiegers were repulsed in every assault. Frequent sallies were made by the garrison; and the
countess herself being the most forward on all occasions, every
one was ashamed not to exert himself to the utmost. The reiterated attacks of the besiegers, however, had at length made several
breaches in the wall; and it was apprehended that a general
assault, which was dreaded every hour, might bear down the
garrison. It became necessary to treat of a capitulation; and
the bishop of Laon was already engaged in a conference on that
subject with Charles of Blois, when the countess, who had
mounted a high tower, and was anxiously looking toward the
sea for relief, descried some sails at a distance. " Behold the
succours!" exclaimed she;—" the English succours!—No capitulation!" They consisted of six thousand archers, and some
cavalry, under the command of sir Walter Manny, one of the

bravest captains of England; and having entered the harbour, and inspired fresh courage into the garrison, immediately sallied forth, beat the besiegers from their posts, and obliged them to decamp[1].

Notwithstanding this success, the troops under sir Walter Manny were found insufficient for the support of the countess of Montfort, who was still in danger of being overpowered by numbers. Edward therefore sent over a reinforcement under Robert of Artois, and afterwards went to her assistance in person. Robert was mortally wounded in the defence of A.D. Vannes; and Edward concluded a truce of three years, 1343. on honourable terms, for himself and the countess.

This truce, however, was of much shorter duration than the term specified in the articles, and each monarch endeavoured to throw on the other the blame of its infraction. The English parliament entered warmly into the quarrel, advised the king A.D. not to be amused by a fraudulent truce, and granted him 1344. supplies for the renewal of hostilities. The earl of Derby was sent over for the protection of Guienne, where he behaved with great gallantry; and Edward invaded Normandy with an army of thirty thousand men. He took several towns, and A.D. ravaged the whole province, carrying his incursions almost 1346. to the gates of Paris. At length Philip advanced against him at the head of about ninety thousand men; and Edward, afraid of being surrounded in the country, retreated towards Flanders[2].

In this retreat happened the famous passage of the Somme, which was followed by the still more celebrated battle of Cressy. —When Edward approached the Somme, he found all the bridges either broken down or strongly guarded. Twelve thousand men, under the command of Godemar de Faye, were stationed on the opposite bank; and Philip was advancing, at the same time, from behind. In this extremity, he was informed of a place that was fordable: he hastened thither, but saw De Faye ready to obstruct his passage. A man of less resolution, or greater caution and coolness, would have hesitated: Edward deliberated not a moment, but threw himself into the river at the head of his troops, drove the French from their station, and pursued them to a distance on the plain. Philip and his forces arrived at the ford, when the rear guard of the English army were passing; and the rising of the tide alone prevented the incensed monarch from following them. On the

---

[1] Froissard, liv. i.   [2] R. de Avesb.—Froissard, ubi sup.

lapse of so few moments depended the fate of Edward!—and these, by his celerity, were turned from ruin into victory! Yet if he had been unfortunate in his passage, or if the French army had arrived sooner, how many pretended philosophers would have told us that he was an inconsiderate prince, and the attempt would have been branded as absurd!—So much, my dear Philip, does the reputation of events depend on success, and the characters of men on the situations in which they are engaged.

Edward by his fortunate passage gained some ground of the enemy, as Philip was obliged to take his route by the bridge of Abbeville; but he still saw the danger of precipitating his march over the plains of Picardy, and of exposing his rear to the insults of the numerous cavalry, in which the French camp abounded. He therefore embraced the prudent resolution of waiting the arrival of the enemy, and chose his ground advantageously near the village of Cressy, where he drew up his army in excellent order. The first line was commanded by the prince of Wales, commonly called the Black Prince, from the colour of his armour; the second by the earls of Arundel and Northampton: and the king himself took the direction of the third. The French army, which now consisted of above a hundred thousand men, was also formed into three lines; but, as Philip had made a hasty and confused march from Abbeville, the troops were fatigued and disordered. The first line, partly consisting of fifteen thousand Genoese cross-bow men, was commanded by Doria and Grimaldi; the second was led by the count d'Alençon; and the king in Aug. person was at the head of the third. The battle began 26. about three o'clock, and continued till towards evening, when the French fled with precipitation. Almost forty thousand of their number were slain, among whom were many of the principal nobility, twelve hundred knights, and fourteen hundred gentlemen. On his return to the camp, Edward embraced and congratulated the prince of Wales, who had distinguished himself in a remarkable manner. " My brave son!" cried he, " persevere in your honourable course. You are my son; for valiantly you have acquitted yourself to-day. You have shown yourself worthy of empire[1]."

This victory is partly ascribed to some pieces of artillery, which Edward is said to have planted in his front, and which gave great alarm to the enemy[2]; but we cannot suppose they did much

[1] Froissard, liv. i.—Walsing.—Avesb.   [2] Villani, lib. xii.

execution. The invention was yet in its infancy; and cannon were at first so clumsy, and of such difficult management, that they were rather incumbrances than those terrible instruments of desolation we now behold them. They had never before been used on any memorable occasion in Europe. This may, therefore, be regarded as the æra of one of the most important discoveries that have been made among men; a discovery which changed by degrees the whole military science, and of course many circumstances in the political government of Europe; which has brought nations more on a level; has made success in war a matter of calculation; and, though seemingly contrived for the destruction of mankind, and the overthrow of empires, has in the issue rendered battles less bloody, and conquests less frequent, by giving greater security to states, and interesting the passions of men less in the struggle for victory.

A weak mind is elate with the smallest success; a great spirit is little affected by any turn of fortune. Edward, instead of expecting that the victory of Cressy would be immediately followed by the total subjection of the disputed kingdom, seemed rather to moderate his views. He prudently limited his ambition to the conquest of Calais; by which he hoped to secure such an easy entrance into France as might afterwards open the way to more considerable advantages. He therefore marched thither with his victorious army, and presented himself before the place.

In the mean time David Bruce, king of Scotland, who had returned from a long residence in France, was strongly solicited by his ally to invade the northern counties of England. He accordingly assembled a great army, and carried his ravages as far as Durham. He was there met by queen Philippa, Oct. at the head of a body of twelve thousand men, which she 17. committed to the command of lord Percy. A fierce engagement ensued; and the Scots were broken and chased off the field with great slaughter. Fifteen thousand of them were slain; and the king was taken prisoner, with many of his chief nobles[1].

As soon as Philippa had secured her royal prisoner, she crossed the sea at Dover, and was received in the English camp before Calais with all the *éclat* due to her rank, her merit, and her success. This was the age of chivalry and gallantry. Edward's courtiers excelled in these accomplishments no less than in policy and war; and the extraordinary qualities of the women

[1] R. de Avesb.—Knight.—Froissard, ubi sup.

of those times, the necessary consequence of respectful admiration, form the best apology for the superstitious devotion which was then paid to the softer sex. Calais was taken, after a blockade of almost twelve months. The inhabitants were expelled; and it was peopled with English subjects, and made the staple of wool, leather, tin, and lead; the four chief commodities of England, and the only ones for which there was yet any demand in foreign markets. A truce was soon afterwards concluded with France, through the mediation of the pope's legate, and Edward returned in triumph to England[1].

A.D.
1347.

Here a few observations seem necessary. The great success of Edward in his foreign wars had excited a strong emulation among the English nobility; and their animosity against France, and respect to their prince, had given a new and more useful direction to that ambition, which had so often been turned by the turbulent barons against the crown, or which discharged its fury on their fellow-subjects. This prevailing spirit was farther promoted by the institution of the military order of the Garter, in emulation of some orders of knighthood, of a like nature, which had been established in different parts of Europe.—A story prevails, though not supported by ancient authority, that Edward's mistress, commonly supposed to be the countess of Salisbury, dropped her garter at a court ball: that the king stooped, and took it up, when, observing that some of his courtiers smiled, as if they had suspected another intention, he held up the trophy, and called out *Honi soit qui mal y pense :* "Evil to him that evil thinks."—And as every incident of gallantry in those times was magnified into a matter of importance, he instituted the order of the Garter in commemoration of this event, though not without political views, and gave those words as the motto of the order. Frivolous as such an origin may seem, it is perfectly suitable to the manners of that age; and, as a profound historian remarks, it is difficult by any other means to account either for the seemingly unmeaning terms of the motto, or the peculiar badge of the garter, which appears to have no reference to any purpose either of military use or ornament[2].

Jan. 19,
1350.

A damp, however, was suddenly thrown over the triumphant festivity of the English court, by a destructive pestilence, which about this time invaded Britain, after having desolated a great portion of the earth. It made its appearance first in the north

---

[1] Knight.—Froissard.   [2] Hume's *Hist. of England*, chap. xv.

of Asia; encircled that vast continent; visited Africa; made its progress from one end of Europe to the other; and is computed to have swept away near a third of the inhabitants in every country through which it passed. Above fifty thousand persons are said to have perished by it in London alone. This grievous calamity more than the pacific disposition of the princes, tended to prolong the truce between England and France.

During this truce Philip de Valois died, without being able to re-establish the affairs of France, which his unsuccessful Aug. war with England had thrown into great disorder. This 22. monarch had, during the first years of his reign, obtained the appellation of *Fortunate*, and acquired the character of *Prudent* : but he ill maintained either the one or the other ; less indeed from his own fault, than because he was overmatched by the superior fortune and genius of Edward. But the incidents in the reign of his son John gave the French cause to regret even the calamitous times of Philip. John was distinguished by many virtues, but particularly by a scrupulous honour and fidelity. He was not deficient in personal courage; but as he wanted that masterly prudence and foresight which his difficult situation required, his kingdom was at the same time disturbed by intestine commotions, and oppressed by foreign wars.

The principal author of these calamities was Charles king of Navarre, surnamed the Bad, and whose conduct fully entitled him to that appellation. He was descended from males of the royal blood of France. His mother was daughter of Louis X., and he had himself married a daughter of the reigning king ; but these ties, which ought to have connected him with the throne, gave him only greater power to shake and overthrow it. He secretly entered into a correspondence with the king of England; and he seduced, by his address, Charles, afterwards surnamed the Wise, the eldest son of the king of France, and the first who bore the title of Dauphin, by the union of the province of Dauphiné with the dominions of the crown. The young prince, however, became sensible of the danger and folly of such connexions, and promised to make atonement for the offence by the sacrifice of his associates. In concert with his father, he accordingly invited the king of Navarre, and other noblemen of the party, to a feast at Rouen, where they were betrayed into the hands of John. Some of the most obnoxious were im- A.D. mediately led to execution, and the king of Navarre was 1355. thrown into prison. But this stroke of severity in the French monarch, and of treachery in the dauphin, was far from proving decisive in restoring the royal authority. Philip of Navarre, brother to Charles the Bad, and Geoffrey d'Harcourt, put all the towns and castles belonging to that prince in a posture of defence ; and they had immediate recourse to England in this desperate extremity [1].

The truce between the kingdoms, which had been ill observed on both sides, had now expired ; so that Edward was at liberty to support the French malecontents. The war was renewed ; and after a variety of fortunes, but chiefly in favour of the English, an event happened which nearly proved fatal to the French monarchy.

The prince of Wales, encouraged by the success of the first campaign, took the field with an army of only twelve thousand men ; and with that small force he ventured to penetrate into the heart of France. John, provoked at the insult offered him by this incursion, collected an army of sixty thousand combatants, and advanced by hasty marches to intercept his enemy. The prince, not aware of John's near approach, lost some days on his march, before the castle of Remorantin, and thereby gave the French monarch an opportunity of overtaking him. The pursuers came within sight at Maupertius, near Poictiers ; and young Edward, sensible that his retreat was now become impracticable, prepared for battle with all the courage of a hero, and all the prudence of an experienced general. No degree of skill or courage, however, could have saved him, had the king of France known how to make use of his present advantages. John's superiority of number might have enabled him to surround the English camp, and, by intercepting all provisions, to reduce the prince to the necessity of surrendering at discretion. But the impatient ardour of the French nobility prevented this idea from striking any of the commanders ; so that they immediately took measures for the assault with full assurance of victory. But they were miserably deceived in their expectations. The English adventurers received them with the most heroic valour, put their army to flight, and took their king prisoner.

The prince was reposing himself after the toils of battle, when he was informed of the fate of the French monarch. John had long refused to surrender himself to any one but his " cousin the prince of Wales." Here commences the real and unexampled heroism of young Edward—the triumph of humanity and

(margin notes: A.D. 1356. — Sept. 19.)

---

[1] Froissard. liv. i.

moderation over insolence and pride, in the heart of a young warrior, elated by as extraordinary and as unexpected success as had ever crowned the arms of any commander. He came forth to meet the captive king with all the marks of regard and sympathy; administered comfort to him amidst his misfortunes: paid him the tribute of praise due to his valour; and ascribed his own victory merely to the blind chance of war, or to a superior Providence, which controls all the efforts of human force and prudence. He ordered a repast to be prepared in his tent for the royal prisoner; and he himself served at the captive's table, as if he had been one of his retinue. All his father's pretensions to the crown of France were now buried in oblivion. John in captivity received the honours of a king, which were refused to him when seated on the throne of Clovis. His misfortunes, not his right, were respected: and the French prisoners, conquered by this elevation of mind, more than by the English arms, burst into tears of admiration; which were only checked by the reflection, that such exalted heroism in an enemy must make him doubly dangerous to the independence of their native country [1].

The prince conducted his royal prisoner to Bordeaux; and, after concluding a truce for two years, brought him over A.D. to England. Here the king of France, besides the gene- 1357. rous treatment which he received, had the melancholy consolation of meeting a brother in affliction. The king of Scotland had remained above ten years a captive in the hands of Edward, whose superior genius and fortune had thus reduced the two neighbouring potentates, with whom he was engaged in war, to the condition of prisoners in his capital. Finding, however, that the conquest of Scotland was not promoted by the captivity of its sovereign, Edward consented to restore David to his liberty, in consideration of the payment of one hundred thousand marks [2].

The captivity of the French monarch, joined to the preceding disorders of the kingdom, had produced an almost total dissolution of civil authority, and occasioned the most horrible and destructive violences ever experienced in any age or country. The dauphin, who was in his twentieth year, had assumed the reins of government; but although he was endowed with an excellent judgment, he possessed not experience or ability sufficient to remedy the prevailing evils. In order to obtain sup-

---

[1] Froissard, liv. i.   [2] Rymer, vol. vi.

plies, he assembled the states of the kingdom.   But the
members of that assembly, instead of supporting his
administration, were themselves seized with the spirit of licentiousness: and they demanded limitations of the regal power,
the punishment of past malversations, and the liberty of the
king of Navarre.   Marcel, chief magistrate of Paris, put himself
at the head of the unruly populace; and from the violence and
temerity of his character, pushed them to commit the most
violent outrages against the royal authority.   They detained the
dauphin in a kind of captivity: they murdered in his presence
Robert de Clermont, and John de Conflans, marechals of
France: they threatened the other ministers with the like fate;
and when Charles, who had been obliged to temporize and dissemble, made his escape from their hands, they openly erected
the standard of rebellion.   The other cities of the kingdom, in
imitation of the capital, shook off the dauphin's authority, took
the government into their own hands, and spread the contagion
into every province.   The wild state of nature seemed to be
renewed in the bosom of society: every man was thrown loose
and independent of his fellow-citizens.

The nobles, whose inclinations led them to adhere to the
crown, and to check these tumults, had lost all their influence.
The troops, who from the want of pay could no longer be retained
in discipline, throwing off all regard to their officers, sought the
means of subsistence by depredation; and associating with them
all the disorderly people, with whom that age abounded, infested
every quarter of the kingdom in numerous bodies.   They desolated the open country; plundered and burned the villages; and,
by cutting off all means of communication or subsistence, reduced
to necessity even the inhabitants of the fortified towns.

The peasants, formerly oppressed, and now left unprotected
by their masters, became desperate from their present misery;
and rising in arms, carried to extremity those disorders which
had arisen from the sedition of the citizens and disbanded soldiers.   The gentry, hated for their tyranny, were exposed to
the violence of popular rage; and instead of meeting with the
respect due to their rank, became only, on that account, the
objects of more wanton insult to the mutinous rustics.   They
were hunted like wild beasts, and put to the sword without
mercy.   Their castles were consumed with fire, and levelled with
the ground: while their wives and daughters were subjected to
violation, and then murdered.

A body of nine thousand of these savage boors broke into Meaux, where the wife of the dauphin, the duchess of Orleans, and above three hundred other ladies, had taken shelter. The most brutal treatment and fatal consequences were apprehended by this fair and helpless company: when the count de Foix and the Captal de Buche, with the assistance of only sixty knights, animated by the true spirit of chivalry, flew to the rescue of the ladies, and beat off the brutal and rapacious peasants with great slaughter [1].

Amidst these disorders the king of Navarre made his escape from prison, and presented a dangerous leader to the furious malecontents. He revived his pretensions to the crown of France; but in all his operations he acted more like a captain of banditti than one who aspired to be the head of a regular government, and who was engaged by his station to aim at the re-establishment of order in the community. All the French, therefore, who wished to restore peace to their desolated country, turned their eyes towards the dauphin; who, though not remarkable for his military talents, daily gained by his prudence and vigilance the ascendency over his enemies. The turbulent Marcel was slain in attempting to deliver Paris to the king of Navarre. The capital immediately returned to its duty; the most considerable bodies of the mutinous peasants were dispersed or put to the sword; some bands of military robbers underwent the same fate, and France began to reassume the appearance of civil government [2].

Edward seemed to have an opportunity of greatly extending his conquests, during the confusion in the dauphin's affairs; but his hands were tied by the truce, and the state of the English finances made a cessation of arms necessary. The truce, however, had no sooner expired than he again invaded France. A.D. He ravaged the country without opposition; pillaged 1359. many towns, and levied contributions upon others; but finding that his army could not subsist in a kingdom wasted by foreign and domestic enemies, he prudently concluded the peace A.D. of Bretigni, which promised essential advantages to his 1360. crown. It was stipulated, that John should pay three millions of crowns of gold for his ransom: that Edward should for ever renounce all claim to the crown of France, and to the provinces of Normandy, Maine, Touraine, and Anjou, possessed by his

[1] Froissard, liv. i.—St. Palaye sur l'Ancienne Chevalerie.
[2] Froissard, ubi sup.

ancestors; in exchange for which he should receive the provinces of Poictou, Saintonge, l'Agenois, Perigord, the Limosin, Quercy, and other districts in that quarter, together with Calais, Guisnes, Montreuil, and the county of Ponthieu, on the other side of France; and that the sovereignty of these provinces, as well as of Guienne, should be vested in the crown of England without homage to France [1].

In consequence of this treaty, the king of France was restored to his liberty; but many difficulties arising with respect to the execution of some of the articles, he took the honourable reso-

A.D. 1363. lution of coming over to England in order to adjust them. His council endeavoured to dissuade him from this design, which they represented as rash and impolitic; and insinuated, that he ought to elude, as far as possible, the execution of so disadvantageous a treaty. " Though justice and good faith," replied John, " were banished from the rest of the earth, they ought still to retain their habitation in the breast of princes!"

April 8, 1364. And he accordingly came over to his former lodgings in the Savoy, where he soon after died [2].

John was succeeded on the French throne by his son, Charles V., a prince educated in the school of adversity, and well qualified, by his prudence and experience, to repair the losses which the kingdom had sustained from the errors of his predecessors. Contrary to the practice of all the great princes of those times, who held nothing in estimation but military courage, he seems to have laid it down as a maxim, never to appear at the head of his armies. He was the first European monarch that showed the advantage of policy and foresight over a rash and precipitate valour.

Before Charles could think of counterbalancing so great a power as England, it was necessary for him to remedy the many disorders to which his own kingdom was exposed. He accordingly turned his arms against the king of Navarre, the great disturber of France during that age: and he defeated that prince, and reduced him to terms, by the valour and conduct of Bertrand du Guesclin, one of the most accomplished captains

A.D. 1365. of those times, whom Charles had the discernment to choose as the instrument of his victories. He also settled the affairs of Bretagne, by acknowledging the title of Montfort, and receiving homage for the duchy. But much was yet to be done.

---

[1] Rymer, vol. vi.   [2] Froissard, ubi sup.

On the conclusion of the peace of Bretigni, a multitude of adventurers, who had served in the war, refused to lay down their arms, or relinquish a course of life to which they were accustomed.   They even associated themselves with the banditti, who were already inured to the habits of rapine and violence, and, under the name of *Companies* and *Companions*, became a terror to the peaceable inhabitants.   Some English and Gascon gentlemen of character were not ashamed to take the command of these ruffians, whose number amounted to near forty thousand, and who bore the appearance of regular armies rather than bands of robbers[1].   As Charles was not able by force to redress so enormous a grievance, he was led by necessity, and by the turn of his character, to correct it by policy; to discover some method of discharging into foreign countries this dangerous and intestine evil.   And an occasion now offered.

Alphonso XI. king of Castile, who took Algesiras from the Moors, after a siege of above nineteen months, had been succeeded, in 1350, by his son Peter I. surnamed the Cruel.   This perfidious and profligate tyrant began his reign with the murder of his father's mistress, Leonora de Gusman : many of his nobles fell victims to his fury : he put to death his cousin, and one of his natural brothers, from groundless jealousy ; and he caused his queen, Blanche de Bourbon, of the royal blood of France, to be thrown into prison, and afterwards poisoned, that he might enjoy in quiet the embraces of Mary de Padilla, of whom he was violently enamoured.

Henry, count of Trastamara, Peter's natural brother, alarmed at the fate of his family, and dreading his own, took arms A. D. against the king; but having failed in the attempt, he 1366. fled into France, where he found the minds of men inflamed against Peter, on account of the murder of the French princess. He asked permission of Charles to enlist the *Companies* in his service, and to lead them into Castile against his brother.   The French monarch, charmed with the project, employed du Guesclin in negociating with the leaders of these banditti.   The treaty was soon concluded ; and du Guesclin, having completed his levies, led the army first to Avignon, where the pope then resided, and demanded, sword in hand, absolution for his ruffian soldiers, who had been excommunicated, and the sum of two hundred thousand livres for their subsistence.   The first was readily promised; but some difficulty being made with respect

---

[1] Froissard, ubi sup.

to the second, du Guesclin replied, " My fellows, I believe, may make a shift to do without your absolution : but the money is absolutely necessary." His holiness now extorted from the inhabitants of the city and its neighbourhood the sum of one hundred thousand livres, and offered it to Guesclin. " It is not my purpose," said that generous warrior, " to oppress the innocent people. The pope and his cardinals can spare me double the sum from their own pockets. I therefore insist that this money be restored to the owners : and if they should be defrauded of it, I will myself return from the other side of the Pyrenées, and oblige you to make restitution." The pope found the necessity of submitting, and paid from his own treasury the sum demanded[1]. Thus hallowed by the blessings, and enriched by the spoils of the church, du Guesclin and his army proceeded on their expedition.

A body of experienced and hardy soldiers, conducted by so able a general, easily prevailed over the king of Castile, whose subjects were ready to join the enemy against their oppressor. A.D. 1367. Peter fled from his dominions, took shelter in Guienne, and craved the protection of the Black Prince, whom the king of England had invested with the sovereignty of the ceded provinces, under the title of the principality of Aquitaine. The prince promised his assistance to the dethroned monarch ; and having obtained his father's consent, he levied an army, and set out on his enterprise.

The first loss which Henry of Trastamara suffered from the interposition of the prince of Wales, was the recal of the *Companies* from his service : and so much reverence did they pay to the name of Edward, that a great number of them immediately withdrew from Spain, and enlisted under his standard. Henry, however, beloved by his new subjects, and supported by the king of Arragon, was able to meet the enemy with seventy thousand men, far beyond the number of those commanded by the Black Prince ; yet du Guesclin and all his experienced officers advised him to delay a decisive action ; so high was their opinion of the valour and conduct of the English hero !— But Henry, trusting to his numbers, ventured to give Edward battle on the banks of the Ebro, near Najara, where he was defeated with the loss of above ten thousand men, and du Guesclin and other officers of distinction became prisoners. All Castile submitted to the victor : Peter was restored to the

[1] *Hist. du Guesclin.*

throne ; and Edward returned to Guienne with his usual glory ; having not only overcome one of the greatest generals of the age, but restrained the blood-thirsty tyrant from executing vengeance on his prisoners[1].

But this gallant warrior had soon reason to repent of his connexions with Peter, who was so ungrateful as to refuse the stipulated pay to the English forces. Edward therefore abandoned him to his fate. As he soon renewed his tyranny over his subjects, their animosity was roused against him ; and du Guesclin, having been restored to liberty, re-appeared with Henry at the head of a body of intrepid warriors. They were joined by the Spanish malecontents ; and having no longer the superior genius and fortune of the Black Prince to encounter, they gained a complete victory over Peter in the neigh- A. D. bourhood of Toledo. The tyrant took refuge in a castle, 1369. where he was soon after besieged by the victors, and made prisoner in endeavouring to escape. He was conducted to his brother, against whom he is said to have rushed in a transport of rage, disarmed as he was. Henry slew him with his own hand, in resentment of his cruelties ; and, though a bastard, was honoured with the crown of Castile, which he transmitted to his posterity[2].

The Black Prince had involved himself so much in debt by his Spanish expedition, that he found it necessary, on his return, to impose on his principality a new tax, which some of the nobility paid with extreme reluctance, and to which others absolutely refused to submit. They carried their complaints to the king of France, as their lord paramount ; and, as the renunciations agreed to in the treaty of Bretigni had never been made, Charles seized this opportunity to renew his claim of superiority over the English provinces[3]. In this resolution he was encouraged by the declining years of King Edward, and the languishing state of his son's health : he therefore summoned the prince to appear in his court at Paris, and justify his conduct towards his vassals. Young Edward replied, that he would come to Paris, but it should be at the head of sixty thousand men. War was renewed between France and England, and with a singular reverse of fortune. The low state of the prince's health not permitting him to exert his usual activity, the French were

---

[1] Froissard, liv. i.   [2] Id. Ibid.—Mariana, lib. xvii.
[3] Walsingham—Froissard, ubi sup.

A.D. victorious in almost every action; and when he was
1370. obliged, by his increasing infirmities, to throw up the
command, and return to his native country, the affairs of the
English on the continent were almost entirely ruined. They
were deprived in a few years of all their ancient possessions in
France, except Bourdeaux and Bayonne; and of all their conquests, except Calais[1].

These misfortunes abroad were followed by the decay of the
king's authority at home. This was chiefly occasioned by his
extravagant attachment to Alice Perrers, a young lady of wit
and beauty, whose influence over him had given such general
disgust, as to become the object of parliamentary remonstrance.
From the indolence naturally attendant on years and infirmities,
Edward had also resigned the administration into the hands of
his son the duke of Lancaster, whose unpopular manners and
proceedings weakened extremely the affections of the English
June 8, to their sovereign. Meanwhile the prince of Wales
1376. died; leaving behind him a character adorned with every
eminent virtue, and which would throw lustre on the most shining period of ancient or modern history. The king survived
that melancholy incident only about twelve months. He ex-
June 21, pired in the sixty-fifth year of his age, and the fifty-first
1377. year of his reign; one of the longest and most glorious
in the English annals. His latter days were indeed somewhat
obscured by the infirmities and the follies of old age; but he
was no sooner dead, than the people of England were sensible
of their irreparable loss; and he is still considered as the greatest
and most accomplished prince of his time.

The domestic government of Edward was even more worthy
of admiration than his foreign victories. By the prudence and
vigour of his administration, England enjoyed a longer time of
interior peace and tranquillity than it had been blessed with in
any former period, or than it experienced for many ages after.
He gained the affections of the great, yet curbed their licentiousness. His affable and obliging behaviour, his munificence and
generosity, inclined them to submit with pleasure to his dominion; his valour and conduct contributed to render them successful in most military enterprises; and their unquiet spirits,
directed against a public enemy, had no leisure to breed those
private feuds to which they were naturally so much disposed.

---

[1] Froissard.

This internal tranquillity was the chief benefit that England derived from Edward's continental expeditions : and the miseries of the reign of his successor made the nation fully sensible of the value of the blessing.

But before I speak of the administration of Richard II., the unhappy son of the Black Prince, I must carry forward the affairs of the German empire. At present, however, it will be proper to observe, that the French monarch, Charles V., whose prudent conduct had acquired him the surname of *Wise*, died in the year 1380, while he was attempting to expel the English from the few places which they still retained in France, and left his kingdom to a minor son of the same name, so that England and France were now both under the government of minors ; and both experienced the misfortunes of a turbulent and divided regency.

LETTER XLII.

Of the German Empire and its Dependencies, from the Election of Louis of Bavaria to the Death of Charles IV.

WE now, my dear Philip, approach that æra in the history of the German empire, when the famous constitution called the Golden Bull was established ; which, among other points, settled the number and the rights of the electors,—as yet uncertain, and productive of many disorders.

Henry VII., as you have already seen, strenuously laboured to recover the sovereignty of Italy ; but he died before he was able to accomplish his purpose. His death was followed by an interregnum of about fourteen months, which were employed in the intrigues of Louis of Bavaria, and of Frederic the A.D. Handsome, duke of Austria. Louis was elected by the 1314. majority of the princes ; but Frederic, being chosen and supported by a faction, disputed the empire with him. A furious civil war, which long desolated both Italy and Germany, was the consequence of this opposition. At last the two com- A.D. petitors met near Muldorff, and agreed to decide their 1319. important dispute by thirty champions, fifteen against fifteen. The champions accordingly engaged in presence of both armies, and fought with such fury, that in a short time not one of them was left alive. A general action followed, in which the Austrians were worsted. But this victory was not decisive. Frederic soon repaired his loss, and even ravaged Bavaria. The Bavarian A.D. assembled a powerful army, in order to oppose his rival; 1322. and the battle of Vechivis, in which the duke of Austria was taken prisoner, fixed the imperial crown on the head of Louis V.[1]

During the course of these struggles was fought, between the Swiss and Austrians, the memorable battle of Morgart, which established the liberty of Switzerland, as the victory of Marathon had formerly done that of Greece ; and Attic eloquence only was wanting to render it equally famous. Sixteen hundred Swiss, from the cantons of Uri, Schwitz, and Underwald, defeated an army of twenty thousand Austrians, in passing the mountains near Morgart, in 1315, and drove them out of the country with terrible slaughter. The alliance into which these three cantons had entered for the term of ten years, was now converted into a perpetual league : and the other cantons occasionally joined in it[2].

Louis V. had no sooner humbled the duke of Austria than a new antagonist started up :—he had the pope to encounter. The reigning pontiff at that time was John XXII., who had been elected at Lyons in 1316, by the influence of Philip the Long, king of France. John was the son of a cobbler, and one of those men who, raised to power by chance or merit, are haughty in proportion to the meanness of their birth. He had not hitherto, however, interfered in the affairs of the empire ; but A.D. now he set himself up as its judge and master. He 1324. declared the election of Louis void ; he maintained, that it was the right of the sovereign pontiff to examine and confirm the election of emperors, and that the government, during a vacancy, belonged to him : and he commanded the Bavarian, by virtue of his apostolic power, to lay aside the imperial ensigns, until he should receive permission from the holy see to reassume them[3].

Several attempts were made by Louis to soothe the pope's spirit, but in vain : the proud pontiff was inflexible, and would listen to no reasonable conditions. The emperor, therefore, jealous of the independence of his crown, endeavoured to

---

[1] Avent. *Annal. Boior.* lib. vii. [2] Simler, *de Repub. Helvetic.*
[3] Steph. Baluzzii, *Vit. Pontif. Avenion.* vol. i.

strengthen his interest both in Italy and Germany. He continued the government of Milan in the family of the Visconti, who were rather masters than magistrates of that city; and he confered the government of Lucca on Castruccio Castruccani, a celebrated captain, whose life is prompously written by Machiavel. The German princes were chiefly in his interest, and no less jealous than he of the dignity of the empire.

Enraged at such firmness, pope John excommunicated and deposed the emperor, and endeavoured to procure the A.D. election of Charles the Fair, king of France. But this 1325. attempt miscarried. None of the German princes, except Leopold of Austria, came to the place appointed for an interview with the French monarch; and the imprudent and ambitious Charles returned, chagrined and disappointed, into his own dominions [1].

Thus freed from a dangerous rival, Louis marched into Italy, in order to establish his authority in that country. He A.D. was crowned at Milan, and afterwards at Rome; where 1327. he ordered the following proclamation to be made three times by an Augustine friar: " Is there any one who will defend the cause of the priest of Cahors, who calls himself pope John ?"— And no person appearing, sentence was immediately pro- A.D. nounced against his holiness. He was declared a heretic, 1328. deprived of all his dignities, and delivered over to the secular power, in order to suffer the punishment of fire; and a Neapolitan friar was created pope, under the name of Nicholas V.[2]

But Louis, notwithstanding this mighty parade, was soon obliged, like his predecessors, to quit Italy, in order to quell the troubles of Germany; and pope John, though a refugee on the banks of the Rhone, recovered his authority in Rome. A.D. The Imperialists were expelled from the city; and the 1330. emperor's pope was carried to Avignon, where, with a rope about his neck, he publicly implored forgiveness of his rival, and ended his days in a prison [3].

The emperor, in the mean time, remained in peace at Munich, having settled the affairs of Germany. But he still lay under the censures of the church, and the pope continued to solicit the princes of the empire to revolt from him. Louis was preparing to assemble a general council, in order to depose his holi- A.D. ness a second time, when the death of John precluded the 1334.

[1] Villani, lib. ix. [2] Baluz. ubi supra.
[3] Baluz. Vit. Pontif. Avenion.

necessity of such a measure, and relieved the emperor from all dread of the spiritual thunder. This turbulent pope, who first invented the taxes for dispensations and mortal sins, died immensely rich. He was succeeded in the papacy by Benedict XII., who seemed desirous of treading in the steps of his predecessor, and confirmed all the bulls which had been issued by John against the emperor. But Louis had now affairs of greater importance to engage his attention than those fulminations. John of Luxemburg, second son of the king of Bohemia, had married Margaret, surnamed Great Mouth, heiress of Carinthia; and that princess accusing her husband of impotency, the bishop of Frisingen dissolved the marriage, and she espoused the margrave of Brandenburg, son of the emperor, who readily consented to a match which added Tyrol and Carinthia to the possessions of his family. This marriage produced a war between the houses A.D. of Bavaria and Bohemia, which lasted only one year, but 1336. occasioned abundance of bloodshed; and the parties came to an extraordinary accommodation. John of Luxemburg confessed that his wife had reason to forsake him, renounced all claim to her, and ratified her marriage with the margrave of Brandenburg [1].

This affair being settled, Louis exerted all his endeavours to appease the domestic troubles of the empire, which were still kept alive by the intrigues of the pope; and notwithstanding all the injuries and insults he had sustained, he made several attempts towards an accommodation with the holy see. But these negociations being rendered ineffectual by the influence of A.D. France, the princes of the empire, ecclesiastical as well as 1338. secular, assembled at Frankfort, and established that famous constitution, by which it was irrevocably decided, "that the imperial dignity might be conferred by a plurality of the suffrages of the electoral college, without the consent of the holy see; that the pope had no superiority over the emperor of Germany, nor any right to approve or reject his election; and that to maintain the contrary was high treason [2]." They also refuted the absurd claim of the popes to the government of the empire during the vacancy; and declared, that this right appertained, by ancient custom, to the count Palatine of the Rhine.

Germany now enjoyed for some years, what it had seldom A.D. known, the blessing of peace, which was again inter-1342. rupted by the court of Avignon. Benedict XII. was suc-

---

[1] *Hist. de Luxembourg.*   [2] Heiss, liv. ii. chap. 26.

ceeded in the papacy by Clement VI., a native of France, who was so haughty and enterprising as to affirm that his " predecessors did not know what it was to be popes." He began his pontificate with renewing all the bulls issued against Louis; with naming a vicar-general of the empire in Lombardy, and endeavouring to make all Italy shake off the emperor's authority.

Louis, still desirous of an accommodation with the holy see, amidst all these acts of enmity, sent ambassadors to the court of Avignon. But the terms prescribed by the pope were so unreasonable, that they were rejected with disdain by a diet of the empire. Clement, highly incensed at this instance of disregard, fulminated new excommunications against the emperor. A.D. " May the wrath of God," says the enraged pontiff in one 1346. of his bulls, " and of St. Peter and St. Paul, crush him in this world, and in that which is to come ! May the earth open and swallow him alive; may his memory perish, and all the elements be his enemies ; and may his children fall into the hands of his adversaries, even in the sight of their father [1] !"

Clement also issued a bull for the election of an emperor; and Charles of Luxemburg, margrave of Moravia, (afterwards known by the name of Charles IV.) son and heir of John, king of Bohemia, having made the necessary concessions to his holiness, was elected king of the Romans by a faction. Louis, Oct. 11, however, maintained his authority till his death, which 1347. happened soon after the election of his rival ; when Charles, rather by his money than his valour, secured the imperial throne.

While these events occurred in Germany, a singular scene was exhibited in Italy. Nicholas Rienzi, a private citizen of Rome, but an eloquent, bold, enterprising man, and a patriot, seeing that city abandoned by the emperors and the popes, set himself up as the restorer of the Roman liberty and the Roman power. Proclaimed tribune by the people, and put in possession of the Capitol, he declared all the inhabitants of Italy free, and denizens of Rome. But these convulsive struggles of long expiring freedom, like many others, proved ineffectual. Rienzi, who styled himself " the severe though merciful Deliverer of Rome, the zealous Asserter of the Liberties of Italy, and the Lover of all Mankind," as he attempted to imitate the Gracchi, met the same fate, being murdered by the patrician faction [2].

A scene no less extraordinary was about this time exhibited at Naples. The kingdoms of Naples and Sicily still continued

---

[1] *Annal. de l'Emp.* tome ii.   [2] Id. ibid.

to be ruled by foreigners. Naples was governed by the house of France, and Sicily by that of Arragon. Robert of Anjou, son of Charles the Lame, though he had failed in his attempt to recover Sicily, had rendered Naples a flourishing kingdom. He died in 1343, and left his crown to Joan his grand-daughter, who had married her cousin Andrew, brother to Louis of Anjou, king of Hungary : a match which seemed to cement the happiness and prosperity of that house, but proved the source of all its misfortunes. Andrew pretended to reign in his own right; and Joan, though but eighteen years of age, insisted that he should only be considered as the queen's husband. A Franciscan friar, called brother Robert, by whose advice Andrew was wholly governed, lighted up the flames of hatred and discord between the royal pair; and the Hungarians, of whom Andrew's court was chiefly composed, excited the jealousy of the Neapolitans, who considered them as barbarians. It was therefore resolved in a council of the queen's favourites, that Andrew should be put to death. He was accordingly strangled in his wife's antechamber; and Joan married the prince of Tarentum, who had been publicly accused of the murder of her husband, and was well known to have been concerned in that bloody deed. How strong a presumption of her own guilt !

The king of Hungary, lamenting his brother's fate, solemnly denounced vengeance against the queen. Having repaired to Rome, he accused her, in form, before the tribune Rienzi; who during the existence of his transitory power, beheld several kings appealing to his tribunal, as was customary in the times of the ancient republic. Rienzi, however, declined giving his decision; a moderation by which he at least gave one example of his prudence : and Louis advanced towards Naples, carrying with him a black standard, on which were painted the most striking circumstances of Andrew's murder. He ordered a prince of the blood, and one of the accomplices in the crime, to be beheaded. Joan and her husband fled into Provence, where finding herself utterly abandoned by her subjects, she visited pope Clement VI. at Avignon, a city of which she was sovereign, as countess of Provence, and which she sold to that pontiff, together with its territories, for eighty thousand florins in gold, which, a celebrated historian tells us, were never paid. Here she pleaded her cause before the pope, and was acquitted. But perhaps the desire of possessing Avignon had some influence upon the judgment of his holiness.

Clement's kindness did not stop here. In order to engage

Louis to quit Naples, he proposed that Joan should pay him a sum of money ; but, as ambition or avarice had no share in the king's enterprise, he generously replied, " I am not come hither to sell my brother's blood, but to revenge it !" and as he had partly effected his purpose, he went away satisfied, though the kingdom of Naples was in his power[1]. Joan recovered her dominions, only to become more wretched. Of her unhappy fate I shall afterwards have occasion to speak.   A.D. 1348.

We must now return to the affairs of the emperor Charles IV. When this prince, who was equally distinguished by his weakness and pride, had settled the affairs of Germany, he went to receive the imperial crown at Rome, where he behaved in a manner more pusillanimous than any of his predecessors. The ceremony was no sooner performed than he retired without the walls, in consequence of an agreement which he had made with the pope ; though the Romans came to offer him the government of their city, as his hereditary right, and entreated him to re-establish their ancient liberty. He told the deputies he would deliberate on the proposal. But being apprehensive of some treachery, he retired in the evening, under pretence of going to take the diversion of hunting ; and he afterwards ratified and confirmed many promises extorted from him by Clement VI., very much to the prejudice of the empire in Italy[2].   A.D. 1355.

The poet Petrarch, so highly celebrated for his love-verses, wrote a letter to Charles upon this occasion, in which are found these spirited words : " You have then promised upon oath never to return to Rome ! What shameful conduct in an emperor, to be compelled by a priest to content himself with the bare title of Cæsar, and to exile himself for ever from the habitation of the Cæsars ! to be crowned emperor, and then prohibited from reigning, or acting as head of the empire !—What an insult upon him who ought to command the universe, to be no longer master of himself, and be subservient to his own vassal[3] !"   A.D. 1356.

This emperor seemed to have entirely renounced the politics of his predecessors ; for he not only discouraged and rejected the proffers of the Ghibellines, but affected to treat them as enemies to religion, and actually supported the Guelphs. By these means he procured the favour of the pope and his dependents,

---

[1] Giov. Villani, lib. xii.   [2] Fleury, tome xx. liv. 96.
[3] *De Vit. Solit.* lib. ii.

who flattered him with the most fulsome adulation; but the Italians, in general, viewed him with contempt, and the greatest part of the towns attached to the empire shut their gates against him.   At Cremona he was obliged to wait two hours without the walls before he received the answer of the magistrates; who, at last, only permitted him to enter as a simple stranger, without arms or retinue [1].

Charles made a more respectable figure after his return to Germany.   The number of electorates had been fixed since the time of Henry VII., more by custom than by laws, but not the number of electors.   The duke of Bavaria presumed that he had a right to elect as well as the Count Palatine, the elder branch of their family; and the younger brothers of the house of Saxony believed themselves entitled to vote as well as the elder.   The emperor resolved to settle these points, that due subordination might take place, and future elections be conducted without confusion or disorder.   For this purpose he ordered a diet to be assembled at Nuremberg, where the famous constitution called the *Golden Bull* was established, in the presence and with the consent of all the princes, bishops, abbots, and the deputies of the imperial cities.

The style of that celebrated charter partakes strongly of the spirit of the times.   It begins with an apostrophe to Satan, anger, pride, luxury; and it says, that it is necessary the number of electors should be seven, in order to oppose the seven mortal sins.   It speaks of the fall of the angels, of a heavenly paradise, of Pompey, and of Cæsar; and it asserts that the government of Germany is founded on the three theological virtues, as on the Trinity.   The seven electors were the archbishops of Mentz, Cologne, and Treves, the king of Bohemia, the Count Palatine, the duke of Saxony, and the margrave of Brandenburg.

The imperial dignity, which of itself then conferred little real power, never showed more of that lustre which dazzles the eyes of the people than on the publication of this edict.   The three ecclesiastical electors, all three arch-chancellors, appeared in the procession with the seals of the empire; the archbishop of Mentz carried that of Germany, the elector of Cologne that of Italy, and the archbishop of Treves that of Gaul; though the empire now possessed nothing in Gaul, except a claim to empty homage for the remains of the kingdom of Provence and the principality of Dauphiné.   How little power Charles had in Italy, we have already

[1] Barre, vol. ii.—Spond. *Contin.* Baron. vol. i.

LETT. XLIII. **MODERN EUROPE.** 367

seen. Besides granting to the pope all the lands claimed by the holy see, he left the family of Visconti in the quiet possession of Milan and the whole province of Lombardy, which they had usurped from him, and suffered the Venetians to retain Padua, Vicenza, and Verona[1]. I must now take notice of the ceremonial.

The duke of Luxemburg and Brabant, who represented the king of Bohemia, as great cup-bearer, delivered to the emperor his drink, which was poured from a golden flagon into a cup of the same metal; the duke of Saxony, as grand marshal, appeared with a silver measue filled with oats; the elector of Brandenburg presented the emperor and empress with water to wash in a golden ewer, placed in a golden basin; and the Count Palatine served up the victuals in golden dishes, in presence of all the great officers of the empire[2].

The latter part of the reign of Charles IV. was distinguished by no remarkable transaction except the sale of the imperial jurisdictions in Italy; which were alternately resumed and sold. Charles, who was reputed a good prince, but a weak em- A.D. peror, was succeeded in all his possessions and dignities 1378. by his son Wenceslaus, whom I shall afterward have occasian to mention.—We must now proceed to the affairs of England; remarking, by the way, that Charles IV. was an encourager of learning, and founded the university of Prague.

LETTER XLIII.

History of England, from the Death of Edward III. to the Accession of Henry V., with some account of the Affairs of Scotland.

AFTER seeing England victorious over France and Spain, you have seen her, my dear Philip, nearly stripped of all her A.D. possesions on the continent, and Edward III. expiring 1377. with much less glory than had distinguished the more early periods of his reign. His successor, Richard II., son of the Black Prince, was little able to recover what had been lost through the

---

[1] Barre, vol. ii.—Spond. *Contin.* Baron. vol. i.
[2] Heiss, liv. ii. chap. 27.

indisposition of his father, and the dotage of his grandfather. Happy would it have been for him, and for his people, if he could have ruled his own kingdom with judgment!

Richard was certainly a weak prince; but his weakness was not immediately perceived or felt by the nation. At his accession he was a boy of eleven years of age, from whom consequently little could be expected. The habits of order and obedience, which the nobles had acquired under the sway of the third Edward, still influenced them; and the authority of Richard's three uncles, the dukes of Lancaster, York, and Gloucester, sufficed to repress for a time that turbulent spirit which the great barons were so ready to indulge during a weak reign. The different characters of those three princes rendered them also a counterpoise to each other; so that there appeared no new circumstance in the domestic situation of England which could endanger the public peace, or give any immediate apprehensions to the lovers of their country.

But this flattering prospect proved delusive. Discontents and dissensions soon arose among all orders of men. The first tumult was of the popular kind. War had been carried on between France and England, after the death of Edward III.; but in so languid a manner as served only to exhaust the finances of both kingdoms. In order to repair the expenses of these fruit-

A.D. 1381. less armaments, the English parliament found it necessary to impose a poll-tax, of three groats a-head, on every person, male and female, above fifteen years of age. The inequality and injustice of this tax were obvious to the meanest capacity; and the rigorous manner in which it was levied made it yet more grievous. The great body of the people, many of whom were still in a state of slavery, became severely sensible of the unequal lot which fortune had assigned to them in the distribution of her favours. They looked up to the first origin of mankind from one common stock, their equal right to liberty, and to all the benefits of nature. Nor did they fail to reflect on the tyranny of artificial distinctions, and on the abuses which had arisen from the degradation of the more considerable part of the species, and the agrandizement of a few individuals [1].

> " When Adam delved, and Eve span,
>   Where was then the gentleman?"

was their favourite distich: and although these verses, when

---

[1] Froissard, liv. ii.—Walsingham.—Knighton.

misapplied, strike at the foundation of all society, they contain a sentiment so flattering to the sense of primitive equality, engraven in the hearts of all men, as never to be repeated without some degree of approbation.

When the discontents of the populace were thus prepared, the insolence of a tax-gatherer, and the spirit of a Kentish blacksmith, blew them into a flame. While the smith was at work, the collector appeared, and demanded payment for his daughter. The father replied, that she was below the age prescribed by the statute: the tax-gatherer affirmed that she was a full-grown woman, and, in proof of his assertion, attempted an indecency, which incensed the smith to such a degree, that he knocked the ruffian dead with his forge-hammer. The bystanders applauded the action, and exclaimed that it was full time for the people to take vengeance on their tyrants, and assert their native rights. They flew to arms: the flame of sedition spread from county to county; and before the government had the least intimation of the danger, the disorder had grown beyond all control or opposition.

These mutinous peasants, who nearly amounted to the number of one hundred thousand, assembled on Blackheath under Wat Tyler the smith (or, as some say, a tiler) and Jack Straw; and sent a message to the king, who had taken refuge in the Tower, that they desired a conference with him. Richard passed down the river in a barge for that purpose; but on approaching the shore he discovered such symptoms of tumult and insolence, that he judged it prudent to return. Finding, however, that the Tower would be no security against the lawless multitude, and afflicted at the ravages and cruelties of the rioters, who had broken into the city of London, plundered the merchants, and cut off the heads of all the gentlemen they could seize, the young king found it necessary to go out and ask their demands. They required a general pardon; the abolition of slavery; freedom of commerce in market-towns, without toll or impost; and a fixed rent on lands, instead of the services due by villanage. These requests were not unreasonable; but the behaviour of Wat Tyler, who, in making his demands, frequently brandished his sword in a menacing manner, so incensed William Walworth, the mayor of London, that he lifted up his mace, or as others say, his spear, and gave Tyler a violent blow which brought him to the ground, where he was instantly pierced through the body by another of the king's train. The mutineers, seeing their leader fall, prepared for revenge ; and the king and his whole company must have perished on the spot, had not Richard discovered an extraordinary presence of mind in that extremity. He ordered his attendants to stop, advanced alone towards the enraged multitude, and accosting them with an affable and intrepid countenance, " What, my good people," said he, " is the meaning of this commotion ?   Be not concerned for the loss of your leader.   I am your king! I will become your leader ; follow me into the fields, and you shall have whatever you desire." Overawed by the royal presence, they implicitly followed him ; and he peaceably dismissed them, after the grant of their demands [1].

This conduct of a prince who was not fifteen years of age, raised great expectations in the nation ; but, in proportion as the king advanced in years, they gradually vanished, and his want of capacity, or at least of solid judgment, appeared in every measure which he adopted.   His first expedition was against Scotland, into which he marched at the head of an army of sixty thousand men.   The Scots did not venture to resist so great a force : they abandoned, without scruple, their rugged territory to be ravaged by the enemy, and made an incursion into the more fertile provinces of England, where they collected a rich booty.   Richard, however, wandered over a great part of the comparatively barren kingdom of Scotland, and led his army back into England, without taking vengeance on the enemy for their devastations [2].   His impatience to return and enjoy his usual pleasures and amusements over-balanced every higher consideration, and made even revenge a motive too feeble to detain him.

A.D. 1385.

Richard, like most weak princes, now resigned himself wholly to the direction of a favourite, Robert de Vere, earl of Oxford, a young nobleman of dissolute manners, whom he loaded with riches, with titles, and with dignities.   He first created him marquis of Dublin, and afterwards duke of Ireland, with a parliamentary grant of the sovereignty of that kingdom for life.   The usual (and too often just) complaints of the insolence of favourites were soon loudly echoed, and greedily received in all parts of England.   A civil war was the consequence ; the royalists were defeated : and Richard was obliged to resign

A.D. 1387.

---

[1] Froissard, liv. ii.—Walsingham.—Knighton.—The grants, except that of pardon, were afterwards revoked.
[2] Walsingham.—Froissard.

the government into the hands of a council of fourteen, appointed by the parliament. The duke of Gloucester A.D. accusing five of the king's ministers of treason against the 1388. state, they were declared guilty; and as many of them as could be seized were executed. The duke of Ireland made his escape beyond sea, as did Michael de la Pole, earl of Suffolk, who had discharged the office of chancellor. Both died abroad.

It might naturally be expected that Richard, thus reduced to a state of slavery by his subjects, and unable to defend his servants from the resentment of his uncles, would remain long in subjection, and never recover the royal power without the most violent struggles; but the event proved otherwise. In the following year he was apparently reconciled to his uncles, and exercised the regal authority in its full extent.

When these domestic disturbances had subsided, and the government had resumed its natural state, there passed an interval of eight years distinguished by no remarkable event; during which the king brought himself into the lowest degree of personal contempt, even while his government appeared in a great measure unexceptionable. Addicted to vulgar pleasures, he spent his whole time in feasting and jollity; and dissipated in idle show, or lavished upon favourites of no reputation, that revenue which the people expected to see him employ in undertakings calculated for the public honour and advantage.

The duke of Gloucester soon perceived the opportunities which this dissolute conduct of his nephew afforded him, of insinuating himself into the affections of the nation; and he now aimed at popularity as the ladder to the throne. He seldom appeared at court or in the council: he never declared his opinion but to testify his disapprobation of the measures embraced by the king and his favourites; and he courted the friendship of every man whom disappointment or private resentment had rendered an enemy to the administration. A.D. Richard, suspecting his ambitious views, ordered him to 1397. be arrested, and carried over to Calais, where he was soon after murdered [1]. The royal vengeance fell also, though with different degrees of severity, on the earls of Arundel and Warwick, the supposed accomplices of the duke, and on the archbishop of Canterbury, Arundel's brother, who was banished. Arundel himself was beheaded, and Warwick was doomed to perpetual confinement in the Isle of Man [2].

---

[1] Cotton's Abridgment.
[2] Walsingham.—Froissard, lib. iv.—Rymer, vol. vii.

A. D.   The ruin of the duke, and of the supporters of his
1398. party, was followed by a misunderstanding among those
noblemen who had joined in the prosecution; and the duke of
Hereford, in particular, went so far as to accuse the duke of
Norfolk in parliament of having spoken " many slanderous words
of the king." Norfolk denied the charge, imputed wilful falsehood to Hereford, and offered to prove his own innocence by
duel. The challenge was accepted: the time and place of the
combat were appointed, and the whole nation seemed anxious
for the event. But when the two champions appeared in the
field, accoutred for the fight, the king interposed, to prevent
both the present effusion of blood and the future consequences
of the quarrel. He stopped the duel, by the advice of the parliamentary commissioners appointed to regulate the combat;
and by the same authority, he ordered both the peers to leave
the kingdom [1]. Hereford was banished for ten years, and Norfolk for life.

This sentence seems to have been impartial; but it surely was
not equitable, as both the dukes were condemned without being
convicted of any crime. It was also unpopular. Richard's conduct in this affair was considered as a mark of the pusillanimity
of his temper: and the weakness and fluctuation of his councils,
at least, appear on no occasion more evident. The duke of
Hereford being a man of great prudence and self-command, behaved with such humility after his condemnation, that the king
promised to shorten the term of his exile by four years, and also
granted him letters patent, empowering him, if any inheritance
should accrue to him during the interval, to enter into immediate possession. But this nobleman, who was the eldest son of
John of Gaunt, duke of Lancaster, had no sooner left the kingdom, than Richard's jealousy of the power and riches of that
family revived; and he became sensible that by Gloucester's
death he had only removed a counterpoise to the Lancastrian
interest, which was now even formidable to the sovereign. He
therefore took every method to sully abroad the reputation of
the duke of Hereford, and to obstruct his alliances, by repre-
A.D.   senting him as guilty of treasonable practices; and when
1399. the father died, he revoked his letters patent to the son,
and took possession of the family estate [2].

These instances of rapacity and severity, and the circumstances

---

[1] Walsingham.—*Parl. Hist.* vol. i.
[2] Tyrrel, vol. iii. from the *Records*.

with which they were accompanied, drew upon Richard the general odium of the people. Hereford, now duke of Lancaster, had acquired the esteem of the public by his valour and abilities. He was connected with the principal nobility by blood, alliance, or friendship; his misfortunes added double lustre to his merit; all men made his case their own : they entered into his resentment ; and they turned their eyes towards him as the only person who could retrieve the lost honour of the nation, or reform the abuses of government.

While the minds of men were thus disposed, Richard went over to quell an insurrection in Ireland, and thereby imprudently afforded his exiled cousin an opportunity of gratifying the wishes of the nation. The duke, landing at Ravenspur in Yorkshire, was joined by the earls of Northumberland and Westmoreland, two of the most potent barons in England; and the malecontents in all quarters flew to arms. He solemnly declared that he had no other purpose in this invasion than to recover the duchy of Lancaster ; and he conjured his uncle, the duke of York, who had been left guardian of the kingdom, not to oppose a loyal and humble supplicant in the recovery of his patrimony. His entreaties had the desired effect. The regent embraced his cause ; and he quickly found himself master of England.

Richard no sooner received intelligence of this invasion, than he hastened from Ireland with twenty thousand men : but he could not confide even in these : and he was soon almost entirely deserted. In this extremity he fled to the isle of Anglesey, where he proposed to embark for France, and there wait the return of his subjects to a sense of their duty. But before he had an opportunity of carrying this scheme into execution, the earl of Northumberland waited upon him from the rebellious duke, with the strongest professions of loyalty and submission ; and Richard was so credulous as to put himself in the power of his enemy. He was carried about in an abject manner, exposed to the insults of the populace; deposed, imprisoned, and murdered [1]. And the duke of Lancaster was proclaimed king, Sept. under the name of Henry IV. 30.

The beginning of the reign of Henry IV., as might be expected from the manner in which he obtained the throne, was stained by many acts of blood and violence. The opposers of

[1] He died on the 6th of January, 1400. The monk of Evesham says, that he was starved to death : but others, among whom we may mention the anonymous author of a curious manuscript in the library of the late king of France, affirm that he was killed by Exton and other ruffians with the stroke of a battle-axe.

his title were cruelly punished; and superstition was called in to swell by new crimes the catalogue of victims. While a subject, Henry was believed to have strongly imbibed the principles of Wickliffe, a secular priest educated at Oxford, who, during the reigns of Edward III. and Richard II., preached the doctrine of reformation; but finding himself possessed of the throne by so precarious a title, this politic prince thought superstition a necessary engine of public authority. There had hitherto been no penal laws enacted against heresy in England. Henry, therefore, who could easily sacrifice his principles to his interest, understanding that the clergy called loudly for the punishment of the disciples of Wickliffe, whose learning and genius had in some measure broken the fetters of prejudice, resolved to procure the favour of the church by the most effectual of all methods, by gratifying her vengeance on those who presumed to A.D. dispute her infallibility. A law was accordingly enacted, 1401. that any heretic who relapsed, or refused to abjure his opinions, should be delivered over to the secular arm by the bishop or his commissaries, and be committed to the flames by the civil magistrate, before the whole people [1]. This weapon did not remain long unemployed in the hands of the clergy. William Sautrè, a clergyman in London, had been condemned by the convocation of Canterbury; his sentence was ratified by the house of peers: and the unhappy sectary suffered the punishment of fire, because he could not think as the church directed.—What a fatal prelude to future horrors, proceeding from the same source!

But all the prudence and precaution of Henry could not shield him from numerous alarms. He was threatened from France with an invasion, which was only prevented by the disorders in that kingdom; and the revolution in England was speedily followed by an insurrection in Wales. Owen Glendour, or Glyndourdwy, descended from the ancient princes of that country, had become obnoxious on account of his attachment to Richard; and Reginald, lord Grey of Ruthyn, who was closely connected with the new king, and who enjoyed a great fortune in the marches of Wales, thought the opportunity favourable for oppressing his neighbour, and taking possession of his estate. Glendour, provoked at the injustice, and still more at the indignity, recovered possession by the sword. Henry sent assistance to lord Grey; the Welsh took part with Glendour: a tedious and troublesome war was kindled, which Glendour long sustained by

---

[1] 2 Hen. IV c. 7.

his valour and activity, aided by the natural strength of the country, and the untamed spirit of the inhabitants.

The Scots were tempted by these disorders to make incursions into England; and Henry, desirous of chastising them, conducted an army as far to the northward as Edinburgh. But, finding that the Scots would neither submit nor give him battle, he returned without effecting any thing of consequence. In the succeeding year, however, Archibald earl Douglas, who, at the head of twelve thousand men, had made an irruption into the northern counties, was overtaken by the earl of Northumberland on his return, at Homeldon, on the borders of England, Sept. 14. where a fierce battle ensued, and the Scots were totally 1402. routed. Douglas himself was taken prisoner; as were the earls of Angus, Murray, Orkney, and many others of the nobility and gentry [1].

When Henry received intelligence of this victory, he sent orders to the victorious earl not to ransom his prisoners; a privilege which that nobleman regarded as his right by the laws of war. The king intended to detain them, that he might be able, by their means, to make an advantageous peace with Scotland. But by this selfish policy he gave great disgust to the family of Percy. The impatient spirit of the earl's son Henry, commonly known by the name of Hotspur, and the factious disposition of the earl of Worcester, younger brother to the powerful peer, inflamed his discontent; and the disputable title of Henry tempted these bold associates to seek revenge, by overturning that throne which they had contributed to establish. The earl entered into a correspondence with Glendour: he set earl Douglas at liberty, and formed an alliance with that martial chieftain. But, when war was ready to break out, he was A.D. seized with a sudden illness at Berwick; and young 1403. Percy, taking the command of the troops, marched towards Shrewsbury to join Glendour.

The king had happily a small army on foot with which he intended to act against the Scots; and knowing the importance of celerity in all civil wars, he instantly hurried down, to give battle to the rebels. He approached Percy near Shrewsbury, before that nobleman was joined by Glendour; and the policy of one leader, and impatience of the other, made them hasten to a general engagement. The armies were nearly equal July. in number, consisting of about twelve thousand men 21.

---

[1] Walsingham.—*Chron.* Otterbourne.

each; and we scarcely find any battle, in those ages, where the shock was more terrible or more constant. Henry exposed his person to all the dangers of the fight; and the prince of Wales, his gallant son, whose military achievements became afterwards so famous, and who here performed his noviciate in arms, signalized himself in a remarkable manner. Percy supported that renown which he had acquired in many a bloody combat; and Douglas, his ancient enemy, and now his friend, still appeared his rival amid the horror and confusion of the fight. This nobleman performed feats of valour which are almost incredible. He seemed determined that the king of England should fall that day by his arm. He sought him all over the field; and as Henry had accoutred several officers in the royal garb, in order to encourage his troops, the sword of Douglas rendered that honour fatal to many. But while the armies were contending in this furious manner, the death of Hotspur, accomplished by an unknown hand, decided the victory. The royalists prevailed, with the slaughter of three thousand of their foes [1].

The earl of Northumberland had levied a fresh army, and was on his march to join his son: but being opposed by the earl of Westmoreland, and hearing of the defeat at Shrewsbury, he dismissed his forces, and came with a small retinue to the king at York. He pretended that his sole intention in arming was to mediate between the parties. Henry thought proper to admit the apology, and even granted him a pardon for his offence. The other rebels seem to have been treated with equal lenity, except the earl of Worcester, lord Kinderton, and sir Richard Vernon, who perished by the hands of the executioner [2].

The suppression of this rebellion did not deter Scrope, archbishop of York, lord Bardolf, and Mowbray, from concerting
A.D. another; but the scheme was discovered before it was
1405. ripe for execution, and the archbishop was beheaded. Northumberland also was concerned in these intrigues, but
A.D. made his escape into Scotland; whence returning to
1408. commit new disorders, he was slain at Bramham, with lord Bardolf. The defeat of Glendour, and the submission of
A.D. the Welsh, which happened soon after, freed Henry
1409. from all his domestic enemies: and a fortunate event, which had thrown the heir of the Scottish crown into his hands, rendered him also secure on that side.

---

[1] *Chron.* Otterbourne.—Walsingham.
[2] Walsingham.—Rymer, vol. viii.

Robert III. king of Scotland, was a prince of slender capacity, and extremely innocent and inoffensive in his conduct. But Scotland, at that time, was still less fitted than England for cherishing a sovereign of such a character. His brother the duke of Albany, a prince of a boisterous and violent disposition, had assumed the government of the state; and, not satisfied with present authority, he entertained the criminal purpose of destroying the king's children, and of acquiring the crown for his own family. He threw into prison his nephew David, who there perished by hunger; and James, the brother of this prince, alone stood between the tyrant and the throne. Robert, aware of his son's danger, resolved to send him into France: but the vessel in which the youth embarked was taken by the English; and although there subsisted at that time a truce between the two kingdoms, Henry refused to restore him to his liberty [1]. But he made ample amends for this want of generosity by bestowing on James an excellent education, which afterwards qualified him, when he mounted the throne, to reform, in some measure, the rude and barbarous manners of his native country.

The remaining part of Henry's reign was chiefly spent in regulating the affairs of his kingdom; which he at length brought into good order, by his valour, prudence, and address. In his latter years, he began to turn his eyes towards those bright projects which his more fortunate son conducted so successfully against the French monarchy; but his declining health prevented him from attempting to put them in execution. Afflicted for some years with violent fits, which deprived him for a time of all sensation, and threatened his existence, he was carried Mar. 20, off by one of them at Westminster, in the forty-seventh 1413. year of his age, and the fourteenth year of his reign [2]. He was considered as a wise prince rather than a good man; and yet if we reflect on the circumstances in which he was involved, we can hardly conceive that a person could carry his ambition to the same height, and transmit a throne to his posterity with less violence to humanity.

We should now examine the affairs of France under Charles VI., as an introduction to the reign of Henry V. of England, who became sovereign of both kingdoms; but we must first carry forward the history of the empire and the church.

---

[1] Buchan, lib. x.—*Scoti-chronicon*, lib. xv.   [2] Walsingham.

LETTER XLIV.

Of the German Empire and its Dependencies, from the Accession of Wenceslaus to the Death of Sigismund.

THE history of the German empire, my dear Philip, becomes always more important to us, in proportion as we advance in the narration, though it seemed at this time to decline in dignity and consequence. We now approach two remarkable events in the history of the church; the great schism in the West, and the council of Constance.

Wenceslaus, at the age of seventeen, succeeded his father A.D. Charles IV. in the government of the empire, and on 1378. the throne of Bohemia, when the church was divided by one of those violent contests so disgraceful to Christianity. The Italians had raised to the pontificate Urban VI., who confirmed the election of the new emperor; and the French had chosen Clement VII. During this schism Wenceslaus appointed Jadoc, marquis of Moravia, his vicar-general in Italy; commanding him to inquire which was the true pope, to acknowledge and protect that pontiff whom he should find to be canonically elected, and to expel by force the other, who had intruded him- A.D. self into the chair. He also held a diet at Nuremberg, 1379. and afterward one at Frankfort; where, the affair of the popes being examined, Urban was acknowledged by the German prelates, and the princes of the empire engaged to protect him in the papacy [1].

After the diet of Frankfort, the emperor repaired to Aix-la-Chapelle, where he resided some time, because the plague raged in Bohemia; and here he gave himself up to gross debauchery, neglecting the affairs of the empire to such a degree, that the princes and towns of Germany were obliged to enter into associations for their mutual defence. At the same time Italy was torn in pieces by the schism in the church. Clement, who had taken Rome from his rival, was expelled in his turn by the citizens, and afterwards settled at Avignon, the former residence of the French pontiffs. Urban used his victory like a tyrant.

---

[1] Du Puy, *Hist. Gen. du Schisme*, &c.—Maimbourg, *Hist. du grand Schisme de l'Occident.*

But all priests in power, it has been said, are tyrants. The famous Joan, queen of Naples, of whom I have spoken in a former letter, first experienced the effects of Urban's vengeance.

This princess, who had imprudently espoused the cause of Clement, had been four times married, but had no children by any of her husbands; she therefore adopted Charles de Durazzo, the regular heir to her kingdom, and the only remaining descendant of the house of Anjou in Naples. But Durazzo, unwilling to wait for the crown till the natural death of his adoptive mother, associated himself with pope Urban, who crowned A.D. him king of Naples at Rome, on condition that he should 1380. bestow the principality of Capua on Francis Prignano, nephew to his holiness. Urban also deposed Joan, and declared her guilty of heresy and high treason.

These steps being taken, the pope and Durazzo marched towards Naples. The church plate and ecclesiastical lands were sold, in order to facilitate the conquest. Joan, on the A.D. other hand, was destitute both of money and troops. In 1382. this extremity, she invited to her assistance Louis of Anjou (brother to Charles V. of France), whom she had adopted in the room of the ungrateful Durazzo; but he arrived too late to defend his benefactress, or dispute the kingdom with his competitor. The pope and Durazzo entered Naples, after having defeated and taken prisoner Otho of Brunswick, the queen's husband. All resistance now appeared to be fruitless, and flight alone seemed practicable. But even in this the unfortunate Joan failed; she fell into the hands of the usurper, who, to give some colour to his barbarity, declared himself the avenger of the murder of her first husband. Louis king of Hungary was consulted in regard to the fate of the captive queen. He replied, that she deserved to suffer the same death which she had inflicted on Andrew; and Durazzo ordered her to be smothered between two mattresses [1]. Thus perished the famous Joan I. queen A.D. of Naples, who was celebrated by Petrarch and Boccace, 1383. and whose life, character, and catastrophe, bear a striking resemblance to those of the unfortunate Mary Stuart, queen of Scotland.

In the mean time Wenceslaus continued immersed in debauchery, and seemed industrious in acquiring the implacable hatred of his subjects, by the extraordinary taxes he imposed, and the cruelties which he exercised upon people of all ranks.

---

[1] Giannone, *Hist. di Nap.*

i

In order to familiarize himself to blood and carnage, he descended so low as to contract an intimacy with the public executioner, whom he distinguished by the appellation of his gossip; and in one of his fits of intoxication, he is said to have ordered his cook to be roasted alive [1].

On account of these atrocities, and of the sale of the rights of the empire, both in Italy and Germany, the electors, assembled A.D. 1400. at Laenstein on the Rhine, justly deposed Wenceslaus, and raised Henry of Brunswick to the imperial dignity; but, he being basely murdered by count Waldeck before his coronation, they elected in his stead Rupert or Robert, count palatine of the Rhine.

Wenceslaus was so little mortified at the news of his deposition, that he is reported to have said, when he received the intelligence, " I am pleased at being delivered from the burthen of the empire, because I shall have more leisure to apply myself to the government of my own kingdom :" and it must be owned that, during the eighteen years which he afterwards reigned in Bohemia, his conduct was much less exceptionable. But although this indolent prince was so unconcerned at the loss of the empire, he appears to have been sensibly affected by some of its probable consequences, though certainly of less moment; for he is said to have desired, as a last mark of the fidelity of the imperial cities, that they would send him " some butts of their best wine [2]."

The first expedition of the new emperor was against Galeazzo Visconti, whom Wenceslaus had created duke of Milan, and who, not content with this promotion, endeavoured by force of arms to obtain possession of Florence, Mantua, Bologna, and other towns and countries. To secure these territories, and A.D. 1402. recover the imperial authority in Italy, Rupert marched into the duchy of Milan; but Galeazzo was so well provided with troops and military stores, that the emperor was obliged to return to Germany without success [2].

The retreat of Rupert left the field open to Galeazzo, who now projected nothing less than the complete conquest of Italy; and fortune at first seemed to second his views. He made himself master of the city of Bologna, and had almost reduced A.D. 1403. Florence, when he was attacked by a malignant fever, which at once put an end to his life and his projects. As

<hr />

[1] Dubrav. lib. xxiii.— *Annal. de l'Emp.* tome ii. [2] Barre, tome vii.
[3] Heiss, lib. ii. cap. xxviii.

he left only one daughter, who was not of age, an opportunity was offered to Rupert of retrieving the affairs of the empire in Italy. But the German princes were so little pleased with his first expedition, that they would not grant him supplies for a second. He therefore employed himself in appeasing the troubles of Germany, and aggrandising his own electorate; to which he added several lordships of Alsace, purchased of the bishop of Strasburg[1].

During the sway of this emperor, Bohemia was involved in disorder by the preaching of John Huss, a theologian of the university of Prague, who had embraced the opinions of Wickliffe, and was excommunicated by the pope. The publication of this sentence was followed by troubles and sedition. Wenceslaus shut himself up in the fortress of Visigrade, and John Huss retired to Hussenitz, the place of his birth; where he appealed from the judgment of the pope to the Holy Trinity, A.D. 1409. and wrote to the cardinals, offering to give an account of his faith, even at the hazard of fire, before the university of Prague, and in the presence of those who had attended his lectures and sermons[2].

The Romish church not only suffered from these innovations, but also continued in a state of distraction from the schism which still remained, and which the emperor attempted in vain to cement. Gregory XII., who was acknowledged pope in Italy, convened a council at Aquileia, to which he invited Rupert, and other Christian princes, to heal the schism. Benedict XIII., who was owned in France, convoked a council at Perpignan : the cardinals held a similar meeting at Pisa, and the emperor appointed a diet for the same purpose at Frankfort ; where, after long debates, the opinions of the assembly were divided between the two popes. The greater part of the archbishops, prelates, and princes, espoused the cause of the cardinals; but the emperor, the archbishop of Treves, the duke of Bavaria, and some others, declared for Gregory, who proposed that a council should be holden at Udina, in Friuli, under the direction of Rupert, by whose decision he promised to abide. The emperor therefore sent an archbishop, two bishops, two doctors, and his chancellor, as ambassadors to Pisa, to prove, by learned arguments, that the cardinals ought not to depose Gregory. But these ambassadors, finding that they could make no converts to their opinion, and that the cardinals, attached to Wenceslaus, would not even ac-

---

[1] Barre, tome vii.   [2] Mosheim, *Hist. Eccles.* vol. iii. et Auct. cit. in loc.

knowledge their master as emperor, appealed from the assembly
at Pisa to an œcumenical council.   The cardinals, however, proceeded to the deposition of the two popes, and raised to the
apostolic chair a native of the island of Candia, who assumed the
appellation of Alexander V.   By this measure the schism was
increased, as three popes ruled at the same time[1].

May 18,   Rupert died soon after this pious negociation, and
1410.   before he was able to settle the affairs of the Holy See.
He was succeeded, after a disputed election, by Sigismund, (brother
to the deposed Wenceslaus,) who had procured the Hungarian
crown by a marriage with the daughter of king Louis.   The new
head of the empire was a prince of experience and abilities, whose
first care was to heal the wounds of the church.   For that purpose he summoned a general council at Constance, with the concurrence of pope John XXIII., successor of Alexander V.

At this council, where Sigismund appeared in all his glory,
were present a great number of cardinals, prelates, doctors;
A.D.   more than a hundred sovereign princes ; one hundred and
1414.   eight counts ;   two hundred barons ;   and twenty-seven
ambassadors from different courts ; who vied with each other in
luxury and magnificence.   There were also five hundred players
on instruments, called in those times minstrels, and seven hundred and eighteen courtezans, who were protected by the
magistrates[2].

In the first session it was maintained that nothing could so
effectually contribute to re-establish the union of the church as
the resignation of the competitors for the papacy.   John, who
presided in the council, assented to this opinion, and promised to
renounce his title, if Gregory and Benedict would imitate him
in that act of self-denial.   This declaration was no sooner made
than the emperor rose from his chair, and ran and embraced the
feet of his holiness, applauding his Christian resignation.   He
A.D.   was also solemnly thanked by the patriarch of Antioch,
1415.   in the name of the whole council.   But John afterwards
repented of this condescension ; and, by aid of Frederic duke of
Austria, fled from Constance in the night, disguised in the habit
of a postillion[3].

This unexpected retreat at first disconcerted the council,
which John declared to be dissolved in consequence of his seces-
sion.   But the members at length agreed, after many learned

[1] Mosheim, *Hist. Eccles.* vol. iii. et Auct. cit. in loc.
[2] *Annal. de l'Emp.* tome ii.   [3] Theod. Niem. *Vit. Jo.* XXIII.

arguments, that a council was superior to the pope; confirmed the sentence of John's deposition; decreed that no other pope should be chosen without the consent of the council; and that the three competitors should be for ever excluded from the papacy. Finding them thus determined, John thought proper to yield to the torrent rather than incur the risk of worse fortune in attempting to oppose it. He acquiesced in the sentence of the council, and renounced the pontificate. Soon after this resignation, Gregory sent a legate to the emperor and council to renounce his title in the same manner; but the proud Spaniard, Peter de Luna, (Benedict XIII.) would not yield: he remained obstinate to the last[1].

The affair of John Huss formed the next subject of discussion. That reformer had found a docile pupil and an able associate in Jerome of Prague, who propagated the new doctrines with great warmth. Both had been summoned to appear before the court of Rome, but refused to obey the citation. They condescended, however, to attend the council of Constance; and Huss, being provided with a safe-conduct from the emperor, resolved to defend the articles of his faith. The assembly seemed inclined to condemn him unheard; but Sigismund opposed that injustice. He was now questioned, and accused of heresy in thirty-nine articles. Some of these he denied, and some he offered to support by argument. But his voice was drowned by the clamours of bigotry; and, on refusing to abjure all the articles, he was declared a propagator of sedition, a hardened heretic, a disciple and defender of Wickliffe. He was degraded by four bishops, stripped of his sacerdotal habit, and clothed in a lay dress. His hair was cut in the form of a cross: upon his head was put a paper mitre, painted with the representation of three devils; and he was delivered over to the secular judge, who condemned him and his writings to the flames. He submitted to his cruel fate with great firmness and resolution[2]. July 16.

After the execution of John Huss, the council resumed the affair of Peter de Luna, who still refused to quit his pretensions to the papacy. On this occasion Sigismund offered to solicit in person the mediation of Ferdinand king of Arragon, with whom Peter had taken refuge. On his arrival at Perpignan, he entered into a negociation with Benedict, the result of which was

---

[1] Platin. *de Vitis Pontificum.*
[2] Laur. Byzinii *Diarium Hussiticum.—Chron. Magdeb.*

sent to the council, though by no means answerable to his expectations. The obstinacy of the priest was insurmountable, and incensed the emperor to such a degree, that he threatened to obtain by force that assent which could not be procured by fair means. Benedict, in consequence of these menaces, retired to the fortress of Paniscola, where he resolved to preserve his pontifical dignity to his latest breath. This unexpected flight deprived him of all his partisans. The king of Arragon, with all the princes and bishops of his party, sent deputies to the emperor at Narbonne; where it was agreed, that the council should invite all the former adherents of Benedict to come to Constance, and join their endeavours for re-establishing the peace of the church; and that, on their arrival, a new pope should be chosen [1].

During the absence of Sigismund, the trial of Jerome of Prague engaged the attention of the council. This man had repaired to Constance, to assist John Huss in making his defence; but perceiving that he had nothing to hope from the clemency of the assembled zealots, he resolved to retire without delay into Bohemia. Being apprehended, however, upon the road, he was loaded with chains, and brought back to Constance, where, in order to avoid the punishment of fire, he solemnly abjured the opinions of Wickliffe and Huss. But, ashamed to survive his master, who had encountered death with so much firmness, or not deriving the advantages which he expected from his submission, he reprofessed the same doctrines, was condemned to the flames, as a wicked apostate, and suffered with great fortitude [2].

A.D. 1416.

Poggio, the Florentine secretary to pope John, and one of the restorers of learning, who was present on this occasion, says he never heard any thing that approached so nearly to the eloquence of the ancient Greeks and Romans as the speech which Jerome made to the judges. "He spoke," exclaims Poggio, "like Socrates; and walked to the stake with as much cheerfulness as that great philosopher drank the cup of hemlock!"

After the return of Sigismund, the council proceeded against Benedict for contumacy; and the definitive sentence of his deposition was pronounced. Their next care was the election of a new pope; and Otho Colonna, who possessed the accomplishments of a prince and the virtues of a prelate, was

A.D. 1417.

---

[1] Theod. Niem. ubi sup.—Heiss, lib. ii. cap. 30.
[2] Mosheim, *Hist. Eccles.* vol. iii.—Spond. *Contin.* vol. ii.

unanimously chosen on St. Martin's day, whence he took the name of Martin V.   Never was the inauguration of any pontiff attended with greater pomp.   He rode in procession to the cathedral, mounted on a white horse; the emperor and the elector of Brandenburg, on foot, leading it by the reins.   A numerous crowd of princes, the ambassadors of all the kings, and the fathers of the council, closed the train.   When he entered the cathedral, the triple crown was placed upon his head, and he returned in the same august manner [1].

The important affair of the schism being thus concluded, other points were regulated by the council, which broke up in its forty-fifth session.   The disputes about religion, however, raged with great and redoubled violence.   The Hussites in   A.D. Prague were so much offended at being debarred from   1419. the use of the cup in the sacrament of the eucharist (contrary, as they affirmed, to the express words of our Saviour, who says, " Except ye eat the flesh of the Son of man, and drink his blood, ye have no life in you"), that they raised a furious tumult, forced the town-house, and murdered the magistrates who were concerned in publishing the order [2].

The news of this massacre filled the court of Wenceslaus with the utmost consternation, and made so strong an impression on that pusillanimous prince, that he was seized with an apoplexy, of which he died in a few days.   He was succeeded in the Bohemian royalty by his brother Sigismund, already emperor, and king of Hungary: yet this powerful prince was several times defeated by Ziska, the general of the Hussites, who revenged the death of their apostle by the most terrible outrages.

A particular account of the war between the emperor and the Hussites would interfere with more important matters, without answering any valuable purpose: I shall therefore only   A.D. observe, that Ziska continued master of Bohemia till his   1424. death, when he ordered a drum to be made of his skin, which was long the symbol of victory.   He was succeeded in the command by Procopius, surnamed the Shaven, because he had been a priest: who supported his party with no less valour than his predecessor.   He boldly defended their cause in the   A.D. council of Basil, where many things were disputed which   1428. it is of little consequence to know; and although he was un-

[1] Barre, tome vii.—*Annal. de l'Emp.* tome ii.
[2] Byzinii *Diarum Hussiticum.*—Mosheim, ubi supra.

successful in that negociation, and also in a battle with the catholics, in which he was mortally wounded, the Hussites at
length obtained a general amnesty, the confirmation of
their privileges, and the right of using the cup in the communion;
a concession which, to them, was a kind of triumph [1].

A.D.
1436.

After this pacification, the emperor enlisted the Hussites in
his army, and led them against the Turks, who had made an
irruption into Hungary, and were defeated with great
slaughter by those hardy veterans. But although Sigismund had been so fortunate as to regain the affections of the
Bohemians, he lost it by attempting again to tyrannize over
their consciences; and his death alone saved him from
a second revolt. He nominated as his successor, in the
kingdoms of Hungary and Bohemia, Albert duke of Austria,
his son-in-law, who was recognised by those states, and also
invested with the government of the empire. The house of
Austria, with the exception of the short reign of Charles VII.,
a Bavarian prince, has ever since filled the imperial throne.

A.D.
1437.

Dec.
8.

Sigismund possessed some respectable qualities: but he was a
narrow-minded bigot; and contrary to the dictates of sound
policy as well as of humanity, was guilty of the most detestable
of all tyranny, that of violence on the will. His wife Barbara
is said to have been a person of a more enlarged way of thinking,
though not more to her honour. She denied a future state,
and held the supreme good to consist in sensual delight.

We must now pass from the empire to other states of the
continent.

LETTER XLV.

*Of the Affairs of Poland, Russia, and the Scandinavian States,
to the Commencement of the Reign of Margaret over the three
Northern Kingdoms.*

WHILE the German empire, under the sway of the fourth
Henry, was convulsed with dissension by the influence and
intrigues of a turbulent pontiff, the intestine disorders of Poland
were aggravated and embittered by the same arbitrary inter-

---

[1] Mosheim, ubi supra.

ference.   After Ladislaus, however, had procured the sovereignty, the papal tyranny was less violently exercised in his
dominions.   That prince, though his natural disposition was
mild and pacific, displayed his courage in some expeditions
against the Prussians and Pomeranians.   In the latter part of
his life, he was cruelly harassed by his aspiring sons; but he
defeated the partisans of one of them, and reclaimed the other.
He died in the year 1103.   The division of his territories produced a sanguinary contest.   Shigneus, his natural son, was
assisted on this occasion by the Bohemians and Saxons; while
Boleslaus procured the aid of the Hungarians and the Russians.
The latter prevailed in several conflicts, and at length obtained
the whole succession.   He was afterwards at war with the emperor Henry IV., whose army he defeated.   In another war,
the Russians were his enemies, and by a victory which they obtained over him, they are said to have hastened his death, in the
year 1139.   Four of his sons shared his dominions; but Ladislaus the eldest had the chief sway, under the title of duke of
all Poland.   The ambition of Christina, the wife of this prince,
soon excited a civil war.   Two of the brothers (Boleslaus and
Henry) were driven from their territories by the duke's forces
and the Russians; but they afterward totally defeated him;
and when they had reduced Cracow, they convoked a diet, by
which, in 1146, the ducal dignity was transferred to Boleslaus,
who gave up the province of Silesia to his deposed brother.
The reign of the new duke was long, and by no means inactive.
He repelled the attacks of the emperor Conrad III., and prevented Frederic Barbarossa from completing the subjugation of
Poland.   He invaded Prussia, and endeavoured to propagate
Christianity among its idolatrous inhabitants; but his success
on this occasion was very imperfect, and his troops were routed
by the incensed pagans.   His brother Mieczslaus, who ruled
after him, was remarkable for the change of character which
followed his elevation to the sovereignty.   He had hitherto appeared as an amiable and respectable prince; but he now became a rapacious and brutal tyrant.   The people therefore
renounced their allegiance to him; and Casimir the Just became
their duke, under whom their chief grievances were redressed,
and their territories augmented at the expense of the Russians.
While his son Lech governed, the country was infested by the
Tartars, whose devastations were followed by famine and pestilence.   After the murder of Lech, 1227, the Tartars renewed
their irruptions with redoubled fury; and intestine war, at the

same time, multiplied the miseries of the people. How calamitous, my dear son, must have been the condition of the inhabitants of the Polish provinces, harassed by the contests of ambitious nobles, and by the most ferocious of all barbarians[1].

After a long course of anarchy, or of government so irregular A.D. and convulsed as to be scarcely superior to anarchy, duke 1295. Premislaus assumed the title of king of Poland; but the splendour of royalty not sufficiently overawing seditious spirits, he was assassinated by conspirators. Ladislaus the Cubit (so called from the shortness of his stature) seized the throne; but he was deposed in 1299, for having invaded the rights of the clergy. Wenceslaus III., king of Bohemia, was then invested with the Polish sovereignty; but he gave such disgust by his partiality to his countrymen, that if he had not died, in 1305, the adherents of Ladislaus would probably have expelled him. This prince now recovered his authority, and reigned with great reputation. His son Casimir acquired still higher fame, by extending his dominions, introducing written laws, restraining the tyranny of the nobles over the peasants, protecting the church, and encouraging the arts[2].

On the decease of Casimir, in 1370, the crown was transferred to his nephew Louis, king of Hungary, but not before he had agreed to some restrictions of authority which had not been included in the pacta conventa between the nation and the princes of the house of Piast. Though Louis was not popular among the Polanders, they chose his daughter Hedwiga for his successor; and her reign was distinguished by the union of Lithuania with Poland, in 1386, in consequence of her marriage with Jagellon, sovereign of the former territory. This event greatly increased the power and respectability of Poland.

With regard to the Russian principality, it appears to have declined in power and importance after the death of Jaroslaus or Yaroslaf, son of Vladimir or Wolodimir the Great, in 1054. Isiaslaf, son of the defunct prince, bore the chief sway; but his government was disturbed by the competition of his brothers, to whom distinct portions of territory had been assigned, and by the ambition of other princes of his family, who wished to rule in different provinces. He was dispossessed of his sovereignty; but recovered it by the aid of the Polanders; he again lost his power, and was again invested with it. He died in 1078, and

---

[1] Matth. Michov. lib. iii.—Guagnini.
[2] Matth. Michov. lib. iv.—Herb. de Pulst.

was succeeded by Wosewolode or Vsevolod, whose administration was not more memorable than that of the next prince or grand duke, Michael Sviatopolk. Vladimir II., who succeeded to the supremacy in 1114, was a prince of considerable merit; and the endeavours of his son Mieczslaus, or Metislaf, were exerted with some effect for the benefit of the state and the improvement of the country. But contests for power, and sanguinary commotions, frequently arose under these and some of the following princes. At length, while George swayed the principality, the horrors of Tartarian devastation were added to the former turmoils of the state [1].

The Tartars made their first appearance in Russia about the year 1223; and their fierce ravages, and barbarous mode of warfare, produced general consternation. In 1237 they attacked the city of Vladimer (then the Russian capital) under the conduct of Batu the grandson of Genghiz Khan; took it by storm, and massacred the greater part of the inhabitants. The grand duke George, bravely defending the place, fell with his sword in his hand. Yaroslaff II. now assumed the sovereignty; and his son Alexander soon after distinguished himself by routing an army of Danish invaders on the banks of the Neva, whence he obtained the surname of Newski, or Nefski. These princes were content to govern as vassals of the khan of the Tartars; and the ignominious yoke continued, for a long period, to wound the pride and check the power and prosperity of the Russians.

The inhabitants of Sweden and Denmark, at this time, were less rude and unpolished, and better governed, than their Russian neighbours. Of the princes who swayed the former kingdom for two centuries from the decease of Alstan, in 1064, the most eminent may here be mentioned. Igno IV. was a just and pious prince; Suercher an able governor. Eric X. established Christianity in Finland, and was an esteemed legislator. Charles VII., who united Gothland to the Swedish crown, was put to death by Canute, who afterwards reigned with ability and moderation. Eric XII., surnamed the Stammerer, acquired popularity by his courage and wisdom.

After some unimportant reigns in Denmark, the enterprising Waldemar, in 1157, put an end to a civil war and to the tyrannic government of Sweyn III., and became sole king. He waged a successful war against the Vandals; and subdued a great part of

[1] Muller, *Sammlung Russ. Gesch.* vol. 1.

Norway, but could not complete the conquest of that realm. He died in 1182, with the fame of a great prince. His son, Canute VI., did not shine as a warrior; but he was not deficient in political talents. Waldemar II. extended his dominions by the sword, and enacted wise laws for the government of the realm. Being inveigled into captivity by Henry, count of Schwerin, he was detained in confinement for three years, and could not procure his liberty without the surrender of some of his German territories. His death was followed by intestine disturbances. His son Eric was murdered, after a reign of eight years, by an inhuman brother, who fell, in his turn, by a violent death. The reign of Christopher I. abounded with faction, and with war both foreign and internal. His son, Eric VII., reigned twenty-seven years, chiefly under the guidance of his mother Margaret, a prudent and politic princess. He lost his life, in 1286, by the fury of conspirators. Eric the Pious was involved in a tedious war with the Norwegians: he was also embroiled with the Swedes, who had expelled the son of their illustrious king, Magnus II. In neither of these wars did he meet with great success. During his reign, the crowns of Sweden and Norway were united in the person of Mag-

A.D. 1319. nus III., a weak and dissolute prince: but he afterwards resigned the latter to his son Haquin, and was deposed from the former sovereignty by his indignant subjects [1].

Christopher II., king of Denmark, having violated the oath which he took at his coronation, was obliged by popular discontent to relinquish the throne. He recovered it in the sequel; but as he had not learned wisdom from adversity, he was again

A. D. 1340. driven from it, and died of grief. After a long *interregnum*, Waldemar III. obtained the crown; and his reign was, in some respects, not inglorious, though his character was a compound of inconsistencies. His chief merit consisted in re-uniting to the crown the petty principalities and divided jurisdictions which distracted the country. At his death, in 1375, the crown of Norway was again joined to that of Denmark, young Olaus having pretensions to both. This prince dying at the age of twenty-two years, an opportunity of royal elevation was afforded to his mother Margaret, the daughter of Waldemar.

The talents and address of this celebrated woman raised her

A. D. 1387. to the Danish throne, though the election of a female was an extraordinary measure. Not content with this dignity,

---

[1] Pontani *Rerum Danic.*—*Hist.*—Meurs.

she aimed at the possession of the crown of Norway, to which, from the authority of a regent, the transition was easy. Albert of Mecklenburgh, king of Sweden, jealous of the power of Margaret, resolved to invade her dominions; but his principal subjects, far from supporting him in such a cause, offered their crown to this princess, that they might be relieved from his tyranny. He was defeated and made prisoner by the malecontents; and though the war was continued by his partisans, he found himself ultimately unable to withstand a torrent which ran so A.D. strongly in favour of the Danish heroine, who thus be- 1390. came sovereign of the three Scandinavian realms [1].

From this survey of the transactions of the North we will now return to the affairs of France.

LETTER XLVI.

History of France, from the Death of Charles the Wise, to the Invasion of that Kingdom, by Henry V. of England.

THE death of Charles V. of France, and the youth of his son put that kingdom in a similar situation with England. A.D. Both realms were under the government of minors; and 1380. the jealousies among the three uncles of Charles VI., the dukes of Anjou, Berri, and Burgundy, distracted the affairs of France even more than the rivalry of the three uncles of Richard II. disordered those of England. But a minute detail of these distractions would be inconsistent with my present purpose, which is only to delineate the great line of history, and make you acquainted with the more remarkable events, or such as have had a particular influence upon government and manners. In the reign of Charles VI. no very memorable enterprise was undertaken; and government and manners, properly speaking, were equally unknown. I shall, therefore, consider the history of France, during this distracted period, as only an introduction to the invasion of that kingdom by Henry V.

As Charles advanced in years, the factions were gradually composed. His uncle, the duke of Anjou, died; and the king, assuming the reins of government, displayed symptoms of genius

[1] Pontan. lib. ix.—Meurs.

and spirit which revived the drooping hopes of his countrymen.
A.D. But this promising state of affairs was of short duration.
1392. Charles fell suddenly into a fit of phrensy, which rendered
him incapable of exercising his authority; and although he
partly recovered from that disorder, he was subject to such frequent relapses, that his judgment was gradually impaired, and
he became incapable of pursuing any steady plan of government [1].

The king's first relapse is said to have been occasioned by the
following accident. The queen having married one of her maids
A.D. of honour to a person of distinction, the nuptials were
1393. intended to be celebrated with great pomp at the palace
of the queen-dowager, relict of Philip of Valois. Among other
amusements there was to be a masquerade—a circumstance
which furnished five young noblemen with the extravagant idea
of appearing as naked savages; and such was the indelicacy of
the times, that the king made one of the party. Their dress,
contrived to sit close to their bodies, was of linen impregnated
with resin, which, while hot, had been covered with fur.   And
the secret was so well kept, that when they appeared, they were
not known; but their whim was highly applauded.   The
duchess of Berri took hold of the king, seeing him robust and
well-made, and told him she would not let him go till she knew
who he was. Some of the party now began to dance ; when
the duke of Orleans, out of levity, making a feint of running a
lighted torch against one of the savages, set his combustible
habit on fire. The flame was quickly communicated to the
rest; and this scene of wanton mirth was instantly changed into
sorrow and distress. But in the midst of their torments the
masks cried out continually, " Save the king ; save the king!"
—And the duchess of Berri, suddenly recollecting that he must
be the mask that stood next to her, immediately threw her
robes over him, and wrapping them close about him, put out
the fire. One of the masks, by jumping into a cistern of water,
saved his life; the other four were so terribly burned that they
died in two days ; and the king was so much affected with the
fright, that it occasioned a return of his disorder, which afterwards generally attacked him four or five times in a year to the
end of his life [2].

History scarcely affords any parallel of a court or country
more corrupt, and more miserable, than that of this unfortunate

---

[1] *Hist. Anonym. de Charles VI.*
[2] Juv. des Urs.—*Hist. Anonym. de Charles VI.*

monarch and his subjects, in consequence of his infirmity.   The administration fell again into the hands of the dukes of Berri and Burgundy, who excluded the duke of Orléans, the king's brother, under pretence of his youth, from any share in the government, and even from the shadow of authority.   The case, however, was very different with regard to the duchess of Orléans. Young, beautiful, and insinuating, she acquired such an ascendant over the king, that she governed him at her pleasure. What is yet more extraordinary, it was she only that could govern him ; for, in the time of his malady, he knew nobody else, not even the queen.   Hence it was rumoured by the duchess of Burgundy, who envied the influence of the young duchess, that she had bewitched the king ; and, to heighten the odium, it was insinuated that the duke of Orléans had bewitched the queen [1].   That both were under the influence of enchantment is not to be doubted ; but it was only that of youth, wit, and beauty, whose assiduities so often fascinate the susceptible heart, and when unrestrained by principle or sentiment, lead it in the chains of loose desire [2].

On the death of Philip duke of Burgundy, his son John disputed the administration with the duke of Orléans, and hoped to govern France as his father had done.   Propinquity to the crown pleaded in favour of the latter ; the former derived consequence from his superior power, the death of his mother having added the county of Flanders to his father's extensive dominions.   The people were divided between these contending princes ; and the king, now resuming and now dropping his authority, kept the victory undecided, and prevented any regular settlement of the state from the final prevalence of either party.

A.D. 1404.

But at length the dukes of Orléans and Burgundy, seemingly moved by the cries of the nation, and swayed by the interposition of common friends, agreed to bury all past quarrels in oblivion, and enter into a league of mutual amity.   They swore before the altar to the sincerity of this friendship ; the priest administered the sacrament to both ; and they exchanged every pledge that could be deemed sacred among men.   All this solemn preparation, however, appears to have been only a cover for basest treachery, deliberately premeditated by the duke of

A.D. 1407.

---

[1] Juv. des Ursins.—Du Tillet.—Le Gendre.
[2] Isabella of Bavaria, queen of France, and Valentina of Milan, duchess of Orléans, were remarkably handsome and accomplished ; and the duke was in a high degree both amorous and ambitious.

Burgundy.   He had hired ruffians, who assassinated his rival in the streets of Paris[1].   The author of the crime was for some days unknown, as the assassins escaped, and the duke endeavoured to conceal the part which he had taken in it; but being detected, he embraced a resolution still more criminal, and more dangerous to society.   He openly avowed and vindicated the action.

This cause was brought before the parliament of Paris; and that august tribunal of justice heard the harangues of the duke's advocate in defence of assassination, which he denominated tyrannicide, without pronouncing any sentence of condemnation against the detestable doctrine.   The same question was afterwards agitated before the council of Constance; and it was with difficulty that a feeble decision in favor of the contrary opinion was obtained from those fathers of the church, the ministers of the Prince of Peace[2].

But the mischievous effects of that tenet, had they been before doubtful, appeared sufficiently from the subsequent incidents. The commission of this crime, which destroyed all trust and security, rendered the war implacable between the French parties, and seemed to cut off all the means of peace and accommodation. The princes of the blood, combining with the young duke of Orléans and his brothers, made violent war on the duke of Burgundy; and the unhappy king, seized sometimes by one party, sometimes by another, transferred alternately to each the appearance of legal authority.   The provinces were harassed by mutual depredations: frequent assassinations arose from the animosity of the several leaders; and executions were ordered without any legal trial, by pretended courts of judicature.

The whole kingdom was divided into two parties, the Burgundians and the Armagnacs; for so the adherents of the young duke of Orléans were called, from the count of Armagnac, father-in-law to that prince.   The city of Paris, distracted between them, but inclining more to the Burgundians, was a perpetual scene of blood and violence.   The king and royal family were

[1] Le Laboureur, liv. xxvii.—Monstrelet, chap. xxxix.   The murder of the duke of Orléans is said to have been occasioned chiefly by his own insolence and licentiousness. (Du Hallan.—Brantome.)   Having succeeded in an amour with the duchess of Burgundy, he had the effrontery to introduce her husband into a cabinet furnished with representations of the women he had enjoyed, among which her portrait occupied a distinguished place.   The duke of Burgundy concealed his emotion, but thirsted for revenge.

[2] Bulay, Hist. Acad. Parisiensis, vol. v.—Mild as this censure was, pope Martin V. refused to ratify it, being afraid of displeasing the duke.   The university of Paris, more just and less timid, boldly condemned the atrocious doctrine and its author.

often detained captives in the hands of the populace : their ministers were butchered or imprisoned before their eyes; and it was dangerous for any man, amidst these enraged factions, to manifest a strict adherence to the principles of probity and honour.

During this scene of general violence, there arose into some consideration a body of men, usually undistinguished in public transactions even during the most peaceful times; namely, the heads of the university of Paris, whose opinions were sometimes demanded, and more frequently offered, in the multiplied disputes between the parties. The schism, by which the church was at that time divided, and which occasioned frequent contests in the university, had raised the professors to an unusual degree of importance; and this connexion between literature and religion had bestowed on the former a consequence which reason and knowledge had seldom been able to obtain among men. But there was another society, whose sentiments were still more decisive at Paris, the fraternity of butchers; who, under the direction of their ringleaders, had declared for the duke of Burgundy, and committed the most violent outrages against the opposite party. To counterbalance this power, the Armagnacs made interest with the fraternity of carpenters : the people ranged themselves on one side or the other : and the fate of the capital depended on the prevalence of either faction [1].

The advantage, which might be taken of these confusions, was easily perceived in England ; and, according to the maxims which generally prevail among nations, the court was inclined to seize so favourable an opportunity. Henry IV., who was courted by both the French parties, fomented the quarrel, by alternately sending assistance to each : and Henry V., impelled by the vigour of youth and the ardour of ambition, re- A. D. solved to push his advantages to a greater length, and 1415. carry war into the heart of France. But before I speak of the success of his great enterprise, I must say a few words on the earlier part of his reign.

[1] Bulay.—Juv. des Ursins.—P. Æmil.—Henault.

LETTER XLVII.

Of the Affairs of England and France, from the Invasion of the latter Kingdom by Henry V. to the Death of Charles VI.

THE precarious situation of Henry IV., with whose character, my dear Philip, you are already acquainted, had so much infected his temper with jealousy, that he entertained unreasonable suspicions with regard to the loyalty of his eldest son; and during the latter years of his life, he excluded that prince from all share in public business. The active spirit of young Henry, restrained from its proper exercise, broke out in extravagancies of every kind. The riot of pleasure, the folly of debauchery, and the outrage of intoxication, filled the vacancies of a mind better adapted to the pursuits of ambition and the cares of government. Such a course of life naturally threw him among companions very unbecoming his rank, whose irregularities, if accompanied with gallantry and humour, he seconded and indulged. And he was detected in many sallies, which to rigid eyes, appeared totally unworthy of his station [1].

But the nation in general considered the young prince with more indulgence. They observed so many gleams of generosity, spirit, and magnanimity, breaking continually through the cloud which a wild conduct threw over his character, that they did not cease to hope for his amendment. And the first steps taken by the youth, after the death of his father, confirmed the prepossessions entertained in his favour. He called together his former companions; acquainted them with his intended reforma-
A.D. 1413.
tion; exhorted them to imitate his example; and strictly prohibited them, until they had given proofs of their amendment, from appearing any more in his presence: while the wise ministers of his father, who had checked his riots, were received with all the marks of favour and confidence. They found that they had unknowingly been paying their court to him. The satisfaction of those who had feared an opposite conduct was augmented by their surprise: so that the character of the young king appeared brighter than if it had never been shaded by any errors.

Henry's first care was to banish, as much as possible, all party distinctions. The instruments of the violences of the preceding reign, who had been advanced from their blind zeal for the Lan-

---

[1] Walsingham.—Hall.—Holinshed.

castrian interest, more than from their integrity or abilities, gave place to men of more honourable characters; and virtue and talents seemed to have a spacious field, in which they might display themselves to advantage. One party distinction, however, remained, which the popularity of Henry was not able to suppress. The Lollards, or disciples of Wickliffe, had extended their influence so as to become a formidable body, which appeared dangerous to the church, and even to the civil power.

The head of this sect was sir John Oldcastle, lord Cobham, a nobleman who had distinguished himself by his military talents, and who had acquired the esteem both of the late and of the present king. His high character, and zeal for the new sect, pointed him out to Arundel, archbishop of Canterbury, as a proper victim of ecclesiastical severity. The primate accordingly applied to the king for permission to indict lord Cobham. The generous nature of Henry was averse from such sanguinary methods of conversion; but, after trying all gentle means in vain, and finding that nobleman obstinate in his opinions, he gave full reins to priestly vengeance against the inflexible sectary. Cobham was condemned to the flames, but made his escape from the Tower before the day appointed for his execution. A.D. 1414. Provoked by persecution, and stimulated by zeal, he was now incited to attempt the treasonable measures which were before imputed to him. The king was informed of his schemes: many of his followers were put to death; and he himself, after a variety of distresses, was hung up by a chain as a traitor, and burned to death as a heretic [1].

When Henry had quelled the conspiracy of the Lollards, he had leisure to consider the dying injunction of his father, not to let the English remain long in peace, which was apt to breed intestine commotions, but to employ them in foreign expeditions, by which the prince might acquire honour, the nobility, in sharing his dangers, might attach themselves to his person, and all the restless spirits find occupation for their inquietude. His natural disposition sufficiently inclined him to follow this advice: and the civil disorders of France, as you have already seen, opened a full career for his ambition. Having prepared a fleet and levied an army, he sailed from Southampton, and landed in Normandy, with six thousand men at arms, and twenty-four thousand foot, chiefly archers [2]. A.D. 1415.

The invaders immediately invested Harfleur, which was taken

---

[1] Walsingham.—Holinshed.   [2] Chron. de Monstrelet.

after a siege of five weeks. The fatigue of the siege, however, and the unusual heat of the season, had so much wasted and enfeebled the English army, that Henry could enter on no other enterprise; and he even sent back a considerable part of his force to England. Fourteen thousand men at arms, and forty thousand foot, were already assembled in Normandy under the constable d'Albret; a force, rightly managed, sufficient either to trample down the English in the open field, or to harass and reduce to nothing their small body, before they could finish a long or difficult march. Henry, therefore, prudently offered to sacrifice his conquest of Harfleur for a safe passage to Calais; but his proposal being rejected by the French court, he determined to make his way by valour and policy through all the opposition of the enemy. And that he might not discourage his troops by the appearance of flight, or expose them to those hazards which naturally attend precipitate marches, he made slow and deliberate journeys [1].

Notwithstanding these precautions, he was continually harassed on his march by flying parties of the enemy; and when he approached the Somme, he saw bodies of men on the opposite bank ready to obstruct his passage. His provisions were cut off; his soldiers languished under sickness and fatigue; and his situation seemed altogether desperate. In this extremity, he was so fortunate as to seize an unguarded ford, over which he safely carried his army, and bent his march towards Calais. But he was still exposed to great and imminent danger from the French army, drawn up in the plains of Azincour, or Agincourt, and posted in such a manner, that it was impossible for him to proceed on his march without coming to an engagement.

Nothing in appearance could be more unequal than the battle, upon which the safety and fortune of Henry now depended. The English army consisted of little more than one half of the number which had disembarked at Harfleur; and the troops laboured under every discouragement and necessity. The French host, at this time, exceeded sixty-five thousand men, headed by the dauphin and all the princes of the blood, and plentifully supplied with provisions. Henry's situation resembled that of Edward III. at Cressy, and of the Black Prince at Poictiers; and the memory of the great victories obtained on those occasions inspired the English with courage, and made them hope for a like deliverance from the present difficulties. The king also

---

[1] Le Laboureur.—Walsingham.

observed the same prudent conduct which had been followed by those illustrious commanders.   He drew up his army on a narrow ground, between woods which guarded each flank; and in that posture he patiently waited the attack of the enemy.

Had the French general been able to reason justly on the circumstances of the two armies, or to profit by past experience, he would have declined a combat, and have waited till necessity had obliged the English to advance, and relinquish the advantages of their situation; but the impetuous valour of the French nobility, and a vain confidence in superior numbers, made him hazard an action, which proved the source of infinite calamities to his country.   The French archers on horseback, and the men at arms, advanced precipitately on the English archers, who had fixed palisades in their front to break the impression of the enemy, and who safely plied them, from behind that defence, with a shower of arrows that nothing could resist. The clayey soil, moistened by rain, proved another obstruction to the force of the French cavalry.   The wounded men and horses discomposed their ranks: the narrow compass in which they were pent prevented them from recovering any order; the whole army was a scene of confusion, terror, and dismay; when Henry, perceiving his advantage, ordered the English archers, who were light and unencumbered, to advance upon the enemy, and seize the moment of victory.   They accordingly fell with their battle axes upon the French, who were now incapable of either flying or defending themselves, and hewed them in pieces without obstruction.   Seconded by the men at arms, who also pushed on against the enemy, they covered the field with the killed, wounded, dismounted, and overthrown.   Every appearance of opposition being now over, the English had leisure to make prisoners; but having advanced to the open plain, they there saw the remains of the French rear-guard, who still maintained the form of a line of battle.   At the same time they heard an alarm from behind.   Some gentlemen of Picardy, having collected about six hundred peasants, had fallen upon the English baggage, and were doing execution on the unarmed followers of the camp, who fled before them.   On this alarm Henry began to entertain apprehensions from his prisoners, and he thought it necessary to issue general orders for putting them to death; but discovering the truth, he stopped the slaughter, and a great number of the captives were saved[1].

Oct. 25.

---

[1] T. Liv. Foro-Jul. *Vit. Hen. V.*—Elmham.—Walsingham.

Few victories were ever more honourable or more complete than this of Azincour. While the loss of the English did not exceed one thousand men, that of the French was enormous. The constable d'Albret and seven princes of the blood were slain: five princes were taken prisoners, with fourteen thousand persons of different ranks; and above ten thousand Frenchmen were left dead on the field of battle[1]. This signal victory, however, was more ostentatious than useful to the conquerors. Henry was obliged to return to England, in order to raise a fresh supply of men and money; and he found it expedient to agree to a cessation of hostilities.

In the mean time France was exposed to all the fury of civil war; and the several parties became every day more enraged against each other. The duke of Burgundy, who had been worsted by his antagonists, attempted to reinstate himself in the possession of the government, as well as of the king's person; and some quarrels in the royal family enabled him to carry his scheme into execution. Louis Bois-Bourdon, favourite to queen Isabella, after the death of the elder duke of Orléans, having been accused by the count d'Armagnac of a commerce of gallantry with that princess, had been put to the torture, and afterwards thrown into the Seine, in consequence of his forced but indis-
A.D. creet confession. The queen herself was sent to Tours, 1416. and confined under a guard. After suffering these multiplied insults, she no longer scrupled to enter into a correspondence with the duke of Burgundy, though hitherto an enemy to that prince; and as her son Charles, the dauphin, was entirely governed by the faction of Armagnac, she extended her animosity even to him, and sought his destruction with the most unrelenting hatred[2]. She had soon an opportunity of rendering her unnatural purpose in some measure effectual.

The duke of Burgundy overran France at the head of a great army of Flemings, and relieved the queen from her confinement. At the same time his partisans raised a commotion in Paris;
A.D. the person of the king was seized; the dauphin made his 1418. escape with difficulty; great numbers of the Armagnac faction were murdered; the count himself, and many persons of note, were confined: and the populace, deeming the course of public justice too dilatory, broke open the prisons, and put to death that nobleman and his friends[3].

---

[1] Le Fevre, *Hist. de Charles VI.*—Elmham.—T. Liv.—Walsingham.
[2] Le Fevre.—Monstrelet.   [3] Le Fevre.

While France was thus torn by civil dissensions, Henry having again invaded the country, met with great success in the reduction of the towns of Normandy.   When the pope's legate attempted to incline him towards peace, he replied, " Do you not see that God has led me hither as by the hand ?   France has no sovereign ;   I have just pretensions to that kingdom :   every thing here is in the utmost confusion ;   no one thinks of resisting me.   Can I have a more sensible proof, that the Being who disposes of empires, has determined to put the crown of France upon my head [1] ?"—Such has ever been the language of force ;   to which weakness, crawling in the dust, has too often listened with an ear of credulity.   Hence conquerors, while living, have been considered as the sons of gods and the delegates of Heaven ;   and after being consigned to that earth which they had desolated, have themselves been exalted into divinities.

But, although Henry seemed so fully assured of the conquest of France, he was induced by prudential motives to negociate with his enemies.   He made at the same time offers of peace to both the French parties ;   to the queen and the duke of Burgundy, on the one hand, who, having possession of the king's person, carried the appearance of legal authority :   and to the dauphin on the other, who, being the rightful heir of the monarchy, was adhered to by all men who paid any regard to the true interests of their country.   These two parties also carried on a continual negociation with each other ;   and all things seemed settled to their mutual satisfaction, when the duke of Burgundy was murdered by the dauphin's party during an interview at Montereau [2]. A.D. 1419.

In consequence of this act of barbarity, and the progress of Henry's arms, the queen, and the new duke of Burgundy, breathing vengeance for the murder of his father, concluded the famous treaty of Troyes, by which the crown of France was transferred to the house of Lancaster.   The principal articles were, that the king of England should espouse the princess Catherine ;   that her father should enjoy for life the title and dignity of king of France ;   that Henry should be declared heir of the monarchy, and be entrusted with the immediate administration of the government ;   that all the princes, peers, vassals, and communities of France, should swear, that they would adhere to the future succession of Henry, and pay him present obedience as regent ;   and that this prince should unite his arms May 21, 1420.

---

[1] Juv. des Ursins.   [2] Monstrelet.—Elmham.

with those of the French king and the duke of Burgundy, in order
to subdue the adherents of Charles the *pretended* dauphin [1].

Henry now espoused the French princess; conducted his
father-in-law to Paris; put himself in possession of that capital;
and obtained from the parliament and the three estates a ratification of the treaty of Troyes.   He supported the duke of Burgundy in procuring a sentence against the murderers of his
father; and he turned his arms with success against the partisans
A.D. of the dauphin, who, as soon as he heard of the late treaty,
1421. assumed the style and authority of regent, and appealed
to God and his sword for the maintenance of his title.   But,
notwithstanding the bravery and fidelity of his officers, young
Charles saw himself unequal to his enemies in the field, and
found it necessary to temporize, and avoid all hazardous action,
with a rival who had acquired so manifest a superiority.

To crown the prosperity of Henry, his queen was delivered of
a son, who was called by his father's name, and whose birth was
celebrated by rejoicings not less pompous (if less sincere) at Paris
than in London.   The infant prince was regarded as the fortunate heir of both monarchies.   But the glory of Henry, when
near its height, was suddenly restrained by the hand of nature,
and all his towering projects vanished into air.   He was seized
with a malady which the surgeons of that age wanted skill to
treat with judgment, namely, a fistula, which proved mortal.
When he found his end approaching, he sent for his brother the
duke of Bedford, the earl of Warwick, and other noblemen whom
Aug. 31. he had honoured with his confidence.   To them he de-
1422. livered, in great composure, his last will with regard to
the government of his kingdom and family.   He left the regency
of France to the duke of Bedford; that of England to his younger
brother the duke of Gloucester; and the care of his son to the
earl of Warwick [2].

Henry V. possessed many eminent virtues, and his abilities
were as conspicuous in the cabinet as in the field.   The boldness
of his plans, and his personal valour in carrying them into execution, were equally remarkable.   He had the talent of attach-
ing his friends by affability, and of gaining his enemies by address
and clemency.   His exterior figure and deportment were engaging; his stature exceeded the middle size; his countenance
was beautiful, his form well proportioned, and he excelled in all
warlike and manly exercises.

---

[1] Rymer, vol. ix.—Monstrelet .   [2] Rymer.

In less than two months after Henry's death Charles VI. terminated his unhappy life.   He had for many years _{Oct. 22.} possessed only the shadow of royalty ; yet was this mere appearance of considerable advantage to the English : it divided the duty and affections of the French between the king and the dauphin, who was now crowned at Poictiers, under the name of Charles VII., Rheims (the usual place of such ceremony) being then in the hands of his enemies.

Henry's widow, soon after his death, married Sir Owen Tudor, a gentleman of Wales, said to be descended from the ancient princes of that country.   She bore him two sons; the elder of whom was created earl of Richmond, the younger earl of Pembroke.   The family of Tudor, first raised to distinction by this alliance, afterwards mounted, as we shall have occasion to see, the throne of England.

LETTER XLVIII.

Continuation of the History of France and England, from the Accession of Charles VII. to the Expulsion of the English from the Continental Territories, in 1453.

IN considering, with a superficial eye, the state of affairs between France and England at the accession of Charles VII., every advantage seems to lie on the side of the latter kingdom ; and the total expulsion of Charles appears an event which might naturally be expected from the superior power of his competitor. Henry VI. was indeed a mere infant; but the duke of Bedford, the most accomplished prince of his age, was entrusted with the administration.   And the experience, prudence, valour, and generosity of the regent qualified him for his high office, and enabled him both to maintain union among his friends, and to gain the confidence of his enemies.   But Charles, notwithstanding the present inferiority of his power, possessed some advantages which promised him success.   As he was the lawful heir of the monarchy, all Frenchmen, who knew the interest or desired the independence of their native country, turned their eyes towards him as its sole resource ; and Charles himself was of a character well calculated to become the object of these benevolent sentiments.   He was a prince of the most friendly and benign disposition; of easy and familiar manners; and of a just and sound, though not a very vigorous understanding. Sincere, generous, affable, he engaged from affection the services of his followers, even while his low fortune might have made it their interest to desert him; and the lenity of his temper could pardon those sallies of discontent to which princes in his situation are naturally exposed. The love of pleasure often seduced him into indolence; but, amidst all his irregularities, the goodness of his heart still shone forth; and by exerting at intervals his courage and activity, he proved that his general remissness proceeded neither from the want of ambition, nor from a deficiency of personal valour [1].

Sensible of these advantages on the side of Charles, the duke of Bedford took care to strengthen the English interest by fresh A.D. alliances with the dukes of Burgundy and Bretagne; and 1423. observing the ardour of the Scots to serve in France, where Charles treated them with great honour and distinction, he persuaded the English council to release James, the heir of the crown, from his long captivity, and to connect him with England, by marrying him to a grand-daughter of John of Gaunt, duke of A.D. Lancaster. The alliance was accordingly formed: James 1424. was restored to the throne of his ancestors; and proved one of the most illustrious princes that ever swayed the Scottish sceptre. His affections inclined to the party of France; but the English had never reason, while he reigned, to complain of any breach of the neutrality by Scotland. He was murdered by his traitorous kinsman the earl of Athol, in 1437.

Bedford, however, was not so much employed in negociation as to neglect the operations of war. He reduced almost every fortress on this side of the Loire; and the battle of Verneuil, in which the French and Scots were defeated, threatened Charles with the total loss of his kingdom, when a succession of remarkable circumstances saved him on the brink of ruin, and disappointed the confident hopes of the English.

Instead of taking any possible advantage of the victory gained at Verneuil, or of the other circumstances that favoured him, the duke was obliged to repair to England, in order to compose some dissensions among the ministry, and to endeavour to moderate the measures of the duke of Gloucester, who had inconA.D. siderately kindled a war in the Low Countries, and car1425. ried thither the troops destined for the reinforcement of

---

[1] P. Æmil.—Du Tillet—Le Gendre.

the English army in France. The affections of the duke of Burgundy were alienated, and his forces diverted by the same war. The duke of Bretagne returned to his allegiance A.D. under Charles. The French had leisure to recollect 1426. themselves, and gained some inconsiderable advantages. .But the regent, soon after his return, retrieved the reputation A.D. of the English arms, by humbling the Breton duke, and 1427. resolved on an undertaking which he hoped would prepare the way for the final conquest of France.

The city of Orléans was so situated between the provinces of Henry and those of Charles, that it opened an easy entrance to either; and as the duke of Bedford intended to make a great effort for penetrating into the south of France, it was necessary to begin with the siege of this place, now become the most A.D. important in the kingdom. The French king used every 1428. expedient to supply the city with a garrison and provisions, and the English left no method unemployed for reducing it. The eyes of all Europe were turned towards the scene of action, where it was reasonably supposed the French were to make their last stand for maintaining the independence of their monarchy and the rights of their sovereign. After numberless feats of valour, performed both by the besiegers and the besieged, the attack was so vigorously pushed by the English, although the duke of Burgundy had withdrawn his troops in disgust, that Charles gave over the city for lost, and even entertained thoughts of retiring into Languedoc or Dauphiné with the remains of his force[1].

But it was fortunate for that gay prince, who lay entirely under the dominion of the softer sex, that the women whom he consulted on this occasion had the spirit to support his sinking resolution. Mary of Anjou, his queen, a princess of great A.D. merit and prudence, vehemently opposed such a measure, 1429. which she foresaw would discourage all his partisans, and serve as a general signal for deserting a prince who seemed himself to despair of success. His mistress, the fair Agnes Sorel, who lived in perfect amity with the queen, seconded all her remonstrances, and threatened, if he thus pusillanimously threw away the sceptre of France, that she would seek in the court of England a fortune more correspondent to her wishes. Love was able to rouse, in the breast of Charles, that courage which ambition had failed to excite. He resolved to dispute every inch of ground

---

[1] Monstrelet. — Hall. — Holinshed.

with an imperious enemy; to perish with honour, in the midst of his friends, rather than yield ingloriously to his ill fortune[1]. And this resolution was no sooner formed than relief was unexpectedly brought to him by another female of a very different character.

In the village of Domremi near Vaucouleurs, on the borders of Lorrain, lived a girl whose name was Joan d' Arc, who had filled the humble station of servant at an inn, and in that capacity had taken care of horses, and performed other offices which usually fall to the share of men. Inflamed by the frequent mention of the rencounters at the siege of Orléans, and affected with the distresses of her country, particularly with those of the youthful monarch, whose gallantry made him the idol of the whole sex, she was seized with a wild desire of procuring relief for her sovereign. Her inexperienced mind, working day and night on this favourite object, mistook the impulses of passion for heavenly inspirations; and she fancied that she saw visions, and heard voices exhorting her to re-establish the throne of France, and expel the foreign invaders. Having an uncommon intrepidity of spirit, she overlooked all the dangers which might attend her in such a path; and the idea of her divine mission dispelled the bashfulness so natural to her sex, her years, and her low condition. She went to Vaucouleurs, procured admission to Baudricourt the governor, and informed him of her inspirations and intentions. Baudricourt observed something extraordinary in the maid, or saw the use that might be made of such an engine, and sent her to the French court at Chinon[2].

Joan was no sooner introduced to the king than she offered, in the name of Heaven, to raise the siege of Orléans, and conduct him to Rheims, to be there crowned and anointed; and she demanded, as the instrument of her future victories, a particular sword which was kept in the church of St. Katherine de Fierbois. The more the king and his ministers were determined to give way to the illusion, the more they pretended to be doubtful and scrupulous. Grave and learned divines were ordered to examine Joan's mission; and they pronounced it divine and supernatural. The parliament also attested her inspirations; and a jury of matrons declared her an unspotted virgin. Her requests were now granted. She was armed cap-à-pie, mounted on horseback, and shown to the people in that martial array. Her dexterity in managing her steed, though acquired in her former station,

---

[1] Monstrelet.—Holinshed.   [2] Hall.—Monstrelet.

was regarded as a fresh proof of her mission ; her former occupation was even denied ; she was converted into a shepherdess,
an employment more agreeable to the imagination than that of
an hostler-wench.   Some years were subtracted from her age, in
order to excite still greater admiration ; and she was received
with the loudest acclamations by persons of all ranks.   A ray of
hope began to break through that cloud of despair in which the
minds of men were involved.   Heaven had now declared itself in
favour of France, and laid bare its out-stretched arm to take
vengeance on her invaders.

The English at first affected to speak with derision of the
Maid and her heavenly commission : but their imagination was
secretly struck with the strong persuasion which prevailed around
them.   They found their courage daunted by degrees, and
thence began to infer a divine vengeance hanging over them.
A silent astonishment reigned among those troops, formerly so
elate with victory, and so fierce for the combat.   The Maid entered
the city of Orléans at the head of a convoy, arrayed in her
military garb, and displaying her consecrated standard.   She
was received as a celestial deliverer by the garrison and inhabitants ; and by the instructions of count Dunois, commonly called
the Bastard of Orléans, who commanded in the place, she
actually obliged the English to raise the siege of that city, May 8.
after driving them from their entrenchments, and defeating
them in several desperate attacks[1].

This success was one part of the Maid's promises to Charles ;
the crowning of him at Rheims was the other ; and she now
vehemently insisted, that he should set out immediately on that
journey.   A few weeks before, such a proposal would have appeared altogether extravagant.   Rheims was then in the power
of victorious enemies ; the whole road that led to it was occupied by their troops ; and no imagination could have been so
sanguine as to hope that such an attempt could be carried into
execution.   But as things had now taken a turn, and it was extremely the interest of the king of France to maintain the belief
of something extraordinary and divine in these events, he resolved to follow the exhortations of his warlike prophetess, and
avail himself of the present consternation of the English.   He
accordingly set out for Rheims, at the head of twelve thousand
men, and scarcely perceived, as he passed along, that he was
marching through an enemy's country.   Every place opened its

---

[1] Monstrelet.—Hall.

gates to him : Rheims sent him its keys; and the ceremony of his inauguration was performed with the holy oil, which a pigeon was said to have brought from heaven to Clovis, on the first establishment of the French monarchy[1].

Charles, thus crowned and anointed, became more respectable in the eyes of all his subjects ; and he seemed to derive from a heavenly commission, a new title to their allegiance. Many places submitted to him immediately after his coronation ; and the whole nation seemed disposed to give him the most zealous testimonies of duty and affection.

The duke of Bedford, in this dangerous crisis, employed every resource which fortune had yet left him. He acted with such prudence and address as to renew his alliance with the duke of Burgundy, who had been long wavering in his fidelity. He seemed present everywhere, by his vigilance and foresight ; and although his supplies from England were very inconsiderable, he attempted to restore the courage of his troops by boldly advancing to face the enemy. But he chose his posts with so much caution as always to decline a combat, and to render it impossible for the French king to attack him. He still attended that prince in all his movements, covered his own towns and garrisons, and kept himself in a posture to reap advantage from every imprudent act or false step of the enemy. He also endeavoured to revive the declining state of his affairs, by bringing over the young king of England, and having him crowned and anointed at Paris. All the vassals of the crown who lived within the provinces possessed by the English, again swore allegiance, and did homage to Henry VI.[2] But this ceremony was cold and insipid, in comparison of the coronation of Charles at Rheims; and the duke of Bedford expected greater advantage from an incident which put into his hands the author of all his misfortunes.

The Maid of Orléans declared, after the coronation of Charles, that her mission was accomplished, and expressed her inclination to retire to the occupations and course of life which became her sex. But Dunois, sensible of the important benefit which might still be derived from her presence in the army, exhorted her to persevere till the final expulsion of the English. In pursuance A.D. of this advice she threw herself into the town of Com-1430. peigne, at that time besieged by the duke of Burgundy, assisted by the earls of Arundel and Suffolk. The defenders on her appearance believed themselves invincible. But their joy

---

[1] Mezeray—Hall.　　　　[2] Rymer, vol. x.

was of short duration.   The Maid was taken prisoner in a sally; and the duke of Bedford, resolved upon her ruin, ordered her to be tried by an ecclesiastical court for sorcery, impiety, and idolatry.   She was found guilty, by her ignorant or iniquitous judges, of these crimes, aggravated by the deep stain of heresy; her revelations were declared to be inventions of the devil to delude the people; and this admirable heroine was cruelly A.D. consigned to the flames, thus expiating by the punish- 1431. ment of fire the signal services which she had rendered to her prince and her native country [1].

The English affairs, however, instead of being advanced by this act of cruelty, daily declined.   The great abilities of the regent were insufficient to repress the strong inclination which had seized the French for returning under the obedience of their rightful sovereign.   The duke of Burgundy deserted the A.D. English interest, and formed an alliance with the French 1435. king; the duke of Bedford died soon after; and the violent factions which prevailed in the court of England, between the duke of Gloucester and cardinal Beaufort, bishop of Winchester, prevented the nation from taking proper measures for repairing these signal losses.

The feeble character of young Henry was now fully known in the court, and was no longer ambiguous to either faction.   Of the most inoffensive and simple manners, but of the most slender capacity, he was fitted, both by the softness of his temper and the weakness of his understanding, to be perpetually governed by those who surrounded him; and it was easy to foresee that his reign would resemble a perpetual minority.   When he reached the age of manhood, it was natural to think of choosing a queen for him; and the leaders of each party earnestly wished to make him receive one from their hand, as it was probable that this circumstance would decide for ever the victory between them. The cardinal proved successful; and Henry was con- A.D. tracted to Margaret of Anjou, daughter of René, titular 1444. king of Sicily, Naples, and Jerusalem, descended from a count of Anjou, who had left these magnificent titles to his posterity, without any real power or possessions in those kingdoms.   She was the most accomplished princess of that age both in body and mind, and seemed to possess those qualities which would enable her to acquire an ascendant over Henry, and to supply

[1] Polyd. Virg.—Monstrelet.

A.D. all his defects and weaknesses. The treaty of marriage 1445. was ratified in England; and Margaret, on her arrival, connected herself with the cardinal and his party; who, fortified by her powerful patronage, resolved on the final ruin of the duke of Gloucester [1].

This generous prince, worsted in all court intrigues, for which his temper was not suited, but possessing in an eminent degree the favour of the public, had already received from his rivals a cruel mortification, which it was impossible a person of his spirit could ever forgive, although he had hitherto borne it without violating public peace. His duchess, the daughter of Reginald lord Cobham, had been accused of the crime of witchcraft; and it was pretended that there was found in her possession a waxen figure of the king, which she and her associates (Bolingbroke, a priest, and a reputed witch named Jourdemain) melted in a magical manner before a slow fire, with an intention of making Henry's force and vigour waste away by the like insensible degrees. The nature of this crime, as the philosophic Hume ingeniously observes, so opposite to all common sense, seems always to exempt the accusers from observing the rules of common sense in their evidence. The prisoners were pronounced guilty : the duchess was condemned to do public penance, and to suffer perpetual imprisonment; and her supposed accomplices were executed. But the people, contrary to their usual practice on such marvellous trials, acquitted the unhappy sufferers, and ascribed these violent proceedings solely to the malice of the duke's enemies. The queen and the cardinal therefore thought it necessary to destroy a man whose popularity made him dangerous, and whose resentment they had so much cause to apprehend. He was accused of treason, and thrown into prison,

A.D. where he was soon after found dead in bed; and although 1447. his body bore no marks of outward violence, no one doubted of his having fallen a victim to the vengeance of his enemies [2].

While England was thus a prey to faction, the king of France employed himself, with great industry and judgment, in removing those numberless ills to which France had been so long exposed from the continuance of wars both foreign and domestic. He restored the regular course of public justice : he introduced order into the finances; he established discipline among his troops; he repressed faction in his court; he revived the languid

---

[1] Grafton's Chronicle.—Holinshed.   [2] Grafton.—Holinshed.

state of agriculture and the arts; and in the course of a few years rendered his kingdom flourishing within itself, and formidable to his neighbours. The English were expelled from all their A.D. possessions on the continent, except Calais; and although 1453. no peace was yet concluded between the two nations, the war was in a manner at an end[1].—England, torn in pieces by civil dissensions, made but one more feeble effort for the recovery of Guienne; and Charles, occupied in regulating the government of his own kingdom, and fencing against the intrigues of his son Louis, scarcely ever attempted to avail himself of her intestine broils. The affairs of the two realms, therefore, became for a while distinct. But before I proceed with the history of either, we must take a view of the state of the German empire.

LETTER XLIX.

Of the German Empire and its Dependencies, from the Election of Albert II. to that of Maximilian.

To the long reign of Sigismund, my dear Philip, succeeded the short sway of Albert. The chief enterprise in which this prince engaged was an expedition against the Turks in Oct. Bulgaria, where he was seized with a violent and fatal 1439. dysentery. He was succeeded on the imperial throne by his cousin Frederic of Austria, the third (sometimes called the Fourth) emperor of that name. The crowns of Hungary and Bohemia were assigned to Ladislaus, Albert's infant son, who was committed to the guardianship of Frederic; but the nobles of the former realm, opposing the will of the defunct prince, transferred the sovereignty to Ladislaus king of Poland.

The emperor's first care was to heal a new schism. With this view he set out for Basil, where a council continued to sit for " the reformation of the church universal, both in its A.D. head and its members." This council had raised to the 1440. papacy Amadeus duke of Savoy, under the name of Felix V., in opposition to Eugenius IV. Frederic exhorted the fathers to concord, and an accommodation with Eugenius. He had also an interview with Felix, whom he refused to acknowledge for pope,

---

[1] Monstrelet.—Henault.—Grafton.

though tempted by an offer of his daughter, a young princess of exquisite beauty, and two hundred thousand ducats as her portion. " This man," said Frederic to one of his courtiers, in a contemptuous tone, " would readily purchase holiness, if he could find a seller." The schism was at length closed, Felix being prevailed upon by the emperor to abdicate the apostolic chair on certain conditions, which were confirmed by Nicholas V. who had succeeded Eugenius [1].

A.D. 1449.

The peace of the church being thus restored, and the affairs of Germany not disordered, Frederic began to turn his eyes towards Italy, where the imperial authority was at a low ebb. Alphonso of Arragon reigned at that time in Naples, and joined the emperor, because he feared the power of the Venetians, who were masters of Ravenna, Bergamo, Brescia, and Cremona. Milan was in the hands of Francis Sforza, a peasant's son, but one of the greatest warriors of his age, and now become the most powerful man in Italy. He had married the natural daughter of Philip Maria Galeazzo duke of Milan, by whom he was adopted. Florence was in league with the pope against Sforza: the Holy See had recovered Bologna; and all the other principalities belonged to different sovereigns, who had mastered them [2]. In this situation were the affairs of Italy, when the emperor resolved upon a journey to Rome, in order to be crowned by the pope, together with Eleonora, sister of the king of Portugal, to whom he was contracted in marriage.

A.D. 1451.

As soon as Frederic had crossed the Alps, he was met by the Venetian ambassadors, who conducted him to their city, where he made his public entry with great magnificence. He thence repaired to Ferrara, where he found ambassadors from Francis Sforza, duke of Milan, inviting him to return by that city, where he should receive the iron crown; and here he also received deputies from Florence and Bologna, soliciting the honour of entertaining him at their respective cities, which he accordingly visited [3]. From Florence he took the route of Sienna, where he gave audience to the pope's legates, who represented to him, that, by ancient custom, the emperors always took an oath to the pope before they entered the territorial patrimony of St. Peter, and requested that he would conform to the same usage.

Frederic, in this particular, complied with the desire of his

[1] Mosheim, *Hist. Eccles.* vol. iii.—Æn. Sylv. *Vit. Fred. III.*
[2] *Annal. de l'Emp.* tome ii.
[3] Machiavel. *Hist. Flor.* lib. vi.

holiness.   The oath which he took was conceived in these terms :
" I Frederic king of the Romans, promise and swear, by the
Father, Son, and Holy Ghost, by the wood of the vivifying cross,
and by these reliques of saints, that if, by permission of the Lord,
I shall come to Rome, I will exalt the holy Roman church, and
his holiness, who presides over it, to the utmost of my power.
Neither shall he lose life, limb, or honour, by my counsel, consent, or exhortation.   Nor will I, in the city of Rome, make any
law or decree touching those things which belong to his holiness
or to the Romans, without the advice of our most holy lord
Nicholas.   Whatever part of St. Peter's Patrimony shall fall
into our hands, we will restore it to his holiness ; and he, to
whom we shall commit the administration of our kingdom of
Italy, shall swear to assist his holiness in defending St. Peter's
Patrimony to the utmost of his power.   So help me God, and
his holy Evangelists [1] !"

The emperor now proceeded to Viterbo, where he was in
danger of his life from a tumult of the populace ; so indifferently
attended was this successor of Charlemagne !—From Viterbo he
repaired to Rome, where he was met by the whole college of
cardinals ; and as it had been customary for the late emperors,
when they went thither to be crowned, to continue some time
without the walls, Frederic ordered tents to be pitched, and
there passed one night.   Having made his public entry, he was
crowned king of Lombardy.   Three days after this ceremony,
he was married to Eleonora, and, with her, received the imperial
crown.   He and the pope then ratified the *Concordata* A.D.
of the German nation, touching the collation to prelacies   1452.
and other benefices, which had some years before been adjusted
by cardinal Carvajal the legate of Nicholas at the imperial
court [2].

Having thus transacted matters at Rome, Frederic set out on
his return to Germany : and in his passage through Ferrara was
visited by Borsi marquis of Este, a prince of extraordinary
merit, whom he created duke of Modena and Reggio.   On
his arrival in Austria he found himself involved in various difficulties, out of which he was never able fully to extricate himself.

After the death of the king of Poland in 1444, the Hungarian
nobles had entreated Frederic to send home Ladislaus, Albert's
son (who, though now elected king, was still detained at the
imperial court) ; and they had earnestly and repeatedly besought

---

[1] Fugger, lib. v.   [2] Barre, tome vii.—Naucleri *Chron.*

him to restore their crown and *regalia*, which were in his custody. But he found means, under various pretences, to postpone his compliance with these demands. The Austrians, joined by a number of Bohemians, and encouraged by several princes of the empire, also sent a deputation to expostulate with Frederic on the same subject; and as he amused them with fresh evasions, they had recourse to arms, and compelled him to sign an accommodation. It was agreed, that Ladislaus, being yet of too tender years to take upon himself the government of his kingdoms, should be put under the tuition of Ulric, count Celley, his uncle by the mother's side, and that the dispute touching the wardship of the emperor, should be determined at Vienna [1].

Count Celley's ambition was elated by the power which he derived from being tutor to Ladislaus. He attempted to make himself absolute master in Austria; he secured the principal fortresses, by giving the command of them to his creatures; and he gradually removed Elsinger (a Bohemian gentleman who had headed the insurrection), and the Austrian nobility, from all offices of importance. His friends and favourites only were trusted. The people were incensed at such proceedings; and Elsinger, profiting by their discontent, roused their resentment to such a degree, that the count was obliged to retire into Hungary, after having delivered up the person of Ladislaus, who consented to take the oath imposed upon him by the Bohemians, and was crowned with great solemnity at Prague [2].

A.D. 1453.

During these contests the city of Constantinople was taken by the Turks, after they had subdued the rest of Greece; and by this blow the Roman empire in the East was entirely subverted, as will be related more at length in its proper place. Here it is only necessary to observe, that the progress of the Mohammedans alarmed all the princes of Christendom, and made them think of uniting, though too late, in order to oppose the common enemy. A diet being convoked at Ratisbon the members unanimously agreed, that there was a necessity of taking some speedy measures to stop the progress of the infidels. But what these measures should be, was a consideration referred to another diet assembled at Frankfort; where, although there was a vast concourse of princes, and great zeal was displayed, very little was done for the common cause.

A.D. 1455.

---

[1] Æn. Syl. *Hist. Boem.*   [2] Id. Ibid.

Other diets discussed the same subject, with no greater effect ; a backwardness which was chiefly ascribed to the timid and slothful disposition of the emperor, who would never heartily embark in the undertaking.

The German princes, however, at the solicitation of the pope's legate, sent a body of troops to the assistance of John Huniades, a famous Hungarian general, who had long gallantly defended his country against the Turks, and gained several advantages over them.   John, thus reinforced, marched to the relief A.D. of Belgrade, which was besieged by Mohammed II., the 1456. conqueror of Constantinople, and the terror of Christendom ; and compelled the sultan, after an obstinate engagement, to raise the siege, and retreat with considerable loss [1].   But the death of Huniades, which happened a few days after the battle, prevented the Christian army from making any progress against the infidels. The fruits of their victory, and their future projects, perished with their illustrious leader.

Ladislaus, king of Hungary and Bohemia, died two years after his illustrious general ; and various competitors arose for A.D. those crowns, as well as for the dominions of Upper 1458. Austria, which belonged to that prince.   The emperor was one of the claimants ; he reaped, however, nothing but damage and disgrace from a civil war which desolated Germany for many years, but which was productive of no event that merits attention.   His son Maximilian was more fortunate, and better deserved success: but he was unable to procure either of the disputed crowns ; for the Hungarian royalty was conferred on Matthias, the brave and respectable son of John Hunaides, while the Bohemians made choice of a nobleman named George Poggebrache, who favoured the propagation of the doctrines of Wickliffe and Huss.

Maximilian, who was as active and enterprising as his father was indolent and timid, married, at eighteen years of age, the only daughter of Charles the Bold, duke of Burgundy.   She brought him Flanders, Franche-Comté, and all the Low Countries.   Louis XI., who disputed some of these territories, and who, on the death of the duke, had seized Burgundy, Picardy, Ponthieu, and Artois, as fiefs of France, which could not A.D. be possessed by a woman, was defeated by Maximilian at 1479. Guinegaste ; and Charles VIII., who renewed the same claims, was obliged to conclude a disadvantageous peace.

---

[1] Æn. Sylv.—Platin. *Vit. Pontif.*

After alternate scenes of peace and war, of tranquillity and Sept. 7, dissension, Frederic died in the seventy-ninth year of 1493. his age, and the fifty-fourth of his reign. No emperor had ever reigned longer, and none less gloriously.

The reign of Maximilian, already elected king of the Romans, introduces a more interesting period than that over which we have now travelled, and opens a vista into some of the grandest scenes of history. But a variety of objects, my dear Philip, must occupy your attention before I treat farther of the concerns of the empire.

LETTER L.

Of the Contest in England between the Houses of York and Lancaster, to its final Extinction in the Accession of the House of Tudor.

I HAVE already had occasion to notice the weakness of Henry VI. His incapacity appeared every day in a stronger light. A.D. The more he was known, the more his authority was de-1450. spised; and when the war in France began to languish, men of restless and ambitious spirits took occasion to disturb his government, and tear with intestine commotions the bowels of their native country.

But the miseries of Henry and of England did not arise solely from these causes: a pretender to the crown appeared; and a title which had never been disputed during the prosperous reign of Henry V. was now called in question under his feeble successor. This competitor was Richard duke of York. He lineally traced his origin from the duke of Clarence, third son of Edward III., and consequently stood in the order of succession before the king, who derived his descent from the duke of Lancaster, fourth son of that monarch.

Such a claim could not, in some respects, have fallen into more dangerous hands. The duke of York was a man of valour and abilities, which he had found frequent opportunities of displaying. In the right of his father, the earl of Cambridge, he bore the rank of first prince of the blood: he possessed an immense fortune; and was connected by marriage and friendship with many of the most powerful nobles. He was generally beloved by the people; whose discontents, at this time, rendered every combination of the great more dangerous to the throne.

The administration of the realm was now in the hands of the queen and William de la Pole, duke of Suffolk, who had attracted universal odium. Margaret was still regarded as a French woman, and a latent enemy to the kingdom, who had betrayed the interest of England, in favour of her family and her country. Suffolk was considered as her accomplice; and the murder of the duke of Gloucester, in which both were known to have been concerned, rendered them yet more obnoxious to the nation.

The partisans of Richard took advantage of these causes of popular discontent, to impeach the duke of Suffolk, in parliament, of various crimes and misdemeanors; and the king, in order to save his minister, banished him for five years. But his enemies, sensible that he still possessed the queen's confidence, and would be recalled on the first opportunity, employed a captain of a ship to intercept him in his passage to France. He was accordingly seized near Dover; his head was struck off on the side of a long-boat, and his body thrown into the sea [1].

The duke of Somerset succeeded to Suffolk's power in the administration, and credit with the queen: and as he was the person under whose government the French provinces had been lost, the people, who always judge by events, soon made him equally the object of their animosity. In consequence of these discontents, the house of commons presented a petition A.D. to the king, praying him to remove the duke of Somerset 1451. for ever from his person and councils. This application was unsuccessful; but when Henry had contracted a disorder A.D. which increased his natural imbecility, the queen and the 1454. council, unable to resist the popular party, were obliged to yield to the torrent. They sent Somerset to the Tower, and appointed the duke of York lieutenant of the kingdom, with power to open and hold a session of parliament: and that assembly created him Protector during pleasure [2].

When the king had so far recovered from his indisposition as to be able to maintain the appearance of authority, his friends urged him to annul the regency of Richard, release Somerset, and commit the administration into the hands of that nobleman. The duke of York, sensible of his danger, levied an army, in order to support his parliamentary commission, but without

---

[1] Hall.—Stow.—*Continuation of Hist. Croyland.*
[2] *Parl. Hist.* vol. ii.—Rymer, vol. xi.

advancing any pretensions to the crown, though his title was
A.D. generally acknowledged.   A battle was risked near St.
1455. Alban's, where the Lancastrians were routed, and the
duke of Somerset fell.   The king himself was made prisoner by
the duke of York, and, while he was treated with apparent kindness, was obliged to resign (what he valued little) the whole
authority of the crown into the hands of his rival [1].

Richard, however, did not yet claim the royalty in form: he
was still content with the title of Protector; and an outward
A.D. reconciliation took place between the parties.   A solemn
1458. procession to St. Paul's was appointed, in order to make
known this amity to the people.   The duke of York led queen
Margaret; and a chieftain of one party marched hand in hand
with a chieftain of the opposite.   But a contest for a crown
could not be thus peaceably accommodated.   Each party watched
only for an opportunity of subverting the other; and the smallest
incident, without any formed design, was sufficient to dissolve
the seeming harmony.   Two servants of the rival houses quarrelled; their companions took part in the fray; a fierce combat
ensued; and both parties, in every county of England, openly
made preparations for deciding the contest by arms [2].

A battle was fought at Blore-heath, on the borders of Staf-
A.D. fordshire, where the royalists were defeated, and chased
1459. off the field with considerable loss.   But this victory was
not sufficient to decide the fate of England; and fortune soon
shifted sides.   When the two armies approached each other
near Ludlow, and a general action was every hour expected, sir
Andrew Trollop, who commanded a choice body of veterans,
deserted to the king; and the Yorkists were so dismayed at this
instance of treachery, which made every man suspicious of his
fellow, that they separated without striking a blow [3].

In this extremity the duke of York fled to Ireland, where he
had formerly acquired great popularity; and his partisans in
England kept themselves in readiness to rise on the first summons from their leaders.   That requisition proceeded from the
earl of Warwick, governor of Calais, the most extraordinary
man of his time, and, from the subsequent events, commonly
A.D. known by the appellation of the *King-Maker*.   He landed
1460. in Kent, where he was joined by several persons of distinction; and as the people bore him an unlimited affection,

---

[1] Stow.—Hall.—Holinshed.   [2] Fabian's *Chron.*—Grafton.
                    [3] Grafton.—Holinshed.

his army increased every day.   He entered London amidst the acclamations of the populace : he advanced to meet the royal army, which hastened from Coventry to attack him ; and a battle ensued at Northampton, where the Lancastrians received a sanguinary defeat.   Henry himself, that empty shadow ^{July 10.} of a king, was again made prisoner, and carried in triumph to his capital [1].

A parliament was now summoned at Westminster, where the duke of York soon appeared from Ireland, and asserted his claim to the crown.   He advanced towards the throne ; and, addressing himself to the house of peers, pleaded his cause before them as his natural and legal judges.   He gave them a deduction of his title by descent ; mentioned the cruelties by which the house of Lancaster had paved its way to sovereign power ; insisted on the calamities which had attended the government of Henry, and exhorted them to return to the right path, by doing justice to the lineal heir : then respectfully left the house, as no one desired him to seat himself upon the throne.

Such a degree of moderation is not perhaps to be paralleled in history, and was little to be expected in those violent and licentious times, from a prince who had a victorious army at his command.   The peers, on their part, discovered an equal share of firmness and composure.   They called in some of the most considerable members among the commons, to assist in their deliberations ; and, after having heard, during six days, the reasons alleged by both parties, they declared the duke's title certain and indefeasible ; but, as Henry had so long enjoyed the crown without dispute or controversy, they determined that he should continue to possess the title and dignity of king during the remainder of his life : that the administration, in the mean while, should remain with Richard, and that he should be acknowledged the true and lawful heir of the monarchy.   The duke acquiesced in this decision ; and Henry himself, being a prisoner, could not well oppose it [2].

The duke of York had a very short enjoyment of the honour of this new settlement, and never attained the envied title of king.   After the battle of Northampton, queen Margaret had fled with her son into Scotland ; but soon returning, she applied to the northern barons of England, and employed every argu-

---

[1] J. de Whethamstede.—Hall.
[2] *Parl. Hist.* vol. ii.—Cotton.—Grafton.—Holinshed.—This account is contradicted in some particulars by Whethamstede, the Abbot of St. Alban's : but a single authority, however respectable, is not sufficient to overthrow general testimony.

ment to procure their assistance.   Her affability, insinuation, and address, aided by caresses and promises, wrought a powerful effect on all who approached her.   The admiration of her great character was succeeded by compassion for her helpless state. The nobility of the north entered warmly into her cause; and she soon found herself at the head of an army of twenty thousand men, collected with a celerity which was neither expected by her friends, nor apprehended by her enemies.

Richard now hastened northward with a body of five thousand men, to suppress, as he imagined, the beginnings of an insurrection.   He met the queen near Wakefield; and though he found himself so much outnumbered by the enemy, his pride would not permit him to retreat before a woman.   He gave battle, and was killed in the action.   His body being found among the slain, his head was cut off by Margaret's order, and fixed on the gates of York, with a paper crown upon it, in derision of his pretended title.   His second son, the earl of Rutland, was taken prisoner, and barbarously murdered in cool blood by lord Clifford, in revenge of the death of his father, who had fallen in the battle of St. Alban's; and the captive earl of Salisbury was beheaded, with several other persons of distinction[1].   This inhuman practice, thus begun, was continued by both parties, from a vindictive spirit, which affected to conceal its enormity under the pretence of retaliation.

Dec. 30.

Elate with this important victory, Margaret advanced towards London where the earl of Warwick was left with the command of the Yorkists.   On the approach of the Lancastrians, that nobleman led out his army, reinforced by a strong body of Londoners, and gave battle to the queen at St. Alban's. Margaret was again victorious, by the treachery of one Lovelace, who commanded a considerable body of the Yorkists, and withdrew from the combat.   She had the pleasure of seeing the formidable Warwick fly before her, and of rescuing the king her husband from captivity.

A.D. 1461.

But the queen's triumph, though glorious, was of short duration, and not altogether complete.   Warwick was still in possession of London, on which she made an unsuccessful attempt; and Edward, earl of March, eldest son of the late duke of York, having gained an advantage over the Lancastrians at Mortimer's Cross, near Hereford, approached her from the other side, and was soon in a condition to give her battle with a superior force.

---

[1] Holinshed.—Grafton.—*Contin. Hist. Croyland.*

She was sensible of her danger, in such a situation, and retreated with her army to the North; while Edward entered the capital amidst the acclamations of the citizens, and immediately opened a new scene to his party.

This young prince, who was remarkable for the beauty of his person, for his bravery, his activity, his affability, and every popular quality, found himself so high in public favour, that, instead of confining himself within those narrow limits which had been found by experience so prejudicial to his father's cause, he determined to assume the name and dignity of king, to insist openly on his claim, and thenceforth to treat the opposite party as traitors and rebels to his lawful authority. But a national consent, or the appearance of it at least, seemed necessary to precede so bold a measure; and for this purpose, as it might have been hazardous to convene a parliament, the populace were assembled in St. John's Fields. When the bishop of Exeter had recommended the claim of Edward, and inveighed against the tyranny and usurpation of the house of Lancaster, the people were asked whether they would have Henry or Edward for their king. They instantly exclaimed, "Edward of York!" This popular election was ratified by an assembly of nobles both spiritual and temporal; and the youth was proclaimed under the title of king Edward IV [1].

March 1.

Edward, who was then in his nineteenth year, was of a temper well fitted to make his way through such a scene of war, havoc, and devastation, as was presented before him. He was not only bold, active, and enterprising, but his hardness of heart, and severity of character, rendered him impregnable to all those movements of compassion which might relax his vigour in the prosecution of the most bloody designs upon his enemies. Hence the scaffold, as well as the field, during this reign, incessantly smoked with the noblest blood of England. The animosity between the contending families had now become implacable; and the nation, divided in its affections, took different symbols of party. The adherents of the house of Lancaster chose, as their mark of distinction, the *Red Rose;* those of York assumed the *White:* and these civil wars were thus known over Europe by the name of the "Quarrel between the *Two Roses.*"

Queen Margaret, as I have observed, had retired to the North. There, such multitudes flocked to her standard, that she was

---

[1] Whethamstede.—Hall.—Stow.

soon furnished with an army of sixty thousand men.   The king
and the earl of Warwick hastened, with above forty thousand,
March to check her progress.   The two armies met at Towton,
29.   and a fierce and bloody battle ensued.   The bow, then
commonly used, was soon laid aside, and the sword decided the
combat, which terminated in a total victory on the side of the
Yorkists.   Edward issued orders to give no quarter; and his
routed enemies were pursued as far as Tadcaster, with great
bloodshed and confusion.   Above thirty-six thousand men are
said to have fallen in the battle and pursuit   Henry and Margaret had remained at York during the action; but learning the
defeat of their army, and being sensible that no place in England could now afford them shelter, they fled with great precipitation into Scotland [1].

I must here say a few words of the state of that country.
The Scots, notwithstanding the animosity between the two
nations, had never made any vigorous attempts to take advantage either of the wars which England caried on with France,
or of the civil commotions which arose from the competition for
the crown.   James I., who had been long a prisoner in England,
and had received his education there (as I have had occasion to
notice), avoided all hostilities with foreign nations.   He was
more laudably employed in civilizing his subjects, and training
them to the salutary restraints of law and justice.   After the
murder of this excellent prince, whose maxims and manners
were too refined for the people whom he had to govern, the
minority of his son James II., and the distractions with which it
was attended, prevented the Scots from molesting England.
But when the quarrel between the houses of York and Lancaster had become incurable, unless by the extinction of one of
the parties, James, who had now risen to manhood, was tempted
to make use of that opportunity, in the hope of recovering those
places which the English had conquered from his ancestors.
He invested the castle of Roxburgh, and had provided himself
with some pieces of cannon in order to forward the siege; but
one of them unhappily bursting, as he was firing it, put an end
to his life.   His son James III. was yet a minor; and the disturbances common to minorities ensued in the government.   The
queen-dowager, Anne of Gueldres, aspired to the regency; the
house of Douglas opposed her pretensions: so that the queen of
England, when she arrived in Scotland, found there a people

---

[1] Whethamstede. — Hall.

little less divided by faction than those from whom she had fled.

The Scottish council, however, agreed to assist Margaret, on her offering to deliver up to them the important fortress of Berwick, and to contract her son in marriage with a sister of their young king. With her northern auxiliaries and A.D. some succours from France, she ventured once more to 1464. take the field, and to make an inroad into England. But, at Hexham, she was attacked by lord Montacute, brother to the earl of Warwick, who totally routed her motley army. All the nobles who were spared in the field suffered on the scaffold [1].

The fate of the unfortunate royal family, after this overthrow, was equally singular and affecting. Margaret fled with her son into a forest, where she endeavoured to conceal herself, but was beset during the darkness of the night by robbers, who despoiled her of her jewels, and treated her with the utmost indignity. She made her escape, however, while they were quarrelling about the booty; and wandered some time with her son in the most unfrequented thickets, nearly exhausted with hunger and fatigue, and ready to sink beneath the load of terror and affliction. In this wretched condition she was met by a robber with his sword drawn, and seeing no means of escape, she suddenly embraced the bold resolution of trusting entirely to his faith and generosity. " Approach, my friend !"—cried she, presenting to him the young prince—" to you I commit the safety of your king's son." Struck with the singularity of the event, and charmed with the confidence reposed in him, the robber became her protector. By his favour she was concealed in the forest till she found an opportunity of escaping into Flanders; whence she passed to her father in Lorrain, where she lived several years in privacy and retirement [3]. Henry was less fortunate in finding the means of escape. He lay concealed during twelve months in Lancashire; but was at last discovered, de- A. D. livered up to Edward, and thrown into the Tower [2].   1465.

The youthful monarch, having thus triumphed over his adversaries, resigned himself freely to those pleasures and amusements which his rank, his time of life, and his natural disposition, no less turned for love than war, invited him to enjoy. The cruel and unrelenting Edward lived in the most familiar and social manner with his subjects. He was the peculiar favourite of the

---

[1] Hall—Stow.   [2] Monstrelet, vol. iii.
[3] Id. Ibid.—Stow.

young and gay of both sexes; and the elegance of his person, as well as the gallantry of his address, which even in the humblest condition would have rendered him acceptable to the fair, facilitated all his applications for their favour. But it is difficult to confine the ruling passion within the bounds of prudence. The amorous and ardent spirit of Edward led him into a snare, which endangered his repose and the stability of his throne.

This prince, while in the height of his dissipation, had resolved to marry, in order to secure his throne by issue, as well as by alliances: and he had cast his eyes on Bona of Savoy, sister to the queen of France. The negociation was committed to the earl of Warwick; the proposals were accepted, and the treaty was concluded. Meanwhile the charms of Elizabeth, the widow of sir John Grey of Groby, had inflamed the amorous heart of Edward. Her husband had been slain, fighting on the side of the house of Lancaster, and his estate confiscated; and when the king came accidentally, after a hunting party, to the house of her father, sir Richard Wideville, she threw herself at his feet, and entreated him to take pity on her impoverished and helpless children.

The sight of so much beauty in distress strongly affected the susceptible Edward. Love insensibly stole into his heart, under the disguise of compassion. He raised the fair suppliant from the ground with assurances of favour; and as his passion was increased by the winning conversation of Elizabeth, he soon found himself reduced to that posture and style of solicitation which had been so lately hers. But all his entreaties were fruitless: she obstinately refused to gratify his passion: and the young and gallant monarch found for once a virtue which his fondest assiduities could not bend. Inflamed by opposition, and filled with veneration for such honourable sentiments, Edward lost sight of all but love. He offered to share his throne, as well as his heart, with the woman whose beauty of person, and dignity of character, seemed so well to entitle her to both: and the marriage was privately celebrated at her father's seat in Northamptonshire [1].

The earl of Warwick no sooner received intelligence of the king's marriage than he returned from France, inflamed with rage and indignation, at being employed in a deceitful treaty, and kept a stranger to the intentions of the prince, who owed

[1] Hall.—Grafton.

every thing to his friendship. The king was sensible that the earl had been ill used; but his pride, or false shame, prevented him from making an apology, or attempting to soothe the incensed peer. The advancement of the queen's relatives to offices of power and trust, to the exclusion of those of Warwick, whom she regarded as her mortal enemy, heightened his discontent, and made him resolve to ruin the king he had made.

In order to effect his purpose, the earl drew over to his interest the king's brother George, duke of Clarence, by offering him in marriage his eldest daughter, co-heiress of his immense fortune. Many of the ancient nobility envied the sudden growth of the Widevilles. They associated themselves with Warwick, who finding his own name insufficient, and being chased into France, after some unsuccessful struggles, entered into a league with queen Margaret, formerly his most determined enemy. A.D. On his return to England, he was joined by the whole 1470. body of Lancastrians. Both parties now prepared for a general decision by arms; but Edward finding himself betrayed by the marquis of Montacute, and suspicious of other noblemen, who pretended to support his title, suddenly abandoned his army, and fled to Holland. Henry VI. was taken from his confinement, and placed once more upon the English throne; and a parliament, called under the influence of Warwick, Oct. 6. declared Edward IV. an usurper [1].

But this revolution was only the effect of the giddiness of faction. Warwick was no sooner at the helm of government, than his popularity began to decline, though he appears to have been guilty of no unpopular act; so fugitive a thing is public favour! The young king was emboldened to return. A.D. He landed at Ravenspur, where Henry IV. had disem- 1471. barked on a similar occasion; and although he brought with him only two thousand men, he soon found himself in a condition to face the earl of Warwick. The gates of London being opened to him, he became at once master of the capital and of the person of his rival Henry, doomed to be the perpetual sport of fortune. Without waiting the return of queen Margaret, whose presence would have been of great service to her party, the earl of Warwick found himself obliged, by the rapid progress of Edward, whom the fickle Clarence had joined with twelve thousand men, to hazard a general engagement. The battle April 14. was fought with great obstinacy on both sides. The two

---

[1] Stow.—Hall.

armies, in imitation of their leaders, displayed uncommon acts of valour, and the contest for victory remained long undecided; but an accident threw at last the balance on the side of the Yorkists. Edward's cognizance was a sun, that of Warwick was a star with rays; and the mistiness of the morning rendering it difficult to distinguish them, a body of the Lancastrians were attacked by their friends, and driven off the field. Warwick did all that experience, conduct, or valour, could suggest, to repair the mistake, but in vain. He had engaged on foot that day, contrary to his usual practice, in order to show his troops that he was resolved to share every danger with them; and now, sensible that all was lost, unless a change of fortune could be wrought by some extraordinary effort, he rushed into the midst of the engagement, and fell covered with wounds. His brother the marquis underwent the same fate; and a great slaughter attended the pursuit[1].

Queen Margaret, and her son Edward, now in his eighteenth year, landed at Weymouth the same day on which that decisive battle was fought. She had hitherto sustained the shocks of fortune with surprising fortitude; but when she received intelligence of her husband's captivity, and of the defeat and death of the earl of Warwick, her courage failed her, and she took sanctuary in the abbey of Beaulieu. Encouraged, however, by the appearance of the earl of Pembroke, and several other noblemen, who exhorted her still to hope for success, she resumed her former spirit, and determined to assert to the last her husband's claim to the crown. She accordingly put herself once more at the head of the army, which increased in every day's march; but the ardent and expeditious Edward overtook her at Tewkesbury, on the banks of the Severn, where the Lancastrians were totally routed. Margaret and her son were taken prisoners, and brought to the king, who asked the prince, in an imperious tone, how he dared to invade his dominions? "I came hither," replied the undaunted youth, more mindful of his high birth than his present fortune, "to revenge my father's wrongs, and rescue my just inheritance out of your hands." Incensed at his freedom, instead of admiring the boldness of his spirit, the ungenerous Edward barbarously struck him on the face with his gauntlet; and the dukes of Clarence and Gloucester, lord Hastings, and sir Thomas Grey, taking this blow as a signal for farther violence, hurried the prince aside, and instantly

---

[1] Grafton.—*Contin. Hist. Croyland.*—*Mémoires de* Phil. de Comines, liv. iii.

dispatched him with their daggers [1].　Margaret was thrown into the Tower, where her husband Henry had recently expired.　It was pretended that he died of grief; but there is little doubt of his having been murdered.

The hopes of the house of Lancaster being thus extinguished, by the death of every legitimate prince of that family, Edward, who had no longer any enemy that could give him anxiety or alarm, was encouraged to resume his habits of pleasure and amusement; and he recovered, by his gay humour and his easy familiar manners, that popularity which must have been in some degree impaired by the cruelties exercised upon his enemies. The example also of his jovial festivity served to abate the acrimony of faction among his subjects, and to restore the social disposition which had been so long interrupted between the opposite parties.　But although Edward was fond of pleasure, he was not deaf to the calls of ambition; and a projected invasion of France, in order to recover the dominions lost under his predecessor, tended to increase his popularity.

The project of a French war has always proved the sure means of uniting the people of England, and of making the members of parliament open their purses.　Edward received a considerable supply, and passed over to Calais with fifteen hundred men at arms, and fifteen thousand archers, besides other troops.　He was attended by his chief nobility, who, animated by former successes, were eager to appear once more on the theatre of honour.　But their ardour was damped when they found, on entering the French territories, that their king's ally, the duke of Burgundy, did not bring the smallest assistance. Transported by his fervid spirit, that prince had carried his troops to the frontier of Germany, where they were employed in hostilities against the duke of Lorrain.　Louis XI., however, alarmed at the presence of so warlike and powerful a monarch as Edward, proposed an accommodation; and a treaty was concluded, by which he agreed to pay the king of England immediately seventy-five thousand crowns, and fifty thousand crowns a-year during their joint lives [2].

A.D. 1475.

This treaty reflected little honour on either of the monarchs. It discovered the imprudence of the one, and the pusillanimity of the other.　But as Louis made interest the sole test of his honour, he thought he had overreached Edward, by sending him out of France on such easy terms.　The most honourable article

---

[1] Hall.—Holinshed.　　　　[2] Rymer, vol. xii.—Phil. de Comines, liv. iv.

on the side of Louis was the stipulation for the liberty of queen Margaret. He paid fifty thousand crowns for her ransom; and this princess, who, in active scenes of life, had experienced so remarkably the vicissitudes of fortune, passed the remainder of her days in tranquillity and privacy. Margaret seems not to have possessed the virtues or to have been subject to the weaknesses of her sex; and she was as much tainted with the ferocity, as endowed with the courage, of the age in which she lived.

The dark and unrelenting disposition of Richard, duke of Gloucester, the future scourge of England, began more particularly to discover itself after Edward's return from France. The duke of Clarence, by his service in deserting Warwick, had not been able to regain the king's friendship, which he had forfeited by his former confederacy with that nobleman. He had also the misfortune to offend his brother Gloucester, who secretly conspired his ruin. Several of his friends were accused and put to death, under frivolous pretences, in hopes that his resentment would betray him into measures which might furnish a ground of impeachment. He fell into the snare. Instead of securing his own life against the present danger by silence and reserve, he was open and loud in asserting the innocence of his friends, and in exclaiming against the iniquity of their prosecutors. The A.D. king ordered him to be committed to the Tower; and he 1478. was sentenced to die by the house of peers, the supreme tribunal of the nation, for arraigning public justice, by maintaining the innocence of men who had been condemned in courts of judicature. The only favour which the king granted him was the choice of his death; and he was privately drowned in a butt of malmsey [1]; a whimsical choice, which leads us to suppose that he was passionately fond of that liquor.

The remaining part of Edward's reign was distinguished by no remarkable event. He relapsed into indolence and pleasure, from which he was again roused by the prospect of a French war. While he was making preparations with that view, he was seized April 9, with a violent distemper, of which he died in the forty-1483. first year of his age. He was a prince of greater vigour than prudence, and consequently less fitted to prevent ills by wise precautions, than to remedy them after they had taken place. As a man he possessed many accomplishments: his virtues were few, his vices were numerous.

He left two sons; namely, Edward V. then in his thirteenth

---

[1] Fabian.—Comines.—Holinshed.

year, and Richard, duke of York, in his ninth.   The duke of
Gloucester, their uncle, soon took them out of the hands of their
reluctant mother, who seemed to forebode their unhappy fate.
He easily procured the appointment of protector ; and his eye
was fixed upon the throne, though not only the sons of Edward,
but those of the duke of Clarence, stood between him and that
pre-eminence.

An attempt to exclude or destroy so many persons possessed
of a preferable right may seem equally imprudent and impracticable.   But a man like Richard, who had abandoned all principles of honour and humanity, was soon carried, by his predominant passion, beyond the reach of fear or precaution.   He
ordered earl Rivers, the queen's brother, sir Richard Grey, her
son by her former husband, and sir Thomas Vaughan, to be
thrown into prison, and put to death, without any form of trial.
His next step was to draw into his views the duke of Buckingham and lord Hastings.   With one he succeeded ; but the other
remained firm in his allegiance to the children of Edward.   His
death was therefore resolved upon ; and for that purpose a
council was summoned in the Tower, whither Hastings, suspecting
no harm, repaired without hesitation.

Richard, on taking his place at the council-board, appeared in
the easiest and most facetious humour imaginable ; but making
a pretence soon after to retire, as if called away by urgent business, he returned knitting his brows, grinding his teeth, and exhibiting, by frequent change of countenance, symptoms of in-
ward perturbation. A general silence ensued, every one dreading
some terrible catastrophe, and all gazing with looks of doubt and
anxiety upon each other.   Richard at last relieved them from
their awful suspense.   " What punishment do they deserve,"
said he, " who have conspired against my life ?"—" The death
of traitors !" replied lord Hastings.   " These traitors," cried
Richard, " are the sorceress, my brother's wife, and that witch
Shore, his mistress, with their associates.   See to what a condition they have reduced me by their spells and incantations!"
uncovering his shrivelled and decayed arm. The amazement of
the council was increased, it being well known that this infirmity
had attended him from his childhood ; and lord Hastings, who
since Edward's death had engaged in an intrigue with Jane
Shore, was naturally alarmed at such an accusation.   " Certainly, my lord," said he, with some hesitation, " if they are
guilty of such a crime, they deserve punishment."—" And do
you," exclaimed Richard, " reply to me with your *ifs?* You

know their guilt: you are yourself a traitor, and the chief abettor of the witch Shore; and I swear by St. Paul, that I will not dine until your head be brought to me!" He struck the table with his hand: armed men rushed in at the signal: Hastings was seized, and instantly beheaded on a log of wood, which accidentally lay in the court-yard of the Tower[1].

The protector then ordered lord Stanley, the archbishop of York, the bishop of Ely, and other counsellors of whom he was suspicious, to be committed to the Tower; and to carry on the farce of accusations, he commanded the goods of Jane Shore to be seized, and summoned her to answer before the council for sorcery and witchcraft. But as beauty was her only witchcraft, and conversation her most dangerous spell, no proofs were produced against her which could be received even in that ignorant age. Her persecution, however, did not end here. Though framed for virtue, she had proved unable to resist temptation, and left her husband, a goldsmith in Lombard-street, to live with Edward. But, while seduced from her fidelity by this gay and amorous monarch, she still made herself respectable by her remaining virtues. She never sold her influence. Her good offices, the genuine dictates of her heart, waited not the solicitation of presents or the hopes of reciprocal benefit; to protect the oppressed, and relieve the indigent, were her highest pleasures. Yet all her amiable qualities could not save her from the bitterness of shame, imposed upon her by a barbarous tyrant. Richard ordered her to be tried, in the spiritual court, for adultery. The charge was too notorious to be denied. She pleaded guilty, and was condemned to do public penance in a white sheet at St. Paul's, after walking bare-footed through the city. Her subsequent life was long and wretched. She experienced in old age and poverty the ingratitude of those courtiers whom she had raised into favour. Not one of the many whom she had obliged had the humanity to bring her consolation or relief. Her frailties as a woman, amidst a court inured to the most atrocious crimes, were thought sufficient to justify all violations of friendship towards her, and all neglect of former obligations; and she was permitted to languish out her days in solitude and want[2].

So many acts of violence, exercised against the relatives and friends of the late king, prognosticated the severest fate to his defenceless children; and after the murder of Hastings, Richard

[1] *Contin. Hist. Croyland.*—Sir T. More's *Hist. of Edward V.*
[2] *Contin. Hist. Croyland.*—Sir T. More.

no longer concealed his intention of usurping the crown.   As a
colour to his pretensions, he not only maintained that his two
nephews were illegitimate, but also his two brothers, Edward
IV. and the duke of Clarence : that his mother had admitted
different lovers into her bed, who were the fathers of these
children ; that their resemblance to those gallants was a sufficient
proof of their spurious birth ; and that he alone of all her sons,
as appeared by his features, was the true offspring of the duke
of York.   The place chosen for promulgating this foul and im-
pudent assertion was the pulpit, before a large congregation, and
in Richard's presence.   Dr. Shaw, a sycophant entirely at his
devotion, was appointed to preach in St. Paul's cathedral ; and
having chosen for his text, from Scripture, " Bastard slips shall
not thrive !" he enlarged on every circumstance that could dis-
credit the birth of Edward IV., the duke of Clarence, and their
children.   He then broke out into a panegyric on the duke of
Gloucester, exclaiming, " It is he who carries in his face, in his
soul, the image of virtue, and the marks of a true descent !"
And it was expected, as soon as the doctor had pronounced these
words, that the audience would cry out, " God save king
Richard !"——a salutation which would immediately have been
construed into a popular consent, and interpreted to be the voice
of the nation.   But the audience kept a profound silence, and
disappointed both the protector and his preacher [1].

Richard, however, had gone too far to recede from his criminal
and ambitious purpose.   Another place was chosen for a
popular harangue ; a place where a popular speaker never fails
to persuade, and where a voice may be obtained for any measure,
however atrocious or absurd.   The citizens of London, with the
rabble at their heels, were assembled at Guildhall, where the
duke of Buckingham addressed them in an eloquent harangue,
setting forth the title and virtues of the protector ; and " God
save king Richard !" was at last returned by the mob.   The
sentiments of the nation were now thought sufficiently declared.
The voice of the people was the voice of God !   Richard was
prevailed upon, though with seeming reluctance, to accept the
crown ; but not before a party of the lords and commons had
invited him to assume the sovereignty, on pretence of the ille-
gality of his brother's marriage with Elizabeth, as a former wife
(lady Eleanor Butler) was at that time living, and of the incapa-

---

[1] Sir T. More.

city to which the attainder of the duke of Clarence subjected his children.

This farce was soon followed by a scene truly tragical—the murder of the two young princes. Richard gave orders to sir Robert Brackenbury, constable of the Tower, to put his nephews to death ; but that gentleman refused to bear any part in the infamous office. The usurper then sent for sir James Tyrrel, who promised obedience, and the government of the Tower was given him for one night. He chose three associates, whom he employed to execute his barbarous commission, and conducted them, about midnight, to the door of the chamber where the princes were sleeping. The ruffians smothered them with bolsters and pillows, and afterwards showed their naked bodies to Tyrrel, who ordered them to be buried at the foot of the stair-case, under a heap of stones[1]. These circumstances were confessed by the perpetrators in the following reign.

Richard, after these cruelties, endeavoured to gain by favours those whom he thought could give stability to his throne. Several noblemen received new honours ; and lord Stanley was set at liberty, and made steward of the household. But Richard's danger arose from a quarter where he least expected it. The duke of Buckingham did not think himself sufficiently rewarded for his services in promoting the usurpation : he observed the general detestation of Richard ; and by the advice of Morton, bishop of Ely, he turned his eyes towards the young earl of Richmond, then resident in Bretagne, as the only person

---

[1] Sir T. More's *Hist.*—A bold attempt has been made by an ingenious but whimsical writer, to invalidate the particulars of this relation, and even to bring into question the fact it tends to establish. But in answer to the *Historic Doubts* of Mr. Walpole, it will be sufficient to reply, in the words of the profound and sagacious Hume, that, from the singular magnanimity, probity, and judgment of sir Thomas More, his narrative and evidence are beyond all exception ; that the testimony of no historian, either of ancient or modern times, can possibly have more weight ; that he may justly be esteemed a contemporary with regard to the murder of the two princes : for although he was not five years of age when that event happened, he lived and was educated among the persons concerned in the principal transactions during the administration of Richard III. And it is plain from his narrative itself, which is often extremely circumstantial, that he had the particulars from eye-witnesses themselves. This authority, therefore, is irresistible, and "*sufficient* to *overbalance* a hundred *little doubts*, and *scruples*, and *objections*." (*Hist. of England*, vol. iii. note M.) All contemporary writers, both English and foreign, charge Richard directly or indirectly, with the murder of his nephews. Comines openly accuses him of it (*Mem.* liv. vi. chap. ix.), and Fabian tells us that, as soon as Richard accepted the sovereignty, " King Edward V., and his brother, the duke of York, *were put under surer keeping* in the Tower, in *such wise* that they *never after came abroad.*" (*Chron.* 225.) Comines supports his accusation with a strong circumstance. The court of France, he tells us, was so much struck with horror at Richard's treason and usurpation, that an audience was refused to his ambassador.

capable of freeing the nation from the tyranny under which it groaned.

Henry, earl of Richmond, was grandson of Sir Owen Tudor, and Catharine of France. By his mother he was descended from John of Gaunt, duke of Lancaster, and was the only remaining branch of that family which had so long contended for the crown. In order to strengthen his interest, a match was concerted between him and Elizabeth, eldest daughter of Edward IV. Money was sent over to him, for the purpose of levying foreign troops; and the queen-dowager promised to join him, on his first appearance, with all the friends and partisans of her family.

But so extensive a conspiracy, though laid on the solid foundations of good sense and sound policy, could not escape the jealous and vigilant eye of Richard. He soon received intelligence that his enemies, headed by the duke of Buckingham, were forming some design against him. The duke, unable to resist the force of Richard, was obliged to seek safety in retreat; he was discovered, condemned, and executed; and the other conspirators, who had taken arms in different parts of the kingdom, desisted from their attempts. The earl of Richmond appeared with an armament on the coast of England; but hearing of the fate of Buckingham, and the dispersion of his friends, he quickly retired [1].

Richard, thus triumphant in every quarter, and fortified by an unsuccessful attempt to dethrone him, ventured at last to summon a parliament; a measure which his multiplied crimes and flagrant usurpation, had hitherto induced him to decline. A.D. 1484. The parliament had no choice left but to recognise his authority, and acknowledge his right to the crown. His son Edward was created prince of Wales; and the king passed some popular laws, in order to reconcile the nation to his government.

Richard's other measures tended to the same object. His queen being now dead, he proposed by means of a papal dispensation to marry the princess Elizabeth, the true heiress of the crown. And strange as it may sound in the ears of civilized persons, the queen-dowager neither scrupled to agree to this alliance, which was very unusual in England, and regarded as incestuous, nor felt any horror at the thought of marrying her daughter to the murderer of her sons and her brother. But the

[1] Sir T. More.—*Contin. Hist. Croyland.*

earl of Richmond, alarmed at an alliance which might prove fatal to all his hopes, and encouraged by the English exiles, resolved upon a new invasion.   All men of probity and honour, he was assured, were desirous of preventing the sceptre from being A.D. any longer polluted by that bloody and faithless hand 1485. which held it.   In consequence of these representations, he set sail with about two thousand men, and landed at Milford Haven.   The Welsh, who considered him as their countryman, flocked to his standard ; and his cause immediately wore a favourable aspect.

Richard was alarmed on this occasion, but not intimidated, though he must have been conscious of his great unpopularity. Scarcely any nobleman was sincerely attached to his cause, except the duke of Norfolk ; and those who professed the greatest loyalty, secretly resolved to betray and abandon him.   Among these was lord Stanley, who raised a numerous body of his friends and retainers in Cheshire and Lancashire, but without openly declaring himself, his son being in the tyrant's power.   And although Henry had received private assurances of Stanley's friendly intentions, the troops on both sides knew not what to infer from his equivocal behaviour, when they met at Bosworth, in Leicestershire.

Aug. 23.   Soon after the battle began, lord Stanley appeared in the field, and declared for the earl of Richmond.   This measure had a proportional effect upon both armies ; it inspired unusual courage into Henry's soldiers ; it threw those of Richard into dismay and confusion.   The intrepid tyrant, now sensible of his desperate situation, cast his eye across the field ; and, descrying his rival at no great distance, attempted to decide the victory by a blow.   He killed with his own hand sir William Brandon, the earl's standard-bearer ; and he was within reach of Henry himself, who declined not the combat, when sir William Stanley broke in between them, and surrounded Richard with his troops.   Though overwhelmed by numbers, he still maintained the combat ; and at last sunk amidst heaps of slain [1].— A life so infamous, it has been said by Voltaire, and by Hume after him, did not merit so glorious a death ; but every man surely merits what his talents enable him to earn.   Richard was a blood-thirsty tyrant ; but he was brave, and he died as a brave man should, with his sword in his hand ; he was brave to the last.   It would, indeed, have been matter of regret had he

[1] *Contin. Hist. Croyland.*—Stow.—Fabian.

died in his bed, after disturbing so cruelly the repose of his fellow creatures; but his death was sufficiently violent to prevent his life from becoming an object of imitation.

This battle was entirely decisive; the king not only being slain, but his whole army routed and dispersed. The victorious troops, in a transport of joy, bestowed on their general the appellation of king; and " Long live Henry the Seventh!" resounded from all quarters, and was continued with repeated acclamations. Thus ended the race of the Plantagenets, who had filled the throne above three hundred and thirty years; and thus were the civil wars extinguished which had so long desolated the kingdom.

We must now return to the history of France.

LETTER LI.

Of the Affairs of France, from the Expulsion of the English by Charles VII. to the Invasion of Italy by Charles VIII. in 1494.

WHILE England, my dear Philip, was convulsed by civil wars, France was increasing both in power and dominion. Most of the great fiefs were united to the crown; the authority of the prince was raised to such a height, as enabled him to maintain law and order; a considerable military force was established, and the finances were able to support it. The means by which these changes were effected require your particular attention.

Charles VII. no sooner found himself in quiet possession of France, by the expulsion of the English, than he devoted himself to the cares of government: he endeavoured to re- A. D. pair the ravages of war by promoting the arts of peace, 1453. and to secure the tranquillity and good order of his kingdom by wise regulations. He established a regular army, instead of the troops required from the vassals of the crown, and levied a tax for its support. Besides this army, each village maintained a free archer, who was exempted from the king's tax; and it was in consequence of this exemption, otherwise peculiar to the nobility, that such a number of persons soon claimed the title of gentlemen, both by name and arms.

These politic measures were followed by the most important consequences. A force always at command, gave vigour to the royal authority; the possessors of fiefs being no longer called upon, had no longer any pretence of arming their followers, to disturb the peace of the state; so that the fedual polity rapidly declined in France, and Charles beheld himself at the head of the largest and best regulated kingdom in Europe.

But all the wisdom and generosity of this great monarch could not secure to him that happiness which he endeavoured to procure for his subjects. His son Louis revolted, and not only embittered his latter days with sorrow, but brought him to an untimely grave : for being informed that this prince intended to July 23, take him off by poison, he long abstained from all food, 1461. and literally died of hunger, that his unnatural son might not be guilty of parricide [1].

Louis XI., so much celebrated as a politician, and despised as a man, now succeeded to that crown, which he had traitorously attempted to seize, in prejudice to the best of kings and fathers. His leading object was the aggrandizement of the monarchy, by depressing the power of the nobles, and re-uniting the great fiefs to the crown. And as he knew that men of honour and character would not be concerned in attempts upon the rights and property of others, he immediately dismissed the respectable ministers who had ably and faithfully served his father, and selected from the lower classes of the people men of a disposition similar to his own—subtle, deceitful, unfeeling, and cruel. But craft may sometimes over-shoot its aim, especially when ac-
A.D. companied with rapacity. The nobles were alarmed;
1465. they entered into an association, and took arms to humble their oppressor. The king also took arms, and prepared to face them. A battle was fought, which decided nothing; and as Louis was more inclined to negociate than to fight, a peace was concluded on terms advantageous to the rebels, but which the perfidious tyrant never intended to fulfil. He took into favour many of those whom he had formerly disgraced; he detached from the confederacy the dukes of Bourbon and Bretagne, and prevailed upon an assembly of the states to annul those articles of the treaty which were most detrimental to his interest [2].

[1] Monstrelet.—Du Tillet.—Mezeray.
[2] By exerting all his power and address in influencing the election of the representatives, by bribing or over-awing the members, and by various changes which be artfully made in the form of their deliberations, Louis acquired such entire direction of the national assemblies, that from being the vigilant guardians of the privileges and property of the people, he rendered them tamely subservient, in protecting the

But although Louis thus artfully defeated a conspiracy that seemed to endanger his throne, his rapacity soon brought him into new troubles: he became the dupe of his own arti- A.D. fice, and had almost perished in his own snare. Philip 1467. the Good, duke of Burgundy, was succeeded in his extensive dominions by his son Charles the Bold. Charles had an antipathy against Louis; and what more alarmed that arch-politician, knew him better than any man in Europe. Both parties assembled forces, and the fate of one was expected to be decided; when the king, who hated coming to extremities, agreed to pay the duke thirty-six thousand crowns to defray his military expenses, and appointed a personal interview at Peronne in Picardy, then in the possession of Charles. The proposal was agreed to; and Louis went to the place of meeting accompanied only by a few domestics. By such an act of confidence he hoped to throw Charles off his guard, and take advantage, during the conferences, of that friendly temper which he had inspired; and to forward his negociation, he even commanded some of his emissaries to enter Liege, and persuade the inhabitants to revolt from the duke. By these arts, he thought himself sure of concluding an advantageous treaty. He was disappointed, however, in his aim. The duke indeed received him with exterior marks of friendship and respect, and seemed highly pleased at the confidence reposed in him by an adversary; but when intelligence arrived that the people of Liege had broken out into open rebellion at the instigation of the French, and had cut the garrison in pieces, Charles, in the first transports of his rage, ordered the king to be shut up in the castle of Peronne, and made him thoroughly sensible that he was a prisoner, at the mercy of his vassal.

In this predicament Louis had continued three days, when he again attempted to set his crooked policy at work, by distributing large sums among the duke's officers. The anger of Charles subsiding, he was induced to enter into a negociation with his prisoner, or rather to prescribe such terms as he thought proper, to a prince whose life and liberty were in his power. The most mortifying condition proposed was, that the king should march with him against Liege, and be active in the reduction of that place, which

most odious measures of his reign. (Phil. de Comines.) He first taught other modern princes the fatal art of becoming arbitrary, by corrupting the fountain of public liberty.

A.D. had revolted at his own request. Liege was reduced;
1468. and Louis, having thus fulfilled the purpose of his vassal, was permitted to depart, before the duke set fire to the
town[1]. This affair was treated with so much ridicule at Paris,
that all the magpies and jays were taught to cry, " Peronne!
Peronne!" a circumstance that proved fatal to many of them; for
the king, after his return, issued an edict for destroying all those
talkative birds, as unnecessary remembrancers of his disgrace[2].

The subsequent part of the reign of this monarch was one
continued scene of executions, wars, and negociations. He and
his infamous ministers divided the possessions of those whom
his tyranny had caused to rebel; his ministers themselves conspired against him; and the bishop of Verdun, and cardinal
Balue, men as wicked as himself, suffered those tortures which
they had invented for others. His brother Charles, who had
been always a thorn in his side, was taken off by poison; the
constable de St. Paul, the count of Armagnac, the dukes of
Alençon and Nemours, lost their heads on the scaffold[3].

With the ignominious but politic treaty by which Louis purchased the retreat of Edward IV., you are already acquainted.
He was always engaged, either in war or negociations, with his
natural enemy, the duke of Burgundy, till the death of that
A.D. prince, who fell at the battle of Nanci, in an unprovoked
1477. attempt to seize the duchy of Lorraine, after having previously exhausted the strength of his dominions, in an equally
unjust and inglorious effort to crush the rising liberties of Switzerland. This was a fortunate event for Louis. As the duke's
daughter Mary was the sole heiress of his extensive dominions,
the king proposed a marriage between this princess and his son
Charles, then only in his seventh year. In the mean time he
seized Burgundy as a male fief, and made himself master of
many of the late duke's towns and fortresses, by atrocious acts of
treachery and cruelty[4]. This was one mode of territorial acquisition, but surely not the most likely to promote a treaty of
marriage; the rapacity of this arch-politician, notwithstanding all
his penetration, once more betrayed him. The princess was
filled with disgust, and her Flemish subjects with detestation.

[1] Phil. de Com. liv. ii. chap. vii.—xiv.
[2] J. Troyes, *Hist. Secrete de Louis XI.*
[3] At the execution of the last-mentioned nobleman, the king ordered his two
sons, yet infants, to be placed beneath the scaffold, that their father's blood might
fall on their heads.—*Mezeray.*
[4] Phil. de Com. liv. v.—Du Clos, *Hist. de Louis XI.*

By their advice, she married the archduke Maximilian [1], son of the emperor Frederic III.; and hence arose new wars, which long desolated the Low Countries, and cherished an implacable animosity between the houses of France and Austria.

Louis, however, put a stop to hostilities by a truce; A.D. and though he could not boast of his success in arms, he 1480. retained Burgundy and some other provinces which he had seized. Anjou, Maine, Provence, and Bar, were soon after left to him by Charles, count of Maine, the last prince of the house of Anjou, who died without issue. He united to the crown Roussillon and Cerdagne, under pretence of mortgage, and the country of Boulogne by purchase. Thus, amidst all his crimes, and after all his struggles and all his blunders, he saw his kingdoms much enlarged, his subjects obedient, and his government firm. But he had only a glimpse of that agreeable prospect; for he was suddenly seized with a fit of apoplexy, which threw him into a lingering illness; and he expected death with all those horrors which a life of such complicated guilt deserved. It at last overtook him; but not before he had suffered Aug. 30, more severe tortures than any criminal punished during 1483. his reign [2].

[1] There is reason, however, to believe, that the heiress of Burgundy was influenced in her choice by other motives than those of policy; for we are informed by Philip de Comines, that, while her marriage with the dauphin was under deliberation, madame Hallouin, first lady of the bed-chamber to the princess, gave it as her opinion, " That there was more need of a man than a boy!" Admitting this to be the case, and the marriage with the dauphin impracticable, Louis might still have prevented the dominions of Burgundy from being conveyed to a rival power, by favouring the suit of the count of Angoulême, (a prince of the blood royal of France, and father of Francis I.) towards whom the princess Mary had indicated her good will. But the rapacious disposition and intriguing spirit of the French monarch, which obscured his naturally clear and sound understanding, with his jealous dread of so highly exalting a subject, made him discourage that alliance, and pursue a line of insidious policy, which contributed, eventually, to raise up in the house of Austria a rival power that thwarted the measures, opposed the arms, and checked, during two centuries, the progress of the successors of a prince, who first united the interior force of France, and established it on such a footing as to render it formidable to the rest of Europe.

[2] Phil. de Com. liv. vi. chap. xii.—Du Clos.—The picture drawn by these two writers of the last scene of this monarch's life, in contrast with his cruelties, is deeply shaded with horror. He put to death, we are told, more than four thousand persons, by different kinds of tortures, and without any form of trial. He was frequently present at their execution, in beholding which he seemed to enjoy a barbarous satisfaction or triumph. Many of the nobility were, by his order, confined in iron cages, invented by the ministers of his tyranny, and carried about like wild beasts; while others were loaded with heavy and galling fetters, with a ring of a particular construction for the feet, called the *King's Nets*. In consequense of these barbarities, and a dread of future punishment, he became greatly afraid of death; and, during his illness, suspicious of every one around him, not excepting his own son, his daughter, and his son-in-law, the lord Beaujeu, afterwards duke of Bourbon; though in the two last he reposed more confidence than in all the others. After often shifting his residence and his domestics, under pretence that nature delights in change, he took up his abode at the castle of Plessiz-les-Tours, which he ordered

The character of Louis XI. is one of the most complicated in history. He obtained the end which he proposed by his policy, but at the expense of his peace and reputation. His life was a jumble of crimes and contradictions. Absolute without dignity; popular (because he humbled the great), without generosity; unjust by system, yet zealous for the administration of justice; living in open violation of the first principles of morals, but resigning himself to the most ridiculous superstitions; the tyrant of his subjects, and the timid slave of his physicians, he debased royalty at the same time that he strengthened it. Yet this prince, who rendered religion contemptible and royalty disgraceful, assumed the title of *Majesty* and *Most Christian*, since given to his successors, and formerly not claimed by the kings of France.

He was succeeded by his son Charles VIII., a young prince, ill educated, rash, and incapable of application. By a law of Charles the Wise, the French kings were of age at the beginning of their fourteenth year. The new king had reached that age; but he was a minor by nature, long after he ceased to be so by law. Louis had wisely entrusted the government, during the youth of the king, to his daughter Anne, lady of Beaujeu, a woman of great spirit and capacity. The administration, however, was disputed by the duke of Orléans, first prince of the blood (afterwards the celebrated Louis XII.), who, proving unsuccessful in his intrigues, betook himself to arms, and entered A.D. into a league with the duke of Bretagne and the arch- 1488. duke Maximilian. The Bretons were defeated in the battle of St. Aubin, and the duke of Orléans was taken prisoner [1].

to be encompassed with large bars of iron, in the form of a grate, with four watch-towers of iron at the four corners of the building. The grates were without the wall, on the farther side of the ditch, and went to the bottom; spikes of iron, set as thick as possible, were fastened into the wall; and cross-bowmen were placed in the ditches and in the watch-towers, to shoot at any man who dared to approach the castle till the opening of the gate. The gate was never opened, nor the draw-bridge let down, before eight in the morning, when the courtiers were permitted to enter. Through the day the captains were ordered to guard their several posts, with a main guard in the middle of the court, as in a town closely besieged. Nor was this all. Every secret of medicine, every allurement of sensuality, and every sacrifice of superstition, were exhausted in order to protract the tyrant's miserable existence, and set at a distance the ills he feared. The pope sent him the vest which St. Peter wore when he said mass; the sacred phial was brought from Rheims to re-anoint him; and he invited a holy hermit from Calabria, at whose feet he kneeled, and whose intercession with Heaven he attempted to purchase, by building him two convents. The most beautiful country girls were procured to dance around him to the sound of music: he paid his physician, whom he feared, the enormous sum of ten thousand crowns a month; and the blood of infants is said to have been spilled with a view of softening the acrimony of his scorbutic humours.

[1] Henault, tome i.—Could the duke of Orléans have flattered the passion of Anne of Beaujeu, he might, if we believe Brantome, not only have escaped this misfortune, but have shared the administration.

The death of the Breton duke, which happened soon after this defeat, threw the affairs of the duchy into the utmost confusion, and seemed to threaten the state with final subjection. It was the only great fief which now remained disunited from the crown of France; and as the duke had died without male heirs, some antiquated claims to its dominion were revived by Charles VIII. But force is the best claim between princes : of that Charles was possessed ; and the conquest of the territory seemed inevitable, unless some foreign power should strenuously interpose.

The prince to whom the distressed Bretons looked up for aid, was Henry VII. of England, who was highly interested in preventing the reduction of their country, as well as bound by ties of gratitude to return that protection to the young duchess, which had been generously yielded to him by her father. But the parsimonious temper of Henry, which disinclined him to warlike enterprises and expeditions, prevented him from sending them any effectual support. They therefore applied to Maximilian of Austria, now king of the Romans, (whose wife, Mary of Burgundy, had lately died,) and offered him their duchess in marriage. The proposal was readily accepted : the A.D. nuptials were celebrated by proxy; and the duchess 1489. of Bretagne assumed the august title of queen of the Romans. But this honour was all she gained by her marriage : for Maximilian, destitute of money and troops, and embarrassed by the continual revolts of the Flemings, was not able to send any succours to his consort. The French made considerable progress ; yet the conquest of the duchy seemed still so distant, and accompanied with so many difficulties, that the court of France changed its measures, and, by a master-stroke in policy, astonished all Europe.

Charles VIII. had been affianced to Margaret, daughter of Maximilian. Though too young for the nuptial union, she had been sent to Paris to be educated, and at this time bore the title of queen of France. Engagements so solemnly formed could not easily be set aside; but the marriage of Charles with the duchess of Bretagne seemed necessary to re-annex that important fief to the crown ; and, as a yet stronger motive for such alliance, the union of Maximilian with this princess seemed destructive to the grandeur, and even to the security, of the French monarchy. It was at length concluded, that all inconveniences would best be obviated by the dissolution of the two marriages, which had been celebrated, but not consummated, and the espousal of the duchess to the king of France.

The measures, by which the French ministry carried this delicate scheme into execution, were wise and politic. While they pressed Bretagne with all the violence of war, they secretly negociated with persons of the greatest influence in the duchy, representing to them that the happiest event, which in their present situation could befall the Bretons, would be a peace with France, though purchased by a final subjection to that monarchy. These arguments had some weight with the barons; but the grand difficulty was, how to obtain the consent of the duchess, who had fixed her affections on Maximilian. In order to subdue her obstinacy, the duke of Orléans was set at liberty; and though formerly her suitor, and favoured with her smile, he now zealously employed all his interest in favour of the king. By his advice, Charles advanced with a powerful army to Rennes, at that time the residence of the duchess. Finding A.D. herself without resource, she opened the gates of the 1491. city, and agreed to the proffered marriage, which was soon after solemnised, and was justly considered as a most fortunate event [1].

The success of Charles in this negociation was the most sensible mortification to the king of the Romans. He was deprived of a considerable territory which he thought he had acquired, and of an accomplished princess, whom he had espoused: he was affronted in the person of his daughter Margaret, who was sent back to him, after she had been treated, during seven years, as queen of France; and he had reason to reproach himself with his own supine security, in neglecting the consummation of his marriage, which was easily practicable for him, and would have rendered the tie indissoluble. The king of England had also reason to accuse himself of misconduct, with regard to this important transaction; for, although the affair terminated in a manner which he could not precisely foresee, his negligence in leaving his most useful ally so long exposed to the invasion of a superior power, could not but appear, on reflection, the result of timid caution, and narrow politics: and, as Henry valued himself on his extensive foresight and sound judgment, the triumph obtained over him by such a youth as Charles, roused his indignation, and prompted him to seek vengeance, after all remedy

---

[1] Mezeray.—Henault.—Bacon's *Hist. of Hen. VII.*

for his miscarriage had become impracticable. He accordingly entered into a league with the king of the Romans, and Ferdinand of Spain, who had also interested himself in this affair: he obtained liberal supplies from his parliament, and he A.D. landed in France with one of the largest and best-appointed 1492. armies that had ever been transported from England [1].

But Charles and his ministers found means to divert the impending storm, by dissolving the confederacy. They drew the Spanish prince into a separate treaty, by restoring the A.D. counties of Roussillon and Cerdagne. As they knew 1493. that Henry's ruling passion was the love of money, he was bought off by the treaty of Estaples, which I shall have occasion to mention in the account of his reign; and the forbearance of Maximilian was procured by the restitution of Artois and other provinces which he had ceded as the dowry of his daughter.

The king's motives for purchasing peace at so high a price were not those of indolence or timidity, but of ambition and youthful ardour. He had determined to vindicate his title to the kingdom of Naples, supposed to descend to him from the second house of Anjou, which ended in the count of Maine, who had bequeathed all his rights and possessions to the crown of France. This project had long engaged the mind of Charles; but, in order to carry it effectually into execution, it was neces- A.D. sary to be at peace with his neighbours; and that being 1494. now secured, he set out for Italy with as little concern as if it had been a mere journey of pleasure.

But, before I speak of the success of that expedition, and the wars in which it involved Europe, several important events merit your notice: particularly the reduction of Constantinople by the Turks, and the expulsion of the Moors from Spain.

LETTER LII.

Of the Progress of the Turks, and the Fall of the Greek Empire.

You have already seen, my dear Philip, the weakness of the empire of Constantinople at the time of the crusades: you have seen the imperial city sacked, and the government seized, by

---

[1] Bacon's *Hist. of Hen. VII.*

the champions of the cross.   The Greeks recovered their empire from the Franks in 1261, but in a mangled and impoverished condition.   It continued in the same weak state.   The monastic passion seemed to have obscured the rays of common sense. Andronicus, son of Michael Palæologus, who had restored the Greek empire, allowed himself to be persuaded, that, as God was his protector, all military force was unnecessary ; and the superstitious Greeks, regardless of danger, employed themselves in disputing about the transfiguration of Jesus Christ, when they should have been studying the art of war, and training themselves to military discipline.   One half of the empire pretended, that the light upon Mount Tabor had been from all eternity ; and the other half affirmed, that it was produced by God only for the purpose of transfiguration.

In the mean time, the Turks, whose force had been broken by the Mogul Tartars, were strengthening themselves near the sea of Marmora, and soon over-ran Thrace.   Othman, from whom the present soltans are descended, and to whom the Ottoman empire owes its establishment, erected a principality in Asia Minor, in the year 1300 ; and having taken Prusa in Bithynia, near the close of his reign, he there fixed the early seat of the Turkish empire.   His son Or-khan extended his territories at the expense of the Greeks, who were exposed to constant danger from the progress of the barbarian infidels.   The emperor John Palæologus, after having in vain implored succours in Italy, and humbled himself at the feet of the pope, was obliged to conclude a shameful treaty with Amurath or Morad, the son of Or-khan, whose tributary he consented to become.   The Turkish army had entered Europe, taken the city of Adrianople, and marched into the heart of Thrace, before the return of the emperor from Italy [1].

Morad first gave to the janisaries that form under which they subsisted for nearly four centuries and a half.   In order to create a body of devoted troops that might serve as the immediate guards of his person and dignity, the soltan commanded his officers to seize annually, as the imperial property, the third part of the young males taken in war.   After being instructed in the Mohammedan religion, inured to obedience by severe discipline, and trained to warlike exercise, these youths were formed into regular bands, distinguished by the name of *janisaries* (yenghisheri) or new soldiers.   And, as every sentiment which enthu-

---

[1] Chalcond. *Annal. Turc.*

siasm could inspire, and every mark of honour that the favour
of the prince could confer, were employed to animate them with
martial ardour, and fill them with a sense of their own pre-
eminence, the janisaries soon became the chief strength and pride
of the Ottoman armies.   By their valour, Morad defeated, on
the plains of Cassova, the united forces of the Wallachians,
Hungarians, Dalmatians, and Triballians, under the conduct of
Lascaris, prince of Servia; but walking carelessly over   A.D.
the field of victory, he was assassinated by a Christian   1389.
soldier, who had concealed himself among the slain.   He was
succeeded by his son Bajazet, or Bayezid, surnamed Ilderim, or
the Thunderbolt, on account of the rapidity of his conquests [1].

The Greeks, though surrounded by such dangerous enemies,
and though their empire was almost reduced to the boundaries of
Constantinople, were not more united among themselves than
formerly.   Discord even reigned in the imperial family.   John
Palæologus had condemned his son Andronicus to lose his eyes:
Andronicus revolted, and by the assistance of the Genoese, who
were masters of the commerce, and even part of the suburbs, of
Constantinople, he threw his father and uncle into prison.   The
latter recovered his liberty, seized the throne, and built a citadel
in order to obstruct the designs of the Turks; but the fierce and
arbitrary Ba-yezid ordered him to demolish his works—and the
works were demolished [2]!—What but destruction could be expected to befall a people, whose timidity induced them to overturn the very column of their security?

In the mean time, the progress of the Turks in Europe alarming the Christian princes, the flower of the French nobility took
arms at the time when Philip the Bold, duke of Burgundy, had
the chief sway in France, and followed the call of his son John
the Fearless, count of Nevers.   The main army (which consisted
of about eighty thousand men, of different nations) was commanded by Sigismund, king of Hungary, afterwards emperor of
Germany. The Christians besieged Nicopolis, upon the Danube.
Ba-yezid came to relieve it.   He examined the disposition of his
enemies; he tried their spirit by skirmishes, and found that they
had courage, but wanted conduct; he drew them into an am-
buscade, and gained a complete victory over them.   He   A.D.
has been justly blamed for massacring his prisoners; but   1396.
it ought to be remembered that the French had shown him the

---

[1] Cantemir, *Hist. Oth Emp.*   [2] Ducas.

example, by putting to death all the Turks whom they had seized before the battle [1].

Constantinople was immediately threatened by the conqueror. But Manuel Palæologus purchased a seeming peace, by submitting to an annual tribute of six hundred pieces of gold; by obliging himself to build a mosque, and receive into the city a cadi, or judge, to decide the differences among the Mohammedans who had settled there on account of trade.   Perceiving, however, a new storm arising, he withdrew, and went to several of the European courts, to seek assistance; but he could procure none. Few princes indeed were in a condition to defend him, almost all Christendom being involved in civil wars.   The Turks, meanwhile, had laid siege to Constantinople, and its ruin seemed inevitable; when the fatal blow was diverted for a time, by one of those great events that fill the world with confusion.

The dominions of the Mogul Tartars, under Genghiz Khan and his immediate successors, extended (as we have had occasion to see) from the frontiers of Russia to India and China. Timour, commonly called Tamerlane, one of the princes of those Tartars, and a descendant of Genghiz Khan by the female line, though born without dominions (in the ancient Sogdiana, at present the country of the Usbecs), subdued almost as great an extent of territory as his victorious ancestor; and, in the sweep of his conquests, gave a blow to the empire of the Turks.   He had subjected Great Tartary, Persia, India, and Syria, when the Greek emperor, and five Moslem princes whom the soltan had stripped of their dominions, invited him into Asia Minor, as the only potentate able to deliver them from the tyranny of Ba-yezid.

Timour was pleased with the opportunity of extending his conquests and his renown: but, as he had still some respect for the laws of nations, he sent ambassadors to the Turkish despot before he commenced hostilities, requiring him to raise the siege of Constantinople, and do justice to those princes whom he had deprived of their territories.   The haughty soltan received these proposals with the highest rage and indignation.   He relinquished his enterprize, and prepared to face his rival.   Timour June 23. continued his march, denouncing vengeance.   They met 1402. near Ancyra; and a great and terrible battle ensued. The dispute was long and obstinate; but fortune at length declared for Timour.   Ba-yezid himself was taken prisoner, and had the

[1] Cantemir, *Hist. Oth. Emp.*

affliction to see one of his sons fall by his side, and the mortification to find another the companion of his chains. They were treated with great humanity by the victor, notwithstanding the vulgar story of the iron cage, in which the captive soltan is said to have been confined [1].

The Tartarian conqueror now took Prusa, pillaged Nice, ravaged all the country as far as the Thracian Bosphorus, and took Smyrna by assault, after one of the most memorable sieges recorded in history. Every place yielded either to the terror of his name or the force of his arms. He soon, however, abandoned his acquisitions in Asia Minor, which he found it would be difficult to preserve against so brave a people as the Turks, and went to secure those conquests which were more likely to prove durable.

Manuel Palæologus, thinking the Turkish power entirely broken, destroyed the mosque in Constantinople, and retook several places in its neighbourhood. The civil wars which arose between the sons of Ba-yezid, after the death of their father, encouraged Manuel in his ill-founded security. But the Greeks were in time made sensible of their mistake. On the death of Mohammed I. (who had dethroned and put to death his brother Mousa) his son Morad II. invested Constantinople.   A.D. 1421. He raised the siege, to quell the revolt of his brother Mustapha : he took Thessalonica, and returned to the imperial city, which was in greater danger than ever. The emperor Manuel had, died in the habit of a monk ; and his successor, John VII., threw himself into the arms of the Latins. He hoped to procure assistance from the West, by uniting the Greek and Roman churches ; but he only gained by this scheme the hatred of his subjects. They considered him, and the bishops of his train, who had assisted at the council of Florence, as no better   A.D. than infidels. The bishops were obliged to retract their   1439. opinions ; and John was much less zealous for the proposed union, when he found that it would not answer his purpose [2].

The Turks, in the mean time, were happily diverted from Constantinople by their wars in Hungary ; where Morad found an antagonist worthy of himself, in the celebrated John Huniades,

---

[1] Sherifeddin, *Hist. de Timur-Bec.* Cantemir, *Hist. Oth. Emp.*
[2] Æn. Sylv. *Europ.*—Mosheim, *Hist. Eccles.* vol. iii. Besides acknowledging that the Roman Pontiff was the supreme judge, the true head of the universal church, the Greek emperor and his bishops were obliged to admit, that the Holy Spirit proceeded from the Son as well as from the Father, and that departed souls are purified in the infernal regions, by a certain kind of fire, before their introduction to the presence, or participation of the vision of the Deity.

vaivode of Transylvania, of whose exploits I have already taken notice.   This great commander, having met with success over the soltan, had constrained him to sue for peace.   Ladislaus, king of Poland and Hungary, accordingly concluded with him a solemn truce of ten years; to which the one swore upon the Koran, the other upon the Gospels: and the soltan, weary of the toils of empire, resigned the sceptre to his son.   But an act of atrocious perfidy, disgraceful to the Christian name, obliged him to resume it, to the confusion of his enemies.

The majority of the Ottoman troops, reposing on the faith of the treaty, which they religiously observed, had retired into Asia. This seemed a very favourable opportunity to attack their countrymen in Europe; and cardinal Julian Cesarini, the pope's legate in Germany, a man of a violent and deceitful character, who had distinguished himself in a crusade against the Hussites, persuaded Ladislaus that the treaty with the Turks was not obligatory, as it had been concluded without the consent of his holiness; and that it not only might, but ought to be violated. The pope confirmed this opinion, ordered the truce to be broken, and released Ladislaus from his oath.   He thus acted in conformity with the maxim, that " no faith is to be kept with heretics," and consequently not with infidels: one of the most pernicious doctrines ever devised by superstition; a doctrine which not only contradicts the first principles of reason and conscience, but which, if carried into practice, must destroy all moral and political order.   It would authorise enemies to sport even with oaths: put an end to public faith; dissolve the links of society; and substitute robbery and bloodshed for the laws of nations and the ties of duty.

The arguments of the pope and his legate, however, prevailed. All the Polish and Hungarian chiefs, except the brave Huniades, suffered themselves to be carried away by the torrent; and La-
A.D.   dislaus, seduced by false hopes, and influenced by false
1444.   principles, invaded the soltan's territories.   The Turks, enraged at such a breach of faith, breathed nothing but vengeance. The janisaries went in a body to urge Morad to quit his retreat, and put himself at their head, his son being yet young and inexperienced.   He consented, and marched in quest of the Christian
Nov. 10.   army, which he found encamped near Varna, in Moldavia.
He had provided himself with a copy of the treaty which had been so solemnly sworn to, and so shamefully violated: he held it up in the height of the engagement, when he found the vigour of his troops beginning to slacken, appealing to God,

as a witness of the perjury of the Christians, and beseeching him to avenge the insult offered to the laws of nations. Perjury for once received its just reward. The Christians were defeated with great slaughter after an obstinate resistance. Ladislaus fell, with his sword in his hand, covered with wounds; cardinal Julian sunk by his side; and ten thousand of his subjects, who guarded their monarch, covered with their dead bodies nearly the same ground on which they were drawn up[1]. Morad, thus victorious, resigned once more the rod of empire—what a rare example of philosophy in a Turk!—and was again induced to resume it.

The person who drew him a second time from his retreat was George Castriot, surnamed Scanderbeg, the son of a prince of Albania or Epirus. This young hero had been delivered as a hostage on the subjection of his father's kingdom; had been educated in the Turkish court, and had risen into favour with Morad by his valour and talents. But he still cherished the idea of becoming one day the deliverer of his country: and an opportunity at last presented itself. He had been sent into Servia with a military force, when he heard of his father's death; and as he understood that a secretary of the Ottoman court was to pass near his camp, he caused him to be loaded with chains, and compelled him to sign and put the soltan's signet to an order, requiring the governor of Croia, the capital of Albania, to deliver up to him the town and citadel. This false order had the desired effect. The place was given up, and Scanderbeg massacred the Turkish garrison. The Albanians crowded to his standard; and he made so good a use of the mountainous situation of his country, as to defy all the efforts of the soltan's power[2].

Morad was succeeded in his extensive dominions by his son Mohammed II., justly surnamed the Great, who had been formerly crowned, and obeyed as emperor, but had re-signed to his parent the reins of government, on account   A.D. 1451. of the exigencies of the times—an example of moderation no less extraordinary than the philosophy of the father in retiring from the honours of empire in the hour of victory, especially as the son was of a fiery and ambitious temper. The character of this prince has been very differently represented by historians. Voltaire is his professed panegyrist; and in order to free him from

---

[1] Mat. Michov. lib. iv.—Fulstin. lib. xiv.—Cantemir.
[2] Cantemir.—Sir Paul Ricaut.

the imputation of certain cruel and ferocious actions, has combated the most incontestable facts. Other writers have gone equal lengths to degrade him : he has been pronounced a rude and ignorant barbarian, as well as a scholar and a patron of the liberal arts. But they who would do justice to his character must trace it by other lineaments. He was both a scholar and a barbarian : he combined the knowledge of the one with the ferocity of the other. He was enlightened, but not civilized. With some taste for the liberal arts, or at least some sense of the value of their productions, he entertained a general contempt for their professors ; the Turk always predominated. He was a warrior and a politician, in the most extensive meaning of the words ; as such he was truly great : and whether we consider the conception or the execution of his enterprises, we shall find reason to admire the extent of his understanding and the vigour of his spirit. His first enterprise was against Constantinople, which had so long been the object of the ambition of his ancestors.

The Greek emperor, John VII., had been succeeded in 1455 by his son Constantine. This prince possessed courage, but little capacity. He took care, however, to strengthen the fortifications of his capital, as soon as he was apprised of the design of Mohammed ; and he made many advances to the soltan, to induce him to lay aside his project ; but nothing could divert him from his purpose. If he sometimes seemed to listen to terms of accommodation, it was only that he might lull his enemies into security, while he carried on his military preparations with unremitted assiduity. At last, he cut off all communication with the city, both by sea and land, and laid siege to it in form.

A.D. Though the garrison was but small, the walls were de-
1453. fended with great gallantry on the land side, the Greeks being actuated by the courage of despair ; and the Turks were incapable of annoying them from the sea, by reason of large chains and booms which secured the mouth of the harbour. But nothing is impossible to human genius, when aided by the necessary force. In order to overcome this difficulty, the besiegers dug a passage of nearly two leagues over land, in the form of a ship's cradle, lined with planks ; and with the aid of engines, they drew up, in the space of one night, eighty galleys, and seventy vessels of smaller size, out of the water, upon these planks, and launched them all into the harbour [1]. What must

---

[1] Ducas.—Cantemir.

have been the surprise of the besieged, in the morning, to behold a large fleet riding in their port, and yet all their booms secure !

The city was now assailed on all sides. Mohammed caused a bridge of boats to be built across the harbour, upon which he raised a battery of cannon. And here I cannot help remarking, that the artillery of the Greeks must have been very indifferent, or very ill served ; otherwise this bridge could never have been built. The cannon employed by the Turks are said to have been of an enormous size, some of them carrying balls of one hundred pounds weight. With these great guns they beat down the walls faster than the besieged could repair them: a body of janisaries entered the breach, with their prince at their head, while another broke in at a sally-port. Constantine, whose valour merited a more distinguished fate, was slain among the crowd, and his capital became a prey to the conqueror. For the honour of Mohammed II. I must observe, that few of the garrison were put to the sword. He arrested the fury of the troops, and granted conditions to the inhabitants, who had sent deputies to implore his clemency [1]. They were allowed to retain a magistrate for the decision of their civil differences, a patriarch, and the public exercise of their religion.

Here I might remark, as has been remarked by graver historians, that Constantinople, (built by the first Christian emperor, whose name it bears,) submitted to the Turks under a Constantine, and Rome to the Barbarians under an Augustus !—but such an accidental coincidence of names and circumstances is more worthy of the notice of a monkish chronologist than an observer of human nature.

Mohammed continued to push his conquests on all sides, and with unvaried fortune, till he received a check from John A.D. Huniades, who obliged him to raise the siege of Belgrade. 1456. The knights of Rhodes opposed him in their island with like success. But he subdued Albania, after the death of Scanderbeg; and Trebisond, where the family of Comnenus had preserved an image of the Greek empire. He carried his arms on the other side as far as Trieste; took Otranto, and fixed the Mohammedan power in the heart of Calabria [2]. He threatened Venice, and Rome itself with subjection ; hoping to make himself master of Italy as well as of Greece; and then the triumph of barbarism would have been complete. All Europe trembled

---

[1] Cantemir.—Ricaut.   [2] Ibid.

at his motions; and not without cause; for Europe, unless united, must have sunk beneath his sword. But death freed Christendom from this terrible conqueror, at an age when he might have executed the greatest enterprises, being only in his fifty-second year. His descendants still possess the finest country in our quarter of the globe. Greece, where civil liberty was first known, and where arts and letters were first brought to perfection, continued long to be the seat of ignorance, barbarism, and despotism: but it has recently thrown off the yoke; and though many years must elapse before the accumulated evils of centuries can be removed, we have grounds for hope that the future fortunes of Greece will be as prosperous as the past have been wretched.

May 4, 1481.

LETTER LIII.

History of Spain, from the Death of Peter the Cruel, in 1369, to the Conquest of Granada, by Ferdinand and Isabella, in 1492.

PETER the Cruel, my dear Philip, after being deserted by the Black Prince, on account of his perfidy, was subdued and slain, as you have already seen, by his illegitimate brother Henry, who succeeded to the throne of Castile. Nothing very remarkable occurred during the reign of this prince, or under his descendants for almost a century. They were engaged in frequent wars with their neighbours, the kings of Portugal and Arragon. But these wars were seldom decisive; so that Spain continued in nearly the same situation, from the death of Peter till the reign of Henry IV. of Castile, whose debaucheries roused the resentment of his nobles, and produced a most singular insurrection, which led to the aggrandisement of the Spanish monarchy.

A.D. 1369.

This prince, who was surnamed the Impotent, was totally enervated by his pleasures; and every thing in his court conspired to set the Castilians an example of the most depraved manners and most abandoned licentiousness. The queen, a daughter of Portugal, lived as openly with her parasites and her gallants as the king did with his minions and his mis-

A.D. 1454.

tresses. Pleasure was the only object, and effeminacy the only recommendation to favour. When the affairs of the state had at length fallen into the greatest disorder, the nobles, with the archbishop of Toledo at their head, formed a combination against the weak and flagitious government of Henry, and arrogated to themselves, as one of the privileges of their order, the right of trying and passing sentence on their sovereign, which they executed in a manner unprecedented in history.

The mal-content nobility met at Avilla. A spacious June 5, theatre was erected in a plain near the town; an image, 1465. representing the king, was seated on the throne, clad in royal robes, with a crown on its head, a sceptre in its hand, and the sword of justice by its side. The accusation against Henry was read, and the sentence of deposition pronounced, in presence of a numerous assembly. At the close of the first article of the charge, the archbishop of Toledo advanced, and tore the crown from the head of the figure; at the close of the second, the condè de Placentia snatched the sword of justice from its side; at the close of the third, the condè de Benevente wrested the sceptre from its hand; and Lopez de Zuniga, when the last article had been adduced, gave the image a blow which hurled it from the throne. At the same moment, Alphonso, Henry's brother, a boy about twelve years of age, was proclaimed king of Castile and Leon [1].

This extraordinary proceeding was followed by all the horrors of civil war, which did not cease till some time after the death of the young prince, on whom the nobles had bestowed the kingdom. The archbishop and his party then continued to carry on war in the name of Isabella, the king's sister; and Henry could not extricate himself out of these troubles, nor remain quiet upon his throne, till he had signed one of the most humiliating treaties ever extorted from a sovereign. He acknowledged Isabella as the only lawful heiress of his kingdom, in prejudice to the rights of his reputed daughter Joan, whom the mal-contents affirmed to be the offspring of an adulterous commerce between the queen and Bertrand de la Cueva [2]. At such a price did this weak prince purchase from his subjects the empty title of king!

The grand object of the mal-content party now was the marriage of the infanta Isabella; upon which it was evident, the

---

[1] Mariana, lib. xxiii.—Diego Henriquez del Castillo.
[2] Rod. Sanctii *Hist. Hisp.* — *Chron. del Rey Don Henric.*

security of the crown and the happiness of the people must in a great measure depend. The alliance was sought by several princes. The king of Portugal offered her his hand; the king A.D. of France demanded her for his brother, and the king of 1469. Arragon for his son Ferdinand. The mal-contents wisely preferred the Arragonian prince, and Isabella prudently made the same choice. Articles were drawn up; and the ceremony of marriage was privately performed by the archbishop of Toledo[1].

Henry was enraged at this alliance, which he foresaw would utterly ruin his authority, by furnishing his rebellious subjects with the support of a powerful neighbouring prince. He disinherited his sister, and established the right of his daughter. A furious civil war desolated the kingdom; but peace was at length A.D. restored. Henry was reconciled to his sister and to 1474. Ferdinand, though it does not appear that he ever renewed Isabella's right to the succession; for he affirmed, in his last moments, that he believed Joan to be his own daughter. The queen swore to the same effect; and Henry left a testamentary deed, transmitting the crown to this princess, who was proclaimed queen of Castile, at Placentia. But the superior fortune, and superior arms of Ferdinand and Isabella prevailed; the king of Portugal was obliged to abandon his niece and intended bride, after many ineffectual struggles and several years A.D. of war. Joan sunk into a convent, when she hoped to 1479. ascend a throne; and the death of Ferdinand's father, which happened about this time, added the kingdoms of Arragon and Sicily to those of Leon and Castile[2].

Ferdinand and Isabella were persons of great prudence, and, as sovereigns, highly worthy of imitation; but they do not seem to have merited all the praises bestowed upon them by the Spanish historians. They did not live like man and wife, having all things in common under the direction of the husband, but like two princes in close alliance. They neither loved nor hated each other; were seldom in company together; had each a separate council, and were frequently jealous of one another, in the administration. But they were inseparably united in their common interests; always acting upon the same principles, and forwarding the same ends. Their first object was the regulation of their government, which the civil wars had thrown into ex-

---

[1] *Zurit. Annal. Arrag.*—Mariana, ubi sup.
[2] *Zurit. Annal. Arrag.*—Mariana, lib. xxiv.

treme disorder. Rapine, outrage, and murder, had become so
common, as not only to interrupt commerce, but in a great
measure to suspend all intercourse between one place and
another. These evils the joint sovereigns suppressed by their
wise policy, at the same time that they extended the royal prerogative.

About the middle of the thirteenth century, the cities in the
kingdom of Arragon, and, after their example, those in Castile,
had formed themselves into an association, distinguished by the
appellation of the *Santa Hermandad*, or the Holy Brotherhood.
They exacted a certain contribution from each of the associated
towns ; they levied a considerable body of troops, in order to
protect travellers, and pursue criminals ; and they appointed
judges, who opened courts in various parts of the kingdom. All
who were guilty of murder, robbery, or any act that violated
the public peace, and were seized by the troops of the Brotherhood, were carried before the judges, who without paying any
regard to the exclusive jurisdiction which the lord of the place
might claim, who was generally the author or abettor of the injustice, tried and condemned the criminals. The nobles often
murmured against this salutary institution ; they complained of
it as an encroachment on one of their most valuable privileges,
and endeavoured to procure its abolition. But Ferdinand and
Isabella, sensible of the beneficial effects of the Brotherhood, not
only in regard to the policy of their kingdoms, but in its tendency to abridge, and by degrees to annihilate, the territorial
jurisdiction of the nobility, countenanced the institution upon
every occasion, and supported it with the whole force of royal
authority. By these means the prompt and impartial administration of justice was restored, and with it tranquillity and order
returned [1].

But, while their *Catholic Majesties* (for such was the title
conferred on them by the pope) were giving vigour to civil
government, and securing their subjects from violence and oppression, an intemperate zeal led them to establish an A.D.
ecclesiastical tribunal, equally contrary to the natural 1480.
rights of mankind, and the mild spirit of the Gospel—I mean
the court of inquisition ; which decides upon the honour, fortune,
and even life of the unhappy wretch who happens to fall under
the suspicion of heresy, or a contempt of any thing prescribed
by the church, without his being confronted with his accusers, or

[1] Zurita.—Mariana.

enjoying the privileges of defence or appeal. Six thousand persons are said to have been burned by order of this infamous tribunal, within four years after the appointment of Torquemada, the first inquisitor-general; and upwards of one hundred thousand felt its fury. The same zeal, however, which led to the depopulation, and the barbarizing of Castile and Arragon, led also to their aggrandizement.

The kingdom of Granada now alone remained, of all the Mohammedan possessions in Spain. Princes equally zealous and ambitious, like Ferdinand and Isabella, were naturally disposed to turn their eyes on that fertile territory, and to think of increasing their dominions by expelling the enemies of Christianity, and extending its doctrines. Every thing conspired to favour their project. The Moorish kingdom was a prey to civil wars, when Ferdinand, having obtained a papal bull authorising a A.D. 1483. crusade, put himself at the head of his troops, and entered Granada. He continued the war with rapid success. Isabella attended him in several expeditions; and they were both in great danger at the siege of Malaga, an important city, which was defended with great courage, and taken in 1487. Baça was reduced in 1489, after the loss of twenty thousand men by disease and the sword. Guadix and Almeria were delivered up by the Moorish king Al-Zagal, who had at first dethroned his brother Aboul-Hassan, and had afterwards been chased from his capital by his nephew Abou-Abdallah. That prince, so blind or so base, as to confound the ruin of his country with the humiliation of his rival, engaged in the service of Ferdinand and Isabella, who, after reducing every other place of eminence, undertook the siege of Granada. Abou-Abdallah made a gallant defence; but all communication with the country being cut off, and all hopes of relief at an end, he capitulated, A.D. 1492. after a siege of eight months, on condition that he should enjoy the revenue of certain places in the fertile mountains of Alpujarras; that the inhabitants should retain the undisturbed possession of their houses, goods, and inheritances; the use of their laws, and the free exercise of their religion[1].

Thus ended the empire of the Arabs in Spain, after it had continued above seven hundred and seventy-seven years. They introduced the arts and sciences into Europe at a time when it was lost in darkness; they possessed many of the luxuries of life,

---

[1] Cardonne, tome iii.—Fran. Bermud. de Pedraza, *Antiq. Excel. de Granad.*—Mariana, lib. xxv.

when they were not even known among the neighbouring nations; and they seem to have given birth to that romantic gallantry which so eminently prevailed in the ages of chivalry, and which, blending itself with the veneration of the Gothic nations for the softer sex, still particularly distinguishes modern from ancient manners. But the Moors, notwithstanding these advantages, and the eulogies bestowed upon them by Voltaire and other writers, appear to have been always destitute of the essential qualities of a polished people—humanity, generosity, and mutual sympathy.

Nor does the boasted literature of the Arabs bear the test of strict examination; their books were more numerous than valuable, their knowledge more extended than profound. Over all their writers a sameness and an uniformity appear, that completely excluded originality. During the whole period of the Moorish dynasty, there flourished no author of sufficient power to stamp his character on the age, no genius that soared above the mediocrity of his compeers. They had no original philosopher, dramatist, or epic poet; and nothing is more certain than the fact that the exact sciences, unaided by inventive literature, contribute but little to the advancement of civilization.

The conquest of Granada was followed by the expulsion, or rather the pillage and banishment, of the Jews, who had engrossed the wealth and commerce of Spain. The inquisition exhausted its rage against these unhappy people, many of whom pretended to embrace Christianity, in order to preserve their property. About the same time, their catholic majesties concluded an alliance with the emperor Maximilian, and a treaty of marriage for their daughter Joan with his son Philip, archduke of Austria, and sovereign of the Netherlands. About this time also the contract was concluded with Christopher Columbus, for the discovery of *new* countries; and the territories of Roussillon and Cerdagne were agreed to be restored by Charles VIII. of France, before his expedition into Italy. But the consequences of these measures, and the interest which Ferdinand took in the Italian wars, must form the subject of future letters.

I should now, my dear Philip, return to the great line of European history; but for the sake of perspicuity, I shall first make you acquainted with the affairs of England under Henry VII., as his son Henry VIII. had a considerable share in the continental transactions, and derived his importance chiefly from the prudent policy of his father.

LETTER LIV.

View of the Reign of Henry VII.

HENRY VII., the first prince of the house of Tudor, ascended the throne of England in consequence of the victory A.D. at Bosworth, and the death of Richard III. His title 1485. was confirmed by the parliament: his merit was known; and his marriage with the princess Elizabeth, eldest daughter of Edward IV., united the jarring claims of the houses of York and Lancaster, and seemed to give great satisfaction to the public. He had therefore every reason to promise himself peace and security.

But Henry, although in many respects a prudent and politic prince, had unhappily imbibed a violent antipathy to the adherents of the house of York, which no time or experience could ever efface. Instead of embracing the present opportunity of abolishing party distinctions, by bestowing his smile indiscriminately on the friends of both families, he carried to the throne all the partialities that belong to the head of a faction. To exalt the Lancastrian party, and depress the retainers of the house of York, were still the favourite ideas of his mind. The house of York was generally beloved by the nation: and, for that very reason, it became every day more the object of Henry's hatred and aversion: hence his amiable consort was treated with contempt, his government grew unpopular, and his reign was filled with plots and insurrections.

The first insurrection was headed by the viscount Lovel, sir Humphry Stafford, and Thomas, his brother, who had all fought in the cause of Richard, and against whom, among many others, the parliament, at Henry's instigation, had passed an act of attainder; though it is not conceivable how men could be guilty of treason for supporting the king in possession, against the earl of Richmond, to whom they had never sworn allegiance, and who had not then assumed even the title of king. Enraged at such A.D. an instance of severity, they left their sanctuary at Col-1486. chester, and flew to arms. The king sent the duke of Bedford against them with a chosen body of troops, and a promise of pardon to such as would return to their duty. Lovel, doubting the fidelity of his followers, privately withdrew, and fled to Flanders. His army submitted to the king's clemency. The two Staffords took sanctuary in the church of Colnham, near Abingdon; but, as it was found that this church had not the privilege of protecting rebels, they were taken thence. The elder was executed at Tyburn, the younger obtained a pardon [1].

This rebellion was immediately followed by another, of a more dangerous nature, as it took firmer hold of the public discontents. Henry's jealousy had confined in the Tower Edward, earl of Warwick, son of the duke of Clarence. This unhappy prince had been formerly imprisoned in Yorkshire by the tyranny of his uncle Richard. A comparison was drawn between Henry and that cruel usurper; and as the Tower was the place where Edward's children had been murdered, a fate not more gentle was feared for Warwick. While the compassion of the nation was thus turned towards youth and innocence, exposed to oppression, a report was spread that Warwick had made his escape. As a general joy communicated itself from face to face, and many seemed desirous of joining him, such an opportunity was not neglected by the enemies of Henry's government.

One Richard Simon, a priest of Oxford, and a zealous partisan of the house of York, endeavoured to gratify the popular wish by holding up an impostor to the nation. For this purpose, he cast his eyes upon Lambert Simnel, a baker's son, who, being endowed with understanding beyond his years, and address above his condition, seemed well calculated to personate a prince of royal extraction. Simnel was taught to assume the name and character of the earl of Warwick; and he soon appeared so perfect in many private particulars relative to that unfortunate prince, to the court of king Edward, and the royal family, that the queen dowager was supposed to have given him a lesson. But how apt soever father Simon might find his pupil, or whatever means he might take to procure him instruction, he was sensible that the imposture would not bear a close inspection; he therefore determined to make trial of it first in Ireland.

That island was zealously attached to the house of York, and bore an affectionate regard to the memory of the duke of Clarence, who had resided there as lord lieutenant: and Henry had been so impolitic as to allow its government to remain in the same state in which he found it. All the officers appointed by his predecessor still retained their authority; so that Simnel no sooner presented himself to the earl of Kildare, the deputy, and

[1] Polyd. Virg. *Hist. Angl.* lib. xxvi.—Bacon's *Hist. of Henry VII.*

claimed his protection as the unfortunate Warwick, than that credulous nobleman believed his tale, and embraced his cause. Other persons of rank were no less sanguine in their zeal and belief: the story diffused itself among the people of inferior condition, naturally more violent and credulous, who listened to it with still greater ardour : the pretended prince was lodged in the castle of Dublin, crowned with a diadem taken from a statue of the blessed Virgin, and publicly proclaimed king, under the appellation of Edward VI.[1]

The king was seriously alarmed, when he received intelligence of this revolt. Though determined always to face his enemies, he scrupled at present to leave England, where he suspected the conspiracy had been framed, and where he knew many persons of all ranks were disposed to give it countenance. After frequent consultations with his ministers, he ordered the queen-dowager to be apprehended, and confined in the nunnery of Bermondsey for life. He then caused the earl of Warwick to be taken from the Tower, led in procession through the streets of London, and exposed in St. Paul's church to public view. This expedient had its full effect in England ; but in Ireland the people persisted in their revolt : and Henry had reason to think, that the attempt to disturb his government was not laid on such slight foundations, as the means employed seemed to indicate.

John, earl of Lincoln, son of John de la Pole, duke of Suffolk, by Elizabeth, eldest sister of Edward IV., was engaged to take part in the conspiracy. This nobleman, alarmed at the king's jealousy of all eminent persons of the York party, and more especially at his rigour towards Warwick, had retired into Flanders, where lord Lovel had arrived before him. He resided some time in the court of his aunt Margaret, duchess-dowager of Burgundy, who, enraged against the oppressor of her family, A.D. hired two thousand German veterans, under Martin 1487. Schwart, and sent them over, with these noblemen, to join Simnel in Ireland.

The courage of the Irish was so elevated by this accession of military force, and the countenance of persons of such high rank, that they formed the bold resolution of invading England, where they believed the spirit of disaffection to be no less prevalent than in Ireland. They accordingly landed in Lancashire, and were joined by sir Thomas Broughton, a man of great interest in that county ; but the people in general, unwilling to associate with

---

[1] Polyd. Virg. lib. xxvi.

Irish and German invaders, convinced of Simnel's imposture, and kept in awe by the king's reputation in arms, either remained inactive or gave assistance to the royal army, which was advancing against the enemy. The earl of Lincoln now found it necessary to bring the contest to a speedy decision; and Henry, emboldened by his native courage, no less than by the superiority of his numbers, intrepidly hastened to the combat. The two armies met at Stoke, in the county of Nottingham, where, after an obstinate battle, the royalists fully prevailed. Lincoln, Broughton, and Schwart, perished in *June 16.* the field, with four thousand of their followers. Lovel is supposed to have undergone the same fate, as he was never more heard of. Simnel and his tutor were taken prisoners. Simon was committed to close custody for life; and his sacred character only could have saved him from a more severe fate. Simnel was too contemptible either to excite apprehension or resentment in Henry: he was therefore pardoned, and employed as a scullion, from which condition he was afterwards advanced to the rank of one of his majesty's falconers [1].

Henry having thus restored tranquillity to his kingdom, and security to his government, had leisure not only to regulate his domestic affairs, but also to look abroad. From Scotland, the most contiguous state, he had nothing to fear. There reigned James III., a prince of little industry, and narrow genius. With him Henry concluded a treaty, when he might have demanded his crown: so truly pacific was the disposition of this monarch! —Of the continental governments I have already spoken. They were hastening to that situation in which they remained, without any very material alteration, for nearly three centuries. The balance of power began to be understood. Spain had rendered herself formidable by the union of the crowns of Arragon and Castile, in the persons of Ferdinand and Isabella; and these princes were employed in wresting Granada from the Moors. France, during the last fifty years, had greatly increased in power and dominion; and she was now attempting to swallow up Bretagne. England alone was both enabled by her power, and engaged by her interests, to support the independence of that duchy: the most dangerous opposition was therefore expected from this quarter. But Henry's parsimonious temper and narrow politics, as I have had occasion to mention in the history of France, prevented him from affording any effectual sup-

[1] Polyd. Virg.—Bacon's *Hist.*

port to the Bretons ; and, as Maximilian, to whom they afterwards applied, was unable to protect them, they were obliged to
submit to the arms of Charles VIII., who prudently married the
heiress of the duchy, in order to conciliate their affections.

Henry, who saw the importance of Bretagne to France, was
mortified and incensed at his disappointment, and talked loudly
of vengeance. The conquest of France, in his language, was
A.D. an easy matter ; and he set out on that enterprise at the
1492. head of a splendid army. The nobility, who had credu-
lously swallowed his idle boasts, were seized with a thirst of
military glory ; they fondly hoped to carry their triumphant banners to the gates of Paris, and put the crown of France on the
head of their sovereign. Henry, in the mean time, had nothing
less at heart than war ; the gratification of his ruling passion
was the only purpose of this great armament—avarice being in
him a more powerful motive than either revenge or glory.
Secret advances had been made towards peace, before the armament was prepared, and commissioners had been appointed to
treat of the terms. His demands were wholly pecuniary ; and
the king of France, who deemed the peaceable possession of
Bretagne an equivalent for any sum, and who was all on fire
for his projected expedition into Italy, readily agreed to the
proposals of the invader. He engaged, by the treaty of Estaples,
Nov. 3. concluded about a month after the English landed in
France, to pay Henry seven hundred and forty-five
thousand crowns ; partly as a reimbursement of the sums advanced to the duchess of Bretagne, partly as arrears of the pension due to Edward IV. ; and he stipulated a yearly pension to
Henry and his heirs of twenty-five thousand crowns [1].

Thus, as lord Bacon observes, the English monarch made
profit upon his subjects for the war, and upon his enemies for
the peace. But although the treaty of Estaples contributed to
fill the coffers of Henry, it did very little honour to England, as
it put a shameful seal to the subjection of Bretagne, which,
properly supported, would have been a continual thorn in
the side of France, and might have prevented that mo-
archy from ever becoming formidable to the liberties of
Europe. The people however agreed, that the king had fulfilled the promise which he made to the parliament, when he
said that he would make the war maintain itself; and all ranks
of men seemed now to be satisfied with his government. He

---

[1] Polyd. Virg.—Bacon's *Hist*.

therefore flattered himself with the hope of durable peace and tranquillity. His authority was fully established at home, and his reputation for policy was great abroad: the hopes of all pretenders to the throne were cut off, as well by his marriage as by the issue which it had brought him; yet, at this height of his prosperity, his indefatigable enemies raised against him an adversary, who long gave him inquietude, and sometimes even brought him into danger.

The old duchess of Burgundy, not discouraged by the ill success of the former conspiracy, resolved to play off another imposture upon Henry. With that view she caused a report to be propagated, that her nephew, Richard duke of York, had made his escape from the Tower, when his elder brother was murdered, and that he was still alive. This rumour being greedily received, her next care was to provide a young man proper to personate the unfortunate prince, and for that purpose she fixed upon Perkin Warbeck, the son of an obscure Fleming. The youth was born in England, and, by some, believed to be the son of Edward IV. on account of the resemblance observable between him and that amorous monarch. A few years after his birth, he was taken by his real father to Tournay, where he did not long remain, but, by different accidents, was carried from place to place; so that his parentage and past life became thereby unknown, and difficult to be traced by the most diligent inquiry. The variety of his adventures had happily favoured the natural versatility and sagacity of his genius, and he seemed to be well qualified to assume any character. In this light he had been represented to Edward's intriguing sister, who immediately desired to see him, and found that he exceeded her most sanguine expectations; so comely did he appear in his person, so graceful in his air, so courtly in his address, so full of dignity in his whole demeanour, and good sense in his conversation!

A young man of such quick apprehension soon imbibed the necessary instructions for personating the duke of York; but, as some time was required before every thing requisite could be prepared for this enterprise, Margaret sent him into Portugal, where he remained a year in obscurity. He then repaired to Ireland, and, assuming the name of Richard Plantagenet, found many partisans among the ignorant and credulous inhabitants. The news of this phenomenon reached France; and Charles VIII., prompted by the secret solicitations of the duchess of Burgundy, sent Perkin an invitation to visit him at Paris. The impostor repaired to the court of France, where he was received with all

the marks of respect due to the duke of York.   The whole
kingdom was full of the accomplishments, as well as the singular
adventures and misfortunes of the young Plantagenet.   From
France the tide of admiration and credulity diffused itself into
England; and sir George Neville, sir John Taylor, and many
other gentlemen, went over to Paris, to offer their services to
the supposed duke of York, and to share his fortunes [1].

Perkin, however, was dismissed from France, in consequence
of the peace of Estaples.   He now retired to the duchess of
Burgundy, craving her protection, and offering to exhibit before
her all the proofs of that birth to which he laid claim.   Margaret affected ignorance of his pretensions, and publicly
desired to learn his reasons for assuming the name which
he bore.   She put many particular questions to him, seemed
astonished at his answers, and at last burst into joy and admiration at his wonderful deliverance, embracing him as her nephew,
the true image of Edward, the sole heir of the Plantagenets, and
the legitimate successor to the English throne.   She assigned
him an equipage suitable to his pretended birth, appointed him
a guard, engaged every one to pay court to him, and on all occasions honoured him with the appellation of *The White Rose of
England.*

The Flemings, swayed by Margaret's authority, readily
adopted the fiction of Perkin's royal descent ; and, in England,
not only the populace, ever fond of novelty, and desirous of
change, but men of the highest birth and quality, disgusted at
the severity of Henry's government, began to turn their eyes
towards this new claimant.   Their passions and prejudices inclined them to give credit to Perkin's pretensions : a regular
conspiracy was formed against the king's authority, and a correspondence settled between the Flemish and English mal-contents [2].

Henry proceeded resolutely, though deliberately, in counter-
working the designs of his enemies.   His first object was to
ascertain the death of the real duke of York, which he was in a
great measure able to do, two of the persons concerned in the
murder being yet alive, and agreeing in the same story.   But
he found it more difficult to discover who the extraordinary
person was that so boldly advanced pretensions to his crown.
For this purpose he dispersed his spies over all Flanders and
England : he engaged many to pretend that they had embraced

A.D.
1493.

[1] Bacon's *Hist.*   [2] Polyd. Virg.—Bacon's *Hist.*

2

Perkin's party ; he bribed the young man's servants, and even his confessor. By these means he at length traced the whole plan of the conspiracy, and the pedigree, adventures, life, and conversation of the pretended duke of York.

The impostor's story was immediately published, for the satisfaction of the nation ; and as soon as Henry's projects A.D. were matured, he made the conspirators feel the weight 1494. of his resentment. Lord Fitzwalter and sir Simon Montfort were arrested, convicted of treason for promisng to aid Perkin, and quickly beheaded. Sir William Stanley, the high chamberlain, was also apprehended ; but great and more solemn preparations were thought necessary for the trial of a man whose authority in the nation, and whose domestic intimacy with the king, as well as his former services, seemed to secure him against any accusation or punishment. Henry, however, was determined to take vengeance on all his enemies. He therefore persuaded sir Robert Clifford, who had learned the youth's secrets, to accuse Stanley of abetting the schemes of the conspirators ; and, after the lapse of six weeks, (a delay which was inter- A.D. posed in order to show the king's lenity and coolness,) 1495. the chamberlain was brought to his trial, condemned, and put to death [1].

The fate of Stanley made great impression on the minds of the people, and struck Perkin's adherents with the deepest dismay, as they found that all their secrets were betrayed. The jealous and severe temper of the king kept men in awe, and quelled not only the movements of sedition, but the very murmurs of faction. A general distrust took place ; all mutual confidence was destroyed, even among particular friends. Henry, not very eager to dispel those terrors, or gain the affections of the nation, continued to indulge his rapacious temper, and employed the arts of perverted law and justice, in order to extort fines and compositions from his subjects. His government was in itself highly oppressive ; but it was so much the less burthensome, as he took care, like Louis XI., to restrain the tyranny of the nobles, and permitted nobody to be guilty of injustice or oppression but himself.

Perkin, finding his correspondence with the nobility cut off by Henry's vigilance and severity, and the king's authority daily gaining ground among the people, resolved to attempt something which might revive the drooping hopes of his party.

---

[1] Polyd. Virg.—Bacon's *Hist*.

With this view he collected a band of outlaws and pirates, put to sea, and appeared off the coast of Kent ; but as the inhabitants were hostile to his cause, he returned to Flanders, and afterwards made a descent upon Ireland. The affairs of that country, however, were now in so good a posture, that he there met with little success ; and being weary of skulking among the wild natives, he bent his course towards Scotland, and presented himself to James IV., who then reigned in that kingdom. Perkin had been recommended to this prince by the king of France ; and James, pleased with the address of the youth, gave him the hand of lady Catharine Gordon, daughter of the earl of Huntley, a young lady eminent both for beauty and virtue.

The jealousy which then subsisted between the courts of England and Scotland was a new recommendation to Perkin ; so that James, who had resolved to make an inroad into England, took the impostor with him, in hopes that the appearance of the pretended prince might raise an insurrection in the northern counties. But the cruelty and rapacity of the Scots roused the hostility of the English people ; even the warmest partisans of the house of York resolved to prevent the desolation of their country, and submit to a usurper, rather than aid a lawful prince supported by such barbarous allies. Consequently, after repeated incursions, James found it expedient to conclude a truce with Henry, Perkin being privately ordered to quit the kingdom [1].

A.D. 1496.

A.D. 1497.

Ireland once more afforded a retreat to the impostor ; but, after a short concealment, he resolved to try the affections of the Cornish malcontents, who had lately risen in rebellion on account of an oppressive tax, and whose mutinous disposition still subsisted, notwithstanding the lenity that had been shown to them. As soon as he appeared at Bodmin he was joined by three thousand men ; and elate with this appearance of success, assumed, for the first time, the appellation of Richard IV. king of England. That the expectations of his followers might not be suffered to languish, he presented himself before Exeter ; and, as the inhabitants shut their gates against him, he laid siege to the place.

Henry was happy to hear that the impostor was in England, and prepared with alacrity to attack him ; for, as he usually said, he desired only to see his enemies. The intimidated youth immediately raised the siege of Exeter : and although his fol-

---

[1] Bacon's *Hist.*—Polyd. Virg.

lowers now amounted to the number of seven thousand, and seemed still resolute to maintain his cause, he himself despaired of success, and retired to the sanctuary of Beaulieu. The Cornish rebels submitted to the king's mercy, and found that it was not yet exhausted in their behalf; a few of their chiefs excepted, they were dismissed with impunity.   Henry was more at a loss how to proceed with regard to Perkin himself.   Some advised him to make the privileges of the church yield to reasons of state; to drag the impostor from the sanctuary, and inflict on him the punishment due to his temerity.   But Henry did not think the evil so dangerous as to require such a violent remedy.   He therefore employed some sagacious persons to persuade A.D. Perkin to deliver himself into the king's hands, under 1498. promise of pardon.   He did so, and Henry conducted him, in a kind of mock triumph, to London.

Although the impostor's life was granted him, he was detained in custody. He escaped from his keepers, but being retaken, was confined in the Tower, where his habits of restless intrigue and enterprise followed him.   He opened a correspondence with the earl of Warwick, and engaged that unfortunate prince to embrace a project for his escape, which Perkin offered A.D. to conduct, by murdering the lieutenant of the Tower. 1499. The conspiracy did not escape the king's vigilance; and Perkin, having thus rendered himself unworthy of mercy, was arraigned, condemned, and hanged at Tyburn.   The earl also was brought to trial and beheaded [1].

This violent act of tyranny, by which Henry destroyed the last prince of the male line of Plantagenet, produced great discontent among the people. They saw, with concern, an unhappy prince, to whom the privileges of his birth had long been denied, and who had even been cut off from the common benefits of nature, now deprived of life itself, merely for attempting to shake off that oppression under which he laboured.   But these domestic discontents did not weaken the king's government; and foreign princes, deeming his throne now perfectly secure, paid him greater deference and attention.

The prince whose alliance Henry valued most was Ferdinand of Spain, whose vigorous and steady policy, always attended with success, had rendered him in many respects the most considerable monarch in Europe.   And the king of England had at

---

[1] Bacon's *Hist.*— Polyd. Virg.

A.D. last the satisfaction of completing a marriage, which had
1501. been projected and negociated during the course of seven
years, between Arthur prince of Wales, and Catharine, daughter
A.D. of Ferdinand and Isabella.   Arthur dying in a few months
1502. after the celebration of the nuptials, the king, desirous of
continuing his alliance with Spain, and also unwilling to restore
Catharine's dowry, obliged his second son Henry to be betrothed
to the Infanta.   The prince made all the opposition of which a
youth under twelve years of age could be supposed capable; but,
A.D. as his father persisted in his resolution, the marriage was
1503. concluded between the parties.   It was productive of the
most important consequences.

Another marriage was celebrated in the same year, which in
the next century gave birth to great events—the union of Margaret, Henry's eldest daughter, with James IV. of Scotland.
When this alliance was discussed in the English council, some
objected that England might, in consequence of such marriage,
fall under the dominion of Scotland.   " No!" replied Henry;
" though Scotland should give an heir to the English crown,
that kingdom will only become an accession to England;" and
the event proved the justice of the observation.

The situation of Henry's affairs was now in every respect fortunate; and, uncontrolled by apprehension or opposition, he was
at liberty to give full scope to his avarice, which being increased
by age, and encouraged by absolute authority, broke through
all restraints of shame or justice.   He found two ministers,
Empsom and Dudley, perfectly qualified to second his rapacious
and arbitrary views; and to prey upon his defenceless people.
These vile instruments of tyranny, by their knowledge of law,
were enabled to pervert the forms of justice to the oppression of
the innocent; and he supported them in all their iniquities [1].

But, while Henry was enriching himself with the spoils of his
oppressed people, he did not neglect the political interests of
the nation.   Philip, archduke of Austria, and his wife Joan,
A.D. heiress of Castile, being thrown upon the English coast,
1506. on their passage to Spain, Henry entertained them with
a magnificence suitable to his dignity, and at an expense by no
means agreeable to his temper.   But, notwithstanding so much
seeming cordiality, interest in this, as in all other things, was
the chief rule of his conduct.   He resolved to draw some advan-

[1] Bacon's *Hist.*

tage from the involuntary visit paid him by his royal guests; and while he seemed only intent on displaying his hospitality, and furnishing the means of amusement, he concluded a treaty of commerce highly beneficial to England [1].

Henry's views did not terminate here: from the interests of the nation he turned them to his own. Edmund, earl of Suffolk, nephew to Edward IV., being an object of royal jealousy, had retired to Flanders in disgust. The king did not neglect the present opportunity of complaining to the archduke of the reception which Suffolk had met with in his dominions. " I really thought," replied Philip, " that your greatness and felicity had set you far above apprehensions from any person of so little consequence: but, to give you satisfaction, I will banish him from my territories."—" I expect that you will carry your complaisance farther," said Henry : " I desire to have Suffolk put into my hands, where alone I can depend on his submission and obedience."—" That measure," observed Philip, " will reflect dishonour upon you as well as myself. You will be thought to have used me as a prisoner."—" Then," replied Henry, " the matter is settled. I will take that dishonour upon myself, and your honour will then be safe." Philip found himself under the necessity of complying; but he first exacted a promise from Henry, that he would spare the earl's life [2].

Henry survived these transactions about three years; but nothing memorable occurred in the remaining part of his reign. His declining health made him turn his thoughts towards that future state of existence, which the severities of his government had rendered a very dismal prospect to him. In order to allay the terrors under which he laboured, he endeavoured to procure a reconciliation with Heaven, by distributing alms and founding religious houses. Remorse even seized him at times for the abuse of his authority by Empsom and Dudley, though not to such a degree as to induce him to stop the rapacious hands of those oppressors, until death, by its nearer approaches, appalled him with new terrors; and then he ordered, by a general clause in his will, that restitution should be made to all those whom he had injured [3]. He died of a consumption at April 21, 1509. his favourite palace of Richmond, in the fifty-third year of his age and the twenty-fourth of his reign. He was a prince of great talents, both civil and military. He put an end to the

[1] Rymer, vol. xiii.
[3] Holinshed.—Polyd. Virg.
[2] Bacon's *Hist.*

civil wars with which the English nation had long been harassed: maintained the most perfect order in the state : repressed the exorbitant power of the barons; and indirectly increased the consequence of the commons, by enabling the nobility to break their ancient entails, as the prodigal were thereby encouraged to dissipate their fortunes and dismember their estates, which were thus transferred to men who had acquired money by trade or industry.   And while he possessed the friendship of some foreign princes, he commanded the respect of all.   Hence his son, as we shall afterward have occasion to see, became the arbiter of Europe.   In the mean time we must take a view of transactions in which England had no share, and which introduced the most important æra in the history of modern Europe.

LETTER LV.

A general View of the Continent of Europe, from the Invasion of Italy by Charles VIII. to the League of Cambray in 1508.

I HAVE hitherto, my dear Philip, generally given you a separate history of the principal European states, because each state depended chiefly on itself, and was in a great measure distinct from every other in its political interests.   But that method will, in future, often be impracticable, by reason of the new system of policy which was adopted about the beginning of the sixteenth century, and in consequence of which an union of interests became necessary in order to form a balance of power. This system took its rise from the political state of Europe at A.D. that time, and was perfected by the Italian wars, which 1494. commenced with the expedition of Charles VIII. in support of his claim to the kingdom of Naples.

The army with which Charles undertook this great enterprise did not exceed twenty thousand men : yet with these he was able to overrun all Italy.   The Italians, who, amid continual wars, had become every day more unwarlike, were astonished to meet an enemy that made the field of battle not a pompous tournament but a scene of blood : they were terrified at the aspect of real war, and shrunk on its approach.   The impetuosity of the French valour appeared to them irresistible.   Pope Alexander VI., of infamous memory, the Venetians, and Ludovico Sforza (surnamed the Moor), duke of Milan, alarmed at the king's progress, which was equally unwished and unexpected, endeavoured to throw obstacles in his way almost as soon as he had crossed the Alps.

All opposition, however, was fruitless. Charles entered in triumph the city of Florence, where the family of Medicis still held the chief authority. He delivered Sienna and Pisa from the Tuscan yoke : he prescribed such terms to the Florentines as their situation obliged them to accept : he marched to Rome, where Alexander had ineffectively intrigued against him ; and he took possession of that city as a conqueror. The pope had taken refuge in the castle of St. Angelo : but no sooner did he see the French cannon pointed against its feeble ramparts, than he offered to capitulate ; and it cost him only a cardinal's hat to make his peace with the king. The president Brisonet, who from a lawyer had become an archbishop, persuaded Charles to this accommodation. In reward for his services, he obtained the purple [1]. The king's confessor was likewise in the secret ; and Charles, whose interest it was to have deposed the pope, forgave him, and afterwards repented of his lenity.

No pontiff surely ever more deserved the indignation of a Christian prince. He and the Venetians had applied to the Turkish emperor, Ba-yezid II., son and successor of Mohammed II., to assist them in driving the French monarch out of Italy. It is also asserted, that the pope had sent one Bozzo in quality of nuncio to the court of Constantinople, and that the alliance between his holiness and the soltan was purchased by one of those inhuman crimes which are not committed without horror even within the walls of the seraglio.

Alexander, by an extraordinary chain of events, had at that time in his possession the person of Zizim, brother to the Turkish potentate. This prince, who was adored by the Turks, had disputed the empire with Ba-yezid, and was defeated. Fortune prevailed over the prayers of the people; and this unhappy son of Mohammed II., the terror of the Christian name, had recourse in his distress to the knights of Rhodes. They at first received him as a prince to whom they were bound to afford protection by the laws of hospitality, and who might one day be of use to them in their wars against the infidels ; but they soon after treated him as a prisoner ; and the soltan agreed to pay them forty thousand sequins annually, on con-

[1] G. Flor. *de Bel. Ital.*—Phil. de Com. liv. vii. chap. xii.

dition that they should not suffer Zizim to return into Turkey. The knights conveyed him to one of their commanders at Poictou in France ; and Charles VIII. received, at the same time, an ambassador from Ba-yezid and a nuncio from pope Innocent VIII., Alexander's predecessor, relative to this valuable captive. The soltan claimed him as his subject ; and the pope desired to have possession of his person, as a pledge for the safety of Italy against the attempts of the Turks. Charles sent him to the pope. The pontiff received him with all the splendour and magnificence which the sovereign of Rome could show to the brother of the sovereign of Constantinople ; and Paul Jovius says, that Alexander sold Zizim's life in a treaty which he negociated with Ba-yezid. Be that as it may, the king of France, full of his vast projects, and certain of the conquest of Naples, now wished to become formidable to the soltan, by having the person of this unfortunate prince in his power. The pope delivered him to Charles, but poisoned, as is supposed. A.D. 1495. It is at least certain that he died soon after ; and the character of Alexander renders it probable, that three hundred thousand ducats, said to have been offered by Ba-yezid, were esteemed an equivalent for such a crime [1].

Matters being thus settled between the king and the pope, who took an oath not to disturb Charles in his conquests, Alexander was set at liberty, and appeared again as pontiff on the Vatican theatre. There, in a public consistory, the French monarch came to pay him what is called the homage of obedience, assisted by John Gannai, first president of the parliament of Paris, who might certainly have been better employed elsewhere than at such a ceremony. Charles now kissed the feet of the person whom, two days before, he would have condemned as a criminal ; and, to complete the ludicrous scene, he served his holiness at high mass [2].

Charle-magne, as we have seen, caused himself to be declared emperor of the West, at Rome : Charles VIII. was, in the same city, declared emperor of the East ; but after a very different manner. One Palæologus, nephew to the prince who lost Constantinople and his life, made an empty cession, in favour of Charles, and his successors, of an empire which could not be recovered [3].

After this ceremony, Charles continued his progress towards

[1] Phil. de Comin.—Paul. Jov.—Arm. Feron.   [2] G. Flor.—Guicciardini.
[3] Phil. de Comin.

Naples ; where Alphonso II., filled with terror at his approach, gave the world an example of a new kind of cowardice and pusillanimity.   He fled privately to Sicily, and took refuge in a cloister ; while Ferdinand his son, who became king by his abdication, finding himself unable to retrieve the public affairs, released his subjects from their oath of allegiance, and retired to the island of Ischia.   Charles, thus left master of his favourite object, the kingdom of Naples, after having marched thither from the bottom of the Alps with as much rapidity, and almost as little opposition, as if he had been on a progress through his own dominions, took quiet possession of the throne, and intimidated, or gave law to, every power in Italy [1].

Such, my dear Philip, was the result of this expedition, which must be considered as the first great exertion of those new powers which the princes of Europe had acquired, and now began to exercise.   Its effects were no less considerable than its success had been astonishing.   The Italians, unable to resist the force of Charles, permitted him to proceed undisturbed.   But they quickly perceived, that although no single power which they could rouse to action was a match for such an enemy, yet a confederacy might accomplish what the separate members durst not attempt.   To this expedient, therefore, they had recourse, the only one that remained, to deliver or preserve them from the French yoke ; and while Charles inconsiderately wasted his time at Naples, in festivals and triumphs on account of his past successes, or was fondly dreaming of future conquests in the East, to the empire of which he now aspired, they formed against him a powerful combination of almost all the Italian princes and states ; the heads of which were the pope, the Venetians, and the duke of Milan, supported by the emperor Maximilian, (who had lately succeeded his father, Frederic III.) and by their catholic majesties [2].

The union of so many powers, who suspended or forgot their particular animosities that they might act with concert against an enemy who had become formidable to them all, awakened Charles from his thoughtless security ; and he saw no prospect of safety but in returning to France.

The confederates had assembled an army of thirty thousand men, in order to obstruct his march. He had only nine thousand men with him.   The two armies met in the valley of Fornova ;

[1] And. de la Vig. *Conq. de Nap.* —Phil. de Comin.
[2] Phil. de Comin.—Mariana.

and though the French, with a daring courage, which more than compensated their inferiority of number, broke the army of the allies, and gained a victory, which opened to their monarch a safe passage into his own territories, he was stripped of all his conquests in Italy in as short a time as he had gained them. Ferdinand, by the help of Gonsalvo de Cordova, surnamed the Great Captain, whom their catholic majesties had sent to his assistance, speedily recovered the whole kingdom of Naples. He died soon after, leaving his uncle Frederic in full possession of the throne [1]; and the political system of Italy resumed the same appearance as before the French invasion.

A.D. 1496.

Charles, after his return to France, gave himself up to those pastimes and pleasures which had been the bane of his Italian expedition. In the mean time his health decayed, and he died without issue in the twenty-eighth year of his age, and the fifteenth of his reign; " a man of small body and short stature (says Comines); but so good that it was not possible to see a better creature; and so sweet and gentle in disposition, that it was not known that he ever either gave or took offence in his life." He was succeeded by the duke of Orleans, under the title of Louis XII., to which was afterward added the most glorious of all appellations, that of *Father of his people.*

April 7, 1498.

Louis was in his thirty-sixth year when he ascended the throne : and from that moment he forgot all his personal resentments. When some of his courtiers reminded him, that certain persons who had formerly been his enemies were now in his power, he made this memorable reply:—" The king of France revenges not the injuries of the duke of Orléans." It is one thing, however, to deliver a fine maxim, and another to make it the rule of one's conduct: Louis did both. But his wild ambition of reigning in Italy brought many misfortunes upon himself and his kingdom, notwithstanding his general prudence, and paternal affection for his subjects.

His claim to Naples was the same with that of Charles, and he demanded the duchy of Milan in right of one of his grand-mothers, daughter of John Galeazzo Visconti, who had stipulated, in the marriage contract of his daughter Valentina, that, on the failure of heirs male in the family of Visconti, the duchy should descend to the posterity of that princess and the duke of Orléans. This event took place. The family of Visconti became extinct in 1447 ; but the house of Orléans had hitherto been prevented, by various accidents, from making good their claim ; and the duchy of Milan was still enjoyed by the descendants of Francis Sforza, a soldier of fortune, who having married the natural daughter of the last legal duke, raised himself by his valour and talents to the ducal throne.   Louis now prepared to assert his right with ardour, and he succeeded.   But before I relate the particulars of that conquest, it will be necessary to say a few words of pope Alexander and his son Cæsar Borgia, on account of their alliance with the king of France, and the share which they had in the wars of Italy, remarking, by the way, that Ludovico Sforza, having murdered his nephew, and taken possession of the duchy of Milan, had been confirmed in it, in 1494, by the investiture of the emperor Maximilian, who married his daughter [1].

Alexander was at that time engaged in two great designs : one was, to recover for the Patrimony of St. Peter the many territories of which it was said to have been deprived; and the other, the exaltation of his son.   Infamous as his conduct was, it did not impair his authority.   He was publicly accused of a criminal correspondence with his own sister, whom he took away from three husbands successively ; and he caused the last to be assassinated, that he might bestow her in marriage on the heir of the house of Estè.   The nuptials were celebrated in the Vatican, with the most shameless diversions that debauch had ever invented for the confusion of modesty.   The duke of Gandia, and Cæsar Borgia, at that time cardinal, are said to have publicly disputed the favours of their sister Lucretia.   The duke of Gandia was assassinated at Rome, and Cæsar Borgia was the supposed author of the murder [2].   The personal estates of the cardinals, at their decease, belong to the pope : and Alexander was strongly suspected of hastening the death of more than one member of the sacred college, that he might become possessed of their treasures.   But, notwithstanding these enormities, the people of Rome obeyed this pontiff without murmuring, and his friendship was courted by all the potentates in Europe.

Louis had several reasons for courting the friendship of Alexander.   He wished to be divorced from his wife Joan, the daughter of Louis XI., who was crooked and ugly, and with whom he had lived in wedlock above twenty-two years, without having any

[1] Du Mont. Corp. Diplom. vol. iii.   [2] Paul. Jov. – Arn. Feron.

children. No law, but the law of nature, could authorise such a separation; and yet disgust and policy rendered it necessary. The king disliked his wife, and was desirous of posterity. Ann of Bretagne, the queen-dowager, still retained that tenderness which she had felt for him when duke of Orléans. His passion for her was not yet extinguished; and unless he married her, or at least if she married another, the province would be for ever dismembered from the French monarchy.

These were powerful motives; but the authority of the holy see was necessary to give a sanction to them. It had long been customary to apply to the pope for permission to marry a relative or put away a wife: Louis applied to Alexander, who never scrupled any indulgence in which he could find his interest. The bull of divorce was issued; and Cæsar Borgia was sent with it into France, with power to negociate with the king on the subject of his Italian claims. But this son of the church, in a double sense, did not leave Rome till he was assured of the duchy of Valentinois, a company of one hundred armed men, and a pension of twenty thousand livres. All these Louis not only agreed to, but also promised to procure for him the sister of the king of Navarre. The ambitious Borgia now changed his ecclesiastical character for a secular one; and the pope granted, at the same A.D. instant, a dispensation for his son to quit the church, and 1499. for the king of France to quit his wife [1]. Affairs were quickly settled between Louis and the queen-dowager; and the French prepared for a fresh invasion of Italy.

In this enterprise Louis had the Venetians on his side, who were to participate in the spoils of the Milanese. Maximilian, whose business it was to have defended the duke of Milan, his father-in-law and vassal, was not at that time in a condition to assist him. He could with difficulty make head against the Swiss, who had entirely freed themselves from the Austrian dominion: he therefore acted, upon this occasion, the feigned part of indifference.

The French monarch amicably terminated some disputes which he had with the archduke Philip, who did homage to him for the counties of Flanders and Artois.. Louis also renewed the treaty concluded by Charles VIII. with England; and being now secure on all sides, he led his army over the Alps. He soon made himself master of the duchy of Milan, while the Venetians

---

[1] Du Clos.—Guicciardini.

occupied the territory of Cremona.   Arrayed in ducal robes, he
entered the city of Milan in triumph; and the duke Lu-   A.D.
dovico Sforza being betrayed soon after by the Swiss in   1500.
his pay, was sent prisoner into France, and shut up in the castle
of Loches, where he lay unpitied during the remainder of
his days [1].

Could Louis here have set bounds to his ambition, satisfied
with the conquest of Milan and with his authority in Genoa
(which he had also reduced under his yoke), he was enabled by
his situation to prescribe laws to all the Italian princes and
states, and to hold the balance among them.   But the desire of
recovering the kingdom of Naples engaged him in new projects;
and as he foresaw opposition from Ferdinand of Spain, who had
formerly expelled the French from that country, and who was
connected both by treaties and affinity with Frederic king of
Naples, he endeavoured, by offers of interest, to which the ears
of that monarch were never deaf, to engage him in an opposite
confederacy.   A plan was accordingly settled for the expulsion of
Frederic, and the partition of his dominions.   Frederic, unable
to resist the force of the combined monarchs, each of whom   A.D.
was far his superior in power, resigned his sceptre.   But   1501.
he had the satisfaction to see Naples prove a source of contention
to his conquerors.   Louis and Ferdinand, though they had concurred in making the conquest, differed about the division of it.
From allies they became enemies; and Gonsalvo de Cordova,
partly by the exertion of those military talents which gave   A.D.
him a just title to the appellation of the Great Captain,   1503.
bestowed on him by his countrymen, partly by such shameless
and frequent violations of the most solemn engagements, as leave
an indelible stain upon his memory, stripped the French of all
they possessed in the Neapolitan dominions, and secured the
entire possession of the disputed kingdom to his no less perfidious master [2].

In the mean time pope Alexander subdued the fiefs in Romagna by the arms of Cæsar Borgia.   There is not one act of
oppression, subtle artifice, heroic courage, or atrocious villany
which his son left unpractised.   He made use of more art and
dexterity to get possession of eight or ten little towns, and to rid
himself of a few noblemen who stood in his way, than Alexander
the Great, Julius Cæsar, Genghiz Khan, or Timour, had employed to subdue the most extensive regions of the globe.   Every

---

[1] Brantome.—Guicciardini.   [2] Paul. Jov.—Guicciardini.—Mezeray.

thing seemed to conspire for his aggrandizement. His father was armed with the spiritual, and he with the temporal power of the church. But his good fortune was of short duration: he laboured, without knowing it, for the Patrimony of St. Peter.

Alexander VI. died in 1503, and left behind him a more detestable memory in Europe than Nero or Caligula had done in the Roman empire; the sanctity of his station adding a double tinge to his guilt. The papacy, however, was indebted to him for an accession to its temporal dominions. Cæsar Borgia lost all the fruits of his crimes, and the church profited by them. Most of the cities which he had conquered chose another master, on the death of his father: and pope Julius II. obliged him to deliver up the rest.

Abandoned by friends, allies, and relations, Borgia, in a short time, had nothing left of all his wicked greatness; and to complete his miserable catastrophe, he who had betrayed so many was at last betrayed. Gonsalvo de Cordova, with whom he had trusted his person, sent him prisoner into Spain. Louis took from him the duchy of Valentinois, and his pension. All the world forsook him. Having found means, however, to escape from prison, he sought refuge in Navarre: and courage, which is not properly a virtue, but a happy qualification, common alike to the wicked and the virtuous, did not desert him in his distresses. While in this asylum, he still maintained every part of his character. He carried on intrigues, and he commanded in person the army of the king of Navarre, his father-in-law, during a war into which that prince entered, by the persuasion of Borgia, against one of his vassals. He was slain fighting[1]. " A glorious end!" says Voltaire; but it is surely only glorious to fall in a good cause, and Borgia's was confessedly a bad one. We have no occasion, therefore, to think his fall too favourable. He wrought his own ruin, after having completed his disgrace; a lesson more striking than if he had suffered by the hands of the public executioner.

Louis made a new attempt to recover the kingdom of Naples, and was again disappointed. This disappointment was A.D. 1504. occasioned by the ambition of his minister the cardinal d'Amboise, (who sold his master's interest for a promise of the papacy,) by the policy of Ferdinand, and by the bravery of A.D. 1505. the Great Captain. The king was now sincerely desirous of peace; and willing to secure the possession of Milan,

---

[1] Paul. Jov.—Guicciardini.—Mezeray.

he engaged by the treaty of Blois to pay Maximilian a large sum for the investiture of that duchy. By this treaty also, he promised his daughter in marriage to Charles of Austria, (grandson of Maximilian and Ferdinand by Philip and Joan,) with Bretagne, Burgundy, and all his Italian dominions, as her dowry, in case of his dying without heirs male. But this stipulation A.D. was wisely opposed by the states of France[1]: and the 1506. princess Anne was given in marriage to the count of Angoulême, first prince of the blood, and presumptive heir to the crown, afterwards Francis I. Thus Bretagne, which had been twice annexed to the French monarchy, and twice near being severed from it, was incorporated with it; and Burgundy also was preserved.

During these transactions, Isabella, queen of Castile, died, and the archduke Philip went to take possession of that kingdom, as heir to his mother-in-law. He also died in a short time; and to the astonishment of all Europe, left the king of France governor to his son Charles.

The balance of power was now happily adjusted among the principal European states, and might long have maintained general tranquillity, had not the active and enterprising genius of an ambitious pontiff excited anew the flames of war and discord among them. But the cause of that discord, and its conquences, must be investigated in a future Letter.

LETTER LVI.

A View of Europe, from the League of Cambray to the Death of Louis XII.

Julius II., to whom the popes are particularly indebted for their temporal dominion, had formed the project of ex- A.D. pelling all foreigners from Italy. But he was desirous, in 1508. the first place, of humbling the Venetians, who not only declined entering into his views, but had refused to restore the places which they had dismembered from the territory of the church. The league of Cambray was the consequence of their refusal.

---

[1] Mezeray, tome iv.—Henault, tome i.

Let us take a view of that republic, which so far excited the jealousy of the European princes and states, as to produce this famous confederacy.

Venice, my dear Philip, took its rise, as I have had occasion to notice, during the inroads of the Barbarians, in the fifth century. The little islands of the Adriatic Gulf afforded an asylum to the neighbouring inhabitants, who originally lived by fishing, and afterwards became rich and powerful by commerce. They again got footing on the Terra Firma ; and Venice now extended her dominion from the lake of Como to the middle of Dalmatia. The Turks had deprived her of what she had taken from the Christian emperors in Greece ; but she still retained the large island of Candia, and soon gained possession of Cyprus.

The civil constitution of Venice, established on a firm basis, had suffered no considerable alteration for several centuries ; and the republic, during the same course of time, had conducted its affairs with an uniform and vigorous spirit of policy, which gave it great advantage over other states, whose views and measures changed with the form of their government, or with the persons by whom it was administered. But the constitution of this republic had one striking fault ; it wanted a counterpoise to the power of the nobles, and did not offer proper encouragement to the common people. No private citizen of Venice could rise to the rank of a senator, or occupy any considerable employment in the state.

Such a partial aristocracy, which commits all power to a few members of the community, is naturally jealous. The Venetian nobles distrusted their own subjects, and were afraid of allowing them the use of arms ; the military force of the republic, therefore, consisted wholly of foreign mercenaries. Nor was the command of these ever trusted to noble Venetians, lest they should acquire such influence as might endanger public liberty. A soldier of fortune was placed at the head of the armies of the commonwealth ; and to obtain that honour was the great object of the Italian *condottieri*, or leaders of bands, who made a trade of war, during the fourteenth and fifteenth centuries, and hired out troops to different princes and states [1].

A republic that disarmed its subjects, and excluded its nobles from military command, must have carried on warlike enterprises at great disadvantage ; but its commerce was an inexhaustible

---

[1] Sandi *Storia Civil. Veneziana.*

source of opulence.   All the nations in Europe depended upon the Venetians, not only for the precious commodities of the East, which they imported by the way of Egypt, but for various manufactures fabricated by them alone, or finished with a dexterity and elegance unknown in other countries.   From this extensive commerce, the state derived such immense supplies as concealed the vices in its constitution, and enabled it to keep on foot such armies as were an overmatch for the force which any of its neighbours could bring into the field.   Venice became an object of terror to the Italian states.   Her wealth was viewed with envy by the greatest monarchs, who could not vie with her private citizens in the magnificence of their buildings, in the richness of their dress and furniture, or in splendour and elegance of living.   And Julius II., whose ambition and abilities were equal to those of any priest who had ever filled the papal throne, by working upon the fears of the Italians, and upon the avarice of the princes beyond the Alps, prompted them to form against this proud republic one of the most extensive confederacies that Europe had ever beheld.

The emperor, the king of France, the king of Spain, and the pope, were principals in the league of Cambray, to which almost all the princes of Italy acceded ; the least considerable of them hoping for some share in the spoils of a state which they deemed to be devoted to inevitable destruction.   The Venetians might have diverted this storm, or have broken its force ; but with a presumptuous rashness, to which there is nothing similar in the course of their history, they waited its approach.   The fury of French courage rendered ineffectual all their precautions for the safety of the republic ; and the battle of Aignadel, fought A.D. near the river Adda, ruined the army on which they relied 1509. for defence.   Julius seized all the towns which they held in the ecclesiastical territories ; and Ferdinand re-annexed to the kingdom of Naples the places which they had taken on the Calabrian coast.   Maximilian, at the head of a powerful army, advanced towards Venice on one side ; the French pushed their conquests on the other ; and the Venetians, surrounded by so many enemies, and left without one ally, sunk from the height of presumption to the depth of despair.   They abandoned their territories on the continent, and shut themselves up in their capital, as their last refuge[1].

---

[1] Guicciardini.—Mezeray.—*Hist. de la Ligue faite à Cambray*, par M. l'Abbé du Bos.

Julius having thus, in the humiliation of the Venetians, attained his first object, began to think of the second, more worthy of his enterprising genius—the expulsion of every foreign power out of Italy. For this purpose it was necessary to dissolve the league of Cambray, and sow dissensions among those princes whom he had formerly united. He absolved the Venetians, on their ceding to him the places claimed by the holy see, from that anathema which had been pronounced against them; and he concluded an alliance with the republic against those very French whom he had invited to oppress it. Their imperious behaviour had rendered them peculiarly obnoxious to the Italians; and Julius, who was a native of Genoa, was greatly desirous of revenging upon Louis the triumphant ostentation with which he had punished the revolt of that city, whose records he caused to be burned, and whose principal citizens he obliged to kneel at the foot of his throne, while he pronounced their sentence; which, after all, was only to pay a trifling fine. On Louis, therefore, the haughty pontiff was determined that the tempest first should fall; and in order to pave the way for this bold project, he at once sought a ground of quarrel with that monarch, and courted the alliance of foreign princes. He declared war against the duke of Ferrara, the confederate of the French; he solicited the favour of Henry VIII. of England, by sending him a sacred rose, perfumed with musk, and anointed with holy oil: he detached Ferdinand from the league, and drew him over to his party, by granting him the full investiture of the A.D. kingdom of Naples; and, what he chiefly valued, he 1510. formed a treaty with the Swiss, whose subsidy Louis had refused to augment, and whom he had offended by some contumelious expressions[1].

The confederacy of Cambray being thus dissolved, affairs soon began to wear a very different aspect in Italy. The Venetians, recovering from their consternation, were able to make head A.D. against the emperor, and even to regain part of the ter-1511. ritory which they had lost. The pope and his allies made war upon the duke of Ferrara. They were compelled by the French to raise the siege of Bologna; but they afterwards formed that of Mirandola, where Julius appeared in person, visited the trenches, hastened the operations, and entered the breach, with all the ardour of a young soldier in pursuit of military glory[2].

Louis was now at a loss how to act; overawed by his venera-

---

[1] Mezeray.—Platin.　　　　　　　　　[2] Guicciardini.

tion for the vicar of Christ, he was afraid to let his generals take those advantages which fortune threw in their way. He therefore wished to divest Julius of that sacred character which chiefly rendered him formidable. With this view, in conjunction with Maximilian, who was himself ambitious of the papacy, and by the authority of some disgusted cardinals, he summoned a general council at Pisa, in order to reform the church, and check the exorbitancies of the sovereign power. But he was as irresolute in supporting the council, as in instructing his generals. Julius saw his timidity, and availed himself of it. He summoned a council at the Lateran; he put Pisa under an interdict, A.D. and all the places that should give shelter to the schisma- 1512. tical council; he excommunicated the cardinals and prelates who attended it; he even pointed his spiritual thunder against the princes who adhered to it; he freed their subjects from all oaths of allegiance, and gave their dominions to every one who could take possession of them[1].

Ambition is ready to seize the slightest pretences to accomplish its designs. The crafty Ferdinand, who, while he bore the surname of the Catholic, regarded the cause of the pope and of religion solely as a cover to his selfish politics, made this anathema of Julius a pretext for robbing the king of Navarre of his dominions, as an abettor of the council of Pisa. The method which he took to effect this conquest was not less remarkable than the measure itself. Henry VIII., his son-in-law, naturally sincere and sanguine in temper, was moved with a hearty desire of protecting the pope from that oppression to which he believed him exposed from the French monarch. Eager also to acquire that distinction in Europe to which his power and opulence entitled him, he could not long remain neuter amidst the noise of arms; he was, therefore, induced to join that alliance, which the pope, Spain, and Venice, had formed against Louis. Ferdinand saw his intemperate ardour, and made him the instrument of his own base ambition.

This artful prince, who considered his close connection with Henry only as the means of taking advantage of his inexperience, advised him not to invade France by the way of Calais, where he himself should not have it in his power to assist him: he exhorted him rather to send forces to Fontarabia, whence he could easily make a conquest of Guienne, a province in which it was imagined the English had still some adherents. He pro-

[1] Spelm. *Concil.*

mised to forward this conquest by the junction of a Spanish army : and so zealous did he seem to promote the interests of his son-in-law, that he even sent vessels to England, in order to transport the forces which Henry had levied for that purpose. But the marquis of Dorset, who commanded this army, had no sooner landed in Guipuscoa, than Ferdinand suggested the necessity of first subduing the kingdom of Navarre.

The marquis refused to take any part in that enterprise, and therefore remained at Fontarabia. But so subtle was the contrivance of Ferdinand, that the English army, even while it lay in that situation, was almost as serviceable to his purpose, as if it had acted in conjunction with his own. It kept the French in awe, and prevented them from advancing to succour the kingdom of Navarre ; so that the duke of Alva, having full leisure to conduct his operations, not only subdued the smaller towns, but reduced Pampeluna, the capital, and obliged John d'Albret, the sovereign, to take refuge in France. Dorset was obliged to return to England, with an army diminished by want and sickness, without being able to effect any thing for the interests of his master ; and Henry, enraged at his ill success, was with difficulty made sensible of the fraudulent conduct of the Spanish prince [1].

These incidents were far from being unimportant ; but events of still greater moment occurred in Italy. Though the war which England waged against France brought no advantage to the former kingdom, it was of much prejudice to the latter ; and by obliging Louis to withdraw his forces from Italy, deprived him of the superiority which his arms, in the beginning of the campaign, had acquired in that country. Gaston de Foix, his nephew, had been entrusted with the command of the French forces ; and at the age of twenty-three, exhibited in a few months such feats of military skill and valour as were sufficient to render illustrious the life of the oldest general. His career

April 11. terminated with the famous battle of Ravenna ; which, after a most obstinate dispute, he gained over the Spanish and papal armies. He perished when his victory was complete, and with him perished the fortune of the French arms in Italy. The Swiss, who had now rendered themselves formidable by their bands of disciplined infantry, invaded the duchy of Milan with a numerous army, and encouraged its inconstant inhabitants to revolt from the dominion of France. Genoa followed the example

---

[1] Lord Herbert's *Hist. of Hen. VIII.*—Polyd. Virg.

of that duchy; and Louis quickly lost all his Italian conquests. Maximilian Sforza, the son of Ludovico, was reinstated in the possession of Milan; and the Genoese recovered their independence[1].

The expulsion of the French gave great pleasure to the pope, the more particularly as he owed it to the Swiss, whom he had honoured with the title of *Defenders of the Holy See*, and whose councils he hoped always to govern. He did not, however, long enjoy this satisfaction. He died suddenly, at an advanced age, and was succeeded in the pontificate by John of Medicis, son of the celebrated Lorenzo, who had governed Tuscany with high reputation, and obtained the appellation of *Father of the Muses*. John took the name of Leo X., and proved one of the most illustrious pontiffs that ever sat on the papal throne. Humane, liberal, affable, the patron of art and genius, he had a soul no less capable of forming great designs than his predecessor; and he was more delicate in employing means for the execution of them. By the negotiations of Leo, who adhered to the political system of Julius, Maximilian was detached from the French interest; and Henry VIII., notwithstanding his disappointments in the former campaign, was still encouraged to prosecute his warlike measures against Louis[2].

A.D.
1513.

To prevent disturbance from Scotland, while the English arms should be employed on the continent, Henry dispatched an ambassador to James IV., his brother-in-law, with instructions to adjust all disputes which had arisen between the two kingdoms. But the projected invasion of France roused the jealousy of the Scottish nation. The ancient league which subsisted between France and Scotland was esteemed the most sacred bond of connection, and believed by the Scots to be essential to the preservation of their independence against a people so superior as the English. Henry's ambassador therefore easily foresaw, though James still made professions of maintaining neutrality, that a war with Scotland would in the end prove inevitable; and he gave warning of the danger to his master, who sent the earl of Surrey to put the borders in a posture of defence, and to resist the expected inroad of the enemy[3].

Thirsting for military fame, Henry invaded France by the way of Calais. But of all the allies, whose assistance he expected, the Swiss alone fully performed their engagements.

---

[1] Guicciardini. [2] Guicciardini.—Herbert.
[3] Buchanan.—Drummond.—Herbert.

Maximilian, among others, failed to perform his; although he had received, in advance, a subsidy of a hundred thousand crowns. That he might make some atonement, however, for this breach of faith, he appeared in person in the Low Countries, and joined the English army with a small body of Germans and Flemings, who were useful in giving an example of discipline to Henry's new-levied forces. The emperor carried his condescension yet farther. He did not pretend, with so few men, to act as an auxiliary, but enlisted himself in the service of the English monarch, wore the cross of St. George, and received a hundred crowns a day for the use of his table [1].

An emperor of Germany, serving under a king of England, and living by his bounty, was surely a spectacle truly extraordinary; but Henry treated him with the highest respect, and he really directed all the operations of the war. The first enterprise which they undertook was the siege of Terouenne, a town situated on the borders of Picardy. During the attack of this place was fought the battle of Guinegate, where the cavalry of France fled at the first onset, and the duke of Longueville, Bussi d'Amboise, the chevalier Bayard, and many other officers of distinction, were made prisoners. This action, or rather rout, is commonly called the *Battle of Spurs*, because the French on that occasion made greater use of their spurs than of their military weapons [2].

After so considerable an advantage, Henry might have made incursions to the gates of Paris; but, instead of pushing his victory, he returned to the siege. Terouenne was soon reduced; and the anxieties of the French were renewed with regard to the motions of the English. The Swiss, at the same time, had entered Burgundy with a formidable army; and the catholic king, though he had made a truce with Louis, seem disposed to seize every advantage which fortune should present to him.

While France was thus endangered, Louis knew not what course to follow, or where to place his safety; his troops were dismayed, and his people intimidated. But he profited by the blunders of his enemies. The Swiss allowed themselves to be seduced into a negotiation by Tremouille, governor of Burgundy, without inquiring whether he had any powers to treat: and that nobleman, who knew that his stipulations would be disavowed by his master, agreed to whatever they were pleased to demand, happy to free the realm from such dangerous invaders at the

---

[1] Herbert.   [2] *Hist. du Chev. Bayard.— Mem. de Bellai.*

expense of a little money and many empty promises. Henry discovered no less ignorance in the conduct of war, than the Swiss in negotiation. By the interested counsel of Maximilian, he laid siege to Tournay, which then belonged to France, and afforded the troops of that kingdom a passage into the heart of the Netherlands. Soon after the reduction of this place, which was of no benefit to Henry, he was informed of the retreat of the Swiss; and as the season was now far advanced, he thought proper to return to England with the greater part of his army. Such, my dear Philip, was the issue of a campaign much boasted of by the English monarch; but which, all circumstances considered, was unprofitable, if not inglorious.

The success which attended the English arms in North-Britain was more decisive. James had crossed the Tweed with fifty thousand men; but, instead of making a vigorous campaign, he wasted his time in the arms of a fair captive. His troops became dissatisfied, and began to be harassed by hunger; and as the authority of the prince was yet feeble amongst the Scots, and military discipline extremely lax, many of them retired from the camp. The earl of Surrey, having collected a body of twenty-six thousand men, advanced to the hills of Cheviot; drew the Scots from their high station, by feigning to enter their country; and defeated them in the field of Flodden, where their Sept. 9. king and the flower of his nobility were slain [1].—Henry, on this occasion, discovered a mind truly great and generous. Though an inviting opportunity was now offered him of extending his dominion over the whole island, he took compas- A.D. sion on the helpless condition of his sister Margaret, and 1514. her infant son; and readily granted peace to Scotland, as soon as it was solicited.

A general accommodation soon followed. Louis, dreading the event of another campaign, sued for peace. He renounced the council of Pisa, now transferred to Lyons; and Leo granted him absolution. Ferdinand the Catholic renewed the truce with France; and he and Maximilian entered into a treaty with Louis for the marriage of his daughter Renée to Charles, prince of Spain. Louis himself espoused the princess Mary of England, and agreed to pay her brother Henry a million of crowns. These two monarchs also entered into an alliance for their mutual defence [2].

The French king, thus rescued from his numerous difficulties,

---

[1] Buchanan.—Drummond.—Herbert.   [2] Du Tillet.

had the happiness of beholding, once more, his affairs in good order, and all Europe in tranquillity.   But he enjoyed this happiness only for a short time.   Enchanted with the beauty and elegant accomplishments of his young queen, he forgot in her arms his advanced age, and was seduced into such a round of gaiety and pleasure as proved very unsuitable to his declining health [1].   He died about three months after the marriage, in his fifty-third year, and when he was meditating anew the conquest of Milan—which was left to immortalize the name, and swell the misfortunes of his successor.

Jan. 1.
1515.

There is no perfection in human beings, my dear Philip, and consequently not in kings, whatever their flatterers may tell them ; but few men, either princes or subjects, seemed to have possessed more social and benevolent virtues than fell to the share of Louis XII.   He was universally beloved by the French ; the populace and the nobility equally adored him, and unanimously called him their Father; a title with which he was particularly pleased, and which he made it the study of his life to deserve. He began his reign with abolishing many taxes ; and at the time of his death, notwithstanding his wars and disasters, he had diminished, by one half, the public burthens.   His very misfortunes, or, in a political sense, his errors, endeared him to his subjects ; for it was well known, that he might have maintained his conquests in Italy, if he would have levied larger sums upon his people.   But his heart would not permit him to distress them : he esteemed any loss trivial, compared with that of their affections.   His moderation was no less remarkable than his humanity.   When informed that some of his courtiers smiled at his economy, which they considered as too rigid, and that certain authors had taken the liberty to ridicule it in their writings, he was by no means displeased.   " I would rather," replied he, magnanimously, " that my people should laugh at my parsimony, than weep at their own oppressions ."

---

[1] Brantome.—*Eloge de Louis XII.*—" The good king," says another writer, " for the sake of his wife, totally altered his manner of living.   Whereas *before* he used to *dine* at *eight* o'clock in the *morning*, he *now* did not *dine* till *noon*.   He had also been *accustomed* to go to *bed* at *six* in the *evening*, and he *now* frequently *sat up* till *midnight*."   (*Hist. du Chev. Bayard.*)   Nothing can mark, more strongly than this passage, the difference between the mode of living in that and the present age.

[2] *Hist. de Louis XII.*—pub. par Theod. Godefroy.

LETTER LVII.

The general View of Europe continued, from the Accession of Francis I. to the Death of the Emperor Maximilian; including the Rise of the Reformation in Germany.

Louis XII. was succeeded by his son-in-law, Francis count of Angoulême, whose military genius, it was foreseen, would soon disturb the peace of Europe. Young, brave, ambitious, A. D. and enterprising, he immediately turned his eyes towards 1515. Italy, as the scene of glory and of conquest. His first object was the recovery of Milan. But before he commenced that expedition, he renewed the treaty which his predecessor had concluded with England; and having nothing to fear from Spain, where Ferdinand was on the verge of the grave, he marched towards the Alps, under pretence of defending his kingdom against the incursions of the Swiss. Informed of his real views, that warlike people had taken arms, at the instigation of the pope, in order to protect Maximilian Sforza, duke of Milan. They took possession of all those passes in the Alps, through which they thought the French would enter Italy; and when they learned that Francis had made his way into Piedmont by a secret route, they descended undismayed into the plain, and gallantly opposed themselves on foot to the heavy-armed cavalry of France. The two armies met at Marignan, near Milan, where ensued one of the most furious and obstinate battles men- Sept. 13. tioned in the history of modern times. The action began towards evening: night parted the combatants; but, the next morning, the Swiss renewed the attack with unabated ardour, and it required all the heroic valour of Francis to inspire his troops with courage sufficient to resist the shock. The Swiss, though at last disordered by the cavalry, and galled by the cannon, long kept their ground, and did not retire till they had lost upwards of twelve thousand of their best troops, about one half of their whole number. The loss of the French was very considerable; twenty thousand men are said to have fallen on both sides; and the old marshal Trivulzio, who had been present at eighteen pitched battles, used to declare, that in comparison of the battle of Marignan every other engagement he had seen was but *the play of children,* but that this was *a combat of heroes* [1].

The surrender of the city of Milan, and the conquest of the whole duchy, were the consequences of this victory. Maximilian Sforza resigned his claim, in consideration of a pension; and Francis, having concluded a treaty with the pope and with the Swiss, returned into France, leaving to Charles duke of Bourbon the government of his Italian dominions [2].

The success and glory of the young monarch began to excite jealousy in the breast of the old emperor Maximilian; nor was the rapid progress of Francis, though in so distant a country, regarded with indifference even by the king of England. Henry dispatched a minister to the court of Vienna, with secret orders to propose certain payments to the emperor; and Maximilian, who was ever ready to embrace any overture to excite fresh troubles, and always necessitous, immediately invaded Italy with a considerable army. But being repulsed before Milan by the French garrison, and hearing that twelve thousand Swiss were advancing to its relief, he retired hastily into Germany, made peace with France and with Venice, ceded Verona to that republic for a sum of money, and thus excluded himself in some measure from future access into Italy [3].

A.D. 1516.

This peace, which restored universal tranquillity to Europe, was preceded by the death of Ferdinand the Catholic, and the succession of his grandson Charles to his extensive dominions, an event which had long been looked for, and from which the most important consequences were expected. Charles, who had hitherto resided in the Low-Countries, which he governed as heir of the house of Burgundy, was now near the full age of sixteen, and possessed a recollection and sedateness much above his years; but his genius had yet given no indications of that superiority which its maturer state displayed. That capacious and decisive judgment, which afterwards directed so ably the affairs of a vast empire, was left to be discovered by those great events to which it gave birth, and those occasions which rendered it necessary. At present there was little call for it.

Jan. 23.

Cardinal Ximenes, archbishop of Toledo, had been appointed sole regent of Castile till the arrival of Charles. This prelate, who united the abilities of a great statesman with the abject de-

---

[1] *Mem. de Fleuranges.*   [2] Guicciardini.—Mezeray.   [3] Guicciardini.

votion of a superstitious monk, and the magnificence of a prime-minister with the austerity of a mendicant, maintained order and tranquillity in Spain, notwithstanding the discontents of turbulent and high-spirited nobles. When they disputed his right to the regency, he coolly showed them the testament of Ferdinand, and the ratification of that deed by Charles ; but these not satisfying them, and arguments proving ineffectual, he led them insensibly towards a balcony, whence they had a view of a large body of troops under arms, and a formidable train of artillery. " Behold," said the cardinal, raising his voice, and extending his arm, " the powers which I have received from his catholic majesty : by these 1 govern Castile, and will govern it, till the king, your master and mine, shall come and take posses- A.D. sion of his realm." A declaration so bold and determined 1517. silenced all opposition [1].

The fate of this minister merits our attention, though not immediately connected with the line of general history. The young king was received with universal acclamations of joy ; but Ximenes found little cause to rejoice. He was seized with a violent disorder, supposed to be the effect of poison; and when he recovered, Charles, prejudiced against him by the Spanish grandees and his Flemish courtiers, slighted his advice, and meanly suffered him to sink into neglect. The cardinal did not bear this treatment with his usual firmness of spirit. He expected a more grateful return from a prince, to whom he delivered a kingdom far more flourishing than it had been in any former age, and authority more extensive and better established than the most illustrious of his ancestors had ever possessed. Conscious of his own integrity and merit, he could not refrain from giving vent, at times, to indignation and complaint. He lamented the fate of his country, and foretold the calamities to which it would be exposed from the insolence, the rapacity, and the ignorance of strangers. These feelings agitated the soul of Ximenes, when he received a letter from the king, dismissing him from his councils, under pretence of relieving his age from that burthen which he had so long and so ably sustained. This epistle proved fatal to the minister. His haughty mind could not endure disgrace, nor his generous heart the stings of ingratitude : he expired a few hours after he had perused the letter [2].

While Charles was taking possession of the throne of Spain, in consequence of the death of one grandfather, another was

[1] Flechier, *Vie de Ximen.*
[2] Marsollier, *Vie de Ximen.*—Baudier, *Hist. de Ximen.*

endeavouring to obtain for him the imperial crown. With this
A.D. view, Maximilian assembled a diet at Augsburg, where
1518. he strove to gain the favour of the electors by many
acts of beneficence, in order to engage them to choose that
young prince as his successor. But Maximilian himself, having
never been crowned by the pope (a ceremony deemed essential
in that age, as well as in the preceding), was considered only as
king of the Romans, or emperor *elect;* and no example occur-
ring in history of any person being chosen successor to a king
of the Romans, the Germans, ever tenacious of their forms,
obstinately refused to confer upon Charles a dignity which was
unknown to their constitution [1].

But the diet of Augsburg had other employment. Thither
was summoned Martin Luther, for " propagating new and dangerous opinions." These opinions, my dear Philip, were the
first principles of the Reformation, which soon diffused themselves through Germany, which were afterwards embraced by
so many nations, and which separated one half of Europe from
the Romish church. Of the origin of this great schism some
account will be necessary ; for, although I would by no means
engage you in theological disputes, you ought to know the
grounds of a controversy, which produced so remarkable a revolution in the creeds and ceremonies of Christians, that you may
be the better enabled to judge of its effects upon society, upon
industry, literature, policy, and morals. In that light only I
mean to consider it : the road to heaven I leave to heavenly
directors.

In the course of these Letters I have had occasion to observe
the rise of the pope's spiritual power, as well as of his temporal
dominion ; to trace the progress, and to remark the abuses of
each. A repetition here would therefore be unnecessary. The
spiritual despotism of Gregory VII.—the temporal tyranny of
Alexander VI.—and the bloody ambition of Julius II.—make
too strong an impression on the mind to be soon effaced. After
that enormous privilege which the Roman pontiffs assumed, of
disposing of crowns, and releasing nations from their oaths of
allegiance, the most pernicious to society was that of absolving
individuals from the ties of moral duty. This dangerous power,
or one equivalent to it, the pope claimed as the successor of St.
Peter, and the keeper of the spiritual treasury of the church,
supposed to contain the superabundant good works of the saints,

[1] Barre, tome vi.

together with the infinite merits of Jesus Christ.   Out of this
inexhaustible storehouse, his holiness might retail, at pleasure,
particular portions to those who were deficient.   He assumed,
in short, and directly exercised, the right of pardoning sins :
which was, in other words, granting a permission to commit
them ; for, if it is known, as had long been the case in the
Romish church, at what price the punishment of any crime
may be bought off, the encouragement to vice is the same as if a
dispensation had been granted beforehand ; and even that was
frequently allowed.

The influence of such indulgences upon morals may easily be
imagined ; especially in ages when superstition had silenced the
voice of conscience, and reason was bewildered in Gothic darkness ; when the church had provided numerous sanctuaries,
which not only screened from the arm of the civil magistrate
persons guilty of the greatest enormities, but often enabled
them to live in affluence.   Yet that great historian and profound
philosopher, Mr. Hume, has endeavoured to prove, that the
protestant writers err in supposing that a dissolution of morals
should ensue, " because a man could purchase for a shilling an
indulgence for the most enormous and unheard-of crimes '!"
But you, I hope, will think otherwise, when you have duly
weighed the foregoing considerations.

Mr. Hume seems here to have forgotten that all men are not
philosophers; or, blinded by the love of paradox, to have lost
sight of common sense.   He seems even to have lost sight of
his argument; for he adds, " that after these indulgences,
there still remained hell-fire, the civil magistrate, and the
remorses of conscience," to awe mankind to their duty.   Now
the first assertion is literally false ; for the very words of an
indulgence imported, that it restored the individual " to that
innocence and purity which he possessed at baptism :" and,
according to the doctrine of the Roman church, the infant is
then fit for heaven.   But the indulgence did not stop here : it
concluded thus ; " so that when you die, the gates of punishment shall be shut, and the gates of the paradise of delight
shall be opened '." The terror of the civil magistrate could
be very small, when, as I have already observed, the church
afforded shelter to every criminal that sought her sanctuaries,
and took into her bosom the whole body of the clergy.   Con-

' *Hist. of England*, vol. iv. note A.
' Seckend, *Comment.* lib. i.—Robertson's *Hist. of Charles V.* book ii.

science, indeed—so often represented by this doubting sage as an erring guide, as a principle superinduced and local—could not be banished from the human breast; but its voice, if not entirely silenced by superstition, was too feeble to be heard by the self-deluding and headstrong passions of man, when flattered by the hope, or encouraged by the assurance, of a papal indulgence.

These indulgences or plenary pardons, of which I have been led insensibly to speak, [and which not only served as a remission of sins to the living, but as a release to the dead from the pains of purgatory,] were first invented by Urban II. as a recompense for those who engaged in the wild expeditions to the Holy Land. They were afterwards granted to such as contributed money for that or any other pious purpose; and the sums so raised were frequently diverted to other uses. They were employed to swell the state, to furnish the luxuries, or accomplish the ambitious enterprises, of the popes. John XXII. reduced this spiritual traffic into a system: and Leo X., the great patron of arts and letters, having exhausted the papal treasury in rewards to men of genius, in magnificent works, and expensive pleasures, thought that he might attempt, without danger, those pious frauds which had been so successfully practised by the most ignorant of his predecessors: Leo published a general sale of *indulgences*.

If any thing could apologize for a religious cheat that tends to the subversion of morals, Leo's apology was ready. He was engaged in the completion of that superb temple, St. Peter's church, founded by his predecessor; and the Turks were preparing to enter Germany. He had no occasion to forge pretences for this extension of papal authority. But Leo, though a polite scholar, and a fine gentleman, was a pitiful pope. Liberal-minded himself, and surrounded by men of liberal minds, he did not foresee that the lamp of knowledge, which he held up to mankind, would illumine the shades of Superstition; would show them her errors, her impostures, her usurpations, and their own slavish condition. He did not reflect, that impositions employed with success in one age may prove dangerous experiments in another. But he had soon occasion to remember it.

The abuse of the sale of indulgences in Germany, where they were publicly retailed in ale-houses, and where the produce of every district was farmed out, in the manner of a toll or custom, awakened the indignation of Martin Luther, an Augustine friar, professor of theology in the university of Wittenberg. Luther was also incensed, it is said, because the privilege of vending this spiritual merchandise had been taken from his order, and given to the Dominicans. Be that as it may, he wrote and preached against indulgences. His writings were read with avidity, and his discourses were listened to with admiration. He appealed to reason and Scripture, for the truth of his arguments, not to the decisions of councils or of popes. A corner of the veil was now happily lifted. The people, ever fond of judging for themselves, (and in matters which concern themselves only, they have an undoubted right,) flattered by this appeal, began to call in question that authority which they had formerly reverenced, which they had blindly adored; and Luther, emboldened by success, extended his views, and ventured to declaim against other abuses. From abuses he proceeded to usurpations; from usurpations to errors; and from one error to another, till the whole fabric of the Romish church began to totter.

Alarmed at the progress of this daring innovater, Leo had summoned him to answer for his doctrines at Rome. But that citation was remitted at the intercession of Frederic the Wise, elector of Saxony, who had hitherto protected Luther; and his cause was ordered to be tried in Germany, by Cardinal Cajetan, a Dominican, eminent for scholastic learning, and the pope's legate at the imperial court. For this purpose, among others, Cajetan attended the diet at Augsburg; and thither Luther repaired without hesitation, after having obtained the emperor's safe-conduct, though he had good reason to decline a judge chosen from among his avowed adversaries. The cardinal received him with decent respect, and endeavoured, at first, to gain him by gentle treatment; but finding him firm in his principles, and thinking it beneath the dignity of his station to enter into any formal dispute, he required him, by virtue of the apostolic powers with which he was invested, to retract his errors (without showing that they were such), and to abstain, for the future, from the publication of new and dangerous opinions. Luther, who had flattered himself with a hearing, and hoped to distinguish himself in a dispute with so able a prelate, was mortified at this arbitrary mode of proceeding; but his native intrepidity of mind did not forsake him. He boldly replied, that he could not, with a safe conscience, renounce opinions which he believed to be true; but offered to submit the whole controversy to the judgment of the learned, naming several universities. This offer was rejected by Cajetan, who still insisted upon a simple recantation; and Luther, by the advice of his friends, after appealing to a general council, secretly withdrew from Augsburg, and returned into Saxony [1]. The progress of this extraordinary man, and of that reformation to which he gave birth, I shall afterwards have occasion to trace.

The diet of Augsburg was soon followed by the death of Jan. 12, Maximilian. This event was, in itself, of little moment, 1519. as that prince had, for some years, ceased to be of any consequence ; but, as it left vacant the first station among Christian princes, of which two great monarchs were equally ambitious, it became memorable by its effects. It gave rise to a competition, and awakened a jealousy, which threw all Europe into agitation : it broke that profound peace which then reigned in Christendom, and excited wars more general, and more mischievously durable, than any which modern times had beheld. —But, before we enter on that interesting æra, I must carry forward the Progress of Society ; notice the improvements in arts and in letters ; and exhibit some account of those great naval discoveries which produced so important a revolution in the commercial world, and gave to Europe a new continent, while religion and ambition were depopulating the old. Meanwhile it will be proper to remark, that, during the reign of Maximilian, Germany was divided into Circles, in each of which a provincial and particular jurisdiction was established, to supply the place of a public and common tribunal. In this reign also was instituted the Imperial Chamber, composed of judges nominated partly by the emperor, partly by the several states, and invested with authority for the final decision of all differences among the members of the Germanic body. The Aulic Council too, which took cognizance of all feudal cases, and such as belong to the emperor's immediate jurisdiction, received under this prince a new form [2]. By these regulations, order was given to that confused government, and some degree of vigour restored to the imperial authority.

---

[1] Sleid. *Hist. Reform.*—Robertson, ubi sup.
[2] Dutt. *De Pace Publicâ Imperii.*

LETTER LVIII.

*Of the Progress of Society in Europe, from the beginning of the
Fourteenth to the middle of the Sixteenth Century, with a
retrospective View of the Revival of Letters.*

WE have already, my dear Philip, traced the progress of
society to the beginning of the fourteenth century. We have
seen corporation charters granted; civil communities formed;
and the great body of the people, released from that servitude
under which they had so long groaned, applying themselves to
trade and industry. We have also seen universities generally
established; the study of the Roman law introducing a more
perfect system of jurisprudence; an acquaintance with the
learned languages awakening an ambition of literary merit;
manners taking a more liberal turn; and commerce beginning
to circulate the conveniences of life. But society had still
many advances to make, before it reached that state of refinement in which we now behold it, or which it had attained under
the pontificate of Leo X.

These advances it is now our business to trace. By the way,
however, I must remind you, that, in the course of the general
narrative, I have taken occasion to notice the progress of society
with respect to the command of national force; the vigour which
government acquired, by the increase of the royal authority;
the alterations which took place in the art of war, in consequence of the invention of gunpowder; the establishment of
standing armies, and the supplies necessary for the support of
such a body of men. I have also had occasion to mention the
new system adopted by princes, for national defence and safety,
by maintaining a balance of political power, and the means by
which that system was perfected. I shall, therefore, devote this
letter solely to such objects as cannot come within the line of
general history; the progress of manners, of arts, and of polite
literature. The sciences, as since cultivated, were not yet
known. True philosophy belongs to a more modern æra.

Mankind are no sooner in possession of the conveniences of
life, than they begin to aim at its elegances. About the commencement of the fourteenth century, such a taste became
general in Europe. The Italian cities, which had early acquired
liberty, and obtained municipal charters, carried on at that time

a flourishing trade with India, through the ports of the Red Sea. They introduced into their own country manufactures of various kinds, and carried them on with great ingenuity and vigour. In the manufacture of silk, in particular, they made so rapid a progress, that about the middle of that century, a thousand citizens of Genoa appeared in procession, clad in silk robes. They attempted new arts; among which may be numbered, the art of taking impressions from engravings on plates of copper, the manufacture of crystal glass for mirrors, of paper from linen rags, and of earthen ware in imitation of porcelain. And they imported from warmer climates the art of raising several natural productions (formerly unknown in Europe), which now furnish the materials of a lucrative and extended commerce; particularly the culture of silk, and the plantation of the sugar cane. Originally the produce of Asia, and esteemed peculiar to the East, the sugar cane was transplanted from the Greek islands into Sicily, thence into Italy, afterwards into Spain and Portugal, and at length into the newly-discovered islands in the Western Ocean [1].

The discovery of those islands, and also of the American continent, was the effect of another modern invention, namely, the mariner's compass; which, by rendering navigation at once more secure and more adventurous, facilitated the intercourse between remote nations, and may be said to have brought them nearer to each other.

But the progress of navigation, and the discoveries to which it gave birth, demand a particular letter. Yet here I must observe, that commerce, during the fourteenth and fifteenth centuries, was by no means confined to the Italian states. Flanders had long been as famous for the manufacture of linen and woollen cloths, as Italy was for that of silk. All the wool of England, before the reign of Edward III., except a small quantity wrought into coarse cloths for home consumption, was sold to the Flemings or Lombards, but chiefly to the former, and manufactured by them; and it was not till the middle of the fifteenth century (so slow were our ancestors in availing themselves of their natural commercial advantages!) that the English were capable of fabricating cloth for foreign markets. Bruges was at once the staple for English wool, for the woollen and linen manufactures of the Netherlands, for the naval stores and other bulky commodities of the North, and for the precious

---

[1] Guicciardini, *Descrit. de' Paesi Bassi.*

commodities of the East, as well as domestic productions, carried thither by the Italian states[1]. It was the greatest emporium in Europe.

Nothing so much advances society as an intercourse with strangers. In proportion as commerce made its way into the different countries of Europe, they successively turned their attention to those objects, and adopted those manners, which occupy and distinguish polished nations. Accordingly we find the Italians and Flemings taking the lead in the liberal as well as in the commercial arts, and exhibiting the first examples of cultivated life.

Painting and architecture revived in Italy towards the close of the thirteenth century. They continued to make rapid progress under different masters, and were both carried to perfection during the period under review. Tapestry, then in high estimation, had long been manufactured with the greatest ingenuity in the Low Countries; and the Flemings, in their turn, became painters and architects, before the rest of Europe were furnished with the necessary arts. Ghent and Bruges, Venice and Genoa, were splendid cities, adorned with stately buildings, while the inhabitants of London and Paris lived in wretched cottages, without even a chimney to carry up the smoke. The fire was made on the ground in the middle of the apartment, and all the family sat round it, like the Laplanders in their huts[2]. This rude method of building and living continued to be common in considerable towns, both in France and England, as late as the beginning of the sixteenth century.

Learning and politeness are supposed to keep pace with each other. But this observation seems to have been made without due attention, to have been formed into a maxim by some dogmatist, and implicitly adopted by succeeding writers; for, if it be applied to the abstract sciences, it seems equally void of foundation, whether we consider the fact itself, the nature of those sciences, or the manners of the *literati* in different ages. Politeness arises from the habits of social life, and the intercourse of men and of nations; it is therefore more likely to accompany commerce than learning. But it must be allowed, that manners received their last polish from works of imagination and sentiment, which soften the mind by pictures of natural and moral beauty, and dispose it to tenderness and social affection.

[1] Ibid.—Anderson's *Hist. of Commerce*, vol. i.   [2] Erasmus.—Holinshed.

These reflections, my dear Philip, naturally lead us to the most curious and interesting inquiries—the revival of letters, and the progress of genius and manners. The method in which you now study history does not permit me to treat those subjects so fully as their importance may seem to require; yet I will take care to omit nothing essential for a gentleman to know, while I studiously avoid every thing that belongs to the mere antiquary. An attempt to trace with critical minuteness, through dark and ignorant ages, the obscure sources of refinement, is like travelling over barren mountains and uninhabited deserts in search of the remote fountain of the Nile, instead of contemplating the accumulated majesty of that river, when, greatly bountiful, its mysterious waters shed health and plenty over an extensive kingdom, and furnish the means of an enriching commerce, which feeds and employs millions, and calls forth every power of the mind, and cherishes every virtue of the heart.

The first permanent step towards the revival of literature in Europe was the erection of schools under lay preceptors. Alfred and Charlemagne, those early luminaries of the modern world, had shed a temporary lustre over the ages in which they lived. They had encouraged learning, both by their example and patronage, and some gleams of genius began to break forth; but the promising dawn did not arrive at perfect day. The schools erected by these great monarchs were confined to the churches and monasteries, and monks were almost the only instructors of youth. The contracted ideas of such men, partly arising from their mode of life, partly from their religious opinions, rendered them utterly unfit for the communication of liberal knowledge. Science, in their hands, degenerated into a barbarous jargon, and genius again sunk in the gloom of superstition. A long night of ignorance succeeded. Learning was considered as dangerous to true piety, and darkness was necessary to hide the usurpations of the clergy, who were then exalting themselves on the ruins of the civil power. The ancient poets and orators were represented as seducers to the path of destruction. Virgil and Horace were the pimps of hell, Ovid a lecherous fiend, and Cicero a vain declaimer, impiously elate with the talent of heathenish reasoning. Aristotle's logic alone was recommended, because it was found capable of involving the simplest arguments, and perplexing the plainest truths. It became the universal science: and Europe, for two centuries, produced no composition that can afford pleasure to a classical reader. Incredible legends, unedifying homilies, and trite expositions of

Scripture, were the only labours of the learned during that dark period. But the gloom at last began to disappear, and the sceptre of Knowledge was wrested from the hand of Superstition. Several enlightened persons among the laity, who had studied under the Arabs in Spain, undertook the education of youth about the beginning of the eleventh century, in the chief cities of Italy, and afterward in those of France, England, and Germany. Instruction was communicated in a more rational manner: more numerous and more useful branches of science were taught: a taste for ancient literature revived; and some Latin poems were written, before the close of the twelfth century, not unworthy of the latter times of the Roman empire[1].

The human soul, during this period, seems to have roused itself as from a lethargy. The same enthusiasm which prompted one set of men to signalise their valour in the Holy Land, inspired another with the ardour of transmitting to posterity the gallant actions of the former, and of animating the zeal of those pious warriors, by the fabulous adventures of former Christian heroes. These performances were composed in verse; and several of them with much elegance, and no small degree of imagination. But many bars were yet in the way of literary refinement. The taste of the age was too rude to relish the beauties of classical composition: the Latin language, in which science was conveyed, was imperfectly known to the bulk of readers; and the scarcity of parchment, together with the expense of transcribing, rendered books so extremely dear, as to be only within the reach of a few. Learning, however, continued to advance, in spite of every obstruction; and the invention of paper in the fourteenth century, and of printing about the middle of the fifteenth, rendered knowledge so general in less than a century after, that Italy began to compare, in arts and in letters, her modern with her ancient state, and to contrast the age of Leo X. with that of the second Cæsar.

In the mean time, an extraordinary revolution had taken place in the empire of Genius, introduced by one no less remarkable in the system of manners. Women, among the ancient Greeks and Romans, seem to have been considered merely as objects of sensuality, or of domestic convenience. They were devoted to a state of seclusion and obscurity, had few attentions offered them, and were permitted to take as little share in the conversation as in the general commerce of life. But the Gothic nations had no

---

[1] Warton's *Hist. of English Poetry*, vol. i.

sooner settled themselves in the provinces of the Roman empire, than the female character began to assume new consequence. Those fierce barbarians, who seemed to thirst only for blood, who involved in one undistinguished ruin the monuments of ancient grandeur and ancient genius, and who devoted to the flames the knowledge of ages, always forbore to offer any violence to the women. They brought with them that respectful gallantry which had power to restrain even their savage ferocity ; and they introduced into the West of Europe a generosity of sentiment, and a complaisance towards the ladies, to which the most polished nations of antiquity were strangers.

These sentiments of generous gallantry were fostered by the institution of chivalry, which lifted woman yet higher in the scale of life. Instead of being nobody in society, she became its *primum mobile.* Every knight devoting himself to danger, declared himself the humble servant of some lady, who was generally the object of his love. Her honour was supposed to be intimately connected with his, and her smile was the reward of his valour : for her he attacked, for her he defended, and for her he shed his blood. Courage, animated by so powerful a motive, lost sight of every thing but enterprise. Incredible toils were cheerfully endured ; incredible actions were performed ; and the boldest inventions of fiction were more than realised. The effect was reciprocal. Women, proud of their influence, became worthy of the heroism they had inspired ; they were not to be approached but by the high-minded and the brave ; and men, in those gallant times, could only hope to be admitted to the bosoms of the chaste fair, after having proved their fidelity and affection, by years of perseverance and of peril.

A similar change took place in the operations of war. The perfect hero of antiquity was superior to fear ; but he made use of every artifice to annoy his enemy : impelled by animosity and hostile passion, like the savage in the American woods, he was only anxious of attaining his end, without regard whether fraud or force were the means. But the true knight or modern hero of the middle ages, who seemed to have had, in all his rencounters, his eye fixed on the judicial combat, or Judgment of God, despised stratagem as much as he courted danger. He disdained to take advantage of his enemy ; he desired only to see him, and to combat him upon equal terms, trusting that Heaven would interpose in behalf of the just : and as he professed only to vindicate the cause of religion, of injured beauty, or oppressed innocence, he was confirmed in this enthusiastic opinion by his own heated imagination. Strongly persuaded that the decision must be in his favour, he fought as if under the influence of divine inspiration rather than of military ardour[1]. Thus the system of chivalry blended the heroic and sanctified characters, united devotion and valour, zeal and gallantry.

From these new manners arose a new species of composition ; namely, the romance, or modern heroic fable. It was originally written in verse, and, by giving a new direction to genius, banished for a time that vein of ancient poetry which had been cultivated with success during the eleventh and twelfth centuries. Modern poetry however lost nothing by this relapse. Had classical taste and judgment been so early established, imagination must have suffered : truth and reason, as an ingenious writer observes, would have chased before their time those visions of illusive fancy which delight to hover on the gloom of superstition, and which form so considerable a part of our polite literature. We should still have been strangers to the beautiful extravagances of romantic fabling.

This new species of composition took its rise in the thirteenth century, among the Troubadours or minstrels of Provence : and was originally written in the Provençal dialect, then the most polished and prevalent of any modern tongue. These Troubadours had followed in crowds to the Holy Land the princes and nobles by whom they were patronised : they had seen the riches and splendour of oriental cities, and the pomp of oriental princes ; they had beheld the greatest scene of war that modern times had yet exhibited. They had seen the combined armies of Europe and of Asia encamp in the plains of Palestine : they had also seen them engaged. Their imagination was inflamed by the sumptuous equipages, gorgeous banners, armorial insignia, and grand pavilions, in which the champions of the cross strove to excel each other ; but still more by the enthusiastic valour of the combatants. They had seen many wonderful things, and heard many marvellous tales ; and they gave to the whole, on their return, the colouring of poetic fancy, heightened by all the exaggerations of Asiatic imagery, and filled with all the extravagances of Asiatic fiction[2].

The ignorance and credulity of the age, the superstitious veneration - paid to the heroes of the crusades, the dreadful ideas

---

[1] *Mem. sur l'Ancienne Chevalerie,* par M. de la Curne de St. Palaye.
[2] Among these may be numbered dwarfs, giants, dragons, and necromancers ; but I am unwilling to give up to the East, with a certain learned critic, the honour of the beautiful invention of fairies. See Warton's *Hist. of English Poetry,* vol. i.

formed of the infidels, and the distance of country, made the wildest conceptions of the poet be received with all the avidity of truth. The romantic became the favourite mode of composition; and as every kingdom in Europe had its valorous knights, every kingdom soon had its romances : and every romance was nearly the same. Whether the scene was laid in ancient or in modern times, in Spain or in Syria, the same set of ideal beings were introduced, the same kind of plot was pursued, and the same manners were painted. A lady miraculously fair and chaste, and a knight more than humanly brave and constant, encountering monsters, and resisting the allurements of enchantresses, formed the groundwork of all those unnatural compositions.

Modern poetry, however, did not long remain in this rude state. The romance which had its rise in the manners of chivalry, and which rendered them still more romantic, fell into disrepute as soon as those manners began to decline. It was succeeded by the allegorical tale ; in which the virtues and vices, appetites and passions, took the place of human beings, and were made subservient to the design of the poet. The shadowy production was followed by the Italian epic ; which, like the heroic poem of the Greeks, consists of a compound of mortal, immortal, and allegorical personages. Dantè, Ariosto, and Tasso, are supposed to have carried it to perfection.

Dantè, the father of Italian poetry, flourished in the beginning of the fourteenth century. His *Inferno*, though full of extravagances, is one of the greatest efforts of human genius. No poem, ancient or modern, affords more striking instances of the true sublime, and true pathetic. He was succeeded by Petrarca and Boccaccio, who perfected the Italian language.

Petrarca was the first modern poet who wrote with classical elegance and purity. He appears to have been intimately acquainted with the beauties of the ancients, and to have studied their graces. His *Canzoni*, or lyric pieces, have often all the ease of Horace, and all the delicacy of Tibullus. In many of them, however, we discover a degree of that puerile conceit or affectation of wit, that perpetual effort to say something brilliant, which seems inseparable from Italian poetry ; and the Platonic ideas with which all his passionate writings abound, though admired by his countrymen as a decent veil to love, give to his celebrated sonnets to Laura too much the air of hymns to a divinity, to interest the human heart. His elegy on the death of that lady, whose story is well known, has been deservedly admired. It partakes of the faults and of the beauties of all his compositions, as will appear from the following lines, translated by sir William Jones in the true spirit of the original :

> " Go, plaintive breeze, to Laura's flow'ry bier,
> Heave the warm sigh, and shed the tender tear.
> There to the awful shade due homage pay,
> And softly thus address the sacred clay :
> Say, envied earth, that dost those charms enfold,
> Where are those cheeks, and where those locks of gold ?
> Where are those eyes, which oft the muse has sung ?
> Where those sweet lips, and that enchanting tongue ?
> Ye radiant tresses, and thou nectar'd smile,
> Ye looks, that might the melting skies beguile,
> You robb'd my soul of rest, my eyes of sleep,
> You taught me how to love, and how to weep !'"

Boccaccio has great and various merit. He is chiefly known as a prose writer; and his prose compositions are superior, in purity of diction, to those of any other Italian author. But if his modesty had not led him to commit to the flames his poetical performances, from an apprehension of their inferiority to those of his master Petrarca, he might possibly have appeared no less considerable as a poet. One piece, which paternal tenderness preserved, and three more that escaped the general ruin, give reason for this opinion. The favourite piece is entitled the *Theseid;* and although, like all the poems of that age, it confounds ancient and modern manners, time, and ceremonies, it possesses so many native beauties as to leave criticism only room for admiration. It is of the heroic kind; and the fable is better constructed, and filled with more interesting incidents, than that of any other Italian poem of the same period. It has been rendered into English, with alterations and additions, by Chaucer, under the name of the *Knight's Tale ;* and, as modernised by Dryden, is perhaps the most animated and truly harmonious piece of versification of the same extent in our language.

The reputation of Boccaccio, however, with the world in general, is chiefly founded on his *Decameron*, which is truly an enchanting work. It contains a greater number of good tales, of the gay and humorous kind, than had ever before appeared. The most celebrated moderns, in that walk, have borrowed from it their best pieces. Chaucer and Fontaine, though they lived at the distance of almost three hundred years from each other, are equally indebted to the *Decameron*. Those tales of Boccaccio, which may be considered as the most early gleanings of popular anecdote, are the first modern compositions that give us any just idea of the manners of domestic life; and both the style in which they are related, and the subjects which they unfold, prove that civilization was then in an advanced state in Italy.

But Italy was not the only country where civilization had made advances. The English court was, in that age, the most splendid in Europe, and one of the most polished. Thither many accomplished foreigners resorted, to behold the grandeur and to enjoy the bounty of the third Edward. The spoils of France swelled the pomp of England in his reign; while a captive king, and his unfortunate nobles, civilized its manners, by accustoming its haughty and insolent barons to the exercise of mutual complaisance. Edward himself, and the Black Prince, were the examples of all that was great in arms, or gallant in courtesy. They were the patrons and the mirrors of chivalry. The stately castle of Windsor, built in this illustrious reign, saw the round table of king Arthur restored, and the order of the Garter instituted; that glorious tribute to gallantry, and sacred badge of honour. Tilts, tournaments, and pageants, were constantly exhibited, and with a magnificence formerly unknown.

The ladies who thronged the court of Edward, and crowded to such spectacles, arrayed in the richest habits, were the judges in those peaceful, though not always bloodless combats; and the victorious knight, in receiving from the hand of beauty the reward of his prowess, became desirous of exciting other passions beside that of admiration. He began to turn his eyes from fancy to the heart. He aspired at an interest in the seat of the affections. Instead of the cold consent of virtue, he sought the warm return of love; instead of acquiescence, he demanded sensibility. Female pride was roused at such a request: assiduities and attentions were employed to soothe it: and nature and custom, vanity and feeling, were long at war in the breast of woman. During this sentimental struggle, which had its rise in a more rational mode of thinking, which opened a greater freedom of intercourse, and terminated in our present familiar manners, the two sexes polished each other; the men acquired more softness and address, the women more knowledge and graces.

In a reign of so much heroism and gallantry, the Muses were not likely to sleep. Geoffrey Chaucer, the Father of English poetry, was the brightest ornament of Edward's court. He added, to a lively genius and a learned education, a thorough knowledge of life and manners. He was perfectly a man of the world; had frequently visited France and Italy, and sometimes with the advantage of a public character. He had studied the

Italian and Provençal poets, was intimately acquainted with both languages, and attempted with success all the kinds of poetry then in use. Beside the *Theseid*, he translated, and greatly improved, the allegorical poem called the *Romance of the Rose*, written by William of Lorris and John of Meun, two celebrated French poets of those times : and he composed the *Canterbury Tales*, after the model of the *Decameron*. They abound with true humour and pleasantry ; and though chiefly borrowed, entitled their author to a distinguished rank among the writers of his age. The Prologues, in particular, which are wholly his own, contain a vein of moral satire that has not hitherto been exceeded.

This eminent poet had several disadvantages to struggle with, particularly that which depended on language. William the Conqueror had attempted to extirpate the English tongue. The Norman language was ordered to be used in all public writings, and taught in all public schools. It was also the dialect of the court. That badge of slavery had remained almost three hundred years, before it was abolished by Edward III. Chaucer had therefore to create, or at least to form a new dialect. This circumstance ought always to be attended to in contemplating the writings of our venerable bard, as it alone can account for the great disparity observable, after all his diligence, between the progress of English manners and of the English language. Had things continued to proceed in their natural order, Chaucer's style would now have been nearly as intelligible as that of Shakspeare.

But this bright dawn of English literature and English refinement, was deeply obscured by the civil wars that followed, and which continued, with little interruption, till the accession of Henry VII. During that long period of anarchy, genius went to decay ; and the animosities of faction had rendered the manners of the people almost altogether savage. The severity of Henry's temper and government was little calculated to promote either letters or politeness ; and the religious disputes which took place under the reign of his son, were a new obstacle to civilization. Chaucer had no successor worthy of himself till the days of Elizabeth.

Similar circumstances obstructed the progress of literature in France till the reign of Francis I., who is deservedly styled the Father of the French Muses. *Chants Royaux, Ballades, Rondeaux*, and *Pastorales*, had taken place of the Provençal poetry about the beginning of the fourteenth century ; but Froissart, who cultivated with success this *New Poetry*, as it was called, cannot be considered equal to William of Lorris, or John of Meun. The *Romance of the Rose* was still the finest French poem.

Genius, in the mean time, continued to advance, with giant strides, in Italy. A succession of great poets followed Dantè in the highest walk of the Muse: at length appeared Ariosto and Tasso, the glory of the sixteenth century, and whose celebrated works are supposed to contain all that is excellent in poetry. The *Orlando* of Ariosto is a wonderful production. It is formed upon the Gothic plan, if it can be said to have any, and consequently is wild and extravagant; but it comprehends so many and such various beauties, that whether considered as a whole or in parts, it commands our fondest admiration. The *Jerusalem* of Tasso is a more classical performance. It is constructed after the Grecian model; and adds, to an interesting and happily conducted fable, a number of striking and well-drawn characters, all operating to one end, together with a profusion of beautiful machinery, affecting situations, sublime images, and bold descriptions. Voltaire prefers the first to the *Odyssey*, and the second to the *Iliad* of Homer; but you, I hope, have a juster taste for solid elegance, and for what is truly great in nature and in poetry, than to be swayed by such an opinion.

The progress of genius in Italy, however, during this period, was not confined to poetry, and still less to one species of it. Petrarca and Boccaccio had their successors, as well as Dantè. The dramatic talent began to disclose itself. Both tragedy and comedy were attempted with success before the middle of the sixteenth century; but that musical drama, which has long been so general in Italy, and which, in excluding too often nature and probability, has enlarged the bounds of harmony, was then in its infancy.

Music is one of the first sciences that are cultivated, and one of the last which are perfected in any country. The rude tale of the bard is accompanied with the wild notes of his voice and harp, to atone for his want of ideas, and engage attention; but as fable becomes more extensive and rich, the legendary poet disdains to court the ear with any thing but the harmony of his numbers. He relies for interest solely on the powers of imagination and sentiment; and these without any adventitious aid, produce their effect upon a people civilized, but not corrupted. The Dramatic writer, in like manner, obtains his end for a time, by the happy disposition of plot, the force of dialogue, and the strength and variety of his characters. But in proportion as mankind become more refined, they become more effeminate, and the luxury of harmony is found necessary to give to theatrical representation its proper influence. Then, and not till then, does the musical science attain perfection; and then poetry begins to decline. Every thing is sung; every thing is composed to be warbled through the eunuch's throat, and sense is sacrificed to sound.

A similar observation may be extended to history. The deeds of the hero are the first objects of human curiosity: yet mankind, in almost every country, have ceased to act with dignity before their actions have been properly recorded. Truth appears cold and insipid to a people inclined to wonder, and wonder is the predominant passion of all uncivilized nations. Fiction is called in to gratify it; and fable is for a time received as history. But when men are more employed in political objects, they become more desirous of being informed than amazed: they wish to know the real actions of their ancestors, and the causes and the consequences of such actions. The historian takes advantage of this disposition of mind to procure admission for his labours: but, as it is more difficult to ascertain facts than to assume them, and easier to assign motives of action and deduce incidents ingeniously from them, than to trace the motives of men in their actions, and give to truth such a degree of colouring as will make it interesting, without rendering its validity suspected, history has every where been later in attaining perfection than the highest works of imagination.

Italy had at last her historians, and excellent ones. Machiavel successfully courted the comic muse, unfolded the principles of a dark and pernicious policy, and digested the annals of his native country with all the discernment of Tacitus; while Guicciardini, a more amiable writer, related the transactions of his own times with the elegance and exactness of Thucydides.

Philosophy only was requisite in the sixteenth century to bring Italy within the line of comparison with ancient Greece, when Greece was in her glory. A number of independent and free states vied with each other in all the elegant and commercial arts; in wealth and in luxury, in manners and in talents, in pomp and in power. Proud of her privileges, and of her liberal acquisitions, she looked down with contempt upon every other country, and branded all other nations with the name of barbarians. Two great monarchs, like those of Persia and Macedon, were contending who should be her master. She wanted only the lights of philosophy to render the parallel complete. Bewildered in the mazes of scholastic reasoning, or lost in the dreams of perverted Platonism, her sages were still alike ignorant of the system of man and of the universe. And before they could know either, it was necessary that the veil of superstition should be rent ; that mankind, beholding the puppet to which they had kneeled, and by which they had been overawed, might fearlessly look through the range of nature, and contemplate its physical and moral order.

LETTER LIX.

Of the Progress of Navigation, particularly among the Portuguese ; the Discoveries and Settlements of that Nation on the Coast of Africa, and in the East Indies, by the Cape of Good Hope ; the Discovery of America by the Spaniards, the Settlement of the West Indies, and the Conquest of Mexico and Peru ; with some Reflections on the moral and political Consequences of those great Events.

FROM the arts that polish nations, my dear son, let us turn our eyes more particularly towards those that aggrandize them ; which supply the wants of one people with the superfluities of another, and make all things common to all. Such are navigation and commerce. By these, and the arts to which they gave birth, the Phœnicians and Carthaginians crowded with cities their barren shores, and attained the first rank among ancient nations : by these, in later times, the Venetians and Dutch, struggling from dirt and sea-weed, crowned with palaces their lakes and marshes, and became, at different æras, the most opulent and powerful people in modern Europe : by these Britain now governs the ocean, while she wafts from pole to pole the luxuries and conveniences of life.

The navigation of Europe, at the beginning of the fifteenth century, though much improved since the age of Charlemagne, was chiefly confined to the Mediterranean and Baltic seas, and was little more than what is now called *coasting.* Flanders was the great theatre of commerce. Thither the Italian states conveyed, from the ports of Egypt, the precious commodities of the East : and thither the Hanseatic merchants carried, from the shores of the Baltic, the naval stores and other rude merchandize of the North. To this common mart all European nations resorted. Here they sold or exchanged the produce of their several countries, and supplied all their wants, without dreaming of new ports, or suspecting that the system of commerce could be altered. Dantzic, Lisbon, and Alexandria, continued to mark the limits of practicable navigation ; when the enlightened and enterprising genius of Don Henry of Portugal extended the views of the mariner, and emboldened him to pilot the Atlantic or great Western Ocean. But before I speak of that prince, and the discoveries which he accomplished, I must say a few words of his country, which I have hitherto considered only as an appendage of Spain.

Portugal had no existence as a separate state till towards the close of the eleventh century. About that time Alphonso VI. king of Castile and Leon, having wrested from the Moors the northern provinces of the present kingdom of Portugal, bestowed them, with his natural daughter, upon Henry of Burgundy, a noble volunteer who had assisted him in his wars. Henry took only the title of count ; but his son Alphonso, having recovered other provinces from the Moors, assumed the regal dignity in 1139. The kings of Portugal, like those of Spain, long spent their force in combating the Moors, and had no connexion with the rest of Europe. A detail of those barbarous wars would be equally void of instruction and amusement. I shall therefore only observe, that the succession continued uninterrupted in the line of Burgundy, till the death of Ferdinand in 1383 ; when John of Castile, who had married the infanta of Portugal, claimed the crown, as the king had left no male issue. But the states of Portugal, after an interregnum of eighteen months, gave it to John, brother of their deceased sovereign, and at that time regent of the kingdom[1]. A.D. 1385.

This John, surnamed the Bastard, no less politic than enterprising, proved worthy of his new dignity. He was the first European prince who formed a respectable navy ; which he employed, with equal success, in annoying his enemies and in protecting his subjects. He took Ceuta from the Moors, and overawed the states of Barbary during his whole reign. He had several sons, who all signalized themselves by their valour and abilities ; but more especially the third, Don Henry, whose bold heart and intelligent mind, influenced by A.D. 1414.

[1] Neufville, *Hist. Gen. de Portugal.*

the reports of travellers, led him to project discoveries in the Western Ocean.

This amiable prince, who joined the virtues of a hero and a patriot to the knowledge of a philosopher, turned to use that astronomy which the Arabs had preserved. He had a considerable share in the invention of the astrolabe, and first perceived the advantage that might be derived from the direction of the magnetic needle to the North; which, though already known in Europe, had not hitherto been employed effectually in navigation. He established an observatory at Sagres, near Cape St. Vincent, where many persons were instructed in astronomy and the art of sailing. The pilots formed under his eye not only

A.D. doubled Cape Nun, long supposed an insurmountable
1420. barrier, but advanced as far as Cape Bajador, and in their return discovered the island of Madeira. Other pilots, yet more bold, were sent out. They doubled Cape Bajador, Cape Blanco, Cape Verd, and at last Cape Sierra Leone, within eight

A.D. degrees of the line, before the death of Don Henry. In
1463. the course of these voyages, the Azores and Cape Verd Islands had been discovered, and the vine and the sugar-cane introduced into the island of Madeira, and there cultivated with success.

In the reign of John II, a prince of profound sagacity and extensive views, who first made Lisbon a free port, the Portuguese prosecuted their discoveries with equal ardour and success.

A.D. The river Zara, on the other side of the line, conducted
1484. them to the kingdom of Congo, in the less known part of Africa, where they made easy conquests, and established an

A.D. advantageous commerce. Captain Diaz passed the ex-
1486. treme point of Africa, to which he gave the name of the *Stormy Cape*; but the king, who saw more fully the importance of that discovery, styled it the *Cape of Good Hope*.

Emmanuel pursued the great projects of his predecessors.

A.D. He sent out a fleet of four ships, under the command of
1497. Vasco de Gama, in order to complete the passage to India by sea. This admiral possessed all the knowledge and talents necessary for such an expedition. After being assailed

A.D. by tempests, he doubled the Cape of Good Hope, and
1498. ranging through unknown seas, happily arrived at the city of Calicut, on the coast of Malabar [1].

---

[1] *Hist. Gen. des Voyages*, tome i.

Calicut was at that time the emporium of India. Thither the Arabs resorted for all the rich products and precious manufactures of the East. These they carried in ships to the ports of the Red Sea, and sold at Alexandria to the Italian merchants. This information Gama had received at Melinda, on the coast of Zanguebar; and he there engaged a pilot, who conducted him into the harbour of Calicut, when the trade was at its height. Here he fortunately met with a native of Barbary, named Monzaida, who understood the Portuguese language, and whose admiration of that people overbalanced the prejudices of religion and country. This admiration determined Monzaida to do every thing in his power to serve strangers who unbosomed themselves to him without reserve. He procured Gama an audience of the *samorin* or emperor, who received him very favourably; and a treaty of commerce was set on foot in the name of the king of Portugal. But this negotiation, when almost completed, was broken off by the jealousy of the Arabs. They represented so strongly the danger of such an alliance, and the ambition of the Portuguese, that the samorin took the ungenerous resolution of putting to death those bold navigators, whom he had lately treated with kindness, and whose friendship he seemed to desire. Informed of his danger by the faithful Monzaida, Gama sent his brother on board of the fleet. "Should you hear," said he, "of my death or imprisonment, I prohibit you, as your commander, from attempting to release me or to avenge my fate. Set sail immediately, and inform the king of the success of our voyage. I am happy in having performed his orders, and discovered a passage to India for Portugal[1]." Fortunately, however, matters were not pushed to that extremity. Gama lived to carry to Portugal the news of his own success. The samorin permitted him to join his fleet, and he departed soon after for Europe.

No language can express the joy of the Portuguese on the return of Gama to Lisbon. They saw themselves, by A.D. one daring enterprise, in possession of the richest com- 1499. merce in the world; and, no less superstitious than avaricious, they flattered themselves with the prospect of extending their religion with their dominion.

The pope farther encouraged this hope. Glad of an occasion of asserting his universal sovereignty, he granted to the Portuguese all the countries which they had discovered, or should

---

[1] Faria y Sousa, *Port. Asia,* vol. i.

discover, in the East, on condition that they should there plant the catholic faith. The whole nation was seized with the enthusiasm of conversion and of conquest. They presented them-

A.D. selves in crowds to man the new fleet destined for India;
1500. and thirteen ships sailed, as soon as the season would permit, from the Tagus to Calicut, under the command of Alvarez de Cabral.

This admiral in his passage keeping out to sea, in order to avoid the calms on the coast of Africa, and the storms which had been met with in doubling the Cape of Good Hope, discovered the rich country now called Brasil, to which he gave the name of the *Land of the Holy Cross*. He took possession of it in the name of the king his master, and proceeded on his voyage. When he arrived at the coast of Malabar, the samorin made him an offer of friendship, and invited him to Calicut, where he had an audience of that Indian prince, and was permitted to open a magazine of commerce. But this good understanding was of short duration. The Arabs again found means to poison the mind of the samorin: the admiral did not behave with the greatest discretion: mutual jealousies and fears arose, and mutual injuries followed. At last the inhabitants of Calicut murdered fifty Portuguese, and burned their magazine. This act of hostility did not escape unpunished. Cabral, in revenge of such a breach of faith, and such undermining perfidy, destroyed all the Arabian vessels in the port, beat down great part of the city, and left it in flames[1].

After this second rupture with the samorin, the measures of the Portuguese in India were totally changed. The peaceful system of Gama was laid aside: the maxims of mutual advantage gave place to those of violence, and commerce was established by the sword. Cabral, leaving Calicut, entered into a negotiation with the kings of Cochin, Cananor, Onor, and other princes, who

A.D. were tributaries of the samorin, and desirous of inde-
1501. pendence. This love of freedom procured the Portuguese the sovereignty of Malabar, and the trade of India. Cabral promised support to those deluded princes, and carried their ambassadors to the court of Lisbon, where such politic steps were taken as rendered success infallible. A force was sent

A.D. out sufficient to combat the samorin. But no prince
1502. could obtain the protection of Portugal without first acknowledging himself its vassal, permitting a fortress to be

---

[1] Maffæi, *Hist. Indic.* lib. ii. cap. iv.

erected in his capital, and selling his commodities to its subjects at their own price.   No foreign merchant might take a cargo, till the Portuguese were served ; nor any mariner cruise in those seas, but with their passports.   They were the terror and admiration of the East, the wonder and envy of the West. All European merchants soon resorted to Lisbon for Indian commodities ; because they could there purchase them at A.D. a much lower rate than at Venice, or any other mart to 1508. which they were brought by the way of Egypt.   And, happily for Portugal, the Venetians were then sinking under the pressure of the League of Cambray.

In order to secure and render perpetual these momentous advantages, the chief command in India was given to Alphonso Albuquerque, a man of uncommon sagacity and penetration, and distinguished by his talents both for war and politics.   He was no sooner invested with the government, than he began to form grand projects, which he executed with astonishing facility. The Arabs settled in India, and their associates, he had long been sensible, were the only power in the East that the Portuguese had to fear.   These traders had secretly entered into a league with the samorin, the soltan of Egypt, and the Venetians, who were gainers by their commerce, and whose interest it was to destroy the trade of Portugal.   The furnishers of the caravans, and navigators of the Red Sea, were the natural enemies of the circumnavigators of the Cape.   Albuquerque saw it early, while a private commander.   He had therefore done every thing in his power to ruin their settlements on the coast of Arabia, and their united naval force had received a signal overthrow in the Indian Ocean.   He now extended his views, and projected the conquest of Ormuz in the Persian Gulf, and of Aden at the mouth of the Red Sea, where Portuguese squadrons stationed, might command the trade of Persia and of Egypt.

The immediate execution of these projects would at once have proved fatal to the commerce of the Arabs and their allies ; but Albuquerque, upon mature deliberation, per- A.D. ceived the expediency of establishing the Portuguese 1509. more fully on the coast of Malabar, before he divided his forces. He accordingly destroyed Calicut ; and observing that the Portuguese had yet no good port in a wholesome air, where they might refit their ships and recruit their seamen after the fatigues of the voyage from Europe, he resolved to procure one.   He found that Lisbon had need of Goa.

Goa, which rises to view in the form of an amphitheatre, is

situate towards the middle of the coast of **Malabar**, in an island detached from the continent by two branches of a river that throws itself into the sea at some distance from the city, after having formed beneath its walls one of the finest harbours in the world. It properly belonged to the king of Deccan ; but a Moor, to whom the government of it had been entrusted, had rendered himself its sovereign. While this usurper was occupied on the continent, Albuquerque appeared before the city, and carried it by assault[1]. It was afterwards recovered, but soon retaken ; and it became the capital of the Portuguese empire in India.

A.D. 1510.

Albuquerque, whose ambition was boundless, attempted next to establish the Portuguese on the coast of Coromandel. With this view he made an attack upon **Malacca**, situated near the Strait of Sincapore, one of the richest cities in India, and the best adapted for commerce. It was the centre of the trade between Japan, China, the Spice-Islands, and the other Indian ports.——When Albuquerque appeared before Malacca, he found it in a posture of defence : and a new obstacle conspired to retard his progress. His friend Araujo was there a prisoner, and was threatened with death the moment the city should be besieged. Deliberating how to act, while the sentiments of friendship and ambition, perhaps of duty, struggled in his breast, he received the following billet from Araujo: " Think only of the glory and advantage of Portugal : if I cannot be an instrument of your victory, let me not retard it." The place was carried by storm, after an obstinate defence and several changes of fortune. The Portuguese found in it an immense booty, both in treasure and valuable commodities. Albuquerque, whose heart was superior to the charms of gold, erected a citadel to secure his conquest, and returned to Goa.

A.D. 1511.

The friendship of the Portuguese was now courted by the most powerful Indian princes, who offered to permit fortresses to be built, and factories to be established in any part of their dominions. Albuquerque did not fail to profit by these offers ; and judging that the season was now arrived for giving the final blow to the Arabian commerce in the East, he commenced the execution of his schemes for the conquest of Aden and of Ormuz. In his attempt upon Aden he miscarried : but he committed so many ravages on the coasts of the Red Sea, and in the Straits of Babelmandeb, that he

A.D. 1513.

---

[1] Lafitau, *Hist. des Conq. des Port.*—*Hist. Gen. des Voyages*, tome i.

ruined the commerce of the Arabs and Egyptians. He was more successful in his expedition against Ormuz, at that time the most opulent and splendid city in the East. It appears to have been nearly equal to ancient Tyre in wealth and in splendour; and, like Tyre, it was seated in a barren isle. Like Tyre, it seemed only to have been disjoined from the land, that it might become queen of the sea. It was one of the greatest marts in the universe. But its voluptuous inhabitants A.D. were little able to withstand the impetuous and hardy 1515. valour of the Portuguese. Albuquerque soon made himself master of the place, and had the honour of there receiving an embassy from the king of Persia [1].

The reduction of Ormuz, with the possession of Goa and Malacca, gave perfect security to the Portuguese commerce in India. The successors of Albuquerque extended it to China and Japan; but it was never more respectable than under him. Yet this founder of his country's greatness died in disgrace, and of a broken heart. That dauntless spirit which had encountered so many enemies, and surmounted so many dangers, could not support the frown of his prince. Emmanuel, jealous of his glory, had listened to the insinuations of his enemies; had appointed another governor in his stead; and promoted those whom he sent home as criminals. When Albuquerque received this intelligence, he sighed, and said, " Can these things be true?— I incurred the hatred of men by my love for the king, and am disgraced by him through his prepossession for other men: to the grave, unhappy old man! to the grave!—thy actions will speak for themselves and for thee [2]!"

While the Portuguese were thus employed in making acquisitions in the East, and appropriating to themselves the most lucrative commerce in the known world, the Spaniards had discovered a new continent toward the West. They had called into existence, as it were, another world: had opened new sources of trade; expanded new theatres of dominion; and displayed new scenes of ambition, of avarice, and of blood.

Christopher Columbus, a Genoese navigator, who resided at Lisbon, and who had devoted himself to the study of astronomy, first conceived the idea of this new continent. Perfectly acquainted with the figure of the earth, the notion of the Antipodes, considered by reason as a chimera, and by religion as

[1] Guyon, *Hist. des Ind. Orient.* tome. i.—*Hist. Gen. des Voyages*, tome i.
[2] *Hist. Gen. des Voyages*, tome i.

impiety, appeared to him an incontestible fact.   But, if he had
not added the stout heart of a hero to the enlightened mind and
persevering spirit of a philosopher, the world might still have
been ignorant of his discoveries.   The Genoese, whom he proposed to put in possession of another hemisphere, treated him
as a dreamer.   He also unfolded his project, the grandest that
human genius ever formed, to the court of Portugal, without
success.   He then communicated it to the court of Spain ; where
he long suffered all that supercilious neglect which unsupported
merit so often meets with from men in office, who are too apt
to despise what they do not understand.

Ferdinand and Isabella were then engaged in the conquest of
Grenada, and the Spanish treasury was nearly exhausted.   But
no sooner were the Moors subdued, than the ambitious mind of
Isabella seemed to sympathize with the bold spirit of Columbus.
She offered to pledge her jewels, in order to furnish him with a
fleet.   Three small vessels were fitted out by other means ; and
Columbus set sail from the port of Palos in Andalusia, on the
third of August 1492, in quest of a western continent, with the
title of Admiral and Viceroy of the Isles and Lands which he
should discover [1].

Transcendent genius and superlative courage experience
almost equal difficulty in carrying their designs into execution,
when they depend on the assistance of others.   Columbus possessed both—he exerted both ; but the concurrence of other
heads and other hearts were necessary to give success to either ;
he had indolence and cowardice to encounter, as well as ignorance and prejudice.   He had formerly been ridiculed as a
visionary enthusiast ; he was now pitied as a desperado.   The
Portuguese navigators, in accomplishing their first discoveries,
had always some reference to the coast ; cape had pointed them
to cape : but Columbus, with no landmark but the heavens, with
no guide but the compass, boldly launched into the ocean,
without knowing what shore should receive him, or where he
could find rest for the sole of his foot. . His crew murmured—
they mutinied : they proposed to commit him to those waves
with which he so wantonly sported, and return to Spain [2].

This was a severe trial to the courage of Columbus ; but the
enthusiasm of genius added strength to his natural fortitude.
Cool and unconcerned himself about every thing but his great

---

[1] *Life of Columbus*, written by his son, chap. xv.
[2] Oviedo, *Hist. de las Indias*, lib. iii.

object, he had recourse to the softest language. He encouraged his men by fair promises; he deceived his officers by false reckonings. But these expedients proving at last ineffectual, he demanded an indulgence of three days; at the end of which, if he did not discover land, he promised to abandon his project. His request was granted; and on the morning of the second day, being the twelfth of October, to his inexpressible joy, he descried one of the Bahama Islands, to which he gave the name of San Salvador [1]. He soon after fell in with several other small islands, to one of which he gave the appellation of Isabella, and to another that of Ferdinand. These he rightly judged to belong to that western continent which he sought, and which he conjectured must reach to the Portuguese settlements in India: hence arose the name of *West Indies.* At length he arrived at the Island of Cuba, where he entered into some correspondence with the natives, and particularly with the women, from whom he learned, that the gold ornaments which they wore came from Bohio, a large island to the south-east. Thither Columbus steered: what heart does not pant for gold? He soon reached Bohio, or Hayti, as it was called by the natives, to which he gave the name of Espagnola, altered by us to Hispaniola. Here he erected a fort, and planted a little colony; after which, having taken a general survey of the island, and settled a friendly intercourse with the inhabitants, he set out on his return to Spain, carrying with him a sufficient quantity of gold to evince the importance of his discoveries, and some of those new people, to complete the astonishment of Europe.

The natives of Hispaniola, and indeed of all the islands which Columbus had visited, were an easy, indolent, harmless race. They were of a copper colour. The men and the girls went entirely naked: the women had a mat of cotton wrapped about their loins. They had no hair on any part of their body but the head: a distinction which also is common to the natives of the American continent. They considered the Spaniards as divinities, and the discharge of the artillery as their thunder: they fell on their faces at the sound. The women, however, seem very early to have had less awful apprehensions of their new guests; for they no sooner saw them than they offered their favours, and courted their embraces as men [2]. Some wicked wit may indeed say, that women from the beginning have been fond of superior beings; and, if we credit ancient story, they have often good

---

[1] *Life of Columbus*, chap. xxiii.   [2] Herrera, dec. i.

reason for such fondness.　　Be that as it may, it is certain that the women of Hispaniola were fonder of the Spaniards than of their husbands.　　Their husbands were not jealous of them. And in the arms of those wantons the companions of Columbus are said to have caught that fatal malady which has strewed with new thorns the paths of love; and which, if human happiness is to be computed by the balance of pain and pleasure, will be found to be more than a counterpoise to all the gold of Mexico, the silver of Peru, and the diamonds of Brazil.

But let not this misfortune be adduced as a charge against the great navigator.　　He could not know that the new hemisphere contained new maladies; he could not foresee, that he should import into Europe a distemper that would poison the springs of life: which would propagate disease from generation to generation, emasculate the vigour of nations, and alarmingly multiply the miseries of mankind!—And, happily for him, his enemies were ignorant of it at his return.　　He re-entered the port of Palos, on the fifteenth of March, 1493, and was received with universal acclamations of joy.　　Those who had ridiculed his project were the most ready to pay court to him.　　In the presence of Ferdinand and Isabella, he was desired to sit covered like a grandee of Spain; and, while royal favour beamed upon him, the church loaded him with its benedictions.　　Superstition lent its sanction to those discoveries, which had been made in its defiance.　　Pope Alexander VI. issued a bull, granting to the sovereigns of Spain all the countries which they had discovered, or should discover, a hundred leagues to the westward of the Azores.　　A fleet of seventeen sail was fitted out in a few months; and Columbus, invested with yet more extensive powers, and furnished with every thing necessary for discovery, colonization, or conquest, again committed himself to the waves in quest of a Western Continent [1].

Great things were expected from this second voyage; and many new islands were discovered: yet it ended in general disappointment, misfortune, and disgust.　　When Columbus arrived at Hispaniola, with a multitude of missionaries, soldiers, and settlers, he found the fortresses utterly ruined, and the garrison all massacred.　　They had drawn upon themselves this untimely fate by their arrogance, licentiousness, and tyranny.　　These particulars he learned from the natives, accompanied with such marked circumstances, as left him no room to disbelieve

---

[1] *Life of Columbus*, chap. xlii. xliii.

them. He therefore entered once more into friendly correspondence with those artless people, established a new colony, and built the town of Isabella—afterwards abandoned for that of St. Domingo, which became the capital of the island. His next care was to discover the mines; near which he erected forts, and left garrisons to protect the labourers. But neither the wisdom nor the humanity of this great man were sufficient to preserve order among his followers, or to teach them fellow-feeling. They roused anew, by their barbarities, the gentle spirit of the natives; they quarrelled among themselves; they rose against their commander. Mortified by so many untoward circumstances, Columbus committed the government of the island to his brother Bartholomew, and returned to Spain in 1496, with some samples of gold dust and ore, pearls, and other precious products [1].

Bartholomew Columbus suffered many hardships, and was on the point of sinking under the mutineers, before he received any assistance from the court of Spain; and although the great Christopher was able to clear himself of all the aspersions of his enemies, some years elapsed before he could obtain a third appointment for the prosecution of his favourite project. At last a small fleet was granted him, and he discovered the continent of America, near the mouth of the river Oronoco, on the first of August, 1498. He carried off six of the natives, and returned to Hispaniola, convinced that he had now reached the great object of his ambition.

But while Columbus was employed in reducing to obedience the mutineers in that island, another navigator unjustly took from him the honour of the discovery of the Western Continent. The merchants of Seville having obtained permission to attempt discoveries, as private adventurers, sent out four ships in 1499, under the command of Alonzo de Ojeda, who had accompanied Columbus in his second voyage, assisted by Americus Vespucius, a Florentine, skilled in the science of navigation. This fleet touched on the part of the western continent already discovered by Columbus, whose course Ojeda followed: and Americus, who was a man of great address, as well as of considerable literary talents, by publishing the first voyages on the subject, and other artful means, gave his name to the New World, in prejudice to the illustrious Genoese [2]. Mankind are now become sensible of the imposture; but time has sanctified the error; and the great Western Continent, or fourth division of the globe, so long un-

---

[1] Herrera, dec. i. lib. iii.   [2] Ibid. lib. iv.

known to the inhabitants of Europe, Asia, and Africa, still continues to be distinguished by the name of AMERICA.

This, however, was but a small misfortune in comparison of what Columbus was doomed to suffer. His enemies having prevailed at the court of Madrid, a new governor was sent out to Hispaniola. The great discoverer and his brother were loaded with irons, and sent home in that condition, in different ships. Touched with sentiments of veneration and pity, Valejo, captain of the vessel on board of which the admiral was confined, approached his prisoner with profound respect, as soon as he was clear of the island, and offered to strike off the fetters with which he was unjustly bound. " No, Valejo !"—replied Columbus, with a generous indignation ; " I wear these fetters in consequence of an order from my sovereigns. They shall find me as obedient to this, as to all their other injunctions. By their command I have been confined, and their command alone shall set me at liberty [1]."

The Spanish ministry were ashamed of the severity of their creature, Bovadilla : Columbus was set at liberty on his arrival, and a fourth command granted him in 1502, for the prosecution of farther discoveries. But this expedition did not prove more fortunate than the former ; for, although Columbus touched at several parts of the American continent, where he exchanged trinkets for gold and pearls, to a considerable amount, he failed in an attempt to establish a colony on the river Yebra or Belem, in the province of Veragua, and lost every thing in his course home. He was shipwrecked on the island of Jamaica : his followers mutinied ; and, after being alternately in danger of perishing by hunger or by violence, he arrived in Spain, in 1505, to experience a more severe fate than either. Queen Isabella was dead at his return. With her all his hopes of future favour perished. The court received him coldly. His services were too great for humility : his proud heart disdained to sue, and his high spirit could not submit to neglect. He retired to Valladolid, where he died, in 1506, a martyr to the ingratitude of that monarch to whom he had given the West Indies, and for whom he had opened a passage into a richer and more extensive empire than was ever subdued by the Roman arms [2].

There is something in true genius which seems to be essentially connected with humanity. Don Henry, Gama, and Columbus, prosecuted their discoveries upon the most liberal prin-

---

[1] *Life of Columbus*, chap. xxxiii.   [2] *Life of Columbus.*—Herrera.

ciples, those of mutual advantage ; they sought to benefit, not to destroy their species.   After the death of Columbus, the maxims of Spain, like those of Portugal, became altogether bloody. Religion, avarice, and violence, walked hand in hand.   The cross was held up as an object of worship to those who had never heard of the name of Jesus : and millions were deliberately butchered, for not embracing tenets which they could not understand, not delivering treasures which they did not possess, or not suffering oppressions which man was never born to bear, and which his nature cannot sustain [1].

The leader who pursued these new maxims with the least violence to humanity, and the greatest advantage to his country, was Fernando Cortez, the conqueror of Mexico.   Before the discovery of that rich and powerful empire, the Spanish colonies of Hispaniola, Cuba, Jamaica, and Port Rico, were in a flourishing condition : frequent expeditions had been made to the continent, and settlements established in Castilla del Oro and on the Isthmus of Darien.   At last a descent was made in the Gulf of Mexico, and information received of the opulence and grandeur of the emperor Montezuma and his capital. A.D. Velasquez, governor of Cuba, immediately resolved upon 1518. the conquest of Mexico, and committed to Cortez the execution of the enterprise ; and that gallant soldier is said to have accomplished, what appears too bold even for fiction, the overthrow of an empire that could send millions into the field, with so small a force as five hundred men [2].

A success so unexampled, in an unknown country, must have been accompanied with many favourable circumstances, independent of the ability of the general, the courage of the troops, and even the superiority of weapons.   Some of these we A.D. know.   When Cortez landed with his little army on the 1519. coast of Mexico, he met with a Spanish captive, who understood the dialect of the country, and whose ransom he obtained.   He also formed an intimacy with a fair American named Mariana, who soon learned the Castilian language, and became both his mistress and counsellor.   Her attachment communicated itself to all the Mexican women, who were generally neglected by their husbands for the most abominable of all debaucheries. While the men opposed their naked breasts to the weapons of the Spaniards, fell by their blows, or fled from their fury, the

---

[1] Bart. de las Casas, *Relat. de la Dest. de las Indias.*
[2] De Solis, lib. ii.—Herrera, dec. ii.

women every where flew to their embrace, and rendered them all the services in their power.

To these fortunate occurrences may be added the arrival of the ambassadors of Montezuma, who endeavoured, by presents, to engage the invaders to re-embark. The delay which this negotiation produced was of infinite service to Cortez. An army, instead of an embassy, on his first landing, might have ruined him. He replied, that he was only an ambassador himself, and as such, could not depart without an audience of the emperor. This answer put the ambassadors of Montezuma to a stand. They reported it to the emperor. He was alarmed at the request. They redoubled their presents: they employed persuasions, but to no purpose. Cortez was inflexible. At last they had recourse to threats, according to their instructions, and talked loudly of the forces and treasures of their country.

"These," said Cortez, turning to his companions, "these are what we seek; great perils, and great riches." Stronger motives could not have been offered to indigent adventurers, burning with the spirit of chivalry and the lust of plunder. Their leader saw conquest in their looks; and having now received the necessary information, and prepared himself against all hazards, he boldly marched toward the seat of empire [1].

The Spanish general, however, though so little diffident of his own strength, prudently negotiated with such princes and states as he found to be enemies of the Mexicans. Among these the most powerful was the republic of Tlascala. Cortez proposed an alliance to the senate; but that assembly resolved, not only to withhold assistance from the Spaniards, but to oppose them. This resolution had almost proved fatal to Cortez and his enterprise. The Tlascalans were a brave people, and brought a formidable army into the field; but by the help of musquetry, artillery, and cavalry, to these republicans above all things tremendous, the Spaniards, after repeated struggles, were enabled to humble them. They saw their mistake; entered into a treaty with Cortez, and were highly serviceable in his future operations.

The invaders now advanced without any interruption to the gates of Mexico. Montezuma was full of irresolution and terror.

That mighty emperor, whose treasures were immense, and whose sway was absolute; who was lord over thirty princes, each of whom could bring a numerous army into the field, was so in-

---

[1] Herrera, dec. ii.—De Solis, lib. iii. iv.

timidated by the defeat of the Tlascalans, that he wanted resolution to strike a blow in defence of his dignity.   The haughty
potentate, who had ordered Cortez to depart from his coast,
introduced him into his capital.   Instead of making use of force,
he had recourse to perfidy.   While he professed friendship to
the Spanish general, he sent an army to attack the Spanish
colony, newly settled at Vera Cruz, and yet in a feeble condition.
Cortez received intelligence of this breach of faith, and took one
of the boldest resolutions ever formed by man.   He immediately
proceeded to the imperial palace, accompanied by five of his principal officers ; arrested Montezuma as his prisoner ; carried him
off to the Spanish quarters, compelled him to deliver to punishment the officer who had acted by his orders, and publicly
acknowledge himself, in the seat of his power, the vassal of the
king of Spain [1].

In the height of these successes, Cortez was informed that a
new general, sent by the governor of Cuba, had arrived with a
superior force to supplant him in the command, and reap the
fruits of his victories.   He marched against his rival ; A.D.
he defeated him ; he took him prisoner ; and the van- 1520.
quished troops, won by the magnanimity and confidence of the
victor, ranged themselves under his standard.   Thus reinforced,
by an occurrence which threatened the extinction of his hopes,
he returned with rapidity to the city of Mexico, where he found
full occasion for this accession of strength.

The Mexicans were all in arms, and had surrounded the party
which Cortes had left to guard the emperor.   This insurrection
was occasioned by the avarice and intemperate zeal of the
Spaniards ; who, on a solemn festival in honour of the gods of
the country, had massacred two thousand of the Mexican nobles,
under pretence of a secret conspiracy, and stripped them of their
precious ornaments.   The spirit of the people was roused ; they
were incensed at the confinement of their prince ; they were
filled with holy indignation at the insult offered to the gods, and
they longed to revenge the fate of their nobility.   Cortez found
it difficult to resist their fury.   They permitted him, however,
to join his detachment, though not from motives of friendship or
generosity ; they hoped to involve the whole body of the Spaniards in promiscuous ruin.   " We have discovered," said they,
" that you are not immortal : and although the death of every
Spaniard should cost us a thousand lives, we are determined to

complete your destruction. After so great a slaughter, there will still remain a sufficient number to celebrate the victory [1]. "

The Mexicans now fiercely attacked the Spanish quarters. They were several times repulsed, and as often returned to the charge with undiminished ardour. They devoted themselves cheerfully to death; boldly advanced in the face of the artillery; threw themselves in crowds upon the musquetry, and fearlessly grappled the mouths of the guns in attempting to ascend the fortifications. Montezuma considered this as a favourable conjuncture for obtaining his freedom and the departure of the Spaniards. On those conditions he consented to employ his good offices with the people. He showed himself on the ramparts, clad in his royal robes, and endeavoured to induce the multitude to retire. They at first seemed overawed by the presence of their sovereign, and ready to obey his commands; but suddenly recollecting the pusillanimity of his behaviour, their love was changed into hate, their veneration into contempt, and a stone launched by an indignant arm at once deprived Montezuma of the empire and his life [2].

That accident gave sincere concern to Cortez, and was a real misfortune to the Spaniards. The successor of Montezuma was a fierce and warlike prince, and resolutely determined to support the independence of his country. Cortez, after several ineffectual struggles, found himself under the necessity of quitting the city. The Mexicans harassed him in his retreat, took from him all his baggage and treasure, and engaged him in the field with an army astonishingly numerous. The ensigns of various nations waved in the air, and the imperial standard of massy gold was displayed. Now was the time for heroism; and stronger proofs of it were never exhibited than in the valley of Otumba. " Death or victory!" was the charge, and the resolution of every Spaniard. The Mexicans were soon thrown into confusion, and a terrible slaughter ensued; but fresh crowds still pressing on, supplied the place of the slain, and the Spaniards must have sunk under the fatigue of continual fighting, had not Cortez, by a happy presence of mind, put an end to the dispute, and rendered the victory decisive. He rushed at the head of his cavalry, towards the imperial standard, closed with the Mexican general who guarded it; and at one stroke of his lance, hurled him from his litter. The standard was seized, and

---

[1] De Solis, lib. iv.—Herrera, dec. ii.
[2] Herrera, dec. ii. lib. viii.—De Solis, lib. iv. cap. xiv. xv.

the consequence proved as Cortez had expected; the Mexicans threw down their arms, and fled with precipitation and terror [1].

This victory, and the assistance of the Tlascalans, encouraged Cortez to undertake the siege of Mexico; and another fortunate circumstance enabled him to complete his conquest. The new emperor Guatimozin was taken prisoner in attempting to A.D. make his escape out of his capital, in order to rouse to 1521. arms the distant provinces of his dominions. The metropolis surrendered, and the whole empire submitted to the Spaniards.

The city of Mexico is represented as one of the most striking monuments of human grandeur. Its spacious squares, its sumptuous palaces, its magnificent temples, are pompously displayed by the Spanish historians; but we must not give entire credit to those splendid descriptions. The mechanical arts could not be carried to great perfection in a country where the use of iron was unknown; nor could the sciences or liberal arts be cultivated with success among a people ignorant of letters. The hieroglyphics, which the Mexicans are said to have used for the communication of their ideas, could but imperfectly answer that end, in comparison with general symbols or signs; and without a facile method of recording past transactions, and of preserving our own thoughts and those of others, society can never make any considerable progress. The ferocious religion of the Mexicans is another proof of their barbarity; for although we frequently find absurd ceremonies prevail among polished nations, we rarely, if ever, meet with those that are cruel. Civilized man has a feeling for man. Human blood was profusely shed upon the altars of the Mexican gods: and, if we believe the most respectable Spanish historians, human flesh (though only that of enemies) was greedily devoured both by the priests and the people. Enormous superstition and excessive despotism always go hand in hand. When the mind is enslaved, it is easy to enslave the body. Montezuma was the most absolute sovereign upon earth, and his subjects the most abject slaves.

The conquest of Mexico was followed by that of Peru, another country in the New World, abounding yet more in precious metals.

Peru had long been governed by a race of emperors, under the name of Incas, who were supposed to be the descendants of the Sun. The name of the Spanish invader was Pi- A.D. zarro, and that of the Inca, in possession of the crown, 1532.

[1] De Solis, lib. iv. cap. xx.

Atahualpa. Alarmed at the ravages of the Spaniards, this prince agreed to an interview with their general, in order to settle the conditions of a peace. Though Pizarro solicited the conference, he had no thoughts but of war. The Inca, it is said, was not more sincere in his professions. He came to the place of meeting carried upon a throne of gold, and attended by upwards of ten thousand men ; twenty thousand more are reported to have waited his signal ; but for this report, or the insincerity of the Inca, there seems to have been no foundation in fact. All the Peruvians were richly dressed, and their arms glittered with gold and precious stones. The avarice of the Spaniards was inflamed. Pizarro disposed his followers, who did not exceed two hundred, in the most advantageous order, while Valverdè, a Dominican friar, advanced towards Atahualpa, with a crucifix in one hand and a breviary in the other. He addressed to the Inca, by the help of an interpreter, a long discourse, unfolding the principles of the Christian faith, and pressing him to embrace that religion, and submit himself to the king of Spain, to whom the pope had given Peru. Atahualpa, who had listened with patience, replied thus to his pious admonisher : " How extravagant is it in the pope, to give away so liberally that which doth not belong to him !—He is inferior, you own, to God the Father, to God the Son, and to God the Holy Ghost : these are all your gods : and the gods only can dispose of kingdoms. I am willing to be a friend to the king of Spain, who has sufficiently displayed his power by sending armies to such distant countries ; but I will not be his vassal. I owe tribute to no mortal prince : I know no superior upon earth. The religion of my ancestors I venerate; and to renounce it would be absurd and impious, until you have convinced me that it is false, and that yours, which you would have me embrace, is true. You adore a God, who died upon a gibbet ; I worship the Sun, who never dies."

" Vengeance !"—cried Valverdè, turning towards the Spaniards : " Vengeance ! my friends ;—kill these dogs, who despise the religion of the cross."

The word of command was given ; the artillery played ; the musquetry fired ; the cavalry spread confusion and terror ; while Pizarro advanced, at the head of a chosen band, and seized the person of the Inca. The slaughter was dreadful, and the pillage immense. The blow was final : Peru ceased to be an empire. The descendants of the Sun, who united in their person both regal and pontifical dignity, sunk under a set of banditti

1

that knew not their birth. After draining Atahualpa of his treasure, under pretence of a ransom for his liberty, Pizarro condemned him to the flames, as an obstinate idolater. A.D. But through the mediation of Father Valverdè, blessed 1533. intercessor! the Inca's sentence was changed into strangling, on condition that he should die in the Christian faith[1]!

The conquest of Mexico and Peru put the Spaniards in possession of more specie than all the other nations of Europe. Yet Spain from that æra has continued to decline. It has declined in population, industry, and vigour. The vices attendant upon riches have corrupted all ranks of men, and enervated the national spirit. From being the first kingdom in Europe, it has become one of the least considerable. Portugal has experienced a like fate, since the discovery of the passage to India by the Cape of Good Hope, and the settlement of Brazil; and, from the same cause, a too great and sudden influx of wealth.

Those reflections lead us to inquire, " How far the discoveries of the Portuguese and Spaniards have been advantageous to Europe or beneficial to mankind?" The subject is complicated, and will best be illustrated by the sequel of events, and the ideas suggested by such a train of particulars. Meanwhile I shall observe, that authors do not judge rightly when they ascribe to those discoveries our present improvements in commerce and civilization. Commerce and civilization were fast advancing in Europe before the beginning of the sixteenth century; and this quarter of the globe would have been nearly in the state in which we now find it, though no such discoveries had been made. We should not indeed have had so much specie, but we should have had less occasion for it; the price of labour would have been lower, and would have borne the same proportion to the price of provisions, which would have answered the purpose of a larger quantity of circulating money. Our resources in war would have been fewer; but our real strength might perhaps have been greater, as we should not have had occasion to colonize and combat at both extremities of the globe.

It must, however, be owned, that the passage by the Cape of Good Hope, in the first instance, has been of singular service to the general commerce of Europe. Our trade with India was formerly conducted by means of the Arabs, who, consequently, had a share in the profits: it is now entirely carried on by

---

[1] Benzoni, *Hist. Nov. Orb.* lib. iii.—Herrera, dec. iii.—Zaret, lib. iii.—Garcilasso, lib. i.

Europeans. European ships and European sailors import the commodities of the East into our harbours. But to counterbalance this advantage, the new passage, by being open to every nation, has increased the taste for Indian commodities, and whetted the avarice of man. It has prompted the nations of Europe to massacre one another in the south of Asia, and rob and murder the industrious natives, without feeling or remorse; while it has hurt the European manufacturer, by furnishing foreign fabrics of superior quality, at a lower price than he can afford to sell. It has encouraged a losing trade; for such, in general, that with India must be accounted;—a trade which continues to drain Europe of its bullion and cash, the commodities of the East being chiefly purchased with gold and silver.

The mines of Mexico and Peru are necessary to supply that drain. So far the discovery of America must be accounted good, or at least the palliation of an evil. Besides, the colonies established on the continent, and in the islands of America, depend chiefly upon Europe for their manufactures, and furnish an honest and comfortable maintenance to millions of our people, who must otherwise have wanted bread, or have lived in the lowest state of wretchedness. In this view, America is favourable both to industry and population. These are solid advantages; and the superabundance of the precious metals alone could make Spain and Portugal overlook them. They are poor amidst their treasures; while other nations, profiting by their indolence, grow wealthy by supplying their wants. The labour of a people is the only desirable source of their riches, and the only certain road to their felicity; though mankind, in general, are so ignorant as to suppose, that they should be happier without toil.

The discovery of America has increased the labour of Europe, and consequently its happiness, collectively considered. It has also augmented the number of the civilized part of the human species, by opening a boundless region for the planting of European colonies, which have greatly flourished in many parts, and supplied the inhabitants of the mother-countries with a variety of commodities, formerly unknown, that contribute to the more comfortable enjoyment of life, and to the extension of trade. But the violent means by which those colonies were generally established, and the outrages which continue to be exercised against the injured natives, as often as they attempt to recover their original rights, together with the brutal slavery to which another race of men are condemned, in order to cultivate the lands so unjustly seized and possessed, are circumstances over which humanity must ever mourn, and which, the heart of every lover of his species will tell him, no commercial, no political, motives can authorize or vindicate.

We must now, my dear Philip, return to the line of general history, and enter upon that important æra, when all the great powers on the European continent made a trial of their strength in Italy; when religion united with ambition to give new energy to the sword; when creeds, no less than kingdoms, became the source of war; and fire and faggot were employed to enforce human belief.

LETTER LX.

A general View of the Affairs of Europe, from the Election of Charles V. in 1519, *to the Peace of Cambray in* 1529; *including the Progress of the Reformation.*

THOUGH Maximilian could not prevail upon the German electors to choose his grandson of Spain king of the Romans, he had disposed their minds in favour of that prince: and other circumstances, on the death of the emperor, conspired to the exaltation of Charles. The imperial crown had so A.D. 1519. long continued in the Austrian line, that it began to be considered as hereditary in that family; and Germany, torn by religious disputes, stood in need of a powerful emperor, not only to preserve its own internal tranquillity, but also to protect it against the victorious arms of the Turks, who, under Selim I., threatened the liberties of Europe. This fierce and rapid conqueror had already subdued the Mamelukes, a barbarous militia that had dismembered the empire of the Arabs, and made themselves masters of Egypt and Syria. The power of Charles appeared necessary to oppose that of Selim. The extensive dominions of the house of Austria, which gave him an interest in the preservation of Germany; the rich sovereignty of the Netherlands and Franche-Comté; the entire possession of the great and warlike kingdom of Spain, together with that of Naples and Sicily; all united to hold him up to the first dignity among Christian princes; and the new world seemed only to be called into existence, that its treasures might enable him to defend Christendom against the Infidels.—Such was the language of his partisans.

Francis I., however, no sooner received intelligence of the death of Maximilian than he declared himself a candiate for the empire, and with no less confidence of success than Charles. He trusted to his superior years and experience, and to his great reputation in arms, acquired by the victory at Marignan, and the conquest of Milan. And it was farther urged in his favour, that the impetuosity of the French cavalry, added to the firmness of the German infantry, would prove irresistible; and not only be sufficient, under a warlike emperor, to set limits to the ambition of Selim, but to break entirely the Ottoman power, and prevent it from ever becoming dangerous again to Germany.

Both claims were plausible. The dominions of Francis were less extensive but more united than those of Charles. His subjects were numerous, active, brave, lovers of glory, and lovers of their king. These were strong arguments in favour of his power, so necessary at this juncture; but he had no natural interest in the Germanic body; and the electors, hearing so much of military force on each side, became more alarmed for their own privileges than the common safety. They determined to reject both candidates, and offered the imperial crown to Frederic the Wise, duke of Saxony. But he, undazzled by the splendour of an object courted with so much eagerness by two great monarchs, rejected it with admirable magnanimity.

"In times of tranquillity," said Frederic, "we wish for an emperor who has no power to invade our liberties; times of danger demand one who is able to secure our safety. The Turkish armies, led by a warlike and victorious prince, are now assembling: they are ready to pour in upon Germany with a violence unknown in former ages. New conjunctures call for new expedients. The imperial sceptre must be committed to some hand more powerful than mine, or that of any other German prince. We possess neither dominions, nor revenues, nor authority, which will enable us to encounter such a formidable enemy. Recourse must be had, in this exigency, to one of the rival monarchs. Each of them can bring into the field forces sufficient for our defence. But, as the king of Spain is of German extraction, as he is a member and prince of the empire by the territories which descend to him from his grandfather, and as his dominions stretch along that frontier which lies most exposed to the enemy, his claim, in my opinion, is preferable to that of a stranger to our language, to our blood, and to our country [1]." Charles was elected in consequence of this speech.

The two candidates had hitherto conducted their rivalry with emulation, but without enmity. They had even softened their competition by many expressions of friendship and regard. Francis in particular declared, with his usual vivacity, that his brother Charles and he were fairly and openly suitors to the same mistress : " The most assiduous and fortunate," added he, " will win her ; and the other must rest contented [2]." But although a generous and high-minded prince, while animated by the hope of success, might be capable of forming such a philosophic resolution, it soon appeared that he had promised a moderation too refined for humanity, and which he was little able to practise. The preference was no sooner given to his rival than Francis discovered all the passions natural to disappointed ambition. He could not suppress his chagrin and indignation at being baffled in his favourite purpose, and rejected in the face of all Europe, for a youth yet unknown to fame. The spirit of Charles resented such contempt ; and from this jealousy, as much as from opposition of interests, arose that emulation between those great princes, which involved them in frequent hostilities, and kept their whole age in agitation.

When princes or private persons are resolved to quarrel, it is easy to find a brand of discord. Charles and Francis had many interfering claims in Italy ; and besides these obvious sources of contention and competition, the latter thought himself bound in honour to restore the king of Navarre to his dominions, unjustly seized by the crown of Spain. They immediately began to negotiate ; and as Henry VIII. of England was the third prince of the age in power and in dignity, his friendship was eagerly courted by each of the rivals. He was the natural guardian of the liberties of Europe. Sensible of the consequence which his situation gave him, and proud of his pre-eminence, Henry knew it to be his interest to keep the balance even between the contending powers, and to restrain both, by not joining constantly with either. But he was seldom able to reduce his ideas to practice ; he was governed by caprice more than by principle ; the passions of the man were an overmatch for the maxims of the king. Vanity and resentment were the great

---

[1] Scard. *Rer. Germ. Script.*—Seckend. *Comment.*—Robertson's *Hist. of Charles V.* book i.

[2] Guicciardini, lib. xiii.

springs of his actions; and his neighbours, by touching these, found an easy way to draw him into their measures.

All the impolitic steps in Henry's government, however, must not be imputed to himself: many of them were occasioned by the ambition and avarice of his prime minister and favourite, cardinal Wolsey. This man, who, by his talents and accomplishments, had risen from one of the lowest conditions in life to the highest employments both in church and state, and who lived with regal splendour, governed the haughty, presumptuous, and intractable spirit of Henry, with absolute ascendency. Equally rapacious and profuse, he was insatiable in desiring wealth; vain and ostentatious, he was greedy of adulation; of boundless ambition, he aspired after new honours with an eagerness unabated by his former success. To these passions he himself sacrificed every consideration, divine and human; and whoever sought to obtain his favour, or that of his master, found it necessary also to sacrifice liberally to them.

Francis was well acquainted with the character of Henry and of his minister. He had successfully flattered Wolsey's pride, by honouring him with particular marks of his confidence, and bestowing upon him the appellations of Father, Tutor, and Governor; and he had obtained the restitution of Tournay, by adding a pension to these respectful titles. He now solicited an

A.D. interview with the king of England near Calais, in hopes
1520. of being able, by familiar conversation, to attach him to his friendship and interest, while he gratified the cardinal's vanity by affording him an opportunity of displaying his magnificence in the presence of two courts, and of discovering to the two nations his influence over their monarchs.

Politic though young, Charles dreaded the effects of this projected interview between two gallant princes, whose hearts were no less susceptible of friendship than their manners were capable of inspiring it. Finding it impossible, however, to prevent a visit, in which the vanity of all parties seemed to be so much concerned, he endeavoured to defeat its purpose, and to pre-occupy the favour of the English monarch, and of his minister, by an act of complaisance still more flattering and more uncommon. Relying wholly upon Henry's generosity for his safety, he landed at Dover, on his way from Spain to the Low Countries. The king of England, who was on his way to France, charmed with such an instance of confidence, hastened to receive his royal guest; and Charles, during his short stay, had the address not only to give Henry favourable impressions of his character and intentions, but to detach Wolsey entirely from the interests of Francis. The tiara had attracted the eye of that ambitious prelate; and as the emperor knew that the papacy was the sole point of elevation, beyond his present greatness, to which he could aspire, he made him an offer of his interest on the first vacancy [1].

The interview between Henry and Francis was in an open plain between Guisnes and Ardres; where the two kings and their attendants displayed their magnificence with such emulation and profuse expense, as procured it the name of the *Field of Cloth of Gold*. Here Henry erected a spacious house of wood and canvas, framed in London, on which, under the figure of an English archer, was inscribed the following motto; " He prevails whom I favour !" alluding to his political situation, as holding in his hands the balance of power between the emperor and French monarch. Feats of chivalry, however, parties of gallantry, and such exercises as were in that age reckoned manly or elegant, rather than serious business, occupied the two courts during the time they continued together, which was eighteen days. And here I cannot help noticing a circumstance that strongly marks the manners of those times, and their contrast to ours, if not their comparative rusticity. After the French and English wrestlers had exercised their strength and agility, which, according to the phrase of the historian, afforded *excellent pastime*, the kings of France and England, says Fleuranges, retired to a tent, where they drank together; and the king of England, seizing the king of France by the collar, said, " My brother, I must wrestle with you !" and attempted once or twice to *trip up his heels;* but Francis, who was *an excellent wrestler*, twisted him round, and threw him on the ground with great violence. Henry endeavoured to renew the struggle, but was prevented [2].

After taking leave of this scene of dissipation, the king of England paid a visit to the emperor and Margaret of Savoy at Gravelines, and engaged them to go with him to Calais; where the artful Charles completed the impression which he had begun to make on Henry and his favourite, and effaced all the friendship to which the frank and generous nature of Francis had given birth. He renewed his assurances of assisting Wolsey in obtaining the papacy; and he put him in present possession of the

---

[1] Polyd. Virg.—Holinshed.—Herbert's *Hist. of Henry VIII.*—Fiddes' *Life of Wolsey.*
[2] *Mem. de Fleuranges.*

revenues of the sees of Badajoz and Palencia. He flattered Henry's pride, by convincing him of his importance, and the justness of the motto which he had chosen; offering to submit to his sole arbitration any difference that might arise between him and Francis [1].

This important point being secured, Charles repaired to Aix-la-Chapelle, where he was solemnly invested with the crown and sceptre of Charle-magne, in presence of a more splendid and numerous assembly than had appeared on any former inauguration. About the same time Solyman the Magnificent, one of the most accomplished, enterprising, and warlike of the Turkish princes, and a constant and formidable rival of the German emperor, ascended the Ottoman throne, in consequence of the death of Selim.

The first act of Charles's administration was the appointment of a diet at Worms, to concert with the princes of the empire proper measures for checking the progress of " those new and dangerous opinions which threatened to dissurb the peace of Germany, and to overturn the religion of their ancestors." The opinions propagated by Luther and his followers were here meant. That bold innovator, after the diet at Augsburg, and the death of Maximilian, had freely promulgated his opinions, under the protection of the elector of Saxony, to whom the vicariate of that part of Germany which is governed by the Saxon laws, was committed, during the interregnum that preceded the election of Charles V. And these opinions were suffered to take root in different places, and to grow up to some degree of strength and firmness. Leo X., though little skilled in such controversies, was now alarmed at Luther's progress; and convinced that all hopes of reclaiming him by forbearance were in vain, he issued a bull of excommunication against him. His books were ordered to be burned, and he himself was delivered over to Satan, as an obstinate heretic, if he should not, within sixty days, publicly recant his errors.

This sentence did not disconcert or intimidate Luther. After renewing his appeal to a general council, he published remarks upon the bull of excommunication, and boldly declared the pope to be the Man of Sin, or Antichrist, whose appearance is foretold in the Revelation of St. John; declaimed against the tyranny and usurpations of the court of Rome with greater vehemence than ever, exhorted all Christian princes to shake off such an

---

[1] Polyd. Virg.—Fiddes.

ignominious yoke, and boasted of his own happiness in being marked out as the object of ecclesiastical indignation, because he had ventured to assert the rights of religion, and the mental liberty of mankind. Nor did he confine his contempt of the papal power to words alone. He assembled all the professors and students of the university of Wittenberg, and with great pomp, and before a vast multitude of spectators, cast the volumes of the canon law, with the bull of excommunication, into the flames: and his example was imitated in several other cities [1].

While the credit and authority of the Roman pontiff were thus furiously shaken in Germany, an attack no less violent, and occasioned by the same causes, was made upon them in Switzerland. The Franciscans being entrusted with the sale of indulgences in that country, executed their commission with the same unblushing rapacity which had rendered the Dominicans so odious in Saxony. They proceeded, however, with uninterrupted success till they arrived at Zurich, where they received a mortal blow from Ulric Zuinglius, a man of extensive learning, uncommon sagacity, and heroic intrepidity of spirit. Animated with a republican boldness, and free from those restraints which subjection to the will of a prince, and perhaps a remnant of original prejudice, imposed upon the German reformer, he advanced with more daring and rapid steps to overturn the whole fabric of the established religion; and the pope's supremacy was soon denied in the greater part of Switzerland [2].

Such was the state of the Reformation, when Charles V. arrived in Germany. No secular prince had yet embraced the new opinions; no change in the established forms of worship had been introduced, nor any encroachments made upon the possessions or jurisdiction of the clergy; a deep impression, however, was made upon the minds of the people; their reverence for ancient institutions and doctrines were shaken; and the materials were already scattered, which produced the conflagration that afterwards spread over Europe. Charles saw the flames gathering; and, as he found it necessary to secure the friendship of Leo X. he cited Luther to appear before the diet at A.D. Worms. Luther did not hesitate a moment about yield- 1521. ing obedience: he accompanied the herald who brought the emperor's letter and safe-conduct. " I am lawfully called to appear in that city," said he to some of his friends, who were

---

[1] Seckend. *Comment.*—Luth. *Oper.* vol. ii.
[2] Ruchart. *Hist. de la Reformat. en Suisse*, liv. i.

anxious for his safety ; " and thither I will go in the name of the Lord, though as many devils as tiles upon the houses were assembled against me [1]."

Had vanity and the love of applause, from which no human heart is free, been the sole principles by which Luther was influenced, his reception at Worms was such as he might have reckoned a full reward for all his labours. Vast crowds assembled to see him whenever he walked abroad; and his apartments were daily filled with princes and personages of the highest rank, who treated him with all the respect that is due to superior merit, but which is more particularly commanded by those who possess the power of directing the understanding and the sentiments of others. Rank or birth can receive no homage so flattering ; for they can receive none so sincere, or which has so immediate a reference to those qualities which men call their own. Luther was not, however, intoxicated: he behaved before the diet with decency and firmness. He readily acknowledged an excess of vehemence and acrimony in his controversial writings; but he refused to retract his opinions while unconvinced of their falsehood, or consent to their being tried by any other standard than the Scripture. Neither threats nor entreaties could prevail on him to depart from this resolution. Some of the fathers, therefore, proposed to imitate the example of the council of Constance, and commit to the flames the author of this pestilent heresy ; but the members of the diet refusing to agree to such a violation of public faith, and Charles not being disposed to bring a stain on the beginning of his administration by such an ignominious measure, Luther was permitted to depart in safety [2]. A few days after he left the city, a severe edict was issued in the emperor's name, and by authority of the diet, forbidding any prince to harbour him, and requiring all to concur in seizing his person as soon as the term of his safe-conduct should expire. But the elector of Saxony, his faithful patron, took him again, though secretly, under protection. Luther, in solitude, propagated his opinions; and Charles, for a time, found other matters to engage his attention.

The Spaniards, displeased at the departure of their sovereign, whose election to the empire they foresaw would interfere with the administration of his own kingdom, and incensed at the avarice of the Flemings, to whom the direction of public affairs had been committed since the death of cardinal Ximenes, broke

[1] Luth. Oper. vol. ii.   [2] F. Paul.—Seckend.

out into open rebellion.　This seemed, to Francis, a favourable conjuncture for reinstating the family of John d'Albret in the kingdom of Navarre.　Charles was at a distance from that part of his dominions, and the troops usually stationed there had been recalled to quell the commotions in Spain.　A French army under Andrew de Foix speedily conquered Navarre; but that young and inexperienced nobleman, dazzled with success, and pushed on by military ardour, ventured to enter Castile. Though divided among themselves, the Spaniards united against a foreign enemy; routed his forces, took him prisoner, and recovered Navarre in a shorter time than he had spent in subduing it.

The hostilities between the rival monarchs soon spread to another quarter.　The king of France encouraged the duke of Bouillon to make war upon the emperor, and invade Luxembourg.　Charles, after humbling the duke, attempted to enter France, but was repelled and worsted before Mezieres, by the famous chevalier de Bayard, distinguished among his contemporaries by the appellation of *The knight without fear and without reproach*, who united the talents of a consummate general to the punctilious honour and romantic gallantry of the heroes of chivalry.　Francis rushed into the Low Countries; where by an excess of caution, an error not natural to him, he lost an opportunity of cutting off the whole imperial army; and, what was still greater misconduct, he disgusted the constable de Bourbon, by giving the command of the van to the duke of Alençon [1].

During these operations in the field, an unsuccessful congress took place at Calais, under the mediation of Henry VIII.　It served only to exasperate those whom it was intended to reconcile.　And a league was soon after concluded at Bruges, through the intrigues of Wolsey, between the pope, Henry, and Charles, against France.　Leo had already entered into a separate league with the emperor; and the French were rapidly losing ground in Italy [2].

The insolence and exactions of Lautrec, governor of Milan, had totally alienated the affections of the people from France. They resolved to expel the troops of that nation, and put themselves under the government of Francis Sforza, brother of Maximilian their late duke.　In this resolution they were encouraged

---

[1] *Œuvr. de Brantome*, tome vi.—*Mém. de* Bellay.
[2] Rymer, *Fœd.* vol. xiii.—Herbert's *Hist. of Henry VIII*.

by the pope, who excommunicated Lautrec, and took into his pay a considerable body of Swiss. The papal army, commanded by Prosper Colonna, an experienced general, was joined by reinforcements from Germany and Naples; while Lautrec, neglected by his court, and deserted by the Swiss in its pay, was unable to make head against the enemy. The city of Milan was betrayed by the inhabitants to the confederates; Parma and Placentia were united to the ecclesiastical state; and of the conquests of the French in Lombardy, only Cremona, the castle of Milan, and a few inconsiderable forts, remained in their power [1].

Leo received the account of this success with such transports of joy as are said to have brought on a fever which occasioned his death. The spirit of the confederacy was broken, and its operations suspended, by that event. The Swiss were recalled: some other mercenaries were disbanded for want of pay; so that only the Spaniards, and a few Germans in the emperor's service, remained to defend the duchy of Milan. But Lautrec, who, with the remnant of his army, had taken shelter in the Venetian territories, destitute both of men and money, was unable to improve this opportunity. All his efforts were rendered ineffectual by the vigilance and activity of Colonna and his associates.

Meantime high discord prevailed in the conclave. Wolsey's name, notwithstanding the emperor's magnificent promises, was scarcely mentioned in the assembly. Julio of Medicis, Leo's
A.D. nephew, thought himself sure of the election; when
1522. by an unexpected turn of fortune, cardinal Adrian of Utrecht, Charles's preceptor, who at that time governed Spain in the character of viceroy, was raised to the papacy, to the great disgust of the Italians.

Francis, roused by the rising consequence of his rival, resolved to exert himself with fresh vigour, in order to wrest from him his late conquests in Lombardy. Lautrec received a supply of money and a recruit of ten thousand Swiss infantry. With this reinforcement he was enabled once more to act offensively, and even to advance within a few miles of the city of Milan; when money again failing him, and the Swiss growing mutinous, he was obliged to attack the Imperialists in their camp at Bicocca, where he was repulsed with great slaughter, having lost his bravest officers and best troops. The Swiss who

---

[1] Guicciardini, lib. xiv.—*Mém. de* Bellay.

survived immediately set out for their own country; and Lautrec, despairing of being able to keep the field, retired into France. Genoa was soon after taken by Colonna; and the authority of the emperor was established in all parts of Italy. The citadel of Cremona was the sole fortress that remained in the hands of the French[1].

The affliction of Francis, for such a succession of misfortunes, was augmented by the unexpected arrival of an English herald, who, in the name of his sovereign, declared war against France. The courage of this high-spirited prince, however, did not forsake him. Though his treasury was exhausted by expensive pleasures no less than by hostile enterprises, he assembled a considerable army, and put his kingdom in a posture for resisting his new enemy, without abandoning any of the schemes which he was forming against the emperor. He was surprised, but not alarmed at such a denunciation.

Willing to derive as much advantage as possible from his powerful ally, Charles paid a second visit to the court of England; and his success exceeded his expectations. He not only gained the entire friendship of Henry, who publicly ratified the treaty of Bruges, but disarmed the resentment of Wolsey, by assuring him of the papacy on Adrian's death; an event seemingly not distant, by reason of his age and infirmities. In consequence of these negotiations, an English army invaded France under the command of the earl of Surrey; who was obliged, however, at the close of the campaign, to retire with diminished forces, without being able to obtain possession of one place within the French frontier.

While the Christian princes were wasting each other's strength, Solyman the Magnificent entered Hungary, and made himself master of Belgrade, reckoned the chief barrier of that kingdom against the Turkish power. Encouraged by this success, he turned his victorious arms against the island of Rhodes, then the seat of the knights of St. John of Jerusalem; and, although every prince in that warlike age acknowledged Rhodes to be the principal bulwark of Christendom in the Levant, so violent was their mutual animosity, that they suffered Solyman without disturbance to carry on his operations against that city and island. L'isle Adam, the grand master, made a gallant defence; but, after incredible efforts of courage, patience, and military skill, during a siege of six months, he was obliged to surrender

---

[1] Guicciardini, ubi sup.

the place, having obtained an honourable capitulation from the soltan, who admired his heroic qualities[1]. Charles and Francis were equally ashamed of having occasioned, through their contests, such a loss to the Christian world; and the emperor, by way of reparation, granted to the knights of St. John the small island of Malta, where they fixed their residence.

Adrian VI., though the creature of the emperor, and devoted to his interest, endeavoured to assume the impartiality which became the common father of Christendom, and laboured to reconcile the contending princes, that they might unite in a league against Solyman, whose conquest of Rhodes rendered him more formidable than ever to Europe. The Italian states were no less desirous of peace than the pope: and so much regard was paid by the hostile powers to the exhortations of his holiness, and to a bull which he issued, requiring all Christian princes to consent to a truce for three years, that the Imperial, French, and English ambassadors at Rome, were empowered to treat of that matter. But while they wasted their time in fruitless negotiations, their masters were continuing their preparations for war.

The Venetians, who had hitherto adhered to the French interest, formed engagements with the emperor for securing Francis Sforza in the possession of the duchy of Milan; and the pope, from a persuasion that the ambition of the French monarch was the only obstacle to peace, acceded to the same alliance. The Florentines, the dukes of Ferrara and Mantua, and other Italian powers, followed this example. Francis was left without an ally to resist the efforts of a multitude of enemies, whose armies every where threatened, and whose territories encompassed, his dominions. The emperor, at the head of a Spanish army, menaced France on the side of Guienne; the forces of England and the Netherlands hovered over Picardy; and a numerous body of Germans prepared to ravage Burgundy[2].

A.D. 1523.

The dread of so many and such powerful adversaries, it was thought, would have obliged Francis to stand wholly on the defensive, or at least have prevented him from entertaining any thoughts of marching into Italy. But it was the characteristic of this prince, who was too apt to become negligent on ordinary occasions, to rouse himself at the approach of imminent danger, and not only to encounter it with spirit and intrepidity, but to

---

[1] Fontan. *de Bell. Rhod.*—Barre, *Hist. d'Allemagne*, tome viii.
[2] Guicciardini, lib. xv.

provide against it with diligence and industry. Before his enemies were able to strike a blow, he had assembled a powerful army, with which he hoped to disconcert all the emperer's schemes, by leading it in person into Italy: and this bold measure could scarcely have failed of the desired effect, had it been immediately carried into execution. But the discovery of a domestic conspiracy, of a very alarming nature, detained him in his kingdom.

Charles duke of Bourbon, high constable of France, was a prince of the most shining talents. His great abilities equally fitted him for the council or the field, while his eminent services to the crown entitled him to its first favour. But, unhappily, Louisa duchess of Angoulême, the king's mother, had contracted a violent aversion against the house of Bourbon; and had taught her son, over whom she had acquired an absolute ascendant, to view the duke's conduct with a jealous eye. After repeated affronts he retired from court, and began to listen to the advances of the emperor's ministers. Meantime the duchess of Bourbon died; and, as the constable was no less handsome than accomplished, the duchess of Angoulême, still susceptible of the tender passions, formed the scheme of marrying him. But Bourbon, who might have expected every thing to which an ambitious mind can aspire, from the doting fondness of a woman who governed her son and the kingdom, incapable of imitating Louisa in her sudden transition from hatred to love, or of meanly counterfeiting a passion for one who had so long pursued him with unprovoked malice, treated the proposal with disdain, and even turned it into ridicule. At once refused and insulted by the man whom love only could have made her cease to persecute, Louisa was filled with all the rage of disappointed woman. She resolved to ruin the duke, and for this purpose commenced an iniquitous suit against him; and by the chicanery of chancellor du Prat, he was deprived of his whole family estate. Driven to despair by this treatment, he had recourse to measures which despair only could have dictated. He entered into a secret correspondence with the emperor and the king of England, and he proposed, as soon as Francis should have crossed the Alps, to raise an insurrection among his numerous vassals, and introduce foreign troops into the heart of France[1].

---

[1] Thuan. *Hist.* lib. i. cap. ii.—*Mém. de* Bellay, liv. ii.

Happily, Francis gained some intimation of this conspiracy before he left the kingdom. But not being sufficiently convinced of the constable's guilt, he suffered that dangerous enemy to escape; and Bourbon, entering into the emperor's service, employed the great resources of his enterprising genius, and his military skill, to the prejudice of his sovereign and his native country. He took a severe revenge for all his wrongs.

Francis now relinquished his intention of leading his army into Italy. He did not know how far the infection had spread among his subjects, and was afraid that his absence might encourage them to make some desperate effort in favour of a man so much beloved. He did not, however, abandon his design on the duchy of Milan; but sent, in order to subdue it, an army of thirty thousand men, under the command of admiral Bonnivet. Colonna, who was entrusted with the defence of that duchy, was in no condition to resist such a force; and the city of Milan must have fallen into the hands of the French, had not Bonnivet wasted his time in frivolous enterprises, till the inhabitants recovered from their consternation. The imperial army was reinforced. Colonna died, and Lannoy, viceroy of Naples, succeeded A.D. him in the command. But the military operations were 1524. chiefly conducted by the duke of Bourbon and the marquis de Pescara, the two greatest generals of their age. Bonnivet, destitute of the talents necessary to oppose such able commanders, was reduced, after various movements and encounters, to the necessity of attempting a retreat into France. He was pursued by the imperial generals, and routed at Biagrassa.

Here fell the chevalier Bayard, whose contempt of the arts of courts prevented him from ever rising to the chief command, but who was always called, in times of real danger, to the posts of difficulty and importance. Bonnivet being wounded, the conduct of the rear was committed to Bayard. He put himself at the head of the heavy-armed cavalry, and, animating them by his presence and example to sustain the whole shock of the imperial army, he gained time for the body of his countrymen to make good their retreat. But in that service he received a mortal wound; and being unable to continue on horseback, he ordered one of his attendants to place him under a tree, where he calmly waited the approach of death. In this situation he was found by Bourbon, who led the van of the Imperialists, and expressed much sorrow for his fate. " Pity not me !" cried the high-minded chevalier: " I die, as a man of honour ought—in the discharge of my duty : but pity those who fight against their king, their country, and their oath [1]."

The emperor and his allies were less successful in their operations on the frontier of France. They were baffled on all sides. And Francis, though stripped of his Italian dominions, might still have enjoyed in safety the glory of having defended his native kingdom against one half of Europe, and have bidden defiance to all his enemies, could he have moderated his military ardour. But, understanding that the king of England, discouraged by his former fruitless enterprises, and disgusted with the emperor, was making no preparations for invading Picardy, his rage for the conquest of Milan returned; and he determined, notwithstanding the approach of winter, to march into Italy.

The French army no sooner appeared in Piedmont, than the whole duchy of Milan was thrown into consternation. The capital opened its gates. The forces of the emperor and Sforza retired to Lodi : and had Francis been so fortunate as to pursue them, they must have abandoned that post, and been totally dispersed. But his evil genius led him to besiege Pavia, a town of considerable strength, well garrisoned, and defended by Antonio de Leyva, one of the bravest officers in the Spanish service. Every thing known to the engineers of that age, or which could be effected by the valour of his troops, was attempted in vain by the French monarch against this important place. Confident of success, he had detached a considerable part of his army to invade the kingdom of Naples : and the main body was much wasted by the fatigues of the siege and the rigour of the season. The imperial generals had not hitherto molested him, but they were not idle. Pescara and Lannoy had assembled forces from all quarters : and Bourbon, having pawned his jewels, had gone into Germany, and levied at his own expense a body of A.D. twelve thousand Lansquenets. The united army advanced 1525. to the relief of Pavia, now reduced to extremity for want of ammunition and provisions. Prudence, and the advice of his most experienced officers, dictated to Francis the propriety of a retreat ; but his own romantic notions of honour, and the opinion of Bonnivet, unhappily determined him to keep his post. Having said that he would take Pavia or perish in the attempt, he thought it ignominious to depart from his resolution ; and he anxiously waited the approach of the enemy.

---

[1] *Mem. de Bellay*, ubi sup.—*Œuvr. de Brantome*, tome vi.

The imperial generals found the French so strongly entrenched, that they hesitated long before they ventured to attack them. But the necessities of the besieged, and the murmurs of their own troops, obliged them at last to put every thing to hazard. Feb. 24. Never did armies engage with greater ardour; never were men more strongly animated with personal emulation, national antipathy, mutual resentment, and all the passions which inspire obstinate bravery. The first efforts of the French valour made the firmest battalions of the Imperialists give ground; but the fortune of the day was soon changed. The Swiss troops in the service of France, unmindful of their national honour, shamefully deserted their post. Pescara fell upon the French cavalry with the imperial horse, and broke that formidable body by a mode of attack with which they were wholly unacquainted[1]: while Leyva, sallying out with his garrison during the heat of action, made a furious assault on the enemy's rear, and threw every thing into confusion. The rout became general. But Francis himself, surrounded by gallant nobles, many of whom fell by his side, long sustained the combat. His horse being killed under him, he fought on foot, undistinguished but by his valour, and killed seven men with his own hand. At last he was observed by Pomperant, a French gentleman, who had followed the fortunes of Bourbon, and who now saved the life of his sovereign, ready to sink beneath an enraged soldiery. By his persuasion Francis was prevailed upon to surrender; yet he obstinately refused, imminent as the danger was, to deliver up his sword to Bourbon. Lannoy received it. But the duke had the cruel satisfaction of exulting over his sovereign's distress, and of repaying, from revenge, the insults offered by jealousy[2].

This great victory, and the captivity of Francis, filled Europe with alarm. Almost the whole French army was cut off; Milan was immediately abandoned; and in a few weeks not a Frenchman was left in Italy. The power of the emperor, and still more his ambition, became the object of universal terror; and resolutions were every where taken to set bounds to it. Meanwhile Francis, deeply impressed with a sense of his misfortune, wrote to his mother Louisa, whom he had left regent of the kingdom, the following short but expressive letter: " All is lost, but honour!"

Charles received the news of the signal and unexpected suc-

---

[1] Pescara had intermingled with the imperial horse a considerable number of Spanish foot, armed with the heavy musquets then in use.   Guicciardini, lib. xv.
[2] Brantome.—Guicciardini.

cess which had crowned his arms with the most hypocritical moderation. He would not suffer any public rejoicings to be made on account of it; and said, he only valued it, as it would prove the occasion of restoring peace to Christendom. Louisa, however, did not trust to those appearances. Instead of giving herself up to such lamentations as were natural to a woman remarkable for maternal tenderness, she discovered all the foresight, and exerted all the activity, of a consummate politician. She took every possible measure for putting the kingdom in a posture of defence, while she employed all her address to appease the resentment and to gain the friendship of¹ England ; and a ray of comfort from that quarter soon broke in upon the French affairs.

Though Henry had not entered into the war against France from any concerted political views, he had always retained some imperfect idea of that balance of power necessary to be maintained between Charles and Francis. By his alliance with the emperor he hoped to recover some part of those territories on the continent which had belonged to his ancestors ; and in that hope he willingly contributed to give Charles the ascendency above his rival. But having never dreamed of any event so apparently decisive as the victory of Pavia, he now became sensible of his own danger, as well as of that of Europe in general, from the loss of a proper counterpoise to the power of Charles. Instead of taking advantage of the distressed condition of France, he therefore determined to assist her in her present calamities. Other causes conspired to enforce this resolution.

The elevation of the cardinal of Medicis (Clement VII.) to St. Peter's chair, on the death of Adrian VI., had made the English minister sensible of the insincerity of the emperor's promises, while it extinguished all his hopes of the papacy ; and Wolsey resolved on revenge. His master too had ground of complaint.

Charles had so ill supported the appearance of moderation which he assumed, when first informed of his good fortune, that he had already changed his usual style to Henry ; and instead of writing to him with his own hand, and subscribing himself " your affectionate son and cousin," he dictated his letters to a secretary, and simply subscribed himself " Charles." Influenced by all these considerations, together with the glory of raising a fallen enemy, Henry listened to the flattering submissions of Louisa ; entered into a defensive alliance with her as regent of

¹ *Mem. de Bellay.*—Brantome.—Guicciardini.

France; and engaged to use his best offices in order to procure a deliverance of her son from a state of captivity [1].

Meanwhile Francis was rigorously confined; and hard conditions being proposed to him, as the price of his liberty, he drew his dagger, and pointing it at his breast, cried, " It were better that a king should die thus!" But flattering himself, when he grew cool, that such propositions could not come directly from Charles, he desired that he might be removed into Spain, where the emperor then resided. His request was complied with; but he languished long before he could obtain a sight of his conqueror. At last he was favoured with a visit; and the emperor, dreading the general combination against him, or that Francis, if driven to despair, might, as he threatened, resign his crown to the dauphin, agreed to abate somewhat of
A.D.
1526. his former demands. A treaty was accordingly concluded at Madrid, in consequence of which Francis obtained his liberty.——The chief articles were, that Burgundy should be restored to Charles as the rightful inheritance of his ancestors, and that the king's two eldest sons should be delivered up as hostages for the performance of the stipulated conditions. The exchange of the captive monarch for his children was made on the frontiers of France and Spain. And the moment that Francis entered his own dominions, he mounted a Turkish horse, and putting it to its speed, waved his hand, and cried aloud several times, " I am yet a king [2]!"

The reputation of the French monarch, however, would have stood in a fairer light had he died a captive; for the unhappy situation of his affairs, delicate as his notions of honour appear to have been, led him henceforth to act a part very disadvantageous to his moral character. He never intended to execute the treaty of Madrid : he had even left a protest in the hands of notaries, before he signed it, that his consent should be considered as an involuntary deed, and be deemed null and void [2]. Accordingly, as soon as he arrived in France, he assembled the states of Burgundy, who protested against the article relative to their province; and when the imperial ambassadors urged the immediate execution of the treaty, the king replied, that he would rigorously perform the articles relative to himself, but in those which affected the French monarchy he must be directed by the sense of the nation. He made the highest acknowledgments to the

[1] Herbert.—Mezeray.—Fiddes' *Life of Wolsey.*
[2] Guicciardini, lib. xvi.
[3] *Recueil de Traitez*, tome ii.

king of England for his friendly interposition, and offered to be entirely guided by his counsels.

Charles and his ministers now saw that they were overreached in those very arts of negotiation in which they so much excelled, while the Italian states observed with pleasure that Francis was resolved to evade the execution of a treaty which they considered as dangerous to the liberties of Europe. Clement VII. absolved him from the oath which he had taken at Madrid; and the kings of France and England, the pope, the Swiss, the Venetians, the Florentines, and the Milanese, entered into an alliance, to which they gave the name of the Holy League, because his holiness was at the head of it, in order to oblige the emperor to deliver up the two sons of Francis on the payment of a reasonable ransom, and to re-establish Sforza in the quiet possession of the duchy of Milan [1].

In consequence of this league, the confederate army took the field, and Italy became once more the scene of war. But Francis, who, it was expected would infuse spirit and vigour into the whole body, had gone through such a scene of distress, that he was become diffident of his talents, and distrustful of his fortune. He had flattered himself, that the dread alone of such a confederacy would induce Charles to listen to what was equitable, and therefore neglected to send sufficient reinforcements to his allies in Italy. In the mean time, the duke of Bourbon, who commanded the imperialists, over-ran the whole duchy of Milan, of which the emperor had promised him the investiture; and his troops beginning to mutiny for want of pay, he May 6, boldly led them to Rome, in spite of every obstacle, by 1527. offering to their avidity the rich spoils of that ancient capital. Nor did he deceive them; for although he himself was slain, while encouraging their efforts by his brave example, in planting with his own hands a scaling-ladder against the walls, they, more enraged than discouraged by that misfortune, mounted to the assault with the greatest ardour; and entering the city sword in hand, pillaged it for many days, and made it a scene of horrid carnage and abominable lust.

Never did Rome experience in any age so many calamities, even from the barbarians by whom she was successively subdued —from the followers of Alaric, Genseric, or Odoacer—as now from the subjects of a Christian and Catholic monarch. Whatever was respectable in modesty, or sacred in religion, seemed

---

[1] Goldast. *Polit. Imperial.*

only the more to provoke the rage of the soldiery. Virgins suffered violation in the arms of their mothers, and upon those altars to which they had fled for safety. Venerable prelates, after being exposed to every indignity, and enduring every torture, were thrown into dungeons, and menaced with the most cruel deaths, in order to make them reveal their secret treasures. Clement himself, who had taken refuge in the castle of St. Angelo, was obliged to surrender at discretion; and found that his sacred character could neither procure him liberty nor respect. He was doomed to close confinement, until he should pay an enormous ransom, imposed by the victorious army, and surrender to the emperor all the places of strength belonging to the apostolic see [1].

Charles received the news of this extraordinary event with equal surprise and pleasure; but, to conceal his joy from his Spanish subjects, who were filled with horror at the insult offered to the sovereign pontiff, and to lessen the indignation of the other powers of Europe, he expressed the deepest sorrow for the success of his arms. He put himself and his whole court into mourning; stopped the rejoicings for the birth of his son Philip; and ordered prayers to be offered in all the churches of Spain for the liberation of the pope, which he could immediately have procured by a letter to his generals [2].

The concern expressed by Henry and Francis, for the calamity of their ally, was more sincere. Alarmed at the progress of the imperial arms, they had, even before the assault upon Rome, entered into a closer alliance, and proposed to invade the Low Countries with a powerful army; but no sooner did they hear of Clement's captivity than they changed, by a new treaty, the scene of the projected war, from the Netherlands to Italy, and resolved to take the most vigorous measures for the release of his holiness. Henry, however contributed only money. A French army crossed the Alps, under the command of Lautrec; Clement obtained his freedom; and war was, for a time, carried A.D. on by the confederates with success. But the death of 1528. Lautrec, and the revolt of Andrew Doria, a celebrated Genoese admiral, at that time in the service of France, changed the face of affairs. He obliged the French garrison in Genoa to surrender, and restored the liberties of his country. The French army was ruined before Naples; and Francis, discou-

---

[1] Onuphr. *Vit. Clem. VII.*—*Mem. de Bellay.*—Guicciardini, lib. xviii.
[2] Muroc. *Hist. Venet.* lib. iii.

raged by unsuccessful enterprises, began at length to think of peace.

At the same time, Charles, notwithstanding the advantages he had gained, had many reasons to wish for an accommodation. Solyman, having overrun Hungary, was ready to break in upon the Austrian territories with a formidable army ; and the progress of the Reformation in Germany endangered the tranquillity of that country. In consequence of this situation of affairs, while pride made both parties conceal or dissemble their real sentiments, two ladies were permitted to restore peace to Europe. Margaret of Austria, the aunt of Charles, and Louisa, the mother of Francis, met at Cambray, and settled the terms of A.D. pacification between the French king and the emperor. 1529. Francis agreed to pay two millions of crowns, as the ransom of his two sons : to resign the sovereignty of Flanders and Artois, and forego all his Italian claims : and Charles ceased to demand the restitution of Burgundy [1].

All the steps of this negotiation had been communicated to the king of England ; and Henry was, on that occasion, so generous to Francis, that he sent him an acquittal nearly of six hundred thousand crowns, in order to enable him to fulfil his agreement with Charles. But the Italian confederates of the French king were less satisfied with the treaty of Cambray. They were almost wholly abandoned to the will of the emperor, and seemed to have no other means of security than his equity and moderation. Of these, from his past conduct, they had not formed the most advantageous idea. But Charles's present circumstances, particularly with regard to the Turks, obliged him to behave with a generosity inconsistent with his character. The Florentines alone, whom he reduced under the dominion of the family of Medicis, had reason to complain of his severity. Sforza obtained the investiture of the duchy of Milan and his pardon : and every other power experienced the lenity of the victor.

Charles who, during this full tide of his fortune, having appeased all the discontents in Spain, had appeared in A.D. Italy with the pomp and power of a conqueror, and 1530. received the imperial crown from the hands of the pope, now prepared to revisit Germany, where his presence was highly necessary ; for, although the conduct and valour of his brother Ferdinand, to whom he had transferred the hereditary dominions

---

[1] Sandov. *Hist. del Emp. Carl. V.*—Robertson, book v.

of the house of Austria, and who had been elected king of Hungary, had obliged Solyman to withdraw his forces, his return was to be feared, and the disorders of religion were daily increasing. But these disorders, and the future exploits of the emperor, must form the subject of another letter.

LETTER LXI.

A general View of the Affairs of Europe, and of the Progress of the Reformation on the Continent, from the Peace of Cambray to that of Crespi, in 1544.

THE Reformation, my dear Philip, had made a great progress in Germany, during that interval of tranquillity which the absence of the emperor, the contests between him and the pope, and his attention to the war with France, afforded to its promoters. Most of the princes who had embraced Luther's opinions had not only established in their territories that form of worship which he approved, but had entirely suppressed the rites of the Romish church. Many of the free cities had imitated their conduct. Almost one half of the Germanic body had revolted from the papal see ; and its dominion, even in that part which had not yet shaken off the yoke of Rome, was considerably weakened by the example of the neighbouring states, or by the secret progress of those doctrines which had undermined it among them.

Whatever satisfaction the emperor, while at open enmity with the pope, might have felt in those events which tended to mortify and embarrass his holiness, he was sensible that the religious divisions in Germany would, in the end, prove injurious to the imperial authority. Accordingly the prospect of an accommodation with Clement no sooner offered itself, than A.D. Charles convoked a diet of the empire at Spire, in order 1529. to take into consideration the state of religion. The diet, after much dispute, issued a decree confirming the edict published against Luther at Worms, and prohibiting any farther innovations in religion, but particularly the abolition of the mass, before the meeting of a general council. Against this decree, as unjust and impious, the elector of Saxony, the landgrave of Hesse, the duke of Lunenburg, and the prince of

Anhalt, together with the deputies of fourteen imperial or free cities, entered a solemn protest. On that account they were called PROTESTANTS[1]; an appellation which has since become common to all the sects, of whatever denomination, that have revolted from the church of Rome.

Such was the state of religious affairs when Charles returned to Germany. He assisted in person at the diet of Augsburg; where the Protestants presented their system of opinions, composed by Melancthon, the most learned and moderate A.D. of all the reformers. This system, known by the name 1530. of the *Confession of Augsburg,* from the place where it was presented, was publicly read in the diet. Some popish divines were appointed to examine it; they brought in their animadversions: a dispute ensued between them and Melancthon, seconded by some of his disciples: and, as in most cases of that kind, nothing was determined. Every one continued in his own way of thinking. From the Protestant divines, Charles turned to the princes, their patrons, but with no better success; they refused to abandon what they deemed the cause of God, for any earthly advantage. Coercive measures were resolved upon. A degree was issued, condemning most of the tenets broached by the Protestants, and withholding all toleration from those who taught them.

In consequence of this decree, which they considered as a prelude to the most violent persecution, the Protestant princes assembled at Smalcalde, and concluded a league of mutual defence; and the emperor's ambition, which led him to procure for his brother the dignity of the king of the Romans, in order to continue the imperial crown in his family, furnished A.D. the confederates with a decent pretence for courting 1531. the alliance of foreign princes. The kings of France and England secretly agreed to support them. Meanwhile many circumstances and reflections convinced Charles, that this was not a proper season to attempt the extirpation of heresy by the sword. He saw Solyman ready to enter Hungary with a prodigious force, in order to wipe off the disgrace which his arms had sustained in a former campaign: he felt the necessity of union, not only for the accomplishment of his future schemes, but for ascertaining his present safety. The peace with France was precarious; and he was afraid that the followers of Luther, if treated with severity, might forget that they were Christians,

---

[1] Sleidan.—Seckend

A.D. and join the infidels. Policy induced him to drop the
1532. mask of zeal. By a treaty concluded at Nuremberg,
and solemnly ratified in the diet at Ratisbon, he granted the
Protestants liberty of conscience until the meeting of a general
council : and they agreed, on their part, to assist him powerfully
against the Turks [1].

This treaty was no sooner signed than Charles received information that Solyman had entered Hungary at the head of two
hundred and fifty thousand men. The imperial army, consisting of eighty thousand disciplined foot, and above twenty
thousand horse, besides a multitude of irregulars, immediately
assembled in the neighbourhood of Vienna. Of this vast body
the emperor, for the first time, took the personal command ; and
Europe waited, in anxious suspense, the issue of a decisive battle
between the two greatest potentates in the universe. But, each
dreading the other's power and good fortune, both conducted
their operations with so much caution, that a campaign, from
which the most important consequences had been expected, was
closed without any memorable event. Solyman, finding it impossible to take advantage of an enemy always on his guard,
marched back to Constantinople ; and Charles, freed from so
dangerous an invader, set out for Spain [2].

During the emperor's absence, great disorders prevailed in
Germany, occasioned by the fanaticism of a sect of reformers
distinguished by the name of Anabaptists, because they contended, that the sacrament of baptism should be administered
only to adults, and performed not by sprinkling them with
water, but by dipping them in it. This tenet was at least harmless : but they held others of a more enthusiastic, as well as
dangerous nature. They maintained, that, among Christians,
who have the precepts of the Gospel to direct, and the Spirit of
God to guide them, the office of magistrate is unnecessary, and
an encroachment on spiritual liberty ; that all distinctions of
birth or rank ought to be abolished ; that a community of goods
should be established, and that every man may lawfully marry
as many wives as he thinks proper.

Tenets so flattering to human weakness and human pride,
produced a number of converts, especially among the lower
classes. The peasants greedily embraced opinions which promised to place them on a level with their imperious masters.

---

[1] Du Mont. *Corps Diplomatique*, tome iv.
[2] Sandov. *Hist. del Emp. Carl. V.* vol. ii.—Robertson, book v.

They assembled in great bodies, and spread devastation where-ever they came.   But being destitute of a skilful leader, they were soon dispersed ; and Muncer, the first Anabaptist prophet, perished on a scaffold at Mulhausen in 1526.   Several of his followers, however, lurked in different places, and secretly pro-pagated the opinions of their sect.   At last two Anabaptist prophets, John Matthias, a baker of Haerlem, and John Bocold, a journeyman tailor of Leyden, possessed with the rage A.D. of making proselytes, fixed their residence at Munster, 1533. an imperial city in Westphalia; and, privately assembling their associates from the neighbouring country, made themselves masters of the town, and expelled the inhabitants.

Here the Anabaptists formed a singular kind of republic, over which Matthias assumed absolute authority, and A.D. wrote to his brethren in the Low Countries, inviting 1534. them to assemble at Mount Sion (so he termed Munster), that they might thence set out in a body to reduce all nations under their dominion. Meanwhile the bishop of Munster, having assembled a considerable army, advanced to besiege the town. On his approach, Matthias sallied out, at the head of a chosen band, forced his camp, and returned to the city loaded with glory and spoil.   But his success proved fatal to him.   Thinking nothing now impossible for the favourites of Heaven, he went out to meet the enemy accompanied by no more than thirty of his followers ; boasting that, like Gideon, he would smite the host of the ungodly with a handful of men.   The prophet and his thirty associates were slain.

The Anabaptists, however, did not despair : John of Leyden, their other light, still remained.   This man, less bold, but more ambitious than Matthias, assumed the title of king : and being young, and of a complexion equally amorous and enthusiastic, he exercised, in their utmost latitude, those principles of his sect which favoured sensual gratification.   He took, in a short time, fourteen wives.   His example was followed by his bre-thren ; no man remained satisfied with a single wife.   The houses were searched ; and young women were instantly seized, and compelled to marry.   Notwithstanding this sensuality, Munster made a gallant defence ; but the bishop's army being reinforced, and the besieged greatly distressed for want of pro-visions, one of their own body deserted, and betrayed A.D. them.   The city was taken by surprise : most of the 1535. Anabaptists were slain : and their king was put to death by the most exquisite and lingering tortures, which he bore with aston-

2

ishing fortitude[1].—So wonderful are the effects of enthusiasm in communicating courage, even to minds naturally the most timid and feeble! and so difficult is it, in such cases, to distinguish between the martyr and the visionary!

During these transactions in Germany, Charles undertook an expedition against the pirates of Africa. Barbarossa, a bold adventurer, had succeeded his brother in the sovereignty of Algiers, which he formerly assisted him to usurp. He regulated with prudence the interior police of his kingdom, and carried on his piracies with great vigour; but perceiving that the natives submitted to his government with impatience, and fearing that his continual depredations might draw upon him a general combination of the Christian powers, he put his dominions under the protection of the Turkish emperor. Solyman, flattered by such an act of submission, and charmed with the spirit of the man, offered him the command of the Ottoman fleet. Proud of this distinction, Barbarossa repaired to Constantinople, and made use of his influence with the soltan to extend his own dominions. Partly by force, partly by treachery, he usurped the kingdom of Tunis; and being now possessed of greater power, he carried on his depredations against the Christian states with more destructive violence than ever.

Daily complaints of the piracies and ravages committed by the galleys of Barbarossa were brought to the emperor by his subjects, both in Spain and Italy; and all Christendom seemed to look up to Charles, as its greatest and most fortunate prince, for relief from this odious and degrading species of oppression. At the same time Muley-Hassan, the exiled king of Tunis, finding none of the African princes able or willing to support him in recovering his throne, applied to the victorious Charles for assistance against the usurper. Equally desirous of delivering his dominions from the dangerous neighbourhood of Barbarossa, of appearing as the protector of an unfortunate prince, and of acquiring the glory annexed in that age to every expedition against the Mohammedans, the emperor readily concluded a treaty with Muley, and set sail for Tunis with a formidable armament.

The Golletta, a strong fortress on an island in the bay of Tunis, and the key of the capital, planted with three hundred pieces of cannon, was taken by storm, together with all Barbarossa's fleet.

---

[1] Ant. Lamb. Hortens. *Tumult. Anabaptist.*—Jo. Bapt. Otii. *Annal. Anabaptist.* —Mosheim, *Hist. Eccles.* vol. v.

He was defeated in a pitched battle; and ten thousand Christian slaves having knocked off their fetters, and made themselves masters of the citadel, Tunis offered to surrender at discretion.

But while Charles was deliberating on the means of preserving the lives of the inhabitants, his troops, fearing that they might be deprived of the booty which they had expected, broke suddenly into the town, and pillaged and massacred without distinction. Thirty thousand persons perished by the sword, and ten thousand were made prisoners. The sceptre, drenched in blood, was restored to Muley-Hassan, on condition that he should acknowledge himself a vassal of the crown of Spain, put into the emperor's hands all the fortified sea-ports in the kingdom of Tunis, and pay annually twelve thousand crowns for the subsistence of a Spanish garrison in the Goletta. These points being settled, and twenty thousand Christian slaves freed from bondage, either by arms or by treaty, Charles returned to Europe; but Barbarossa, who had retired to Bona, soon recruited his strength, and again became the tyrant of the ocean[1].

The king of France took advantage of the emperor's absence, to revive his claims in Italy. The treaty of Cambray had covered up, but not extinguished, the flames of discord. Francis in particular, who waited only for an opportunity of recovering the territories and reputation which he had lost, continued to negociate against his rival with different courts. But all his negociations were disconcerted by unforeseen accidents. The death of Clement VII. (whom he had fixed in his interest by marrying his son the duke of Orléans, afterwards Henry II., to Catharine of Medicis, the niece of that pontiff,) deprived him of all the support which he hoped to receive from the court of Rome. The king of England, occupied with domestic cares and projects, declined engaging in the affairs of the continent; and the princes of the league of Smalcalde, to whom Francis had applied, being filled with indignation and resentment at the cruelty with which some of their reformed brethren had been treated in France, refused to have any connexion with the enemy of their religion.

The particulars of this persecution it will be proper to relate, as they serve to illustrate the manners of the times. Francis was neither cruel nor bigoted. His levity and love of pleasure allowed him little leisure to concern himself about religious disputes; but his principles becoming suspected, at a time when the emperor was gaining immortal glory by his expedition against

---

[1] Sandov. vol. ii.—Robertson's *Hist. Charles V.* book v.

the infidels, he resolved to vindicate himself by an extraordinary demonstration of reverence for the established faith. The indiscreet zeal of some Protestant converts furnished him with the occasion. They had fixed to the gates of the Louvre, and other public places, papers containing indecent reflections on the rites of the Romish church. Six of the persons concerned in this rash action were seized; and the king, pretending to be struck with horror at their blasphemies, appointed a solemn procession, in order to avert the wrath of Heaven. The host was carried through the city of Paris in great pomp; Francis walked uncovered before it, bearing a torch in his hand; the princes of the blood supported the canopy over it; the nobles walked behind. In presence of this numerous assembly, the king declared, that if one of his hands should be infected with heresy, he would cut it off with the other; "and I would sacrifice," added he, "even my own children, if found guilty of that crime." As an awful proof of his sincerity, the six unhappy persons who had been seized were publicly burned before the procession was finished, and in the most cruel manner. They were fixed upon a machine which descended into the flames and retired alternately, until they expired [1].—Can we wonder that the Protestant princes were incensed at such barbarity?

But Francis, though unsupported by any ally, commanded his army to advance toward the frontier of Italy, under pretence of chastising the duke of Milan for a breach of the law of nations, in putting to death his ambassador. The operations of war, however, soon took a new direction. Instead of marching directly to the duchy of Milan, Francis commenced hostilities against the duke of Savoy, with whom he had cause to be dissatisfied, and on whom he had some claims; and before the end of the campaign, that feeble prince saw himself stripped of all his dominions except the province of Piedmont. To complete his misfortunes, the city of Geneva, the sovereignty of which he claimed, and where the reformed religion was already established, threw off his yoke; and its revolt was attended with the loss of the adjacent territory. Geneva was then an imperial city, and now became the capital of an independent republic.

In this extremity the duke of Savoy saw no resource but in the emperor's protection; and as his misfortunes were chiefly occasioned by his attachment to the imperial interest, he had a claim to immediate assistance. But Charles, who had recently

---

[1] Belcarii *Comment. Rer. Gallic.*—Sleid. *Hist. Reformat.*

returned from his African expedition, was not able to lend him the necessary support. His treasury was entirely drained, and he was obliged to disband his army, until he could raise new supplies. So wasting is the continued practice, even of successful war, to the most opulent princes and states !

Meantime the death of the duke of Milan changed the nature of the war, and afforded the emperor full leisure to prepare for action. The French monarch's pretext for taking up arms was at once cut off; but as the duke had died without issue, all the rights of Francis to the duchy of Milan, which he had yielded only to Sforza and his descendants, returned to him in full force. He accordingly renewed his claim to it; and if he had ordered his army immediately to advance, he might have made himself master of it. But he unfortunately wasted his time in fruitless negotiations, while his more politic rival took possession of the long-disputed territory, as a vacant fief of the empire. And although Charles seemed still to admit the equity of the claim of Francis, he delayed granting the investiture under various pretences, and was secretly taking every possible measure to prevent the success of that prince in Italy.

During the time gained in this manner, Charles had recruited his finances, and of course his armies; and finding himself in a condition for war, he at last threw off the mask, under which he had so long concealed his designs from the court of France. A.D. Entering Rome with great pomp he pronounced, before 1536. the pope and cardinals assembled in full consistory, a violent invective against Francis, by way of reply to his propositions concerning the investiture of Milan. Yet the French king, by an unaccountable fatality, continued to negotiate, as if it had still been possible to terminate their differences in an amicable manner; and Charles finding him so eager to run into the snare, favoured the deception, and, by seeming to listen to his proposals, gained yet more time for the execution of his own ambitious projects [1].

If misfortune had rendered Francis too diffident, success had made Charles too confident. He even presumed on the subversion of the French monarchy, and seemed to consider it as an infallible event. Having chased the forces of his rival out of Piedmont and Savoy, he pushed forward at the head of fifty thousand men, against the advice of his most experienced

[1] *Mem. de* Bellay.

ministers and generals to invade the southern provinces of France, while two other armies were ordered to enter that kingdom, one on the side of Picardy, the other on the side of Champagne. He thought it impossible for Francis to resist so many attacks ; but he was too sanguine in his expectations.

The French monarch fixed upon the most effectual plan for defeating the invasion ; and he prudently persevered in following it, though it was contrary to his natural temper and to the genius of his people. He determined to remain altogether upon the defensive, and to deprive his enemies of subsistence, by laying waste the country before them. The execution of this plan was committed to the marechal de Montmorency, its author, a man happily fitted for such service, by the inflexible severity of his disposition. He made choice of a strong camp, near the walls of Avignon, where he assembled a considerable army, while the king, with another body, encamped at Valence. Marseilles and Arles were the only towns he thought it necessary to defend ; and each of these he furnished with a numerous garrison of his best troops. The inhabitants of the other towns were compelled to abandon their habitations ; the fortifications of such places as might have afforded shelter to the enemy were thrown down ; corn, forage, and provisions of every kind, were carried off or destroyed ; the mills and ovens were ruined, and the wells filled or rendered useless.

This devastation extended from the Alps to Marseilles, and from the sea to the confines of Dauphiné ; so that the emperor, when he arrived with the van of his army on the borders of Provence, instead of that rich and populous country which he expected to enter, beheld nothing but one vast solitude. He did not, however, despair of success ; and, as an encouragement to his officers to continue the invasion, he held out the prospect of lands and honours in France. But all the land which any of them obtained was a grave ; and their master lost much honour by this rash enterprise. After unsuccessfully investing Marseilles and Arles ; after attempting in vain to draw Montmorency from his camp, and not daring to attack it, Charles, having spent two inglorious months in Provence, and lost one half of his troops by famine or disease, was under the necessity of ordering a retreat :—and although he was some time in motion before the enemy suspected his intention, his retreat was conducted with such precipitation and disorder as to deserve the name of a flight, the light troops of France having turned his march into a rout. The invasion of Picardy was not more effectual; the imperial forces were obliged to retire without achieving any con quest of importance [1].

Francis now gave himself up to that vain resentment which had formerly disgraced the prosperity of his rival. They had frequently, in the course of their quarrels, given each other the lie, and mutual challenges had been sent, which, though productive of no' serious consequences between the parties, had a powerful tendency to encourage the pernicious practice of duelling. Charles, in his invective pronounced at Rome, had publicly accused Francis of perfidy and breach of faith : Francis now exceeded Charles in the indecency of his accusations. The dauphin dying suddenly, his death was imputed to poison; Montecuculi, his cup-bearer, was put to the rack; and that unhappy nobleman, in the agonies of torture, accused the emperor's generals, Gonzaga and De Leyva, of instigating him to the detestable act. The emperor himself was suspected; this extorted confession, and some obscure hints, were even considered by many as proofs of his guilt; though it was evident that neither Charles nor his generals could have any inducement to perpetrate such a crime, as Francis was still in the vigour of life himself, and had two sons besides the dauphin [2]. A.D. 1537.

But the incensed monarch's resentment did not stop here. He was not satisfied with endeavouring to blacken the character of his rival by an ambiguous testimony, which led to the most injurious suspicions, and upon which the most cruel constructions have been put: he was willing to add rebellion to murder. For this purpose he went to the parliament of Paris; where, when he was treated with the usual solemnities, the advocate-general appeared, and accused Charles of Austria (so he affected to call the emperor) of having violated the treaty of Cambray, by which he was freed from the homage due to the crown of France for the counties of Artois and Flanders; adding, that this treaty being now void, he was still to be considered as a vassal of France, and consequently had been guilty of rebellion, in taking arms against his sovereign. The charge was sustained by the court, and Charles was summoned to appear before the parliament. On his non-appearance at the appointed time, the court gave judgment that he had forfeited those counties by rebellion and contumacy [3].

---

[1] Sandov. *Hist. del Emp. Carl. V.*—Robertson, book vi. [2] Sandoval.
[3] *Mem. de* Ribier.

Francis, after this vain display of his animosity, marched into the Low Countries, as if he had intended to seize the forfeited provinces. But a suspension of arms soon took place, through the interposition of the queens of France and Hungary; and it A.D was followed by a regular truce, concluded at Nice, 1538. through the mediation of the reigning pontiff, Paul III., of the family of Farnesè, a man of venerable character and pacific disposition.

Each of these rival princes had strong reasons for being desirous of peace. The finances of both were exhausted; and the emperor, the more powerful of the two, was deeply impressed with the dread of the Turkish arms, which Francis had drawn upon him by a league with Solyman. In consequence of this league, Barbarossa, with a great fleet, appeared on the coast of Naples; filled that kingdom with consternation; obliged Castro, a place of some strength, to surrender; plundered the adjacent country, and was taking measures for securing and extending his conquest, when the sudden arrival of Doria with a respectable fleet induced him to retire. The soltan's forces also invaded Hungary, where, after gaining several inferior advantages, they defeated the Germans in a great battle at Essek, on the Drave.

Happily for Charles and for Europe, it was not in the power of Francis, at this juncture, either to join the Turks, or to assemble an army strong enough to penetrate into the duchy of Milan. The emperor, however, was sensible that he could not long resist the efforts of two such potent confederates, nor expect that the same fortunate circumstances would concur a second time in his favour. He, therefore, thought it necessary, both for his safety and reputation, to give his consent to a truce: and Francis chose rather to incur the risk of disobliging his Ottoman ally, than draw on himself the indignation, and perhaps the arms of all Christendom, by obstinately obstructing the re-establishment of tranquillity, and contributing to the aggrandizement of the Infidels [1].

These considerations inclined the contending monarchs to listen to the arguments of the pope: but his holiness found it impossible to bring about a final accommodation between them, each inflexibly persisting in the assertion of his own claims. Nor could he prevail on them to see one another, though both came to the place of rendezvous, so great were the remains of distrust and rancour, or such the difficulty of adjusting the cere-

---

[1] Jovii *Hist.* lib. xxxv.

monial! Yet, improbable as it may seem, a few days after signing the truce, the emperor in his passage to Barcelona being driven on the coast of Provence, Francis invited him to come on shore; frankly visited him in his galley, and was received and entertained with exterior marks of esteem and affection. Charles, with an equal degree of confidence, paid the king a visit at Aiguesmortes; where these two hostile rivals, and vindictive enemies, who had accused each other of every kind of baseness, seemed to vie in expressions of respect and friendship [1]!—Such sudden transitions from enmity to affection, and from suspicion to confidence, can only be accounted for from that spirit of chivalry, with which the manners of both princes were strongly tinctured.

Besides the glory of having restored tranquillity to Europe, Paul III. secured a point of much consequence to his family: he obtained in marriage, for his grandson, the emperor's natural daughter, formerly wife to Alexander de Medicis, whom Charles had raised to the supreme power in Florence. Lorenzo de Medicis, the kinsman and intimate companion of Alexander, had assassinated him by one of the blackest treasons recorded in history. Under pretence of having secured him an assignation with a lady of great beauty, and of the highest rank, he drew him into a secret apartment of his palace, and there stabbed him, as he lay carelessly on a couch, expecting the presence of the lovely fair, whom he had often solicited in vain. Lorenzo, however, did not reap the fruits of his crimes; for, although some of his countrymen extolled him as a third Brutus, and endeavoured to seize this occasion for recovering their liberties, the government of Florence passed into the hands of Cosmo II. another kinsman of Alexander [2]. Cosmo was desirous of marrying the widow of his predecessor; but the emperor chose rather to oblige the pope, by bestowing his daughter upon Octavio Farnesè, son of the duke of Parma, and grandson of his holiness.

Charles had soon farther cause to be sensible of his obligations to Paul for negotiating the truce of Nice. His troops mutinied for want of pay; and the ability of his generals only could have prevented a total revolt. He had depended upon the subsidies which he expected from his Castilian subjects for discharging the arrears of his army. He accordingly assembled the Cortès of Castile at Toledo; and having represented to them the great expense of his military operations, he proposed to levy such supplies as the present state of his

A.D. 1539.

---

[1] Sand. *Hist. del Emp. Carl. V.*　　　　[2] *Lett. di Princip.*

affairs demanded, by a general excise on commodities.   But the Spaniards, who already felt themselves oppressed with a load of taxes unknown to their ancestors, and who had often complained that their country was drained of its wealth and its inhabitants, in order to prosecute quarrels in which they had no interest, determined not to add voluntarily to their own burthens.   The nobles, in particular, inveighed with great vehemence against the measure proposed, as it would encroach on the most valuable and distinguished privilege of their order, that of being exempted from the payment of any tax.   After employing arguments and promises in vain, Charles dismissed the assembly with indignation; and from that period neither the nobles nor the prelates have been called to the cortès, on pretence that such as pay no part of the public taxes should not claim a vote in imposing them. These assemblies have since consisted merely of the procurators or representatives of eighteen cities, two from each ; in all thirty-six members, who are absolutely at the devotion of the crown[1].

The citizens of Ghent, still more bold, broke out into open rebellion against the emperor's government, on account of a tax which they judged contrary to their ancient privileges, and a decision of the council of Mechlin in favour of the imperial authority.   Enraged at an unjust imposition, and rendered desperate on seeing their rights betrayed by that very court which was bound to protect them, they flew to arms, seized several of the emperor's officers, and expelled such of the nobility as resided among them.   Sensible, however, of their inability to support what their zeal had prompted them to undertake, and desirous of securing a protector against the formidable force by which they might expect soon to be attacked, they offered to acknowledge the king of France as their sovereign ; to put him into immediate possession of their city, and to assist him in recovering those provinces in the Netherlands which had anciently belonged to his crown.   True policy directed Francis to comply with this proposal.   The counties of Flanders and Artois were more valuable than the duchy of Milan, for which he had so long contended ; and their situation in regard to France made it more easy to conquer or to defend them.   But we are apt to estimate the value of things by the trouble which they have cost us.   Francis, computing in this manner, overrated the territory of Milan.   He had lived in friendship with the emperor ever since their interview at Aigues-mortes, and Charles had pro-

---

[1] *La Science de Gouv.* par. M. de St. Real.—Robertson's *Hist. Charles V.* book vi.

mised him the investiture of that duchy.   Forgetting, therefore, all his past injuries, and the deceitful promises by which he had been so often duped, the credulous, generous, but unprincipled Francis, not only rejected the proposition of the citizens of Ghent, but communicated to the emperor his whole negotiation with the malecontents [1].

Judging of Charles's heart by his own, Francis hoped, by this seemingly disinterested proceeding, to obtain at once the investiture of Milan : and the emperor, well acquainted with the weakness of his rival, flattered him in this hope, for his own selfish purposes.   His presence being necessary in the Netherlands, he demanded a passage through France.   It was immediately granted him ; and Charles, to whom every moment was precious, set out, notwithstanding the remonstrances of his council, and the fears of his Spanish subjects, with a small but splendid train of a hundred persons.   He was met on the frontiers of France by the dauphin and the duke of Orléans, who offered to go into Spain, and remain there as hostages, till he should reach his own dominions ; but Charles replied, that the king's honour was sufficient for his safety, and prosecuted his journey without any other security.   The king entertained him with the utmost magnificence at Paris, and the two young princes did not take leave of him till he entered the Low Countries ; yet he still found means to evade his promise, and Francis continued to believe his professions sincere [2].

The inhabitants of Ghent, alarmed at the approach of the emperor, who was joined in the Netherlands by three armies, sent ambassadors to implore his mercy, and offered to throw open their gates.   Charles only condescended to reply, that he would appear among them, as a " sovereign and a judge with the sceptre and the sword."   He accordingly entered the place of his nativity on the anniversary of his birth ; and instead of that lenity which might have been expected, exhibited an awful example of his severity.   Twenty-six of the principal citizens were put to death ; a greater number were banished ; the city was declared to have forfeited its privileges ; a new system of political administration was prescribed ; and a large fine was imposed on the inhabitants, in order to defray the expense of erecting a citadel, together with an annual tax for the support of a garrison.   They were not only despoiled of

A.D. 1540.

---

[1] Sandoval.—*Mem. de* Bellay.   [2] *Mem. de* Ribier.—Thuan. lib. i.

their ancient immunities, but obliged to pay, like conquered people, for the means of perpetuating their own slavery [1].

Having thus re-established his authority in the Low Countries, and being now under no necessity of continuing that scene of falsehood and dissimulation with which he had amused the French monarch, Charles began gradually to throw aside the veil under which he had concealed his intentions with respect to the duchy of Milan, and at last peremptorily refused to give up a territory of such value, or voluntarily to make such a liberal addition to the strength of an enemy, by diminishing his own power. He even denied, that he had ever made any promise which could bind him to an action so unnecessary, and so contrary to his own interest [2].

This transaction exposed the king of France to as much scorn as it did the emperor to censure. The blind credulity of Francis, after he had experienced so often the duplicity and artifices of his rival, seemed to merit no other return. He remonstrated, however, and exclaimed, as if this had been the first instance in which the emperor had deceived him. The insult offered to his understanding affected him even more sensibly than the injury done to his interest; and he discovered such resentment as made it obvious that he would seize the first opportunity of revenge, and that a new war would soon desolate the European continent.

Charles, in the mean time, was obliged to turn his attention towards the affairs of Germany. The Protestants, having in vain demanded a general council, pressed him earnestly to appoint a conference between a select number of divines of each party, in order to examine the points in dispute. For this purpose a diet was assembled at Ratisbon; and such a conference, notwithstanding the opposition of the pope, was maintained A.D. with great solemnity in the presence of the emperor. 1541. But the divines chosen to manage the controversy, though men of learning and moderation, were only able to settle a few speculative opinions, all points relative to worship and jurisdiction serving only to inflame the minds of the disputants. Finding his conciliatory endeavours ineffectual, Charles prevailed on a majority of the members to approve the following edict of recess: That the articles concerning which the divines had agreed should be treated as points decided; that those about which they had differed should be referred to the deter-

---

[1] Harœi *Annal. Brabantiœ.* [2] *Mem. de* Bellay.

mination of a general council, or, if that could not be obtained, to a national synod; and should it prove impracticable to assemble a synod of Germany, that a general diet of the empire should be called within eighteen months, in order to give final judgment on the whole controversy; and that, in the mean time, no innovations should be made, nor any means employed to gain proselytes [1].

This edict gave great offence to the pope. The bare mention of allowing a diet, composed chiefly of laymen, to pass judgment in regard to articles of faith, appeared to him no less criminal and profane than the worst of those heresies which the emperor seemed so zealous to suppress. The Protestants also were dissatisfied with it, as it considerably abridged the liberty which they at that time enjoyed. They murmured loudly against it; and Charles, unwilling to leave any seeds of discontent in the empire, granted them a private declaration, exempting them from whatever they thought injurious or oppressive in the edict of recess, and ascertaining to them the full possession of all their former privileges.

The situation of the emperor's affairs at this juncture made these extraordinary concessions necessary. He foresaw a rupture with France, and was alarmed at the rapid progress of the Turks in Hungary. A great revolution had happened in that kingdom. John Zapol Scæpius, by the assistance of Solyman, had wrested from the king of the Romans a considerable part of the country. John died, and left an infant son. Ferdinand attempted to take advantage of the minority, in order to repossess himself of the whole kingdom: but his ambition was disappointed by the activity and address of George Martinuzzi, bishop of Waradin, who shared the regency with the queen. Sensible that he was unable to oppose the king of the Romans in the field, Martinuzzi satisfied himself with holding out the fortified towns: and he sent ambassadors to Solyman, beseeching him to extend toward the son that protection by which he had so generously maintained the father on the throne. Ferdinand used his utmost endeavours to thwart this negotiation, and even meanly offered to hold the Hungarian crown on the same ignominious conditions by which John had obtained it, that of paying tribute to the Porte. But the soltan saw such advantages in espousing the interest of the young king, that he instantly marched into Hungary; and the Germans, having formed the siege of Buda, were defeated with great slaughter before that city. Solyman,

---

[1] Sekend. lib. iii.—Du Mont. *Corps Diplom.* tome iv.

however, instead of becoming the protector of the infant sovereign whom he had relieved, made use of this success to extend
his own dominions : he sent the young prince into Transylvania,
and added the greater part of Hungary to the Ottoman empire[1].

Charles had received intelligence of this revolution before
the close of the diet at Ratisbon ; and, in consequence of his
concessions to the Protestants, he obtained liberal supplies,
both of men and money. He now hastened to join his fleet
and army in Italy, with a view of executing a great and favourite
enterprise which he had concerted against Algiers ; though it
would certainly have been more consistent with his dignity to
have conducted the forces of the empire against Solyman, the
common enemy of Christendom, who was preparing to enter the
Austrian dominions.

Algiers, from the time that Barbarossa commanded the Turkish
fleet, had been governed by Hassan, a renegado eunuch, who,
if possible, outdid his master in boldness and cruelty. The commerce of the Mediterranean was greatly interrupted by his galleys :
and such frequent alarms were given to the coasts of Spain,
that there was a necessity for erecting watch-towers at certain
distances, and keeping a guard constantly employed, in order to
descry the approach of his squadrons, and to protect the inhabitants from the depredations of the rapacious ruffians by
whom they were manned.

Charles was extremely eager to humble this daring corsair,
and to exterminate the lawless crew who had so long infested
the ocean ; and although the autumn was now far advanced, he
obstinately persisted in his purpose, notwithstanding the remonstrances of Andrew Doria, who conjured him not to expose
his armament to the hazard of destruction, by venturing, at so
late a season, to approach the stormy coast of Algiers.   Doria's
words proved prophetical.

No sooner had the emperor landed in Barbary, than a hur-
ricane dispersed and shattered his fleet ; while he and his land
forces were exposed to all the fury of the elements, in an
enemy's country, without a hut or a tent to shelter them, or
even a spot of firm ground on which they could rest their
wearied bodies. In this calamitous situation they continued
for several days, harassed at the same time by the attacks of the
Algerines.   At last, Doria being able to assemble the remains
of the fleet, Charles was glad to re-embark, after having lost the

---

[1] Istuanhaffi, *Hist. Reg. Hung.* lib. xiv.

greater part of his army, by the inclemency of the weather, famine, or the sword of the enemy.   And the men who yet survived were doomed to encounter new miseries in their return, the fleet being scattered by a fresh storm[1].

Such, my dear Philip, was the result of the emperor's pompous expedition against Algiers, the most unfortunate enterprise of his reign, and that on which he built the highest hopes.   But if he failed to acquire the glory which ever attends success, he secured that which is more essentially connected with merit. He never appeared greater than amidst his misfortunes.   His firmness and constancy of spirit, his magnanimity, fortitude, humanity, and compassion, were eminently conspicuous.   He endured as severe hardships as the meanest soldier ; he exposed his own person to whatever danger appeared ; he encouraged the desponding, visited the sick and wounded, and animated all by his words and example[2].   He paid dearly for his obstinacy and presumption : but he made mankind sensible, that he possessed some valuable qualities, which an almost uninterrupted flow of prosperity had hitherto afforded him little opportunity of showing.

The loss which the emperor suffered in this calamitous enterprise encouraged the king of France to begin hostilities, an action dishonourable to civil society having furnished him with a pretence for taking arms.   The marquis del Guasto, governor of the duchy of Milan, had gained intelligence of the motions and destination of two ambassadors whom Francis had dispatched to the Porte and to the Venetian state ; and knowing how much his master wished to discover the intentions of the French monarch, and of what consequence it was to retard the execution of his measures, he employed some soldiers to lie in wait for these envoys as they sailed down the Po.   The ambassadors and most of their attendants were murdered, and their papers seized[3].

Francis immediately demanded reparation for that barbarous violence ; and as Charles endeavoured to amuse him with an evasive answer, he appealed to all the courts of Europe, setting forth the heinousness of the injury, the iniquity of the emperor in disregarding his just request, and the necessity of vengeance. But Charles, who was a more profound negotiator, defeated in a great measure the effects of these spirited representations.   He secured the fidelity of the Protestant princes in Germany, by

[1] Nic. Villag. *Expedit. Car. V. Argyriam.*—Sandov. vol. ii.—Robertson, book vi.
[2] Id. ibid.
[3] *Mem. de* Bellay.

gratifying them with new concessions; and engaged the king of England to espouse his cause, under pretence of defending Europe against the Infidels; while Francis was only able to form an alliance with the kings of Denmark and Sweden, and to renew his treaty with Solyman, which drew on him the indignation of Christendom.

But the activity of Francis supplied all the defects in his negotiation. Five armies were soon ready to take the field, under different generals, and with different destinations. Nor was Charles slow or negligent in his preparations. He and Henry, a second time, made an ideal division of the kingdom of France. But as the hostilities that ensued were followed by no important consequence, nor distinguished by any memorable event, except the battle of Cerisoles, gained by the count d'Enghien over the imperialists, of whom nearly ten thousand fell, I shall not enter into particulars. It will be sufficient to observe, that, after France, Spain, Piedmont, and the Low Countries, had been alternately, or at once, the scenes of war; after the Turkish fleet, under Barbarossa, had ravaged the coasts of Italy, and the lilies of France and the crescent of Mohammed had appeared in conjunction before Nice, where the cross of Savoy was displayed, Francis and Charles concluded at Crespi a treaty of peace, in which the king of England was not mentioned; and, from being implacable enemies, became once more, in appearance, cordial friends, and even allies by the ties of blood[1].

The chief articles of this treaty were, that all the conquests which either party had made since the truce of Nice should be restored; that the emperor should give in marriage to the duke of Orléans, either his eldest daughter, with the Low Countries, or the second daughter of his brother Ferdinand, with the investiture of the duchy of Milan; that Francis should renounce all pretensions to the kingdom of Naples, as well as to the sovereignty of Flanders and Artois, and Charles resign his claim to the duchy of Burgundy; and that both should unite in making war against the Turks[2].

The emperor was chiefly induced to grant conditions so advantageous to France, by a desire of humbling the Protestant princes in Germany. With the papal jurisdiction, he foresaw they would endeavour to throw off the imperial authority; and he had determined to make his zeal for the former a pretence for

A.D. 1542.

A.D. 1544.

---

[1] *Mem. de Bellay.*   [2] *Recueil des Traitez*, tome i.

enforcing and extending the latter. But before I speak of the wars in which that resolution involved him, I must carry forward the domestic history of England, the knowledge of which will throw light on many foreign transactions.

Meanwhile I shall observe, for the sake of perspicuity, that the death of the duke of Orléans, before the consumma- A.D. tion of his marriage, released the emperor from the most 1545. unpleasing stipulation in the treaty of Crespi; and that the French monarch, being still engaged in hostilities with England, was unable to obtain any reparation for the loss which he suffered by this unforeseen event. These hostilities, like those between Charles and Francis, terminated in nothing decisive. Equally weary of a struggle, attended with no glory or ad- vantage to either, the contending parties concluded at A.D. Campe, near Ardres, a treaty of peace in which it was 1546. stipulated that Francis should pay the arrears due by former treaties to England. But these arrears did not amount to more than one-third of the sum expended by Henry on his military operations; and Francis, being in no condition to discharge them, Boulogne (a chargeable pledge) was left in the hands of the Eng- lish monarch as a security for the debt[1]. Such was the result of a war which had considerably diminished the wealth and im- paired the strength of both kingdoms.

LETTER LXII.

The domestic History of England during the Reign of Henry VIII., with some Account of the Affairs of Scotland, and of the Rise of the Reformation in both Kingdoms.

No prince ever ascended the throne of England with greater advantages than Henry VIII. You have already had A.D. occasion, my dear Philip, to observe his fortunate situation 1509. with respect to the great powers of the continent: he was no less happy in regard to the internal state of his kingdom, and other domestic circumstances. His title to the crown was un-

---

[1] Herbert.—Stow.

disputed ; his treasury was full ; his subjects were in tranquillity ; and the vigour and comeliness of his person, his freedom of manners, his love of show, and his dexterity in every manly exercise, rendered his accession highly popular, while his proficiency in literature and his reputation for talents, made his character respectable.   Every thing seemed to prognosticate a happy and prosperous reign.

The first act of Henry's administration confirmed the public hopes : it was the prosecution of Empsom and Dudley, the unfeeling ministers whom his father had employed in his extortions. They insisted, and perhaps justly, that they had acted solely by royal authority : but the jury gave a verdict against them ; and Henry, at the earnest desire of the people, granted a warrant for their execution[1].

Having punished the instruments of past oppression, the king's next concern was to fulfil his former engagements.   He had been long betrothed to his brother's widow ; and notwithstanding some scruples, he now agreed that the nuptials should be celebrated.   We shall afterwards have occasion to observe the extraordinary effects of this marriage, and of the king's remorse, either real or pretended.

Some princes have been their own ministers ; but almost every one has either had a minister or a favourite : Wolsey, whose character has already been delineated, was both to Henry. Being admitted to the youthful monarch's pleasures, he took the lead in every jovial conversation, and promoted, notwithstanding his religious habit, all that frolic and gaiety, which he found to be agreeable to the age and inclinations of the king. During the intervals of amusement, he introduced politics, and insinuated those maxims of conduct which he was desirous his master should pursue[2].   By these means he insensibly acquired that absolute ascendant over Henry, which distinguished his administration : and the people saw with concern very frequent instances of his uncontrolled authority.

The duke of Buckingham, high constable of England, the first nobleman in the kingdom both in family and fortune, having wantonly given disgust to Wolsey, soon found reason to repent his imprudence.   He was descended by a female from the duke of Gloucester, son of Edward III., and being infatuated with judicial astrology, he consulted a Carthusian friar, named Hopkins, who flattered him with the hope of ascending the English

---

[1] Hollinshed's *Chron.*   [2] *Life of Wolsey, by* Cavendish.

throne.　He had even been so unguarded as to utter some expressions against the king's life.　The cardinal made these the grounds of an impeachment; and although the duke's threats seem to have proceeded more from indiscretion than de- A.D. liberate malice, he was brought to trial, condemned, and 1521. executed[1].　The office of high constable, which this nobleman inherited from the Bohuns, earls of Hereford, being forfeited by his attainder, was never afterwards revived in England.

The next memorable event in the domestic history of this reign, was the divorce of queen Catharine.　The king's scruples in regard to the lawfulness of his marriage increased with the decay of the queen's beauty.　She had borne him several children; but they were all dead except the princess Mary; and Henry was passionately desirous of male issue.　He consulted his confessor, the bishop of Lincoln, on the legality of marrying a brother's widow, and found that prelate possessed with some doubts and difficulties.　He next proceeded to examine the question by his own learning and study, being himself a great divine and casuist; and having had recourse to the works of his oracle, Thomas Aquinas, he discovered that this celebrated doctor had expressly declared against the lawfulness of such marriages.　The archbishop of Canterbury was now applied to, and desired to consult his brethren.　All the prelates of England, except Fisher, bishop of Rochester, declared, under their hands and seals, that they deemed the king's marriage unlawful[2]. Wolsey also fortified his master's scruples; and the bright eyes of Anne Boleyn, maid of honour to the queen, carried home every argument to the heart of Henry, more forcibly than even the suggestions of that powerful favourite.

This young lady was a daughter of sir Thomas Boleyn, who had been employed by Henry in several embassies.　She had been carried over to Paris in early youth, by the king's sister, when espoused to Louis XII. of France; and the graces of her mind, no less than the beauty of her person, had distinguished her even in that polished court.　The time at which she returned to England is not certainly known; but it appears to have been after the king had entertained doubts of the lawfulness of his marriage.　She immediately caught the roving and amorous eye of Henry; and as her virtue and modesty left him no hope of licentious indulgence, he resolved to raise her to the throne,

---

[1] Herbert.　　　　[2] Burnet's *Hist. Reformat.* book i.

which her accomplishments, both natural and acquired, seemed equally fitted to adorn.

But some obstacles were yet in the way of Henry's wishes. It was necessary to obtain a divorce from the pope, as well as a revocation of the bull which had been granted for his marriage with Catharine, before he could marry Anne : and he had to combat all the interest of the emperor, whose aunt he was going to degrade. He did not, however, despair of success. He was in high favour with the court of Rome, and he deserved to be so. He had not only opposed the progress of the Lutheran tenets, by all the influence which his extensive and almost absolute authority conferred upon him ; but he had even written a book against them ; a performance in itself not contemptible, and which gave so much pleasure to Leo X., that he conferred upon Henry the title of *Defender of the Faith*. Sensible therefore of his importance, as one of the chief pillars of the church, at a time when it stood in much need of support, he confidently applied to Clement VII. for a dissolution of his marriage with Catharine.

The pope seemed at first favourable to Henry's inclinations ; but his dread of displeasing the emperor, whose prisoner he had lately been, prevented him from coming to any fixed determination. He at last, however, empowered Campeggio and Wolsey, A.D. his two legates in England, to try the validity of the 1529. king's marriage. They accordingly opened their court at London, and proceeded to the examination of the affair. The first point which came before them, and that which Henry chiefly endeavoured to establish, was Arthur's consummation of his marriage with Catharine ; and although the queen protested that her virgin honour was yet untainted, when the king married her, and even appealed to his Grace (the title then borne by our kings) for the truth of her asseveration, stronger proofs than were produced could not be expected of such a fact, after so long an interval. But when the business seemed drawing to a close, and while Henry was in anxious expectation of a sentence in his favour, all his hopes were suddenly blasted. Campeggio, on the most frivolous pretences, prorogued the court : and Clement, at the request of the emperor, evoked the cause soon after to Rome [1].

This finesse occasioned the fall of Wolsey. Anne Boleyn

---

[1] Herbert.—Burnet.

imputed to him the failure of her expectations ; and Henry, who entertained the highest opinion of the cardinal's capacity, ascribed his miscarriage in the present undertaking not to misfortune or mistake, but to the malignity or infidelity of that minister. The great seal was taken from him, and given to Sir Thomas More, a man of learning, virtue, and capacity. He was indicted in the Star-Chamber ; his lands and goods were declared to be forfeited ; his houses and furniture were seized ; and he was pronounced to be out of the protection of the laws [1]. The king's heart, however, relented, and the prosecution was carried no farther ; but the cardinal was ordered to remove from court, and his final ruin was hanging over him.

The parliament seized the present opportunity to pass several bills, restraining the impositions of the clergy ; and Henry was not displeased, that the pope and his whole militia should be made sensible of their dependence upon him, and of the willingness of his subjects, if he was so disposed, to reduce the power and privileges of ecclesiastics. Amidst the anxieties with which he was agitated, he was often tempted to break off all connexion with Rome : and Anne Boleyn used every insinuation to induce him to take that bold step, both as the readiest and surest means of her exaltation to the royal dignity, and of spreading the new doctrines, in which she had been initiated under the duchess of Alençon, a warm friend to the Reformation. But Henry, having been educated in a superstitious veneration for the holy see, dreaded the reproach of heresy ; and he abhorred all alliance with the Lutherans, the chief opponents of the papal power, because Luther, their apostle, had handled him roughly, in an answer to his book in defence of the Romish communion.

While Henry was fluctuating between contrary opinions, two of his courtiers accidentally met with Dr. Thomas Cranmer, fellow of Jesus College, in Cambridge, a man distinguished by his learning, but still more by his candour ; and as the affair of the divorce became the subject of conversation, he observed, that the best way, either to quiet the king's conscience or obtain the pope's consent, would be to consult all the universities in Europe with regard to that controverted point. When A.D. 1530. Henry was informed of this proposal, he was delighted with it, and swore with great vehemence, " By God ! Cranmer has got

---

[1] Strype.—Cavendish.—The richness of Wolsey's furniture was such as must astonish even the present age. The principal apartments of his palace were lined with cloth of gold, or cloth of silver ; he had a side-board of plate of massy gold ; and every other article for domestic use or ornament was proportionably sumptuous.

the right sow by the ear." The doctor was immediately sent for, and taken into favour; the universities were consulted according to his advice; and all of them declared the king's marriage invalid [1].

Clement, however, being still under the influence of the emperor, continued inflexible; and as Henry was sensible that the extremities to which he was proceeding, both against the pope and the ecclesiastical order, must be disagreeable to Wolsey, whose opposition he dreaded, he renewed the prosecution against his ancient favourite.

The cardinal, after his disgrace, had remained for some time at Richmond; but being ordered to remove to his see of York, he took up his residence at Cawood, in Yorkshire, where he rendered himself extremely popular in the neighbourhood, by his affability and hospitality. In this retreat he lived, when the earl of Northumberland received orders to arrest him for high treason, and conduct him to London, as a prelude to his trial. On his journey he was seized with a disorder, which turned into a dysentery; and it was with much difficulty that he was able to reach Leicester-abbey. "I am come to lay my bones among you," said Wolsey to the abbot and monks, who came out to receive him; and he immediately retired to bed, whence he never rose more. "O had I but served my God," cried he, a little before he expired, "as diligently as I have served my king, he would not have deserted me in my grey hairs [2]." His treason, indeed, seems rather to have been against the people than the prince, or even the state; for, although the violence and obstinacy of Henry's character may serve as apologies for many of the cardinal's public measures, his iniquitous extortions, in what he called his legatine court, admit of no alleviation.

Thus freed from a person whom he considered as an obstacle to his views, and supported by the opinion of the learned in the step which he intended to take, Henry ordered a parliament and convocation to meet, in which he was acknowledged "the Protector and supreme Head of the Church and Clergy of England." And having now satisfied his mind on the subject, without dreading the consequences, he privately celebrated his marriage with Anne Boleyn, whom he had created marchioness of Pembroke.

A.D. 1531.

A.D. 1532.

Cranmer, who had been promoted to the see of Canterbury, annulled, soon after, the king's marriage with Catharine (a step

---

[1] Herbert.—Burnet.　　　　[2] Cavendish.

which ought to have preceded his second nuptials), and ratified that with Anne, who was publicly crowned queen, with all the pomp and dignity suited to such a ceremony. And to complete the satisfaction of Henry on the conclusion of this troublesome business, the queen was safely delivered of a daughter, who received the name of Elizabeth, and whom we shall afterwards see swaying the English sceptre with equal glory to herself and happiness to her people. A.D. 1533.

When intelligence was conveyed to Rome of these transactions, the pope was urged by the cardinals of the imperial faction to dart his spiritual thunders against Henry. But Clement was still unwilling to proceed to extremities; he only declared Cranmer's sentence null, and threatened the king with excommunication, if he would not restore things to their former condition, before a day named. In the mean time Henry was prevailed upon, by the mediation of the king of France, to submit his cause to the Roman consistory, provided the cardinals of the imperial faction were excluded from it. The pope consented; and promised, that if the king would sign an agreement to this purpose, his demands should be fully complied with. But on what slight incidents often depend the greatest events! The courier appointed to carry the king's written promise was detained beyond the day fixed; news arrived at Rome, that a libel had been published in London against the holy see, and a farce acted before the king in derision of the apostolic body [1]. The pope and cardinals entered into the consistory inflamed with rage; the marriage between Henry and Catharine was pronounced valid; the king was declared excommunicated, if he refused to adhere to it, and the rupture with England was rendered final.

The English parliament, soon after this decision of the court of Rome, conferred on the king the title of " The *only* *supreme* HEAD of the Church of England *upon earth*," as they had already invested him with all the real power belonging to it; a measure of the utmost consequence to the kingdom, whether considered in a civil or ecclesiastical view, and which forms a memorable æra in our constitution. The legislature, by thus acknowledging the king's supremacy in ecclesiastical affairs, and uniting the spiritual with the civil power, introduced greater simplicity into government, and prevented all future disputes about the limits of contending jurisdictions. A door was also A.D. 1534.

[1] Paolo Sarpi, lib. i.

opened for checking the exorbitancies of superstition, and breaking those shackles by which human reason, policy, and industry, had so long been circumscribed; for, as an able historian has justly observed, the prince being head of the religious, as well as of the temporal jurisdiction of the kingdom, though he might sometimes be tempted to employ the former as an engine of government, could have no interest, like the Roman pontiff, in encouraging its usurpations [1].

But England, though thus happily released from the oppressive jurisdiction of the pope, was far from enjoying religious freedom.   Liberty of conscience was, if possible, more confined than ever.   Henry not only retained his aversion against Luther and his doctrines; but so many of his early prejudices hung about him, that the idea of heresy still filled him with horror. Separate as he stood from the Catholic church, he continued to value himself on maintaining its dogmas, and on guarding with fire and sword the imaginary purity of his speculative opinions. All who denied the king's supremacy, or the legitimacy of his daughter Elizabeth, or who embraced the tenets of the reformers, were equally the objects of his vengeance.   Among the latter were many unhappy persons, who had greedily imbibed the Lutheran doctrines, during Henry's quarrel with Rome, in hopes of a total change of worship; and who, having gone too far to recede, fell martyrs to their new faith.   Among the former were the bishop of Rochester, and Sir Thomas A.D. More, who died upon the scaffold with heroic con-
1535. stancy.   More retained to the last moment his facetious humour.   When he laid his head on the block, and saw the executioner ready with his weapon, " Stay, friend," said he, " till I put aside my beard; for," added he, " it never committed treason [2]."   What pity, and what an instance of the inconsistency of human nature, that the man who could make a jest of death should make a matter of conscience of the pope's supremacy!

Although Henry thus punished both Protestants and Catholics, his most dangerous enemies, he was sensible, were the zealous adherents to the ancient religion, and more especially the monks, who, having their immediate dependence on the Roman pontiff, apprehended that their own ruin would be the consequence of the abolition of his authority in England.   The king therefore determined to suppress the monasteries, as so many nurseries of rebellion, as well as of idleness, superstition, and folly, and

---

[1] Hume's *Hist. Eng.* chap. xxx.   [2] Herbert.

to put himself in possession of their ample revenues.   In order to effectuate this robbery with some colour of justice, he appointed commissioners to visit all religious houses; and these men, acquainted with the king's design, brought reports, whether true or false, of such frightful disorders, lewdness, ignorance, priest-craft, and unnatural lusts, as filled the nation with horror against institutions which had long been objects of profound veneration.   The smaller monasteries, said to have been the most corrupted, to the number of three hundred and seventy-six, were at once suppressed by parliament; and their A.D. revenues, goods, chattels, and plate, were granted to the 1536. king [1].

The convocation, at this time, passed a vote for a new translation of the Bible, none being yet published, by authority, in the English language; and the Reformation seemed to gain ground rapidly in the kingdom, though the king still declared himself its enemy; when its promoters, Cranmer, Latimer, and others, met with a severe mortification, which seemed to blast all their hopes, in the untimely fate of their patroness, Anne Boleyn.

This lady now began to experience the decay of the king's affections, and the capriciousness of his temper.   That heart, whose allegiance she had withdrawn from another, revolted at last against herself.   Henry's passion, which had subsisted in full force during the prosecution of the divorce, and seemed only to increase under difficulties, had scarcely attained possession of its object, when it sunk into languor, succeeded by disgust.   His love was suddenly transferred to a new mistress.   The charms of Jane Seymour, a young lady of exquisite beauty, had entirely captivated him; and as he appears to have had little idea of any other connexion than that of marriage, he thought of nothing but how to raise her to his bed and throne.

This peculiarity in Henry's disposition, proceeding from an indolence of temper, or an aversion against the vice of gallantry, involved him in crimes of a blacker dye, and in greater anxieties, than those which he sought to avoid by forming a legal connexion.   Before he could marry Jane, it was necessary to remove his once beloved Anne, now a bar in the way of his felicity.   The heart is not more ingenious in suggesting apologies for its deviations, than courtiers in finding expedients to

---

[1] Burnet.—Stow.

gratify the inclinations of their prince. The queen's popish enemies, sensible of the alienation of the king's affections from her, accomplished her ruin by flattering his new passion. They represented that freedom of manner which Anne had acquired in France as a dissolute levity; they directly accused her of a criminal correspondence with several gentlemen of the bedchamber, and even with her own brother! and they extolled the virtues of Jane Seymour. Henry believed all, because he wished to be convinced. The queen was committed to the Tower; impeached; brought to trial; condemned without evidence, and executed without remorse. History affords us no reason to call her innocence in question; and the king, by marrying her known rival the day after her execution, made the motives of his conduct sufficiently evident, and left the world in little doubt about the iniquity of the sentence [1].

If farther argument, my dear Philip, should be thought necessary in support of the innocence of the unfortunate Anne Boleyn, her serenity, and even cheerfulness, while under confinement and sentence of death, ought to have its weight, as it is perhaps unexampled in a woman, and could not well be the associate of guilt. " Never prince," says she, in a letter to Henry, " had wife more loyal in all duty, and in all true affection, than you have ever found Anne Boleyn; with which name and place I could willingly have contented myself, if God, and your grace's pleasure, had been so pleased; neither did I at any time so far forget myself in my exaltation, or received queenship, but that I always looked for such an alteration as I now find; for the ground of my preferment being on no surer foundation than your grace's fancy, the least alteration I knew was fit and sufficient to draw that fancy to some other object." In another letter to the king she says, " You have raised me from a private gentlewoman to a marchioness; from a marchioness to a queen: and since you can exalt me no higher in this world, you are resolved to send me to heaven, that I may become a saint." This gaiety continued to the last. On the morning of her catastrophe, while she was calmly conversing with the lieutenant of the Tower on what she was going to suffer, he endeavoured to comfort her by the shortness of its duration. " The executioner, indeed," replied she, " I am told, is very expert, and I have but a slender neck;" grasping it with her hand, and

---

[1] Burnet.

smiling [1]. The queen's brother, and three gentlemen of the bed-chamber, also fell victims to the king's suspicions, or rather were sacrificed to hallow his nuptials with Jane Seymour.

The Catholics, who had been the chief instruments of these tragical events, did not reap so much advantage from the fall of Anne as they expected. The friends of the Reformation still maintained their credit with the king; and articles of faith were drawn up by the convocation under Henry's eye, more favourable to the new than the old religion, but still more conformable to the ideas of the royal theologist than agreeable to the partisans of either. Prudence, however, taught the Protestants to be silent, and to rest satisfied with the ground which they had gained. The disappointed Catholics were less quiet. The late innovations, particularly the dissolution of the smaller monasteries, and the imminent danger to which all the rest were exposed, had bred discontents among the people. The Romish religion, suited to vulgar capacity, took hold of the multitude by powerful motives: they were interested for the souls of their forefathers, which they believed must now lie during many ages in the torments of purgatory, for want of masses to relieve them. The expelled monks, wandering about the country, encouraged these prejudices, to rouse the populace to rebellion; and they assembled in large bodies, in different parts of the kingdom, particularly in Lincolnshire and the northern counties. But by the prudent conduct of the duke of Norfolk, who commanded the king's forces, and who secretly favoured the cause of the rebels, though he disapproved their rebellious measures, tranquillity was restored to the kingdom with little effusion of blood [2].

The suppression of these insurrections was followed by an event which completed Henry's domestic felicity, the birth of a son, who was baptized under the name of Edward. But this happiness was not without allay; the queen died two days after. A son, however, had been so long and so ardently desired by Henry, and was now become so necessary, in order to prevent disputes with regard to the succession, the two princesses being declared illegitimate, that the king's sorrow was drowned in his joy. And his authority being thus confirmed at home, and his consideration increased abroad, he carried into execution a measure on which he had been long resolved, the utter destruction of the monasteries.

A.D.
1537.

[1] Strype.- Burnet.   [2] Burnet.

The better to reconcile the minds of the people to this great A.D. innovation, the impostures of the monks were zealously 1538. brought to light. Among the sacred repositories of convents were found the parings of St. Edmund's toes; some coals that roasted St. Laurence; the girdle of the blessed Virgin, shown in eleven different places; two or three heads of St. Ursula; and part of the shirt of St. Thomas à Becket, much reverenced by pregnant women. Some impostures of a more artificial nature also were discovered, particularly a miraculous crucifix, which had been kept at Boxley in Kent, and bore the appellation of the *Rood of Grace*, the eyes, lips, and head of which moved on the approach of its votaries. The crucifix was publicly broken at St. Paul's Cross, and the springs and wheels by which it had been secretly moved were shown to the people. The shrine of Becket was likewise destroyed, much to the regret of the populace. So superstitious was the veneration for this saint, that it appeared in one year, not a penny had been offered at God's altar; at the Virgin's only four pounds one shilling and eight-pence; but at that of St. Thomas, nine hundred and fifty-four pounds six shillings and three pence [1].

The exposure of such enormous absurdities and impieties took off much of the odium from a measure in itself rapacious, violent, and unjust. The acquiescence of the nobility and gentry was farther procured by grants of the revenues of convents, or leases of them at a reduced rent: and the minds of the people were quieted by being told, that the king would have no future occasion to levy taxes, but would be able, during war as well as peace, to defray from the abbey lands the whole expense of government [2]. Henry also settled pensions on the ejected monks, and erected six new bishoprics, which silenced the murmurs of such of the secular clergy as were not altogether wedded to the Romish communion.

After renouncing the pope's supremacy, and suppressing monasteries, the spirit of opposition, it was thought, would lead the king to declare war against the whole doctrine and worship, as well as discipline, of the church of Rome. But although Henry, since he came to years of maturity, had been gradually changing the tenets of that theological system in which he had been educated, he was no less dogmatical in the few which yet remained to him, than if the whole fabric had been preserved entire; and so great was his scholastic arrogance, that he thought himself entitled to

[1] Burnet.—Stow.   [2] Coke's *Inst*. fol. 44.

regulate, by his own particular standard, the religious faith of
the nation.   The chancellor was therefore ordered to   A.D.
state to the parliament, that it was his majesty's earnest   1539.
desire to extirpate from his kingdom all diversity of opinion in
matters of religion.   A bill, consisting of six articles, called by
the Protestants the *Bloody Bill*, was drawn up according to the
king's ideas: and having passed through both houses, received
the royal assent.   This statute tended to establish the doctrine
of the real presence, or transubstantiation ; the communion in one
kind, or with bread only ; the perpetual obligation of vows of
chastity ; the utility of private masses ; the celibacy of the clergy,
and the necessity of auricular confession.   The violation of any
of these articles was made punishable with death ; and a denial
of the real presence, to the disgrace of common sense, could not
be atoned for by the most humble recantation [1]—an instance of
severity unknown even to the inquisition !

The affairs of religion being thus settled, the king began to think
of a new wife ; and as the duke of Cleves had great interest
with the princes of the Smalcaldic league, whose alliance was
considered as advantageous to England, Henry solicited the
hand of Anne, daughter of that duke.   A flattering picture of
this princess, drawn by Hans Holbein, co-operated with these
political motives to determine the king in his choice, and Anne
was sent over to England.   But Henry, though fond of large
women, no sooner saw her, than (so devoid was she of beauty
and grace) he swore she was a great Flanders mare, and declared
he never could bear her any affection.   He resolved, however,
to consummate his marriage, notwithstanding his dislike, sensible
that a contrary conduct would be highly resented by her friends
and family.   He therefore told Cromwell, his minister since
the death of Wolsey, and who had been instrumental in   A.D.
forming the match, that, "as matters had gone so far, he   1540.
must put his neck into the yoke."

But although political considerations had induced Henry to
consummate, at least in appearance, his marriage with Anne of
Cleves, they could not save him from disgust.   His aversion increased every day ; and Cromwell, though still seemingly in
favour, saw his own ruin, and the queen's disgrace, hastily approaching.   An unforeseen cause accelerated both.   The king
had fixed his affections on Catharine Howard, niece to the duke

---

[1] *Stat.* 31 *Hen. VIII.* cap. xiv.

2

of Norfolk ; and, as usual, he determined to gratify his passion, by making her his royal consort. The duke who had long been at enmity with Cromwell, made use of his niece's insinuations against that minister, who was a promoter of the Reformation, as he formerly had used those of Anne Boleyn against Wolsey. Cromwell was accused of heresy and treason, committed to the Tower, condemned, and executed [1].—He was a man of low birth, but worthy, by his integrity and abilities, of the high station to which he was raised ; worthy of a better master and a better fate.

The measures for divorcing Henry from Anne of Cleves were carried forward at the same time with the bill of attainder against Cromwell. Henry pleaded, that when he espoused Anne, he had not *inwardly* given his consent ; and that, notwithstanding the near approach he had made, he had not thought proper to *consummate* the marriage. The convocation sustained these reasons, and solemnly annulled the engagements between the king and queen. The parliament, ever obsequious to Henry's will, ratified the decision of the church [2].

The marriage of the king with Catharine Howard, which quickly followed his divorce from Anne of Cleves, was regarded as a favourable incident by the Catholic party ; and the subsequent events corresponded with their expectations. The king's councils being now directed by the duke of Norfolk and bishop Gardiner, a furious persecution arose against the Protestants. The *Law of the Six Articles*, which Cromwell had, on all occasions, taken care to soften, was executed with rigour : and Dr. Barnes, and several other clergymen, were prosecuted, and brought to the stake.

But Henry's attention was soon turned to prosecutions of a A.D. different kind, and to a subject which affected him still 1541. more sensibly than even the violation of his favourite theological statute. He had thought himself extremely happy in his new consort. The elegant person and agreeable manners of Catharine had captivated his heart ; and he had publicly, in his chapel, returned thanks to Heaven for the felicity which the conjugal state afforded him. This happiness, however, was of short duration. It disappeared like a gaudy meteor, almost as soon as it was perceived ; and its loss keenly afflicted the king. The queen had led a dissolute life before marriage ; the proofs of her licentiousness were positive; and there was reason to believe, notwithstanding her declaration to the contrary, that she had not been faithful to the king.

When the proofs of her incontinence were communicated to him, he was so deeply affected, that he remained for some moments speechless, and at last burst into tears. The natural ferocity of his temper, however, soon returned; and he A.D. assembled a parliament, the usual instrument of his 1542. tyranny, in order to satiate his vengeance. A bill of attainder was voted against the queen and the viscountess of Rochford, who had conducted her criminal amours. A singular bill was also passed at the same time, making it treason in any person to conceal the incontinence of a queen of England; and farther enacting, that if a king of England should marry any woman who had been incontinent, taking her for a true maid, she likewise should be deemed guilty of treason, in case she did not previously reveal her shame to him.—And the queen and lady Rochford were beheaded on Tower-hill, though their guilt had preceded the framing of that statute [1].

Henry now reverted to the concerns of religion, altering the national creed according to his own capricious humour. And he afterwards turned his arms against James V. of Scotland, because that prince had refused to imitate his conduct, in throwing off the jurisdiction of the pope.

The principles of the Reformation had already found their way into Scotland. Several persons there had fallen martyrs to the new faith; and the nobility, invited by the example of England, had cast a wishful eye on the ecclesiastical revenues; hoping, if a change in religion should take place, to enrich themselves with the plunder of the church. But the king, though very poor, not superstitious, and somewhat inclined to magnificence, fortified by the arguments of the clergy, and guided by the inclinations of his queen, a daughter of the duke of Guise, resisted every temptation to such robbery, and continued faithful to the see of Rome. This respect for the rights of the church proved fatal to James, and brought many miseries on his kingdom, both before and after his death.

Had the king of Scotland flattered the pride of Henry by following his example in ecclesiastical affairs, he would have been supported in his measures with the whole force of England; whereas he now had that force to oppose, and a dissatisfied people to rule. Flushed, however, with an advantage gained over a detachment from the English army by lord Hume, he marched at the head of thirty thousand men to meet the main body, commanded by the duke of Norfolk, who had advanced as far as Kelso; and as that nobleman retreated on the approach of the Scottish army, the king resolved to enter England, and take vengeance on the invaders. But his nobility, dissatisfied on account of the preference shown to the clergy, opposed his resolution, and refused to attend him. Equally enraged and surprised at this mutiny, he reproached them with cowardice, he threatened punishment, and still hoping to make some impression on the enemy's country with the forces that adhered to him, he dispatched ten thousand men to ravage the western border. They entered England near Solway Frith, while he himself followed, at a small distance, ready to join them upon occasion.

But this expedition also proved unsuccessful, and even highly unfortunate; and from a cause allied to that which had ruined the former enterprise. The king, rendered peevish by disappointment, and distrustful of his nobles, deprived lord Maxwell of the command of the army, and conferred it on Oliver Sinclair, a private gentleman. The Scots, displeased with this alteration, were preparing to disband, when a small body of English appearing, they suddenly retreated, and were all either killed or made prisoners [1].

Nov. 24.

This disaster had such an effect on the haughty mind of James, that he would admit of no counsel or consolation, but abandoned himself wholly to despair. All the passions that are inimical to human life, shame, rage, and despondency, took hold of him at once. His body wasted daily by sympathising with his anxious mind; and he was brought to the verge of the grave, when his queen was safely delivered of the celebrated and unfortunate Mary Stuart. Having no former issue living, he anxiously inquired whether his consort had brought him a son or a daughter; and being informed that it was a female, he said, " The crown came with a woman, and it will go with a woman! Many woes await this unhappy kingdom : Henry will make it his own, either by force of arms or by marriage." He soon after expired.

Dec. 14.

Henry was no sooner informed of the victory at Solway, and the death of his nephew, than he formed the project of uniting

[1] Buchan. lib. xiv.

Scotland to his own dominions, by marrying prince Edward to the heiress of that kingdom. For this purpose he called together such of the Scottish nobility as were his prisoners, and offered them their liberty without ransom, provided they would second his views. They readily agreed to a proposal so favourable to themselves, and which seemed so natural and so advantageous to both kingdoms; and by their means, notwithstanding the opposition of cardinal Beaton, archbishop of St. Andrews, who had placed himself at the head of the regency, by forging a will in the name of the late king, the parliament of Scotland consented to a treaty of marriage and union with England [1]. The stipulations in that treaty it would be of little consequence to enumerate, as they were never executed. A.D. 1543.

Henry now finding himself at peace with all his neighbours, began to look out for another wife; and by espousing Catharine Parr, relict of lord Latimer, he confirmed what had been foretold in jest, that he would be obliged to marry a widow, as no reputed maid would ever be persuaded to incur the penalty of his statute respecting virginity. Catharine was a woman of virtue and good sense; and, though inclined to promote the Reformation, a circumstance which gave great joy to the Protestant party, she delivered her sentiments with much caution in regard to the new doctrines. Henry, however, whose favourite topic of conversation was theology, by engaging her frequently in religious disputes, found means to discover her real principles; and his unwieldy corpulence and ill health having soured his temper, and increased the severity of his naturally passionate and tyrannical disposition, he ordered an impeachment to be drawn up against her: and nothing but the greatest prudence and address could have saved her from the block.

Having gained some information of the king's displeasure, Catharine replied, when he again offered to converse with her on theological subjects, that such profound speculations were little suited to the natural imbecility of her sex; observing, at the same time, that though she declined not to discourse on any topic, however sublime, when proposed by his majesty, she well knew that her conceptions could serve no other purpose than to afford him a momentary amusement; that she found conversation apt to languish when not revived by some opposition, and had ventured, at times, to feign a contrariety of sentiment, in order to afford him the pleasure of refuting her. And A.D. 1546.

[1] Buchan. lib. xv.—Sir Ralph Sadler's *Letters.*

she ingeniously added, that she also proposed by this innocent artifice to engage the king in arguments, whence she had observed, by frequent experience, that she reaped much profit and instruction. " And is it so, sweetheart?" said Henry; " then we are friends again !" embracing her tenderly, and assuring her of his affection. The chancellor, ignorant of this reconciliation, came the next day to arrest Catharine, but was dismissed by Henry with the opprobrious appellations of *knave, fool,* and *beast* [1]. So violent and capricious was the temper of that prince !

But although the queen was so fortunate as to appease Henry's resentment against herself, she could not save those whom she most respected. Catharine and Cranmer excepted, the king punished with unfeeling rigour all who presumed to differ from him in religious opinions, particularly in the capital tenet, transubstantiation. Among the unhappy victims committed to the flames for denying that absurd doctrine, was Ann Ascue, a young woman of extraordinary beauty and merit, connected with the principal ladies at court, and even with the queen. She died with great tranquillity and fortitude, refusing to earn a pardon by recantation, though it was offered to her at the stake [2].

Nor did Henry's tyrannical and persecuting spirit confine its vengeance to religious offenders : it was no less severe against such as excited his political jealousy. Amongst these were the duke of Norfolk and his gallant son the earl of Surrey. The duke had rendered considerable services to the crown ; and although understood to be the head of the Catholic party, he had always conformed to the religion of the court. He had acquired an immense fortune in consequence of the favours bestowed upon him by Henry, and was confessedly the first subject in England. That eminence drew upon him the king's jealousy. As Henry found his death approaching, he was afraid that Norfolk might disturb the government during his son's minority, or alter his religious system.

The earl of Surrey was a young nobleman of the most promising hopes, distinguished by every accomplishment which could adorn a scholar, a courtier, or a soldier of that age. But he did not always regulate his conduct by the caution and reserve which his situation required ; and as he had declined all proposals of marriage among the nobility, Henry imagined that he entertained hopes of espousing his eldest daughter, the

[1] Burnet. vol. i.—Herbert.   [2] Burnet.

princess Mary. The suspicion of such a dangerous ambition was enough. Both he and his father, the duke of Norfolk, were committed to the Tower; tried for high treason, and condemned to suffer death, without any evidence of guilt being produced against either of them : unless that the earl had quartered the arms of Edward the Confessor on his escutcheon, which was considered as a proof of his aspiring to the crown, although the practice and privilege of so doing had been openly avowed by himself, and maintained by his ancestors. The earl was beheaded; and an order was issued for the execution of the duke; but he was saved by the death of the tyrant [1]. A.D. 1547.

Henry's health had long been declining, and his approaching dissolution had been foreseen by all around him for some days ; but as it had been declared treason to foretell the king's death, no one durst inform him of his condition, lest he should, in the first transports of his fury, order the author of such intelligence to immediate punishment. Sir Anthony Denny, however, at last ventured to make known to him the awful truth. He intimated his resignation, and desired that Cranmer might be sent for. The archbishop came, though not before the king was speechless; but as he still seemed to retain his senses, Cranmer desired him to give some sign of his dying in the faith of Christ. He squeezed the primate's hand, and immediately expired [2], in the fifty-sixth year of his age, and thirty-eighth of his reign ; affording, in his end, a striking example, that composure in the hour of death is not the inseparable characteristic of a life well spent, nor vengeance in this world the universal fate of blood-thirsty tyrants. Happily, we know that there is a state beyond the grave, where all accounts will be settled, and a tribunal before which every one must answer for the deeds done in the flesh ; otherwise, we should be apt to conclude, from seeing the same things happen to the just and to the unjust, to the cruel and the merciful, that there was no eye in heaven that regarded the actions of man, nor any arm to punish. Jan. 28.

But the history of this reign, my dear Philip, yields other lessons than those of a speculative morality ; lessons which come home to the breast of every Englishman, and which he ought to remember every moment of his existence. It teaches us the most alarming of all political truths : " That absolute despotism may prevail in a state, and yet the form of a free constitution remain." It even leads us to a conjecture still more inter-

---

[1] Burnet, vol. i.　　　　　[2] Burnet.

esting to Britons, " That, in this country, an ambitious prince may most successfully exercise his tyrannies under the shelter of those barriers which the constitution has placed as the security of national freedom—of our lives, our liberty, and our property."

Henry changed the national religion, and, in a great measure, the spirit of the laws of England. He perpetrated the most enormous violences against the first men in the kingdom; he loaded the people with oppressive taxes, and pillaged them by loans which it was known he never meant to repay; but he never attempted to abolish the parliament, or even to retrench any of its doubtful privileges. The parliament was the prime minister of his tyrannical administration: it authorised his oppressive taxes, and absolved him from the payment of his debts: it gave its sanction to his most despotic and sanguinary measures: to measures, which, of himself, he durst not have carried into execution; or which, if supposed to be merely the result of his own arbitrary will, would have so far roused the spirit of the nation to assert the rights of humanity and the privileges of a free people, that some arm would have been found bold enough to rid the world of such a scourge, by carrying vengeance to his heart.

The conclusion which I mean to draw from these facts and reasonings (and it deserves our most serious attention) is this— that the British constitution—though so happily poised, that no one part of it seems to preponderate; though so admirably constructed that every one of the three estates is a check upon each of the other two, and both houses of parliament upon the crown; though the most rational and perfect system of freedom that human wisdom has framed—is no positive security against the despotism of an artful or tyrannical prince; and that, if Britons should ever become slaves, such an event is not likely to happen, as in France, by the abolition of our national assembly, but by the corruption of its members; by making that proud bulwark of our liberty, as in ancient Rome, the means of our slavery. Our admirable constitution is but a gay curtain to conceal our shame, and the iniquity of our oppressors, unless our senators are animated by the same spirit which gave it birth. If they can be overawed by threats, seduced from their duty by bribes, or allured by promises, another Henry may rule us with a rod of iron, and drench once more the scaffold with the best blood of the nation: the parliament will be the humble and secure instrument of his tyrannies.

We must now, my dear son, return to the continent, where we left Charles V. attempting that despotism which Henry VIII. had accomplished.

———

[LETTER LXIII.

A General View of the Continent of Europe, including the Progress of the Reformation in Germany, from the first Meeting of the Council of Trent, in 1546, to the Peace of Religion concluded at Passau, in 1552.

IN consequence of the resolution of the emperor to humble the Protestant princes, his chief motive, as has been observed, for concluding a disadvantageous peace with Francis, he sent ambassadors to Constantinople, and agreed to a dishonourable truce with Solyman. He stipulated, that his brother A.D. Ferdinand should pay an annual tribute to the Porte for 1546. that part of Hungary which still acknowledged his sway, and that the soltan should retain the imperial and undisturbed possession of the other [1]. He, at the same time, entered into an alliance with Paul III. for the extirpation of heresy ; or, in other words, for oppressing the liberties of Germany, under pretence of maintaining the jurisdiction of the Holy See.

A general council had been assembled at Trent, by the authority of the pope, in order to regulate the affairs of religion. But the Protestants, though they had appealed to a general council, refused to acknowledge the legality of this, which they were sensible was convoked to condemn, not to examine, their opinions. The proceedings of the council confirmed them in this resolution ; they therefore renounced all connexion with it ; and as they had discovered the emperor's ambitious views, they began to prepare for their own defence.

The emperor, whose schemes were not yet ripe for execution, again had recourse to that dissimulation which he had so often practised with success. He endeavoured to persuade the princes of the Smalcaldic league, that he had no intention of abridging their spiritual liberty. It being impossible, however, to conceal his military preparations, he declared that he took arms, not in

———

[1] Barre, tome viii.—*Mem. de* Ribier.

a religious, but in a civil, quarrel; not to oppress those who continued to behave as quiet and dutiful subjects, but to humble the arrogance of such as had thrown off all sense of that subordination in which they were placed under him, as the head of the Germanic body.   But the substance of his treaty with the pope coming to light, these artifices did not long impose on the greater and sounder part of the Protestant confederacy.   Its more intelligent members saw, that he not only aimed at the suppression of the reformed religion, but at the extinction of the German liberties; and, as they would neither renounce those sacred truths, the knowledge of which they had attained by means so wonderful, nor abandon those civil rights which had been transmitted to them from their ancestors, they immediately had recourse to arms [1].

Feb. 18   In the mean time the death of Luther, their great apostle, threw the German Protestants into much consternation, and filled the Catholics with excessive and even indecent joy; neither party reflecting that his opinions were now so firmly rooted, as to stand in no further need of his fostering hand.   The members of the Smalcaldic league were also discouraged by the little success of their negotiations with foreign courts; having applied in vain for assistance, not only to the republic of Venice, and to the Swiss cantons, but to the kings of France and England.   But they found at home no difficulty in bringing a great force into the field.

Germany at that time abounded with inhabitants.   The feudal institutions subsisted in full force, and enabled the nobles to call out their numerous vassals, and to put them in motion on the shortest notice.   The martial spirit of the people, not broken or enervated by the prevalence of commerce and arts, had acquired additional vigour during the frequent wars in which they had been employed.   On every opportunity of entering upon action, they were accustomed to run eagerly to arms; and, to every standard that was erected, volunteers flocked from all quarters.   Zeal seconded on this occasion their native ardour. Men, on whom the doctrines of the Reformation had made that deep impression which accompanies truth when first discovered, prepared to maintain it with proportional courage; and among a warlike people, it appeared infamous to remain inactive, when the defence of religion and liberty invited them to draw the sword.   The confederates were therefore able, in a few weeks, to

[1] Sl..l.— Thuan.—Paolo Sarpi.

assemble an army of seventy thousand foot and fifteen hundred horse, provided with every thing necessary for the operations of war[1].

The emperor was in no condition to resist such a force : and, had the Protestants immediately proceeded to hostilities, they might have dictated their own terms. But they imprudently negotiated instead of acting, till Charles received supplies from Italy and the Low Countries. He still, however, cautiously declined a battle, trusting that discord and the want of money would oblige the confederates to disperse. Meantime, he himself began to suffer from the want of forage and provisions. Great numbers of his foreign troops, unaccustomed to the climate and the food of Germany, had become unfit for service; and it was a doubtful point, whether his steadiness was most likely to fail, or the zeal of the confederates to be exhausted, when an unexpected event decided the contest, and occasioned a fatal reverse in their affairs.

Several of the Protestant princes, overawed by the emperor's power, had remained neutral; while others, allured by the prospect of advantage, had voluntarily entered into his service. Among the latter was Maurice, marquis of Misnia and Thuringia, of the house of Saxony; a man of bold ambition, extensive views, and profound political talents. After many conferences with Charles and his ministers, he concluded a treaty, by which he engaged to concur in assisting the emperor as a faithful subject; and Charles, in return, engaged to bestow on him all the spoils of his relative and benefactor, the elector of Saxony, his dignities as well as territories.

These stipulations, however, so contradictory to all that is just and honourable among men, Maurice was able to conceal, as they had been formed with the most mysterious secrecy. And so perfect a master was he in the art of dissimulation, that the confederates, notwithstanding his declining all connexion with them, and his singular assiduity in paying court to the emperor, seemed to have entertained no suspicion of his designs! The elector, when he marched to join his associates, even committed his dominions to the protection of Maurice, who undertook the charge with an insidious appearance of friendship. But scarcely had the confederates taken the field, when he began to consult with the king of the Romans, how to invade those dominions which he had engaged to defend; and no sooner did he receive

---

[1] Seckend, lib. iii.—Thuan. lib. i.

a copy of the imperial ban denounced against his cousin and his father-in-law, the elector of Saxony and the landgrave of Hesse, as leaders of the confederacy, than he suddenly entered one part of the electoral territories, at the head of twelve thousand men; while Ferdinand, with an army of Bohemians and Hungarians, overran the other [1].

The news of this violent invasion, and the success of Maurice, who in a short time made himself master of the whole electorate of Saxony, except Wittenberg, Gotha, and Eisenach, no sooner reached the camp of the confederates, than they were filled with astonishment and terror. The elector immediately proposed to return home with his troops, in order to recover his hereditary dominions; and his associates, forgetting that it was the union of their forces which had hitherto rendered the confederacy formidable, and more than once obliged the imperialists to think of quitting the field, consented to his proposal of dividing the army.

Ulm, one of the chief cities of Suabia, highly distinguished by its zeal for the Smalcaldic league, submitted to the emperor. An example being once set for deserting the common cause, the rest of the members were eager to follow it, and seemed afraid that others, by anticipating their intentions, should obtain more favourable terms. All the conditions, however, were sufficiently severe. Charles, being in great want of money, not only imposed heavy fines upon the princes and cities that had taken arms against him, but obliged them to deliver up their artillery and warlike stores, and to admit garrisons into their principal towns and places of strength [2]. Thus a confederacy, so powerful lately as to shake the imperial throne, fell to pieces, and was dissolved in the space of a few weeks; scarcely any of the associates remaining in arms, except the elector of Saxony and the landgrave of Hesse, whom the emperor was at no pains to conciliate, having marked them out as the victims of his vengeance.

A.D.
1547.

Meanwhile the elector, having expelled the invaders from Saxony, not only recovered in a short time possession of his own territories, but overran Misnia, and stripped his rival of all that belonged to him, except Dresden and Leipsic; while Maurice, obliged to abandon the field to superior force, and to shut himself up in his capital, dispatched courier after courier to the emperor, representing his dangerous situation, and soliciting

[1] Seckend, lib. iii.—Thuan. lib. i.   [2] Sleidan.—Thuan.

him with the most earnest importunity to march immediately to his relief.

But various causes conspired to prevent the emperor from instantly taking any effectual step in favour of his ally. His army was diminished by the departure of the Flemings, and by the garrisons which he had been obliged to throw into the towns that had capitulated; and the pope now perceiving that ambition, not religion, was the chief motive of Charles's hostilities, had weakened the imperial army still farther by unexpectedly recalling his troops.

Alarmed at the rapid progress of Charles, Paul began to tremble, and not without reason, for the liberties of Italy. Francis also observed with deep concern the humiliation of Germany, and became sensible, that if some vigorous and timely effort should not be made, Charles would soon acquire such a degree of power as might enable him to give law to the rest of Europe. He therefore resolved to form such a combination against the emperor as should put a stop to his dangerous career. He accordingly negotiated for this purpose with Solyman II., with the pope, the Venetians, and with England. He encouraged the elector of Saxony and the landgrave of Hesse, by remitting to them considerable sums, to continue the struggle for their liberties; he levied troops in all parts of his dominions, and contracted for a body of Swiss mercenaries[1].

Measures so complicated could not escape the emperor's observation, nor fail to alarm him: and the news of a conspiracy at Genoa, where Fiesco, count of Lavigna, an ambitious young nobleman, had almost overturned the government in one night, contributed yet farther to divert Charles from marching immediately into Saxony, as he was uncertain how soon he might be obliged to lead his forces into Italy. The politic Maurice, however, found means to save himself during this delay, by a pretended negotiation with his injured kinsman; while the death of Francis I., which happened before he was able to carry his schemes into execution, together with the final extinction of Fiesco's conspiracy by the vigilance of the celebrated Andrew Doria, equally a friend to the emperor and the republic, encouraged Charles to act with vigour in Germany.   March 31.

Intent upon vengeance, the emperor now marched into Saxony at the head of sixteen thousand veterans. The elector's forces were more numerous, but they were divided. Charles did

---

[1] Sleidan.—Thuan.

not allow them time to assemble. He attacked the main body at Mulhausen, defeated it after an obstinate dispute, and took the elector prisoner. The captive prince was immediately conducted to the emperor, whom he found standing on the field of battle, in the full exultation of victory. The elector's behaviour, even in his present unfortunate and humbling condition, was decent, and even magnanimous. It was worthy of his gallant resistance. He alike avoided a sullen pride and a mean submission. "The fortune of war," said he, "most gracious emperor, has made me your prisoner, and I hope to be treated"—Here Charles rudely interrupted him :—"And am I then, at last, acknowledged to be emperor? Charles of Ghent was the only title you lately allowed me. You shall be treated as you deserve!" turning from him with a haughty air. To this cruel repulse the king of the Romans added reproaches in his own name, using expressions still more harsh and insulting. The elector made no reply; but, with an unaltered countenance, accompanied the Spanish soldiers appointed to guard him[1].

The emperor speedily marched towards Wittenberg (the capital, in that age, of the electoral branch of the Saxon family,) hoping that, while the consternation occasioned by his victory was still recent, the inhabitants would submit as soon as he appeared before their walls. But Sibylla of Cleves, the elector's wife, a woman equally distinguished by her virtue and abilities, instead of obeying the imperial summons, or abandoning herself to tears and lamentation on account of her husband's misfortunes, animated the citizens by her example, as well as exhortation, to a vigorous defence; and Charles, finding that he could not suddenly reduce the place by force, had recourse to means both ungenerous and unwarlike, but more expeditious and certain. He summoned Sibylla a second time to open the gates; informing her, that, in case of refusal, the elector should answer with his head for her obstinacy. And to convince her that he was in earnest, he brought his prisoner to an immediate trial, subjecting one of the greatest princes in the empire to the jurisdiction of a court-martial composed of Spanish and Italian officers; who founding their charge against him upon the imperial ban, a sentence pronounced by the sole authority of Charles, and destitute of every legal formality which could render it valid, presumed the elector convicted of treason and rebellion, and condemned him to suffer death by being beheaded[2].

[1] Hortens. *de Bell. Germ.*—Robertson's *Hist. Charles V.* book ix.   [2] Id. ibid.

Frederic was amusing himself at chess with his fellow-prisoner, Ernest of Brunswick, when this decree was intimated to him. He paused for a moment, though without any symptom of surprise or terror; and after taking notice of the irregularity as well as injustice of the proceedings against him, " It is easy," said he, " to comprehend the emperor's scheme. I must die because Wittenberg refuses to surrender: and I will lay down my life with pleasure, if by that sacrifice I can preserve the dignity of my house, and transmit to my posterity the inheritance which I received from my ancestors. Heaven grant," continued he, " that this sentence may affect my wife and children no more than it does me! that they may not, for the sake of adding a few years to a life already too long, renounce honours and territories which they were born to possess!" He then turned to his antagonist, challenged him to continue the game, and played with his usual attention and ingenuity [1].

It happened as the elector had feared: the account of his condemnation was not received with the same indifference at Wittenberg. Sibylla, who had supported with such undaunted fortitude her husband's misfortunes while she imagined his person was free from danger, felt all her resolution fail the moment his life was threatened. Anxious for his safety, she despised every other consideration; and was willing to make any sacrifice, in order to appease the rage of an incensed conqueror. Meantime, Charles, perceiving that the expedient he had tried began to produce the intended effect, fell by degrees from his former firmness, and allowed himself to soften into promises of clemency and forgiveness, if the elector would show himself worthy of favour, by submitting to certain conditions. Frederic, on whom the consideration of what he himself might suffer had made no impression, was melted by the tears of a wife whom he loved. He could not resist the intreaties of his family. In compliance with their repeated solicitations, he agreed to articles of accommodation which he would otherwise have rejected with disdain; —to resign the electoral dignity, to put the imperial troops immediately in possession of his capital, and to remain the emperor's prisoner. In return for these important concessions, Charles promised, not only to spare his life, but to settle on him and his posterity the city of Gotha and its territory, with a revenue of fifty thousand florins [2]. The Saxon electorate was instantly bestowed upon Maurice. This sacrifice, though with

[1] Thuan. lib. i. [2] Du Mont. Corps Diplom. tome iv.

no small reluctance, Charles was obliged to make, as it would not have been safe or prudent to violate his engagements with a warlike prince, whom he had seduced by ambitious hopes to abandon his natural allies, and whose friendship was still necessary.

The landgrave of Hesse, Maurice's father-in-law, was still in arms; but he thought no more of resistance. Alarmed at the fate of the elector of Saxony, his only care was how to procure favourable terms from the emperor, whom he now viewed as a conqueror to whose will there was a necessity of submitting. Maurice encouraged this tame spirit, by magnifying Charles's power, and boasting of his own interest with his victorious ally. The landgrave accordingly threw himself at the emperor's feet, after ratifying what terms he was pleased to impose, Maurice and the elector of Brandenburg being sureties for his personal freedom. But his submission was no sooner made, than Charles put him under the custody of a Spanish guard; and when the elector and Maurice, filled with indignation at being made the instruments of deceiving and ruining their friend, represented the infamy to which his detention would expose them, after they had pledged their faith for his release, the emperor, who no longer stood in need of their services, coolly replied, that he was ignorant of their particular or private transactions with the landgrave, nor was his conduct to be regulated by theirs. " I know," added he, in a decisive tone, " what I myself have promised; for that alone I am answerable [1]." These words put an end to the conference, and all future entreaties proved ineffectual.

Charles having now in his power the two greatest princes of the empire, carried them about with him in triumph; and having humbled all whom he had not attached to his interest, proceeded to exercise the rights of a conqueror. He ordered his troops to seize the artillery and military stores of all who had been members of the Smalcaldic league; and he exacted large sums by his sole authority, both from those who had served him with fidelity, and from such as had appeared in arms against him : from the former, as their contingent towards a war undertaken, as he pretended, for the common benefit; from the latter, as a penalty for their rebellion. His brother Ferdinand tyrannized with still greater severity over his Bohemian subjects, who had taken arms in support of their civil and religious liber-

---

[1] Thuan. lib. iv.—Struv. *Corp. Hist. Germ.* vol. ii.

ties: he deprived them of their ancient privileges, and loaded them with oppressive taxes [1].

The good fortune, or, as it has been called, the STAR of the house of Austria, was now at its height. The emperor having humbled, and, as he imagined, subdued the independent spirit of the Germans, summoned a diet to meet at Augsburg, " in order to compose finally the controversies with regard to religion, which had so long disturbed the empire;" or, in other words, to enslave the minds of those whose persons and property were already at his disposal. He durst not, however, commit to the free suffrage of the Germans, broken as their spirit was by subjection, the determination of a matter so interesting. He therefore entered the city at the head of his Spanish troops; cantoned the rest of his army in the adjacent villages; and took forcible possession of the cathedral, and one of the principal churches, where his priests re-established with great pomp the rites of the Romish worship. He then opened the diet with a speech, pointing out the fatal effects of the religious dissensions which had arisen in Germany, and exhorting the members to recognise the authority of the general council which he had taken such pains to procure.

But the council to which Charles wished to refer all controversies, had undergone by this time a violent change. The same jealousy which had made the pope recall his troops, had also prompted him to transfer the assembly to Bologna, a city subject to his own jurisdiction. The diet of Augsburg, overawed by threats, and influenced by promises, petitioned the pope, in the name of the whole Germanic body, to order the prelates of his party to return to Trent. But Paul eluded the demand. He persuaded the fathers at Bologna, to whom he referred the petition of the diet, to put a direct negative upon the request; and Charles, no longer expecting to acquire such an ascendant in the council as to render it subservient to his ambitious aims, yet wishing to prevent the authority of so venerable an assembly from being turned against him, sent A.D. two Spanish lawyers to Bologna, who, in presence of the 1548. legates, protested, that the removal of the council to that place had been unnecessary, and founded upon false or frivolous pretexts; that while it continued to meet there, it ought to be considered as an unlawful and schismatical conventicle, and all its decisions deemed null and void; and that, as the pope, with the

---

[1] Thuan. lib. iv. Struv. *Corp. Hist. Germ.* vol. ii.

corrupt ecclesiastics who depended upon him, had abandoned the care of the church, the emperor, as its protector, would employ all the power which God had committed to him, in order to preserve it from those calamities with which it was threatened.

In consequence of this resolution, Charles employed some able divines to prepare a system of doctrine, which he presented to the diet, as what all should conform to, " until a council, such as they wished for, could be called."—Hence the name *Interim*, by which this system is known. It was conformable in almost every article to the tenets of the Romish church, and the Romish rites were enjoined; but all disputed doctrines were expressed in the softest words, in phrases of Scripture, or in terms of studied ambiguity. In regard to two points only, some relaxation of popish rigour was granted, and some latitude in practice admitted. Such ecclesiastics as had married, and did not choose to part from their wives, were yet allowed to perform their sacred functions; and those provinces which had been accustomed to partake of the cup as well as of the bread in the communion, were still indulged with the privilege of receiving both .

This treatise being read in presence of the members, the archbishop of Mentz, president of the electoral college, rose up hastily, as soon as it was finished, and having thanked the emperor for his unwearied endeavours to restore peace to the church, signified the diet's approbation of the system of doctrine which his imperial majesty had prepared, and its resolution of conforming to it in every particular. And although the whole assembly was amazed at a declaration so unprecedented and unconstitutional, as well as at the archbishop's presumption, in pretending to deliver the sense of the diet upon a point which had not hitherto been the subject of consultation or debate, not one member had the courage to contradict what he had said. Charles therefore held the archbishop's declaration to be a ratification of the *Interim*, and prepared to enforce the observance of it as a decree of the empire [1].

The Interim, like all conciliating schemes proposed to men heated with disputation, pleased neither party. The Protestants thought it granted too little indulgence; the Catholics, too much : both were dissatisfied. The emperor however, fond of his plan, adhered to his resolution of carrying it into effect. But

---

[1] Paolo Sarpi, lib. iii.—Goldast, *Const. Imp.* vol. i.   [2] Id. Ibid.

this proved one of the most difficult and dangerous undertakings in his reign; for although three Protestant princes, Maurice, the elector Palatine, and the elector of Brandenburg, agreed to receive the Interim, several others remonstrated against it : and the free cities joined in refusing to admit it, till force taught them submission. Augsburg and Ulm being barbarously stripped of their privileges, on account of their opposition, many other cities feigned compliance. But this obedience, extorted by the rigour of authority, produced no change in the sentiments of the Germans. They submitted with reluctance to the power that oppressed them; and although for a time they concealed their resentment, it was daily gathering force, and soon broke forth with a violence that shook the imperial throne.

In this moment of general submission, it is worthy of remark, that the elector of Saxony, though the emperor's prisoner, and tempted both by threats and promises, refused to lend his sanction to the Interim. His reasons were those of a philosopher, not of a bigot. After declaring his fixed belief in the doctrines of the Reformation, " I cannot now," said he, " in my old age, abandon the principles for which I early contended ; nor, in order to procure freedom during a few declining years, will I betray that good cause, on account of which I have suffered so much, and am still willing to suffer. It is better for me to enjoy, in this solitude, the esteem of virtuous men and the approbation of my own conscience, than to return into the world with the imputation and guilt of apostasy, to disgrace and embitter the remainder of my days [1]."

The contents of the Interim were no sooner known at Rome than the members of the sacred college were filled with rage and indignation. They exclaimed against the emperor's profane encroachment on the sacerdotal function, in presuming, with the concurrence of an assembly of laymen, to define articles of faith, and regulate modes of worship. They compared this rash deed to that of Uzzah, who with an unhallowed hand had touched the ark of God. But the pope, whose judgment was improved by longer experience in great transactions, and more extensive observation of human affairs, though displeased at the emperor's encroachment on his jurisdiction, viewed the matter with great coolness. He perceived that Charles, by joining any one of the contending parties in Germany, might have had it in his power to crush the other, but that the presumption of suc-

---

[1] Sleid. p. 462.—Robertson, book ix.

cess had now inspired him with the vain thought of being able to domineer over both; and he foresaw that a system which all attacked and none defended, could not be of long duration [1]. He was more sensibly affected by the emperor's political measures, and his own domestic concerns.

Charles, as I have already had occasion to notice, had married his natural daughter to the pope's grandson Octavio. On his own son Ludovico, Octavio's father, whose aggrandizement he had sincerely at heart, Paul bestowed the duchies of Parma and Placentia. But the emperor, less fond of aggrandizing his daughter, whose children were to succeed to the inheritance, refused to grant to Ludovico the investiture of those territories, under pretence that they were appendages of the duchy of Milan. Enraged at such ungenerous conduct, the pope undertook to bestow himself that investiture which he craved; but the emperor persisted in refusing to confirm the deed. Hence a secret enmity took place between Paul and Charles, and one still stronger between Charles and Ludovico. To complete the pope's misfortunes, his son became one of the most detestable tyrants that ever disgraced human nature; and justly fell a sacrifice to his own crimes, and to the injuries of his oppressed subjects. Gonzaga, governor of Milan, who had watched for such an opportunity, and even abetted the conspirators, immediately took possession of Placentia, in the emperor's name, and reinstated the inhabitants in their ancient privileges. The Imperialists likewise attempted to surprise Parma, but were disappointed by the vigilance and fidelity of the garrison [2].

Paul was deeply afflicted for the loss of his son, whom, notwithstanding his vices, he loved with an excess of parental affection, and immediately demanded of the emperor the punishment of Gonzaga, and the surrender of Placentia to Octavio. But Charles evaded both demands; he chose rather to bear the infamy of defrauding his son-in-law of his patrimonial inheritance, and even to expose himself to the imputation of being accessary to the crime which had given him an opportunity of seizing it, than quit a possession of such value. An ambition so rapacious, and which no considerations either of decency or justice could restrain, transported Paul beyond his usual moderation. Eager to take arms against the emperor, but conscious of his inability to contend with such an enemy, he warmly solicited the king of France,

[1] Paolo Sarpi, lib. iii.—Pallavincini, lib. ii.
[2] Thuan. lib. iv.—*Mém. de* Ribier.

and the republic of Venice to take part in his quarrel; but finding all his negotiations ineffectual, he endeavoured to acquire
by policy what he could not recover by force.   Upon a supposition that Charles would not dare to detain the possessions of
the Holy See, he proposed to re-unite to it Parma and Placentia, by recalling his grant of Parma from Octavio, whom he
could indemnify by a new establishment in the ecclesias-   A.D.
tical state, and by demanding Placentia from the em-   1549.
peror, as part of the patrimony of the church.   But while Paul
was priding himself in this happy device, Octavio, an ambitious
and high-spirited young man, having little faith in such refinement of policy, and not choosing to abandon certainty for hope,
applied to the emperor to protect him in his duchy [1].

This unexpected defection of one of his own family, of the
grandson whose fortune it had been the care of his declining
years to build, to an enemy whom he hated, agitated the venerable pontiff beyond his strength, and is said to have occasioned
that illness of which he soon after died [2].   We must not, however, on this account stigmatize Octavio as a parricide ; for as
the pope had now attained his eightieth year, a very little excite-
ment was required to accelerate the natural effect of old age.

Paul was succeeded by the cardinal de Montè, Julius III.,
who, as he owed his election to the Farnesè party, put Octavio
in full possession of Parma.   " I would rather," replied   A.D.
he, when told what injury he did the Holy See by   1550.
alienating a territory of such value, " be a poor pope with the
reputation of a gentleman, than a rich one with the infamy of
having forgotten the obligations conferred upon me, and the
promises I made [3]."   He discovered less inclination, however, to
observe the oath which each cardinal had taken when he entered
the conclave, that if the choice should fall on him, he would immediately call a general council to resume its deliberations.   He
knew by experience, how difficult it was to confine the inquiries,
or even the decisions of such a body of men, within the narrow
limits which it was the interest of the court of Rome to prescribe.   But, as the emperor persisted in his resolution of forcing
the Protestants to return into the bosom of the church, and
earnestly solicited that a council might be called, in order to
combat their prejudices, and support his pious intentions, Julius

---

[1] Thuan. lib. vi.—Pallav. lib. ii.   [2] Id. Ibid.
[3] *Mém. de* Ribier.

could not with decency reject his request ; and, willing to assume to himself the merit of a measure which seemed now to be necessary, and also to ingratiate himself more particularly with Charles, he pretended to deliberate on the matter, and afterwards issued a bull for the council to reassemble at Trent [1].

In the meantime, the emperor held a diet at Augsburg, to enforce the observation of the Interim, and procure a more authentic act of the empire, acknowledging the jurisdiction of the council, as well as an explicit promise of conforming to its decrees.   And such absolute ascendancy had he acquired over the members of the Germanic body, that he procured a Recess, in which the authority of the council was recognised, and declared to be the proper remedy for the evils which afflicted the church. The observation of the Interim was more strictly enjoined than ever; and the emperor threatened all who neglected or refused to conform to it with the severest effects of his vengeance.

During the meeting of this diet, a new attempt was made to procure liberty for the landgrave.   Having often applied to his sureties, Maurice and the elector of Brandenburg, who took every opportunity of soliciting the emperor in his behalf, though without effect, he now commanded his sons to summon them, with legal formality, to perform their engagements, by surrendering themselves to be treated as the emperor had treated him. Thus pushed to extremity, the sureties renewed their application to Charles.   He endeavoured to prevail on the landgrave to give up the obligation which he had received from them ; and when that prince refused to part with a security which he deemed essential to his safety, Charles, by a singular act of despotism, cut the knot which he could not untie.   As if faith, honour, and conscience, had been subjected to his sway, he, by a public deed, annulled the bond which Maurice and the elector had granted, A.D. and absolved them from all their obligations to the land- 1551. grave [2]!   A power of cancelling those solemn contracts which are the foundation of that mutual confidence whereby men are held together in social union, was never claimed by the most despotic princes or arrogating priests of heathen antiquity : that enormous usurpation was reserved for the Romish pontiffs, who had rendered themselves odious, by the exercise of such a pernicious prerogative.   All Germany was therefore filled with astonishment when Charles assumed the same right.   The

---

[1] Paolo Sarpi, lib. iii.   [2] Thuan. lib. vi.

princes who had hitherto contributed to his aggrandizement began to tremble for their own safety, and to take measures for preventing the danger.

The first check which Charles met with in his ambitious projects, and which convinced him that the Germans were not yet slaves, was in his attempt to transmit the empire, as well as the kingdom of Spain and his dominions in the Low Countries, to his son Philip. He had formerly assisted his brother Ferdinand in obtaining the dignity of king of the Romans; and that prince had not only studied to render himself acceptable to the people, but had a son, who was born in Germany, grown up to the years of manhood, and who possessed in an eminent degree such qualities as rendered him the darling of his countrymen. The emperor, however, warmed with contemplating this vast design, flattered himself that it was not impossible to prevail on the electors to cancel their former choice of Ferdinand, or at least to elect Philip a second king of the Romans, substituting him as next in succession to his uncle. With this view he took Philip, who had been educated in Spain, to the diet at Augsburg, that the Germans might have an opportunity of becoming acquainted with the prince in whose behalf he solicited their interest; but all the electors concurred in expressing such strong disapprobation of the measure, that Charles was obliged to drop his project as impracticable [1]. They foresaw, that by continuing the imperial crown, like an hereditary dignity, in the same family, they should give the son an opportunity of carrying on that system of oppression which the father had begun, and put it in his power to overturn whatever was yet left entire in the ancient and venerable fabric of the German constitution.

This plan of domestic ambition, which had long engrossed his thoughts, being laid aside, Charles imagined he should now have leisure to turn all his attention towards his grand scheme of establishing uniformity of religion in the empire, by forcing all the contending parties to acquiesce in the decisions of the council of Trent. But the machine which he had to conduct was so great and complicated, that an unforeseen irregularity, or obstruction in one of the inferior wheels, often disconcerted the motion of the whole, and disappointed him of the effect upon which he depended. Such an occurrence now happened, and created new obstacles to the execution of his religious plan.

Though Julius, during the first effusions of joy and gratitude

---

[1] Thuan. lib. vi.—*Mém de* Ribier.

on his promotion to the papal throne, had confirmed Octavio in the possession of Parma, he soon began to repent of his generosity. The emperor still retained possession of Placentia; and the governor of Milan, a sworn enemy to the family of Farnesè, was preparing, by Charles's permission, to seize Parma. Octavio saw his danger; and, sensible of his inability to defend himself against the imperial troops, he applied to the pope for protection, as a vassal of the Holy See. But the imperial minister having already pre-occupied the ear of Julius, Octavio's petition met with a cold reception. Despairing, therefore, of support from his holiness, he requested aid from Henry II. of France, who, having not only settled his domestic concerns, but brought his transactions with the two British kingdoms, which had diverted his attention from the affairs of the continent, to such an issue as he desired, was at full leisure to pursue the measures which his hereditary jealousy of the emperor's power naturally suggested. He accordingly listened to the overtures of Octavio, and furnished him with the desired assistance.

The war of Parma, in which the French took the field as the allies of the duke, and the Imperialists as the protectors of the Holy See, the pope having declared Octavio's fief forfeited, was distinguished by no memorable event; but the alarm which it occasioned in Italy prevented most of the Italian prelates from repairing to Trent on the day appointed for re-assembling the council; so that the legate and nuncios found it necessary to adjourn to a future day, hoping that such a number might then assemble as would enable them in decency to begin their deliberations. When that day came, the French ambassador demanded audience, and protested, in his master's name against an assembly called at such an improper juncture; when a war, wantonly kindled by the pope, rendered it impossible for the deputies of the Gallican church to resort to Trent in safety, or to deliberate upon articles of faith and discipline with the requisite tranquillity. He declared, that Henry did not acknowledge this to be an œcumenic council, but must consider and would treat it as a partial convention [1].

This declaration gave a deep wound to the credit of the council, at the commencement of its deliberations. The legate, however, affected to despise Henry's protest; the prelates proceeded to determine the great points in controversy concerning the sacrament of the Lord's supper, penance, and extreme unction;

[1] Paolo Sarpi, lib. iv.—Robertson, book x.

and the emperor strained his authority to the utmost in order to establish the reputation and jurisdiction of that assembly. The Protestants were prohibited from teaching any doctrine contrary to its decrees, or to the tenets of the Romish church: and, on their refusing compliance, their pastors were ejected and exiled; such magistrates as had distinguished themselves by their attachment to the new opinions were dismissed; their offices were filled with the most bigoted of their adversaries; and the people were compelled to attend the ministration of priests whom they regarded as idolaters, and to submit to the authority of rulers whom they detested as usurpers [1].

These tyrannical measures fully opened the eyes of Maurice of Saxony and other Lutheran princes, who, allured by the promise of liberty of conscience, and the prospect of farther advantages, had assisted the emperor in the war against the confederates of Smalcalde. Maurice, in particular, who had long beheld with jealous concern the usurpations of Charles, now saw the necessity of setting bounds to them; and he who had perfidiously stripped his nearest relative and benefactor of his hereditary possessions, and been chiefly instrumental in bringing to the verge of ruin the civil and religious liberties of his country, became the deliverer of Germany. Or, we should rather say, finding a new opportunity of personal aggrandizement, deserted the imperial party with as little scruple as he had formerly shown in quitting the cause of his religion and his country.

The policy with which he conducted himself in the execution of his design was truly admirable. He was so perfect a master of address and dissimulation, that he retained the emperor's confidence, while he recovered the good opinion of the Protestants. As he knew Charles to be inflexible with respect to the submission which he required to the Interim, he did not hesitate a moment whether he should establish that form of doctrine and worship in his dominions: he even undertook to reduce to obedience the citizens of Magdeburg, who persisted in rejecting it; and he was chosen general, by a diet assembled at Augsburg, of the imperial army levied for that purpose. But he at the same time issued a declaration, containing professions of his zealous attachment to the reformed religion, as well as of his resolution to guard against all the errors and encroachments of the papal see; and he entered his protest against the authority of the council of Trent, unless the Protestant divines should have a full hearing

---

[1] Paolo Sarpi, lib. iv. — Robertson, book x.

granted them, and be allowed to have an operative voice in that assembly; unless the pope should renounce his pretensions to preside in it, should engage to submit to its decrees, and to absolve the bishops from their oath of obedience, that they might deliver their sentiments with greater freedom. He reduced Magdeburg, after a siege of twelve months,—protracted by design, in order that his schemes might be ripened before his army was disbanded [1]. The public articles of capitulation were perfectly conformable to the emperor's views and sufficiently severe. But Maurice gave the magistrates secret assurances that their city should not be dismantled, and that the inhabitants should neither be disturbed in the exercise of their religion, nor deprived of any of their ancient privileges; and they, in their turn, elected him their burgrave—a dignity which had formerly belonged to the electoral house of Saxony, and which entitled its possessor to every ample jurisdiction both in the city and its dependencies.

Far from suspecting any thing fraudulent or collusive in the terms of accommodation, the emperor ratified them without hesitation, freely absolving the Magdeburgers from the sentence of ban denounced against them; and Maurice, under various pretences, kept his veteran troops in pay; while Charles, engaged in directing the affairs of the council, entertained no apprehension of his views. But before we state the result of these schemes, some account must be given of a new revolution in Hungary, which contributed not a little toward the extraordinary success of Maurice's operations.

When Solyman deprived the young king of Hungary of his realm, he allowed him to retain Transylvania. The government of this province was committed to Isabella the queen-mother, and Martinuzzi, bishop of Waradin, whom Zapol had appointed his son's guardians, and regents of his dominions. This co-ordinate jurisdiction occasioned the same dissensions in a small principality which it would have excited in a great monarchy. The queen and bishop grew jealous of each other's authority; both had their partisans amongst the nobility; but as Martinuzzi, by his superior talents, began to acquire the ascendant, Isabella courted the protection of the Turks. The politic prelate saw his danger; and through the mediation of some of the nobles, who were solicitous to save their country from the calamities of civil war, he concluded an agreement with the queen. But, he

[1] Sebast. Besselm. *Obsid. Magdeb.*—Arnoldi *Vit. Maurit.*

at the same time entered into a negotiation with the king of the Romans, whom he offered to assist in expelling the Turks, and in recovering possession of the Hungarian throne.

Allured by such a flattering prospect, Ferdinand agreed, notwithstanding his truce with Solyman, to invade the principality of Transylvania. The troops destined for that service, consisting of veteran Spanish and German soldiers, were commanded by Castaldo marquis de Piadena, an officer of great knowledge in the art of war, who was powerfully seconded by Martinuzzi and his faction; and the soltan being then at the head of his forces on the borders of Persia, the Turkish governors and officers could not afford the queen such immediate or effectual assistance as the urgency of her affairs required. She was, therefore, obliged to listen to such conditions as she would at any other time have rejected with disdain. She agreed to give up Transylvania to Ferdinand, and to make over to him her son's title to the crown of Hungary, in exchange for the principalities of Oppelen and Ratibor in Silesia.

Martinuzzi, as the reward of his services, was appointed governor of Transylvania, with almost unlimited authority; and he proved himself worthy of it. He conducted the war against the Turks with equal ability and success; and he established the dominion of the king of the Romans, not only in Transylvania, but in several of the adjacent countries. Always, however, afraid of the talents of Martinuzzi, Ferdinand now became jealous of his power; and Castaldo, by imputing to the governor designs which he never formed, and charging him with actions of which he was not guilty, at last convinced the king of the Romans that in order to preserve his Hungarian crown, he must cut off that ambitious prelate. The fatal mandate was accordingly issued: Castaldo willingly undertook to execute it; Martinuzzi was assassinated. But Ferdinand, instead of the security which he expected from that barbarous measure, found his Hungarian territories only exposed to more certain danger. The nobles, detesting such jealousy and cruel policy, either retired to their own estates, or grew cold in the service, if they continued with the Austrian army; while the Turks, encouraged by the death of an enemy, whose vigour and abilities they dreaded, prepared to renew hostilities with fresh vigour [1].

Maurice, in the mean time, having almost finished his in-

---

[1] Istuanhaffi, *Hist. Reg. Hung.* lib. xvi.—*Mem. de* Ribier, tome ii.

trigues and preparations, was on the point of taking the field against the emperor. He had concluded a treaty with the French king, who wished to distinguish himself, by trying his strength against the same enemy whom it had been the glory of his father's reign to oppose. But as it would have been indecent in a popish prince to undertake the defence of the Protestant church, the interests of religion, how much soever they might be affected by the treaty, were not mentioned in any of the articles. The only motives assigned for now leaguing against Charles were to procure the liberation of the landgrave, and to prevent the subversion of the ancient constitution and laws of the German empire. Religious concerns the confederates pretended to commit entirely to the care of Providence.

Having secured the protection of the French monarch, Maurice proceeded with great confidence, but equal caution, to execute his plan. As he judged it necessary to demand once more, before he took off the mask, that the landgrave should be set at A.D. liberty, he sent a solemn embassy, in which most of the 1552. German princes joined, to the emperor at Inspruck, in order to enforce his request. Constant to his system in regard to the captive prince, Charles eluded the demand, though urged by such powerful intercessors. But this application, though of no benefit to the landgrave, was of infinite service to Maurice. It served to justify his subsequent proceedings, and to demonstrate the necessity of taking arms, with a view of extorting that equitable concession which his mediation or entreaty could not obtain. He accordingly dispatched Albert of Brandenburg to Paris, to hasten the march of the French army : he took measures to bring his own troops together on the first summons ; and he provided for the security of Saxony, while he should be absent.

These complicated operations were carried on with such secrecy, as to elude the observation of Charles, whose sagacity in observing the conduct of all around him commonly led him to excess of distrust. He remained in perfect tranquillity at Inspruck, solely occupied in counteracting the intrigues of the pope's legate at Trent, and in settling the conditions on which the Protestant divines should be admitted into the council. Even Granville, bishop of Arras, his prime minister, though one of the most subtle statesmen of that, or perhaps of any age, was deceived by the exquisite address with which Maurice concealed his designs. " A drunken German head," replied he to the doubts expressed by the duke of Alva, concerning the

2

elector's sincerity, "is too gross to form any scheme which I cannot easily penetrate and baffle." Granville was on this occasion,
however, the dupe of his own artifice. He had bribed two of
Maurice's ministers, on whose information he depended for their
master's intentions; but that prince having fortunately discovered their perfidy, instead of punishing them for their crime,
dexterously availed himself of the fraud. He affected to treat
these ministers with greater confidence than ever : he admitted
them into his consultations, and seemed to lay open his heart to
them; while he really informed them of nothing but what it
was his interest should be known; and they transmitted to
Inspruck such accounts as lulled the crafty Granville into
security [1].

At last, Maurice's preparations were completed : and he had
the satisfaction to find, that his intrigues and designs were still
unknown. But although ready to take the field, he did not yet
lay aside the arts he had hitherto employed. Pretending to be
indisposed, he dispatched one of the ministers whom Granville
had bribed, to inform the emperor that he meant soon to wait
upon him at Inspruck, and to apologise for his delay. When he
had assembled his army, which amounted to twenty thousand
foot and five thousand horse, he announced in form his reason
for taking arms; namely, to secure the Protestant religion, to
maintain the German constitution, and deliver the landgrave of
Hesse from the miseries of a long and unjust imprisonment.
To this the king of France, in his own name, added a manifesto,
in which he assumed the extraordinary appellation of *Protector
of the Liberties of Germany and its captive Princes* [2].

No words can express the emperor's astonishment at events
so unexpected. He was not in a condition to oppose such formidable enemies. His embarrassment increased their confidence : their operations were equally bold and successful. The
king of France immediately entered Lorrain, and made himself
master of Toul, Verdun, and Metz; while Maurice, no less
intrepid and enterprising in the field than cautious and crafty
in the cabinet, traversed all Upper Germany, reinstating the
magistrates whom Charles had deposed, and putting the ejected
Protestant ministers in possession of the churches.

The emperor had recourse to negotiation, the only resource
of the weak; and Maurice, conscious of his own political talents,
and willing to manifest a pacific disposition, agreed to an inter-

---

[1] Melvil's *Memoirs.*   [2] *Mém. de* Ribier, tome ii.

view with the king of the Romans at Lintz, leaving his army to proceed on its march, under the command of the duke of Mecklenburg. Nothing was determined in the conference at Lintz, except that another should be holden at Passau. Meanwhile Maurice continued his operations with vigour. He marched directly towards Inspruck; and, hoping to surprise the emperor in that town, he advanced with the most rapid motion that could be given to so great a body of men, forcing several strong passes, and bearing down all resistance.

Charles was happily informed of his danger a few hours before the enemy's arrival; and although the night was far advanced, dark, and rainy, he immediately fled over the Alps, in a litter, being so much afflicted with the gout as to be incapable of any other mode of travelling. Enraged at the escape of his prey, when he was on the point of seizing it, Maurice pursued the emperor and his attendants some miles; but finding it impossible to overtake men whose flight was hastened by fear, he returned to Inspruck, and abandoned the emperor's baggage to the pillage of the soldiers. Charles pursued his journey, and arrived in safety at Villach in Carinthia, where he continued till the disputes were finally adjusted with the Protestant princes [1].

In consequence of Maurice's operations, the council of Trent broke up. The German prelates, anxious for the safety of their territories, returned home; the rest were extremely desirous of departing; and the legate, who had hitherto disappointed all the endeavours of the imperial ambassadors to procure the Protestant divines an audience in the council, gladly made use of such a plausible pretext for dismissing an assembly, which he had found it so difficult to govern [2]. The breach which had been made in the church, instead of being closed, was widened; and all mankind became sensible of the inefficacy of a general council for reconciling the contending parties.

The victorious Maurice repaired to Passau, on the day appointed for the second conference with the king of the Romans; and as points of the greatest consequence to the future peace and independence of the empire were then to be agitated, thither resorted the ministers of all the electors, together with deputies from most of the considerable princes and free cities. The elector limited his demands to three articles set forth in his manifesto; namely, the liberty of the landgrave, the public

---

[1] Arnoldi *Vit. Maurit.*   [2] Paoli Sarpi, lib. iv.

exercise of the Protestant religion, and the re-establishment of the ancient constitution of Germany.

These demands, which seemed extravagant to the imperial ambassadors, were presented by Ferdinand to the emperor, in the name of all the princes of the empire, Popish as well as Protestant ; in the name of such as had assisted in forwarding his ambitious schemes, as well as of those who had viewed the progress of his power with jealousy and dread.　　Unwilling, however, to forego at once objects which he had long pursued with ardour and hope, Charles, notwithstanding his need of peace, was deaf to the united voice of Germany.　　He rejected the proffered terms with disdain : and Maurice, well acquainted with the emperor's arts, suspecting that he meant only to amuse and deceive by a show of negotiation, immediately rejoined his troops, and laid siege to Frankfort on the Maine.　　This measure had the desired effect.　　Firm and haughty as his nature was, Charles found it necessary to make concessions ; and Maurice thought it more prudent to accept conditions less advantageous than those he had proposed, than again commit all to the doubtful issue of war[1].　　He therefore repaired once more to Passau, renewed the congress, and concluded a peace on the following terms :—" The confederates shall lay down their arms before the 12th day of August ; the landgrave shall be restored to liberty on or before that day ; a diet shall be holden within six months, in order to deliberate on the most effectual method of preventing for the future all dissensions concerning religion ; in the mean time, no injury shall be offered to such as adhere to the Confession of Augsburg, nor shall the Catholics be molested in the exercise of their religion ; the imperial chamber shall administer justice impartially to persons of both parties, and Protestants be admitted indiscriminately with Catholics to sit as judges in that court ; the encroachments, said to have been made upon the constitution and liberties of Germany, shall be referred to the consideration of the approaching diet of the empire ; and if that diet should not be able to terminate the disputes respecting religion, the stipulations in the present treaty, in behalf of the Protestants, shall continue for ever in full force[2].

Such, my dear Philip, was the memorable treaty of Passau, which set limits to the authority of Charles V., overturned the vast fabric which he had employed so many years in erecting,

July 17.

---

[1] Thuan. lib. x.　　　　[2] *Recueil des Traitez*, tome ii.

and established the Protestant church in Germany upon a firm and secure basis. It is remarkable that in this treaty no article was inserted in favour of the king of France, to whom the confederates had been so much indebted for their success. But Henry II. experienced only the treatment which every prince, who lends his aid to the authors of a civil war, may expect[1]. As soon as the rage of faction began to subside, and any prospect of accommodation to open, his services were forgotten, and his associates made a merit with their sovereign of the ingratitude with which they had abandoned their protector.

The French monarch, however, sensible that it was more his interest to remain on good terms with the Germanic body than to resent the indignities offered by any particular members of it, concealed his displeasure at the perfidy of Maurice and his associates. He even affected to talk, in the same strain as formerly, of his zeal for maintaining the ancient constitution and liberties of the empire; and he prepared to defend, by force of arms, his conquests in Lorrain, which he foresaw Charles would take the first opportunity of wresting from him. But before I relate the events of the new wars to which those conquests gave birth, we must take a view of the affairs of our own island; a more contracted but not less turbulent scene, and more discoloured by horrors and cruelties than the continent, during the dark and changeable period that followed the death of Henry VIII. and terminated in the steady government of Elizabeth.

LETTER LXIV.

History of England, from the Death of Henry VIII. to the Accession of Elizabeth, in 1558, with an account of the Affairs of Scotland, and of the Progress of the Reformation in both the British Kingdoms.

HENRY VIII. by his will, left the crown, first to prince Edward his son by Jane Seymour; then to the princess Mary A.D. his daughter by Catharine of Arragon; and lastly to 1547. Elizabeth, his daughter by the unfortunate Anne Boleyn, though both princesses had been declared illegitimate by parliament. These particulars, my dear Philip, are necessary to be mentioned here, that you may better understand the disputes which arose with regard to the succession.

Edward VI. being only nine years of age at the time of his father's death, the government of the kingdom was committed to sixteen executors, among whom were the archbishop of Canterbury, and all the great officers of state. They chose one of their number, namely, the earl of Hertford, the king's maternal uncle, instantly created duke of Somerset, to represent the royal majesty, under the title of Protector; to whom despatches from English ministers abroad should be directed, and whose name should be employed in all orders and proclamations. Him they invested with all the exterior symbols of regal dignity; and he procured a patent from the young king, investing him also with regal power [1].

This patent (in which the executors are not even mentioned) being surreptitiously obtained from a minor, the protectorship of Somerset was a palpable usurpation; but as the executors acquiesced in the new establishment, and the king discovered a strong attachment to his uncle, who was a man of moderation and probity, few objections were made to his power or title. Other causes conspired to confirm both. Somerset had long been regarded as the secret partisan of the reformers, who had become the most numerous, and respectable body of men in the kingdom; and, being now freed from restraint, he scrupled not to disclose his intention of correcting all abuses in the ancient religion, and of adopting still more of the Protestant innovations. He also took care that the king should be educated in the same principles. To these Edward soon discovered a zealous attachment; and as the people foresaw, in the course of his reign, the total abolition of the Catholic faith in England, they began early and very generally to declare themselves in favour of those tenets, which were likely to become in the end triumphant, and of that authority by which they were propagated.

In his schemes for advancing the progress of the Reformation, the protector had always recourse to the counsels of Cranmer, whose moderation and prudence disinclined him to all violent changes, and determined him to draw over the people, by insensible gradations, to that system of doctrine and discipline which he esteemed the most pure and perfect [2]. And to these

---

[1] Burnet's *Hist. Reformat.* vol. ii.   [2] Id. ibid.

moderate counsels we are indebted, not only for the full establishment of the Protestant religion in England, but also for that
happy medium between superstition and enthusiasm observable
in the constitution of the English church.   The fabric of the
secular hierarchy was left and maintained entire; the ancient
liturgy was preserved, as far as it was thought consistent with
the new principles; many ceremonies, venerable from age and
preceding use, were retained; and the distinctive habits of the
clergy, according to their different ranks, were continued.   No
innovation was admitted merely from a spirit of opposition or a
fanatical love of novelty.   The establishment of the Church of
England was a work of reason.

As soon as the English government was brought to some
degree of composure, the protector made preparations for a war
with Scotland; determined to execute, if possible, that project
of uniting the two kingdoms by marriage, on which the late king
had been so intent, and which seemed once so near a happy
issue, but which had been defeated by the intrigues of cardinal
Beatoun.   This politic and powerful prelate, though not able
to prevent the parliament of Scotland from agreeing to the
treaty of marriage and union with England, being then in the
hands of the Protestant party, afterwards regained his authority,
and acquired sufficient influence, not only to oblige the earl of
Arran, who had succeeded him in the regency, to renounce his
alliance with Henry VIII., but also to abjure the principles of
the Reformation, to which he seemed zealously attached, and
reconcile himself, in 1543, to the Romish communion, in the
Franciscan church at Sterling[1].

The fatal effects of this change in the religious and political
sentiments of the regent were long felt in Scotland.   Arran's
apostacy may even perhaps be considered as the remote cause of
all the civil broils which afflicted both kingdoms in the subsequent century, and which terminated in the final expulsion of
the house of Stuart, of which the infant queen of Scots was now
the sole representative.   The southern and most fertile parts of
the kingdom were suddenly ravaged by an English army.   Desultory hostilities ensued with various success, and without any
decisive event.   At length an end was put to that ruinous and
inglorious warfare, by the peace concluded between Henry VIII.
and Francis I. at Campe, in 1546; the French monarch gene-

---

[1] Robertson's *Hist. Scot.* book ii.

rously stipulating, that his Scottish allies should be included in the treaty. The religious consequences were more serious and lasting, and their political influence was great.

The Scottish regent consented to every thing that the zeal of the cardinal thought necessary for the preservation of the established religion. The reformers were cruelly persecuted, and many were condemned to that dreadful punishment which the church has appointed for its enemies. Among those who were committed to the flames was a popular preacher named George Wishart; a man of honourable birth, and of primitive sanctity, who possessed in an eminent degree the talent of seizing the attention and engaging the affections of the multitude. Wishart suffered with the patience of a martyr; but he could not forbear remarking the barbarous triumph of his insulting adversary, who beheld from a window of his sumptuous palace the inhuman spectacle:—and he foretold, that, in a few days, the cardinal should, in the same place, lie as low as he now stood high, in opposition to true piety and religion[1].

This prophecy, like many others, was probably the cause of the event which it foretold. The disciples of Wishart, enraged at his cruel execution, formed a conspiracy against Beatoun; and having associated with them Norman Leslie, eldest son of the earl of Rothes, who was instigated by revenge on account of private injuries, they surprised the cardinal in his palace or castle at St. Andrews, and instantly put him to death. One of the assassins, named James Melvil, before he struck the fatal blow, turned the point of his sword towards Beatoun, and in a tone of pious exhortation called to him, " Repent, thou wicked cardinal! of all thy sins and iniquities, but especially of the murder of George Wishart, that instrument of Christ for the conversion of these lands. It is his death which now cries for vengeance. We are sent by God to inflict the deserved punishment upon thee[2]."

The conspirators took possession of the castle, prepared for a vigorous defence, and sent a messenger to London, craving assistance from Henry VIII. The death of that prince, which happened soon after, blasted all their hopes. They received, however, during the siege, supplies both of money and provisions from England; and if they had been able to hold out only a few weeks longer, they would have escaped that severe capitulation

[1] Spotswood.—Buchanan.   [2] Knox.—Keith.

to which they were reduced, not by the regent alone, but by a body of troops sent to his assistance from France.

Somerset entered Scotland at the head of eighteen thousand men; while a fleet of sixty sail, one half of which consisted of ships of war, and the other of vessels laden with provisions and military stores, appeared on the coast, in order to second his operations, and supply his army. The earl of Arran had for some time observed this storm gathering, and was prepared to meet it. His army, double in number to that of the enemy, was posted to the greatest advantage on a rising ground, guarded by the banks of the river Eske, a little above Musselburgh, when the Protector came in view. Alarmed at the sight of a force so formidable, and so happily disposed, Somerset made an overture of peace to the regent, on conditions very admissible. He offered to withdraw his troops, and compensate the damage he had done by his inroad, provided the Scots would engage to keep their young queen at home, and not contract her to any foreign prince, until she should attain the age of maturity, when she might choose a husband without the consent of her council. But this moderate demand was rejected by the regent with disdain, and merely on account of its moderation. It was imputed to fear; and Arran, confident of success, was afraid of nothing but the escape of the English army. He therefore left his strong camp as soon as he saw the Protector begin to move toward the sea, suspecting that he intended to embark on board his fleet; and passing the river Eske, advanced into the plain, and attacked the English army near the village of Pinkey with no better success than his rashness deserved.

Having drawn up his troops on an eminence, Somerset had now the advantage of ground on his side. The Scottish army consisted chiefly of infantry, whose principal weapon was a long spear, and whose files for that reason were as deep as their ranks were close. A body so compact and firm easily resisted the attack of the English cavalry, broke them, and drove them off the field. Lord Grey, their commander, was dangerously wounded; lord Edward Seymour, son of the protector, had his horse killed under him, and the royal standard was near falling into the hands of the enemy. But the Scots being galled by the protector's artillery in front, and by the fire from the ships in flank, while the English archers, and a body of foreign fusileers, poured in volleys of shot from all quarters, they at last began to give way: the rout became general, and

Sept. 10.

the whole field was soon a scene of confusion, terror, and flight. The pursuit was long and bloody. Ten thousand of the Scots are said to have fallen, and a very inconsiderable number of the conquering enemy [1].

This victory, however, which seemed to threaten Scotland with final subjection, was of no real utility to England. It induced the Scots to throw themselves into the arms of France, and send their young queen to be educated in that kingdom; a measure universally regarded as a prelude to her marriage with the dauphin, and which effectually disappointed the views of Somerset, and proved the source of Mary's accomplishments as a woman, and of her misfortunes as a queen. The Scottish nobles, in taking this step, hurried away by the violence of resentment, seem to have forgotten that zeal for the independence of their crown which had made them violate their engagements with Henry VIII. and oppose with such ardour the arms of the protector.

The cabals of the English court obliged the duke of Somerset to return before he could take any effectual measures for the subjection of Scotland; and the supplies which the Scots received from France, enabled them in a great measure to expel their invaders, while the protector was employed in re-establishing his authority, and quelling domestic insurrections. His brother, lord Seymour, a man of insatiable ambition, had married the queen-dowager, and openly aspired at the government of the kingdom. In order to attain this object, he endeavoured to seduce the young king to his interests; found means to hold a private correspondence with him, and publicly decried the protector's administration. He had brought over to his party many of the principal nobility, together with some of the most popular persons of inferior rank; and he had provided arms for ten thousand men, whom it was computed he could muster from among his own domestics and retainers [2].

A.D. 1548.

Though apprised of all these alarming circumstances, Somerset showed no inclination to proceed to extremities. He endeavoured by the most friendly expedients, by reason, entreaty, and even by loading Seymour with new favours, to make him desist from such dangerous politics. But finding all his endeavours ineffectual, he began to think of more serious remedies: and the earl of Warwick, who hoped to raise his fortune on the ruin of both,

---

[1] Patten.—Holinshed.   [2] State Papers published by Haynes, p. 105, 106.

A.D. inflamed the quarrel between the brothers.   By his ad-
1549. vice lord Seymour was committed to the Tower, attainted
of high treason, condemned, and executed [1].

The protector had now leisure to complete the Reformation,
which was the chief object of concern throughout the nation.   A
committee of bishops and divines had been appointed by the
privy council to compose a liturgy; they had executed the work
committed to them, as already observed, with judgment and
moderation : and they not unreasonably flattered themselves,
that they had framed a service in which every denomination of
Christians might concur.   This form of worship, nearly the
same with that which is at present authorised by law, was established by parliament in all the churches, and uniformity was
ordered to be observed in all the ceremonies [2].

Thus, my dear Philip, in the course of a few years, was the
Reformation happily completed in England ; and its civil and
religious consequences have since been deservedly valued.   But
there is no abuse in society so great as to be destitute of some
advantages ; and in the beginnings of innovation the loss of
those advantages is always sensibly felt by the bulk of a nation,
before it can perceive the benefits resulting from the desirable
change.

No institution can be imagined less favourable to the interests
of mankind than that of the monastic life ; yet was it followed
by some effects which, having ceased at the suppression of monasteries, were much regretted by the people of England.   The
monks, by always residing at their convents, in the centre of
their estates, spent their money in the country, and afforded a
ready market for commodities.   They were also acknowledged
to have been in England, what they still are in kingdoms where
the Romish religion is established, the best and most indulgent
landlords ; being restricted by the rules of their order to a certain
mode of living, and consequently having fewer motives for ex-
tortion than other men.   The abbots and priors were besides
accustomed to grant leases at an under value, and to receive a
present in return.   But the abbey-lands fell under different
management, when distributed among the principal nobility and
gentry ; the rents of farms were raised, while the tenants found
not the same facility in disposing of the produce.   The money
was often spent in the capital ; and, to increase the evil, pas-

---

[1] Burnet, vol. ii.   [2] Stat. 2 & 3 Edw. VI. cap. i.

turage in that age being found more profitable than tillage, whole estates were laid waste by inclosure. The farmers, regarded as an useless burthen, were expelled from their habitations; and the cottagers, deprived even of the commons, on which they had formerly fed their cattle, were reduced to beggary [1].

These grievances of the common people occasioned insurrections in several parts of England; and Somerset, who loved popularity, imprudently encouraged them, by endeavouring to afford that redress which was not in his power. Tranquillity, however, was soon restored to the kingdom by the vigilance of lord Russel and the earl of Warwick, who slew many of the unhappy malcontents, and dispersed the rest. But the protector never recovered his authority. The nobility and gentry were in general displeased with the preference which he seemed to have given to the people; and as they ascribed all the insults which they had suffered during the insurrections to his procrastination, and to the countenance shown to the multitude, they apprehended a renewal of the same disorders from his passion for popular fame. His enemies even attempted to turn the rage of the populace against him, by working upon the lower class among the Catholics; and having gained over to their party the mayor of London, the lieutenant of the Tower, and many of the great officers of state, they obliged Somerset to resign the protectorship, and committed him to custody. A council of regency was formed, in which the earl of Warwick, who had conducted this revolution, bore the chief sway; and he actually governed the kingdom without the invidious title of protector [2].

The first act of Warwick's administration was the negotiation of a treaty of peace with France and with Scotland. Henry II. had taken advantage of the disturbances in A.D. 1550. England to recover several places in the Boulonnois, and even to lay siege, though without effect, to Boulogne itself. He now took advantage, in treating, of the state of the English court. Sensible of the importance of peace to Warwick and his party, he refused to pay the two millions of crowns which his predecessor had acknowledged to be due to the crown of England, as arrears of former stipulations. He would never consent, he said, to render himself tributary to any prince, alluding to the reversion of annual payments demanded; but he offered a large

---

[1] Strype, vol. ii.　　　　[2] Stow.—Burnet.

sum for the immediate restitution of Boulogne and its territory. Four hundred thousand crowns were agreed on as the equivalent. Scotland was comprehended in this treaty. The English stipulated to restore some fortresses, which they still held in that kingdom [1].

Having thus established his administration, freed the kingdom from all foreign danger, and gained partisans, who were disposed to second him in every domestic enterprise, the earl of Warwick began to think of carrying into execution those vast projects which he had formed for his own aggrandisement. The last earl of Northumberland had died without issue; and as his brother, sir Thomas Percy, had been attainted on account of the share which he took in the Yorkshire insurrection during the late reign, the title was at present extinct, and the estate was vested in the crown. Warwick procured for himself a grant of that A.D. large estate, which lay chiefly in the North, the most 1551. warlike part of the kingdom; and he was dignified with the title of duke of Northumberland. This was a great step; but there was yet a strong bar in the way of his ambition. Somerset, though degraded, and lessened in the public esteem in consequence of his spiritless conduct, continued to possess a considerable share of popularity. Northumberland, therefore, resolved to ruin that unfortunate peer. For this purpose, he employed his emissaries to suggest desperate projects to the A.D. duke, and afterwards accused him of high treason for 1552. seeming to acquiesce in them. Somerset was tried, condemned, and executed on Tower-hill; and four of his friends shared the same unjust and unhappy fate. His death was sincerely lamented by the people, who regarded him as a martyr in their cause. Many of them dipped their handkerchiefs in his blood, which they long preserved as precious relics [2].

The duke of Northumberland might seem to have now attained the highest point of elevation to which a subject could aspire, and the greatest degree of power. His rank was second only to that of the royal family, his estate was one of the largest in the kingdom, and the government was entirely under his direction. But he aimed at yet greater power and consequence: his ambition knew no bounds. Having procured a parliament, which ratified his most despotic measures, and regulated its proceedings according to his will, he endeavoured to ingratiate himself more particularly with the young king, by manifesting an un-

---

[1] Rymer, vol. xv.   [2] Hayward's Life of Edward VI.—Holinshed.

common zeal for the reformed religion; to which the opening mind of Edward was warmly devoted, and the interests of which more sensibly touched him than all other objects.

In his frequent conversations on this subject, Northumberland took occasion to represent to that pious prince, whose A.D. health began visibly to decline, the danger to which the 1553. Reformation would be exposed, should his sister Mary, a bigoted Catholic, succeed to the throne of England; that, although no such objection lay against the princess Elizabeth, he could not, with any degree of propriety, exclude one sister, without also excluding the other; that both had been declared illegitimate by parliament; that the queen of Scotland was excluded by the late king's will, and was besides attached to the church of Rome; that these princesses being set aside for such solid reasons, the succession devolved on the marchioness of Dorset, eldest daughter of Charles Brandon, duke of Suffolk, and the French queen, Henry the Eighth's youngest sister; and that the apparent successor to the marchioness was her daughter, lady Jane Grey, who was every way worthy of a crown.

These arguments made a deep impression upon the mind of Edward. He had long lamented the obstinacy of his sister Mary in adhering to the Romish communion, and seemed to foresee all the horrors of her reign. He respected and even loved Elizabeth. But lady Jane Grey, being of the same age, had been educated with him, and had commanded his esteem and admiration by the progress which she made in every branch of literature. He had enjoyed full opportunity of becoming acquainted with the purity of her religious principles, a circumstance that weighed with him above every other consideration in the choice of a successor; and it also seems probable, that her elegant person and amiable disposition had inspired his heart with a tender affection. He therefore listened to the proposal of disinheriting his sisters with a patience which would otherwise have been highly criminal.

In the present languishing state of the king's health, after all the arguments that had been used, it was not a very difficult matter to obtain a deed from him in favour of lady Jane, whom the duke had married to his fourth son, lord Guildford Dudley. Greater opposition arose from the judges, and other persons necessary to the execution of such a deed. But they, at last, were all silenced, either by threats or promises; and the great seal was affixed to the king's letters patent, settling the crown on the heirs of the marchioness of Dorset, then duchess of Suffolk, she herself being content to give place to her daughters, or, in other words, to lady Jane.

The king died soon after this singular transaction; and so much the sooner by being put into the hands of an igno- rant woman, who undertook to restore him, in a little time, to his former state of health. Most of our historians, but especially such as were well affected to the reformation, dwell with peculiar pleasure on the excellent qualities of this young prince, whom (as an elegant writer observes) the flattering pro- mises of hope, joined to many real virtues, had made an object of fond regard to the public; and if we make allowance for the delicacy of his frame, and the manners of the age in which he lived, he seems to have possessed all the accomplishments that could be expected in a youth of fifteen.

July 6.

Aware of the opposition that would be made to the concerted change in the succession, Northumberland had carefully con- cealed the destination of the crown signed by Edward. He even kept that prince's death secret for a while, in hope of getting the two princesses into his power. With this view, he engaged the council to desire their attendance at court, under pretence that the king's infirm state of health required the assistance of their advice, and the consolation of their company. They in- stantly left their several retreats in the country, and set out for London; but happily, before their arrival, they gained intelli- gence of their brother's death, and of the conspiracy formed against themselves. Mary, who had advanced as far as Hoddes- don when she received this notice, made haste to retire, and wrote letters to the nobility and most considerable gentry in every county of England, commanding them to assist her in the defence of her crown and person [1].

Farther dissimulation, Northumberland now saw, would be fruitless; he therefore went to Sion-house, where lady Jane Grey resided, accompanied by a body of the nobles, and, ap- proaching her with the respect usually paid to the sovereign, informed her of her elevation to the throne. Lady Jane, who was in a great measure ignorant of the intrigues of her father-in- law, received this information with equal grief and surprise. She even refused to accept the crown; pleaded the preferable title of the two princesses; expressed her dread of the consequences attending an enterprise so dangerous and so criminal, and begged to remain in that private station in which she was born. Her

---

[1] Burnet.—Fox.

heart, full of the passion for literature and the elegant arts, and of affection for her husband, who was worthy of all her regard, had never opened itself to the flattering allurements of ambition. Subdued, however, by the entreaties, rather than the reasons of her relatives, she submitted to their will; and the duke immediately conveyed her to London, where she was proclaimed queen, but without one applauding voice. The people heard the proclamation with silence and concern; the very preachers employed their eloquence in vain to convince their auditors of the justice of lady Jane's title. Respect for the royal line, and indignation against the Dudleys, were stronger, even in the breasts of Protestants, than the dread of popery [1].

When Mary appeared in Suffolk, the inhabitants resorted to her in crowds; and when she assured them that she did not intend to alter the laws of Edward VI. concerning religion, they zealously enlisted themselves in her cause. The nobility and gentry daily flocked to her with reinforcements. Sir Edward Hastings, brother to the earl of Huntingdon, carried over to her four thousand men, levied for the support of her rival. The fleet declared for her. Even the duke of Suffolk, who commanded in the Tower, finding resistance fruitless, opened the gates of the fortress; and lady Jane, after the vain pageantry of wearing a crown during nine days, returned without a sigh to the privacy of domestic life. The council ordered Mary to be proclaimed; and Northumberland, deserted by his followers, and despairing of success, complied with that order with exterior marks of joy and satisfaction. He was brought to trial, however, condemned, and beheaded, for high treason. Sentence was also pronounced against lady Jane Grey, and lord Guildford Dudley, but they were respited on account of their youth, neither of them having attained the age of seventeen [2].

No sooner had Mary ascended the throne than a total change of men and measures took place. They who had languished in confinement were lifted to the helm of power, and entrusted with the government of the church as well as of the state. Gardiner, Bonner, and other Catholic bishops, were restored to their sees, and admitted to the queen's favour and confidence; while the most eminent Protestant prelates and zealous reformers, Ridley, Hooper, Latimer, Coverdale, and Cranmer, were thrown into prison. The men of Suffolk were browbeaten,

[1] Burnet.—Fox.—Heylin.   [2] Heylin.—Burnet.

because they presumed to plead the queen's promise of maintaining the reformed religion; and one, more bold than the rest, for recalling to her memory the engagements into which she had entered when they enlisted themselves in her service, was exposed in the pillory. A parliament was procured entirely conformable to the sentiments of the court, and a bill passed declaring the queen to be legitimate; ratifying the marriage of Henry VIII. with Catharine of Arragon, and annulling the divorce pronounced by Cranmer. All the statutes of Edward VI. respecting religion were repealed; and the queen sent assurances to the pope of her earnest desire of reconciling herself and her kingdoms to the Holy See, and requested that cardinal Pole might be appointed legate for the performance of that pious office [1].

Reginald Pole was descended from the royal family of England, being grandson of George duke of Clarence. He gave early indications of that fine genius, and generous disposition, by which he was so much distinguished during his more advanced age; and Henry VIII., having conceived a great friendship for him, proposed to raise him to the highest ecclesiastical dignities. As a pledge of future favours, Henry conferred on him the deanery of Exeter, the better to support him in his education. But when that monarch was at variance with the court of Rome, Pole refused to second his measures, and even wrote against him in a treatise on the *Unity of the Church*. This performance produced an irreparable breach between the young ecclesiastic and his sovereign, and blasted all Pole's hopes of rising in the English church. He was not, however, allowed to sink. The pope and the emperor thought themselves bound to provide for a man of such eminence, who, in support of their cause, had sacrificed all his pretensions to fortune in his own country. Pole was created a cardinal, and sent legate into Flanders. But he took no higher than deacon's orders, which did not condemn him to celibacy; and he was suspected of having aspired to the English crown, by means of a marriage with the princess Mary, during the life of her father. The marquis of Exeter, lord Montacute, the cardinal's brother, and several other persons of rank, suffered for this conspiracy, whether real or pretended. To hold a correspondence with that obnoxious fugitive was deemed sufficient guilt. It was enough, at least,

---

[1] Burnet, vol. ii.

to expose them to the indignation of Henry; and his will, on many occasions, is known to have usurped the place both of law and equity.

But whatever doubt may remain of Pole's intrigues for obtaining the crown of England, through an alliance with Mary, it is certain that she was no sooner seated upon the throne than she thought of making him the partner of her sway. The cardinal, however, being now in the decline of life, was represented to the queen as unqualified for the bustle of a court, and the fatigues of business. She therefore relinquished all thoughts of him as a husband; but, as she entertained a high esteem for his wisdom and virtue, she still proposed to reap the benefit of his counsels in the administration of the realm;—and hence arose her request to the pope.

This alliance, and one with the earl of Devonshire, being rejected for various reasons, the queen turned her eye toward the house of Austria, and there found a ready correspondence with her views. The ambitious Charles no sooner had heard of the accession of his kinswoman Mary to the crown of England, than he formed the scheme of obtaining the kingdom for his son Philip; hoping by that acquisition to balance the losses he had sustained in Germany: and Philip, although eleven years younger than Mary, who was destitute of every external beauty or grace, gave his consent without hesitation to the match proposed by his father. The emperor, therefore, immediately sent over an agent to signify his intentions to the queen of England; who, flattered with the prospect of marrying the presumptive heir of the greatest monarch in Europe, pleased with the support of so powerful an alliance, and happy to unite herself more closely to her mother's family, to which she had always been warmly attached, gladly embraced the proposal. The earls of Norfolk and Arundel, lord Paget, and bishop Gardiner, then prime-minister, finding how Mary's inclinations leaned, gave their opinion in favour of the Spanish alliance; but as they were sensible that the prospect of it diffused general apprehension and terror for the liberty and independence of the kingdom, the articles of marriage were drawn up with all possible attention to the interest and security, and even to the grandeur of England. The emperor agreed to whatever was thought A.D. necessary to soothe the fears of the people, or quiet the 1554. jealousies of the nobility. The chief articles were, that Philip, during his marriage with Mary, should bear the title of king, but that the administration should be vested solely in the queen;

that no foreigner should be capable of holding any office in the kingdom; that no innovation should be made in the English laws, customs, or privileges; that Philip should not carry the queen abroad without her consent, nor any of her children, without the consent of the nobility; that the male issue of the marriage should inherit, together with England, Burgundy and the Low Countries; that if Don Carlos, Philip's son by a former marriage, should die without issue, Mary's issue, whether male or female, should succeed to the crown of Spain, and all the emperor's hereditary dominions; and that Philip, if the queen should die before him without issue, should leave the crown of England to the lawful heir, without claiming any right of administration whatsoever[1].

But this treaty, though framed with so much caution and skill, was far from reconciling the English nation to the Spanish alliance. It was properly observed, that the emperor, in order to get possession of England, would agree to any terms; and that the more favourable were the conditions which he had granted, the more certainly might it be concluded he had no serious intention of observing them. His general character was urged in support of these observations; and it was added, that Philip, while he inherited his father's vices, fraud, and ambition, united to them more dangerous vices of his own, sullen pride and barbarity. England seemed already a province of Spain, groaning under the load of despotism, and subjected to all the horrors of the inquisition. The people were every where ripe for rebellion, and wanted only an able leader to have subverted the queen's authority. No such leader appeared. The more prudent part of the nobility thought it would be soon enough to correct ills when they began to be felt. Some turbulent spirits, however, judged it more safe to prevent than to redress grievances. They accordingly formed a conspiracy to rise in arms, and declare against the queen's marriage with Philip. Sir Thomas Wyat proposed to raise Kent; sir Peter Carew, Devonshire; and the duke of Suffolk was engaged, by the hope of recovering the crown for his daughter, to attempt raising the midland counties. But these conspirators, imprudently breaking concert, and rising at different times, were soon humbled. Wyat and Suffolk lost their heads, as did lady Jane Grey and her husband, to whom the duke's guilt was imputed.

This fond and unfortunate couple died with much piety and

[1] Rymer, vol. xv.—Burnet, vol. ii.

fortitude.   It had been intended to execute them on the Feb. 12.
same scaffold on Tower-hill; but the council, dreading
the compassion of the people for their youth, beauty, and innocence, changed its orders, and gave directions that lady Jane
should be beheaded within the verge of the Tower.   She refused
to take leave of her husband on the day of their execution;
assigning as a reason, that the tenderness of parting might un-
bend their minds from that firmness which their approaching
doom required of them.   " Our separation," added she, " will
be but for a moment; we shall soon rejoin each other in a scene
where our affections will be for ever united, and where death,
disappointment, and misfortune, can no longer disturb our felicity[1]."   She saw lord Guildford led to execution, without discovering any sign of weakness.   She even calmly met his headless
body, as she was going to execution herself, and intrepidly desired to proceed to the fatal spot, emboldened by the report
which she had received of the magnanimity of his behaviour.
On that occasion she wrote in her table-book three sentences;
one in Greek, one in Latin, and one in English.   The meaning
was, that although human justice was against her husband's
body, divine mercy would be favourable to his soul; that if her
fault deserved punishment, her youth and inexperience ought to
plead her excuse; and that God and posterity, she trusted,
would show her favour.   On the scaffold she behaved with great
mildness and composure, and submitted herself to the stroke of
the executioner with a steady and serene countenance[2].

The queen's authority was considerably strengthened by the
suppression of this rebellion; and the arrival of Philip in England gave still greater stability to her government.   For although
that prince's behaviour was ill calculated to remove the prejudices which the English nation had entertained against him,
being distant in his address, and so intrenched in form and ceremony as to be in a manner inaccessible, his liberality, if money
disbursed for the purposes of corruption can deserve that name,
procured him many friends among the nobility and gentry.   Cardinal Pole also arrived in England about the same time, with
legatine powers from the pope; and both houses of parliament
voted an address to Philip and Mary, acknowledging that the
nation had been guilty of a most horrible defection from the
true church; declaring their resolution to repeal all laws enacted
in prejudice to the Romish religion; and praying their majesties

[1] Heylin, p. 167.—Fox, vol. iii.   [2] Id. ibid.

(happily uninfected with that criminal schism!) to intercede with the Holy Father for the absolution and forgiveness of their penitent subjects. The request was readily granted. The legate, in the name of his holiness, gave the parliament and kingdom absolution, freed them from ecclesiastical censures, and received them again into the bosom of the church[1].

In consequence of this reconciliation with the see of Rome, the punishment by fire, that dreadful expedient of super- A.D. stition for extending her empire and preserving her 1555. dominion, was rigorously employed against the most eminent reformers. The mild councils of cardinal Pole, who was inclined to toleration, were overruled by Gardiner and Bonner; and many persons of all conditions, both sexes, and various ages, were committed to the flames. The persecutors made their first attack upon Rogers, prebendary of St. Paul's; a man equally distinguished by his piety and learning, but whose domestic situation, it was hoped, would bring him to compliance. He had a wife whom he tenderly loved, and ten children; yet did he continue firm in his principles; and such was his serenity after condemnation, that the gaolers, it is said, waked him from a sound sleep, when the hour of his execution approached. He suffered in Smithfield. Hooper, bishop of Gloucester, was condemned at the same time with Rogers, but was sent to his own diocese to be punished, in order to strike the greater terror into his flock. The constancy of his death, however, had a very contrary effect. It was a scene of consolation to Hooper to die in their sight, bearing testimony to that doctrine which he had formerly taught among them. He continued to exhort them, till his tongue, swollen by the violence of his agony, denied him utterance: and his words were long remembered[2].

Ferrar, bishop of St. David's, also suffered this terrible punishment, in his own diocese. And Ridley and Latimer, who had been bishops of London and Worcester, two prelates venerable by their years, their learning, and their piety, perished in the same fire at Oxford, supporting each other's constancy by their mutual exhortations. Latimer, when tied to the stake, called to his companion, "Be of good cheer, my brother! We shall this day kindle such a flame in England, as, I trust in God, will never be extinguished[3]."

Sanders, a respectable clergyman, was committed to the flames

[1] Burnet, vol. ii.—Fox, vol. iii.   [2] Id. ibid.
                         [3] Id. ibid.

at Coventry. A pardon was offered him if he would recant: but he rejected it with disdain, and embraced the stake, saying, " Welcome, cross of Christ! welcome, everlasting life!" Cranmer had less courage at first. Overawed by the prospect of those tortures which awaited him, or overcome by the fond love of life, and by the flattery of artful men, who pompously represented the dignities to which his character still entitled him, if he would merit them by a recantation, he agreed, in an unguarded hour, to subscribe the doctrines of the papal supremacy and the real presence. But Mary and her council, no less perfidious than cruel, determined that this recantation should not avail him ; that he should acknowledge his errors in the church before the people, and afterward be led to execution. He soon repented, however, of his weakness, and surprised the audience by a declaration very different from that which was expected from him. After explaining his sense of what he owed to God and his sovereign, " There is one miscarriage in my life," said he, " of which above all others, I severely repent—the insincere declaration of faith which I had the weakness to subscribe ; but I take this opportunity of atoning for my error by a sincere and open recantation, and am willing to seal with my blood that doctrine which I firmly believe to have been communicated from Heaven."

As his hand had erred, by betraying his heart, he resolved that it should first be punished by a severe but just doom. He accordingly stretched out his arm, as soon as he came to the stake ; and without discovering, either by his looks or motions, the least sign of compunction, or even of feeling, he held his right hand in the flames, till it was utterly consumed. His thoughts appeared to be totally occupied in reflecting on his former fault ; and he called aloud several times, " This hand has offended!" When it dropped off, he discovered a serenity in his countenance, as if satisfied with sacrificing to Divine justice the instrument of his crime ; and when the fire attacked his body, his soul, wholly collected within itself, seemed fortified against every external accident, and altogether inaccessible to pain [1].

It would be endless, my dear Philip, to enumerate all the cruelties practised in England during this bigoted reign, near three hundred persons having been brought to the stake in the

[1] Fox, vol. iii.—Burnet, vol. ii.

first rage of persecution.   Besides, the savage barbarity on one hand, and the patient constancy on the other, are so similar, in all those martyrdoms, that a narration, very little agreeable in itself, would become altogether disgusting by its uniformity.   It is sufficient to have mentioned the sufferings of our most eminent reformers, whose character and condition make such notice necessary.   I shall therefore conclude this subject with observing, that human nature appears on no occasion so detestable, and at the same time so absurd, as in these religious horrors, which sink mankind below infernal spirits in wickedness, and beneath the brutes in folly.   Bishop Bonner seemed to rejoice in the torments of the victims of persecution.   He sometimes whipped the Protestant prisoners with his own hands, till he was tired with the violence of the exercise : he tore out the beard of a weaver who refused to relinquish his religion, and, in order to give the obstinate heretic a more sensible idea of burning, he held his finger to the candle, till the sinews and veins shrank and burst [1]. All these examples prove that no human depravity can equal revenge and cruelty, inflamed by theological hate.

But the members of the English parliament, though so obsequious to the queen's will in re-uniting the kingdom to the see of Rome, and in authorising the murder of their fellow-subjects who rejected the Catholic faith, had still some regard left both to their own and the national interest.   They refused to restore the possessions of the church ; they would not declare her husband presumptive heir to the crown, or vest the administration in his hands ; and she could not even procure their consent to his coronation.

The queen likewise met with long opposition from parliament in another favourite measure ; namely, in an attempt to engage the nation in a war which was kindled betwen France and Spain. The motion was suspended ; and Philip, disgusted with Mary's importunate love, which was equal to that of a girl of eighteen, and with her jealousy and spleen, which increased with her declining years and her despair of having issue, had gone over to his father in Flanders.   The voluntary resignation of the emperor, soon after this visit, put Philip in possession of the wealth of America, and of the richest and most extensive dominions in Europe.   He did not, however, lay aside his attention to the affairs of England, of which he still hoped to have the direction ;

---

[1] Fox, vol. iii.

and he came over to London, in order to support his A.D.
parliamentary friends in a new motion for a French war. 1557.
This measure was zealously opposed by several of the queen's
most able counsellors, and particularly by cardinal Pole, who,
having taken priest's orders, had been installed in the see of
Canterbury on the death of Cranmer. But hostilities having
commenced in France, as was pretended, war was at last denounced against that kingdom ; and ten thousand men were sent
over to the Low Countries, under the command of the earl of
Pembroke [1].

An attempt was made in Scotland by the French monarch to
engage that kingdom in a war with England. Mary of Guise,
the queen dowager, had obtained the regency through the intrigues of the court of France; and Henry II. now requested
her to take part in the common quarrel. She accordingly summoned a convention of the states, and asked their concurrence
for a war with England. But the Scottish nobles, who had become as jealous of the French as the English were of Spanish
influence, refused their assent: and the regent had in vain recourse
to stratagem, in order to accomplish her purpose.

The French monarch, however, without the assistance of his
ancient allies, and notwithstanding the unfortunate battle of St.
Quintin, of which I shall afterward have occasion to speak, made
himself master of Calais, which the English had possessed above
two hundred years ; and which, as it opened to them an easy and
secure entry into the heart of France, was regarded as the most
valuable foreign territory belonging to the crown. This important
place was recovered by the vigilance and valour of the duke of
Guise ; who, informed that the English, trusting to the strength
of the town, deemed in that age impregnable, were accustomed
to recall, towards the close of summer, great part of the garrison,
and replace it in the spring, undertook the enterprise in the
depth of winter. As he knew that success depended upon A.D.
celerity, he pushed his attacks with such vigour, that 1558.
the governor was obliged to surrender on the eighth day of
the siege [2].

The joy of the French on this occasion was extreme. Their
vanity indulged itself in the utmost exultation of triumph, while
the English gave vent to all the passions which agitate a high-
spirited people, when any great national misfortune is evidently

---

[1] Burnet, vol. ii.—Strype, vol. ii.   [2] Thuan. lib. xx. cap. ii.

the consequence of the misconduct of their rulers. They murmured loudly against the queen and her council, who, after engaging the nation in a fruitless war, for the sake of foreign interest, had thus exposed it, by their negligence, to so severe a disgrace.

This event, with the consciousness of being hated by her subjects, and despised by her husband, so much affected the queen of England, whose health had long been declining, that she fell Nov. 17. into a low fever, which put an end to her short and inglorious reign. "When I am dead," said she to her attendants, "you will find Calais at my heart." Mary possessed few qualities either estimable or amiable. Her person was as little engaging as her manners; and amidst that complication of vices which entered into her composition, namely, obstinacy, bigotry, violence, and cruelty, we scarcely find any virtue but sincerity.

Before the queen's death, negotiations had been opened for a general peace. Among other conditions, the king of France demanded the restitution of Navarre to its lawful owner; the king of Spain, that of Calais and its territory to England. But the death of Mary somewhat altered the firmness of the Spanish monarch in regard to that capital article. And before I speak of the treaty which was afterwards signed at Château Cambresis, and which restored tranquillity to Europe, I must carry forward the affairs of the continent. In the mean while, it will be proper to say a few words of the princess Elizabeth, who now succeeded to the throne of England.

The majority of the English were under great apprehensions for the life of this princess, during her sister's whole reign. The attachment of Elizabeth to the reformed religion offended Mary's bigotry; and menaces had been employed to bring her to a recantation. The violent hatred which the queen entertained against her broke out on every occasion; and all her own distinguished prudence was necessary, in order to prevent the fatal effects of it. She retired into the country; and knowing that she was surrounded by spies, she passed her time chiefly in reading and study. She complied with the established mode of worship, and eluded all questions in regard to religion. When asked, on purpose to gather her opinion of the *real presence*, what she thought of these words of Christ, "This is my body,"— and whether she believed it the *true* body of Christ, that was in the sacrament of the Lord's supper,—she replied thus:

> " Christ was the word that spake it ;
> He took the bread and brake it ;
> And what the word did make it,
> That I believe and take it [1]."

After the death of her sister, Elizabeth delivered her sentiments more freely ; and an early act of her administration was
the re-establishment of the Protestant religion.　The liturgy
was again introduced in the English tongue, and the oath　A.D.
of supremacy was tendered to the　clergy.　The number　1559.
of bishops had been reduced to fourteen, by a sickly season
which preceded this change ; and all these (except the bishop of
Llandaff,) having refused compliance, were deprived of their sees.
But of the great body of the English clergy, only eighty rectors
and vicars, fifty prebendaries, fifteen heads of colleges, twelve
archdeacons, and as many deans, sacrificed their livings for their
theological opinions [2].

This change in religion completed the joy of the people on
account of the accession of Elizabeth ; the auspicious commencement of whose reign may be said to have prognosticated that
felicity and glory which uniformly attended it.　These particulars,
my dear Philip, will make all retrospect in the affairs of England
unnecessary, beyond the treaty of Château Cambresis.

LETTER LXV.

*View of the Continent of Europe, from the Treaty of Passau, in
1552, to the Peace of Château Cambresis, in 1559.*

THE negotiations at Passau were no sooner completed, than
Maurice, the deliverer of Germany, marched into Hungary
against the Turks, at the head of twenty thousand men, in
consequence of his engagements with Ferdinand, whom　A.D.
the hopes of such assistance had rendered a zealous　1552.
advocate of the confederates.　But the vast superiority of the
Turkish armies, together with the dissensions between Maurice
and Castaldo, the Austrian general, who was piqued at being

---

[1] Strype.—Camden.　　　　　[2] Id. Ibid.

superseded in the command, prevented the elector from perform-ing, on this occasion, any exploits worthy of his former fame, or of much benefit to the Romans.

In the mean time Charles V., deeply affected by the loss of Metz, Toul, and Verdun, which had formed the barrier of the empire on the side of France, and would now secure the frontier of Champagne, left his inglorious retreat at Villach, and put himself at the head of those forces which he had assembled against the confederates, for the recovery of the three bishoprics. To conceal the destination of his army, he circulated a report that he intended to lead it into Hungary, to second Maurice in his operations against the infidels ; and as that pretext failed him, when he began to approach the Rhine, he pretended that he was marching first to chastise Albert of Brandenburg, who had refused to be included in the treaty of Passau, and whose cruel exactions in that part of Germany called loudly for redress.

The French, however, were not deceived by these artifices. Their sovereign immediately guessed the true object of the emperor's armament, and resolved to defend his conquest with vigour. The defence of Metz, against which it was foreseen the chief weight of the war would be turned, was committed to Francis of Lorrain, duke of Guise, who possessed in an eminent degree all the qualities that render men great in military com-mand. To courage, sagacity, fortitude, and presence of mind, he added that magnanimity which delights in bold enterprises, and aspires after fame by splendid and extraordinary actions. He repaired with joy to the dangerous station ; and many of the French nobility, and even princes of the blood, eager to dis-tinguish themselves under such a leader, entered Metz as volun-teers. They were all necessary. The city was of great extent, ill fortified ; and the suburbs were large. For these incon-veniences the duke endeavoured to provide a remedy. He re-paired the old fortifications with all possible expedition, labour-ing with his own hands : the officers imitated his example ; and the soldiers, thus encouraged, cheerfully submitted to the most severe toils. He erected new works, and levelled the suburbs with the ground. At the same time he filled the magazines with provisions and military stores, compelled all useless persons to leave the place, and laid waste the neighbouring country; yet such were his popular talents, and his power of acquiring an ascendant over the minds of men, that the citizens not only refrained from murmuring, but seconded him with no less ardour than the soldiers, in all his operations—in the ruin of their estates, and in the havoc of their public and private buildings [1].

Meanwhile the emperor continued his march toward Lorrain at the head of sixty thousand men. On his approach, Albert of Brandenburg, whose army did not exceed twenty thousand, withdrew into that duchy, as if he intended to join the French king; and Charles, though the winter was approaching, laid siege to Metz, contrary to the advice of his most experienced officers.

The attention, both of the besiegers and the besieged, was turned for a time to the motions of Albert, who still hovered in the neighbourhood, undetermined which side to take, though resolved to sell his services. Charles at last came up to his price, and he joined the imperial army. The emperor now flattered himself that nothing could resist his force, but he found himself deceived. After a siege of almost sixty days, during which he had attempted all that was thought possible for art or valour to effect, and had lost about thirty thousand men by the inclemency of the weather, diseases, or the sword of the enemy, he was obliged to abandon the enterprise. " Fortune," said Charles, " I now perceive, like other fine ladies, chooses to confer her favours on young men, and forsake those who are in the decline of life [2]."

This saying has been thought gallant, and perhaps it is so; but the occasion merited more serious reflections. When the French sallied out to attack the enemy's rear, a spectacle presented itself to their view, which extinguished at once all hostile rage, and melted them into compassion. The imperial camp was filled with the sick and wounded, with the dead and the dying. All the roads by which the army retired were strewed with the same miserable objects; who having made an effort beyond their strength to escape, and not being able to proceed, were left to perish without assistance. Happily, that, and all the kind offices which their friends had not the power to perform, they received from their enemies. The duke of Guise ordered that they should be supplied with every necessary. He appointed physicians to attend, and direct what treatment was proper for the sick and wounded, and what refreshments for the feeble: and such as recovered he sent home, under a safe escort, with money to bear their charges [3]. By these acts of humanity, less common in that age than in the present, the

---

[1] Thuan. lib. xi.   [2] Id. Ibid.
[3] Thuan. lib. vi.—Daniel, *Hist. de France*, tome iv.—Father Daniel's account of this siege is copied from the Journal of the Sieur de Salignac, who was present at it.

duke completed that heroic character which he had acquired by his brave and successful defence.

The emperor's misfortunes were not confined to Germany. During his residence at Villach he had been obliged to borrow two hundred thousand crowns from Cosmo of Medicis; and so low was his credit, that he was obliged to put that prince in possession of the territory of Piombino, as a security for the repayment of the money. By this step he lost the footing he had hitherto maintained in Tuscany; and, nearly at the same time he lost Sienna. The Siennese, who had long enjoyed a republican government, rose against the Spanish garrison, which they had admitted as a check upon the tyranny of the nobility, but which they now found was meant to enslave them. Forgetting their domestic animosities, they recalled the exiled nobles, demolished the citadel, and put themselves under the protection of France [1].

These unfortunate events were followed by the most alarming dangers. The severe administration of the viceroy of Naples had filled that kingdom with dissatisfaction. The prince of Salerno, the head of the malcontents, fled to the court of France. The French monarch, after the example of his father, had formed an alliance with the grand seignior; and Solyman, at that time highly incensed against the house of Austria, on account of the proceedings in Hungary, sent a powerful fleet into the Mediterranean, under the command of the corsair Dragut, an officer trained up under Barbarossa. Dragut appeared on the coast of Calabria, where he expected to be joined by a French squadron; but not meeting with it according to concert, he returned to Constantinople, after plundering and burning several places, and filling Naples with consternation [2].

While Charles, who had retired into the Low Countries, A.D. breathed vengeance against France, Germany was still 1553. disturbed by the restless ambition of Albert of Brandenburg; and as that prince obstinately continued his violences, notwithstanding a decree of the imperial chamber, a league was formed against him by the most powerful princes of the empire, of which Maurice was declared the head. This confederacy, however, wrought no change in the sentiments of Albert. As he knew that he could not resist so many princes if they had leisure to unite their forces, he marched directly against Maurice, whom he dreaded most, and hoped to crush before he could re-

---

[1] *Mém. de* Ribier.　　　　　　　　　[2] Id. ibid.

ceive support from his allies; but he found that prince ready for conflict.

These hostile chiefs, whose armies were nearly equal in number, met at Siverhausen, in the duchy of Lunen- July 9. burg. There an obstinate battle was fought, in which the combat long remained doubtful, each gaining ground upon the other alternately; but at last victory declared for Maurice. Albert's army fled in confusion, leaving four thousand men dead on the field, and their baggage and artillery in the hands of the enemy. But the allies bought their victory at a dear rate. Their best troops suffered greatly; several persons of distinction fell; and Maurice himself received a wound of which he died two days after, in the thirty-second year of his age. No prince, ancient or modern, ever perhaps discovered such deep political sagacity at so early a period of life. As he left only one daughter (afterwards married to the famous William, prince of Orange), John Frederic, the degraded elector, claimed the electoral dignity, and that part of his patrimonial estate of which he had been stripped during the Smalcaldic war; but the states of Saxony, forgetting the merits and sufferings of their former master, declared in favour of Augustus, Maurice's brother. The unfortunate, but magnanimous, John Frederic died soon after this disappointment, which he bore with his usual firmness[1]; and the electoral dignity is still possessed by the descendants of Augustus.

The consternation which Maurice's death occasioned among his troops prevented them from making a proper use of their victory; so that Albert, having re-assembled his broken forces, and made fresh levies, renewed his depredations with additional fury. But being defeated in a second battle Sept. 12. by Henry of Brunswick, who had taken the command of the allied army, he was driven from all his hereditary dominions, as well as from those which he had usurped; was subjected to the ban of the empire, and obliged to take refuge in France, where he lingered out a few years in indigence[2].

During these transactions in Germany, war was carried on in the Low Countries with considerable vigour. In the hope of effacing the stain which his military reputation had received before Metz, Charles laid siege to Terouenne; and the fortifications being out of repair, that important place was carried by

---

[1] Arnoldi *Vit. Maurit.*—Robertson's *Hist. Charles V.* book x.
[2] Id. ibid.

assault. Hesden also was invested and taken in the same manner. The king of France was too late in assembling his forces, to afford relief to either of those towns; and the emperor cautiously avoided an engagement during the remainder of the campaign.

The imperial arms were less successful in Italy. The viceroy of Naples failed in an attempt to recover Sienna; and the French not only established themselves more firmly in Tuscany, but conquered part of the island of Corsica. Nor did the affairs of the house of Austria wear a better aspect in Hungary during the course of this year. Isabella and her son appeared once more in Transylvania, at a time when the people were ready for revolt, in order to revenge the death of Martinuzzi, whose loss they had severely felt. Some noblemen of eminence declared in favour of the young king: and as the pasha of Belgrade, by Solyman's order, espoused his cause, the Austrians were obliged to abandon Transylvania to Isabella and the Turks [1].

To counterbalance these and other losses, the emperor, as has
A.D. been already related, concerted a marriage between his
1554. son Philip and Mary of England, in the hope of adding this kingdom to his other dominions. Meanwhile the war between Henry and Charles was carried on with various success in the Low Countries, and in Italy, much to the disadvantage of France. The French, under the command of Strozzi, a Florentine nobleman, were defeated in the battle of Marciano; and Sienna being reduced after a siege of ten months, the brave
A.D. inhabitants were again harassed by Spanish tyranny.
1555. Nearly at the same time a plot was formed by the Franciscans, but was discovered before it could be carried into execution, for betraying Metz to the imperialists. The father-guardian and twenty other monks received sentence of death on account of this conspiracy; but the guardian, before the time appointed for his execution, was murdered by his incensed accomplices, whom he had seduced from their allegiance, and six of the youngest were pardoned [2].

While war thus raged in Italy and the Low Countries, accompanied with all its train of miseries, and all the crimes to which ambition gives birth, Germany enjoyed such tranquillity as afforded the diet full leisure to confirm and perfect the plan of religious pacification agreed upon at Passau, and referred to the consideration of the next meeting of the Germanic body. For

---

[1] Thuan. lib. xv.   [2] Ibid.

this purpose a diet had been summoned to meet at Augsburg, soon after the conclusion of the treaty; but the commotions excited by Albert of Brandenburg, and the attention which Ferdinand was obliged to pay to the affairs of Hungary, had hitherto obstructed its deliberations. The following stipulations were at last settled, and formally published: " Such princes and cities as have declared their approbation of the Confession of Augsburg, shall be permitted to profess and exercise, without molestation, the doctrine and worship which it authorises: the popish ecclesiastics shall claim no spiritual jurisdictions in such cities or principalities, nor shall the Protestants molest the princes and states that adhere to the church of Rome: no attempt shall be made to terminate religious differences, except by the gentle and pacific methods of persuasion and conference: the supreme civil power in every state may establish what form of worship it shall deem proper, but shall permit those who refuse to conform to remove their effects: all who seized the benefices or revenues of the church, before the treaty of Passau, shall retain possession of them, and be subject to no persecution in the imperial chamber on that account; but if any prelate or ecclesiastic shall hereafter abandon the Romish religion, he shall instantly relinquish his diocese or benefice, and it shall be lawful for those in whom the right of nomination is vested to proceed immediately to an election, as in the case of death, or translation [1]."

These were the principal articles in the Recess of Augsburg, the basis of religious peace in Germany. The followers of Luther were highly pleased with the security which it afforded them, and the Catholics seem to have had no less reason to be satisfied. That article which preserved entire to the Romish church the benefices of such ecclesiastics as should hereafter renounce its doctrines, at once placed a barrier around its patrimony, and effectually guarded against the defection of its dignitaries. But cardinal Caraffa (who was now raised to the papal throne, under the name of Paul IV.), full of high ideas of his apostolic jurisdiction, and animated with the fiercest zeal against heresy, regarded the indulgence given to the Protestants, by an assembly composed of laymen, as an impious act of usurped power. He therefore threatened the emperor and the king of the Romans with the severest effects of his vengeance, if they did not immediately declare the Recess of Augsburg illegal and void; and as

[1] Father Paul, lib. v.—Pallavicini, lib. xiii.

Charles showed no disposition to comply with his demand, the pope entered into an alliance with the French king, in order to ruin the imperial power in Italy.

That negociation was depending, when an event occurred which astonished all Europe, and confounded the reasonings of the wisest politicians.   Charles, though only in his fifty-sixth year, an age when objects of ambition operate with full force on the mind, and are generally pursued with the greatest ardour, had for some time formed the resolution of resigning his hereditary dominions to his son Philip.   He now prepared to put it into execution.   Various have been the opinions of historians respecting the motives of this extraordinary determination; but the most probable seem to be, the disappointments which Charles had met with in his ambitious hopes, and the daily decline of his health.   He had early in life been attacked with the gout; and the fits had become so frequent and severe, that not only the vigour of his constitution was broken, but the faculties of his mind were sensibly impaired.   He therefore judged it more decent to conceal his infirmities in some solitude than to expose them to the public eye; and as he was unwilling to forfeit the fame, or lose the acquisitions of his better years, by attempting to guide the reins of government when he was no longer able to hold them with steadiness, he prudently resolved to seek in the tranquillity of retirement that happiness which he had in vain pursued amidst the tumults of war and the intrigues of state.

Having already ceded to Philip the kingdom of Naples and the duchy of Milan, he assembled the sates of the Netherlands at Brussels : and seating himself for the last time in the chair of state, he explained to his subjects the reasons of his resignation, and solemnly devolved his authority upon his son.   He recounted with dignity, but without ostentation, all his great enterprises; and that enumeration gives us the highest idea of his activity and industry.   " I have dedicated," observed he, " from the seventeenth year of my age, all my thoughts and attention to public objects, reserving no portion of my time for the indulgence of ease, and very little for the enjoyment of private pleasure.   Either in a pacific or hostile manner, I have visited Germany nine times; Spain six times; France four times; Italy seven times; the Low Countries ten times; England twice; Africa as often; and while my health permitted me to discharge the duties of a sovereign, and the vigour of my constitution was not unequal to the arduous office of governing such extensive dominions, I never shunned labour or repined under fatigue:

but now, when my health is broken, and my vigour exhausted by the rage of an incurable distemper, my growing infirmities admonish me to retire ; nor am I so fond of reigning as to retain the sceptre in an impotent hand which is no longer able to protect my subjects.

"Instead of a sovereign worn out with diseases," continued he, "and scarcely half alive, I give you one in the prime of life, already accustomed to govern, and who adds to the vigour of youth all the attention and sagacity of maturer years." Then turning towards Philip, who fell on his knees and kissed his father's hand, "It is in your power," said Charles, "by a wise and virtuous administration, to justify the extraordinary proof which I give this day of my paternal affection, and to demonstrate that you are worthy of the confidence which I repose in you. Preserve," added he, "an inviolable regard for religion ; maintain the Catholic faith in its purity ; let the laws of your country be sacred in your eyes ; encroach not on the rights of your people ; and if the time should ever come, when you shall wish to enjoy the tranquillity of private life, may you have a son to whom you can resign your sceptre with as much satisfaction as I give mine to you !" A few weeks after, the emperor also resigned to Philip the Spanish crown, with all the dominions depending upon it, in the Old as well as in the New World ; reserving nothing to himself, out of all those vast possessions, but an annual pension of one hundred thousand ducats[1].

Charles was now impatient to embark for Spain, where he had fixed on a place of retreat. But, by the advice of his physicians, he deferred his voyage for some months, on account of the severity of the season ; and, by yielding to their judgment, he had the satisfaction, before he left the Low Countries, of taking a considerable step towards a peace with France. Of this he was ardently desirous, not only on his son's account, whose administration he wished to commence in quietness, but that he might have the glory, when quitting the world, of restoring to Europe that tranquillity which his ambition had banished from it almost during his whole reign.

The great obstacle to such a pacification on the part of France, was a treaty which had been concluded with the court of Rome ; and the emperor's claims were too numerous to admit any hope of rapid adjustment. A truce of five years was therefore pro-

[1] Godlev. *Relat. Abdicat. Car. V.*—Thuan. lib. xvi.—Sandov. vol. ii.—Robertson, book ix.

posed by Charles, during which term, without discussing their respective pretensions, each should retain what was in his possession ; and Henry, through the persuasion of the constable Montmorency, who represented the imprudence of sacrificing the true interests of his kingdom to his rash engagements with the pope, authorised his ambassadors to sign at Vaucelles a treaty which would ensure to him, for so considerable a period, the important conquests which he had made on the German frontier, together with the greater part of the dominions of the duke of Savoy.

Paul IV., when informed of this transaction, was filled no less with terror and astonishment than with rage and indignation. But he took equal care to conceal his fear and his anger. He affected to be highly pleased with the truce ; and he offered his mediation as the common father of Christendom, for the adjustment of a permanent peace. Under this pretext, he dispatched cardinal Rebiba, as his nuncio, to the court of Brussels ; and his nephew, cardinal Caraffa, to that of Paris. The public instructions of both were the same ; but, Caraffa, besides these, received a private commission, to spare no entreaties, promises, or bribes, in order to induce the French monarch to renounce the truce, and renew his engagements with the court of Rome. He flattered Henry with a hope of the conquest of Naples : he gained to his interest, by his address, the Guises, the queen, and even the famous Diana of Poictiers, duchess of Valentinois, the king's mistress : and they easily swayed the king himself, who had already leaned to that side toward which they wished to incline him. All Montmorency's prudent remonstrances were disregarded. The nuncio, by powers from Rome, absolved Henry from his oath of truce ; and that rash prince signed a new treaty with the pope, which rekindled with fresh violence the flames of war, both in Italy and the Low Countries.

A.D. 1556.

No sooner was Paul acquainted with the success of this negotiation, than he proceeded to the most indecent extremities against Philip II. He ordered the Spanish ambassador to be imprisoned : he excommunicated the Colonnas, because of their attachment to the Imperial house ; and he declared that Philip was guilty of high treason, and had forfeited his right to the kingdom of Naples, which he was supposed to hold of the Holy See, for afterward affording them a retreat in his dominions[1].

Alarmed at a quarrel with the pope, whom he had been

---

[1] Pallav. lib. xiii.

taught to regard with the most superstitious veneration, as the vicegerent of Christ, and the common father of Christendom, Philip tried every gentle method before he made use of force. He even consulted some Spanish divines on the lawfulness of taking arms against a person so sacred. They decided in his favour, and Paul continuing inexorable, the duke of Alva, to whom the conduct of the negotiation as well as of the war had been committed, entered the ecclesiastical state at the head of ten thousand veterans, and carried terror to the gates of Rome.

The haughty pontiff, though still obstinate and undaunted himself, was forced to give way to the fears of the cardinals; and a truce was concluded for forty days. But, when the duke of Guise arrived with twenty thousand men, Paul be- A.D. came more arrogant than ever, and banished from his 1557. mind all thoughts except those of war and revenge. The duke, however, who is supposed to have given his voice for this war, chiefly from a desire of displaying his military talents, was able to perform nothing in Italy worthy of his former fame. He was obliged to abandon the siege of Civitella: he could not bring the duke of Alva to a general engagement; a multitude of his men perished by disease; and the pope neglected to furnish the necessary reinforcements. He requested to be recalled, and France stood in need of his abilities.

Philip, though willing to have avoided a rupture, was no sooner informed that Henry had violated the truce of Vaucelles, than he determined to act with such vigour as should convince all Europe that his father had not erred in resigning to him the reins of government. He immediately assembled in the Low Countries a body of fifteen thousand men: he obtained a supply of ten thousand from England, which he had engaged, as we have seen, in this quarrel; and not being ambitious of military fame, he gave the command of his army to Emanuel Philibert, duke of Savoy, one of the greatest generals of that warlike age.

The duke of Savoy kept the enemy for a time in utter ignorance of his destination. At length he seemed to threaten Champagne, toward which the French drew all their troops; a motion which he no sooner perceived, than turning suddenly to the right, he advanced by rapid marches into Picardy, and laid siege to St. Quintin. It was deemed in that age a place of considerable strength; but the fortifications had been neglected, and the garrison did not amount to a fifth part of the number requisite for its defence: it must therefore have surrendered in a few days, if the admiral de Coligny had not taken the gallant resolution of throwing himself into it with such a body of men as could be suddenly collected for that purpose. He effected his design in spite of the enemy, breaking through the main body with seven hundred horse, and two hundred foot. The town, however, was closely invested ; and Montmorency, anxious to extricate his nephew out of that perilous situation in which his zeal for the public good had engaged him, as well as to save a place of great importance, rashly advanced to its relief with forces inferior by one half to those of the enemy. He was totally defeated, and made prisoner[1].

The cautious temper of Philip, on this occasion, saved France from devastation, if not ruin. The duke of Savoy proposed to overlook all inferior objects, and march directly to Paris—of which, in its present consternation, he could not have failed to make himself master. But the Spanish monarch, afraid of the consequences of such a bold enterprise, desired him to continue the siege of St. Quintin, in order to secure a safe retreat, in case of any disastrous event. The town, long and gallantly defended by Coligny, was at last taken by storm ; but not before France was in a state of defence.

Philip was now sensible he had lost an opportunity, that could never be recalled, of distressing his enemy, and contented himself with reducing Ham and Catelet, two petty towns, which, with St. Quintin, were the sole fruits of one of the most complete victories gained in the sixteenth century. The Catholic king, however, continued in high exultation, on account of his success ; and as all his passions were tinged with superstition, he vowed to build a church, a monastery, and a palace, in honour of St. Laurence, on the day sacred to whose memory the battle of St. Quintin had been fought. He accordingly laid the foundation of an edifice in which all those buildings were included, and which he continued to forward, at a vast expense, for twenty-two years. The same principle that dictated the vow directed the construction of the fabric. It was so formed as to resemble a gridiron !—on which culinary instrument, according to the legendary tale, St. Laurence had suffered martyrdom[2]. Such, my dear Philip, is the origin of the famous Escurial, near Madrid, the royal residence of the kings of Spain.

The earliest account of the great blow which France had received at St. Quintin was carried to Rome by the courier

---

[1] Thuan. lib. xix.   [2] Colmenar, *Annal. d'Espagna*, vol. ii.

whom Henry had sent to recall the duke of Guise. Paul remonstrated warmly against the departure of the French army; but Guise's orders were peremptory. The arrogant pontiff, therefore, found it necessary to acommodate his conduct to the exigency of his affairs, and to employ the mediation of the Venetians, and of Cosmo of Medicis, in order to obtain peace from Spain. The first overtures to this purpose were easily listened to by the Catholic king, who still doubted the justice of his cause, and considered it as his greatest misfortune to be obliged to contend with the pope. Paul agreed to renounce his league with France; and Philip stipulated, on his part, that the duke of Alva should repair to Rome, and, after asking pardon of the holy father, in his own name, and in that of his master, for having invaded the patrimony of the church, should receive absolution for that crime!—Thus the pope, through the superstitous timidity of Philip, not only finished an unpropitious war without any detriment to the apostolic see, but saw his conqueror humbled at his feet; and so excessive was the veneration of the Spaniards in that age for the papal character, that the duke of Alva, the proudest man perhaps of his time, and acccustomed from his infancy to converse with princes, acknowledged, that, when he approached Paul, he was so much overawed, that his voice failed, and his presence of mind forsook him [1].

But although this war, which at its commencement threatened mighty revolutions, was terminated without occasioning any alteration in those states which were its immediate object, it produced effects of considerable consequence in other parts of Italy. In order to detach Octavio Farnese, duke of Parma, from the French interest, Philip restored to him the city of Placentia and its territory, which had been seized, as we have seen, by Charles V., and he granted to Cosmo of Medicis the investiture of Sienna, as an equivalent for the sums due to him [2].

By these treaties the balance of power among the Italian states, was poised more equally, and rendered less variable than it had been since it received the first violent shock from the invasion of Charles VIII.; and Italy henceforth ceased to be the theatre on which the sovereigns of Spain, France, and Germany, contended for fame and dominion. Their hostilities, excited by new objects, stained other regions of Europe with

[1] Pallav. lib. xiii.　　　[2] Thuan. lib. xviii.

blood, and made other states feel, in their turn, the calamities of war.

The duke of Guise, who left Rome the same day that his adversary the duke of Alva made his humiliating submission to the pope, was received in France as the guardian-angel of the kingdom. He was appointed commander-in-chief, with a jurisdiction almost unlimited; and, eager to justify the extraordinary confidence which the king had reposed in him, as well as to perform something suitable to the high expectations of his country-

A.D. 1558.

men, he undertook the siege of Calais. Of the complete success of that enterprise, and its different effects upon the English and French nations, we have already had occasion to take notice. The duke next invested Thionville, in the duchy of Luxembourg, one of the strongest towns on the frontier of the Netherlands, and forced it to capitulate after a siege of three weeks. But the advantages in this quarter were more than balanced by an event which happened in another part of the Low Countries. The marechal de Termes, governor of Calais, who had penetrated into Flanders, and taken Dunkirk, was totally routed near Gravelines by count Egmont, and made prisoner [1]. This disaster obliged the duke of Guise to relinquish all his other schemes, and hasten to the frontier of Picardy, that he might there oppose the progress of the enemy.

The eyes of France were now anxiously turned toward the operations of a general on whose arms victory had always attended, and on whose conduct, as well as good fortune, his countrymen could confide in every danger. Guise's strength was nearly equal to that of the duke of Savoy, each commanding about forty thousand men. They encamped at the distance of a few leagues from each other; and the French and Spanish monarchs having joined their respective armies, it was expected that, after the vicissitudes of war, a signal victory would at last determine which of the rivals would take the ascendant for the future in the affairs of Europe. But both princes, as if by agreement, stood on the defensive; neither of them discovering any inclination, though each had it in his power, to rest the decision of a point of such importance on the issue of a single battle.

During this state of inaction, peace began to be mentioned in each camp, and both Henry and Philip discovered an equal disposition to listen to any overture that tended to re-estab-

[1] Thuan. lib. xx.

lish it.   The private inclinations of both kings concurred
with their political interests and the wishes of their people.
Philip languished to return to Spain, the place of his nativity;
and peace only could enable him, either with decency or safety,
to quit the Low Countries.   Henry was no less desirous of
being freed from the avocations of war, that he might have
leisure to turn the whole force of his government to the suppression of the opinions of the reformers, which were spreading with
such rapidity in Paris and the other great towns, that the Protestants began to grow formidable to the established church.
Court intrigues conspired with these public and avowed motives
to hasten the negociation, and the abbey of Cercamp was fixed
on as the place of congress [1].

While Philip and Henry were making these advances toward
a treaty which restored tranquillity to Europe, Charles V.,
whose ambition had so long disturbed it, but who had been for
some time dead to all such pursuits, ended his days in the
monastery of St. Justus, in Estremadura, which he had chosen
as the place of his retreat.   It was seated in a valley of no great
extent, watered by a small brook, and surrounded by rising
grounds, covered with lofty trees.   In this solitude Charles
lived on a plan that would have suited a private gentleman of
moderate fortune.   His table was plain, his domestics few, and
his intercourse with them familiar.   Sometimes he cultivated
the plants in his garden with his own hands, sometimes rode out
to the neighbouring wood on a little horse, the only one which
he kept, attended by a single servant on foot; and when his
infirmities deprived him of these more active recreations, he
admitted a few gentlemen who resided near the monastery to visit
him, and entertained them as equals; or he employed himself
in studying the principles, and in framing curious works of
mechanism, of which he had always been remarkably fond, and
to which his genius was peculiarly turned.   But, however he
was engaged, or whatever might be the state of his health, he
always devoted a considerable portion of his time to religious
exercises.

In this manner, not unbecoming a man perfectly disengaged
from the affairs of the world, did Charles pass his time in retirement.   But, some months before his death, the gout, after a
longer intermission than usual, returned with a proportional increase of violence, and enfeebled both his body and mind to such

---

[1] Robertson's *Hist. Charles V.* book xii.

a degree as to leave no traces of that sound and masculine understanding which had distinguished him among his contemporaries. He sunk into a deep melancholy. An illiberal and timid superstition depressed his spirit. He lost all relish for amusements of every kind, and desired no other company than that of monks. With them he chanted the hymns of the missal, and conformed to all the rigours of monastic life, tearing his body with a whip, as an expiation for his sins! Not satisfied with these acts of mortification, and anxious to merit the favour of Heaven by some new instance of piety, he resolved to celebrate his own obsequies. His tomb was according erected in the chapel of the monastery: his attendants walked thither in funeral procession. Charles followed them in his shroud. He was laid in his coffin, and the service of the dead was chanted over him; he himself joining in the prayers that were put up for the repose of his soul, and mingling his tears with those which his attendants shed, as if they had been solemnizing a real funeral [1].

The fatiguing length of this ceremony, or the awful sentiments which it inspired, threw Charles into a fever, of which he died in the fifty-ninth year of his age. His enterprises speak his most eloquent panegyric, and his history forms his highest character. As no prince ever governed so extensive an empire, including his American dominions, no one seems ever to have been endowed with a superior capacity for sway. His abilities as a statesman, and even as a general, were of the first class; and he possessed in the most eminent degree the science which is of the greatest importance to a monarch, that of discerning the characters of men, and of adapting their talents to the various departments in which they are to be employed. But unfortunately for the reputation of Charles, his insatiable ambition, which kept himself, his neighbours, and his subjects, in perpetual inquietude, not only frustrated the chief end of government, the felicity of the nations committed to his care, but obliged him to have recourse to low artifices, unbecoming his exalted station, and led him into such deviations from integrity as were unworthy of a great prince. This insidious policy, in itself sufficiently detestable, was rendered still more odious by a comparison with the open and undesigning character of Francis I.; and served, by way of contrast, to turn on the French monarch a degree of admiration to

Sept. 21.

---

[1] Zuuig. *Vida de Carlos.*—Robertson, ubi sup.

which neither his talents nor his virtues as a sovereign seem to
have entitled him.

Before Charles left the Low Countries, he had made a second
attempt to induce his brother to give up his title to the imperial
throne to Philip, and to accept the investiture of some provinces,
either in Italy or the Netherlands, as an equivalent. But finding Ferdinand inflexible on that point, he finally desisted from
his scheme, and resigned to him the government of the empire.
The electors made no hesitation in recognizing the king of the
Romans, whom they put in possession of all the ensigns of the
imperial dignity, as soon as the deed of resignation was presented
to them; but Paul IV., whose lofty ideas of the papal prerogative
neither experience nor disappointments could moderate, refused
to confirm the choice of the diet. He pretended that it belonged alone to the pope, from whom, as vicegerent of Christ, the
imperial power was derived, to nominate a person to the vacant
throne : and this arrogance and obstinacy he maintained during
his whole pontificate. Ferdinand I., however, did not enjoy
the less authority as emperor.

Soon after the death of Charles, Mary of England ended her
disgraceful reign; and her sister Elizabeth, as we have already
seen, succeeded to the throne, to the general joy of the nation,
notwithstanding some supposed defects in her title. Henry and
Philip beheld Elizabeth's elevation with equal solicitude; and,
equally sensible of the importance of gaining her favour, both
courted it with emulative zeal. Henry endeavoured, by the
warmest expressions of regard and friendship, to detach her
from the Spanish alliance, and to engage her to consent to a
separate peace with him; while Philip, unwilling to lose his
connexion with England, not only vied with Henry in declara-
tions of esteem for Elizabeth, and in professions of his resolution
to cultivate the strictest amity with her; but, in order to confirm
and perpetuate their union, he offered himself to her in marriage,
and undertook to procure a dispensation from the pope for that
purpose.

Elizabeth weighed the proposals of the two monarchs with
that provident discernment of her true interests which was conspicuous in all her deliberations ; and, while she intended to
yield to the solicitations of neither, she continued for a time to
amuse both. By this happy artifice, as well as by the prudence
with which she at first concealed her intentions concerning religion, the young queen so far gained upon Philip, that he warmly

2

A.D. espoused her interest in the conferences at Cercamp, and
1559. afterwards at Château Cambresis, whither they were removed. The earnestness, however, with which he seconded the
arguments of the English plenipotentiaries, began to relax in
proportion as his prospect of espousing the queen became more
distant; and the vigorous measures that Elizabeth took, as soon
as she found herself firmly seated on the throne, not only for
overturning all that her sister had done in favour of popery, but
for establishing the Protestant church on a sure foundation, convinced Philip that his hopes of an union with her had been from
the beginning vain, and were now desperate. Henceforth, decorum alone made him preserve the appearance of interposing in
her favour. Elizabeth, who expected such an alteration in his
conduct, quickly perceived it. But as peace was necessary to
her, instead of resenting this coolness, she became more moderate in her demands in order to preserve the feeble tie by which
she was still united to him; and Philip, that he might not seem
to have abandoned the English queen, insisted that the treaty of
peace between Henry and Elizabeth should be concluded in
form, before that between France and Spain [1].

The treaty between Henry and Elizabeth contained no article
of importance, except that which respected Calais. It was stipulated that the king of France should retain possession of that
town with all its dependencies, during eight years, at the expiration of which term he should restore it to England. But as the
force of this stipulation was made to depend on Elizabeth's preserving inviolate, during the same number of years, the peace
both with France and Scotland, all men of discernment saw, that
it was but a decent pretext for abandoning Calais; and, instead
of blaming her, they applauded her wisdom, in palliating what
she could not prevent.

The expedient which Montmorency employed, in order to
facilitate the conclusion of peace between France and Spain, was
the negociation of two treaties of marriage; one between Elizabeth, Henry's eldest daughter, and Philip II.; the other between Margaret, Henry's only sister, and the duke of Savoy.
The principal articles of the treaty of peace were, that all conquests made by either party, on this side of the Alps, should
be mutually restored; that the duchy of Savoy, the principality
of Piedmont, the county of Bresse, and all the other territories

---

[1] Strype's *Annals*, vol. i.—Forbes' *Full View*, vol. i.

formerly subject to the dukes of Savoy, should be restored to Emanuel Philibert, immediately after the celebration of his marriage with Margaret of France, (a few towns excepted, which Henry should retain till his claims on that prince were decided in a court of law ;) that the French king should immediately evacuate all the places which he held in the duchy of Tuscany and the territory of Sienna, and renounce all future pretensions to them ; that he should receive the Genoese into favour, and give up to them the towns which he had conquered in the island of Corsica.　But he was allowed to keep possession of Metz, Toul, and Verdun, because Philip was not very studious of the interests of his uncle Ferdinand.　All past transactions, either of his princes or subjects, it was agreed should be buried in oblivion [1]. Thus the great causes of discord that had so long embroiled the powerful monarchs of France and Spain seemed to be wholly removed, or finally annihilated, by this famous treaty, which fully restored peace to Europe ; almost every prince and state in Christendom being comprehended in the treaty of Château Cambresis, as allies either of Henry or of Philip.

The French king did not long survive the pacification.　He was mortally wounded in a tournament, while he was celebrating the marriage of his sister ; and his son Francis II., a weak prince, succeeded to the crown.　A few weeks after, Paul IV. ended his violent and imperious pontificate :—and thus, as a learned historian observes [2], all the personages who had long sustained the principal characters on the great theatre of Europe disappeared nearly at the same time. *July 10.*

At this æra, my dear Philip, a more known period of history opens.　Other actors appeared on the stage, with different views and passions ; new contests arose ; and new schemes of ambition occupied and disquieted mankind.——But before we enter on that period, we must take a view of the affairs of Poland and the northern states.

---

[1] *Recueil des Traitez*, tome ii.　　　　　　[2] Robertson, book xii.

LONDON :
GILBERT & RIVINGTON, PRINTERS,
ST. JOHN'S SQUARE.

LONDON:
GILBERT & RIVINGTON, PRINTERS,
ST. JOHN'S SQUARE.

Check Out More Titles From HardPress Classics Series In this collection we are offering thousands of classic and hard to find books. This series spans a vast array of subjects – so you are bound to find something of interest to enjoy reading and learning about.

Subjects:
Architecture
Art
Biography & Autobiography
Body, Mind &Spirit
Children & Young Adult
Dramas
Education
Fiction
History
Language Arts & Disciplines
Law
Literary Collections
Music
Poetry
Psychology
Science
…and many more.

Visit us at www.hardpress.net

CPSIA information can be obtained
at www.ICGtesting.com
Printed in the USA
BVHW080222190819
556172BV00015B/1647/P